Fiscal Policy Developments in India

1947 to 2007

Fiscal Policy Developments in India
1947 to 2007

Incorporating

A Comprehensive Description and Review of Trends and Policies Pertaining to Government Budgeting, Taxation, Public Expenditure, Subsidies, Public Debt and Fiscal Federalism in India

▼

Appendices Containing Material on Indian Fiscal System

▼

Glossary of Fiscal Terms

▼

Time-series Public Finance Data on India

By

M.M. Sury

Indian Tax Foundation
New Delhi

in association with

NEW CENTURY PUBLICATIONS

NEW DELHI, INDIA

NEW CENTURY PUBLICATIONS
4800/24, Bharat Ram Road,
Ansari Road, Daryaganj,
New Delhi-110 002

Tel.: 23247798, 65396605
Telefax: 011-41017798
E-mail: indiatax@vsnl.com
www.newcenturypublications.com

Editorial office:
34, Gujranwala Town, Part-2,
Delhi - 110 009
Tel.: 27247805, 27464774

First Published 2007

ISBN: 81-7708-135-7

Published by New Century Publications and printed at Singhal Print Media, New Delhi -110 005

PRINTED IN INDIA

The Book

Fiscal policy is an important instrument of the general economic policy of a government. It is concerned with the use of a government's taxation and expenditure powers to influence economic activities in an economy at the aggregate level. It also deals with financial relations between different tiers of government in a federal polity. Through the medium of budget, fiscal policy determines the level of taxation, public expenditure, borrowings and the issue of additional currency by a government.

The external payments crisis of 1991 in India, which led to the initiation of economic reforms, was the result of deteriorating fiscal situation during the latter half of 1980s. Fiscal imbalance was identified as the underlying cause of the twin problems of inflation and the difficult balance of payments position.

This book provides an exhaustive and analytical account of fiscal developments in India since Independence in 1947 with focus on post-1991 reforms. The book is organised into 10 parts, each part containing chapters/information dealing with some aspect of fiscal policy in India.

Part I is introductory in nature. It explains the economic role of governments in modern societies and the policy instruments available to them to influence the working of an economy, particularly the role of fiscal policy.

Part II is devoted to Government budgeting in India. It explains (a) the mechanics of government budgeting, (b) constitutional provisions regarding Government budgeting in India, (c) structure of the Central Government budget and (d) functional, economic and cross-classification of the budget.

Part III deals with Indian tax system. It is sub-divided into 5 Sections. Section A describes pre-Independence tax system. Section B explains trends in combined (Centre and State) tax revenues. Section C examines Central taxes. Section D is devoted to State taxes. Section E relates to international aspects of Indian taxation.

Part IV covers public expenditure in India. It presents a theoretical insight into the issues involved in public expenditure and explains the structure of Central Government expenditure. It specially focuses on subsidies which form a significant part of the revenue non-plan expenditure of the Government.

Part V focuses on public debt. It explains constitutional provisions regarding public borrowings in India and the main instruments of Government borrowings. Besides, it highlights the debt problems of the State Governments and the restructuring of public debt suggested by the Twelfth Finance Commission.

Part VI discusses Centre-State financial relations (fiscal federalism) in India. It provides a detailed description and analysis of the evolution of Centre-State financial relations in India during the post-Independence period and examines the existing arrangements for intergovernmental financial transfers. It also explains the role of the Finance Commission and the Planning Commission in effecting these transfers, particularly the principles followed by these agencies to reduce vertical and horizontal imbalances in the availability of resources to various tiers of the Government in India.

Part VII relates to local bodies in India. It describes the functional responsibilities and sources of revenue of local bodies, explains the present constitutional arrangements relating to state-local financial relations, and examines the role of various statutory bodies in this regard.

Part VIII consists of 12 appendices which provide supplementary information related to public finance in India.

Part IX contains glossary of fiscal terms.

Part X provides time-series public finance data on India.

The book is designed to interest a cross-section of readers, viz. teachers and students of economics, commerce, law, public administration, business management, chartered accountancy and company secretaryship. It will also serve the needs of legislators, business executives, entrepreneurs and investors, and others interested in fiscal policy developments in India.

Author's Profile

M.M. Sury received his B.A. (Hons.), M.A., and Ph.D. degrees in economics from the University of Delhi. Specialising in fiscal economics, he has published widely on the Indian fiscal system in national and international journals. He was a Visiting Fellow at the International Bureau of Fiscal Documentation, Amsterdam (May 1989), a Fellow at the Indian Institute of Advanced Study, Shimla (1991-92) and a Visiting Fellow in the Department of Law and Management, University of Mauritius, Mauritius (September-October, 2000). He was Economic Adviser, Delhi State Finance Commission (1996-97). Presently, he is a Reader in the Department of Economics, A.R.S.D. College, University of Delhi. He is also the President of the Indian Tax Foundation.

About the Indian Tax Foundation

Indian Tax Foundation was started in June 2000 by a team consisting mainly of teachers and researchers of the University of Delhi and Indira Gandhi National Open University, New Delhi. It is an independent, non-profit, non-governmental research organisation devoted to the study of Indian taxation and allied subjects. It records and reviews tax policy developments in India and examines their impact on different sectors of the economy. It undertakes its own and contractual research in these areas. It also provides consultancy and database services on Indian taxation. Publications of the Foundation, authored by experts/research teams contain both theoretical and empirical analysis. Occasionally, the Foundation also brings out special reports on subjects of topical interest concerning Indian economy.

Results of research conducted at the Foundation are given wider dissemination through its publications to create public awareness, update information and improve ideas. The Foundation provides facilities for knowledge on taxation to meritorious students and researchers, irrespective of caste, creed, sex or religion.

Indian Tax Foundation, based in Delhi, is registered with the Registrar of Societies, Delhi under the Indian Societies Registration Act (XXI) of 1860.

Registration No.: S 37728	Date of Registration: 24th August 2000

Author's Note on the Book

Fiscal policy is an important instrument of the general economic policy of a government. It is concerned with the use of a government's taxation and expenditure powers to influence economic activities in an economy at the aggregate level. It also deals with financial relations between different tiers of government in a federal polity. Through the medium of budget, fiscal policy determines the level of taxation, public expenditure, borrowings and the issue of additional currency by a government.

It may be recalled that the external payments crisis of 1991 in India, which led to the initiation of economic reforms, was the result of deteriorating fiscal situation during the latter half of 1980s. This period was marked by high and persistent fiscal deficits, accompanied by large revenue deficits. This had led to a significant enlargement of Government borrowings from financial intermediaries and increased financing of Government deficit through automatic monetisation which aggravated price rise. When the Indian economy faced an unprecedented macroeconomic crisis in 1991, fiscal consolidation constituted a major objective of the policy response. This consolidation was to be achieved through reduction in the size of budget deficit and public debt in relation to GDP. For this purpose, it became necessary to (a) enhance tax and non-tax revenue, (b) curtail current expenditure growth, (c) restructure public sector undertaking, including disinvestment, (d) improve fiscal-monetary co-ordination, and (e) deregulate financial system.

Apart from these reforms aimed at fiscal consolidation, a number of institutional measures were also taken during the 1990s. Public sector restructuring and disinvestments were undertaken with a view to increase the efficiency of the public sector undertakings and also to provide additional resources to the Government. The need for improvements in budgetary practices led to the enactment of the Fiscal Responsibility and Budget Management (FRBM) Act, 2003 which ushered the Indian economy in an era of fiscal consolidation based on fiscal policy rules.

The financing of fiscal deficit is another area, which underwent significant changes in the post-reform period. With the discontinuation of *ad hoc* 91-day Treasury Bills in April 1997, automatic monetisation of deficits was eliminated. Greater reliance on borrowing at market-related interest rates since 1992 led to a substantial lowering of statutory pre-emption of institutional resources for the Government. This has also facilitated development of the market for Government securities, which has witnessed remarkable changes since the latter half of the 1990s.

This book provides an exhaustive and analytical account of fiscal developments in India since Independence in 1947 with focus on post-1991 reforms. The book is organised into 10 parts, each part containing chapters/information dealing with some aspect of fiscal policy in India.

Part I is introductory in nature. It explains the economic role of governments in modern societies and the policy instruments available to them to influence the working of an economy, particularly the role of fiscal policy.

Part II is devoted to Government budgeting in India. As a financial blueprint of a government, budget is an important instrument to carry out its policies and programmes. It is through the budget that a government arranges financial resources and allocates them among competing uses. Budget is also the chief source of government finance statistics to facilitate research and decisions on fiscal and economic matters.

Government budgeting is a subject of increasing importance and interest in India. The high level of administrative, welfare and developmental activities of the Central Government entail colossal amounts of both receipts and disbursements. Such large-scale public transactions through the medium of the budget affect the economy in various ways. For example, the level and composition of taxes influence the allocation of resources among various sectors of the economy, distribution of income among different economic classes, and macro management of the economy. Similarly, the borrowing policy of the Central Government affects the amount of national savings available to the private sector for consumption and investment. No less important are the effects of massive public expenditure on production, distribution and economic stabilisation.

In India, the Central budget is designed mainly to ensure Parliamentary control and accounting scrutiny. Each year the Government has to obtain the authority of Parliament to raise revenues to meet its expenditure. Budget of the Government is perhaps the most important annual item on the agenda of the Parliament. It is an instrument of financial control, economic and social development and administrative delegation. It is prepared in financial terms and the intention is to facilitate itemised financial control. Thus, the budget is accountability-oriented without much emphasis on the results of proposed outlays.

This part explains (a) the mechanics of government budgeting, (b) constitutional provisions regarding Government budgeting in India, (c) structure of the Central Government budget and (d) functional, economic and cross-classification of the budget.

Although in the context of India's federal structure, the budgetary trends and procedures should be examined at both the Central and State levels, the present exercise is confined to Central budget only which forms the nerve centre of the financial activities of the economy.

Part III deals with Indian tax system. It is sub-divided into 5 Sections. Section A describes pre-Independence tax system. Section B explains trends in combined (Centre and State) tax revenues. Section C examines Central taxes. Section D is devoted to State taxes. Section E relates to international aspects of Indian taxation.

The Indian tax system has undergone major structural changes since Independence. It has become comprehensive and complicated over the years. It has successfully mobilised resources to finance administrative and developmental activities of public authorities. Besides being the main source of revenue, both for the Central and State Governments, it is an effective instrument to realise various socio-economic objectives of national policies. However, it has been relying heavily on indirect taxes and suffering extensively from fiscal malady called tax evasion.

Restructuring of the tax system has constituted a major component of fiscal reforms initiated since 1991. The main focus of the tax reforms has been on simplification and rationalisation of both direct and indirect taxes with the objective of augmenting revenues and removing anomalies in the tax structure. Tax reforms since 1991 have brought the tax system much closer to international tax practices. Government's concern with tax reforms is reflected in the appointment of a number of committees in the last few years to review the tax system. These have, *inter alia*, included:

- Tax Reforms Committee (Chairman: Raja Chelliah), 1991.
- Advisory Group on Tax Policy and Tax Administration for the Tenth Plan (Chairman: Parthasarathi Shome), 2001
- Inter-ministerial Working Group on Customs Tariff (Chairman: Arvind Virmani), 2002.
- Task Force on Direct Taxes (Chairman: Vijay Kelkar), 2002.
- Task Force on Indirect Taxes (Chairman: Vijay Kelkar), 2002.
- White Paper on State-Level Value Added Tax (Chairman: Asim Kumar Dasgupta), 2005.
- Rationalisation of Customs and Excise Duties on Edible Oils and Oilseeds (Chairman: Ashok Lahiri), 2006.

In fact, tax reforms are a part of the package to liberalise and globalise the Indian economy. The post-1991 period has witnessed a sharp decline in the rates of income tax, excise duty and customs tariff. The theory that high rates of duty lead to higher revenue collection has been discarded in favour of lower rates with fewer exemptions and concessions.

Tax reforms undertaken by the Government in tandem with economic reforms since 1991 have helped to rationalise and simplify the tax system considerably. The rates have been moderated and many exemptions and concessions have been weeded out.

The Union Budget for 2006-07 emphasised the need to increase the tax/GDP ratio without impeding the growth momentum. The strategy in respect of direct taxation is to minimise distortions in tax structure by expanding the tax base and moderating tax rates on the one hand and improving the efficiency of tax administration and increasing the deterrence level on the other, so as to encourage voluntary compliance. The strategy in respect of indirect taxes is to continue the tariff reform process towards mean ASEAN levels of customs tariff, convergence towards CENVAT rate for excise duty, widening of service tax base and phased move towards a fully integrated goods and services tax by April 1, 2010. In his 2006-07 budget speech, the Union Finance Minister observed, "It is my sense that there is a large consensus that the country should move towards a national level Goods and Services Tax (GST) that should be shared between the Centre and the States. I propose that we set April 1, 2010 as the date for introducing GST. World over, goods and services attract the same rate of tax. That is the foundation of a GST. People must get used to the idea of a GST."

Part IV covers public expenditure in India. Public expenditure is an important instrument of the economic policy of the government. The size and pattern of public spending has great relevance in the growth process and in the reduction of economic disparities. The pressure on public expenditure in India is particularly heavy because of growing population and the consequent need for medical, educational, housing and employment facilities. In the emerging economy of India, people have great aspirations of achieving a better standard of living and public expenditure is an effective means to realise their hopes.

This Part of the book presents a theoretical insight into the issues involved in public expenditure and explains the structure of Central Government expenditure. It specially focuses on subsidies which form a significant part of the revenue non-Plan expenditure of the Government.

Part V focuses on public debt. The Government of India borrows heavily both internally and externally. Internal borrowings of the Government are chiefly meant to meet budgetary deficit. External borrowings are meant to meet deficit in the balance of payments.

The main sources of internal borrowings are: individuals, commercial banks, financial institutions and the Reserve Bank of India (RBI). Borrowings from the

RBI are through ways and means advances (WMA). Under statutory liquidity ratio (SLR), commercial banks and other financial institutions are required to invest prescribed proportions (presently 25 per cent) of their assets/liabilities in Government securities. Government also raises loans from the general public through regular floatation of securities and bonds like Kisan Vikas Patras and various other small saving schemes. The major sources of external borrowings are the international agencies like the IMF and the World Bank, foreign governments, and foreign private sources.

This Part of the book explains constitutional provisions regarding public borrowings in India and the main instruments of Government borrowings. Besides, it highlights the debt problems of the State Governments and the restructuring of public debt suggested by the Twelfth Finance Commission.

Part VI discusses Centre-State financial relations (fiscal federalism) in India. A federal set up creates a dual polity based on divided governmental functions and powers. Fiscal federalism, as a branch of public finance, deals with financial arrangements and their working in a federal polity.

Centre-State financial relations in India is a subject of topical interest in view of some recent developments of historical importance. The Constitution (Eightieth Amendment) Act, 2000, significantly changed the manner of distribution of Central tax collections between the Central and State Governments. Prior to Constitution (Eightieth Amendment) Act, 2000, income tax and Union excise duties were the only taxes shared with the States. The aforesaid Amendment altered the pattern of sharing of Central taxes between the Centre and the States by providing for the sharing of the net proceeds of all Union taxes and duties with the States. Furthermore, the Constitution (Eighty-eighth Amendment) Act, 2003 has included 'taxes on services' under entry 92C in the Union List (List I) in the Seventh Schedule of the Constitution.

This Part of the book provides a detailed description and analysis of the evolution of Centre-State financial relations in India during the post-Independence period and examines the existing arrangements for intergovernmental financial transfers. It also explains the role of the Finance Commission and the Planning Commission in effecting these transfers, particularly the principles followed by these agencies to reduce vertical and horizontal imbalances in the availability of resources to various tiers of Government in India.

Part VII relates to local bodies in India. The passage of the Constitution (Seventy-third Amendment) Act, 1992 marked a watershed in the history of modern India. With this amendment, a uniform structure of *panchayats* emerged throughout the country. Similarly, the passage of the Constitution (Seventy-fourth

Amendment) Act, 1992 was a landmark in the history of municipal administration in India. *Panchayats* and municipalities are now constitutional bodies forming third tier to the federal polity of India. India's decentralisation initiative in the form of Seventy-third and Seventy-fourth Amendments poses challenges and offers opportunities.

This Part describes the functional responsibilities and sources of revenue of local bodies, explains the present constitutional arrangements relating to state-local financial relations in India, and examines the role of various statutory bodies in this regard.

Part VIII consists of 12 appendices which provide supplementary information related to public finance in India. Part IX contains glossary of fiscal terms. Part X provides time-series public finance data on India.

The overall approach to the subject is descriptive, analytical and at places normative.

New Delhi
April 27, 2007

M.M. Sury

Contents

Part III: Tax Structure Developments

Part IV: Public Expenditure

Part VII: State-Local Financial Relations in India

Part VIII: Appendices

List of Tables in the Text

Key to Numeration

1 lakh	=	0.1 million
10 lakh	=	1.0 million
1 crore	=	10.0 million
100 crore	=	1.0 billion

Exchange Rate

The unit of currency in India is Indian Rupee

As on 28.3.2007

1 US Dollar	= 43.04 Rupees
1 UK Pound	= 84.52 Rupees
1 Euro	= 57.44 Rupees

Fiscal Year

Fiscal year in India runs from April 1 to March 31 of the following year

anna = 1/16th of a rupee before the introduction of the metric system of currency in India from April 1, 1957

Naya paisa = 1/100th of a rupee after the introduction of the metric system of currency.

Part I: Economic Role of the Government and Fiscal Policy

This introductory Part examines the economic role of modern governments, particularly in developing countries. It highlights various reasons for state intervention in the working of an economic system with special reference to the provision of public goods. Modes of state intervention are also explained with special reference to fiscal policy.

1

Economic Role of the Government and Fiscal Policy

Fiscal policy is an important instrument of the general economic policy of a government. It is concerned with the use of a government's taxation and expenditure powers to influence economic activities in an economy at the aggregate level. It also deals with financial relations between different tiers of government in a federal polity. Through the medium of budget, it determines government expenditure, borrowing requirements and issue of new currency. It also determines private spending through taxation measures.

1.1 Economic Responsibilities of the State

The government is big and important in our times. We depend on the government to protect ourselves against external aggression, internal disorders, pollution, epidemics, social injustice, exploitation, unemployment and poverty. Furthermore, a government is expected to do the following.

- Provide educational, medical and housing facilities.
- Build roads, bridges and communication networks.
- Ensure personal freedom and enforcement of contracts.
- Maintain democratic institutions and cordial relations with foreign countries.

Though the list is not exhaustive, it does provide an idea of the amplitude of the multifarious activities of modern governments.

Present day economies are complex and hence need constant monitoring on the part of the government to deal with such economic problems as inflation, recession, and deficit in the balance of payments. The widening of the scope of governmental economic activities is the result of diversified and interdependent nature of modern economies. The concepts of welfare state [1] and economic planning have made modern governments active partners in the growth process. Hence, active participation of the government in the economic life of a country is recognised by economists the world over.

1.1.1 Views of Classical Economists: The very best of all financial plans is to spend little. This famous dictum of Jean Baptiste Say (1767-1832) aptly summarises the views of classical economists who dominated European economic thinking during the 18th and 19th centuries. Their leader Adam Smith (1723-1790) restricted the duties of a government to the following activities in his epoch-making book, *The Wealth of Nations* (1776).

1. The duty of protecting the society from violence and invasion by other independent societies; this, of course, is the function of national defence.
2. The duty of protecting every member of society from injustice or oppression by every other member of society. This reflects the obligation of establishing an administration of justice which provides law and order within the society so that market economy may function.
3. The duty of establishing and maintaining highly beneficial public institutions and public works which are of such nature that the profits they could earn would never repay the expense to any individual or small number of individuals to provide them.
4. The duty of meeting the expenses necessary for support of the sovereign, which vary depending on the form of political structure.

Other activities, such as government enterprise, were declared unjustifiable by Adam Smith. He maintained, "No two characters seem more incongruous than those of the trader and the sovereign." Excessive public expenditure leads to excessive taxation and the latter was considered an obstacle to a country's march towards industrialisation.

The classical ideas had always been based on the hypothesis that an economic system, via price mechanism, normally tends to equilibrium, i.e. full employment of all the productive forces. Any deviation from the equilibrium was attributed to incidental and temporary friction, which could ultimately be eliminated by the automatic working of price mechanism. Classical economists postulated full employment because they believed that unlimited wants created unlimited possibilities of production. There was no room for permanent instability in their system. They also assumed that the productivity of government services was nil. In short, they believed that the best government is that which does the least.

Classical economists were preoccupied mainly with the relationship between business firms and various economic classes participating in production: landowners, investors and wage earners. This micro level approach had led them to an examination of prices, land, rent, interest, wages and profits. The classical economists paid no attention to the solution of problems created by business depressions and unemployment. They believed that the influences of demand and supply would bring about such an adjustment of individual relationships that the economy would tend to a high level of activity and full employment on its own accord. Occurrence of depressions and unemployment would be temporary in character and self-correcting. They firmly believed in Say's law [2] that there was always enough demand for all the goods that could be produced. They reasoned that there must be enough demand for all the labour and all the capital that was available to produce goods. The economic process tends towards a condition of full employment. However, there could be unemployment of labour or capital at local levels of the economy because of lack of adjustment between specific demands and specific supplies. The possibility of prolonged general unemployment was ruled out.

The theory of employment propounded by classical economists was based on the assumption that receipts of money income by factor suppliers were approximately equal to their spending on consumption or investment goods. This assumption, they believed, was close enough to the facts of real life. However, the occurrence of serious business depressions from time to time belied their thinking.

The ideas of the classical school were respected and followed by the European statesmen up to the first half of the 19th century. However, as the Western economies grew complex in the wake of Industrial Revolution, it became increasingly difficult to maintain the rigidities of classical prescriptions. Rapid industrialisation was accompanied by its own problems like unemployment, exploitation of labour, trade cycles and balance of payments difficulties. Governments could no longer afford to remain silent spectators. Faith in economic automatism was shaken and that in intervention started growing. European governments started drifting away from classical ideals in the latter half of the 19th century. The First World War aggravated the urgency of state interference, and the depression of the 1930s proved to be the last straw on the camel's back. The entire philosophy of the classical economists crumbled like a house of cards.

1.1.2 Keynesian Economics and Compensatory Finance: From the chaos of the depression grew the economic ideas of British economist John Maynard Keynes (1883-1946) as propounded in his path-breaking work *The General Theory of Employment, Interest and Money* (1936) and other writings.

Keynes rejected outright the classical reasoning that working of price mechanism would always bring economic activities to a level of full employment. He believed that in the modern day economic life aggregate demand could be insufficient to absorb all the products that industry would produce if the factors of production were fully employed. If the continuity of the circular flow of money is broken, a tendency towards under-employment of labour and capital emerges with a correspondingly low level of national income.

Keynes developed a new theory which was concerned with certain economic aggregates. He stressed the relationship between total income, total consumption, total saving and investment, and total employment. As a result of his work, new tools of analysis were introduced into economics which are valid till date to a large extent.

During times of depression, production, national income and employment are at a low level. The functioning of price mechanism is imperfect and consequently the ill-effects of depression cannot be successfully tackled at the micro level. The most efficient way to obtain or to maintain full employment is to use government's financial policy. Keynes believed that government intervention in a free enterprise economy was necessary to ensure sustained economic development. He maintained that insufficient aggregate demand causes unemployment and excessive demand results in inflation. Therefore, a government should manipulate the level of aggregate demand by varying the level of its own expenditure and taxation. For example, to avoid a recession, the government should increase spending on public works, reduce taxes and provide easy credit. These measures would lead to more investment, higher employment and increased private spending. All this can be achieved through the medium of the budget. Hence, the importance of budgetary policy and government intervention is clear.

1.1.3 Limitations of Market Mechanism: Indeed, the classical concept of passive public finance has given way to functional finance to deal with the complexities of modern economies which require constant monitoring on the part of fiscal authorities to avoid various disequilibria. Furthermore, there is increasing realisation that left to itself, market mechanism cannot perform all economic functions optimally. The premise that market mechanism leads to efficient use of resources, i.e. it produces in the cheapest way what consumers want the most, is based on the following assumptions.

- There is perfect competition in the factor market as well as in the commodity market.
- Individuals can be excluded from consuming goods if they do not pay for them.

These conditions are rarely fulfilled in practice. Monopolistic and oligopolistic tendencies replace competitive forces to rob capitalism of its virtues. To quote, "In reality, various difficulties arise. Markets may be imperfectly competitive, production may be subject to decreasing cost, consumers may lack sufficient information or be misled by advertising, and so forth. For these reasons, market mechanism is not as ideal a provider of private goods as it might be." [3]

State intervention becomes necessary to curb such tendencies to protect consumers' interests. Even if it is assumed that competition is assured in the factor and commodity markets, still certain goods, because of their peculiar production and consumption characteristics, cannot be provided through market mechanism. In view of the problem of externalities, certain services (like defence, and street lighting) have to be provided through the public sector. This leads us to the discussion of public or social goods. [4]

A. Market Failure for Social Goods: Market mechanism operates almost successfully in the case of private goods. The two chief characteristics of private goods are: (a) Benefits derived are internalised and (b) consumption is rival. In other words, market for private goods functions on the basis of exclusion principle. According to this principle, he who pays the price gets the commodity, and he who does not pay the price is denied the same. The principle applies in the case of private goods like food, furniture, houses, cycles, and hundreds of other marketable goods. As we see in our daily life, the nature of these goods is such that the exclusion principle can be readily applied. When A pays the price, he is handed over the shirt but B is refused the same if he fails to make the payment. This is so because benefits derived are internalised and consumption is rival.

However, market mechanism fails in the case of public goods. The production and consumption characteristics of social goods are such that they cannot be provided through the market economy. To quote, "Social goods are goods the consumption of which is non-rival. That is, they are goods where A's partaking of the consumption benefits does not reduce the benefits derived by all others." [5] Two appropriate examples of non-rival consumption are: (a) defence services and (b) anti-pollution measures. It would be inefficient to apply exclusion principle in the case of such services. Efficient resource use requires that price should equal marginal cost. Since the marginal cost in this case is zero, the additional consumer should be admitted even if he pays zero price. It is noteworthy that exclusion, even if desired, is not possible in the case of services mentioned above. In short, market may fail due to non-rival consumption or due to non-excludability or both of these reasons.

1.1.4 Special Economic Role of the State in Developing Countries: Economic role of governments is all the more important in less developed countries of Asia and Africa. These countries have inherited from the colonial rulers economically weak and socially unjust economies. Political awakening and growing awareness of high living standards in developed countries have made rapid economic growth the most important politico-economic objective of developing countries. The role of government is particularly to be viewed in the context of the urgency to tackle the twin formidable problems of widespread unemployment and poverty. This scenario calls for massive efforts on the part of national governments to provide economic and social justice to the masses which have suffered centuries of deprivation. For this purpose many of the former colonies have embarked upon ambitious programmes of planned economic development the benefits of which are widespread. In many cases, state participation has been direct, resulting in the emergence of mixed economies of which India is a typical example.

1.2 Modes of State Intervention

Granted that state intervention is necessary in the economic system, the next question relates to the techniques of such intervention. Modern governments are equipped with several powers to influence the working of an economy directly and indirectly.

1.2.1 Direct Intervention: A government may participate in economic activities directly by assuming the role of a producer, banker, transporter and distributor. It may influence the production and consumption of commodities through regulatory measures. For instance, it can discourage the consumption of liquor through prohibition. Similarly, minimum wage legislation, mine safety rules, child labour laws, anti-trust legislations, foreign exchange regulations are some other examples of the regulatory powers of the government.

State regulations require the citizens to follow a course of action which they probably would not otherwise take. In this sense, regulatory policies of a government restrict personal freedom in as much as they require or prohibit certain behaviour. In the context of situations which call for immediate and definite action, regulatory policies prove more effective than monetary and fiscal policies. Direct controls become immediately effective and are preferred during emergencies like a war. Such controls interfere ruthlessly with individual preferences and require administrative resources for their implementation.

1.2.2 Indirect Intervention: Governments may influence the level and pattern of production and consumption indirectly through fiscal, monetary, industrial and commercial policies. Indirect controls distort consumer preferences more gently through the price mechanism and need fewer administrative resources for their operation. Monetary policy regulates money supply and the structure of interest rates. Fiscal policy controls the flow of income between public and private sectors and the relative prices of goods and services. Public subsidies may be given to increase output of goods and services which would otherwise be under-produced. Similarly, progressive taxation based on the principle of ability-to-pay is a typical measure to reduce economic inequalities. On the expenditure side, the distributive objective is served either by the direct transfer of money to the needy or through the funding of programmes designed to benefit the poor.

A. Fiscal Policy: See section 1.3 below.

B. Monetary Policy: Monetary policy refers to the expansion or contraction of money and credit supply in an economy. Since monetary policy includes the regulation of both the volume and allocation of credit therefore credit policy is a part of the overall monetary policy.

Monetary policy operates through changes in the stock of money and changes in the cost and availability of credit. The operation of monetary policy rests on the interrelationship between the stock of money, output and prices. Through money creation, credit is made available to productive enterprises. The availability of credit has favourable impact on output. Simultaneously, increase in money supply raises demand, exerting pressure on prices. The output effect and the price effect must be considered together to assess the overall effect of a monetary measure on the economy.

Monetary policy is of crucial importance in the context of the overall development of a country. The objectives of monetary policy are, by and large, the same as those of general economic policy.

Price stability is of prime concern for a developing country like India. Since price rise is closely linked with the supply of money therefore monetary policy holds the key to price stability. This is why the economists stress growth with stability as the ideal objective of economic policy of a country. Domestic price stability is a precondition for increasing exports. Monetary policy becomes relevant in this connection.

The need for monetary resources is linked with the increase in output and the desire for investment. Monetary policy should react to such changes in time and adequately. It should ensure proper balance between the monetary needs of the economy and money supply. Monetary policy, by influencing the cost, volume and direction of credit, contributes to the achievement of general objectives of economic policy.

C. Industrial Policy: A government can influence the operation of an economy through its industrial policy which has the following ingredients.

1. Attitude towards foreign participation in industrial initiatives.
2. Determination of the relative roles of public and private sectors.
3. Relative emphasis on consumer goods and capital goods industries.
4. Role of large vis-à-vis small-scale industries.
5. Location of industries: economic versus social criteria. [6]
6. Concentrated versus broad-based entrepreneurship.
7. Licensing policy, procedures, rules and regulations to control industrial activities.

D. Commercial Policy: It refers to a country's official policy towards foreign trade, tariffs, quotas and non-tariff barriers. It also deals with the composition and direction of a country's foreign trade.

1.3 Fiscal Policy

Fiscal policy refers to the use of a government's taxation and expenditure policies to influence the level of economic activities at the macroeconomic level. Export-import duties, subsidies etc. are important instruments of fiscal policy on the external front. The broad objectives of fiscal policy are detailed below.

1.3.1 Resource Mobilisation: There are several ways through which resources can be acquired for public use. A government may resort to the following alternatives or a judicious mix of all of them.

1. Through deficit financing, it can purchase a part of the goods and services available in the economy. Since such a policy usually leads to price rise, it is called *inflation tax*, the effects of which are very disorderly in the sense that the burden of inflation falls inequitably on different classes.
2. A government can raise resources by charging for the goods and services it provides. This is possible where it operates like a commercial enterprise but not in the case of many other services like defence, and law and order.
3. A government may raise loans internally as well as externally. However, public borrowings involve problems of debt management, debt servicing, and increase in government's liabilities besides burdening future generations.
4. A government can, and usually does, impose taxes to finance public expenditure.

In fact, the first and foremost objective of tax policy in a country is to raise resources for public authorities for administration and development. Taxes are the main instrument for transferring resources from private to public use. By designing an appropriate tax structure, resources can be raised from those who are holding them idly or squandering them on luxury consumption. According to Roy Gobin, "the revenue criterion is usually the dominant consideration, since governments in LDCs have become increasingly aware of the active role which budgetary measures can play not only in initiating and promoting growth but also in maintaining political power. Not only are higher revenue levels needed, but also tax yields should be increased at a faster rate than income, if infrastructural investments and social welfare expenditures are to be financed without generating unacceptable inflationary pressures and/or increasing reliance on foreign assistance." [7]

Revenue performance, i.e. resource mobilisation function of a tax system may be judged in terms of responsiveness of the tax yield to changes in macroeconomic aggregates like national income. Two widely-accepted measures of revenue performance are buoyancy and elasticity of tax revenue.

1.3.2 Resource Allocation: Scarcity of real resources in developing countries calls for their optimum utilisation. Since the composition of investment is an important determinant of the growth rate of an economy, public policy must discourage the flow of resources to low priority areas so that they could be diverted to vital sectors of the economy. By imposing high tax rates on luxuries and other low priority items (such as motor cars, air conditioners, and jewellery) a government can discourage the consumption and production of such items, ensuring in the process the release of resources for high priority sectors. Conversely, production of necessities of life and employment-oriented industries can be encouraged by offering tax concessions or even subsidies.

1.3.3 Distributive Justice: Distributive justice or economic justice is an important function of budgetary policy. Economic justice relates largely to distribution of tax burden and benefits of public expenditure. It is a component of the broader concept of social justice which encompasses, besides distributive justice, such questions as treatment of women and children, and racial and religious tolerance in a society.

A. Determinants of Economic Power: Distribution of economic power in a society depends on two factors.

1. Distribution of factor endowments which include
   - personal earning abilities and
   - ownership of accumulated and inherited wealth.
2. Prices of these factors in the market.

In other words, in a free enterprise economy, an individual's income is determined by the factors of production owned by him and the prices of those factors in the market. An individual who has no capital or land and is unable to work will receive no income. Distribution of income and wealth based on this method is socially undesirable. Moreover, the development process generally brings in its wake proportionately large benefits for certain select groups like industrialists, real estate owners, exporters and importers, traders, speculators, big landlords, and the like. If no corrective measures are adopted, the gulf between the rich and the poor goes on widening, threatening political stability and social order.

How should economic power be distributed? It should be distributed as fairly or justly as possible. Unfortunately, it is difficult to define what is precisely meant by fairness or justness. These ideas involve considerations of value judgement and social philosophy.

Tax policy is a democratic method to influence the distribution of income and wealth on desired lines. The main ingredients of this policy can be the following.

1. Progressive direct taxation of income, wealth and property transactions.
2. Taxation of commodities (customs duties, excise levies, and sales taxes) purchased largely by high-income groups.

3. Subsidies (negative taxation) on goods purchased by low-income groups.

It might be argued that taxation of the rich will reduce savings and thus retard developmental efforts. The conflict between equity and growth can be reduced by incorporating suitable provisions in tax laws to encourage savings and investments. Highlighting the importance of taxation and public expenditure policies in the context of redistribution of economic power, Alejandro Foxley has opined, "modern public finance studies have de-emphasised the analysis of the normative considerations of theory and focused on the very basic question of incidence; who pays and who benefits from government action? Thus, we can say that focus has shifted from the question of 'What should the State do?' to the question of knowing 'What in fact it has been doing'?" [8]

The present upsurge of interest in the distributional aspects of fiscal policy in developing countries is a reaction against the growth-oriented development theories propounded by Western economists. The state, far from being a neutral entity, has to act to correct distortions, and to change the distributive content of the development efforts.

1.3.4 Stabilisation: Initial developmental efforts are generally marked by inflationary tendencies in an economy. Inflation, if uncontrolled, may thwart all development plans and bring misery to the poor. A reasonable degree of price stability should be a primary concern of a government's economic policies.

The overall level of economic activities in an economy depends upon aggregate demand, relative to capacity output. At times, the level of aggregate demand may be insufficient to secure full employment of labour and other factors of production. At other times, aggregate demand may exceed available output at full employment level. Government intervention in both the cases becomes essential to correct such disequilibria in an economy.

Monetary and fiscal policies are important instruments available to a government to ensure smooth functioning of the economy. Reduction in taxes during deflation would leave greater disposable incomes with the people, giving boost to aggregate demand. The reverse is true in times of inflation.

1.4 Fiscal Policy-Monetary Policy Interaction

Monetary policy and fiscal policy are two important instruments of the general economic policy of a government. Although fiscal and monetary policies are complementary to each other in promoting the objectives of economic policy, the former is generally considered more effective. It straightway determines government expenditure and affects private expenditure through taxation measures. Fiscal policy, through budgetary deficits or surpluses, determines changes in government debt and hence issue of new currency. Contrarily, monetary policy has no direct spending and income effects. The effects of monetary policy are indirect and depend on the reactions of lenders and borrowers to the changes brought about by monetary policy. Monetary policy is less effective if an economy is less monetised and financial institutions are underdeveloped. Changes in the monetary policy are more frequent and can be made at any time during a year. However, changes in fiscal policy are less frequent and may require parliamentary approval.

Notes

1. It refers to an economy in which large-scale government action takes place for social benefit, particularly for the labour class. These benefits include free or subsidised health and educational facilities, retirement benefits and protection of environment.

2. Say's law, a proposition propounded by French classical economist Jean Baptiste Say (1767-1832), maintains that every supply creates its own demand. This proposition occupied an important place in the thinking of classical economists. Say believed that aggregate supply of goods produced is the same thing as the aggregate demand. In other words, total demand and total supply are identical. His reasoning was as follows:

In the course of producing goods, business firms incur money costs in the form of payments for the use of land, labour, capital and some profit for the entrepreneur. Money paid out by business firms becomes the purchasing power in the hands of different factors of production. They may either spend it in consumption or save it, putting the savings into some kind of investment goods. By this process of spending for consumption or for the purchase of investment goods, the money flows back into the hands of business firms who have these goods for sale. It follows that the recipients of money incomes must always have enough to buy all the goods produced at prices which will cover their costs. It is not possible to produce more than the people have the means to pay for. There could never be a lack of sufficient demand for all the goods that the economy could produce. Or, to put it differently, a general over-production of goods is impossible.

3. Richard Musgrave and Peggy Musgrave, *Public Finance in Theory and Practice* (New York: McGraw-Hill Book Company, 1985), p. 48.

4. The terms public goods and social goods are used interchangeably here. For niceties of the distinction between the two, see *ibid*, pp. 50-51.

5. *Ibid.*, p. 49.

6. Economic criteria include availability of raw materials, nearness to market and infrastructural facilities. These may be available in already developed areas. Social criteria include employment opportunities and laying of social and economic overheads in backward areas.

7. Roy T. Gobin, "An Analysis of the System of Sales Taxation in Caribbean Market", *Public Finance*, Vol. XXXV, No. 2, 1980, pp. 272-73.

8. Alejandro Foxley, Eduardo Aninat, and J.P. Arellano, *Redistributive Effects of Government Programmes - The Chilean Case* (Pergamon Press, 1979), p. 18.

Part II: Government Budgeting in India: Procedures and Structure

This part explains (a) the mechanics of government budgeting, (b) constitutional provisions regarding Government budgeting in India, (c) structure of the Central Government budget and (d) functional, economic and cross-classification of the budget.

2

Government Budgeting: Theoretical Settings

2.1 Significance of Government Budgeting

Budgetary operations of the government have an important bearing on the functioning of an economy. The ideals of welfare state and economic planning have tremendously increased the magnitude of public spending, resulting in the emergence of the government as an important sector of the economy. This sector has its own money inflows and outflows. Government collects huge sums of money through taxation, borrowings, and printing of additional currency. The manner of collection of these monetary funds and the pattern of their spending influences saving and investment levels, distribution of income and wealth, allocation of resources, and the consumption behaviour of the people.

Modern economies are frequently beset with problems like inflation, excessive fluctuations in economic activities, and deficit in the balance of payments. Budget is an important instrument to carry out corrective operations. Budget is not merely an exercise in matching expenditure to income but a powerful medium to realise objectives of public policy. Budget is a description of both the fiscal policies of the government and the financial plans corresponding to them.

It is necessary for governments to have a planned appraisal of their earnings and proper means of controlling the channels of spending them. Absence of such exercises may lead to corruption, inefficiency, and even bankruptcy of the government. Hence, planned earnings and wise spending are prerequisites for the stability of a government. The medium for fulfilling these requirements is the budget. Public budgeting is desirable from government's point of view because it can answer its critics squarely and prove its honesty in financial matters. It is also important for the legislators because they can ensure that all is well with public money.

2.2 Government Budgeting versus Private Budgeting

Neither a government nor an individual can function without finance. Individuals and governments both have sources of receipts and heads of expenditure and face the problem of adjustment between the two. Both entities try to maximise welfare with limited means. In spite of these few points of similarities, public budgeting is an altogether different exercise in nature and scope as compared to private budgeting.

Individuals, unlike governments, may, at their own risk, earn and spend without planning, foresight, and proper recording of their transactions. Governments in democracies are answerable for their actions to the legislators who in turn enjoy the mandate of the electorate. A private individual may prefer to keep his financial transactions a secret whereas financial activities of the government get wide publicity and are subject to audit and inspection.

Financial resources at the disposal of individuals are far less than those available to a government. Like a government, a private organisation cannot impose taxes nor can it print currency. It has to cut its coat according to cloth. However, this is not a limitation with the government. Public authorities first determine the volume of expenditure and then arrange resources to meet it. In most cases, public expenditure is inelastic and has to be incurred, e.g. on defence, law and order, and general administration.

An individual regards surplus budget as a virtue and a means to accumulate capital and become rich. Contrarily, deficit budgeting is more a rule than an exception for the government.

Private budget-making is guided exclusively by profit motive while public budgeting has social welfare as the objective function. While performance of all private activities is capable of measurement with the standard of money, most public activities defy such measurement. In the absence of market mechanism, government services are determined not by profit expectations but by decisions arrived at through political and administrative procedures and based on common social objectives.

2.3 Canons of Government Budgeting

It is difficult to formulate a universally acceptable set of public budgeting principles because of the differing nature of world economies, their socio-economic objectives and political set-ups. Nevertheless, some general guidelines can be provided to government authorities in-charge of spending public funds. The list of these guidelines is as follows.

1. Although a budget can be prepared for any length of time, it is a common convention to frame it on an annual basis. It is believed that one year is an optimum period for which a legislature should give financial sanction to a government and it is also a reasonable duration for the government to execute budgetary provisions.
2. Budget-making involves extensive estimates of revenue and expenditure for the ensuing financial year. The actuals or accounts represent the figures available after the expiry of the financial year under consideration.

Obviously, there is bound to be some divergence between the estimates and the actuals. However, the nature and the degree of this divergence is of considerable importance because it has far-reaching implications in terms of resource mobilisation, economic planning, financial stability and tax burden.

The degree of deviation between the estimates and the actuals reflects upon the skill and competence of budget makers. Excessive divergence reveals poor financial predictability of the experts. Divergence has two aspects: (a) over-estimation and (b) under-estimation. Over-estimation of revenue ends up with shortages of funds, leading to curtailment or even exclusion of certain development projects. Under inflationary conditions, it may further worsen the situation. In case public expenditure is inelastic, over-estimation of revenue will necessitate deficit financing. Also, over-estimation may slacken government efforts at additional resource mobilisation.

Conversely, under-estimation of revenues leads to unwarranted tax doses. Apart from antagonising the public, it complicates the tax structure and increases administrative costs. Unexpected resources available to public authorities generally go into unproductive projects formulated at short notice. Under- estimation also induces a government to resort to public borrowing thereby unnecessarily increasing liabilities of the public exchequer.

In countries where the process of economic planning is linked with annual budgets, the need for close relation between the budget agency and the planners is all the more important. Surplus in the revenue account of the budget is the first major source of funds available for capital expenditure. Budget-plan integration will become difficult in the face of inaccurate revenue estimates. When the emphasis is on self-reliance, i.e. dependence on internal resources, the importance of accurate revenue estimation assumes unique relevance.

3. Government transactions, both on receipt and expenditure sides, should be shown on gross basis rather than net basis. It will be an unsound budgetary practice if receipts are deducted from charges and expenditure is shown on a net basis in the budget estimates. Under this faulty practice, government will approach legislature for authorisation of only that part of expenditure which cannot be met from receipts. This would render legislature's control over government expenditure meaningless. Therefore, budget estimates ought to be presented on gross basis.
4. It is always desirable to have one budget for a government. If different ministries/departments have their separate budgets, it would become difficult to evaluate the true financial position of a government. Furthermore, the government should try, as far as possible, to prepare a balanced budget.

Surplus budgets raise doubts among people regarding the desirability of levying additional taxes. Contrarily, a deficit budget erodes government's confidence and the will to execute budgetary plans. It will be under strain all the time to look for additional funds.

5. A good budgetary practice is one which makes provision for the expiry of all appropriations at the close of the financial year. This is necessary to prepare and balance the accounts and also to ascertain surpluses or deficits for each year.
6. The estimates and accounts of budgetary transactions should be prepared on a cash basis. This system facilitates transactions of a year to be closed soon after their termination so that the actual trends in government finances are available to legislature and government departments for scrutiny and forecasting. The form in which budget estimates are presented should conform to that of accounts. If the scheme of classification of estimates is different from that of accounts, confusion will arise, making the task of government officials and legislators difficult.

2.4 Zero-base Budgeting (ZBB)

Credit for this fiscal innovation goes to Peter Pyhrr who propounded it in the early 1970s in the context of corporate industrial organisations. The idea soon caught the fancy of Jimmy Carter, the then Governor of Georgia, who became the first to adopt the ZBB approach to government budgeting in the 1973 budget of that State. When he became President, he mandated the Federal bureaucracy to prepare the United States budget for the year 1979 on the basis of ZBB. Since then a number of state governments in the United States have followed suit by adopting ZBB in varying degree depending upon their local requirements and conditions.

Under ZBB, each item of expenditure is challenged for its very existence in every budget cycle and no base or minimum expenditure level is presumed for any activity. Zero-base budgeting means the past is cut off, the present is regarded as a clean slate and all departments have to start from a scratch (hence zero-base). It is also called sunset budgeting meaning that the sun would set on each governmental activity after a specified period. Before the sunset date, each department would be required to present a ZBB, indicating the achievements of its activities and what would result if the activities were not renewed.

2.4.1 Essential Elements of ZBB: There are three essential elements which distinguish ZBB from conventional budgeting.

Firstly, under the conventional system, departments (called budget units) prepare and submit budgets which group many important activities under one head, making it difficult to scrutinise each activity closely. As against this aggregative approach, ZBB requires budget units which are small enough to allow close examination of their programmes. ZBB puts under magnifying glass the nature of activity of each budgetary unit. For example, in the case of health department, a separate budget needs to be prepared for controlling each disease instead of for the whole department. Once the budget unit's activity is identified, the ZBB procedure asks: what if the activity were not funded at all? Are there other ways to perform the activity and meet the unit's objectives? The onus of explanation lies squarely on the departmental heads who are responsible for the activity and for preparing its budget. For instance, the Health Department of Delhi Administration may be asked what if malaria eradication programmes were not funded. A possible answer from the Department could be: 'Mosquitoes would thrive'. However, under a system of ZBB more definite and quantitative answers are sought such as the estimated increase in the incidence of malaria, likely number of man days lost, increase in public and private medical bills, and possibility of fatalities. In essence, it becomes an exercise in social cost-benefit analysis involving strenuous exercises at each departmental level.

Secondly, ZBB assumes that even if an activity needs to be financed it can be financed at a lower-than-current level. In other words, economy in public expenditure on acceptable public activities is at the heart of ZBB's second essential rule. It requires evaluation and review of all programmes and activities, current as well as new, and believes that those who are in-charge of public spending have the capacity to cut down expenditure without adversely affecting the current level of public services.

Thirdly, ZBB requires priority-ranking among competing services of a budgetary unit. This ranking is done by listing all elements of a decision package in order of decreasing benefits to the community. High-priority services are ranked at the top followed by low-priority services until all are ranked. The list so prepared is used to fund services in order of priority until available resources are exhausted. Many of the services at the fag end of the list may just be eliminated for want of funds.

In brief, the three essential principles of ZBB are the following: (a) Should we spend? (b) How much should we spend? and (c) Where should we spend?

2.4.2 Limitations of ZBB: Application of ZBB has various limitations. Many activities of the government may be mandatory within the existing political framework and may even lie outside the jurisdiction of the legislature. For example, in India emoluments and allowances of the President, the Speaker and Deputy Speaker of the Lok Sabha, the Chairman and Deputy Chairman of the Rajya Sabha, and the Supreme Court and High Court Judges are beyond the vote of the Parliament. Furthermore, ZBB becomes unrealistic in case of many other public services which defy application of cost-benefit analysis owing to their very nature. Defence services, law and order, and maintenance of foreign relations are cases in point. It would obviously be ridiculous to ask: What if India's membership of the UNO were not funded? and are there other ways to achieve objectives of this membership? It is clear that the application of ZBB has to be selective rather than government-wide. ZBB is an approach not a fixed procedure to be applied uniformly from one type of expenditure to another or one level of government to another. The procedure must be adapted to suit specific needs of each department.

The major threat to the ZBB approach emanates from bureaucrats because it evaluates the effectiveness of their decisions and exposes their programmes to critical public review. This new idea in public budgeting requires effective administration, communication, and training of personnel involved in the analysis. It increases paperwork considerably and one frequent complaint against ZBB is that legislators seldom find time to scrutinise the analytical exercises done by the bureaucracy. In any event, ZBB is a long-term budgetary reform and its introduction has to be done in a phased manner.

3

Government Budgeting in India: Constitutional Provisions and Procedures

As in other democratic societies, government budgeting is a constitutional obligation in India.

3.1 Annual Financial Statement

Under Article 112 of the Constitution, a statement of estimated receipts and expenditures of the Central Government has to be laid before Parliament in respect of every financial year which runs from April 1 to March 31. The document titled *Annual Financial Statement* is the basic budget document. [1] It sets forth receipts and expenditures of the Government for three consecutive years. It gives details of the actual receipts and expenditures for the preceding year, revised estimates for the current year and causes for such revisions, and the budget estimates for the ensuing year.

3.2 Accounts of the Government

Articles 266 and 267 of the Constitution define the three parts in which Government accounts are kept. The *Annual Financial Statement* shows the receipts and payments of the Government under the following three parts.

3.2.1 Consolidated Fund of India: This is the reservoir into which all revenues received by the Government, all loans raised by the Government, and all money received by the Government in repayment of loans are paid. All expenditure of the Government is incurred from this Fund and no amount can be withdrawn from this Fund without authorisation from the Parliament. Whether the expenditure is charged on the Consolidated Fund or it is an amount voted by the Lok Sabha, no money can be issued out of this Fund unless the expenditure is authorised by an Appropriation Act.

3.2.2 Contingency Fund: This Fund is like an imprest placed at the disposal of the Government to meet urgent unforeseen expenditures which cannot be delayed. Parliamentary approval for such expenditure and for withdrawal of an equivalent amount from the Consolidated Fund is subsequently obtained and the amount spent from Contingency Fund is recouped to the Fund. From 1976, the corpus of the Fund authorised by the Parliament remained at the level of Rs. 50

crore. However, in the wake of Tsunami experience, the corpus of the Fund was raised from Rs. 50 crore to Rs. 500 crore as part of the budgetary exercise for the year 2005-06.

3.2.3 Public Account: Apart from the normal receipts and expenditures of the Government which relate to the Consolidated Fund, certain other transactions enter Government accounts. For instance, transactions relating to provident funds, small saving collections etc. belong to this category where the Government acts more as a banker. These moneys, as a matter of fact, do not belong to the Government and have to be paid back sometime or the other to the persons who deposited them. Therefore, moneys thus received are kept in the Public Account and the concerned disbursements are also made therefrom. Parliamentary authorisation for payments from the Public Account is, therefore, not required.

3.3 Financial Emergency

The normal financial relations between the Union and the States under Articles 268 to 279 are subject to modifications in different kinds of emergencies. Thus, while an emergency (security of India) under Article 352(1) is in operation, the President may suspend, for a period not extending beyond the expiration of the financial year in which the emergency ceases to operate, all or any of the provisions relating to the division of taxes between the Union and the States and grants-in-aid (Article 354). In that event, the States will be left with their revenue under List II (State List) of the Seventh Schedule.

Under Article 360(1) of the Constitution, if the President is satisfied that a situation has arisen whereby the financial stability or credit of India or any part of the territory is threatened, he may make a proclamation of financial emergency. During the period of operation of such a proclamation:

1. The executive authority of the Union shall extend to the giving of directions to any State to observe such canons of financial propriety as may be specified in the directions.
2. Any such direction may also include

(i) a provision requiring the reduction of salaries and allowances of all or any class of persons serving in connection with the affairs of the State,

(ii) a provision requiring all money bills or other financial bills to be reserved for the consideration of the President after they are passed by the State Legislature.

3. The President may also issue directions for the reduction of salaries and allowances of all or any class of persons serving in connection with the affairs of the Union including the judges of the Supreme Court and High Courts.

3.4 Phases of Budgetary Cycle

The budgetary process in India involves the following four operations.

1. Preparation of the budget.
2. Legalisation of the budget.
3. Execution of the budget.
4. Auditing of accounts.

3.4.1 Preparation of the Budget: Preparation of the budget involves considerable efforts on the part of the Ministry of Finance, other Ministries/ Departments and the Planning Commission. It is sometime in the month of September every year that the Budget Division of the Department of Economic Affairs of the Ministry of Finance sends a circular to various Ministries/ Departments, requesting them to prepare estimates of expenditure to be incurred by them in the following year. Specific information is sought on the following matters.

- Actuals of the previous year.
- Sanctioned budget estimates for the current year.
- Revised estimates for the current year.
- Proposed estimates for the next financial year with explanation for any increase or decrease in estimates.

With the help of their financial advisers, individual Ministries/Departments formulate their spending plans on the basis of their previous year spending and the new schemes and projects which they intend to take up. These estimates of expenditure are furnished to the Ministry of Finance during December/January for screening and integration into the main budget.

The Ministry of Finance, after having scrutinised the estimates, embarks upon the process of compilation and co-ordination of estimates of expenditure of different Ministries/Departments. It may prune excessive demands because there are limits to financial resources available to the Government. It also ensures that the estimates conform to the various economy instructions issued from time to time. Before the expenditure estimates are finalised, discussions take place between the Secretary (Expenditure), Ministry of Finance, and the financial advisers of the Ministries/Departments concerned. However, the Ministry of Finance has the final say in regard to all estimates.

Estimates of revenue are prepared by the Department of Revenue, Ministry of Finance. The Department remains equipped with records of yields of various taxes for previous years and on that basis it prepares estimates for the ensuing year. It also undertakes quick estimates of non-tax revenue and non-RBI (Reserve Bank of India) funded borrowings including external aid. A view is then taken on the likely total resources including additional resource mobilisation and RBI credit to the Government. The RBI credit to the Government has to be consistent with the current state of the economy and fiscal consolidation policy (i.e. restraint on both fiscal deficit and monetised deficit). Based on these projections of resources and the non-Plan expenditure commitments, an idea of likely availability of budgetary resources for financing the Plan is conveyed to the Planning Commission.

The Plan expenditure of the Centre comprises (a) Central assistance for the Plans of the States and Union Territories and (b) budget support for Central Plan and Centrally sponsored Plan schemes. The Central Plan sector includes activities of national and strategic importance such as steel, cement, coal, petrochemicals, railways, ports, airways and telecommunications

Estimates of Plan outlay are scrutinised by the Planning Commission. It commences discussion on the Annual Plan with the State Governments and Central Ministries/Departments in November/December regarding availability of resources—States' own resources and the Central assistance that can be made available. An attempt is made to match the needs of various projects and schemes to available resources and fix the size of the annual Plans of each of the States. Similarly, discussions are held with each of the Central Ministries on the fund requirements of various programmes.

After the discussions are completed, a tally is made of the total budgetary support required. Generally, the support required is in excess of the total fund availability as intimated by the Ministry of Finance. Meetings are then held between the Ministry of Finance and the Planning Commission to explore the extent to which resources can be improved and/or the fund requirements can be reduced. Finally, an agreement is reached regarding the approved size of the Plan for the year.

During this period, the Finance Minister remains in close touch with the secretaries of revenue, expenditure, and economic affairs in the Ministry of Finance. The budget proposals prepared by the Ministry are examined by the Finance Minister and he may make changes in them in consultation with the Prime Minister.

Budget-making in India is a highly secretive exercise. The team of officials working on the budget go almost underground for weeks preceding the presentat'on of the budget to the Parliament. In line with the British tradition of parliamentary privilege, details of the budget proposals must be kept secret before they are made known to the legislators. Changes in rates of taxes and duties constitute the most sensitive part of the budgetary proposals. Any leakages of these proposals can have unsettling effect on the product as well as the capital market. Hoaders and speculators swing into action on hearing rumours of duty cuts or hikes. In case the leakage is actual and comes to the notice of opposition party members, it can even cost the Finance Minister his job. To prevent such eventualities, elaborate security arrangements are made which, *inter alia*, include transportation of budget documents to Parliament in heavily guarded vehicles.

On the budget day (generally the last working day of February), the Finance Minister calls on the President to apprise him of the budget proposals. Similarly, the Finance Minister briefs the Cabinet about the budget shortly before it is presented to Parliament.

3.4.2 Legalisation of the Budget: Once the budget is prepared, it has to pass through the following review and approval stages in the Parliament.

1. Presentation of the budget by the Finance Minister in both the Houses of Parliament.
2. General discussion on revenue and expenditure proposals.
3. Presentation, discussion and voting on demands for grants.
4. Voting and passing of the Appropriation Bill.
5. Passing of the Finance Bill.

A. Presentation of the Budget [2]: The budget is presented in the Lower House, viz. Lok Sabha (House of the People) on such a day as the President may direct. By convention, the budget is presented on the last working day of the month of February each year. [3] Simultaneously, a copy of the budget is laid on the table of the Upper House, viz. Rajya Sabha (House of the States).

The proceedings of the day start and end with the budget speech of the Finance Minister. Conventionally, the Finance Minister will start with a review of the economic situation in the current year. He will inform the House about the Economic Survey (generally laid on the table of the House a couple of days before the presentation of the budget). However, he will highlight the major points of the Economic Survey or other economic developments such as agricultural production; price situation, balance of payments situation or any other international development (say oil crisis) which has bearing on the Indian economy. In a way he prepares the background for his budget proposals.

He then outlines the economic policy of the government in the ensuing year. What will be emphasized (infrastructure, agriculture, power etc.), what new schemes will be launched for various sections of society (generally for rural areas and poor people). In short, the presentation of the budget offers an opportunity to the Government to review and explain its financial and economic policies and programmes to the Legislature.

Then he presents the revised estimates for the current year and reasons for changes in receipts/expenditure, if any. Then he presents the budget estimates for the ensuing year. Generally, estimated expenditure is more than estimated receipts, leaving a deficit (or gap) in budget.

Then he proposes measures for Additional Resource Mobilisation (ARM). This may include new taxes or enhancement of rates on existing taxes. He also proposes tax concession wherever required.

He then summarises the net effect of his tax proposals. By ARM he reduces the gap between expenditure and receipts. Some gap still remains (deficit financing) which he considers reasonable and believes will not have undue adverse effect on price level.

The budget papers are made available to members after the Finance Minister's speech is over, the Finance Bill has been introduced, and the House has adjourned for the day. No discussion on the budget takes place on the day it is presented to the House.

B. General Discussion: The Government has to approach the Parliament for approval of its plans to collect, keep and spend money. The budget presented to the House by the Finance Minister is discussed in two stages: the general discussion followed by a detailed discussion, and voting on the demands for grants.

The general discussion, in both the Houses of Parliament, relates to budget as a whole (or any question of principle involved therein), a review and criticism of the administration but no motion is moved at this stage nor is the budget submitted to vote. The scope of discussion is confined to an examination of the general scheme and structure of the budget, items of expenditure and tax policy as expressed in the budget and in the speech of the Finance Minister. The Finance Minister has the general right to reply at the end of the discussion. The Rajya Sabha has no further business with the budget beyond the above general discussion.

Presentation of the budget in itself does not authorise the Government to collect taxes/additional taxes or incur expenditure. For giving effect to tax proposals contained in the budget, a bill called Finance Bill [explained below in section 2.4.2 (E)] is introduced in the Parliament immediately after the budget speech of the Finance Minister.

C. Demands for Grants: Under Article 113 of the Constitution, the financial initiative is the executive's privilege. The Article reads, 'no demand for a grant shall be made except on the recommendation of the President'. The implication is that only the Government can present a demand for grant and not the private members. The purpose of this restriction is obvious because the balancing of revenue and expenditure is the job of the executive and if private members were to propose fresh items of expenditure and the Parliament were to approve of them, the Government finances will fall into disarray. Thus, limiting financial initiative to the Government protects taxpayers against improper appropriation of public funds. It is noteworthy that when a demand for a grant is presented, the Parliament can object to it, refuse it, reduce it but cannot increase it.

The estimates of expenditure for various Departments which need to be voted by the Parliament are submitted in the form of demands for grants. In case a Ministry/Department is in-charge of a number of distinct services, a separate demand for each of the major services is presented. Each demand for grant shows the total amount required for a service during the year showing revenue and capital expenditure separately. Furthermore, they are presented for gross amounts of expenditure. The demands for grants are presented to the Lok Sabha along with the budget statement. They are generally not moved in the House by the Minister concerned. The demands are assumed to have been moved and are proposed from the Chair to save the time of the House.

The demands for grants of the Posts and Telegraphs Department are presented to the Parliament along with the other demands of the Central Ministries. The financial results of the working of Posts and Telegraphs Department are summarised in one of the statements appended to the Central budget. Proposals for increase in postal, telegraph and telephone charges, if any, are explained in a separate memorandum presented along with other budget documents. [4]

(i) Voted and Charged Expenditures: Under Article 112 (2), estimates of expenditure contained in the budget show separately (i) the sums required to meet expenditure described by the Constitution as expenditure charged upon the Consolidated Fund of India and (ii) the sums required to meet other expenditure proposed to be made from the Consolidated Fund. The estimates of expenditure charged upon the Consolidated Fund are not submitted to the vote of Parliament (non-votable expenditure) but each House is competent to discuss any of these estimates. The estimates relating to other expenditure are submitted in the form of demands for grants to the Lok Sabha, and it has the power to accept, or reject any such demand, or to accept any such demand subject to a reduction of the amount specified therein.

Thus, the demands for grants indicate separately the *voted* and the *charged* items of expenditure. Though normally the Government cannot spend any money without the authorisation of the Parliament, certain items of expenditure have been allowed to be incurred even without the Parliament's vote. Such items are called *charged items*. [5] These are indispensable items of expenditure. Lest they should be subjected to changing political fortunes, they have been placed beyond the vote of the Parliament. If Parliament does not vote an item of expenditure, the Government falls immediately. But the President has to carry on, the Supreme

Court has to function and liabilities of the Government have to be cleared.

(ii) Plan and Non-Plan Expenditures: Out of the total expenditure of the Central Government, a significant proportion is incurred as Plan expenditure. Therefore, the demands for grants show separately the Plan and Non-Plan expenditures of the Ministry/Department. The document *Expenditure Budget* (Vol. 1) gives the total Plan provisions for each of the Ministries arranged under various heads of development and highlights the budget provisions for the more important plan programmes and schemes. The document titled *Plan Budget* indicates the total provision for the Central Plan, Plans of Union Territories, and Central assistance for State Plans. The details of Plan outlay at both the Central and the State levels are contained in the document titled *Annual Plan* prepared separately by the Planning Commission.

A significant proportion of Plan expenditure by the Central Government is incurred on public sector undertakings through investment in shares and loans. Public sector enterprises contribute to budgetary receipts by transferring surpluses to the budget (non-tax revenue) and thereby helping Government savings in the form of balance from current revenues. The retained profits of public sector undertakings and deposits accepted from the public represent internal and extra-budgetary resources of the public sector. A detailed survey of the working of public sector undertakings is given in the document titled *Public Enterprises Survey* brought out by the Ministry of Industry. A report on the working of enterprises under the charge of various Ministries is also given in the *Annual Reports* of the various Ministries. The *Annual Reports* along with the audited accounts of each of the Government companies are also separately presented to the Parliament. Moreover, the reports of the Comptroller and Auditor-General of India on the working of various public sector enterprises are also laid before Parliament.

Non-Plan expenditure is a generic term used to cover all government expenditure not included in the Plan. It includes both revenue and capital expenditure, developmental and non-developmental expenditure. A part of the expenditure is obligatory in nature as, for example, interest payments, pensions and statutory transfers to the States. A part of the expenditure is essential such as defence and internal security. Expenditure on the maintenance of assets (buildings, roads etc.) created in previous Plans is also treated as non-Plan expenditure. A large part of resources of the Government is pre-empted by various items of non-Plan expenditure.

(iii) Cut Motions: At the time of discussion on the demands for grants, copies of the *Annual Reports* and *Performance Budgets* of the Ministries are made available to the Members of Parliament. The presentation of demands for grants by a Ministry is an occasion to review the working of that Ministry by the Members of Parliament. The scope of discussion at this stage is confined to matters falling under the administrative purview of the Ministry. It is open to members to disapprove policies of a Ministry or to suggest measures for economy in the administration of that Ministry.

At this stage, a *cut motion* can be moved to reduce any demand for grant but no amendments to a motion seeking to reduce any demand are permissible. The motions to reduce amounts of demands for grants are called *cut motions*. The object of a cut motion is to draw the attention of the House to the matter specified therein. Cut motions can be classified into three categories.

1. **Disapproval of Policy Cut:** A cut motion which says "that the amount of the demand be reduced to Re. 1" implies that the mover disapproves of the policy underlying the demand.
2. **Economy Cut:** Where the object of the motion is to effect economy in the expenditure, the form of the motion is "that the amount of the demand be reduced by Rs...(a specified amount)." The amount suggested for reduction may be either a lump sum reduction in the demand or omission or reduction of an item in the demand.
3. **Token Cut:** Where the object of the motion is to ventilate a specific grievance within the sphere of responsibility of the Government of India, the form of the motion is "that the amount of demand be reduced by Rs. 100." Discussion on such a cut motion is confined to the particular grievance specified in the motion and which is within the sphere of responsibility of the Government of India.

(iv) Principle of Guillotine: Discussion on the demands for grants in the Lok Sabha has to be completed in the budget session. These discussions take place under pressure of time and in practice only a limited number of demands are discussed in the Lok Sabha. As the budget session draws to a close, the principle of guillotine is applied, i.e. demands are passed without any detailed discussion or scrutiny.

In the Constitution of India, the real power in relation to financial matters rests with the Lok Sabha. The voting of demands takes place in this House only. Rajya Sabha can discuss the demands, if it so chooses, but it does not vote the demands.

D. Appropriation Bill: After the demands for grants are voted by the Lok Sabha, the Appropriation Bill is introduced, considered, and passed by it. The Bill incorporates all moneys required to meet (i) charged expenditure and (ii) grants made by the Lok Sabha. This Bill is then passed as a Money Bill subject to the condition that no amendment is proposed to it in either House which has the effect of varying the amount or altering the destination of any grant or varying the amount of any expenditure charged on the Consolidated Fund (Article 114). No money can be withdrawn from the Consolidated Fund, either with respect to voted grants or the non-votable *charged* items of expenditure, except under an Appropriation Act passed by the Parliament. It provides the legal authority for the withdrawal of sums from the Consolidated Fund. In other words, the passing of the Appropriation Bill completes the authorisation by Parliament of Government expenditure. The Parliament then goes to consider the Finance Bill.

The Appropriation Bill is first passed by the Lok Sabha and then transmitted to the Rajya Sabha. If the Rajya Sabha does not return the Bill within 14 days the Bill is deemed to be passed by both Houses. If the Rajya Sabha makes some changes and the Lok Sabha does not accept them, then also the Bill is deemed to be passed by both the Houses in the form in which the Lok Sabha had passed it.

After the Appropriation Bill is passed in the foregoing manner, the various Ministries/Departments inform the respective spending agencies and project authorities the amount allocated in the budget to each of them.

Normally, the budget of the Government is presented by the end of February. The Parliament has to discuss the budget, vote the demands for grants, and finally pass the Appropriation Bill. The Appropriation Bill has to be passed before 31st March so as to enable the Government to incur expenditure from the beginning of the ensuing financial year. Since the presentation, discussion, and voting of demands for grants and passing of Appropriation Bill generally go beyond the current financial year, a provision exists in the Constitution empowering the Lok Sabha to make any grant in advance through a *Vote on Account* to enable the Government to carry on until the voting of demands for grants and the passing of the Appropriation Bill. This enabling authorisation gets enacted before March 31.

(i) Vote on Account: A vote on account (Article 116) may be sought when a change in Government takes place shortly before the end of a financial year. The new Government may wish to recast taxation and expenditure proposals to reflect its own policies through the budget and it may find the time at its disposal inadequate to effect the desired changes. Under such circumstances, the Parliament may be approached to pass a vote on account providing sufficient grants to enable the Government to incur expenditure till the Appropriation Bill is passed. In this case, a vote on account becomes a mere statement of estimated revenues and expenditures at the existing rates of taxation. In other words, it does not contain any taxation proposals. It just enables the government to withdraw funds from the Consolidated Fund of India till a regular budget is presented and passed by the Parliament.

Under normal circumstances, the vote on account is sought for two months for a sum equivalent to one-sixth of the estimated expenditure for the entire year.

However, during an election year the vote on account may be taken for a longer period, say 3 to 4 months if it is anticipated that the Appropriation Bill will take longer than 2 months to be passed by the House. A vote on account is passed by the Lok Sabha after the general discussion on the budget is over and before the discussion on demands for grants is taken up. Traditionally, vote on account is treated as a formal matter and passed by the Lok Sabha without discussion. [6]

(ii) Vote of Credit: Situations may arise when the Government requires huge amounts of money urgently, e.g. if the country is threatened with war. Under such extraordinary situations the Government may not be in a position to furnish details of expenditure to be incurred. To deal with such circumstances, the Parliament may grant a sum in gross to the Government on a vote called a *Vote of Credit* and leave the responsibility of distributing the money to the executive (Article 116).

(iii) Excess Grant: At the end of the financial year, all voted amounts lapse. If the Government incurs expenditure on any service during a financial year in excess of the grant voted by the Parliament, a demand for such excess has to be presented to the House which may vote on *excess grant* [Article 115(1)(b)]. All such cases are brought to the notice of the Parliament by the Comptroller and Auditor-General through his report on Appropriation Accounts. The excess grants are then examined by the Public Accounts Committee which makes recommendations regarding their regularisation in its report to the House. The demands for excess grants are made after the expenditure has actually been incurred and after the financial year to which it relates has ended.

E. Finance Bill: It is expressly laid down in the Constitution that no tax shall be levied or collected except by the authority of law (Article 265).

The regular budget contains proposals with regard to both direct and indirect taxes. These proposals regarding the levy of new taxes, modifications in the existing tax structure or continuance of existing rates of taxation for a further period are presented through the Finance Bill.

Taxation proposals take effect the moment the Finance Bill is presented, indirect taxes immediately and direct taxes on a date specified in the Bill (normally the first day of the ensuing financial year, i.e. April 1). The introduction of the Finance Bill cannot be opposed and it may be introduced without prior circulation of copies to Members. The scope of discussion on the Finance Bill is vast and the whole administration comes under review.

The procedure in respect of the Finance Bill is the same as in the case of other money bills. Only after the Finance Bill is passed and becomes the Finance Act, does the collection of revenues get legislative authority. A document titled *Memorandum Explaining the Provisions in the Finance Bill* is also presented along with the Finance Bill to facilitate easy appreciation of the taxation proposals made in the Finance Bill. As in the case of other bills, the presentation and passing of the Finance Bill involves a time lag. However, as the Finance Bill contains, *inter alia*, changes in duty rates on commodities, economic activities in the economy will get disrupted if these changes are made public but not implemented immediately. Hence, a mechanism exists under which those taxation proposals, where it will not be in public interest to defer bringing them into force forthwith, take effect immediately pending the passing of the Finance Bill. Under the Provisional Collection of Taxes Act, 1931, the Government is empowered to collect taxes for a period of 75 days or taking of decision by Parliament on the Bill, whichever is earlier. In a way, it sets out the time frame within which the budget authorisation process has to be completed in the Parliament.

(i) Money Bills: Under Article 110(1), bills dealing with imposition, abolition, remission, alteration, or regulation of any tax or the regulation of the borrowing of money by the Government or the custody and payment of Government money are all money bills. [7] Money bills can be introduced only in the Lok Sabha. After a money bill has been passed by the Lok Sabha, it is sent to the Rajya Sabha for its recommendations. The Rajya Sabha cannot reject, amend or vote upon money bills. It can only offer recommendations which may or may not be accepted by the Lok Sabha. Also, the Rajya Sabha cannot take more than 14 days for considering the return of a money bill. Thus, in case a money bill is not returned to the Lok Sabha within 14 days, the bill is considered to have been passed by both the Houses. Therefore, the power of voting on money bills is limited to the directly elected Lok Sabha. Similarly, although the budget is presented before both Houses of Parliament, the demands for grants are submitted only to the Lok Sabha.

F. Supplementary Budget: It is likely that the forecasts on the basis of which the original budget was prepared go haywire due to exogenous factors (international economic crisis) and/or internal disturbances like industrial unrest, political instability etc. Government may then present to the Parliament a supplementary budget to deal with such shocks.

Furthermore, if a grant voted by the Parliament in accordance with the estimates presented in the budget for a particular service for the current financial year is found to be insufficient for the purpose of that year, the Government presents a *supplementary estimate* [Article 115(1)(a)] and the Parliament may make a *supplementary grant.* Also, the Government may approach the Parliament when a need has arisen during the current financial year for supplementary or additional expenditure on some *new service* not contemplated in the budget of that year. The supplementary demands for grants are presented to and passed by the House before the end of the financial year.

3.4.3 Execution of the Budget: Once the Appropriation Bill and the Finance Bill are passed, the executive departments get a green signal to collect revenue and spend money on approved schemes. Collection of revenue is the duty of the Revenue Department of the Ministry of Finance. This Department has two wings: the Central Board of Direct Taxes and the Central Board of Excise and Customs. There are detailed departmental rules governing the mode of assessment, collection and remittance of various taxes into Government treasury.

More important, however, is the executive control of public expenditure. Once the appropriations are voted and approved by the Parliament, spending authorities are authorised to draw the necessary amounts and spend them. Individual Ministries/Departments are informed by the Ministry of Finance about their respective budget allocations. All appropriated amounts lapse at the end of the financial year. Hence, they must be spent during the current financial year. Reappropriation between expenditure heads is allowed subject to prescribed rules in this regard. However, reappropriation between voted and charged items of expenditure is not allowed. Similarly, reappropriation is not permitted for meeting expenditure on a new service not provided for in the budget.

A. Maintenance of Accounts: The system of government accounts is a matter of great significance in any democratic country. The primary objective of government accounts is to facilitate the formulation, authorisation and the execution of the budget. The manner in which various items of receipt and expenditure are grouped and presented plays an important role in determining the character and quality of the decisions at various stages of the budgetary process. The adequacy and effectiveness of legislature over financial administration is chiefly determined by the form and contents of consolidated and classified financial statements.

In India, the budget is presented to Parliament and the State Legislatures in terms of the various sections and major heads of account grouped under them as prescribed by the Comptroller and Auditor General (CAG) with the approval of the President. The structure of the accounting system of the Central Government is primarily meant to satisfy the needs of Parliament and the executive including its subordinate agencies. The system ensures that the Parliament receives a full and reliable account of the funds provided to the executive.

An important feature of the accounting structure in India is its uniformity as between the transactions of the Central and the State Governments. This uniformity is intended to facilitate understanding and comparison of the variety of financial transactions both of the Centre and the States from one financial year to another.

Article 149 of the Constitution prescribes duties and powers of the CAG. Under Article 150, the CAG is required to prescribe the format in which the accounts of the Union and the States are to be kept. Similarly, Article 151 requires the CAG to present reports relating to the accounts of the Union and the States.

The CAG performs such duties and exercises such powers in relation to the accounts of the Union and of the States as may be prescribed by the Parliament. In exercise of this power, the Parliament enacted the Comptroller and Auditor-General (Duties, Powers, and Conditions of Service) Act, 1971 which after amendment in 1976, relieved him of his duty to prepare the accounts of the Union. The other important provisions relating to his duties are as follows.

- To audit and report on all expenditure from the Consolidated Fund of India and of each State as to whether such expenditure has been in accordance with the law.
- To audit and report on all expenditure from the Contingency Fund and the Public Account of the Union and of the States.
- To audit and report on all trading, manufacturing, profit and loss accounts kept by any Department of the Union or a State.

Constitutional provisions have safeguarded the independence and freedom of the CAG and have placed him beyond political influences. He is an officer of the Constitution. Though appointed by the President, he may be removed on an address from both the Houses of Parliament on grounds of *proved misbehaviour* or *incapacity*. His salary and conditions of service are statutory, i.e. as laid down by the Parliament by law and are not liable to variations to his disadvantage during his term of office.

As already noted, the CAG continued to maintain accounts of the Central Government as well as of all the State Governments until 1976 when it was decided to relieve him of this responsibility in respect of Central Government accounts. Under a new system of *Integrated Financial Administration,* introduced with effect from October 1, 1976, the Secretary of a Ministry/Department acts as the chief accounting authority. He discharges his responsibilities through and with the assistance of the *Integrated Financial Adviser* of the Ministry/Department. It is the responsibility of the Integrated Financial Adviser to render financial advice, prepare the budget, distribute budget allocations among the various sections of the Ministry, arrange payments, compile and consolidate accounts, and also to ensure accuracy in accounts on the part of various sections of the Ministry/Department. Under the Integrated Financial Adviser, there is a Controller of Accounts for each Ministry. The latter has under him, the Regional Pay and Accounts Officers functioning in various parts of the country. The banking business of each Ministry/Department is conducted by a designated public sector bank nominated by the RBI as its agent. The account of the Ministry/Department is operated with a branch of that public sector bank by the Pay & Accounts Officer of the Ministry/Department.

This departmentalised system of payments and accounts separates accounts from audit and provides for a separate Controller of Accounts for each Ministry. Under the old system, prevalent in the States, the primary responsibility for incurring and controlling expenditure and for maintaining accounts, rests with the departmental officers. The final accounts are compiled by the Indian Audit and Accounts Department from the initial accounts submitted by the departmental officers.

Under Article 150 of the Constitution, estimates of receipts and disbursements in the budget have to conform to the accounting classification prescribed by the CAG. The estimates of receipts and disbursements in the budget and of expenditure in the demands for grants are shown according to this classification. The prescribed classification is intended to help the Parliament and the public to meaningfully scrutinise the allocation of resources and the purposes of Government expenditure.

The accounting classification of the Central budget has undergone two major changes, once in 1974-75 and again in 1987-88. Besides, there have been regrouping and reclassification of certain receipts and expenditure items between revenue and capital accounts. These regroupings and reclassifications, *inter alia*, included (a) external grants which were treated as capital receipts prior to 1991-92, are now reclassified under revenue receipts since then and (b) beginning 1987-88, the budgetary classification has been changed by regrouping the expenditures into plan and non-plan heads from the classification of developmental and non-developmental heads followed then. This was done to bring about correspondence with the Plan heads of development.

In October 1976, an organisation named Controller-General of Accounts (CGA) was set up to administer matters pertaining to the departmentalisation of accounts of the Union Government. This organisation which works as part of the Ministry of Finance performs, *inter alia*, the following main functions.

1. Prescribing the form of accounts relating to the Union and the State Governments.
2. Laying down accounting procedures.
3. Overseeing the maintenance of adequate standards of accounting by Central Accounts Offices.
4. Consolidation of the monthly and annual accounts of the Government of

India.

5. Administration of rules under Article 283 of the Constitution relating to the custody of the Consolidated Fund of India, the Contingency Fund, and the Public Account.

The CGA prepares a condensed form of the Appropriation Accounts and the Finance Accounts of the Union Government.

3.4.4 Auditing of Accounts: Audit of public expenditure is an ex-post check to ensure that the spending was within the budgeted amount and for the purpose intended. Audit in relation to government accounts has, at least, the following four functions:

- **Appropriation Audit:** Its objective is to ascertain whether the amounts spent by the government have been applied to the purposes and within the limits set by the appropriations authorised by the legislature.
- **Regulatory Audit:** It is concerned with ensuring that the various rules and regulations are fully adhered to by the spending agencies.
- **Propriety Audit:** It includes within its scope an examination of the propriety (wisdom) of executive actions even where their legality is not in question.
- **Efficiency Audit:** It examines the efficiency (economy) with which the agency under audit is discharging its financial responsibilities.

The institution of CAG in India has already been mentioned in section 2.4.3 (A) above. The appropriation audit and regulatory audit are the statutory duties of the CAG. The other two types of audit (propriety and efficiency) are discretionary in nature in the sense that it is left largely to CAG to determine whether and to what extent he should extend his audit into these areas.

Preparation of accounts by CGA is not enough. It is necessary to verify the accuracy and completeness of the accounts and to ensure that the expenditure incurred has been sanctioned by the Parliament and that it has taken place in conformity with the rules sanctioned by the Parliament. Thus, the accounts prepared by CGA are audited by the CAG. The audited accounts are placed on the table of both the Houses of Parliament along with the CAG report. The CAG is responsible for auditing all expenditure of the Central and State Governments and submitting his audit reports to the President or the Governor for being placed before the appropriate legislature. The report of the CAG amounts to the issuance of a *certificate*. The *observations* of the CAG summarise objections and irregularities in relation to voted and charged expenditures in the budget.

Thus, the audit department scrutinises, independently and fearlessly, the expenditure incurred by the Central and State Governments and seeks to ensure that expenditure is not irregularly and wastefully incurred. In this manner it assists the legislature in exercising financial control over the executive.

3.5 Performance Budgets

In the context of India's economic plans, accountability is not merely confined to ensuring spending of funds for the various purposes and within the limits laid down in the budget. It also extends to ensure that the expected results are achieved. The budget should help to reveal that whatever was proposed to be done during the year has actually been achieved both in financial and physical terms. Performance budgeting shifts the emphasis from the means of accomplishment to the accomplishment itself. With this intention in view, performance budgets were introduced in India as an adjunct to the Central budget in 1968-69. Initially, these were prepared and circulated to Members of Parliament in respect of a few Departments/organisations. Since 1975-76, all the Central Ministries and Departments dealing with developmental activities prepare performance budgets which are presented to the Parliament as a supplementary document to the traditional budget. Performance budgets are meant to serve as an instrument of administrative and financial control in the implementation of development programmes. They supplement the conventional budgeting done by Ministries/Departments.

Performance budgets of the various Ministries/Departments are documents in terms of their functions, programmes, and activities/projects. For example, health is a function, malaria eradication a programme, and training of personnel for this purpose an activity. Projects generally refer to activities of capital nature, e.g. construction of a hospital building.

Performance budgets explain the scope and objectives of the schemes, their estimated cost, physical targets, achievements, reasons for shortfalls if any, cost-benefit analysis, standards of performance, and a summary of staff employed for the purpose. Moreover, performance budgets of the various Ministries/ Departments also contain statements of various public sector undertakings under the charge of respective Ministries. These statements show physical targets, achievements, details of inventory, sources of funds and their utilisation, return on capital, details of installed and utilised capacity. In short, performance budgets provide a link between financial allocations and physical achievements by the concerned spending agency.

Unfortunately, implementation of performance budgeting has not been very successful in India. As a pre-requisite for success, performance budgeting requires determination of norms and standards of performance on a scientific basis so that performance could be measured without any arbitrariness. This task has proved difficult with regard to many activities undertaken by the Government. There is a view that very few of governmental activities are susceptible of any physical measurement. Performance budgets can be most appropriately associated with things which government does, rather than the things which government buys. Moreover, it is difficult to evolve norms and standards for uniform application in a vast country like India with geographical variations.

As a result, performance budgets are merely an annual ritual much less a management tool for monitoring of various projects and schemes of the Government.

3.6 Outcome Budget

Beginning 2007-08, the Performance Budget and the Outcome Budget hitherto presented to Parliament separately by Ministries/Departments, were merged and presented as a single document titled "Outcome Budget" by each Ministry/Department in respect of all Demands/Appropriations controlled by them, except those exempted from this requirement. Outcome Budget broadly indicates physical dimensions of the financial budget of a Ministry/Department, indicating actual physical performance in the preceding year, performance in the first nine months of the current year and the targeted performance during the next year.

Outcome Budget contains a brief introductory note on the organization and function of the Ministry/Department, list of major programmes/schemes implemented by the Ministry/Department, its mandate, goal and policy framework, budget estimates, scheme-wise analysis of physical performance and linkage between financial outlays and outcome, review covering overall trends in expenditure vis-à-vis budget estimates in recent years, review of performance of statutory and autonomous bodies under the administrative control of the Ministry/Department, reform measures, targets and achievements and plan for future refinements. As far as feasible, coverage of women and SC/ST beneficiaries under various developmental schemes and schemes for the benefit of North Eastern Region are also separately indicated.

3.7 Other Supplementary Documents on the Budget

3.7.1 Medium-term Fiscal Policy Statement: The Medium-term Fiscal Policy Statement, as enjoined by the Fiscal Responsibility and Budget Management Act, 2003 (FRBM Act) sets forth a three year rolling target for specific fiscal indicators along with underlying assumptions. The statement includes an assessment of sustainability relating to balance between revenue receipts and revenue expenditure and the use of capital receipts including market borrowings for generation of productive assets.

3.7.2 Fiscal Policy Strategy Statement: The Fiscal Policy Strategy Statement, as enjoined by the FRBM Act, contains the policies of the Central Government for the ensuing financial year relating to taxation, expenditure, lending and investments, administered pricing, borrowings and guarantees. It outlines the strategic priorities of the Government in the fiscal area, how the current policies are in conformity with sound fiscal management principles and rationale for any major deviation in key fiscal measures.

3.7.3 Macro-economic Framework Statement: The Macro-economic Framework Statement, as enjoined by the FRBM Act, contains an assessment of the growth prospects of the economy with specific underlying assumptions. It contains assessment regarding the GDP growth rate, fiscal balance of the Central Government and the external sector balance of the economy.

3.8 Parliamentary Control over the Budget

As already noted, the Parliament exercises control over both receipts and expenditure of the Central Government. By passing Appropriation Bill and the Finance Bill, the Parliament authorises the Government to collect revenues and spend money. However, the authority of the Parliament is not limited only to sanctioning appropriations. Rather, it has the means to ensure that the appropriations have been applied towards the purposes approved and within the limits imposed. For the sake of this completeness of legislative control, the Parliament constitutes its three financial committees, viz. the Public Accounts Committee, the Estimates Committee, and the Committee on Public Undertakings. A brief description of the functions of each of these committees is as follows.

3.8.1 Public Accounts Committee: After the report of the Comptroller and Auditor-General (CAG) is laid before the Parliament, it is examined by the Public Accounts Committee. It is a Parliamentary Committee with a non-official chairman appointed by the Speaker from amongst the members elected to the Committee. The Committee consists of 22 members: 15 members elected by the Lok Sabha from amongst its members, and 7 members of the Rajya Sabha elected by that House from amongst its members every year. To ensure that each party/group is represented on the Committee, the election is held on the basis of proportional representation system by means of single transferable vote. The term of office of the members of the Committee is one year.

Being an all-party Committee, it scrutinises the accounts and audit reports prepared by the CAG to satisfy itself that (a) the moneys shown in the accounts as having been disbursed were legally available for, and applicable to, the service or purpose for which they have been applied or charged, (b) the expenditure conforms to the authority which governs it and (c) every reappropriation has been made in this behalf under the rules framed by a competent authority.

The Committee also examines two reports of the CAG on revenue receipts: one relating to direct taxes, and the other pertaining to indirect taxes. While scrutinising these reports, the Committee examines cases involving under-assessments, tax evasion, and also identifies loopholes in tax laws and procedures, and makes recommendations to plug leakages of revenue.

Though normally the Committee confines itself to matters contained in audit reports, it can of its own accord inquire into irregularities which may be brought to its notice or which become of wider public interest. The Committee, however, does not examine the accounts relating to such public undertakings as are allotted to the Committee on Public Undertakings.

Since the work of the Committee is normally confined to the various matters referred to in the audit reports and appropriations accounts, its functions start only after these reports and accounts are laid on the table of the House. In view of the time constraint, the Committee selects important paragraphs from these reports for examination during its term of office. A number of working groups are constituted by the Chairman from amongst the members of the Committee for detailed examination of the subjects selected by the Committee and for considering procedural matters. A sub-committee is also constituted for scrutiny of the action taken by the Government on the recommendations contained in the previous reports of the Committee.

The Committee calls for advance information from the Ministries/Departments with regard to subjects selected by it for examination. It may also undertake on-the-spot study tours of various Departments connected with the subjects taken up for examination. For this purpose, members of the Committee are divided into study groups and each study tour is undertaken with the specific approval of the Speaker.

One of the important functions of the Committee is to find out whether any money has been spent on a service in excess of the amount granted by the House for the purpose. If so, the Committee examines the same with reference to the facts of each case, and the circumstances leading to such excess expenditure. Such excess expenditures are brought up before the House by the Government for regularisation in the manner prescribed in Article 115 of the Constitution. Similarly, the findings of the Committee on a subject are contained in its report which is presented by the Chairman to the Lok Sabha so that the irregularities noticed are discussed and remedial steps taken thereof. A copy of the report is also laid on the table of the Rajya Sabha. After presentation to the Lok Sabha, the report is forwarded to the Ministry/Department concerned which is required to take action on the findings/recommendations contained in the report and furnish Action Taken Replies thereon within six months. Action Taken Notes received from the Ministries/Departments are examined by the Action Taken Sub-Committee. The Action Taken Reports of the Committee are presented to the House. Furthermore, replies received from the Government in respect of recommendations contained in the Action Taken Reports are also laid on the table of the House in the form of statements.

3.8.2 Estimates Committee: To suggest economy and efficiency in public expenditure, the Lok Sabha constitutes the Estimates Committee every year. The first such Committee was constituted in 1950. The members of the Committee are elected every year from amongst the members of the Lok Sabha according to the principle of proportional representation by means of single transferable vote. Originally, the Committee consisted of 25 members but from the year 1956-57 the membership was raised to 30 to facilitate the constitution of sub-committees and study groups for taking up intensive examination of various estimates. The Chairman of the Committee is appointed by the Speaker from amongst the members of the Lok Sabha elected to the Committee. The term of office of the members of the Committee is one year.

Though the Committee is known as Estimates Committee, it does not examine the budget estimates presented to Parliament. It is concerned with *estimates* only after they have been presented to the House. The purpose of the Estimates Committee is to ensure that public expenditure is incurred in a judicious manner and that the objectives underlying the plans and schemes are effectively achieved. In a sense, it is a mechanism to extend parliamentary control over Government expenditure beyond the granting of appropriations. Thus, the Committee examines in detail the estimates presented to the House, makes appraisals of the plans and programmes, and reviews the performance of public expenditure in various fields. In view of these objectives, it has to discharge the following responsibilities.

- To report what economies, improvements in organisational efficiency, or administrative reforms consistent with the policy underlying the estimates, may be effected.
- To suggest alternative policies in order to bring about efficiency and economy in administration.
- To examine whether the money is well laid out within the limits of the policy implied in the estimates.
- To suggest the form in which the estimates shall be presented to the Parliament.

Public undertakings allotted to the Committee on Public Undertakings are outside the purview of the Estimates Committee.

The scrutiny by the Committee of the estimates for the various Ministries/Departments is a continuing exercise throughout the financial year and the Committee reports to the House as its scrutiny proceeds. It is not incumbent on the Committee to examine the entire estimates of the Union Government in its term of one year. Therefore, it takes up only selected subjects for examination which are of current importance or which it may consider necessary to bring to the notice of the House. The subjects selected by the Committee are widely publicised in newspapers, and experts and the general public are invited to send memoranda to the Committee giving their views and suggestions on these subjects.

A number of study groups are constituted by the Chairman from amongst the members of the Committee for detailed scrutiny of the subjects selected by the Committee. The Committee calls for preliminary material from Ministries/ Departments concerned in regard to the subjects selected by it for scrutiny and it also undertakes on-the-spot study tours, with the specific approval of the Speaker, of various institutions/organisations connected with the subjects taken up for examination. The findings of the Committee on a subject are contained in its report which is presented by the Chairman to the Lok Sabha. After presentation to the Lok Sabha, the report is forwarded to the Ministry/Department concerned which is required to take action on the recommendations contained in the report and furnish Action Taken Replies within six months. The Action Taken Notes received from the Ministries/Departments are examined by the Action Taken Study Group, and Action Taken Reports of the Committee are, in turn, presented to the House. Replies received from the Government in respect of the recommendations contained in the Action Taken Reports are laid on the table of the Lok Sabha in the form of statements.

3.8.3 Committee on Public Undertakings: In the wake of Industrial Policy Resolution of 1948 and the subsequent Five Year Plans, public sector in India has grown tremendously. Industries of basic and strategic importance and of public utility are mostly under the ownership and control of the Government. Unlike Railways and Posts and Telegraphs, which are departmental undertakings, most of the public sector undertakings are statutory corporations or Government companies enjoying autonomy and flexibility in their day-to-day operations. This freedom from the usual red-tapism of Government procedures is necessary to ensure their smooth and efficient working in a business-like manner.

Soon after the commencement of the Constitution in 1950, there grew a demand for a separate Parliamentary Committee to review the working of public sector undertakings which were being financed from out of the Consolidated

Fund of India. After a long debate, the Committee was ultimately set up in 1964. The Committee on Public Undertakings consists of 22 members: 15 elected by the Lok Sabha and 7 by the Rajya Sabha from amongst their members according to the principle of proportional representation by means of single transferable vote. The Chairman of the Committee is appointed by the Speaker from amongst the members of the Lok Sabha elected to the Committee. The term of office of the members of the Committee is one year.

The Committee is charged with the task of scrutinising the reports and accounts of public undertakings, the reports of the CAG on such undertakings, and to suggest economies, improvements in organisation/management and production that could be effected in various undertakings. Keeping in mind issues of current interest regarding public sector, the Committee selects for detailed examination such undertakings as it may deem fit. It pays particular attention to those undertakings which come under a cloud in the audit reports of the CAG. The Committee may also examine such subjects or matters which may be specifically referred to it by the House or by the Speaker. However, it is barred from examining and investigating matters of major Government policy as distinct from business or commercial functions of public undertakings.

A number of study groups are constituted by the Chairman from amongst members of the Committee for carrying out detailed examination of various subjects selected by the Committee. The Committee calls for preliminary material from the Ministries/Public Undertakings regarding the working of public undertakings selected for examination. The Committee may also call for memoranda on the subject under examination from non-official organisations and individuals who are knowledgeable in the subject under examination by the Committee. It may also undertake on-the-spot study tours of various public undertakings connected with the subjects taken up for examination.

The findings of the Committee on a subject are contained in its report which is presented by the Chairman to the Lok Sabha. A copy of the report is also laid on the table of the Rajya Sabha. After presentation to the Lok Sabha, the report is forwarded to the Ministry/Department concerned which is required to take action on the recommendations contained in the report and furnish Action Taken Replies thereon within six months. These replies are examined by the Action Taken Sub-Committee, and the Action Taken Reports of the Committee are presented to the House. Replies received from Government in respect of recommendations contained in the Action Taken Reports are also laid on the table of the house in the form of statements.

The three Committees mentioned above are instruments of Parliamentary control over Government finances. However, it is noteworthy that this control is indirect in the form of influence, advice, scrutiny and criticism.

Notes

1. Under Article 202 of the Constitution, a similar type of financial statement for each State is presented before the legislature of that State.

2. The procedure for presentation of the budget in and its passing by the Lok Sabha is as laid down in Articles 112-117 of the Constitution. The budgets of the Union Territories and States under President's rule are also presented to the Lok Sabha.

3. The long-standing tradition of British Raj of presenting the budget at 5.00 P.M. was discarded in 1999. It is now presented in the morning at around 11.00 A.M.

4. Although Railways are a Department of the Government, traditionally the detailed railway budget is presented separately to the Parliament about 2 to 3 days in advance of the General Budget. However, the total of the receipts and expenditure of the Railways is incorporated in the budget statement of the Government of India.

5. Under Article 112(3) of the Constitution, the following expenditure is charged on the Consolidated Fund: (a) Emoluments and allowances of the President and other expenditure relating to his office, (b) the salaries and allowances of the Chairman and the Deputy Chairman of the Council of States (Rajya Sabha), and the Speaker and the Deputy Speaker of the House of People (Lok Sabha), (c) debt charges for which the Government of India is liable, (d) (i) salaries, allowances and pensions payable to or in respect of judges of the Supreme Court, (ii) the pensions payable to or in respect of judges of the Federal Court, (iii) the pensions payable to or in respect of judges of any High Court, (e) the salary, allowances and pensions payable to or in respect of the Comptroller and Auditor-General of India, (f) any sums required to satisfy any judgement, decree or award of any court or arbitral tribunal, (g) any other expenditure declared by the Constitution or by the Parliament by law to be so charged.

6. In the case of Railway budget which is passed before March 31, a vote on account is not sought except, if necessary, in an election year.

7. If any question arises whether a bill is a money bill or not, the decision of the Speaker of the Lok Sabha is final in this regard. When a bill is sent to the Rajya Sabha or is presented for the assent of the President it bears the endorsement of the Speaker that it is a money bill. This is one of the special powers of the Speaker.

4

Structure of the Central Government Budget

Under Article 112(2) of the Constitution, the budget of the Government has to distinguish expenditure on revenue account from other expenditure. In other words, the Constitution requires revenue and capital expenditures to be shown separately in the budget. The Article states: "The estimates of expenditure embodied in the annual financial statement shall show separately - (a) the sums required to meet expenditure described by this Constitution as expenditure charged upon the Consolidated Fund of India; and (b) the sums required to meet other expenditure proposed to be made from the Consolidated fund of India, and shall distinguish expenditure on revenue account from other expenditure."

The distinction between revenue and capital expenditures is not only a constitutional requirement but also an essential ingredient for policy formulation and efficient resource allocation. Therefore, the budget is presented in two parts: revenue budget and capital budget.

4.1 Revenue Budget

Revenue budget shows revenue receipts of the Government and the expenditures met from these revenues. It thus consists of (a) revenue receipts and (b) revenue expenditure.

4.1.1 Revenue Receipts: All those receipts of the Government which are non-redeemable may be termed as revenue receipts. These receipts are divided under two heads: (i) tax revenues and (ii) non-tax revenues. Tax revenues comprise proceeds of taxes and duties levied by the Union. Estimates of tax revenue take into account the effects of taxation proposals made in the Finance Bill. Non-tax revenue of the Government mainly consists of interest and dividends on investments made by the Government, and fee and other receipts for services rendered by it.

A. Tax Revenue: It comprises proceeds of taxes and other duties levied by the Centre. Tax revenue has always occupied a dominant place in the revenue receipts of the Government. It accrues to the Government through a variety of taxes imposed by it. From revenue angle, there are three important Central taxes, viz. income tax, customs duties, and excise duties. The proceeds of these taxes are shared with the States. The relative importance of different taxes and duties is shown in Table 4.1. Gross tax revenue was estimated at Rs. 5,48,122 crore in the budget for 2007-08. Net tax revenue of the Centre (i.e. net of States' share) was placed at Rs. 4,03,872 crore and the non-tax revenue of the Centre at Rs. 82,550 crore in the same budget. The two items put together composed the revenue receipts of the Central Government (Rs. 4,86,422 crore), giving a ratio between tax and non-tax revenue of 83:17 (Table 4.1).

B. Non-Tax Revenue: Non-tax revenue is classified under three broad heads: (a) interest receipts, (b) dividends and profits, and (c) other non-tax revenue.

Receipts on account of interest on loans by the Central Government represent the most important source of non-tax revenue. These receipts comprise interest on loans to State Governments and Union Territories, interest payable by the Railways, the Department of Telecommunications, and *other interest receipts* which include interest on loans advanced to public sector enterprises, port trusts and other statutory bodies, co-operatives and Government servants.

Table 4.1: Composition of the Revenue Budget of the Central Government, 2007-08

(Rs. crore)

Revenue receipts		**Revenue expenditure**	
Gross tax revenue, of which	5,48,122	A. Revenue Non-Plan expenditure, of which	3,83,546
1. Corporation tax	1,68,401	1. Interest payment	1,58,995
2. Income tax	98,774	2. Defence	54,078
3. Customs duties	98,770	3. Major subsidies	54,330
4. Excise duties	1,30,220	B. Revenue Plan expenditure, of which	1,74,354
A. Net tax revenue*	4,03,832	1. Central Plan	1,28,727
B. Non-tax revenue, of which	82,550	2. Central assistance for State Plans	45,627
1. Interest receipts	19,308	A+B Total revenue expenditure	5,57,900
2. Dividends and profits	33,925		
A+B Total revenue receipts	4,86,422		
Revenue deficit = 5,57,900 − 4,86,422 = 71,478			

* Net of States' share.

Source: Government of India, Ministry of Finance, *Budget at a Glance*, 2007-08.

The main items under the head *dividends and profits* include profits of the

Reserve Bank of India, profits from nationalised banks, and the Life Insurance Corporation of India, dividends from the General Insurance Corporation, the Industrial Development Bank of India, and from other public sector companies and financial institutions.

The category *other non-tax revenue* includes a number of sub-heads, each comprising a large number of items. The sub-heads are: fiscal services, *other general services*, social services, economic services, and grants-in-aid and contributions.

Revenues from *fiscal services* include profits from circulation of coins, representing the difference between the face value of coins and their manufacturing cost, receipts relating to refining and assaying charges levied by the mints, and penalties realised against economic offences.

Receipts from *other general services* include examination fees of the Union Public Service Commission, receipts of police on account of Central Police Forces supplied to State Governments, sale of forms, gazettes, audit fees, passport and visa fees.

Then there are receipts from various social and community services, e.g. receipts from commercial services of Akashvani and Doordarshan, entry fees at museums and ancient monuments, and charges realised from patients for hospital and dispensary services.

Receipts under the head *economic services* relate to animal husbandry, dairy development, fisheries, forests, transport and communications, ports, lighthouses, tourism, roads and bridges, and import and export licence application fees. Lastly, there are cash grants-in-aid from foreign countries and international organisations.

The lack of attention paid to non-tax revenue of the Government was well brought out by the Ninth Five Year Plan when it observed, "Sufficient attention has not been paid to realisation of non-tax revenues. Areas from where non-tax revenues can be augmented are irrigation charges, royalties on minerals and revision of user charges on services rendered by the Government. There is an urgent need for more frequent revision of water rates and effective water rate administration. The approach should be to collect at least enough revenues to meet the full O&M expenditures of the irrigation department. There is also urgent need to raise the efficiency of irrigation systems by reducing costs and supplying water in time and in adequate measure." [1]

4.1.2 Revenue Expenditure: Revenue expenditure relates to the normal running of Government departments and various services, interest charges on debt incurred by the Government, and grants given to State Governments and other parties. Broadly speaking, all those expenditures of the Government which do not result in the creation of physical or financial assets may be treated as revenue expenditures.

A. Revenue Non-Plan and Plan Expenditure: Budget documents classify total revenue expenditure into revenue non-Plan and revenue Plan expenditure. Out of an estimated total revenue expenditure of Rs. 5,57,900 crore for the year 2007-08, the shares of revenue non-Plan and revenue Plan expenditures were Rs. 3,83,546 crore (68.7 per cent), and Rs. 1,74,354 crore (31.3 per cent) respectively (Table 4.1).

Revenue Plan expenditure pertains to Central Plan and Central assistance for State and Union Territory Plans. However, the more important revenue non-Plan expenditure covers a wide variety of general, social, and economic services of the Government.

B. Functional Categories of Revenue Non-Plan Expenditure: Revenue non-Plan expenditure is classified under the following four categories.

1. General Services: This category includes both civil and defence services. Civil services include (a) *Organs of State* like the Parliament, the President, the Vice-President, and the Council of Ministers, administration of justice, elections, and audit, (b) *Fiscal Services* like collection of customs duties, Union excise levies, income tax, wealth tax and other taxes levied by the Government, currency, coinage and mint, (c) *Interest Payments* on market loans, external loans, and loans from various reserve funds, (d) *Administrative Services* like Union Public Service Commission, police, jails, public works, external affairs, pensions and secretariats and attached offices of the Ministries of Finance, Home Affairs, Law, Justice and Company Affairs, Defence and External Affairs. In short, expenditure on general services relates to the maintenance of law and order, defence of the country, and upkeep of the general organs of the Government.

2. Social and Community Services: This category includes expenditure incurred on basic social amenities to benefit citizens as consumers. It relates to expenditure on education, art and culture, scientific services and research, medical services, family planning, public health, sanitation, water supply, housing, urban development, information and publicity, broadcasting, labour and employment, and social security and welfare. Expenditure on the secretariat and attached offices of the various Ministries dealing with these services are also included under this head.

3. Economic Services: This category includes all such expenditures which promote productive activity within the economy. In other words, benefits of expenditure under this category accrue to citizens as producers. The major heads of expenditure of this sector are: (a) *General Economic Services* like foreign trade and export promotion, co-operation and secretariats and attached offices of the various Ministries dealing with programmes of economic development, (b) *Agriculture and Allied Services* like irrigation schemes, soil and water conservation programmes, animal husbandry, dairy development, fisheries, forestry, community development, food subsidy to Food Corporation of India and other services related to agriculture, (c) *Industry and Minerals* which include large-scale industries, village and small industries, and development of mines and minerals, (d) *Water and Power Development* including navigation, drainage, flood control, power houses, (e) *Transport and Communications* such as ports, light houses, shipping, civil aviation, roads and bridges, tourism and other transport and communication services.

4. Unallocable: Expenditures which cannot be related to specific purposes are included under this head. The main items are: statutory grants-in-aid, ways and means advances, ad hoc loans, grants to Nepal and Bhutan, technical and other loans to foreign countries.

The rationale underlying the categorisation of Government expenditure into the above-mentioned four categories is that while general services relate to the defence of the country and the general upkeep of the Government, social services provide basic amenities to citizens as consumers, economic services extend benefits to citizens as producers, and unallocable expenditures signify lack of specific purpose.

C. Major Items of Revenue Non-Plan Expenditure: The three main items of revenue non-Plan expenditure are: (a) interest payments, (b) defence services and (c) subsidies. These three items put together accounted for Rs. 2,67,403 crore (69.7 per cent) out of a total revenue non-Plan expenditure of Rs. 3,83,546 crore budgeted for the year 2007-08 (Table 4.1).

1. Interest Payments: Interest payments constitute the single largest component of revenue non-Plan expenditure. It is in the nature of committed expenditure arising out of past profligacy. In the 2007-08 budget, interest payments accounted for Rs. 1,58,995 crore, constituting 41.4 per cent of the revenue non-Plan expenditure of the Government (Table 4.1). The high level of interest payments is directly linked to high reliance on borrowings.

The increased reliance on borrowings has directly multiplied the debt servicing liabilities of the Government. Fiscal experts have warned against an internal debt trap, a situation in which borrowings have to be resorted to just to keep up with debt servicing.

Reduction in interest rates is one alternative to arrest the rising debt servicing obligations of the Government. However, cuts in interest rates will provide only short-lived relief. For a long-term solution of the problem, the borrowed funds must be used for productive purposes and for projects which ensure reasonable rates of return. This is also the underlying philosophy of public debt.

2. Defence: The allocation for defence represents the second largest component of revenue non-Plan expenditure. In the 2007-08 budget, defence expenditure was placed at Rs. 54,078 crore, accounting for 14.1 per cent of revenue non-Plan expenditure of the Government. Defence expenditure started increasing steadily after the Chinese aggression in 1962, and the Indo-Pak conflicts in 1965 and 1971.

Defence expenditure, chiefly determined by the geo-political situation, is almost a committed expenditure. In view of growing global tensions there is little scope for stabilisation much less reduction in defence expenditure. Defence expenditure is a sacred cow in India and any suggestion to control or reduce it is construed as almost unpatriotic. However, restraining defence expenditure should not be understood in terms of weakening defence preparedness. It simply means exploring the possibilities of achieving the existing level of defence preparedness at reduced costs. As a result of the implementation of the recommendations of various pay commissions, the wage component of the defence budget has increased disproportionately.

3. Subsidies: Subsidies [2] represent a sizeable item of the Centre's revenue non-Plan expenditure. In the 2007-08 budget, they accounted for Rs. 54,330 crore (14.2 per cent) out of a total revenue non-Plan expenditure of Rs. 3,83,546 crore. Food, and fertilisers are the two main items subsidised by the Government through budgetary support.

(i) Food Subsidy: Food subsidy is designed to help the producers (farmers) and the consumers of cereals (wheat and rice). The Food Corporation of India procures foodgrains from the market at prices (support prices) fixed by the Government. To these prices are added the handling costs (transportation, storage etc.) to arrive at the economic cost of procuring foodgrains. The procured foodgrains are then released to the public through the public distribution system. The issue price of foodgrains is less than the economic cost to the Government. The difference between the two is reimbursed to the Food Corporation of India as subsidy. The major determinants of food subsidy are (a) cost of procurement, (b) storage and distribution, (c) foodgrain stocks and (d) issue price of cereals.

The basic purpose of food subsidy is to help the weaker sections of population to obtain cereals at reasonable prices. Presently, every citizen of India, irrespective of his economic circumstances, is entitled to draw subsidised items (cereals, sugar, kerosene) from fair price shops. This is also true in case of subsidised educational and medical facilities. There is hardly any justification for this non-discriminatory treatment of every section of society and some eligibility criterion based on income needs to be fixed. If the cut-off income level is kept low, it will exclude a large section of deserving population. A high cut-off level will have marginal effect. The administrative and enforcement costs of implementing such measures should also be borne in mind.

In his 2000-01 budget speech, the Finance Minister announced the exclusion of income tax assessees from the purview of PDS but only in respect of sugar. The same should have been done in respect of cereals and kerosene. The basic purpose of food subsidy is to help the weaker sections of population to obtain cereals at reasonable prices.

(ii) Fertiliser Subsidy: Use of fertilisers is necessary to improve yield of various crops. Fertiliser consumption has been on the increase in India. In November 1977, the Government introduced the Fertiliser Retention Price and Subsidy Scheme under which fertilisers are supplied at subsidised prices to farmers throughout the country. Some idea of the extent of fertiliser subsidy can be had from the following facts, "The average urea price based on domestic cost of production of urea was Rs. 6,720 per tonne in 1998 as against the current selling price of Rs. 4,000 per tonne fixed on 29.1.1999. The Hanumantha Rao Committee (1998) had estimated the long-run marginal cost of domestic urea at Rs. 6,500 per tonne. Total fertiliser subsidy in 1999-2000 was estimated at Rs. 13,250 crore (BE)." [3]

The issue price of fertilisers is revised from time to time. In spite of this, subsidy on fertilisers is an important item of non-plan expenditure. While it is desirable that small and marginal farmers should continue to enjoy the benefits of subsidised fertilisers, it is questionable if such benefits should continue to be extended to big farmers as well.

The Finance Commissions have emphasised, from time to time, the need to curtail fertiliser subsidy. The Seventh Finance Commission assumed a progressive decrease in fertiliser subsidy and its complete elimination by 1983-84. The Eighth Finance Commission regretted that the stipulations of the previous Commission did not materialise. The Ninth Finance Commission also felt that further growth in fertiliser subsidy should be severely restricted.

The Ninth Five Year Plan also criticised the present system of subsidies when it observed, "It, therefore, becomes essential that the Government gradually shifts its expenditure patterns away from providing non-transparent and non-targeted subsidies. Unfortunately, the beneficiaries of the present system of subsidies are much more organised and politically more vocal than the vast majority of our common citizens who silently suffer the lack of even the basic amenities of a decent and healthy existence." [4]

4.2 Capital Budget

Capital budget comprises capital receipts and capital expenditures of the Government. It shows capital requirements of the Government and their financing patterns. Among the principal sources of meeting these requirements are: revenue surplus, regular floatation of loans in the domestic market, small savings, and external borrowings. To the extent that these receipts fall short of capital requirements, the deficit is made good by borrowings from the Reserve Bank of India and drawing down of cash balances. Capital account signifies that the economic role of the Government extends far beyond collecting and spending tax revenue. It reflects Government's influence over the economy through its acquisition and disposition of a significant portion of the annual savings of the people. The amount of savings available to the private sector for investment is reduced by the amount of capital raised by public authorities.

4.2.1 Capital Receipts: Those receipts of the Government which create liability or reduce financial assets may be called capital receipts. The main components of such receipts are borrowings of different kinds and repayment of loans and advances by other parties. These receipts totalled Rs. 1,94,099 crore in the 2007-08 budget (Table 4.2). They are classified under the following heads.

Table 4.2: Composition of Capital Budget of the Central Government, 2007-08

(Rs. crore)

Capital receipts		Capital expenditure	
A. Non-debt receipts, of which	43,151	A. Capital non-Plan expenditure, of which	91,875
1. Recoveries of loans	1,500	1. Defence	41,922
2. Miscellaneous capital receipts	41,651	2. Loans to public enterprises	767
B. Debt receipts to finance fiscal deficit, of which	1,50,948	B. Capital Plan expenditure, of which	30,746
1. Market loans	1,09,579	1. Central Plan	26,212
2. External assistance (net)	9,111	2. Central assistance for State Plans	4,534
3. State provident funds (net)	5,000	A+B Total capital expenditure	1,22,621
A+B Total capital receipts	1,94,099		

Source: Government of India, Ministry of Finance, *Budget at a Glance*, 2007-08.

A. Market Loans: These include the regular market floatations by the Government. They are taken on net basis, i.e. gross borrowings minus repayment of loans.

B. Special Deposits: These relate to investments with the Government of net accretions by non-Government provident funds, superannuation and gratuity funds, and of surplus funds of the Life Insurance Corporation, General Insurance Corporation, Employees' State Insurance Corporation, Power Finance Corporation etc.

C. External Assistance: Self-explanatory as it is, this category shows loans received from friendly foreign countries and international organisations.

D. Recovery of Loans and Advances: Under the Five Year Plans, the Centre has been giving liberal loans to State and Union Territory Governments and other parties. The receipts under this head pertain to the recoveries of loans and advances made by the Central Government to State and Union Territory Governments, foreign governments, industrial and commercial undertakings and financial institutions in the public sector, municipalities, port trusts, companies and institutions in the private sector, co-operative societies, and Government employees.

E. Small Savings: These comprise Post Office Savings Accounts, Post Office Time Deposits, Recurring Deposits, National Saving Certificates, Social Security Certificates, Kisan Vikas Patra, National Saving Scheme, and Post Office Monthly Income Scheme.

F. Provident Funds: Receipts under this head relate to State Provident Funds and Public Provident Funds. Credit assumed is net of the deposits into the fund including interest on balances and withdrawals including temporary advances therefrom. Also taken into account are net accretions under the Public Provident Fund Scheme launched in 1968.

G. Other Receipts: This head shows the net effect of transactions occurring under other funds and accounts some of which are as follows: (i) Railway reserve funds like Railway Pension Fund, Railway Depreciation Reserve Fund, Railway Revenue Reserve Fund, Railway Development Fund, Railway Accident Compensation, Safety, and Passenger Amenities Fund. (ii) Telecommunication reserve funds like Telecommunication Revenue Reserve Fund. (iii) International financial institutions. This head represents liabilities assumed in respect of special securities issued in payment of India's subscription/contribution to (a) International Monetary Fund, (b) International Development Association, (c) International Fund for Agricultural Development, (d) Asian Development Bank, (e) International Bank for Reconstruction and Development. It also represents certain transactions involving use of Special Drawing Rights with International

Monetary Fund.

4.2.2 Capital Expenditure: Those expenditures of the Government which lead to the creation of physical or financial assets or reduction in recurring financial liabilities fall under the category of capital expenditure. Such expenditures pertain to payments on acquisition of assets like land, buildings, machinery, equipment, as also investments in shares, and loans and advances given to State Governments, public sector enterprises and other parties. Capital disbursements are of two kinds: those spent directly (capital outlays) and those spent indirectly by extending loans and advances.

A. Capital Non-Plan and Capital Plan Expenditure: Budget documents categorise total capital expenditure into capital non-Plan and capital Plan expenditure. Out of an estimated total capital expenditure of Rs. 1,22,621 crore budgeted for the year 2007-08, the shares of capital non-Plan and capital Plan expenditures were Rs. 91,875 crore (74.9 per cent) and Rs. 30,746 crore (25.1 per cent) respectively (Table 4.2). Plan capital expenditure relates to Central Plan and Central assistance for State and Union Territory Plans.

B. Functional Categories of Capital Non-Plan Expenditure: Capital non-Plan expenditure covers various general, social, and economic services provided by the Government. The four broad categories of this expenditure are the following.

1. General Services: This sector includes capital expenditure on civil and defence services. It accommodates capital outlay on all non-residential buildings, e.g. office and administrative buildings, other than those for functional purposes like hospitals, schools and godowns. Regarding defence services, provision for capital expenditure on acquisition of land and construction works, machinery and equipment, military farms etc. is included under this sector of expenditure.

2. Social and Community Services: This sector includes capital expenditure on buildings for schools, technical institutions (mainly in Union Territories), scientific research organisations, hospitals, dispensaries, medical stores and research laboratories. Also included under this sector are capital outlays on studios, transmitters, machinery and equipment, and buildings for All India Radio and Doordarshan. Still further, this sector also accommodates capital outlays and loans granted under various schemes for the resettlement of displaced persons as well as other social security and welfare programmes.

3. Economic Services: This sector includes capital outlays and loans granted for various schemes of economic development in the field of agriculture and allied services, industry and minerals, petroleum, chemical and fertiliser industries, aircraft and ship building industries, telecommunication and electronics industries, mining and metallurgical industries, water and power development, roads and bridges and other economic services.

4. Loans and Advances: Loans and advances are given to State Governments, Union Territories, foreign governments (like Nepal, and Bhutan), and Central Government employees for various purposes.

4.3 Various Measures of Budget Deficit and Their Significance

Budget deficit is a multi-dimensional concept. It may refer to overall deficit, fiscal deficit, revenue deficit, primary deficit, monetised deficit or some other mismatch between receipts and expenditures of the Government. The various measures of budget deficit have their own relevance for different purposes. This will be explained after describing the different measures of budget deficit used in India as indicators of the financial health of the Central Government.

4.3.1 Overall Deficit (or Budgetary Deficit): This conventional measure of budget deficit represents the excess of aggregate disbursements over aggregate receipts, both revenue and capital. In other words, it shows the gap in the total receipts and total disbursements of the Government. This gap is financed by (a) increase in ways and means advances by the RBI (prior to April 1, 1997, it was financed by borrowings from the RBI through the issue of 91 days treasury bills i.e. net increase in the RBI's holdings of treasury bills), and (b) draw down of cash balances of the Government. This deficit determines the growth of liquidity and inflationary pressure in the economy.

Overall budget deficit = Aggregate disbursements – Aggregate receipts

The overall deficit does not fully capture the structural imbalances in the fiscal operations of the Government as it depicts only that part of the resource gap in current fiscal operations which is financed by the foregoing two methods.

A. Treasury Bills Replaced by Ways and Means Advances (WMA): The system of ad hoc treasury bills or simply *ad hocs* to finance the budgetary deficit was discontinued from April 1, 1997. Instead, a scheme of ways and means advances (WMA) by the Reserve Bank of India to the Central Government was introduced to accommodate temporary mismatches in the Government's receipts and payments. This will not, however, be a permanent source of financing the Government's deficit. These advances have to be fully repaid within a period not exceeding three months from the date of making such advance. This temporary accommodation, however, is outside the RBI's support to the Government borrowing programme during the year. With the discontinuance of *ad hocs* and the introduction of WMA (floating debt), the concept of overall deficit lost its relevance as an indicator of short-term requirement of funds by the Government or the extent of automatic monetisation. Thus, beginning with the 1997-98 budget, the practice of showing overall deficit was discontinued.

The size and the cost of WMA are decided through agreement between the RBI and the Government of India. The RBI provides WMA to the Government, as and when required, at an interest rate mutually agreed upon from time to time. Amounts drawn beyond the WMA limit are treated as overdraft. Overdrafts on WMA attract a higher interest rate, i.e. mutually agreed upon rate plus two percentage points. Thus, if the agreed upon rate is 8 per cent, the interest rate on overdrafts beyond the WMA limit would be 10 per cent.

The introduction of WMA imparted a new dimension to the concept of deficit in that the conventional budgetary deficit which comprised changes in ad hoc treasury bills net of changes in cash balances was rendered redundant. In its place, the concept of fiscal deficit is now the key measure of deficit. The introduction of WMA is intended to strengthen fiscal discipline and provide greater autonomy to the RBI in its conduct of monetary policy. It will also strengthen the fiscal-monetary co-ordination and debt management.

4.3.2 Fiscal Deficit: Fiscal deficit, an internationally used concept, shows the excess of all expenditure, both revenue and capital, plus loans net of repayments (net lending) *over* total revenue receipts plus non-debt capital receipts.

Fiscal deficit measures the entire shortfall in the non-debt resources for financing the Central Government expenditure and fully reflects the impact of fiscal operations on the indebtedness of the Government by quantifying the total borrowing by the Government. In short, it indicates the total borrowing requirements of the Government from all sources. These borrowings are from (a) the public under various small saving schemes, (b) commercial banks, and other financial institutions, mainly through Statutory Liquidity Ratio (SLR) instrument, and (c) the Reserve Bank of India. Fiscal deficit makes no distinction between different types of borrowings although the implication of borrowings from the Reserve Bank of India is different compared to borrowings from other sources.

Fiscal deficit = Total expenditure – (Revenue receipts + Recoveries of loans + Other receipts)

In the 2007-08 budget, fiscal deficit was shown at a figure of Rs. 1,50,948 crore, which was 3.3 per cent of GDP (Table 4.3).

Fiscal deficit is met by borrowings which lead to internal debt of the Government. The servicing of this debt has become a serious problem. Public debt in India is mostly subscribed to by commercial banks and financial institutions. A judicious macro-management of the economy requires progressive reduction in the fiscal deficit and revenue deficit of the Government. With the discontinuance of the concept of overall deficit, fiscal deficit is now the key indicator of deficit.

Table 4.3: Summary Statement of the Central Government Budget, 2007-08

(Rs. crore)

Receipts		Expenditure	
1. Revenue receipts	4,86,422	4. Non-Plan expenditure	4,75,421
2. Capital receipts	1,94,099	4.1 On revenue account	3,83,546
2.1 Recoveries of loans	1,500	4.1.1 Interest payments	1,58,995
2.2 Other receipts	41,651	4.2 On capital account	91,875
2.3 Borrowings	1,50,948	5. Plan expenditure	2,05,100
3. Total receipts (1+2)	6,80,521	5.1 On revenue account	1,74,354
		5.2 On capital account	30,746
		6. Total revenue expenditure (4.1 + 5.1)	5,57,900
		7. Total capital expenditure (4.2 + 5.2)	1,22,621
		8. Total expenditure (6+7)	6,80,521
9. Revenue deficit = 71,478; (6 – 1)	10. Fiscal deficit = 1,50,948; [8 – (1+2.1+2.2)]	11. Primary deficit = – 8,047 (10 – 4.1.1)	

Source: Government of India, Ministry of Finance, *Budget at a Glance*, 2007-08.

Till recently, a major worry of policy makers in India was the growing fiscal deficit in the budgets of the Central and State Governments. Stressing the need to reduce fiscal deficit to a sustainable level, the Ninth Five Year Plan (1997-2002) observed, "The success of any development strategy depends critically upon the ability of the Government to maintain a stable macro-economic environment in which the fiscal deficit is kept at a reasonable level. Unfortunately, this is an area where the experience of the Eighth Plan has been disappointing. The combined fiscal deficit of the Central and State Governments has remained between 6 and 7 per cent over the past several years, which is very high by international standards. Continued deficits at these levels will either mean continued high rate of interest, or a constant threat of over monetisation and consequent inflation." [5]

A. Is Fiscal Deficit Always Worrisome? There is a view that higher fiscal deficits should not be a matter of much concern. Taking clue from Keynesian economics, it is argued that fiscal deficits would be inflationary only if the economy is at full employment or is characterised by supply constraints in certain crucial sectors. Given the present buoyant nature of the Indian economy marked by excess industrial capacity, large food stocks, enormous foreign exchange reserves, and low/moderate inflation, a monetised deficit is not only non-inflationary, but virtuous for sustaining high growth rate.

4.3.3 Revenue Deficit: Revenue deficit refers to the excess of total revenue expenditure over total revenue receipts. Revenue deficit means dissavings on government account and the use of the savings of other sectors of the economy to finance a part of the consumption expenditure of the government. An important objective of fiscal policy should be to ensure surplus in the revenue budget so that the government also contributes to raising the rate of savings in the economy.

Revenue deficit = Total revenue expenditure – Total revenue receipts

In the 2007-08 budget, revenue deficit of the Central Government was shown at Rs. 71,478 crore, which was 1.5 per cent of GDP (Table 4.3).

A. Revenue Surplus Turned into Revenue Deficit: Till the year 1978-79, it was almost customary that Central budgets recorded a surplus on revenue account, representing a measure of savings on the part of the Government. The surplus on revenue account used to offset, though partially, deficit on capital account and, therefore, the overall deficit. The deficit on capital account indicated the excess of capital expenditure over various types of capital receipts. Since capital expenditure is mainly developmental in nature, leading to creation of physical and financial assets, the budgetary trend was generally welcome except for the magnitude of the overall deficit.

However, beginning with the year 1979-80, revenue account assumed a reversal of role by registering regular and in some years growing deficits. As already noted, the revenue deficit was placed at Rs. 71,478 crore in the 2007-08 budget (Table 4.3). Revenue deficit is met by using a part of the borrowed resources to finance a portion of the consumption expenditure of the Government. Increased borrowings lead to increased interest payments which, in turn, necessitate still larger borrowings, landing the economy in a vicious circle of deficit and debt.

It is interesting to note the reasons responsible for the change from surplus to deficit in the revenue account. The main contributory factor for this change may be traced back to the recommendations of the Seventh Finance Commission which doubled the States' share in Union excise duties from 20 per cent to 40 per cent, and increased their share in income tax from 80 per cent to 85 per cent for the period of its award (1979-84). The Eighth Finance Commission further enhanced the share of States in excise revenue from 40 per cent to 45 per cent, and the Tenth Finance Commission from 45 per cent to 47.5 per cent. However, the Tenth Finance Commission decreased the share of States in income tax from 85 per cent to 77.5 per cent. The Eleventh Finance Commission fixed the share of States at 28 per cent of the net proceeds of all Central taxes/duties. The recommendations of the recent Finance Commissions have considerably eroded the current revenues of the Central Government.

The non-tax revenue of the Government has also suffered on account of shortfalls in surplus generation by public sector undertakings. Emergence of revenue deficits in the government's budgets has resulted, to a considerable extent, from the manner of plan budgeting and financing. At the time when planning was initiated, the expectation was that the finances for the plan would come out of surpluses to be generated by the public sector, although some draft on the private sector savings was not ruled out. This expectation did not materialise as the public sector savings turned out to be inadequate and the bulk of the requirements for the plans were made out of borrowings.

While the Centre's share in divisible taxes has shrunk, several factors have contributed to the faster growth of its revenue expenditure, particularly interest payments, staff salaries and pension payments. It may be recalled that Government gave 25 per cent more to its employees than what was recommended by the Fifth Central Pay Commission. This *magnanimity* of the Government was rightly termed as fiscal suicide by no less a person than Professor Suresh Tendulkar who himself was a member of the Commission. His prophecy has come true if one looks at the unmanageable levels of fiscal and revenue deficits in the recent budget. It is noteworthy that consequent upon the implementation of the recommendations of the Fifth Pay Commission, the salary bill and pension outgo of the Central Government increased sharply, straining its fiscal position. In 1996-97, salaries accounted for 13.5 per cent and pensions 4.0 per cent of revenue receipts (net of States' share) of the Central Government. In 1997-98, the figures stood at 16.4 per cent and 5.0 per cent respectively. [6] Expressing concern at this sharp rise the *Economic Survey*, 1998-99 observed, "Salary and pension payments being in the nature of contractual obligations divert resources away from vital social and infrastructure sectors.... The pension obligations are likely to rise further as life expectancies improve and the ratio of pensioners to work force in Central Government increases in the coming years. The direct expenditure on salaries does not fully reflect the true cost of work force employed since there are large associated costs in consumption of goods and services by those employed in the government. The implementation of the Fifth Central Pay Commission recommendations at the Centre also provides a bench mark for pay revision at State level. This has led to a substantial increase in their salary and pension outgo thereby adversely affecting the fiscal health." [7] In short, one wrong decision of the Central Government, under pressure from a handful of bureaucrats, not only upset its own apple cart but that of the State Governments too. Any talk of fiscal correction/fiscal responsibility is meaningless in the absence of downsizing the government which means reducing the government staff by one-third as recommended by the Fifth Pay Commission.

Strong measures on the part of the Government are needed to curtail revenue deficit. These should aim at (a) improving tax and non-tax revenue and (b) controlling non-Plan revenue expenditure. The Long Term Fiscal Policy had indicated that it would be possible for the Government to balance its revenue budget in 1987-88 and actually attain a revenue surplus in 1988-89. [8] Regrettably, it could not be achieved.

4.3.4 Primary Deficit: The fiscal deficit, as already explained, does not necessarily reflect the extent to which current discretionary fiscal actions improve or worsen the Government's net indebtedness. In particular, interest payments in the current period are obligatory but reflect the impact of debt increased by past budgets. Hence, the concept of primary deficit, indicating the precise extent to which current fiscal action affects the indebtedness of the Central Government. It is measured by deducting interest payments from fiscal deficit.

Primary deficit = Fiscal deficit – Interest payments

In the 2007-08 budget, primary deficit was shown at a figure of Rs. – 8,047 crore (Table 4.3).

4.3.5 Monetised Deficit: Besides ways and means advances, the RBI also supports the Government's borrowing programme. In India, the management of public debt and the floatation of market loans are entrusted to the RBI. Monetised deficit represents changes in the borrowings of the Central Government from the RBI. In other words, it indicates the level of support extended by the RBI to the Government's borrowing programme. Hence, it captures the monetary impact of fiscal operations. This is measured by increase in net RBI credit to the Government which is the sum of increases in the RBI's holding of (a) Central Government dated securities, (b) treasury bills and (c) loans and advances, adjusted for changes in Centre's cash balances with the RBI. In the case of State Governments, monetised deficit refers to ways and means advances given to them by the RBI net of their deposits with the RBI.

The foregoing account of the various kinds of deficit in the budget indicates different aspects of budgetary imbalance. Overall deficit determines the growth of liquidity and inflationary pressure in the economy. Fiscal deficit indicates the extent of Government borrowings from all sources necessary to balance the budget. It encompasses the revenue deficit. Revenue deficit measures Government's negative contribution to domestic savings. In other words, it indicates the extent of borrowing required to finance current expenditure. The large interest payments are the main cause of revenue deficit. This deficit highlights the need to bring down expenditure and augment tax revenue, preferably through better compliance. Thus, various measures of budget deficit help to identify areas of weaknesses in the budget.

4.4 Fiscal Responsibility and Budget Management Act (FRMBA), 2003

It may be recalled that the external payments crisis of 1991, which led to the initiation of economic reforms in India, was the result of deteriorating fiscal situation during the latter half of 1980s. Fiscal imbalance was identified as the underlying cause of the twin problems of inflation and the difficult balance of payments position.

To promote the conduct of prudent and accountable fiscal policy, the Government introduced in the Lok Sabha in December 2000 the Fiscal Responsibility and Budget Management Bill, 2000. The Bill provided for a legal and institutional framework to (a) eliminate revenue deficit, (b) bring down fiscal deficit, (c) contain the growth of public debt and (d) stabilise debt as a proportion of GDP within time frame. The Bill, covering only the finances of the Central Government, defined the principles of fiscal responsibility in terms of budgetary deficit, government borrowings and public debt.

Two indicators of budgetary deficit, namely revenue deficit and fiscal deficit, were the focus of the Bill. Thus, the Bill proposed elimination of revenue deficit and progressive reduction of the fiscal deficit to not more than 2 per cent of GDP within a period of 5 financial years following the promulgation of the law. However, the proposed legislation contained provisions to ensure flexibility in fiscal management under emergency situations like war and natural calamities.

Under borrowing-related norms, the Bill proposed to prohibit certain types of borrowing from the Reserve Bank of India. Similarly, under debt-related norms, it proposed to prescribe a limit on the debt stock. Thus, the Bill envisaged that within a period of 10 financial years, the total liabilities (including external debt at current exchange rate) would not exceed 50 per cent of the estimated GDP.

Emphasising the importance of the Bill, the *Economic Survey*, 2000-01 observed, "The introduction of Fiscal Responsibility and Budget Management Bill, 2000 in Lok Sabha in December, 2000 is a historic step in our fiscal history. It shifts the emphasis of fiscal management from a purely short term perspective to a longer time horizon for conduct of prudent and accountable fiscal policy. Introduction of rule based budget management practices will also enable the economic agents and the community at large to take informed decisions. Besides, its enactment is likely to be seen as a demonstration of our country's resolve to maintaining macro economic stability. Placing limits on the Central Government borrowings, debt and deficits and emphasising greater transparency in fiscal operations would also greatly facilitate effective conduct of monetary policy." [9]

In an unexpected move, the Central Government decided on February 4, 2003 to dilute the Bill, dispensing with the proposed reduction in fiscal deficit by 0.5 per cent annually. The diluted Bill did not have a provision on reducing revenue and fiscal deficits. It emphasised the need to uphold the spirit of sound fiscal management rather than achieve it through legislative measures. The Bill was passed by the Lok Sabha on May 7, 2003. The Act was enacted on August 26, 2003.

The Fiscal Responsibility and Budget Management Act, 2003 and the Fiscal Responsibility and Budget Management Rules, 2004 made under Section 8 of the Act came into force on July 5, 2004. The salient features of the Act are as under.

1. Rules to be made under the Act to specify the annual targets for reduction of fiscal deficit and revenue deficit, contingent liabilities and total liabilities.
2. The revenue deficit and fiscal deficit may exceed the targets specified in the rules only on grounds on national security or national calamity or such other exceptional grounds as the Central Government may specify.
3. The Central Government shall not borrow from the Reserve Bank of India except by way of advances to meet temporary excess of cash disbursements over cash receipts.
4. Reserve Bank of India not to subscribe to the primary issues of the Central Government securities from the year 2006-07.
5. Central Government to take suitable measures to ensure greater transparency in its fiscal operations.
6. Central Government to lay in each financial year before both Houses of Parliament three statements viz., Medium Term Fiscal Policy Statement, Fiscal Policy Strategy Statement and Macroeconomic Framework Statement along with the Annual Financial Statement and Demands for Grants.
7. Finance Minister to make a quarterly review of trends in receipts and expenditure in relation to the Budget and place the review before both Houses of Parliament.

Highlighting the importance of FRBMA, the *Economic Survey*, 2006-07 noted, "FRBMA is an important institutional expression to ensure fiscal prudence and support for macroeconomic balance. With the enactment of the FRBMA, the traditional annual budgeting moved to a more meaningful medium-term fiscal planning framework. According to the Rules, revenue deficit is to be reduced by an amount equivalent to half per cent or more of the estimated GDP at the end of each financial year and eliminated by March 31, 2009. Fiscal deficit is to be reduced by an amount equivalent to 0.3 per cent or more of the estimated GDP at the end of each financial year and reduced to no more than three per cent of the estimated GDP by the financial year ending on March 31, 2009." [10]

4.5 Deficit Financing: Magnitude and Timing

Deficit financing is a kind of forced saving. When all types of receipts of a government fall short of its stipulated total expenditure, then the only alternative left with it is to print more currency. The net effect of deficit financing is an increase in the money supply in the economy. When money supply in the economy increases, it puts pressure on the supply of goods and services. Since supply cannot be increased easily, prices have a tendency to rise. Rise in prices is accompanied by its own adverse effects which are very disorderly because the burden of price rise falls inequitably on different classes. Deficit financing is a kind of *inflation tax* which compels people to save involuntarily.

Magnitude, timing, and consequences of deficit financing are subjects of controversy among economists. In developing countries, governments are always looking for more and more resources to finance development schemes. Taxes are by far the most important source of public revenue but a great part of revenue from taxes goes to meet the administrative expenditure of the governments. Next in importance are borrowings, internal as well as external. When this source is also exhausted, then a government resorts to deficit financing in order to claim a part of the real resources in the economy.

Deficit financing is generally resorted to during war or for development purposes. Apparently, if deficit financing is for development purposes, its ill-effects will be short-lived because when the development schemes mature, the improved production level will reduce inflationary pressure in the economy. Contrarily, if it is for war purposes, the adverse consequences are long-drawn, causing widespread dislocation in the economy.

In the initial stages of development, a modest dose of deficit financing may be justified on grounds of monetisation of the economy. When developmental activities pick up, the demand for money also increases because of increasing transactions. A controlled and gradual increase in money supply plays an important role by boosting investment in the economy. However, a reckless monetary expansion may prove dangerous by aggravating inflationary tendencies. In a supply-constrained economy, the Keynesian investment multiplier operates more in money terms than in real terms. During inflation, fixed income groups are adversely affected and the poor suffer the most. Producers, distributors, speculators, and hoarders are the gainers. In the extreme case, if inflation becomes uncontrolled, people may lose faith in the currency itself. Thus, no society can afford a continuous and significant rise in the general price level. It is rightly said that deficit financing, like fire, is a good servant but a bad master.

The continuous expansion of the administrative, welfare and developmental activities of the Government since Independence has led to a steady upward trend in both receipts and disbursements. The Government has always felt the need for additional resources and has quite often spent more than what it could collect from normal sources.

Should there be a limit on the deficit financing by the Government? In this regard the Ninth Finance Commission recommended, "that a convention should, therefore, be developed limiting the extent of deficit financing by Central Government, in any given year, to an amount to be determined in consultation with the Governor of the Reserve Bank of India on the basis of certain objective economic criteria to be clearly laid down in advance. We would urge that suitable guidelines and criteria for determining the permissible amount of net RBI credit to Government be devised jointly by the Union Ministry of Finance and the Reserve Bank of India." [11]

4.6 Budget-Plan Integration

Economic development of India since Independence in 1947 is unique in several ways. In an innovative effort the founding fathers adopted the middle course of a mixed economy, assigning a pivotal role to public sector and economic planning. This new approach to socio-economic growth was set within a framework of parliamentary democracy guaranteeing universal franchise.

Soon after Independence, India launched an ambitious programme of planned economic development. The Planning Commission was constituted in March 1950 by an executive order of the Government of India. The broad functions of the Planning Commission are: assessment of material capital and human resources; formulation of a plan for their most effective and balanced utilisation; determination of priorities and allocation of resources for completing each stage of the plan; determination of machinery for securing successful implementation of the plan; appraisal of progress and recommending adjustments in policies and measures during the execution of the plan; and making of interim and ancillary recommendations on current development policies.

The Planning Commission prepares the blueprint of economic plans in consultation with the States and in accordance with the guidelines provided by the National Development Council (NDC). A Five Year Plan is broken into 5 Annual Plans. After the draft plan is approved by the NDC and finalised by the Central Government, it is implemented, to a substantial extent, through the state machinery. Apparently, successful execution of a plan presupposes co-operation between the Central and the State Governments.

In India, a plan is a consultative document and does not have the force of law. It is merely a statement of intent and not an authorisation for the executing authorities to go ahead. The plan is a blue print for action but its actual implementation is done through the budget duly approved by the legislature. Budget-Plan integration is important in that while the Plan defines the society's desired ends, the budget allocates and authorises funds for achieving these ends. Hence, the plan and the budget are required to be inter-linked properly to ensure translation of the intentions of the planners into operational realities for achieving the planned objectives.

To facilitate translation of plan into action, it is necessary that the budget distinguishes the plan programmes of expenditure from other (i.e. non-plan) expenditure. The *Annual Financial Statement* does not show the break up of expenditure between plan and non-plan. However, this deficiency is made good through separate presentation of plan and non-plan expenditures in the demands for grants. The annual plan which establishes yearly segments of programmes and projects to be completed is thus dovetailed into the framework of the budget.

In one respect, the planning process has a wider coverage as it deals with developments in the entire economy, encompassing both the public and the private sectors. On the other hand, budgetary process is restricted to the activities of the government sector. In another respect, however, the budgetary process covers more than the planning process as it includes both developmental activities and current activities of the government while planning relates essentially to developmental activities only.

4.7 Budget and the External Sector

Budgetary operations of the Government get linked up with the external sector through the imposition of import duties, tax concessions and/or subsidies on exports, and plan financing through foreign aid.

If the import duties are too high (i.e. high tariff wall), domestic industries get undue protection, resulting in general inefficiency, high production cost and inferior production. Low level of import duties exposes the domestic industries to international competition which may prove beneficial in the long-run. Similarly, if import duties on raw materials and machinery are reduced, the production cost of domestic industries will be lowered. However, lowering of import duties can adversely affect domestic industry if it leads to dumping by the foreigners.

4.8 Budgetary Reforms Suggested by the Eleventh Finance Commission

The Eleventh Finance Commission dealt at length with the current budgetary practices and made valuable suggestions to improve the situation. It observed, "A major weakness of the budgetary process of governments in the States and also at the Centre is the practice of spreading resources over too many projects. Often only a token amount is provided in the year in which the project is announced but this commits the future budgets also for which no detailed estimates are provided in the current year's budget and the projects remain incomplete for years for lack of adequate funds. For government expenditure to be brought under the discipline of resource availability and efficiency in resource use, proper budgeting and strict discipline in matters of launching new projects is required. Also there should be a commitment to completion of projects within the stipulated period and to provide necessary funds.

Another necessary reform in budgeting is to do a way with the dichotomy between 'plan' and 'non-plan' in expenditure. With the introduction of planning, budget heads have come to be divided under 'plan' and 'non-plan' and the distinction runs through all items of expenditure on revenue as well as capital accounts. Apart from creating problems in keeping the revenue deficits and thereby fiscal deficit in control, as pointed out earlier, the distinction has had a deleterious effect on the quality of public services. Essential maintenance has been neglected as they do not come under the plan and existing assets including schools and hospitals are starved of much needed support for their running." [12]

4.9 Budgetary Reforms Suggested by the Twelfth Finance Commission

In the context of the current budgetary practices in India, the Twelfth Finance Commission observed, "The conventional budget exercises have focused on allocation of resources to different heads, without taking into account how these government expenditures get translated into outputs and outcomes. Outputs are the direct result of government expenditure and outcomes are the final results. Thus, in the context of education, opening a new school or appointing a new teacher is an output and reduction in the rate of illiteracy is an outcome. Issues of efficiency require consideration whether the same outcome can be achieved at lower costs and whether the same costs can produce better outcomes. A critical part of budgetary reforms must include information on the relationship between expenditures and the corresponding performance in producing real results as in determining the size of the budget and its allocation among different heads. Although in the past there have been attempts at introducing performance budgeting, such endeavors have receded in importance. There is need to bring back performance budgeting as an integral part of the preparation and evaluation of budgets, both for the centre and the states. Thus, the management of public expenditures should be guided by economy, efficiency, and effectiveness. [13]

4.10 Budgetary Reforms Suggested by the Committee on Capital Account Convertibility (Chairman: S.S. Tarapore), 2006

It may be recalled that in August 1994, by accepting obligations under Article VIII of the articles of agreement of the IMF, India made the Rupee convertible for current account transactions. As regards capital account convertibility, a committee was constituted in 1997 under the chairmanship of S.S. Tarapore which chalked out a phased road map for making the capital account convertible. The East Asian crisis intervened soon thereafter, leading to lack of popular enthusiasm for capital account convertibility.

In view of external sector remaining robust and gaining strength every year and the relative macro economic stability, the Government set up another committee headed by S.S. Tarapore on March 20, 2006 for setting out a roadmap towards fuller capital account convertibility. The Committee submitted its Report on July 31, 2006.

After reviewing the existing capital controls, it detailed a broad five-year time frame for movement towards fuller convertibility in three phases:

Phase I (2006-07).

Phase II (2007-08 to 2008-09).

Phase III (2009-10 to 2010-11).

The Committee recommended the meeting of various indicators/targets as a concomitant to the movement towards fuller capital account convertibility. Some of these recommendations, which pertained to current budgetary practices, were the following.

1. Meeting targets under the Fiscal Responsibility and Budget Management Act (FRMBA), 2003.
2. Shifting from the present measure of fiscal deficit to a measure of the Public Sector Borrowing Requirement (PSBR).
3. Segregating Government debt management and monetary policy operations through the setting up of the Office of Public Debt independent of the RBI.
4. Imparting greater autonomy and transparency in the conduct of monetary policy.

Notes

1. Government of India, Planning Commission, *Approach Paper to the Ninth Five Year Plan* (1997-2002), pp. 42-43.

2. Subsidies are generally classified into the following three categories: (a) public goods, (b) merit goods and (c) non-merit goods.

The best examples of public goods are defence, internal security and general administration. These services are characterised by non-rivalry and non-excludability in consumption. Such services are available to all citizens and cannot be priced. Hence, they are not included in the calculation of subsidies.

Merit goods encompass a large variety of services like anti-pollution measures, malaria eradication programme, primary education and health, roads and bridges, scientific research, flood control, and soil and water conservation. The social benefits resulting from these services are much greater than the sum of private benefits to individual consumers. This is so because these services contain elements of *externality* beneficial to the society as a whole. Subsidies on these services are justified because of availability of benefits in the form of externality.

Non-merit goods include, *inter alia*, food, fertilisers, higher education. The element of externality is either absent or limited. Social and equity objectives are generally the ground for subsidising these services. Considerable controversy exists about such subsidies.

3. Government of India, *Economic Survey*, 1999-2000, p. 140.
4. Government of India, Planning Commission, *Ninth Five Year Plan* (1997-2002, Preface.
5. Government of India, Planning Commission, *Ninth Five Year Plan* (1997-2002), Vol. I, p. 8.
6. Government of India, *Economic Survey*, 1998-99, p. 23.
7. *Ibid.*, 23.
8. Government of India, *Long-term Fiscal Policy*, December 1985, p. 13.
9. Government of India, *Economic Survey*, 2000-01, p. 52.
10. Government of India, *Economic Survey*, 2006-07, p. 18.
11. *Second Report of the Ninth Finance Commission*, p. 41.
12. Report of the Eleventh Finance Commission, June 2000, p. 33.
13. Report of the Twelfth Finance Commission, November 2004, p. 79.

5

Functional, Economic and Cross-classification of the Budget

Budgetary transactions of a government can be delineated and analysed in a number of ways. A functional classification of budgetary data groups items of government expenditure in terms of broad purposes to be served, e.g. defence, health, education, agriculture and industry. Economic classification of the budget involves rearrangement of government's receipts and expenditures into meaningful economic categories. A cross-classification of the budget provides information on government's expenditure by economic categories as well as functions.

5.1 Functional Classification of the Budget

Functional classification of the budget groups government expenditure according to purposes to be served by such expenditure, e.g. administration, defence, education, health, economic services etc. This type of budgeting is done for administrative accountability, parliamentary control, and booking and auditing of transactions. The scheme of functional classification relates essentially to expenditure side of the budget.

5.1.1 Uses and Limitations: Functional classification is defined to include all types of expenditure which are determined by political bodies and which are related in a meaningful way to specific purposes. It ensures that receipts are collected in the manner and the form authorised by law, and expenditures are incurred by the specific authority and on specified items sanctioned by Parliament. This classification is useful for providing general information to the public on the nature of government services and the share of public expenditure devoted to a particular service.

Functional classification facilitates formulation, implementation, and review of the broad policy objectives of the government. Under this classification, a distinction is made between development and non-development expenditure. In India, decisions regarding allocation of resources under the Five Year Plans are based on the objectives prescribed for specific functional categories. It is in this context that functional classification of expenditure becomes relevant for our planners, legislators, and the general public.

Although functional classification of government expenditure has its own uses, it does not furnish suitable information for analysis of government's economic policy. The purpose of such classification is primarily to ensure accountability of those spending public money to those authorising the expenditure and thus facilitating budgetary control. It does not throw light on such economic magnitudes as consumption expenditure, saving, investment, and income generation on the part of government. Pointing out the limitations of functional classification of expenditure, a document of the Economic and Social Council of the United Nations observed, "(Under this classification) the accounts may have different classifications and not be all for the same accounting period. They may not reflect transactions at the time they take place and in some accounts appropriations may be found covering no fixed period.., it is not only difficult to obtain a complete picture of government transactions from existing accounts but also difficult to put it into perspective for policy use. This is not because there is too much detail in the accounts, but because the detail is not always of the right kind nor is it summarised in suitable ways." [1]

5.2 Economic Classification of the Budget since 1957-58

To overcome the deficiencies of functional classification, the United Nations Manual suggested an economic classification of budgetary data. To quote, "(Economic classification provides) an analysis of the transactions of government bodies according to homogenous economic categories of transactions with the other sectors of the economy directly affected by them." [2]

5.2.1 Meaning and Rationale: Economic classification splits government's total expenditure into meaningful economic aggregates, viz. how much is consumed, how much is saved, how much is invested, and how much is transferred to other sectors of the economy. Economic classification of budgetary data is necessary for the following reasons.

1. Economic classification of the budget is necessary because the activities of all government departments do not have the same economic significance. Thus, current transactions of the commercial departments of the government are on par with those of producers in the private sector while current transactions of administrative departments of the government are akin to that of private consumers. Similarly, current receipts of departmental commercial undertakings are sale proceeds of goods and services supplied to the rest of the economy whereas administrative departments have little or no income of their own and largely draw upon the incomes of other sectors to meet their expenditures. Likewise, current expenditures of the departments like Railways, Posts, and Telecommunications are intermediate expenditures

reflected in the prices of goods and services supplied by them. Apparently, these are different in nature from current expenditures on goods and services purchased by the administrative departments which represent demand for goods and services for final consumption.

2. Budget distinguishes revenue receipts and revenue expenditures from capital receipts and capital expenditures. However, in reality, revenue expenditure may include certain items which are capital expenditure from economic point of view. Revenue expenditure on education and training centres is a case in point. Contrarily, certain expenditures on capital account may, in fact, be current expenditures from a purely economic angle, e.g. capital outlay on defence.
3. Revenue expenditure, as shown in the budget, groups together direct expenditure on goods and services and expenditure of the nature of mere transfers (like pensions) intended to add to incomes of others. These have to be isolated and treated separately. Similarly, capital outlays in the budget group together capital grants, investment in shares, and direct outlays by the government on construction, machinery and equipment. These categories, however, have different significance and therefore need to be viewed separately. Thus, capital grants are outright transfers intended to add to the investible resources of the rest of the economy, investment in shares increases government's claim against enterprises falling outside the government sector, and direct outlays increase stock of physical assets in the government sector.

With the above rationale in view, the Economic Division of the Ministry of Finance prepared and issued for the first time an Economic Classification of the Central Government Budget in 1957-58. Ever since, this exercise is regularly done shortly after the presentation of the budget every year. To quote, "in brief, this classification involves arranging the expenditures and receipts of the Central Government including those of Railways and Post and Telegraphs by significant economic categories, distinguishing current from capital outlays, spending for goods and services from transfers to individuals and institutions, tax receipts by kind from other receipts and from borrowing and intergovernmental loans and grants etc." [3]

Therefore, to understand and analyse the economic impact of Government transactions, particularly in the context of the Five Year Plans, it is necessary to regroup budgetary data into meaningful economic categories. The methodology of economic classification of the budget is explained below.

5.3 Methodology of Economic Classification of the Budget

Economic classification of the budget is prepared by regrouping government transactions in a set of six accounts. In this system of six accounts a distinction is drawn between transactions in goods, services, and transfers (accounts 1 to 3) and financial transactions which affect the net claims of the government on the rest of the economy. (accounts 4 to 6). Transactions in goods, services, and transfers are again divided into current transactions (accounts 1 and 2) and capital transactions (account 3). Finally, a distinction is drawn between current transactions of government administration (account 1) and the current transactions of departmental commercial undertakings (account 2).

A brief description of each of the six accounts with reference to the 2006-07 budget of the Central Government is given below.

Account 1: Transactions in Commodities and Services and Transfers: Current Account of Government Administration

The expenditure side of this account (Table 5.1) is concerned with Government consumption expenditure and current transfers to others. On the revenue side, it indicates current receipts from taxation, fees and the property incomes of the government. If total revenue is more than the total expenditure, the difference will be represented as savings on the current account. Together with the savings of the departmental commercial undertakings it represents the savings of the Central Government available for capital formation.

Table 5.1: Account 1: Transactions in Commodities and Services and Transfers: Current Account of Government Administration: Budget 2006-07

(Rs. crore)

Expenditure		Revenue	
1. Consumption expenditure	1,27,078	6. Tax receipts	3,27,205
1.1 Wages and salaries	49,066	7. Income from property and enterprises	49,436
1.2 Commodities and services	78,012	8. Fees and miscellaneous receipts	21,200
2. Transfer payments	3,37,030	9. Total	3,97,842
3. Total expenditure (1+2)	4,64,109		
4. Saving on current account	(-) 66,267		
5. Total	3,97,842		

Source: Government of India, Ministry of Finance, *An Economic and Functional Classification of the Central Government Budget*, 2006-07.

Government's consumption expenditure shown in this account comprises wages and salaries paid to employees, and current expenditure incurred on the purchase of commodities and services. In other words, it indicates the value of goods and factors drawn into Government's current use, for development as well as non-development purpose.

Transfer payments shown in this account are of the nature of mere transfers intended to add to the incomes of others. A distinction is drawn between current transfers and capital transfers on the ground that current transfers supplement the income accounts of the recipients while capital transfers are intended to assist capital expenditure. This account deals with current transfers only which comprise current grants to States, subsidies, pensions etc.

Account 2: Transactions in Commodities and Services and Transfers: Current Account of Departmental Commercial Undertakings

This account (Table 5.2) gives components of the costs and incomes of departmental commercial undertakings like Railways, Posts, and Telecommunications.

Table 5.2: Account 2: Transactions in Commodities and Services and Transfers: Current Account of Departmental Commercial Undertakings: Budget 2006-07

(Rs. crore)

Expenditure		Receipts	
1. Wages and salaries	16,778	10. Gross sale proceeds	85,457
2. Pension payments	9,296	(a) Railways	61,834
3. Commodities and services	30,704	(b) Manufacturing activities of railway workshops and production units	8,556
4. Repairs and maintenance	12,794	(c) Posts	4,999
5. Interest	4,085	(d) Others	10,068
6. Provision for depreciation	4,441	11. Interest receipts	730
7. Profits transferred to C/A of Govt. (administration)	1,540	12. Total	86,188
8. Retained profits of depart. Commercial undertakings	6,549		
9. Total	86,188		

Source: Same as for Table 5.1.

The activities of these departments are entrepreneurial in nature. Current expenditure of these undertakings constitutes intermediate expenditure that enters into prices of goods and services as they are sold to other sectors of the economy. Thus, they are different in character from final outlays by administrative departments. Similarly, sale proceeds of these undertakings are different from tax receipts of purely administrative departments which have no income of their own. In short, account 2 is profit and loss account of departmental commercial undertakings.

Account 3: Transactions in Commodities and Services and Transfers: Capital Account of Government Administration and Departmental Commercial Undertakings

This account (Table 5.3) shows total capital outlay representing physical asset formation by administration and departmental commercial undertakings and capital transfers. A distinction between administration and commercial departments is not meaningful in respect of capital expenditure because the entire expenditure on capital formation is a final expenditure which is a charge on the national product and for which Government has to find resources either from its own savings or by drawing on private savings. The balancing item of this account represents deficit on all transactions in commodities and services and transfers.

Table 5.3: Account 3: Transactions in Commodities and Services and Transfers: Capital Account of Government Administration and Departmental Commercial Undertakings: Budget 2006-07

(Rs. crore)

Disbursements		Receipts	
1. Gross fixed capital formation	37,388	5. Gross savings	(-) 55,277
1.1 Buildings and other construction	31,316	5.1 Savings on C/A (item 4 in a/c 1)	(-) 66,267
(a) New outlays	28,276	5.2 Retained profits of departmental commercial undertakings (item 8 in a/c 2)	6,549
(b) Renewals and replacements	3,039	5.3 Depreciation provision (item 6 in a/c 2)	4,441
1.2 Machinery and equipment	6,072	6. Capital transfers	2,617
(a) New outlays	4,909	7. Balance: deficit on all transactions in commodities and services and transfers	1,33,655
(b) Renewals and replacements	1,162	8. Total	80,995
2. Increase in work stores	1,227		
3. Capital transfers	42,380		
3.1 Grants for capital formation	39,547		
3.2 Gratuities etc.	2,833		
4. Total	80,995		

Source: Same as for Table 5.1.

Account 4: Changes in Financial Assets: Capital Account of Government Administration and Departmental Commercial Undertakings

This account (Table 5.4) deals with transactions in financial assets, i.e. investment in shares, and loans granted to rest of the economy. Loans are sub-divided into those meant for capital formation and those for other purposes. Investment in shares and loans for capital formation indicate the extent to which the Central Government promotes capital formation through financial assistance. This is in addition to the capital formation directly undertaken by it. The balancing item of this account, representing net outlay on financial investments and loans together with the deficit in account 3 represents the total requirement of finance to be met out of net domestic and net foreign borrowings and by deficit financing.

Table 5.4: Account 4: Changes in Financial Assets: Capital Account of Government Administration and Departmental Commercial Undertakings: Budget 2006-07

(Rs. crore)

Outgoings		Incomings	
1. Investment in shares	9,052	7. Repayment of loans by States and others	7,999
2. Loans for capital formation	7,038	8. Disinvestment in shares	3,840
3. Other loans	1,823	9. Balance: Net increase in financial assets	6,202
4. Subscription to international financial organisations	128	10. Total	18,041
5. Net purchase of domestic gold and silver	0		
6. Total	18,041		

Source: Same as for Table 5.1.

Account 5: Changes in Financial Liabilities: Capital Account of Government Administration and Departmental Commercial Undertakings

This account (Table 5.5) is the borrowing account of the Government. It deals with the provision of finance for meeting the deficit emerging from accounts 3 and 4. Incomings show gross market borrowing, gross borrowing from abroad, net accretions to small savings, provident funds and other debt. The outgoings on this account include repayments on account of market borrowings and foreign loans. The balance emerging from this account represents net increase in financial liabilities and together with adjustment in cash balance is equivalent to the sum of balancing items in accounts 3 and 4.

Table 5.5: Account 5: Changes in Financial Liabilities: Capital Account of Government Administration and Departmental Commercial Undertakings: Budget 2006-07

(Rs. crore)

Outgoings		Incomings	
1. Repayment of market loans	39,079	5. Market loans	1,52,856
2. Repayment of external debt	7,741	6. External debt	16,065
3. Balance: Net increase in financial liabilities	1,39,857	7. Small savings (net)	4,523
4. Total	1,86,677	8. State provident funds	6,000
		9. Deposit of non-government PF (net)	0
		10. Treasury bills (net)	(-) 110
		11. Miscellaneous capital receipts	7,342
		12. Total	1,86,677

Source: Same as for Table 5.1.

Account 6: Cash and Capital Reconciliation Account of Government Administration and Departmental Commercial Undertakings

This is the reconciliation account (Table 5.6) summing up the net position in respect of accounts 3, 4 and 5 and showing the effect of all transactions of the Government on its cash position. The net variation in the cash balance read with net sales of treasury bills in account 5 provides a conventional measure of the Central Government's budgetary deficit.

Table 5.6: Account 6: Cash and Capital Reconciliation Account of Government Administration and Departmental Commercial Undertakings: Budget 2006-07

(Rs. crore)

Outgoings		Incomings	
1. Deficit on all transactions in commodities and services and transfers (balancing item in a/c 3)	1,33,655	5. Net increase in financial liabilities (balancing item in a/c 5)	1,39,857
2. Net increase in financial assets (balancing item in a/c 4)	6,202	6. Decrease in cash balance	0
3. Increase in cash balance	0	7. Total	1,39,857
4. Total	1,39,857		

Source: Same as for Table 5.1.

It will be observed that each of the six accounts explained above is intended to bring out a meaningful set of totals. Thus, account 1 shows, on the expenditure side, Government's consumption expenditure and current transfers to others, and on the revenue side it indicates current receipts from taxation, fees and the property income of the Government.

Account 2 highlights components of costs and incomes of departmental commercial undertakings.

Account 3 deals with gross capital formation by the Central Government and its departmental undertakings and capital transfers to others. On receipt side it indicates Government savings as emerging from accounts 1 and 2. Account 4 explains changes in financial assets of the Government and their breakdown into investment in shares, loans for capital formation and other purposes and repayment of loans. Accounts 5 and 6 explain the manner in which Government draws upon the saving of other sectors to meet the net requirement for financing transactions detailed in the first four accounts.

5.3.1 Derivation of Significant Economic Aggregates: The six accounts presented above contain reclassified data of the Central Government budget. From these accounts are derived certain economic magnitudes to understand the economic impact of Government's budgetary transactions on the economy.

These economic aggregates are:

A. Government's total expenditure.
B. Government's final outlays.
C. Capital formation out of the budgetary resources of the Government.
D. Net capital formation and savings of the Government.
E. Various measures of deficit in the Government's budgetary transactions.
F. Income generation by the Government.

A brief description and the method of derivation of each of these aggregates with reference to the 2002-03 budget of the Central Government of India is as follows.

A. Total Expenditure of the Government: Total expenditure of the Government is composed of final outlays, disbursements by way of transfer payments, financial investments, and loans to the rest of the economy. Details of total expenditure are given in Table 5.7.

B. Final Outlays of the Government: These outlays represent direct demand for goods and services for consumption and capital formation. In a system of national accounts these final outlays get linked up with the consumption expenditure and capital formation in other sectors of the economy. Details of final outlays are given in Table 5.7.

Table 5.7: Central Government's Total Expenditure: Budget 2006-07

(Rs. crore)

1. Final outlays	1,65,694	= Direct demand for commodities and services
(a) Government's consumption expenditure (item 1 in a/c 1)	1,27,078	= Direct demand for consumption goods and services
(b) Gross capital formation (items 1 and 2 in a/c 3)	38,615	= Direct demand for capital goods and services
2. Transfer payments to the rest of the economy	3,79,410	= Addition to incomes of other sectors
(a) Current transfers (item 2 in a/c 1)	3,37,030	= Addition to income accounts of other sectors
(b) Capital transfers (item 3 in a/c 3)	42,380	= Addition to capital accounts of other sectors
3. Financial investments in shares and loans to rest of the economy (a/c 4)	18,041	= Assistance for capital formation (only items 1 and 2 in a/c 4)
4. Total expenditure (1+2+3)	5,63,145	

Source: Same as for Table 5.1.

C. Capital Formation Out of the Budgetary Resources of the Government: Capital formation by the Government out of its budgetary resources may be classified into two categories: (a) capital formation directly undertaken by it, and (b) capital formation through assistance to the rest of the economy in the form of grants, loans, and investment in shares. The components of this aggregate are given in Table 5.8.

Table 5.8: Gross Capital Formation Out of the Budgetary Resources of the Central Government: Budget 2006-07

(Rs. crore)

1. Gross capital formation by the Central Government	38,615
1.1 Gross fixed capital formation (item 1 in a/c 3)	37,388
1.2 Increase in works store (item 2 in a/c 3)	1,227
2. Financial assistance for capital formation to the rest of the economy	55,637
2.1 Grants for capital formation (item 3.1 in a/c 3)	39,547
2.2 Investments in shares (item 1 in a/c 4)	9,052
2.3 Loans for capital formation (item 2 in a/c 4)	7,038
3. Gross capital formation out of the budgetary resources of the Central Government (1+2)	94,252

Source: Same as for Table 5.1.

D. Net Capital Formation and Net Savings by the Government: Gross capital formation denotes the resources utilised for maintaining and expanding the capital base of the economy. Net capital formation then means expanding the capital base of the economy.

(i) Net Capital Formation. For understanding the expansionary impact of budgetary operations, the magnitude of net capital formation and net savings are more relevant. The difference between net capital formation and net savings represents the expansionary effect. Net capital formation by the Government means net addition to the stock of fixed assets and inventories. This figure is arrived at by deducting from gross fixed capital formation (i.e. investment in buildings, public works, equipment and other fixed assets) the provision for expenditure on renewals and replacements by departmental commercial undertakings.

The composition of net capital formation is shown in Table 5.9.

(ii) Gross and net Savings. Gross and net savings of the Government and its departmental commercial undertakings are shown in Table 5.10.

Table 5.9: Central Government's Net Capital Formation: Budget 2006-07

(Rs. crore)

1. Construction works (item 1.1(a) in a/c 3)	28,277
2. Machinery and equipment (item 1.2(a) in a/c 3)	4,910
3. Increase in works stores (item 2 in a/c 3)	1,227
4. Net capital formation by the Central Government (1+2+3)	34,414

Source: Same as for Table 5.1.

Table 5.10: Gross and Net Savings of the Central Government: Budget 2006-07

(Rs. crore)

1. Savings of Government Administration (item 5.1 in a/c 3)	(-) 66,267
2. Retained profits of departmental commercial undertakings (item 5.2 in a/c 3)	6,549
3. Depreciation provision of departmental commercial undertakings (item 5.3 in a/c 3)	4,441
4. Gross savings by the Government (1+2+3)	(-) 55,277
5. Expenditure on renewals and replacements of departmental commercial undertakings (items 1.1(b) and 1.2(b) in a/c 3)	4,202
6. Net savings by the Government (4-5)	(-) 59,479

Source: Same as for Table 5.1.

E. Various Measures of Deficit in the Central Government's Budgetary Transactions: The excess of direct net capital formation over net savings measures the *income deficit* of the Government (Table 5.11). In other words, it measures the gap between the Government's net savings and net capital formation.

Table 5.11: Income Deficit of the Central Government: Budget 2006-07

(Rs. crore)

1. Net capital formation, i.e. net investment by the Central Government (item 4 in Table 5.9)	34,414
2. Net savings by the Central Government (item 6 of Table 5.10)	(-) 59,479
3. Income deficit of the Central Government (1-2)	93,892

Source: Same as for Table 5.1.

This gap, when adjusted with net capital transfers (i.e. item 3 in account 3 minus item 6 in account 3) gives the balancing item in account 3 which represents the deficit on all transactions in commodities and services and transfers. When this is added to the deficit arising out of Government's net transactions in financial assets (balancing item in account 4), it represents another measure of deficit denoting Government's total requirement of finance (Table 5.12). In other words, this requirement is the sum of the balancing items in accounts 3 and 4.

The financing pattern of the deficit indicated in Table 5.12 is given in Table 5.13.

Table 5.12: Central Government's Total Requirement of Finance: Budget 2006-07

(Rs. crore)

1. Deficit on all transactions in commodities and services and transfers (balancing item in a/c 3)	1,33,655
2. Net increase in financial assets (balancing item in a/c 4)	6,202
3. Total requirement of finance (1+2)	1,39,857

Source: Same as for Table 5.1.

Table 5.13: Sources for Meeting Government's Total Requirement of Finance: Budget 2006-07

(Rs. crore)

1. Net borrowings	139857
1.1 Market loans (net)	113778
1.2 External debt (net)	8324
1.3 Small savings (net)	4523
1.4 State/public provident funds (net)	6000
1.5 Special deposits of non-government provident funds	--
1.6 Medium and long-term loans	--
1.7 Miscellaneous capital receipts (net)	(-) 30208
1.8 Sales of treasury bills to the rest of the economy (net)	37440
2. Draw down of cash balance	--
3. Total (1+2)	139857

Source: Same as for Table 5.1.

F. Income Generation by the Government: Yet another significant economic aggregate is income generation out of the budgetary operations of the Government. The procedure to derive this aggregate is detailed in Table 5.14.

5.3.2 Limitations of Economic Classification: Economic classification of the budget, though useful in various respects, has limitations of its own. The economic classification of the budget discussed above pertains to Central Government transactions and does not include the transactions of non-departmental public undertakings, State Governments, and local bodies. Thus, it presents a partial assessment of the role of Government vis-à-vis the rest of the economy in promoting economic development and stability.

Table 5.14: Income Generation Out of the Budgetary Operations of the Central Government: Budget 2006-07

(Rs. crore)

1. Wages & salaries paid by the Governmentadministration (item 1.1 in a/c 1)	49,066
2. Net output of departmental commercial undertakings	35,588
(a) Wages and salaries (item 1 in a/c 2) and wages and salaries component of repairs and maintenance (1/2 of item 4 in a/c 2)	23,176
(b) Interest (item 5 in a/c 2)	4,085
(c) Profits transferred to administration and retained (items 7 and 8 in a/c 2) plus excess of depreciation provision over renewals and replacement (item 6 in a/c 2 minus the sum of items 1.1(b) and 1.2(b) in a/c 3)	8,328
3. Wages and salaries component of Government outlays on construction [1/3 of item 1.1 (a) in a/c 3]	9,426
4. Total (1+2+3)	94,080

Source: Same as for Table 5.1.

Another limitation of economic classification of the budget is that it can record only those governmental influences which can be measured by changes in the volume and composition, e.g. Government expenditure. The regulatory activities of the Government which may effectively influence the level of economic activities are not revealed in this classification. Furthermore, economic classification of the budget does not provide estimates of the effects of governmental activities on the distribution of income or the effects of this distribution among various sectors of the economy.

5.4 Cross-classification of the Budget since 1967-68

An economic-cum-functional classification of the Central Government's budgetary transactions is annually prepared by the Ministry of Finance since 1967-68. Table 5.15 presents a summarised version of this classification for the year 2006-07. Columns in the Table correspond to the functional categories and rows indicate their economic character. Thus, reading along columns one gets the break-up of each functional category under economic heads. For example, it would show as to how much of the total expenditure on social services is in the form of direct current expenditure, how much in the form of grants and loans, and how much in the form of capital formation. Reading row-wise, one finds the break-up of each economic category of expenditure into functional heads. For example, one can understand the break-up of consumption expenditure into civil,

Table 5.15: Economic-cum-Functional Classification of the Central Government Expenditure: Budget 2006-07

(Rs. crore)

Functional → Economic ↓	Services other than defence	Defence services	Social & economic services	Unallocable	Total
1. Consumption expenditure	24,408	88,888	13,782	--	1,27,078
2. Transfer payments	16,240	0	1,12,354	2,08,435	3,37,030
3. Gross capital formation	4,392	0	34,223	0	38,615
4. Capital transfers	1,623	0	37,924	2,833	42,380
5. Investment in shares	3,901	0	5,151	0	9,052
6. Loans for capital formation	65	0	6,973	0	7,038
7. Other loans	28	0	1,495	300	1,823
8. Subscription to international financial organisations	128	0	0	0	128
9. Net purchase of gold and silver	0	0	0	0	0
Total	50,786	88,888	2,11,902	2,11,568	5,63,144

Source: Government of India, Ministry of Finance, *An Economic and Functional Classification of the Central Government Budget*, 2006-07, pp. 22-23 (rearranged data).

defence, social, and economic services.

Cross or economic-cum-functional classification provides the break-up of Government expenditure not only by economic categories but also by functional heads. This classification is important to understand the economic significance of Government expenditure for various purposes. Thus, expenditure on medical facilities (a functional head) is split between economic categories such as current expenditure, capital expenditure, and various types of transfers and loans. Conversely, cross-classification shows how expenditure on a particular economic category, say capital formation is divided according to different purposes of public activities like education, labour welfare, family planning, sanitation etc.

Thus, under a scheme of cross classification, functional classification of expenditure can be analysed according to its economic character and economic classification of expenditure can be analysed according to the functions performed by it. Therefore, the two types of classification supplement each other and they need to be shown together for purposes of general budgeting.

Cross-classification of expenditure presents in one statement basic information on public expenditure both by economic character and by the function of the expenditure. Such a classification is particularly helpful in drawing up a programme of projected expenditure covering a period of years, and in evaluating the progress of actual expenditure.

Notes

1. United Nations, Department of Economic Affairs, *A Manual for Economic and Functional Classification of Government Transactions* (New York, 1958), p. 4.
2. *Ibid.*, p. 33.
3. Government of India, Ministry of Finance, *An Economic and Functional Classification of the Central Government Budget,* 1979-80, p. 111.

Part III: Tax Structure Developments

This Part consists of the following 5 sections.

Section A: Pre-Independence Tax System
Chapter 6: Pre-Independence Tax System

Section B: Trends in Combined (Centre and State) Tax Revenues
Chapter 7: Constitutional Provisions Pertaining to Taxes
Chapter 8: Trends in Tax-GDP Ratio
Chapter 9: Direct and Indirect Taxes
Chapter 10: Buoyancy and Elasticity of Tax Revenue
Chapter 11: Distribution of Tax Burden (Tax Incidence)
Chapter 12: Tax Evasion: Magnitude, Causes and Remedial Measures

Section C: Central Taxes
Chapter 13: Trends in Central Taxes
Chapter 14: Income Tax
Chapter 15: Wealth Tax
Chapter 16: Union Excise Duties
Chapter 17: Taxation of Services
Chapter 18: Customs Duties

Section D: State Taxes
Chapter 19: Trends in State Taxes
Chapter 20: Taxation of Agricultural Income
Chapter 21: Sales Tax

Section E: International Aspects of Indian Taxation
Chapter 22: International Aspects of Indian Taxation (Double Taxation)

Section A: Pre-Independence Tax System

This Section gives a brief account of tax system in ancient India, during Mughal period and subsequently during British rule. It provides the necessary backdrop to the post-Independence evolution of the present structure of taxation in India. It contains the following chapter

6

Pre-Independence Tax System

Taxes are as old as civilizations. Taxes are imposed so that a government may perform its traditional functions (defence, and maintenance of law and order), undertake welfare and developmental activities, and make provision for public goods to satisfy collective needs of the people. It has also to pay for its own administration. It needs financial resources for these purposes and taxation is one method of transferring money from private to public hands. Taxation is necessary because what the government gives it must first take away.

6.1 Taxes in Ancient India

References to taxes in ancient India are found in *Arthashatra* the famous work of Kautilya (also known as Chanakya and Vishnugupta). He wrote, "Extract taxes just as bees extract honey from the flowers without hurting the flowers."

Arthashatra embodies values, norms, and beliefs pertaining to public administration, economics, ethics and diplomacy. Taxes in ancient India were levied both in cash and in kind and were collected by local officers. Major sources of revenue for the king included land tax, octroi, taxes on liquor shops, gambling houses and on professionals like dancing girls.

In his work *Raghuvansa*, Kalidasa, the greatest Sanskrit scholar of ancient India, observed, "Just as the sun extracts water from the reservoirs and gives it back in the form of showers, so does the ruler extract tax from his subjects and give it back to them in the form of prosperity."

6.2 Taxes during Mughal Period

Vivid accounts of tax system during Mughal rule are found in contemporary court chronicles, particularly *Ain-i-Akbari* (the official chronicler of the reign of Emperor Akbar) compiled by Abul Fazl, one of Akbar's courtiers. The work describes, *inter alia*, matters pertaining to taxes, other revenues, expenditure, salaries of public officers etc. Travel accounts of visitors, especially those who came from the West, also throw light on the Mughal system of revenue administration.

In fact, Babur, founder of the Mughal rule in India, had no tax policy as such. To quote, "Babur did not even have an orderly tax system. Plundering was his main source of state income, and he wrote very frankly in his diary that he had decided to advance on an area to the west of Agra at a time when he needed money, because there were some pickings left for him there. In October 1528, he had to levy a tax on his amirs of 30 per cent of their salaries, since he had given away everything in India and did not have enough funds at his disposal for war equipment, gunpowder and the operation of cannons." [1]

Land revenue by far was the most important source of income for the Mughal rulers. Other means of lining the emperor's treasury were gifts, import and export duties and *jizya* (or *zazia*). [2] That the tax policy of the Mughals was guided by religious considerations also is clear from the following account, "In the large market cities, in the sea harbours and at the borders of the Empire, import and export duties of 2.5 per cent ad valorem were levied; later on Aurangzeb doubled this percentage for Hindus who had to make use of Muslim friends to evade this taxation. There were monopolies on some goods, for instance on salt and saltpetre. The monopoly on indigo yielded a few million rupees to the Treasury.

Jizya, the tax on non-Muslims, abolished by Akbar, was reintroduced by Aurangzeb in 1679 in the form of a degressive income tax. Those who had more than 2,500 rupees per year paid 48 dirhams (tax sums were expressed in dirhams in accordance with the words of the shariah; 48 dirhams was about 13 rupees), those with an income between 250 and 2,500 rupees paid 24 dirhams (about 6.5 rupees), those of limited means, who had an income of at least 52 rupees and could support a wife and children, paid 12 dirhams (about 3.25 rupees) and the real minimum wage earners paid nothing at all (Table 6.1). For the levying of the *jizya* a special service with new collectors of taxes was created. This service was led by a high official who had to control whether the colleting was taking place and whether it was done in a regular way. It is not known how much the new tax yielded, but that was not very important either, for the religious motive – encouraging Hindus to convert to Islam – prevailed over the financial objective." [3] The discriminatory tax policy based on religion adopted by some of the Mughal rulers was a contributory factor to the decline of Mughal empire after the death of Aurangzeb in 1707.

6.3 Taxes during British Rule

Prior to 1947, India was a dependency of the United Kingdom and encompassed the entire area which now forms the three countries of India, Pakistan, and Bangladesh. It consisted of the British Indian Provinces, and the Indian Princely States. The political and economic scene changed greatly after 1947 when India emerged as an independent country merging with itself the former Princely States (called Part B States), but excluding areas of the other two countries mentioned above. Although it is desirable to trace historical developments of a subject to understand its present features and trends, the changed circumstances noted above fail to provide comparable data for the purpose. Therefore, only a brief account of the tax system prevailing prior to Independence is presented here. However, historical account of individual taxes has been attempted at relevant places. It is noteworthy that consequent upon the financial integration of Part B States with the Indian Union from April 1, 1950, comparable data of public revenues for the whole country are available from 1950-51 onwards and the same have been used in this book.

Table 6.1: Rate of Zazia during the Rule of Aurangzeb

Income level per year	Rate of Zazia
More than 2,500 rupees	48 dirhams (or 13 rupees)
Between 250 and 2,500 rupees	24 dirhams (or 6.5 rupees)
Between 52 and 250 rupees	12 dirhams (or 3.25 rupees)
Less than 52 rupees	Exempted

Ferdinand H.M. Grapperhaus has noted, "According to *The Cambridge Economic History of India, Volume I*, the value of the rupee in 1600 should be equated with twelve rupees in 1970. Considering the inflation since then, which made the price index for commodities rise by a factor of six, we may equate a rupee in 1600 to seventy rupees in 1995." (Ferdinand H.M. Grapperhaus, *Tax Tales from the Second Millennium* (International Bureau of Fiscal Documentation (Amsterdam), 1998, p. 110.

Source: 1. Ferdinand H.M. Grapperhaus, *Tax Tales from the Second Millennium* (International Bureau of Fiscal Documentation (Amsterdam), 1998, pp. 143-144.

The tax system of British India reflected characteristics of a traditional agricultural economy. Revenues of the Central Government were dominated by customs duties as domestic requirements for manufactured goods were met mostly by imports, chiefly from Britain and other Commonwealth countries. Import duties were levied on almost all items of imports whereas major items subject to export duties were jute and tea in which India enjoyed near-monopoly in the world market. Various customs and tariff enactments were passed from time to time but the following two were the main: 1. The Sea Customs Act, 1878, and 2. The Tariff Act, 1934. After Independence, the Sea Customs Act and other allied enactments were repealed by a consolidating and amending legislation entitled the Customs Act, 1962. Similarly, the Tariff Act of 1934 was repealed by the Customs Tariff Act, 1975.

Another important source of tax revenue for the Central Government was excise duty levied on a few commodities. Excise taxation in its modern form dates back to 1894 when for the first time a duty at the rate of 5 per cent *ad valorem* was imposed on cotton yarn of more than twenty counts. Excise at the rate of 6 *annas* [4] per Imperial Gallon was imposed on motor spirit in 1917 and on kerosene at the rate of one *anna* per Imperial Gallon in 1922. Another landmark in the history of excise taxation was the year 1934 when excise duties were imposed on sugar, matches, and steel ingots. Duties were imposed on tyres in 1941 and on vegetable products, and tobacco in 1943, mainly to meet the exigencies of war finances. The year 1944 saw excise duties being imposed on coffee, tea and betel nut. Cigarettes came within the excise net in 1948 and mill-made cotton cloth in 1949. Before 1944, excise duties were levied under separate enactments for different goods, e.g. tobacco levies were imposed under the Tobacco (Excise Duty) Act, 1943. About 16 such separate laws were in force till 1944. However, in that year the various enactments were consolidated into the Central Excises and Salt Act and the Central Excise Rules, 1944.

Among the direct taxes, the only important source of revenue was the income tax introduced in India by the British in 1860 to overcome the financial difficulties created by the events of 1857. Out of a Central tax revenue of Rs. 73.90 crore in 1938-39, customs accounted for Rs. 40.51 crore, Central excises Rs. 8.66 crore, and income tax Rs. 13.74 crore (Table 6.2).

Table 6.2 Structure of Central and Provincial Tax Revenues: 1938-39

(Rs. crore)

Central tax revenue		Provincial tax revenue*	
Total taxes	73.90	Total taxes	56.07
of which		of which	
Customs	40.51	Land revenue	25.40
Taxes on income	13.74	State excises	13.08
Corporation tax	2.04	Stamps	9.53
Central excise duties	8.66	Registration	1.09
Salt duty	8.12	Devolution of taxes from the Centre	3.98

Note: Figures relate to undivided India.
* Data refer to nine Provinces including Sind and N.W.F.P. (now in Pakistan).
Source: Government of India, Ministry of Finance, *Report of the Taxation Enquiry Commission*, 1953-54, Vol. I, Tables 4 (p. 20), 5 (p. 23), and 7 (p. 25).

As for the British Indian Provinces, the chief source of income was land revenue followed by Provincial excises, mainly on liquor (Table 6.2). Although under the Government of India Act, 1935, Provincial Governments had been authorised to levy sales tax, it formed a very low component of their revenue till Independence. The Province of Bombay levied a tax on the sale of tobacco in

1938. A retail sales tax on motor spirit and lubricants was imposed by Central Provinces (now Madhya Pradesh) in the same year. A multi-point general sales tax was levied in Madras Province at the rate of half per cent in 1939 under the Madras General Sales Tax Act.

The Princely States did not form part of the structure of public finance of British India. They had separate budgets and separate sources of revenue. The maritime States imposed their own customs duties.

Notes

1. Ferdinand H.M. Grapperhaus, *Tax Tales from the Second Millennium* (International Bureau of Fiscal Documentation (Amsterdam), 1998, pp. 113-14.

2. It is an Islamic direct tax of the nature of a poll tax. In India, under some Mughal emperors, *zazia* or capitation tax was levied on all non-Muslims in lieu of military service which was required of all Mohammedans.

3. Ferdinand H.M. Grapperhaus, *Tax Tales from the Second Millennium, op. cit.*, pp. 143-44.

4. One *anna* was equal to 1/16th of a rupee before the introduction of the metric system of currency from April 1, 1957.

Section B: Trends in Combined (Centre and States) Tax Revenues

This Section describes constitutional provisions relating to taxation powers of the Central and State Governments, and critically evaluates post-Independence developments in the combined tax revenues of the two tiers of the Government. Other aspects covered are: trends in tax-GDP ratio, relative roles of direct and indirect taxes, buoyancy and elasticity of tax revenue, distribution of tax burden (tax incidence), and the problem of tax evasion.

7

Constitutional Provisions Pertaining to Taxes

This chapter explains the complex nature of constitutional provisions pertaining to taxation powers of different tiers of Governments in India.

7.1 India: A Federal Polity

The Constitution of India adopted on November 26, 1949, became operative on January 26, 1950. It provides for two layers of Government, one at the Central level, and the other at the level of the States. A federal polity of this kind requires division of powers and responsibilities between the Centre and the States and generally brings in its wake problems and conflicts in Centre-State relations. Other important countries of the world with federal set up of government are: U.S.A., Canada, Australia, Brazil, and Nigeria.

Why did the framers of the Constitution opt for a federal set up? Answering this question, the Commission on Centre-State Relations, 1988, observed, "In a country too large and diverse for a unitary form of Government, they envisaged a system which would be worked in co-operation by the two levels of government - national and regional - as a common endeavour to serve the people. Such a system, it was conceived, would be most suited to Indian conditions as it would at once have the advantages of a strong unified central power, and the essential values of federalism." [1]

The Constitution describes in detail the legislative powers and functions of the two tiers of Government. Under Article 246 read with Seventh Schedule of the Constitution, these powers have been defined through precise entries in the three lists in the Schedule. Thus, the Centre has exclusive powers to legislate in respect of matters contained in List I (Union List) such as defence, foreign affairs, citizenship, railways, posts and telegraph, telephones, broadcasting, airways, banking, coinage and currency. Entries 82 to 92C of this list pertain to taxation powers. Similarly, the States enjoy the power to legislate on matters mentioned in List II (State List) such as public order, police, public health, local government, agriculture and fisheries. Entries 45 to 63 of this list relate to taxation powers of the States. The Parliament and the State Legislatures have concurrent powers to make laws on any matters in List III (Concurrent List). The framers of the Constitution recognised that there was a category of subjects of common interest which could not be allocated exclusively either to the Union or the States. Some of the items included in the Concurrent List are: marriage and divorce, forests, economic and social planning, population control and family planning, legal, medical, and other professions. This list does not contain any head of taxation which means the Centre and the States have no concurrent powers of taxation. Residuary powers of legislation including taxation belong to the Centre as per Entry 97 of List I.

The foregoing three-fold division of subjects of legislation rests on the ground that matters of national concern are placed in the Union List and those of purely State or local significance in the State List. Matters of common Centre-State interest are included in the Concurrent List.

7.2 Centrally Biased Constitution and its Justification

From its very inception, the Constitution is loaded in favour of the Centre. Constitutional amendments effected subsequently have tilted the balance further in favour of the Centre. The concept of a strong Centre has been incorporated in the anatomy of the Constitution through a variety of devices, among which the following are noteworthy.

7.2.1 Supremacy of Union Legislative Power: Article 246 (2) and (3), and Article 254 (1) establish the supremacy of Union legislative power. Thus, where with respect to a matter, there is irreconcilable conflict or overlapping as between the three lists of the Seventh Schedule, the legislative power of the States must yield to that of the Union. This is how the non-obstante provisions of clauses (1) and (2) of Article 246 are interpreted. Similarly, Article 254 (1) states that a law made by a State legislature, repugnant to a law made by the Parliament or an existing law applicable in that State, in regard to any matter enumerated in the Concurrent List, shall be void to the extent of repugnancy.

7.2.2 Union Control over State Legislation: Articles 200 and 201 establish control of the Union executive over State legislation. Article 200 provides that a Bill passed by a State Legislature shall be presented to the Governor who may give his assent, withhold his assent or return the same for reconsideration by the legislature. However, if it is again passed by the State legislature, with or without amendment, he shall not withhold his assent. The Governor may also reserve the Bill for consideration of the President (in effect the Union Council of Ministers) who may in turn signify his assent, withhold the same or return it for reconsideration. However, in contrast to the position of the Governor, the President need not give his assent when such a Bill is returned with or without amendment after reconsideration by the legislature of the State (Article 201).

7.2.3 Emergency Provisions: Articles 352 and 360 provide for certain emergency provisions. Article 352 provides for proclamation by the President of a grave emergency whereby the security of India is threatened by war or external aggression or armed rebellion. When such a proclamation is in operation, the Union may assume for its organs all the legislative and executive powers of the States. A proclamation of emergency has the effect of converting the State List into Concurrent List and, therefore, if the Parliament legislates on any subject in the State List, the State laws, to the extent of repugnancy, shall be null and void and the law made by the Parliament shall prevail.

Article 360 envisages yet another type of emergency, i.e. financial emergency. If the President is satisfied that a situation has arisen whereby the financial stability or credit of India or of any part of its territory is threatened, he may proclaim a financial emergency. When such an emergency is in operation, the executive authority of the Union extends to directing any State for the purpose of securing observance of canons of financial propriety.

7.2.4 Restrictions on States' Taxation Powers: Constitution also imposes certain restrictions on the taxation powers of the States. Although a State legislature enjoys the power to levy any of the taxes mentioned in List II, in the case of certain taxes, this power is subject to restrictions imposed by substantive provisions of the Constitution. Some examples of these restrictions are as follows.

1. The power to impose taxes on the sale or purchase of goods other than newspapers belongs to the States vide entry 54 of List II. However, Article 286 ensures that sales taxes imposed by the States do not interfere with imports and exports or inter-State trade and commerce which are matters of national importance. In view of this, Article 286 places the following restrictions on the power of the States to enact sales tax legislation.

(a) No law of a State shall impose a tax on the sale or purchase of goods where such sale or purchase takes place (i) outside the State; or (ii) in the course of import into or export out of the territory of India; (b) with regard to inter-State trade, there are two restrictions (i) the power to tax sales taking place in the course of inter-State trade and commerce belongs to the Union vide entry 92A of List I in the Seventh Schedule, and (ii) the sales tax on intrastate sales of 'declared goods' (i.e. goods of special importance in inter-State trade) is subject to certain restrictions in terms of the nature of the levy and the rate of tax.

2. A State legislature is empowered to levy a tax on professions, trade, calling or employment vide entry 60 of List II. However, the total amount payable in respect of any one person to the State by way of such tax is not to exceed Rs. 2,500 per annum [Article 276(2)].

7.2.5 Restrictions on the Borrowing Powers of the State Governments: Under Article 292 the executive power of the Centre extends to borrowing, either within or outside India, upon the security of the Consolidated Fund of India, within such limits, if any, as may from time to time be fixed by Parliament. However, the borrowing power of a State (Article 293) is subject to a number of restrictions: (i) it cannot borrow outside India; (ii) it can borrow within the territory of India subject to the following conditions (a) limitations as may be imposed by the State Legislature, (b) consent of the Union Government to raise fresh loan if the Union has guaranteed an outstanding loan of the State, (c) consent of the Union to raise fresh loan if a Union loan to the State remains outstanding. Since all the States are in debt to the Centre, they have to obtain Centre's permission for raising loans. These restrictions are meant to avoid uncontrolled borrowings by the States and thus to prevent the possibility of any State becoming defaulter or insolvent.

7.2.6 President's Rule: Lastly, there is the controversial Article 356. According to it, if the President on receipt of a report from the Governor of a State, or otherwise, is satisfied that a situation has arisen in which the Government of the State cannot be carried on in accordance with the provisions of the Constitution, he may by proclamation assume to himself all or any of the functions of the State Government. He may also declare that the powers of the Legislature of the State shall be exercised by or under the authority of the Parliament.

In view of the above provisions of the Constitution, some experts call it unitary in extraordinary situations, such as war (or emergency), and federal in normal times. It is also called as a quasi-federal Constitution.

Similarly, a scrutiny of the taxation powers contained in the Union List and the State List reveals that major and elastic sources of tax revenue belong to the Centre while relatively inelastic sources of revenue come under the purview of State Governments. Moreover, the Centre enjoys almost unlimited powers to borrow from internal and external sources while the borrowing powers of the States are subject to various restrictions.

Why is there a need for a strong Centre? According to the Commission on Centre-State Relations, 1988, "The primary lesson of India's history is that, in this vast country, only that polity or system can ensure and protect its unity, integrity and sovereignty against external aggression and internal disruption, which ensures a strong Centre with paramount powers, accommodating, at the same time, its traditional diversities. This lesson of history did not go unnoticed by the framers of the Constitution. Being aware that, notwithstanding the common cultural heritage, without political cohesion, the country would disintegrate under the pressure of fissiparous forces, they accorded the highest priority to the ensurance of the unity and integrity of the country." [2] Moreover, the founding fathers were aware that several regions or areas of India were economically and industrially far behind in relation to others, a situation which exists even today. Revenue-raising capacities and revenue needs of various States also differ. To reduce these economic disparities, a policy of regional balanced development was necessary, and which could be effectively implemented by a financially and otherwise strong Centre.

7.3 Constitutional Provisions Pertaining to Taxes

The Constitution makes elaborate and complex arrangements relating to the distribution, between the Union and the States, of taxes, the power of borrowing, and provision for grants-in-aid by the Union to the States. The underlying philosophy of these arrangements is to place at the disposal of the two tiers of Government adequate financial resources to enable them to discharge their respective responsibilities under the Constitution.

7.3.1 Distribution of Taxation Powers: Article 265 of the Constitution specifically states that no taxes shall be levied or collected except by the authority of law. Entries 82 to 92B of List I in the Seventh Schedule refer to the taxation powers of the Union Government (Table 7.1). Entries 45 to 63 of List II in the same Schedule specify the taxation powers of the State Governments (Table 7.2). List III does not contain any head of taxation which means the Union and the States have no concurrent powers of taxation. The absence of joint occupancy of tax fields is meant to avoid duplication in tax administration, and minimise tax rivalry between the Centre and the States, and among the States themselves. [3] The residual powers of taxation, as in general legislation, belong to the Union vide entry 97 of List I in the Seventh Schedule. For example, gift tax (abolished in 1998) was imposed by the Union Government under these residual powers. Similarly, prior to the Constitution (Eighty-eighth Amendment) Act, 2003, service tax was imposed under these residual powers.

The Constitution does not provide for any taxation powers to local governments. However, the implication of Article 276 is that the taxes on professions, trades, callings or employment are for the benefit of a State or of a municipality, district board, local board or any other local authority. The States on their own may assign any of the taxes in the State List to the local bodies. The taxes generally assigned to local governments are property taxes, octroi, and taxes on vehicles.

The property of the Centre is exempt from State taxation under Article 285(1). Likewise, the property and incomes of the States are exempt from Union taxes [Article 289 (1)], except that Parliament may by law provide for Central taxation of any trading activities of a State which are not incidental to the ordinary functions of Government [Article 289(2)]. As regards Union Territories, the Parliament has the power to impose any tax included in the State List.

Table 7.1: Taxes within Union Jurisdiction as Enumerated in List I in the Seventh Schedule of the Constitution of India

S. No.	Entry No. in List I	Description of the tax/duty
1.	82	Taxes on income other than agricultural income.
2.	83	Duties of customs including export duties.
3.	84	Duties of excise except on alcoholic liquors and narcotics but including medicinal and toilet preparations containing alcohol.
4.	85	Corporation tax.
5.	86	Taxes on the capital value of assets, exclusive of agricultural land, of individuals.
6.	87	Estate duty in respect of property other than agricultural land.
7.	88	Duties in respect of succession to property other than agricultural land.
8.	89	Terminal taxes on goods and passengers carried by railway, sea or air; taxes on railway fares and freights.
9.	90	Taxes other than stamp duties on transactions in stock exchanges and future markets.
10.	91	Rates of stamp duty in respect of bills of exchange, cheques, promissory notes, bills of lading, letters of credit, policies of insurance, transfer of shares, debentures, proxies, and receipts.
11.	92	Taxes on the sale or purchase of newspapers and on advertisements published therein.
12.	92A*	Taxes on the sale or purchase of goods other than newspapers, where such sale or purchase takes place in the course of inter-State trade or commerce.
13.	92B**	Taxes on the consignment of goods (whether the consignment is to the person making it or to any other person), where such consignment takes place in the course of inter-State trade or commerce.
14.	92C***	Taxes on services
15.	97	Any tax not enumerated in List II or List III of the Seventh Schedule.

* Inserted by the Constitution (Sixth Amendment) Act, 1956.

** Inserted by the Constitution (Forty-sixth Amendment) Act, 1982.

*** Inserted by the Constitution (Eighty-eighth Amendment) Act, 2003.

Source: Government of India, Ministry of Law, Justice and Company Affairs, *The Constitution of India,* Seventh Schedule, List I.

Table 7.2: Taxes within State Jurisdiction as Enumerated in List II in the Seventh Schedule of the Constitution of India

S. No.	Entry No. in List II	Description of the tax/duty
1.	45	Land revenue.
2.	46	Taxes on agricultural income.
3.	47	Duties in respect of succession to agricultural land.
4.	48	Estate duty in respect of agricultural land.
5.	49	Taxes on lands and buildings.
6.	50	Taxes on mineral rights subject to any limitations imposed by Parliament by law relating to mineral development.
7.	51	Duties of excise on alcoholic liquors and narcotics manufactured or produced in the State but not including medicinal and toilet preparations containing alcohol.
8.	52	Taxes on the entry of goods into a local area for consumption, use or sale therein.
9.	53	Taxes on the consumption or sale of electricity.
10.	54*	Taxes on the sale or purchase of goods other than newspapers, subject to the provisions of Entry 92A of List I.
11.	55**	Taxes on advertisements other than advertisements published in the newspapers (and advertisements broadcast by radio or television)
12.	56	Taxes on goods and passengers carried by road or on inland waterways.
13.	57	Taxes on vehicles, whether mechanically propelled or not, suitable for use on roads, including tram-cars subject to the provisions of Entry 35 of List III.
14.	58	Taxes on animals and boats.
15.	59	Tolls.
16.	60***	Taxes on professions, trades, callings and employment.
17.	61	Capitation taxes.
18.	62	Taxes on luxuries, including taxes on entertainment, amusements, betting and gambling.
19.	63	Rates of stamp duty in respect of documents other than those specified in the provisions of List I with regard to rates of stamp duty.

*Substituted by the Constitution (Sixth Amendment) Act, 1956: ** The words 'and advertisements broadcast by radio or television' inserted by the Constitution (Forty-second Amendment), Act, 1976: *** The scope of these taxes is spelt out in Article 276, the clause (2) of which fixes the amount payable by a person on account of these taxes.

Source: Government of India, Ministry of Law, Justice and Company Affairs, *The Constitution of India*, Seventh Schedule, List II.

7.3.2 Restrictions on the Taxation Powers of the States: see section 7.2.4 of this chapter.

7.3.3 Rationale for Constitutional Arrangements: Constitutional division of taxation powers between the Union and the States rests on economic and administrative considerations. Taxes with an inter-State base, and those in the case of which uniformity in rates is desirable, are vested in the Central Government. Also, taxes which the taxpayer can evade by shifting his habitat, or where the place of residence is not a correct guide to the true incidence of the tax, belong to the Centre. Taxes which are location-specific and relate to subjects of local consumption are with the States. Broadly speaking, taxes on production, with some exceptions, are levied by the Centre, and taxes on sales by the State Governments. The distribution of taxation powers between the Centre and the States is meant to minimise tax problems in a federal set up such as double taxation, tax rivalry among States, duplicate tax administration, and tax evasion.

Commenting upon the soundness of the constitutional arrangements regarding division of taxation powers, the Commission on Centre-State Relations, 1988, observed, "A well balanced distribution of heads of taxation based on economic and administrative rationale between the Union and the States and adequate arrangements for sharing of resources is vital for the proper functioning of the two-tier polity. We are of the firm view that the basic scheme of the Constitution dividing the field of taxation between the Union and the States and incorporating adequate arrangements for sharing of resources between them, is sound and no major modifications in it are called for." [4]

7.3.4 Sharing of Central Taxes: Although the taxation powers allocated to the Union and the States are mutually exclusive, all the taxes and duties levied by the Union are not meant entirely for the purpose of the Union. Revenues from certain taxes and duties leviable by the Union are totally assigned to or shared with the States to supplement their revenues in accordance with their needs. It is a tribute to the foresight of the founding fathers that they realised that the sources of revenue allocated to the States may not prove sufficient in view of their growing welfare, maintenance, and developmental activities. Hence, specific provisions were made to set apart a portion of Central revenues for the benefit of States. These provisions indicate the flexibility of India's Constitution in terms of distribution of financial resources between different layers of the Government. They also make a distinction between the legislative power to *levy* a tax and the power to *appropriate* the proceeds of a tax so levied.

Prior to the eightieth amendment of the Constitution, two main Central taxes were shared with the states, namely income tax other than corporation tax and the Union excise duties. The sharing of the income tax was mandatory under Article

270 while that of the Union excise duties was discretionary under Article 272. There were also two tax rental arrangements with the States, where the Union Government collected the tax on behalf of the States and then distributed the proceeds among the States on the basis of criteria recommended by the Finance Commission. These were (i) additional duties of excise in lieu of sales tax on textiles, tobacco and sugar and (ii) grant in lieu of the tax on railway passenger fares.

The Constitution (Eightieth Amendment) Act, 2000, significantly changed the manner of distribution of Central tax collections between the Central and State Governments. Following this amendment, all central taxes were brought into a shareable pool and it became mandatory to assign a share from each central tax to the States. The amended article 270 provided for the sharing of all central taxes except taxes under Articles 268 and 269, earmarked cesses, and surcharges under Article 271. Only *net proceeds* are to be shared, and as such *cost of collection* has to be deducted to obtain the net proceeds as prescribed under Article 279. The proceeds are to be distributed among the States where the central taxes are *leviable* in *that year*. Article 269 was also amended and it now contains only central sales tax and consignment tax, which is not levied.

The objective of the Constitution (Eightieth Amendment) Act, 2000 was to construct a pool of all central taxes for sharing so that a holistic view can be taken and both sides could share in the aggregate buoyancy of the central tax revenues.

Furthermore, Constitution (Eighty-eighth Amendment) Act, 2003 placed service tax under the Union List in the Seventh Schedule and was brought under the purview of Article 268A which provides as follows:

"(1) Taxes on services shall be levied by the Government of India and such tax shall be collected and appropriated by the Government of India and the States in the manner provided in clause (2).

(2) The proceeds in any financial year of any such tax levied in accordance with the provisions of clause (1) shall be

(a) collected by the Government of India and the States;

(b) appropriated by the Government of India and the States;

in accordance with such principles of collection and appropriation as may be formulated by Parliament by law."

Thus, Article 268A specifies that the principles of collection and appropriation of taxes on services will be determined by Parliament. Prior to Eighty-eighth Amendment, the Central Government levied the service tax on specific services under its residual powers (vide entry 97 of List I in the Seventh Schedule). The sharing of this revenue was on the basis of the recommendations of the Finance Commission, as applicable to other central taxes. However, revenues from taxation of services that are taxed by the centre under article 268A rather than under article 270 is now excluded from the purview of the Finance Commission. In this connection, the Twelfth Finance Commission remarked, "With service taxes having been excluded from the ambit of the recommendations of the finance commission, the idea of an overall shareable pool of central taxes appears to be in the process of being reversed. While service taxes are likely to prove highly buoyant in the near future, these will not be subjected to sharing with the states under the Constitution, although other statutory arrangements can be made, which can include sharing as well as assignment. It may be noted that hitherto items under articles 268 and 269 were subjects that were generally of inter-state nature with limited revenue importance. These were wholly assigned to the states. In this context, it needs to be stressed that any legislation passed by Parliament with respect to appropriation of service tax proceeds must take care to ensure that the revenue accruing to the states through any proposed changes should not be less than the share that would accrue to them, had the entire service tax proceeds been part of the shareable pool." [5]

In short, after the Constitution (Eighty-eighth Amendment) Act, 2003, the Central taxes can be classified into the following categories.

Duties Levied by the Union but Collected and Appropriated by the States (Article 268): These include duties of excise on medicinal and toilet preparations containing alcohol, and stamp duties on bills of exchange etc. as mentioned in entries 84 and 91 of the Union List respectively.

Service Tax Levied by the Union and Collected and Appropriated by the Union and the States (Article 268A).

Taxes Levied and Collected by the Union but Assigned to the States (Article 269): These are: taxes on the sale or purchase of goods other than newspapers, where such sale or purchase takes place in the course of inter-State trade or commerce, and taxes on the consignment of goods (whether the consignment is to the person making it or to any other person), where such consignment takes place in the course of inter-State trade or commerce. These taxes correspond to entries 92A and 92B in the Union List. [6]

Taxes Levied and Distributed Between the Union and the States (Article 270): All taxes and duties referred to in the Union List shall be levied and collected by the Government of India and shall be distributed between the Union and the States with the following exceptions: (a) duties and taxes referred to in Articles 268 and 269, (b) surcharge on taxes and duties referred to in Article 271 and (c) any cess levied for specific purposes under any law made by Parliament.

7.3.5 Philosophy of Articles 268 and 269: Taxation arrangements under

Articles 268 and 269 of the Constitution are of special importance. They place under the charge of the Union the taxes and duties which have inter-State character and require uniformity in rate structure for the smooth conduct of business and trade activities throughout the country. These two Articles mention taxes/duties which shall be levied by the Centre but assigned completely to the States within which they are leviable.

A. Duties under Article 268: Article 268 mentions duties which shall be levied by the Union but collected and appropriated by the States within which they are leviable. These are duties of excise on medicinal and toilet preparations containing alcohol, and stamp duties, and correspond respectively to entries 84, and 91 of the Union List with corresponding qualification of entry 51 of the State List in the Seventh Schedule of the Constitution. The Eighth Finance Commission was asked for the first time to examine the scope for enhancing revenues from these duties.

Duties on medicinal and toilet preparations are imposed under the Medicinal and Toilet Preparations (Excise Duties) Act, 1955. It includes a range of medicinal items which are important from the viewpoint of public health policy. They have inter-State significance and therefore uniformity in regard to taxation is in larger national interest. Since the rates of duty on these preparations were increased in 1982 (the year in which the Commission was constituted), the Commission did not find any scope for enhancing this duty at that time.

Stamp duties are leviable on bills of exchange, cheques, promissory notes, bills of lading, letters of credit, policies of insurance, transfer of shares, debentures, proxies, and receipts. These documents are executed in the course of business and trade and they find place in the Union List to ensure uniformity of rates throughout the country for the smooth conduct of commercial and related transactions. Inter-State disparities in their rates and tax regulations can hinder, and even disrupt, the free flow of trade and commercial activities. The levy and collection of stamp duty is governed by the Indian Stamp Duty Act, 1899 which was last amended in 1976 when rates of stamp duty on certain instruments were revised.

After ascertaining the views of States and other relevant agencies, the Eighth Finance Commission did not think it desirable to raise the rates of stamp duty on bills of exchange, promissory notes, life insurance policies, transfer of shares, debentures, proxies, and receipts. Raising duty on these instruments was considered to be detrimental to the growth of trade and industry. The Commission also disfavoured reimposition of stamp duty on cheques. [7] However, the Commission opined that scope for raising the rates of duty exists in respect of bills of lading, letters of credit, and policies of general insurance.

B. Taxes and Duties under Article 269: Article 269 mentions taxes which shall be levied and collected by the Union but assigned completely to the States, in which they are leviable. These taxes are: (a) taxes on the sale or purchase of goods other than newspapers, where such sale or purchase takes place in the course of inter-State trade or commerce, and (b) taxes on the consignment of goods where such consignment takes place in the course of inter-State trade or commerce. These taxes correspond to entries 92A and 92B in the Union List in the Seventh Schedule of the Constitution. It is noteworthy that out of these two taxes only one is being levied at present, viz. inter-State sales tax (entry 92A).

7.3.6 Taxes and Duties in the Union List not being Levied at Present: These taxes/duties are discussed below individually along with the logic for retaining them with the Centre.

A. Entries 87 and 88: These two entries pertain to estate duty, and succession duty in respect of property other than agricultural land respectively. Since the incidence of both estate duty, and succession duty is on the same object, viz. property passing on the death of the owner to his successors, they are essentially similar in nature. However, while in the case of the estate duty, the value of the whole estate, even if situated in more than one State, is the base for taxation, the succession duty is relatable to the value of individual shares (i.e. parts of an estate) passing on to the successors.

The desirability of retaining both these duties with the Centre is self-evident. An individual may have properties located in more than one State and a total assessment of his estate can better be undertaken by the Union Government. Similarly, if succession duty is levied by the States, the persons inheriting properties in different States will have to deal with different tax rates and procedures. Moreover, if estate/succession duties are levied by the States, it may trigger unhealthy competition among the States, resulting into harassment of the assessees and hence litigation. On efficiency criterion (i.e. cost of collection) also it is desirable if these duties are levied and administered by the Union, thus avoiding duplication of tax administration. Moreover, the Union has better access to information and otherwise also it is in larger national interest to ensure uniformity with respect to these duties. It may be noted that estate duty was first imposed in India in 1953 when the Estate Duty Act of that year imposed a duty on the capital value of all property passing on the death of any person on or after October 15, 1953. It was abolished with effect from March 16, 1985.

B. Entry 89: It relates to terminal taxes on goods and passengers carried by railway, sea or air. However, by virtue of entry 52 of List II, States are competent to impose octroi (terminal tax) on entry of goods into a local area for consumption, use or sale. Likewise, under entry 56 of List II, States are empowered to levy taxes on goods and passengers carried by road or on inland waterways. Thus, the taxation powers in regard to the services of the major means of transport rest with the Union.

In a developing and diversifying economy like India, the importance of transport sector is self-evident. The growth of this vital infrastructure enlarges the size of the market and determines, *inter alia*, the level of private enterprise. Lest the free flow of inter-State trade should be hampered by differential State levies, the taxation of transport services is, by and large, with the Union Government. The Fifth and the Eighth Finance Commissions examined the scope for levying these taxes but expressed themselves against their imposition on grounds of administrative difficulties and meagre revenue potential. It is noteworthy that there already exists a terminal tax on passengers carried by railway from or to certain places of pilgrimage or where fairs or exhibitions are held. The proceeds of the tax are credited to the Consolidated Fund of the concerned States. The tax is restrictive and limited in scope and not a general terminal tax on passengers carried by railways to all places.

Entry 89 also refers to taxes on railway fares and freights. The Eighth Finance Commission favoured levying tax on railway passenger fares but not until the present arrangement of giving grants in lieu of such a tax continues to exist.

C. Entry 90: It pertains to 'taxes other than stamp duties on transactions in stock exchanges and future markets.' Since stock exchanges and future markets [8] are at a formative stage and have an inter-State character therefore it is desirable to retain these taxes with the Union. The Eighth Finance Commission did not think it advisable to levy taxes on transactions in stock exchanges and future markets.

D. Entry 92: It refers to 'taxes on the sale or purchase of newspapers and on advertisements published therein.' This tax is retained with the Union to protect the freedom of the press, and avoid undue tax burden on newspaper industry, particularly the regional language newspapers. Since newspaper reading habit is not sufficiently developed and widespread in the country, it is not desirable to impose a tax on the sale or purchase of newspapers.

Both the Fifth and the Eighth Finance Commissions did not recommend a tax on the sale or purchase of newspapers. However, both the Commissions opined that there was scope for tax on advertisements published in newspapers. The Eighth Commission cautioned that a tax on advertisement, if levied, should be borne by the advertisers themselves and not passed on to the newspapers and journals.

7.3.7 Freedom as to Payment of Taxes for Promotion of any Particular Religion: According to Article 27 of the Constitution of India, "No person shall be compelled to pay any taxes, the proceeds of which are specifically appropriated in payment of expenses for the promotion or maintenance of any particular religion or religious denomination."

Notes

1. Government of India, *Report of the Commission on Centre-State Relations* (Chairman: Justice R. S. Sarkaria) Part I, 1988, p. 8.

2. *Ibid.*, p. 7.

3. Concurrent taxation powers are a characteristic feature of federal set up in USA, Canada, and Australia. Most tax fields in these countries are jointly occupied by the federal and provincial governments. The overlapping taxation powers have often caused frictions not only between the federal and provincial governments but also among the provinces *inter se.* Tax problems owing to joint occupancy of tax fields are solved through tax rental and tax sharing negotiations and agreements.

4. *Report of the Commission on Centre-State Relations*, Part I, 1988, op. cit., p. 271.

5. Report of the Twelfth Finance Commission (2005-10), November 2004, pp. 15-16.

6. Prior to the Eightieth Amendment of the Constitution, provisions of Article 269 were as follows.

Taxes Levied and Collected by the Union but Assigned to the States (Article 269): These were: (a) duties in respect of succession to property other than agricultural land, (b) estate duty in respect of property other than agricultural land, (c) terminal taxes on goods or passengers carried by railway, sea or air, (d) taxes on railway fares and freights, (e) taxes other than stamp duties on transactions in stock exchanges and future markets, (f) taxes on the sale or purchase of newspapers and on advertisements published therein, (g) taxes on the sale or purchase of goods other than newspapers, where such sale or purchase takes place in the course of inter-State trade or commerce, and (h) taxes on the consignment of goods (whether the consignment is to the person making it or to any other person), where such consignment takes place in the course of inter-State trade or commerce. These taxes corresponded to entries 87, 88, 89, 90, 92, 92A and 92B in the Union List.

7. Stamp duty was payable on cheques prior to 1927 but was withdrawn in that year.

8. Future trading refers to contracts for sale and purchase of goods at a future date primarily with a view to avoid price fluctuations. Presently, future trading is allowed at specific centres in respect of four commodities, viz. jute products, paper, turmeric, and *gur*.

8

Trends in Tax-GDP Ratio

8.1 Tax-GDP Ratio: Meaning and Significance

The primary objective of tax policy in developing countries is to mobilise resources for the public sector to finance welfare and developmental plans. The extent to which tax policy is used for this purpose is a matter of interest for national policymakers and foreign aid donors. Foreign governments and international organisations usually assess the efforts made by recipient countries to raise resources domestically.

Level of taxation in a country is traditionally judged in terms of the ratio which taxes bear to some measure of national income. This ratio is called tax-GDP ratio and the change in it is determined by variations in both the numerator (total tax revenue) and the denominator (national income).

There are various problems associated with the definitions of numerator and denominator of tax-GDP ratio. For example, should profits/losses of public monopolies form part of the numerator? Should social security contributions be included in tax receipts? The denominator of the ratio suffers from more ambiguities because there are various measures of national income. Among the alternative measures of national income, the important ones are: Gross Domestic Product (GDP), Gross National Product (GNP), and Net National Product (NNP). [1] Should taxes be related to GDP or GNP or NNP, and whether at market prices or at factor cost?

In choosing from the alternative measures of national income, the important considerations are: (a) the measure chosen should be readily available, (b) it is widely understood, and (c) it is reliable. In view of these considerations, it is a common practice to use GDP at market prices as the denominator of the tax-GDP ratio. GDP is preferred because it avoids estimation of depreciation which is subject to various statistical and conceptual problems. For example, the Organisation for Economic Co-operation and Development uses GDP at market prices as the denominator for comparing tax-GDP ratios among its member countries.

The study of tax-GDP ratio is important because trends in taxation in a country or a group of countries are analysed mainly in terms of this ratio, and the composition of tax revenues. The latter may change owing to variations in tax-GDP ratio.

Tax-GDP ratio is generally regarded as an index of relative tax burden in a country over a period of time (time-series analysis) or when countries are compared for the same period (cross-section analysis). To describe tax burden in terms of tax-GDP ratio can be misleading because taxes, though burden for individuals, are used to finance vital governmental activities and to make transfers to needy sections of society.

What does then tax-GDP ratio signify? Since tax-GDP ratio indicates the percentage of national income that is compulsorily transferred from private pockets to public exchequer, and hence the relative share of government in the disposition of national income, it signifies the economic role of a government in the national economy. The ratio, however, does not reflect the importance of government sector as a final purchaser of goods and services because a part of tax revenue is returned to the private sector in the form of transfer payments like pensions and scholarships. If such transfer payments are deducted from the total tax revenue, the ratio of the remaining tax revenue to GDP will show importance of government as a final purchaser of goods and services. Since tax-GDP ratio reflects movements in both tax receipts and GDP, any significant revision in GDP figures will affect the ratio. Such revisions are not uncommon, particularly in developing countries, and therefore they indicate a limitation of the use of tax-GDP ratios. These cautions must be kept in mind while interpreting tax ratios.

8.2 Determinants of Tax-GDP Ratio/Taxable Capacity

Tax-GDP ratio varies from country to country. What explains inter-country variations in tax ratios? The list of factors affecting tax ratio is almost inexhaustible. It includes a wide variety of economic, social, cultural, and political factors. Broadly speaking, the variables explaining inter-country variations in tax ratio may be grouped under two categories: 1. Quantitative or statistical factors, and 2. Qualitative or institutional factors.

Among the quantitative factors, the important ones are the following. These factors are crucial as they determine the tax bases which governments use to raise tax revenues. They are also the determinants of tax levels most widely used in empirical studies. They are believed to exert a strong influence over the tax ratio through their effect on what are called capacity factors.

8.2.1 Stage of Development: Stage of economic development is the first and foremost determinant of tax ratio. Economic development is a multi-faceted phenomenon affecting quality of life and therefore cannot be measured precisely by a single variable. Still, a variable frequently used as a proxy is per capita income which, though incomplete, is by far the single best indicator of the stage of economic development attained by a country.

It is usually hypothesised that per capita income and tax ratio move in the same direction, i.e. they are positively related. Presumably, people in countries with high per capita income require a smaller proportion of their incomes to meet their basic needs, and hence are left with a surplus which may be conveniently taxed. It is also argued that income elasticity of demand for public goods is high at high levels of per capita income. Moreover, since development process is normally accompanied by increasing urbanisation, high literacy rate, widespread monetisation, public consciousness, and improved administration, the scope for taxation, particularly direct taxation, increases because all these factors are conducive to tax collection. However, in the context of inter-country comparisons, the use of per capita income as a determinant of tax ratio is subject to errors owing to the conversion of domestic currencies into US dollars. Moreover, the relationship between tax ratio and per capita income becomes decisive only after the latter has reached a minimum level, though it is difficult to define that level.

8.2.2 Composition of GDP: Another determinant of taxation level is the composition of GDP or the industrial origin of national output. Normally, a higher agricultural share in GDP is indicative of a lower per capita income, and hence a low stage of economic development. Thus, the proportion of income generated in the agricultural sector provides another index of the stage of development. Two countries may have the same level of per capita income but differences in the composition of their national output will affect their taxable capacities and tax ratios. Preponderance of agricultural sector means lack of industrialisation, existence of a large subsistence sector, and administrative difficulties in implementing tax laws. Moreover, there is effective political resistance to taxation of agricultural sector. All these factors explain the negative influence of the agricultural sector on tax ratio.

Contrarily, the relative share of mining sector has a positive influence on tax ratio. As Roy Bahl has opined, "the mining sector generally produces a larger surplus than any other sector, and therefore it is a positive determinant of taxable capacity. Because of the heavy fixed investment associated with mining industries, operations will tend to be confined to a few large firms, and accordingly it will be administratively easier to levy income or export taxes." [2]

Tax potential is greatly increased where industrial production dominates other sources of national income. Industrialisation is associated with urbanisation, banking transactions, accounting practices, all of which facilitate levy and collection of taxes. Some taxes (e.g. corporation tax) are directly linked with industrial activities.

8.2.3 Foreign Trade: Another determinant of tax level is the size of the foreign trade sector. It is presumed that taxable capacity increases with the expansion of external trade because it is administratively easier to tax trade inflows and outflows than internal transactions. Moreover, a relatively large size of external sector is indicative of greater degree of monetisation and organised industrial sector, both of which are favourable conditions for taxation.

There are three alternative measures of the size of foreign trade sector based on combinations of import and/or export share of GNP. These are: (a) import ratio (My), (b) export ratio (Xy), and (c) openness ratio, i.e. the ratio of imports plus exports (My + Xy) to GNP. Theoretically, the use of openness ratio is justified because it reflects the total trade base available for taxation.

8.2.4 Composition of Government Expenditure: If public expenditure pertains mainly to welfare activities (educational and medical services), it will favourably influence the general standard of living and hence the taxpaying capacity of the citizens. Conversely, if a large proportion of expenditure is devoted to defence, and law and order, the taxpaying capacity will be reduced.

8.2.5 Pattern of Income Distribution: Two countries with the same level of per capita income may have different taxable capacities if the pattern of income distribution differs. Thus, size distribution of income becomes another determinant of tax ratio. It is widely believed that scope for taxation is greater when degree of concentration of income and wealth is higher. This is not always true because economic concentration implies more political power with the rich who effectively resist additional tax burdens upon themselves. For example, in India the near absence of agricultural income tax is mainly due to the preponderance of landlords and other vested interests in state legislatures.

Among the qualitative factors, the important ones are: efficiency of tax administration, attitude of the citizens towards government and its laws, and ideology of the ruling party (e.g. left wing governments prefer a larger public sector). It is difficult to quantify the influence of socio-political factors on taxable capacity.

Vito Tanzi has called to attention the connection between tax levels and macroeconomic policies such as exchange rate, import substitution, trade liberalisation, inflation, public debt, and financial policies. [3] He believes that changes in tax levels cannot be attributed to traditional determinants alone, and greater attention should be devoted to the relationship between these macroeconomic variables and tax levels.

Factors influencing tax-GDP ratio are many and a variety of permutations and combinations can be used in empirical analysis. The choice of factors and their application is, however, constrained by the availability of data in a country.

8.3 Trends in Tax-GDP Ratio: Post-liberalisation Slippage and Recovery

In 1950-51, total tax collections in India were a mere 6.31 per cent of GDP. With the launching of the Five Year Plans in 1951, and expansion in administrative and welfare activities of the Government at different levels, the need for revenue increased and it was met mainly by additional tax efforts. Consequently, tax-GDP ratio started increasing from decade to decade, being 7.86 per cent in 1960-61, 10.40 per cent in 1970-71 and 13.80 per cent in 1980-81. [4] It stood at 15.43 per cent in 1990-91 and after that it declined to as low as 13.38 per cent in 1998-99. Lately, an upward trend is noticeable in tax-GDP ratio (Table 8.1).

Table 8.1: Combined Tax Revenue as Per Cent of GDP: 1990-91 to 2004-05

(Rs. crore)

Year	Combined tax revenue*	Col. 2 as % of GDP
1	2	3
1990-91	87,722	15.43
1991-92	1,03,198	15.80
1992-93	1,14,166	15.26
1993-94	1,21,961	14.19
1994-95	1,47,849	14.60
1995-96	1,75,259	14.75
1996-97	2,01,056	14.69
1997-98	2,20,659	14.49
1998-99	**2,33,017**	**13.38**
1999-00	2,74,583	14.02
2000-01	3,05,320	14.49
2001-02	3,14,535	13.79
2002-03	3,56,277	14.54
2003-04	4,14,084	15.00
2004-05	4,94,016	15.83
2005-06	5,85,626	16.58

* Total tax revenue of the Central and State Governments.

2004-05= Revised estimates; 2005-06 – Budget estimates

Note: The ratios of GDP since 1950-51 are with reference to new series GDP (Base: 1993-94) at current market prices.

Source: Rearranged data from Government of India, Ministry of Finance, *Indian Public Finance Statistics*, 2005-2006, Tables 1.7 and 1.8.

The slippage in tax-GDP ratio was confirmed by the Twelfth Finance Commission. To quote, "Taking the 15-year period from 1987-88 to 2001-02, and comparing three-year averages at both ends, that is for 1987-90 and 1999-2002, we note that the tax-GDP ratio fell from a level of about 16 per cent relative to GDP by 1.6 percentage points to reach an average level of 14.4 per cent of GDP." [5] Stating the reasons for the slippage, the Commission noted, "As a result of tax reforms, the indirect taxes relative to GDP started coming down whereas that of direct taxes started increasing. But the magnitude of increase in the direct taxes was less than the fall in indirect taxes. In consequence, the overall tax-GDP ratio fell from its peak in 1987-88 to 14.4 per cent in 2001-02." [6] It is noteworthy that rates of excise and customs duties have gradually been lowered during the post-1991 period.

Emphasising the need to increase tax-GDP ratios, the Commission suggested ratios for the year 2009-10 (Table 8.2).

Table 8.2: Tax-GDP Ratios Suggested by the Twelfth Finance Commission for the Year 2009-10

	2004-05	2009-10
Combined tax revenue	15.6	17.6
Centre's gross tax revenue	9.7	10.9
States' own tax revenues	5.9	6.8

Source: Report of the Twelfth Finance Commission (2005-10), November 2004, Tables 4.12 and 4.13 (excerpted).

8.4 Tax-GDP Ratios in Developed and Developing Countries

There has been a good deal of literature on ranking countries according to tax ratio relative to their taxable capacity to measure national tax performance. These inter-country comparisons of tax levels have been attempted by individual scholars, and international agencies from time to time. Much of the research work in this area has been done by the Fiscal Affairs Department of the International Monetary Fund. [7]

Tax-GDP ratio is generally high in developed countries as compared to developing countries. In Denmark, the tax-GDP ratio was as high as 47.75 per cent in 2004. For the same year, it was 36.25 per cent in Sweden, 35.16 per cent in Norway, and 30.68 per cent in Australia. Table 8.3 records tax-GDP ratios for important developed countries of the world and compares them with tax-GDP ratios in some developing countries. It is found that tax-GDP ratios in developing countries are far low as compared to developed countries.

Table 8.3: Tax-GDP Ratios in Selected Developed and Developing Countries: 2004 (in per cent)

Countries (in descending order of Tax-GDP Ratio)	Tax-GDP Ratio	Countries (in descending order of Tax-GDP Ratio)	Tax-GDP Ratio
Developed countries		9. Netherlands	23.29
1. Denmark	47.75	10. Germany	21.91
2. Sweden	36.25	**Developing countries**	
3. Norway	35.16	11. Malaysia	18.57
4. Australia	30.68	12. Thailand	17.19
5. Italy	29.68	13. Mauritius	17.11
6. United Kingdom	29.20	14. India	15.15
7. Canada	28.98	15. Nepal	9.7
8. France	26.95		

Sources: International Monetary Fund, *Government Finance Statistics Yearbook* 2005. For India, Government of India, Ministry of Finance, *Indian Public Finance Statistics*, 2004-05, Table 1.8.

From the foregoing analysis it can be inferred that the level of taxation is linked with the stage of development. More specifically, tax-GDP ratio is positively related to per capita income, i.e. higher the per capita income, greater is the tax-GDP ratio and *vice versa.* In poor countries, the taxpaying capacity of the people is less owing to low levels of per capita income.

8.4.1 Limitations of Inter-country Tax Comparisons: Are inter-country comparisons of taxation levels meaningful? Some fiscal experts have sharply criticised these attempts. [8] According to critics, the economic, political, and institutional characteristics of individual countries are so different that neither theoretical nor empirical studies provide useful information of policy relevance. Tax-GDP ratios do not consider the fact that some countries are more favourably placed to levy and collect taxes than others. For example, Lotz and Morss [9] analysed a sample of 72 developed and developing countries to examine the relationship between tax ratio variations and differences in per capita income and degree of openness. The sample included a wide spectrum of dissimilar economies ranging from Nepal to Singapore. It is *prima facie* erroneous to compare Nepal's traditional rural and agricultural economy with a highly commercial and industrial city state of Singapore.

According to critics, the actual tax-to-income ratio is a vague concept because the definitions of numerator and denominator are debatable. In spite of these limitations, international tax comparisons are useful so far as they process and condense a large amount of otherwise incomprehensible information. However, it must be emphasised that such comparisons are more meaningful if attempted among countries having similar socio-economic circumstances.

Notes

1. GDP includes income produced locally including income accruing to non-residents but excluding foreign income of residents. GNP, on the other hand, excludes local income of non-residents but includes foreign income of residents. NNP excludes depreciation (capital consumption) and signifies a measure of output available for private and government consumption and investment without reducing the capital stock.

2. See Roy W. Bahl (1971, p. 590) in note 7.

3. See Vito Tanzi in note 7.

4. See Table 1 in Part X of this book.

5. *Report of the Twelfth Finance Commission* (2005-10), November 2004, p. 22.

6. Ibid,, p. 63.

7. Studies pertaining to international tax comparisons conducted by International Monetary Fund include: (1) Jorgen R. Lotz and Elliott R. Morss, 'Measuring 'Tax Effort' in Developing Countries', *IMF Staff Papers*, Vol. 14, November 1967, pp. 478-99; (2) Raja J. Chelliah, 'Trends in Taxation in Developing Countries', *IMF Staff Papers*, Vol. 18, July 1971, pp. 254-331; (3) Roy W. Bahl, 'A Regression Approach to Tax Effort and Tax Ratio Analysis', *IMF Staff Papers*, Vol. 18, November 1971, pp. 570-612. (4) Roy W. Bahl, 'A Representative Tax System Approach to Measuring Tax Effort in Developing Countries', *IMF Staff Papers*, Vol. 19, March 1972, pp. 87-123; (5) Raja J. Chelliah, Hessel Bass and Margaret Kelly, 'Tax Ratios and Effort in Developing Countries, 1969-71', *IMF Staff Papers*, Vol. 22, March, 1975, pp. 187-205; (6) Alan Tait, Wilfrid Gratz, and Barry Eichengreen, 'International Comparisons of Taxation for Selected Developing Countries, 1972-76', *IMF Staff Papers*, Vol. 26, March 1979; (7) Vito Tanzi, 'The Impact of Macroeconomic Policies on the level of Taxation and the Fiscal Balance in Developing Countries', *IMF Staff Papers*, Vol. 36, No. 3, September 1989, pp. 633-656.

8. See contributions of R.M. Bird, B. R. Bolnick, and A. R. Prest in J.F.J. Toye (ed.) *Taxation and Economic Development* (London: Frank Cass and Company).

9. See Lotz and Morss in note 7.

9

Direct and Indirect Taxes

9.1 Direct versus Indirect Taxes: Theoretical Considerations

The distinction between direct and indirect taxes has been a subject of long-drawn debate in public finance literature.

A direct tax is one the ultimate burden of which falls on the person on whom it is levied. In other words, it is a tax that cannot be shifted from the original payer to someone else. It is contrasted with indirect tax which can readily be shifted to ultimate consumers of the commodity or service taxed.

John Stuart Mill, the celebrated British economist of the nineteenth century, distinguished between direct and indirect taxes as follows. "A direct tax is one which is demanded from the very person who, it is intended or desired, should pay it. Indirect taxes are those which are demanded from one person in the expectation and intention that he shall indemnify himself at the expense of another." [1]

Income tax, wealth tax, and estate duty are generally considered direct taxes. Some economists believe that it is possible to pass on certain direct taxes under special circumstances. Corporate income tax, a supposedly direct tax, is known to be shifted to consumers in many countries. [2]

Direct taxes, though administratively inconvenient, are preferred because they (a) can be related to ability-to-pay, (b) satisfy the principle of certainty, and (c) create civic consciousness.

An indirect tax is one which can be shifted from the original payer to the ultimate consumer of the commodity or service taxed. Import duties, excise levies, and sales taxes are generally regarded as indirect taxes. Thus, an excise duty on cigarettes levied on producers is usually passed on to the consumers in the form of higher prices.

Indirect taxes (also called hidden taxes) are convenient to collect but lack equity attribute. They do not allow considerations for the personal circumstances of taxpayers as do direct taxes. It is not possible to grant exemptions or allow deductions or to have a progressive rate schedule. Indirect taxes are borne in relation to the consumption expenditure which constitutes a higher percentage of income for lower income groups than for persons in higher income brackets. It is true that incidence of indirect taxes depends on (a) the selection of commodities for taxation and (b) the rate of tax on them. It is desirable that luxuries and comforts are chosen for heavy taxation with necessities of life either exempted or moderately taxed. However, in poor countries the demand for luxury items is limited apart from being price elastic. Conversely, the demand for necessities is vast and price inelastic, obliging tax authorities to extend the tax net to daily needs. This has a tendency to fuel inflation.

In short, it is almost universally accepted that indirect taxes are inferior to direct taxes in terms of equity attribute. The distribution of indirect tax burden is often, though not always, regressive and even the poorest of the poor are made to contribute to public exchequer. The chief advantage of indirect taxes is that they are convenient to collect.

The demarcation between direct and indirect taxes is ambiguous because of conflicting empirical evidence of tax incidence studies. Direct taxes can be shifted under certain circumstances while taxes on commodities may stick on the producers finally. [3]

9.2 Trends in the Relative Significance of Direct and Indirect Taxes in India

There is no legal definition of direct and indirect taxes in India. Taxes under the charge of Central Board of Direct Taxes are direct taxes while those administered by the Central Board of Excise and Customs are indirect taxes. The classification adopted in this book is the same as followed in the documents of the Government of India.

In 1950-51, direct taxes accounted for a sizeable 36.8 per cent of total tax collections: Rs. 231 crore out of Rs. 627 crore. Within a span of 35 years the proportionate share dropped to less than half at 14.4 per cent in 1985-86, and stood at 13.1 per cent in 1987-88. The declining trend of direct taxes led to a rising share of indirect taxes. The ratio between direct and indirect taxes which stood at 36.8:63.2 in 1950-51 worsened with every passing decade, recording 29.8:70.2 in 1960-61, 21.2:78.8 in 1970-71, 16.5:83.5 in 1980-81 and 13.1:86.9 in 1987-88. [4]

The declining share of direct taxes was not consistent with the norms of tax theory. It is well-known that as an economy experiences modernisation, diversification, and expansion of corporate sector, the scope for direct taxes widens. [5]

It is customary to explain the limited role of direct taxes in developing countries in terms of their peculiar circumstances which include large agricultural sector of subsistence nature, small-scale industrial activities, lack of monetisation and accounting practices, and low levels of income. Even a modest exemption limit of personal income tax keeps the vast majority of income earners outside the income tax net. In addition to these underlying reasons, a host of specific factors also contributed to the reduced role of direct taxes. These included: (a) scaling down rates of direct taxes, (b) plethora of exemptions/concessions, (c) abolition of estate duty in 1985, and (d) large-scale tax evasion.

The declining share of direct taxes caused concern in Government circles and this feeling was expressed in official documents. The Long Term Fiscal Policy (LTFP) while seeking to correct the imbalance maintained, "While the predominance of indirect taxes in the present situation is unavoidable, it cannot be gainsaid that a certain balance has to be maintained between direct and indirect taxes. Taxes like the personal income tax have an important role in the tax structure and cannot be substituted by taxes on commodities. It is not easy to tailor commodity taxes to the circumstances of the taxpayers in the same way as is possible with the personal income tax. Hence, although reliance on indirect taxation cannot be avoided in the foreseeable future, it is necessary to make a transition to a system whereby income tax makes a larger contribution to revenue. Such transition is not possible without a distinct improvement in the buoyancy of the income tax in response to growth in incomes. An important objective of fiscal policy must be to reverse the decline in the share of direct taxes over the long term." [6]

9.2.1 Reversal of Roles: After the tax reforms initiated in 1991, the decline in the relative share of direct taxes has not only been arrested but reversed. The ratio between direct and indirect taxes which stood at 14.0:86.0 in 1990-91 was estimated at 31.1:68.9 in the budget estimates for 2005-06 (Table 9.1).

Stating the reasons for fall in the share of indirect taxes and increase in the share of direct taxes, the Tenth Five Year Plan (2002-07) observed, "The reasons for this steep fall in the indirect tax revenue are obvious. The structural and administrative reforms in the Indian tax system during the Nineties characterised by scaling down of the tax rate, reduction in number of slabs, introduction of modified value added tax system, etc, among others, were not necessarily aimed at raising revenue productivity. Rather, the purpose was to improve efficiency in production and trade by removing market distortion. The analysis of data in the post -reform period exposes several issues worth mentioning. First, the value of imports has not responded to tariff reduction in equal proportion, i.e. import elasticity with respect to tariff has not been very high. Second, a host of tariff exemptions still exists on substantial proportion of imports ranging from 60 per cent to 80 per cent. Third, the excise duty has not been structured to lead to a revenue-neutral tax system under MODVAT/CENVAT. Fourth, the tax base for excise revenue (manufacturing sector) is gradually shrinking as a proportion of GDP. Our projections of the tax buoyancy for the Tenth plan have considered all these issues.

The improvement in direct tax collection, which has been experienced despite the scaling back of income tax rates in India during the post-reform period, could be attributed to expansion in the tax base through introduction of innovative schemes, extension of the base for tax deduction at source and improvement in direct tax administration etc. Continuous efforts towards improvement in the direct tax administration and its re-structuring, and introduction of information technology on a large scale to facilitate tax administration are expected to further enhance revenue collection under direct tax." [7]

Table 9.1: Combined Tax Revenue, Breakdown between Direct and Indirect Taxes with Percentage Shares: 1990-91 to 2005-06

(Rs. crore)

Year	Combined tax revenue* (3+4)	Direct taxes	Indirect taxes	Col. 3 as % of Col. 2	Col. 4 as % of Col. 2
1	2	3	4	5	6
1990-91	87,722	12,260	75,462	14.0	86.0
1991-92	1,03,198	16,657	86,541	16.1	83.9
1992-93	1,14,166	19,387	94,779	17.0	83.0
1993-94	1,21,961	21,713	1,00,248	17.8	82.2
1994-95	1,47,849	28,878	1,18,971	19.5	80.5
1995-96	1,75,259	35,777	1,39,482	20.4	79.6
1996-97	2,01,056	41,061	1,59,995	20.4	79.6
1997-98	2,20,659	50,538	1,70,121	22.9	77.1
1998-99	2,33,017	49,119	1,83,898	21.1	78.9
1999-00	2,74,583	60,864	2,13,719	21.4	78.6
2000-01	3,05,320	71,762	2,33,558	23.5	76.5
2001-02	3,14,535	73,108	2,41,427	23.2	76.8
2002-03	3,56,277	87,365	2,68,912	24.5	75.5
2003-04	4,14,084	1,09,546	3,04,538	26.5	73.5
2004-05	4,94,016	1,39,017	3,55,000	28.1	71.9
2005-06	5,85,626	1,82,134	4,03,492	31.1	68.9

* Total tax revenue of the Central and State Governments.

2003-04 = Revised estimates; 2004-05 = Budget estimates.

Source: Rearranged data from Government of India, Ministry of Finance, *Indian Public Finance Statistics*, 2005-2006, Table 1.7. Columns 5 and 6 calculations own.

9.3 Equity Implications

Though, of late, the share of direct taxes has increased, they are still far below the contribution made by indirect taxes. The subdued role of direct taxes or the dominance of indirect taxes in India's tax structure has serious equity implications. Indirect taxes do not allow considerations for personal circumstances of taxpayers as do direct taxes. It is not possible to grant exemptions or allow deductions or to have a progressive rate schedule, e.g. in the case of excisable goods. Commodity taxes are borne in relation to consumption expenditure which constitutes a higher percentage of income for lower income groups than for persons in higher income brackets.

Moreover, a substantial amount of indirect taxes is paid by the Government to itself. Broadly speaking, public expenditure at all levels forms one-fourth of the total spending in India. Customs duties, excise levies, and sales taxes and the hikes in them entail additional expenditure on the part of Central and State Governments to maintain their existing command over real resources of the economy. Commodities like motor vehicles, petrol, air conditioners, water coolers, and steel furniture are favourite items for heavy and additional taxation and these are also the items extensively used by civil and defence establishments of the Government. Therefore, a substantial part of indirect tax revenue including the additional tax effort is merely a book transfer and does not reflect increase in real resources at the command of the Government. This argument can also be extended to increase in the prices of goods produced by public sector enterprises. Any such increase and the resultant additional proceeds may improve the finances of an individual public enterprise but not necessarily of the Government of India because the various Ministries and Departments will be required to spend more to purchase the same volume of goods and services from the concerned enterprise. Thus, in any reform of indirect tax structure it is important to emphasise, apart from quantity, the quality of revenue, i.e. who pay the taxes to the Government.

With the growth of corporate sector and the rise in income levels, India is showing signs of modernisation, reflecting increased scope for direct taxes. For widening the direct tax base, effective measures are needed to tap the unincorporated industrial sector and the affluent agricultural class.

Notes

1. *Collected Works of John Stuart Mill*, University of Toronto Press, 1965, Vol. III, Book V, Chapter 3, p. 825.

2. For United States, see M. Krzyzaniak and R. A. Musgrave, *The Shifting of the Corporation Income Tax* (Baltimore: John Hopkins University Press, 1963); For India, see G.S. Laumas, 'The Shifting of Corporation Income Tax - A Study with Reference to Indian Corporations', *Public Finance*, Vol. 21, No. 4, 1966, pp. 462-73.

3. For a detailed discussion on the distinction between direct and indirect taxes, see I. Ursula K. Hicks, "The Terminology of Tax analysis," in *Readings in the Economics of Taxation*. The

American Economic Association (London: George Allen and Unwin Ltd., 1959), pp. 214-16; 2. D. Walker, "Direct versus Indirect Taxes," in *Public Finance* edited by D. W. Houghton (England: Penguin Books Ltd., 1972), pp. 349-75.

4. See Table 1 in Part X of this book.

5. According to a study conducted by Raja Chelliah and others for a group of 47 developing countries for the average of the period 1969-71, the average share of indirect taxes was 64 per cent of the total tax revenue. As for developed economies, the share of indirect taxes ranged between 45-50 per cent of the total tax revenues. [See R.J. Chelliah, H.J. Bass, and M.R. Kelly, "Tax Ratios and Tax Efforts in Developing Countries, 1969-71", *I.M.F. Staff Papers,* Volume 22, No. 1, March 1975, Table 2]. It is noteworthy that in India the proportion of indirect taxes stood at 78.8 per cent in 1970-71, much higher than the international average of the developing world.

6. Government of India, Ministry of Finance, *Long Term Fiscal Policy* (December 1985), p.23.

7. Government of India, Planning Commission, *Tenth Five Year Plan* (2002-07), Vol. I, p. 61.

10

Buoyancy and Elasticity of Tax Revenue

10.1 Conceptual Framework

High degree of responsiveness of tax yield to changes in national income is a desirable characteristic of any tax system. If a government depends on tax revenue to finance a large part of its expenditure, then it is necessary to ensure that an increasing proportion of national income flows into the public treasury as taxes. In other words, the requirement is to increase the incremental tax ratio. Computation of tax buoyancy and elasticity becomes relevant in this context.

10.1.1 Automatic Response versus Discretionary Changes: Tax revenue may change through *automatic* response of the tax yield to changes in national income and/or through the imposition of new taxes, revision of the rates and/or the bases of the existing taxes, tax amnesties, stricter tax compliance and other administrative measures backed by legal action. Changes in the tax yield resulting from modifying such tax parameters (i.e. rate, base etc.) are called *discretionary changes* which are the result of legislative action.

With tax parameters held constant (i.e. discretionary changes being removed), automatic changes in the tax yield resulting from variations in the national income measure the elasticity or built-in-flexibility of a tax or a tax system. It is the ratio of percentage change in tax revenue (adjusted for discretionary changes) to the percentage change in national income. Changes in the tax yield flowing from the combined effect of automatic response and discretionary changes measure the buoyancy of a tax. It is computed by dividing the percentage change in tax yield by the percentage change in the national income. [1]

Buoyancy coefficient compares the actual growth of tax revenue with the growth in national income. It assesses the overall success of government measures to increase tax revenue. Elasticity coefficient, on the other hand, indicates the inherent responsiveness of a tax system to changes in national income. It reflects the revenue potential of the tax system.

If a tax system lacks elasticity, the government will have to make frequent changes in tax laws to boost revenue. This will cause legal complications, reduce administrative efficiency and prove to be politically inexpedient. Therefore, while casting the tax net, tax bases should be so selected and rate structure so designed that reasonable degree of elasticity is imparted to the tax system.

Buoyancy and elasticity attributes of a tax system assume varying importance during the course of development process. As economic activities pick up and monetisation spreads, more and more tax handles become available to the government. To extend and intensify the tax structure, new taxes are imposed, rates of existing taxes are revised, tax bases are widened and administrative machinery is toned up. These discretionary changes, which are part of the buoyancy concept, play the dominant role and in a sense initiate the process towards higher tax-to-national income ratio. When tax revenue forms quite a high ratio of national income, further legislative action becomes politically disadvantageous in view of tax payers' resistance. Moreover, frequent changes in tax parameters create confusion and uncertainty harming the smooth growth of trade and industry. Thus, discretionary changes, though never coming to a halt in an expanding economy, lose significance in course of time. Elasticity of the tax system becomes more important at this stage. If a tax system is sufficiently elastic, the process initiated by discretionary changes will be kept up automatically.

10.1.2 Choice of Appropriate Base: Should tax yield be related to national income or to the appropriate tax base? As early as 1937, R. F. Bretherton in his classic article on the question of sensitivity of tax revenue (the first of its kind in public finance) observed, "Since money income is the ultimate source from which all taxes must be paid, it seems desirable to measure fluctuations in the yield of particular taxes against fluctuations in the total of national social income." [2] In modern societies, most taxes are either based on, or in some ways related to, production, income, expenditure, wealth or transactions which tend to increase with the growth of national income. Hence, taxes should be so devised as to grow automatically with increase in national income.

J. Maxwell, however, holds the contrary view and maintains, "When measurement of overall built-in-flexibility is in question, it seems proper to take national or gross national product as the base. But when particular taxes are being examined, it may seem appropriate to relate changes in tax yield to changes in the precise base upon which the tax is levied." [3] In view of the current practice of relating tax yield to national income as well as to appropriate base, the problem of choosing the variables for comparison has considerably eased. [4]

If the tax system as such is related to national income, it is important to relate individual taxes also to national income to facilitate comparisons. If the elasticity of the tax system is 1 and that of a particular tax is less than 1, it is clear that that particular tax is a weakling in the system, the exact weakling influence being determined by its relative revenue significance in the tax system.

10.2 Buoyancy and Elasticity Estimates of Tax Revenue in India

Several studies have computed the buoyancy and elasticity attributes of the Indian tax system since Independence. Estimates of some of these studies are summarised in Table 10.1.

In the early 1960s, G.S. Sahota made the first systematic and comprehensive attempt to compute buoyancy and elasticity of the tax revenue. For the period 1951-52 to 1957-58, Sahota estimated the buoyancy of Union and State taxes taken together at 1.69 while for Union taxes taken separately at 2.39. The crucial elasticity coefficient for the same period was found to be 0.83 for Union and State taxes considered together and 0.61 for Union taxes considered separately.

Another notable study was undertaken by V.G. Rao who estimated the buoyancy and elasticity of all Central and State taxes at 1.22 and 0.82, all Central taxes at 1.22 and 0.74, and all State taxes at 1.27 and 1.01 respectively for the period 1960-61 to 1973-74.

The computations of the Indirect Taxation Enquiry Committee, 1978, also revealed poor elasticity of the indirect tax system, except import duties. For the Union excise duties, accounting for nearly half of Centre's total tax collections, the Committee estimated the buoyancy and elasticity coefficients at 1.31 and 0.75 respectively for the period 1963-64 to 1974-75.

In another study, I.K. Khadye estimated the buoyancy and elasticity of combined tax revenue (Centre and States) at 1.25 and 0.88 respectively for the period 1960-61 to 1978-79. For the same period, the buoyancy and elasticity coefficients of Central taxes taken separately were found to be 1.25 and 0.83 respectively.

In yet another attempt, M.M. Sury estimated buoyancy and elasticity of Union excise duties for two sub-periods, 1950-51 to 1964-65, and 1965-66 to 1980-81 separately. For the period 1950-51 to 1964-65, the buoyancy and elasticity coefficients turned out to be 3.02 and 1.86 respectively. However, for the period 1965-66 to 1980-81, the values of both the buoyancy and elasticity coefficients were relatively low at 1.27 and 0.73 respectively. It is noteworthy that these estimates (1.27 and 0.73) were very close to the estimates of ITEC (1.31 and 0.75) for Union excise duties for the period 1963-64 to 1974-75.

The buoyancy estimates of various Central taxes made by the Tenth Finance Commission (1995-2000) for the period 1983-84 to 1992-93 were as follows: Union excise duties (1.01), income tax (1.10), corporation tax (1.31), and customs duties (1.38).

The Eleventh Finance Commission's calculations showed, "The buoyancy of gross tax revenue of the Centre with respect to GDP works out to 0.91 during the nineties, as compared to 1.15 in the eighties. In the case of the States, the

Table 10.1: Buoyancy and Elasticity of Tax Revenue in India in Relation to National Income

Author	Period for which computations made	Tax group	Buoyancy	Elasticity
G.S. Sahota	1951-52 to 1957-58	1. All Central and State taxes 2. All Central taxes	1.69 2.39*	0.83 0.61
V.G. Rao	1960-61 to 1973-74	1. All Central and State taxes 2. All Central taxes 3. All State taxes	1.22 1.22 1.27	0.82 0.74 1.01
Indirect Taxation Enquiry Committee	1963-64 to 1974-75	1. Union excise duties	1.31	0.75
I.K. Khadye	1960-61 to 1978-79	1. All Central and State taxes 2. All Central taxes	1.25 1.25	0.88 0.83
M.M. Sury	1950-51 to 1964-65 and 1965-66 to 1980-81	1. Union excise duties	3.02 and 1.27	1.86 0.73
Tenth Finance Commission (1995-2000)	1983-84 to 1992-93	1. Union excise duties 2. Income tax 3. Corporation tax 4. Customs duties	1.01 1.10 1.31 1.38	--- --- --- ---
Eleventh Finance Commission (2000-05)	1980-81 to 1989-90 and 1990-91 to 1998-99	1. Central taxes: Gross revenues 2. States own tax revenues 3. Combined tax revenues	1.15 and 0.91 1.12 and 1.04 1.14 and 0.96	--- --- ---
Tenth Five Year Plan (2002-07)	8th Plan, 9th Plan and 10th Plan	1. Central tax revenue 2. Direct taxes 3. Indirect taxes 4. Customs 5. Excise	0.9, 0.8, 1.26 1.3, 1.3, 1.5 0.7, 0.6, 1.1 0.9, 0.1, 0.96 0.6, 1.0, 1.16	--- --- --- --- ---

Contd...

Twelfth Finance Commission (2005-2010)	1950-51 to 2001-2002	1. Central taxes: Gross revenues	1.14	---
		2. States own tax revenues	1.17	---
		3. Combined tax revenues	1.15	---

* For the period 1953-54 to 1957-58.

Sources: 1. G.S. Sahota, *Tax Structure and Economic Development* (Bombay: Asia Publishing House, 1961), Tables IV and VI; 2. V. G. Rao, *Responsiveness of the Indian Tax System,* 1960-61 to 1973-74 (New Delhi: Allied Publishers Pvt. Ltd., 1979), Tables 4.1 and 4.4; 3. Government of India, Ministry of Finance, *Report of the Indirect Taxation Enquiry Committee,* Part II, January 1978, p. 399; 4. I. K. Khadye, "The Responsiveness of Tax Revenue to National Income in India, 1960-61 to 1978-79", RBI *Occasional Papers,* Vol. 2, No. 1, June 1981; 5. M M. Sury, "Buoyancy and Elasticity of Union Excise Revenue in India: 1950-51 to 1980-81", *Margin,* Vol. 18, No. 1, October, 1985, p. 55; 6. *Report of the Tenth Finance Commission*, December 1994, p. 168; 7. *Report of the Eleventh Finance Commission*, June 2000, p. 10; 8. Government of India, Planning Commission, *Tenth Five Year Plan* (2002-07), Vol. I, Table 2.25, p. 61; 9. *Report of the Twelfth Finance Commission* (2005-10), November 2004, Table 4.9, p. 64.

buoyancy coefficients were 1.04 in the nineties as against 1.12 in the eighties. The slump in the buoyancy of Central taxes in the nineties occurred despite a smart rise in the growth of revenue from direct taxes, as the revenue growth from the two major indirect taxes - customs and Union excises - sharply decelerated. Tax reform, while no doubt helping to introduce some rationality in the tax structure apparently had a dampening effect on the Centre's revenue, as the impressive growth of direct taxes could not fully compensate for the drop in customs and Union excises that took place in the post-reform period. On the States' side, the dip in tax buoyancy occurred as revenue from sales tax, the principal component of their own tax sources, showed a declining growth trend owning to tax competition among the States to attract trade and industry." [5]

For more recent periods, two estimates of buoyancy of tax revenue in India are noteworthy: one by the Tenth Five Year Plan (2002-07) and the other by the Twelfth Finance Commission (2005-10). Tenth Plan estimated the buoyancy of Central tax revenue at 0.9, 0.8 and 1.26 for Eighth Plan, Ninth Plan, and Tenth Plan respectively. Buoyancy of direct tax revenue of the Centre was estimated at 1.3, 1.3 and 1.5 for the three Plans respectively. For the same Plans, buoyancy estimates for other categories of taxes were as follows: Centre's indirect taxes (0.7, 0.6, 1.1); customs duties (0.9, 0.1, 0.96); and excise duties (0.6, 1.0, 1.16). Buoyancy estimates of the Twelfth Finance Commission (2005-10) of various groups of taxes for the period 1950-51 to 2001-02 were as follows: gross Central taxes (1.14), States own tax revenue (1.17) and combined tax revenue (1.15).

The relatively high buoyancy of the tax system revealed by the foregoing estimates indicates the success of tax policy as a tool of resource mobilization in India. However, the same studies show a relatively low elasticity of the tax system, indicating lack of inherent response of tax yield to changes in national income. Weakness of the elasticity characteristic of the tax system is generally attributed to lax administration and large-scale tax evasion.

Notes

1. If there are several discretionary changes of revenue significance during the reference period, the elasticity coefficient would be much lower than the buoyancy coefficient.
2. R. F. Bretherton, 'The Sensitivity of Taxes to Fluctuations of Trade'. *Econometrica*, Vol. V, 1937, p. 171.
3. J. Maxwell, *Fiscal Policy*, 1954, p. 105.
4. Since information on the true base of a tax is often inaccessible, proxy bases are often used.
5. Report of the Eleventh Finance Commission, June 2000, p. 11.

11

Distribution of Tax Burden (Tax Incidence)

11.1 Meaning of Tax Incidence

Incidence in economics refers to the distributional effects of a fiscal measure. Thus, tax incidence means *who bears the burden of taxes* while expenditure incidence means *who benefits from public expenditure*? Similarly, budget incidence relates to the combined effects of an equal increase in tax and public expenditure on the distribution of income. It is also called net incidence and is obtained by summing, algebraically, both the tax incidence (negative) and expenditure incidence (positive) for each of the income/expenditure classes.

Incidence of a tax is on the person who ultimately pays it, i.e. who cannot shift it any further. Hence, tax incidence relates to the final resting place of the tax burden as against the impact which means the first place where a tax is imposed. Due to economic transactions, a tax percolates through many parts of the economy and the burden of it can be shifted, forward or backward, by the original taxpayer to other entities. [1]

11.2 Methodological Issues

Analysis of the incidence of direct taxes is comparatively simple because the burden by income groups is indicated by the schedule of rates. Moreover, in poor countries direct taxes cover a very small fraction of the community so that in a classification of the population into a few broad income categories, the class of direct taxpayers will easily belong to the highest income category. In the case of indirect taxes, the problem is difficult. To analyse the incidence, one has to trace the consumption of taxed commodities to the family budgets of people in different income/expenditure classes. Income distribution data are required to estimate the liability of households for direct taxes while expenditure data are needed for ascertaining the burden of indirect taxes on households.

A tax incidence study aims at obtaining a quantitative basis for examining equity attribute of a tax system. For example, we may like to know the distribution of the money burden of excise duties among different economic classes in India in a particular year. The following points need to be kept in view before surveying tax incidence studies in India.

1. It is generally assumed that commodity taxes levied on the producers are shifted in full to the consumers who bear them in proportion to their consumption

of the various commodities taxed. However, the theory of tax incidence states that the burden of a commodity tax is shared between the consumers and producers in the ratio of elasticity of supply to elasticity of demand of the taxed commodity.

The full shifting assumption would be valid if the supply of the taxed commodity is perfectly elastic. This is not likely to be the case in the short-run in view of certain fixed costs of production. However, in the long-run when all costs become variable (i.e. factors of production can move in and out of the industry freely), the supply can be assumed to be perfectly elastic. The whole burden of the tax will get shifted to the consumers.

2. Evasion of commodity taxes (customs duties, excise levies and sales taxes) by importers, manufacturers and sellers is not uncommon in India. For example, while producers evade excise duty, in part or in full, they nevertheless 'recover' the same from the consumers. It means excise duty paid by consumers is not reflected, in such cases, in the tax collections of the Government. Estimates of tax incidence are understated to this extent.

3. A part of actual collection of commodity taxes represents tax element in the Government's consumption expenditure. This part of collections is a mere book adjustment and should be excluded from the purview of the study to avoid overestimation of tax burden. For this purpose the share of Government (at all levels) in the consumption of taxed commodities has to be found out so that that portion of revenue which the Government pays to itself could be taken out. [2] It means the money burden of commodity taxes is taken to be equivalent to revenue collections realised from non-Government sector.

4. It is desirable if the incidence analysis estimates the burden of commodity taxes on rural and urban sectors separately. This inter-sectoral approach provides a measure of horizontal equity of the tax under consideration. The rural-urban classification is important because it reflects the nature of economic activity in which people are engaged - the former primarily in agriculture and the latter in industry and services.

5. For the purpose of the study of tax incidence, researchers generally use the consumer expenditure data collected by the National Sample Survey (NSS) periodically. The NSS data splits total expenditure of a class into cash and non-cash expenditure. The important items in which non-cash expenditure (for which values are imputed) predominates are foodgrains, pulses, milk and milk products, fuel and light. These items are supplied from own-farms, kitchen gardens or free sources. The ratio of non-cash expenditure to total expenditure is high in rural sector as compared to urban sector due to obvious reasons. The non-cash expenditure is not subject to taxation.

Should incidence of taxation he expressed in relation to cash consumer expenditure only or to total consumer expenditure? One view can be that since only cash purchases are subject to taxation therefore the burden of the latter should be expressed in relation to the total cash purchases. Relating tax burden to total expenditure, will underestimate the incidence in cases where the ratio of cash purchases to total expenditure is lower as, for example, in rural areas. The other view is that since total consumption expenditure and not cash expenditure only is the appropriate index of taxpaying capacity therefore tax burden should be related to the total expenditure. As already pointed out, non-cash expenditure mainly pertains to the value imputed to consumption of home produce, goods supplied in kind (e.g. to agricultural workers) and articles acquired by barter.

6. Another issue is whether to work out incidence per capita or per household in urban and rural areas. Though estimates are available for both per household and per capita expenditure, there is no standard definition of a household in NSS data. NSS defines household as a group of persons normally living together and taking food from common kitchen. Now the ratio of tax incidence for each income/expenditure class represents the 'average' burden on that class. If these classes consist of families with different sizes, there would naturally be variations in the tax incidence on the households within each class. Therefore, the Indirect Taxation Enquiry Committee preferred monthly per capita expenditure groups "because the relative economic positions of different households are more accurately reflected by per capita expenditure levels." [3]

7. Should the burden of commodity taxes be related to income or expenditure of various economic classes? Preferably, it should be estimated with reference to both income and expenditure to present a comparative view of tax progressivity. While expenditure data are actuals as provided by NSS, income data could be derived with the help of available saving estimates of different classes.

We now turn to the estimates of various studies regarding incidence of indirect taxes in India during the post-Independence period. The findings of these studies are helpful in assessing the equity attribute of the Indian tax system.

11.3 All-India Level Studies

11.3.1 Findings of the Taxation Enquiry Commission (Chairman: John Matthai), 1953-54: Taxation Enquiry Commission (TEC), 1953-54, was the first to undertake a systematic and comprehensive study of the incidence of Central and State indirect taxes on rural and urban households in different expenditure groups. [4] TEC study was based on the consumer expenditure data collected by the National Sample Survey (NSS) in the 4th round (April-September 1952). These data were assumed to hold good for the year 1953-54 for which TEC worked out the incidence of indirect taxes. The burden of indirect taxes was worked out in terms of percentages of expenditure in different monthly expenditure classes by rural and urban areas. In the absence of data on income distribution, the expenditure was assumed to be equal to income and this presumption constituted a serious limitation of the study. The main findings of the TEC study were: (a) 3.6 per cent of consumer expenditure was paid in indirect taxes by all households in the country, (b) urban households paid twice the proportion of consumer expenditure paid in indirect taxes by rural households, and (c) among different expenditure groups in rural and urban households, the money burden of indirect taxes was mildly progressive (Table 11.1).

11.3.2 Studies by the Ministry of Finance: The incidence of Central and State indirect taxes in India was examined twice later by the Union Ministry of Finance. The first study which may be called in short as MF-I related to the year 1958-59 [5], and the second called MF-II to the year 1963-64. [6]

MF-I study was based on the NSS data on consumer expenditure collected in the 13th round (September 1957 to May 1958). Similarly, MF-II study was based on NSS data on consumer expenditure collected during the 18th round (February 1963 to January 1964). Results of these two studies are summarised in Table 11.1.

MF-I provided a comparative analysis of the distribution of money burden of all indirect taxes among rural and urban households in different expenditure groups during 1953-54 and 1958-59. The comparison brought out the change in the distribution of tax burden produced by the increase in indirect taxation during the period between the mid-points of the First and the Second Five Year Plans. The main findings of MF-I study were as follows: (a) In 1953-54, indirect taxes accounted for 3.6 per cent of consumer expenditure of all households in the country. By 1958-59, the proportion went up to 5.7 per cent, mainly on account of expansion of Central excises, and sales taxes. (b) This was true for both rural and urban households. The proportion of consumer expenditure paid in indirect taxes by rural households increased from 2.9 per cent in 1953-54 to 4.4 per cent in 1958-59, and by urban households from 5.9 per cent to 9.3 per cent over the same period. (c) In 1953-54, urban households paid twice the proportion of consumer expenditure paid in indirect taxes by rural households while by 1958-59 the proportion paid by urban households became 2.1 times that paid by rural households, implying a slightly higher relative burden on urban households. (d) the distribution of money burden of indirect taxes among different expenditure groups was progressive both in 1953-54, and 1958-59. (e) In 1958-59, the distribution of money burden of indirect taxes among different expenditure groups was more progressive at the all-India level and also separately for rural and urban households.

Table 11.1: Indirect Taxes as Per Cent of Consumer Expenditure

	TEC 1953-54			MF-I 1958-59			MF-II 1963-64		
Monthly household expenditure groups (Rs.)	Rural	Urban	All-India	Rural	Urban	All-India	Rural	Urban	All-India
1 - 50	2.2	3.3	2.4	2.5	5.8	3.1	5.8	11.1	6.5
51 - 100	2.3	4.4	2.7	3.6	7.1	4.3	6.1	11.6	7.0
101 – 150	2.7	5.1	3.1	4.1	8.0	5.1	6.8	12.6	8.0
151 – 300	2.8	5.1	3.3	4.8	9.0	5.9	8.8	14.0	10.1
301 and above	4.4	8.3	5.6	6.9	13.8	9.3	11.9	24.6	16.6
All households	2.9	5.9	3.6	4.4	9.3	5.7	8.0	16.6	10.1

Note: In the MF-II study, the lowest monthly group consisted of Rs. 0-50 and the highest Rs. 501 and above whereas in the case of the earlier studies the lowest group comprised Rs. 0-50, and the highest Rs. 301 and above. To facilitate comparison, groups Rs. 301-500 and Rs. 501 and above in the MF-II study were combined and the results for the merged group Rs. 301 and above are set out in the above table.

Sources: For TEC, Government of India, Ministry of Finance, *Report of the Taxation Enquiry Commission, 1953-54,* Vol. I, p. 69, Table 7; for MF-I, Government of India, Ministry of Finance, *Incidence of Indirect Taxation 1958-59* (New Delhi, 1961), p. 10; and for MF-II, Government of India, Ministry of Finance, *Incidence of Indirect Taxation, 1963-64* (New Delhi, 1969), Table VI.

MF-II study pertained to the incidence of indirect taxes for the year 1963-64. According to MF-II study, the proportion of indirect taxes in the total consumer expenditure increased from 3.6 per cent in 1953-54 to 5.7 per cent in 1958-59, and 10.1 per cent in 1963-64. In the case of urban households, the tax element as a percentage of per capita consumer expenditure rose from 5.9 per cent in 1953-54 to 9.3 per cent in 1958-59, and further up to 16.6 per cent in 1963-64. In the case of rural households, the corresponding increase in the tax element was from 2.9 per cent in 1953-54 to 4.4 per cent in 1958-59, and 8.0 per cent in 1963-64. Thus, as in the case of TEC and MF-I studies, the tax incidence on the urban households in 1963-64 was a little more than two times the incidence on rural households. Finally, the incidence of indirect taxation continued to remain progressive in 1963-64, both in the case of urban and rural households, judging by the proportion paid in indirect taxes by the households in different expenditure groups.

11.3.3 Estimates of Indirect Taxation Enquiry Committee (Chairman: L.K. Jha), 1978: Indirect Taxation Enquiry Committee (ITEC), 1978, undertook a comprehensive study of the incidence of indirect taxes for the year 1973-74. It was based on NSS data of consumer expenditure collected in the 28th round (October 1973 to June 1974). [7] Taking into account all indirect taxes which amounted to 11.2 per cent of national income in 1973-74, the ITEC arrived at the following main conclusions, "of this 11.2 per cent, 1.65 percentage points could be said to have fallen on the Government sector and on the investors, and the rest to have been shifted to the private consumers. The portion falling on the consumers is estimated to have amounted to 10.54 per cent of household consumption expenditure. This is an average of the burden on rural and urban households, which differed considerably in percentage terms. While the burden on rural households amounted only to 8.0 per cent of their consumption, that on the urban households amounted to 18.0 per cent. The rural sector accounted for 77 per cent of private consumption, and bore 57 per cent of the indirect taxes allocable to consumers. The share of rural sector in total population is estimated to have been 80.1 per cent in that year." [8]

Table 11.2 shows indirect taxes paid as per cent of consumer expenditure by different per capita expenditure groups ranging from the poorest group with a monthly per capita expenditure not exceeding Rs. 15 to the highest expenditure group with a monthly per capita expenditure above Rs. 100.

Table 11.2: Indirect Taxes as Per Cent of Total Expenditure by Per Capita Expenditure Groups (1973-74)

Monthly per capita expenditure group (Rs.)	Taxes as per cent of Total Expenditure		
	Rural	Urban	All-India
0 - 15	2.91	3.63	2.96
15 - 28	3.33	6.31	3.63
28 - 43	4.45	7.36	4.89
43 - 55	6.18	9.66	6.85
55 - 75	6.71	11.86	7.92
75 - 100	10.02	14.80	11.40
100 and above	16.17	30.19	21.96
All Households	8.03	17.96	10.54

Source: Government of India, Ministry of Finance, *Report of the Indirect Taxation Enquiry Committee*, Part II (January 1978), p. 90 (excerpted).

The table reveals a progressive distribution of the tax burden in terms of percentage of total expenditure at the all-India level. It increases progressively from 2.96 per cent for households with per capita monthly expenditure not exceeding Rs. 15 to 21.96 per cent for the group with per capita expenditure of Rs. 100 and above. Thus, even the poorest section of the society was found to be paying about 3 per cent of its expenditure as taxes to the Government.

Table 11.2 further reveals that the incidence of indirect taxes on different per capita expenditure groups in both rural and urban households was progressive but more so in urban than in rural area. In rural area, the lowest expenditure group (Rs. 0-15) paid 2.91 per cent of its expenditure as indirect taxes and the highest expenditure group (Rs. 100 and above) paid 16.17 per cent. In urban area, the proportion varied from 3.63 per cent (for Rs. 0-15) to 30.19 per cent (for Rs. 100 and above). The higher burden of taxes on urban households was explained by differences in the pattern of consumption between rural and urban households and also by the higher proportion of non-cash expenditures of rural households.

The ITEC study concluded also that per capita indirect tax payment per annum for urban and rural households was Rs. 174.50 and Rs. 57.30 respectively in 1973-74, giving an approximate ratio of 3:1 (Table 11.3).

Apart from the combined burden of indirect taxes, ITEC studied also the incidence of individual taxes on various expenditure groups. Table 11.3 shows the relative incidence of Central indirect taxes vis-à-vis State indirect taxes as also the incidence of Central excise duties. The last column of the table reveals that Central taxes accounted for a larger share of incidence in both urban and rural sectors. Out of 8.03 per cent, Central taxes accounted for 4.99 percentage points in rural areas and in urban areas their share was 12.03 percentage points out of a total tax burden of 17.96 per cent of expenditure. It is also observed that Central indirect taxes were more progressive than State taxes.

The share of Central excises hovered around half of the total incidence of indirect taxes. Their burden on the lowest expenditure group (Rs. 0-15), middle expenditure group (Rs. 43-55) and the highest expenditure group (Rs. 100 and above) was estimated to be 1.47 per cent 3.31 per cent and 11.55 per cent of expenditure respectively at all-India level; 1.42 per cent, 2.92 per cent and 7.87 per cent for rural sector; and 2.42 per cent, 4.94 per cent and 16.78 per cent for urban sector. The incidence of Central excises was quite progressive (Table 11.3).

In a first attempt of its kind in India, ITEC worked out the incidence of indirect taxes on major types of goods separately. The goods subject to taxes were classified into three main groups according to the nature of use, viz. (a) consumption goods, (b) intermediate goods and (c) capital goods.

Table 11.3: Per Capita Per Annum Consumer Expenditure, Indirect Tax Burden and Indirect Tax Burden as Per Cent of Consumer Expenditure, 1973-74

	RURAL							
Monthly Per Capita Expenditure Group (Rs.)	0-15	15-28	28-43	43-55	55-75	75-100	100 and above	All Households
Per Capita Per Annum Total Consumer Expenditure (Rs.)	164.66	311.20	478.55	653.01	855.11	1146.46	1907.89	713.74
Amount of Indirect Taxes Per Capita Per annum (Rs.)	4.79	10.37	21.28	40.34	57.39	114.86	308.44	57.30
Central Taxes	2.76	5.80	12.36	24.04	36.37	72.48	196.45	35.58
Central Excises	2.34	4.66	9.60	19.07	27.93	55.56	150.17	27.46
States Taxes	2.03	4.57	8.92	16.30	21.02	42.38	111.99	21.72
Tax as Percentage of Consumer Expenditure								
All Indirect Taxes	2.91	3.33	4.45	6.18	6.71	10.02	16.17	8.03
Central Taxes	1.68	1.86	2.58	3.68	4.25	6.32	10.30	4.99
Central Excises	1.42	1.50	2.01	2.92	3.27	4.85	7.87	3.85
States Taxes	1.23	1.47	1.86	2.50	2.46	3.70	5.87	3.04
	URBAN							
Per Capita Per Annum Total Consumer Expenditure (Rs.)	166.73	329.49	497.05	671.74	879.75	1179.35	2164.41	971.86
Amount of Indirect Taxes Per Capita Per annum (Rs.)	6.05	20.80	36.59	64.89	104.33	174.59	653.38	174.52
Central Taxes	4.04	12.32	22.67	40.11	66.95	110.92	454.33	116.87
Central Excises	4.04	10.25	18.65	33.18	55.00	91.68	363.12	94.54
States Taxes	2.01	8.48	13.92	24.78	37.38	63.67	199.05	57.65
Tax as Percentage of Consumer Expenditure								

Contd...

All Indirect Taxes	3.63	6.31	7.36	9.66	11.86	14.80	30.19	17.96
Central Taxes	2.42	3.74	4.56	5.97	7.61	9.41	20.99	12.03
Central Excises	2.42	3.11	3.75	4.94	6.25	7.77	16.78	9.73
States Taxes	1.21	2.57	2.80	3.69	4.25	5.40	9.20	5.93
	ALL INDIA							
Per Capita Per Annum Total Consumer Expenditure (Rs.)	164.75	312.91	481.29	656.57	860.75	1156.78	2006.09	765.13
Amount of Indirect Taxes Per Capita Per annum (Rs.)	4.87	11.35	23.55	45.00	68.13	131.81	440.44	80.65
Central Taxes	2.83	6.41	13.88	27.10	43.37	83.38	295.14	51.77
Central Excises	2.43	5.18	10.94	21.76	34.13	65.80	231.67	40.82
States Taxes	2.04	4.94	9.67	17.90	24.76	48.43	145.30	28.88
Tax as Percentage of Consumer Expenditure								
All Indirect Taxes	2.96	3.63	4.89	6.85	7.92	11.40	21.96	10.54
Central Taxes	1.72	2.05	2.88	4.13	5.04	7.21	14.71	6.77
Central Excises	1.47	1.66	2.27	3.31	3.97	5.69	11.55	5.34
States Taxes	1.24	1.58	2.01	2.73	2.88	4.19	7.24	3.77

Source: Government of India, Ministry of Finance, *Report of the Indirect Taxation Enquiry Committee*, Part II, January 1978, Appendix 10, Table 1 (excerpted).

Table 11.4 shows that out of the total incidence of 10.54 per cent of consumption expenditure for all households at all-India level, the share of consumption goods was 5.34 percentage points, amounting to half of the total incidence. Intermediate goods accounted for 4.53 percentage points and the remaining 0.63 percentage point was accounted for by capital goods. In sharp contrast to this pattern, the incidence of Central excises according to type of goods showed a totally different distribution. Intermediate goods claimed the largest share of the incidence of Central excises i.e. out of a total incidence of 5.34 per cent of consumption expenditure attributable to Central excises in respect of all households at all-India level, the incidence of Central excises on intermediate goods accounted for 2.95 percentage points which was 55 per cent of 5.34 per cent.

The ITEC also estimated the distribution of the burden of indirect taxes on certain selected commodities among various expenditure groups of urban household. It is interesting to note that the expenditure group Rs. 15-28 was made to pay 1.77 per cent of its total expenditure as tax on the six commodities (Table 11.5, col. 3, last row) while the burden on the highest expenditure group (Rs. 100 and above) was just 1.57 per cent of its expenditure (col. 8, last row). It points to the regressive nature of indirect taxes on commodities listed in Table 11.5.

A. Critical Assessment: The estimates of incidence by ITEC indicated that the overall indirect tax structure was quite progressive. However, before drawing any conclusions the following points should be noted. In its study, all households with per capita monthly expenditure of Rs. 100 and above were lumped together into one class. This was too broad a group to understand the distribution of tax burden on the middle and the rich classes.

Furthermore, the study expressed the burden of indirect taxes as a ratio of expenditure, rather than income of different economic groups. It is generally accepted that income of an individual is a better index of his ability-to-pay taxes. What percentage of income do people surrender as taxes shows the real sacrifice on their part. The law of marginal propensity to consume states that consumption expenditure, as a proportion of income, tends to fall as one moves up the income scale. Thus, at very low levels of income, consumption might be as much as the income whereas it might account for an insignificant proportion of income at high income levels. For instance, it can safely be assumed that for the lowest two or three expenditure groups the distinction between income and expenditure is not significant in view of the high marginal propensity to consume amongst these groups.

Therefore, the percentage of consumption expenditure paid as taxes virtually represents the percentage of income. This, however, is not true at higher levels of

Table 11.4: Burden of all Indirect Taxes and Central Excises as per cent of Consumer Expenditure According to Type of Goods

	Monthly per capita Expenditure Groups (Rs.)							
	0-15	15-28	28-43	43-55	55-75	75-100	100 and above	All Households
All India **All Indirect Taxes**	2.95	3.63	4.89	6.85	7.92	11.40	21.96	10.54
1. Consumption Goods	1.32	1.66	2.31	3.58	3.91	6.10	11.11	5.34
2. Intermediate Goods	1.47	1.75	2.30	2.91	3.59	4.75	9.17	4.53
3. Capital Goods	0.16	0.22	0.28	0.36	0.42	0.55	1.68	0.67
Central Excises	1.47	1.66	2.27	3.31	3.97	5.69	11.55	5.34
1. Consumption Goods	0.41	0.46	0.74	1.37	1.63	2.62	5.03	2.25
2. Intermediate Goods	1.06	1.19	1.52	1.92	2.31	3.01	6.01	2.95
3. Capital Goods	---	0.01	0.01	0.02	0.03	0.06	0.51	0.14

Source: Compiled from Government of India, Ministry of Finance, *Report of the Indirect Taxation Enquiry Committee*, Part II, (January 1978), Chapter 6, Tables 3 and 4, pp. 96 and 98.

Table 11.5: Distribution of the Burden of Indirect Taxes on Certain Selected Commodities Among Various Expenditure Groups of Urban Households as per cent of Total Consumption Expenditure (1973-74)

Commodities	Monthly per capita Expenditure Groups (Rs.)							
	0-15	15-28	28-43	43-55	55-75	75-100	100 and above	All Households
	Percentages							
Total Incidence for All Indirect Taxes	3.63	6.31	7.36	9.66	11.86	14.80	30.19	17.96
Foodgrains and *Atta**	0.30	0.37	0.36	0.33	0.28	0.24	0.18	0.26
Sugar	0.61	0.46	0.60	0.55	0.54	0.51	0.38	0.47
Vegetable Product, Oil and Fats	0.00	0.33	0.46	0.52	0.50	0.50	0.40	0.47
Kerosene	0.00	0.48	0.51	0.54	0.51	0.50	0.45	0.50
Matches	0.00	0.05	0.07	0.10	0.09	0.06	0.05	0.07
Soaps and Detergents	0.00	0.08	0.11	0.11	0.12	0.12	0.11	0.11
Total for the 6 items	0.91	1.77	2.11	2.15	2.04	1.93	1.57	1.88

* Taxes on these commodities are levied only by the State Governments.

Source: Compiled from Government of India, Ministry of Finance, *Report of the Indirect Taxation Enquiry Committee*, Part II (January 1978), Chapter 6, Table 7, pp.102-3.

income where the amount of taxes forms a higher percentage of expenditure but quite a low percentage of income. Thus, a progressive system of taxation with reference to expenditure may turn out to be less progressive or even regressive when related to income. Or, putting it differently, the studies which relate tax burden to expenditure overstate the progression (or understate the regression) of the tax system. Therefore, it is difficult to conclude on the basis of ITEC findings whether the indirect tax system is equitable or not.

11.3.4 Findings of the Study by National Institute of Public Finance and Policy (NIPFP): This study of incidence of indirect taxes in India was sponsored by the Ministry of Finance, Government of India. It was conducted at the National Institute of Public Finance and Policy (NIPFP) by Pawan K. Aggarwal. The study, which has recently been published in the form of a book [9], estimated the incidence of major indirect taxes, viz. customs duties and excise duties levied by the Central Government, and sales taxes levied by the State Governments.

Major findings of the study which pertained to the fiscal year 1989-90 are the following, "(i) a large variation in the tax incidence across commodities with high incidence of tax on some commodities, (ii) moderately high tax incidence on necessities, (iii) substantial input taxation (accounting for more than 30 per cent of tax incidence on most commodities), (iv) sales tax contributing the highest to input taxation, (v) tax incidence on consumers in rural areas lower than that in urban areas, (vi) progresssivity of taxes in rural areas higher than that in urban areas, (vii) tax incidence on food items lower than that on non-food items, and (viii) tax incidence on cereals lower than that on other food items." [10]

Based on the consumer expenditure data of the National Sample Survey in the 44th round (July 1988 - June 1989), the study estimated the combined effective tax rates for rural and urban areas at 11.2 per cent and 12.2 per cent respectively, indicating lower tax burden on consumers in rural areas than in urban areas. The distribution of tax burden with reference to consumer expenditure was found to be progressive in both rural and urban areas, though tax progressivity was higher in rural areas vis-à-vis urban areas. The effective tax rate increased along low to high expenditure classes from 9.8 per cent to 13.7 per cent in rural areas, and from 10.2 per cent to 13.4 per cent in urban areas (Table 11.6).

By relating tax burden to monthly per capita expenditure, the study repeated the mistake committed by the Indirect Taxation Enquiry Committee. Hence, its conclusions suffer from limitations. By its own admission, the study observed "It may, however, be noted that the tax progressivity would not have been so pronounced if it was viewed with reference to income instead of expenditure as the rich has a lower propensity to spend. If we assume zero savings by an average person in the lowest expenditure class and a 30 per cent savings rate for an average person in the top expenditure class, then their effective tax rates with respect to income will be approximately equal even in the rural areas." [11] More appropriately, the expenditure classes should have been converted into income classes by using estimates of savings of different income groups, periodically brought out by NCAER. This was actually done by the Orissa Taxation Enquiry Committee while estimating incidence of taxation in that State.

Table 11.6: Combined Effective Rates of Major Indirect Taxes by 5 Expenditure Classes: 1988-89

		All Commodities		
S. No.	Monthly Per Capita Expenditure (Rs.)	Rural Areas	Urban Areas	All Areas
1	< 110	9.81	10.25	9.85
2	110 - 160	10.27	10.82	10.36
3	160 – 215	10.94	11.21	11.00
4	215 - 385	11.74	11.78	11.75
5	Above 385	13.75	13.45	13.59

Source: Pawan K. Aggarwal, *Who Pays the Tax* (Gayatri Publications, Delhi, 1998), p. 63, Table 5.3 (excerpted).

11.4 State-Level Studies

Among the State-level tax incidence studies, the following are noteworthy: one by the Orissa Taxation Enquiry Committee [12] and two studies by National Council of Applied Economic Research (NCAER) for the States of Gujarat, and Mysore (now Karnataka). [13]

11.4.1 Orissa Taxation Enquiry Committee: The Orissa Taxation Enquiry Committee was appointed by the Government of Orissa in 1959 under the chairmanship of P.S. Lokanathan. One of the terms of reference of the Committee was, 'to assess and advise on the incidence of the present structure and level of taxation on the people of different classes with particular reference to conditions in other States.'

For analysing the tax burden vis-à-vis the pattern of consumption expenditure of different income groups in the rural and urban sectors in Orissa, the Committee conducted a family budget enquiry in 1960 on the basis of stratified sampling. Households were classified and calculations of incidence made on the basis of monthly expenditure, instead of on the basis of monthly income. However, a procedure was devised to compute average income of each of the expenditure groups so that the burden of taxation could be related to income rather than expenditure of the household. It was assumed that the three expenditure groups (Table 11.7) did not have any savings, i.e. their income was the same as expenditure. In regard to the remaining groups it was assumed that there were some savings, and the higher the group the greater would be the rate of saving. The average propensity to save would be different for urban and rural households in the same expenditure level. Generally speaking, urban households can save less than their counterparts in rural areas in the same expenditure group. On the advice of NCAER, the average propensity to save in Orissa was assumed to be 5 per cent in rural areas and 11 per cent in urban areas. The rate of saving assumed for each group may be seen in Table 11.7.

Table 11.7: Incidence of Taxes in Orissa, 1960

Expenditure Group	Taxes as % of consumption expenditure		Average propensity to save		Taxes as percentage of income	
	Rural	Urban	Rural	Urban	Rural	Urban
1 - 50	1.9	3.6	---	---	1.9	3.6
51 – 100	2.2	4.1	--	---	2.2	4.1
101 – 150	2.7	4.3	---	--	2.7	4.3
151 – 300	3.3	4.7	7.0	7.0	3.1	4.3
301 – 500	3.0	5.7	12.0	10.0	2.7	3.2
501 – 1000	2.8	8.2	25.0	20.0	2.3	6.8
1000 and above	2.6	14.6	35.0	25.0	1.9	11.7
All Groups	2.6	5.8	5.0	11.0	2.5	5.2

Source: Government of Orissa, *Orissa Taxation Enquiry Committee Report*, Bhubaneshwar, 1961.

The following information was revealed by the Orissa Committee: (1) Incidence of direct taxes per person per year was Rs. 1.56 in the rural areas against Rs. 8.64 in the urban areas. This disparity was due to the fact that income tax did not touch the rural taxpayers; (2) among indirect taxes, those of Central origin were found to claim a larger share than State taxes in rural as well as urban sectors. Rural incidence was Rs. 5.40 per annum while the urban incidence was Rs. 13.68; (3) by relating tax burden to income, the Committee found that in rural areas people paid 2.5 per cent of their income towards taxes against 5.2 per cent in urban areas; (4) the Committee found that the more well-to-do households in rural areas pay comparatively less tax than their counterparts in the urban areas or even the poorer households in the rural areas.

11.4.2 NCAER Study on Gujarat: The NCAER study of tax incidence in Gujarat pertained to the year 1967-68. It was an attempt to estimate the incidence of all taxes (Central and State) on households by income/expenditure groups. In order to measure the distribution of the burden of taxation among different income/expenditure classes of households, a sample survey was specially designed to collect data regarding family budgets and incomes of households. The actual tax liability of each household was calculated by applying the tax rates to the expenditure and income data collected through the survey.

The distribution of the money burden of the tax system as a whole was found to be progressive. Taxes as a proportion of income increased from 8 per cent in the lowest income group (less than Rs. 1,200 per annum) to 22 per cent in the highest group (above Rs. 24,000 per annum). This progression was attributed to the Central income tax, particularly at the higher income levels. The Study, however, found the incidence of individual taxes on commodities and services, such as Union excise and sales tax, to be regressive throughout the income ranges. The incidence of taxes on commodities and services was also studied with reference to expenditure. It was found that the overall burden of these taxes did not vary significantly at lower expenditure ranges although it became markedly progressive in the higher expenditure groups mainly due to the Central excise duty and State sales tax.

Two limitations of this study may particularly be noted. The Gujarat study was confined to the urban sector of that State. This partial analysis robbed the study much of its usefulness. Not only this, the survey sample (1000 households in five towns) was too inadequate for a State like Gujarat. Moreover, the incidence of Union excises on consumer goods only was taken into account, i.e. the duty on producer goods used for the production of consumer goods was not covered due to difficulties of calculating the tax element in the prices of consumer goods that might have been shifted from the excise duties on raw materials and other intermediate goods.

11.4.3 NCAER Study on Mysore (Now Karnataka): The NCAER study of tax incidence for the State of Mysore related to the year 1968-69. It examined the tax burden in relation to household income and analysed the pattern of its distribution among different income groups, both in the urban and in the rural sectors of the State of Mysore. A representative sample survey of incomes and expenditures of households, stratified separately for urban and rural areas was undertaken to collect the necessary data.

For estimating the incidence of income tax, the tax revenue realised in the State from incomes arising during the year 1968-69 was allocated to the different income classes in the proportion of their tax liability calculated on the basis of the survey data. For indirect taxes, incidence was calculated separately for taxes on final consumer goods and producer goods.

The study showed contrasting effects of the tax system on the urban and the rural sectors. The tax system as a whole was found to be progressive in the urban sector but regressive in the rural sector (Table 11.8). Thus, in the urban sector, the tax-income ratio was found to rise from 10.1 per cent in the lowest income class to 18.3 per cent in the highest income group. Conversely, the ratio declined from 9.0 per cent to 5.7 per cent in the rural sector. The regressivity of the tax system in the rural sector was attributed to the absence of a progressive income tax. A marked disparity between the tax incidence on the urban and the rural sectors was also noticed throughout the entire range of household incomes. The inter-sectoral disparity was found to increase sharply with increase in income and the tax burden on the highest income class in the urban sector was more than three times that on the comparable level in the rural sector (18.3:5.7). However, the average incidence on households in the urban areas was less than twice than in the rural sector (11.4:6.7). It was observed that even in the urban sector the tax system was not strictly progressive throughout the range of household incomes. It was regressive in the lowest income classes due to exemption from income tax at that income level. [14]

Table 11.8: Incidence of Tax System as a whole in the State of Mysore (now Karnataka), 1968-69

Annual Household Income Groups (Rs.)	Urban (per cent)	Rural (per cent)	Ratio of Urban/Rural Tax incidence
Up to 1,200	10.1	9.0	1.12
1,201 - 2,400	9.0	6.5	1.37
2,401 - 4,800	8.8	6.6	1.35
4,801 - 9,000	9.3	7.0	1.33
9,001 – 18,000	10.3	7.1	1.46
18,001 – 36,000	14.1	5.7	2.47
Over 36,000	18.3	5.7	3.21
All Groups	11.4	6.7	1.70

Source: National Council of Applied Economic Research, *Incidence of Taxation in Mysore State* (1972), p. 6.

11.5 Sectoral Studies

Tax incidence studies pertaining to particular sectors of the Indian economy have also been attempted. Agricultural sector has received the maximum attention owing to the long-standing controversy regarding tax burden on Indian agriculture. The controversy was further aggravated by the Report of the

Committee on Taxation of Agricultural Wealth and Income. [15] The Committee recommended the levying of Agricultural Holdings Tax (AHT) on operational holdings and on a family basis. Incidence studies on Indian agriculture have been of all-India as well as State-level character. [16]

Most of the tax incidence studies have pointed out that the agricultural sector is relatively undertaxed and thus has the potential to bear a larger share of the tax burden. However, it must be noted that aggregative estimates of tax incidence of these studies have not taken into account the pattern of distribution of income in the two sectors. The greater the unequal distribution of income, the higher the tax yield under a system of progressive taxation. Furthermore, differences in the incidence of indirect taxes on the same expenditure groups in the rural and in the urban sectors are not due to deliberate manipulations in the tax system but are the result of differing characteristics of the two sectors. As Anand P. Gupta observed, "But what must be noted is that this horizontal inequity in the incidence of Central taxes is not due to any formal bias of these taxes in favour of the expenditure groups in the rural areas. In effect, the reasons for the inequitable incidence of Central indirect taxes, which are formally uniform throughout the country, lie in (a) the differences in the relative shares of cash and non-cash expenditures in the total consumer expenditures, with the ratio of cash purchases to total consumer expenditures for the same expenditure groups being lower in the rural sector than in the urban sector and (b) the differences in the expenditure patterns of the same rural and urban expenditure groups and the failure of the tax system to adapt itself to these differences." [17]

Incidence of individual taxes has also attracted a lot of attention, the prominent being the corporation tax which has become an issue of fierce controversy as regards the possibility of its being shifted to consumers. Traditionally, this tax, on the earnings of companies, has been accepted as a direct tax but lately this belief has come in for sharp criticism in view of the empirical evidence produced by some studies. [18] While V. D. Lall and G. S. Laumas have concluded that company taxes are shifted to consumers, Ved. P. Gandhi has come to the opposite conclusion that company taxes are not shifted to the consumers. In view of the conflicting evidence, the issue can be regarded as wide open.

Notes

1. When taxes are imposed, disposable real income of the people is reduced. Real income may be reduced due to reduction in disposable money income because of direct taxes and/or increase in the prices of products purchased due to indirect taxes. To use the Musgravian formula, the disposable real income (DRY) of a household may be defined as

$$DRY = \frac{E - Ty}{P + Ts} = \frac{DY}{GP}$$

where E is earning, Ty is income tax, P is the price (at factor cost) of products bought, and Ts is the sales tax (or some other commodity tax) addition thereto. DY is disposable or after-tax money income, and GP is the gross (or market) price (R. A. Musgrave and P. B. Musgrave, *Public Finance in Theory and Practice*, Third edition, p. 263).

Changes in Ty operate on the earnings (as producers) side of the household account. Changes in Ts operate on the expenditure (as consumers) side of the account. Thus, an increase in income tax lowers DRY via an increase in Ty and hence a fall in DY. An increase in sales tax lowers DRY via an increase in Ts and hence in GP. It is clear now how disposable real income of a household is subject to the effects of both direct and indirect taxes . The total incidence of a tax system on an individual is equal to the sum of tax burden borne by him as a producer and as a consumer.

For every rupee raised as tax, there is a corresponding reduction in the disposable real income of someone. Reduction in one's disposable real income is taken to be equivalent to the tax realisation by the government. Incidence analysis attempts to track down individuals/households whose real incomes are truncated when taxes are imposed. Incidence analysis deals with the diffusion of tax burden among different economic classes in a country.

Various Types of Tax Incidence

Statutory versus Economic Incidence: Persons who have legal responsibility of paying taxes to the government suffer statutory incidence (or impact) of a tax. In other words, statutory incidence refers to the legal placing of the tax liability, i.e. who bears the tax burden in the first instance. For example, the statutory incidence of excise duty on sugar is on the producer of sugar.

Those who suffer statutory incidence of a tax are not necessarily the ultimate bearers of the tax burden. Very often, persons who have the legal obligation of paying taxes to the government shift, in part or in full, the tax burden to consumers or other entities. This shifting becomes possible through economic transactions in an economy. Hence, those who bear the tax burden ultimately suffer the economic incidence of a tax. It refers to the final resting place of a tax. If excise duty on sugar is shifted by the producers to the consumers, the latter suffer the economic incidence of the duty.

Absolute versus Relative Incidence: The extent to which persons in different economic groups are hurt as a result of the imposition of taxes is generally measured in terms of money burden of taxes as a percentage of money income/expenditure of various groups. The amount of income surrendered as taxes by the income receivers is the absolute measure of tax burden while the proportion of income paid as taxes is a relative measure of this burden. Obviously, it is the relative burden which is relevant for comparing money burden of taxes on households in different income/expenditure groups.

Formal versus Effective Incidence: Formal incidence means the money burden of taxes as resting with the subject on whom the burden is intended by the tax authority to fall. In other words, it refers to the statistical estimate of tax payments by income groups

In addition to imposing direct money burden (formal incidence), taxes also generate effects which may affect the relative economic positions of different individuals/ households. Effective incidence refers to the economic effects of taxation.

Differential Tax Incidence: It is the study of the effects of a tax that has been substituted for another tax yielding equal revenue.

Factors Determining Extent of Tax Shifting

Tax shifting means the transfer of tax burden from the original payer to some other entity. Tax shifting is the study of ways in which the burden of taxation is shifted among persons and organisations in an economy. For example, excise duty on producers of sugar can be shifted forward to the consumers by increasing the price of sugar by the amount of duty. The burden of excise duty can be shifted backward also by reducing the price paid to sugarcane suppliers or factors of production hired. Forward shifting or backward shifting may be full or partial.

Is it always possible for the producers to shift the burden of a commodity tax to the consumers? The degree and the direction to which a tax can be shifted depends on a host of factors including elasticity of demand and supply, coverage of the tax, and the time period allowed for adjustments. The study of tax shifting and the estimation of the final distribution of the tax burden is an essential component of tax analysis.

Elasticity of Demand and Supply: As for the elasticity factor, the general rules are: 1. Higher the elasticity of demand, greater is the tax burden on producers, and 2. Higher the elasticity of supply, greater will be the tax burden on consumers. In technical terms, the ratio in which tax burden is divided between the consumers and the producers is given by the ratio of elasticity of supply to elasticity of demand.

Coverage of the Tax: If excise duty is imposed on tea and not on coffee, then it would be difficult for producers to shift the duty on tea to consumers. If they try to do so, consumers have the option to switch over to the consumption of coffee. However, if excise duty is imposed on both tea and coffee, it would be difficult for the consumers to escape the tax burden. Thus, wider the coverage of a tax, the greater will be the burden on consumers and vice versa. Hence, selective taxes are more likely to be avoided by the consumers than broad-based taxes.

Time Period: Distribution of the burden of an indirect tax between producers and consumers is governed also by the time period allowed for adjustment. In the short-run, it is difficult for the producers to adjust their supplies in response to fluctuating demand because of certain fixed costs of production. Technically, the supply curve in the short-run is less elastic. Under such circumstances, it would be difficult for the producers to pass on the tax burden to the consumers. However, in the long-run, the distinction between fixed and variable costs vanishes. Producers can adjust the supplies in tune with demand conditions. Technically, the supply curve is elastic, may be perfectly elastic. Thus, the burden of a commodity tax can be passed on to the consumers.

The time factor is important from demand side also. If a commodity is taxed, it may have to be purchased in the short-run in the absence of substitutes. However, in the long-run substitutes of the taxed commodity become available. Moreover, consumption habits may also change. Hence, consumers are in a better position to avoid the tax in the long-run. Since both demand and supply become more elastic in the long-run, it is difficult to say as to what extent producers and consumers would be able to avoid the tax burden.

2. Government here means Government Administration as defined in Account 1 of the economic classification of the Central Government budget. In other words, departmental and non-departmental industrial and commercial activities of the Government are not considered. This distinction is important because all Governmental activities do not have the same economic significance. Thus, expenditure of Government administration is in the nature of consumer outlays and represents demand for goods and services for final consumption. Contrarily, expenditure of public sector undertakings is intermediate expenditure forming part of the prices of goods and services supplied by them.

3. Government of India, Ministry of Finance, *Report of the Indirect Taxation Enquiry Committee* (Chairman: L. K. Jha) Part II, 1978, p. 105.

4. Government of India, Ministry of Finance, *Report of the Taxation Enquiry Commission* (Chairman: John Matthai) 1953-54, Vol. I, chapters 4 and 5.

5. Government of India, Ministry of Finance, *Incidence of Indirect Taxation, 1958-59* (New Delhi, 1961).

6. Government of India, Ministry of Finance, *Incidence of Indirect Taxation, 1963-64* (New Delhi, 1969).

7. The procedures adopted by the National Sample Survey (NSS) to collect consumer expenditure data in the 28th round are explained hereunder.

NSS collected in its 28th round (October 1973 to June 1974) data on *consumer expenditure per person* for 30 days on *broad groups of items by monthly per capita expenditure classes* in rural and urban areas. It also prepared estimates of quantity of consumption of cereals per person for 30 days by the same expenditure classification. The information was collected both at State and all-India level. The period of 30 days for which data were collected preceded the date of survey. No account was taken of any expenditure incurred towards the productive enterprises of the household. The survey extended over the whole of the rural and urban areas of the Indian Union except certain inaccessible parts like Ladakh or disturbed areas like parts of Tripura. The survey period of 9 months was divided into 3 sub-rounds of 3 months each.

Some of the important concepts and definitions followed in the 28th round were as follows:

Household. A household was defined as a group of persons normally living together and taking food from common kitchen. A boarding house, a hotel or a hostel was treated as a cluster of households, where each individual boarder formed a separate household. Households maintained and fed directly by government such as those in prisons, police quarters, cantonments, hospitals, relief camps were excluded from the scope of the enquiry.

Cash Purchase. This referred to all cash purchases except for enterprise purposes of the household during the reference period. Only such purchases as were made for non-productive domestic purposes were considered for this purpose.

Homegrown Stock: Homegrown stock included commodities produced at home like from kitchen garden and household livestock products and produce from household industries. Produce brought from village home was also included in this. Homegrown stocks were imputed ex-farm price or ex-factory rate which was free from distribution cost or middle man's profit or other trade margins.

Household Consumer Expenditure: Consumer expenditure of a household comprised all expenditure incurred by the household during a reference period of 30 days preceding the date of survey exclusively towards its non-productive domestic consumption. Transfer payments in *kind* like loans advanced, charities, gifts and other payments in kind, if any, were not considered as consumer expenditure. But any consumption out of transfer receipts in kind like borrowing, gifts, charities, perquisites received by the household, free collection and other receipts in kind, if any, were considered for determining total consumption of the household.

Data on consumer expenditure were collected by NSS for a large number of items. But in presenting the results similar items were merged to form homogeneous groups (21 such groups were formed in the 28th round).

The results were presented in the form of detailed tables in respect of rural and urban areas for each State and Union Territory, all-India, Union Territories pooled, and for four big cities (Bombay, Calcutta, Delhi and Madras) separately and combined.

The following information was provided by the 28th round.

(a) Distribution of sample households, percentage distribution of estimated number of households and estimated number of adult males, adult females and children per household *by monthly per capita expenditure classes.*

(b) Consumer expenditure (in Rs.) per person for a period of 30 days by broad groups of items and by monthly per capita expenditure classes.

(c) Quantity (in Kg.) and value (in Rs.) of consumption per person for a period of 30 days on items cereals, gram and cereal substitutes by monthly per capita expenditure classes.

The general sample design in the NSS 28th round was stratified with two-stage selection within each stratum; the first stage units were villages/blocks in the rural/urban areas and the second stage units the households. The sample design was made self-weighting for all the household schedules at stage level separately by rural and urban sectors.

In the sample there were 8730 villages in rural areas and 4944 blocks in urban areas.

Rural Sample Design: The sampling frame used for selection was the list of villages as per 1971 population census stratification. The whole of India was divided into a number of basic strata so that the basic strata did not cut across district boundaries. Districts with more than 1.5 million 1971 census rural population were divided into two or more basic strata by grouping contiguous tehsils, homogeneous as far as possible with respect to density of rural population and crop pattern, so that the population of each basic stratus was less than 1.5 million. Each district with less than 1.5 million 1971 census rural population formed one basic stratum by itself. Basic strata so formed were treated as basic strata both for rural and urban sectors.

Allocation: Within each State and Union Territory, the allocated number of villages was distributed over the constituent basic strata in proportion to their rural population.

Selection of Villages: The 1971 census list of villages was used as the sampling frame for selection of villages. Sample villages within each basic stratum were selected with probability proportional to 1971 population and with replacements.

Selection of household: All households in a sample village were arranged into six classes on the basis of their means of livelihood and visit to health centre or not. From the arranged frame in a village, a sample of households was selected linear systematically using the intervals and random starts specified for the purpose. The list of 1971 census enumeration blocks was used as the sampling frame.

Stratification: Basic strata as described in rural sample design were treated as basic strata for urban sector also.

Allocation: Within each State and Union Territory, the allocated number of blocks was distributed over the constituent basic strata in proportion to their urban population.

Selection of Households: All households in a sample block were arranged into six classes by occupations. From the arranged frame in a block a sample of households was selected linear systematically with specified interval and random start.

8. Government of India, Ministry of Finance, *Report of the Indirect Taxation Enquiry Committee* (Chairman: L. K. Jha), Part II, January 1978, p. 89.

9. Pawan K. Aggarwal, *Who Pays the Tax*? (Delhi: Gayatri Publications, 1998).

10. *Ibid*, pp. i-ii.

11. *Ibid*, p. 61.

12. Government of Orissa, *Report of the Orissa Taxation Enquiry Committee* (Bhubaneshwar, 1961).

13. National Council of Applied Economic Research, *Incidence of Taxation in Gujarat* (New Delhi, 1970); and *Incidence of Taxation in Mysore State* (New Delhi, 1972). See also A. C. Angrish, "Agricultural and Non-Agricultural Taxation: An Estimate of Their Burden in Rajasthan', in *Economic and Political Weekly*, Vol. V, January 10, 1970.

14. It is a general phenomenon that the tax system as a whole is regressive in the lowest ranges, proportional in the middle ranges and progressive in the upper ranges of income. Thus, continuous progressivity is a rare occurrence when both direct and indirect taxes are taken into account.

15. Government of India, Ministry of Finance, *Report of the Committee on Taxation of Agricultural Wealth and Income*,(Chairman: K. N. Raj) October 1972.

16. Major among these are: Ved P. Gandhi, *Tax Burden on Indian Agriculture* (Cambridge, Massachusetts, 1966); Mahesh T. Pathak and Arun S. Patel, *Agricultural Taxation in Gujarat* (Bombay: Asia Publishing House, 1970); Hemlata Rao, "Tax Incidence on Agricultural Sector in Uttar Pradesh", in *Economic and Political Weekly*, Vol. VI, September 11, 1971; S. L. Shetty, "An Inter-Sectoral Analysis of Taxable Capacity and Tax Burden", in *Indian Journal of Agricultural Economics* (Bombay), Vol. XXVI, July-September 1971 and "Inter-Class Incidence of Taxation in Farm and Non-Farm Sectors in India", in *Economic and Political Weekly* (Bombay), Vol. VI, December 25, 1971; C. H. Hanumantha Rao, *Taxation of Agricultural Land in Andhra Pradesh* (Bombay, Asia Publishing House, 1964).

17. Anand P. Gupta, *Fiscal Policy and Employment Generation in India* (New Delhi: Tata McGraw-Hill, 1977), p. 37.

18. The Chief among these are: Ved P. Gandhi, *Some Aspects of India's Tax Structure* (Bombay: Vora and Co., 1970); A. Ambirajan, *The Taxation of Corporate Income in India* (Bombay: Asia Publishing House, 1964); V. D. Lall, "Shifting and Incidence of Direct Taxes on Companies", *Fiftieth Annual Conference Papers of Indian Economic Association*, Part III (Bombay, 1967); Gurcharan S. Laumas, "The Shifting of the Corporation Income Tax - A Study with Reference to Indian Corporations", in *Public Finance*, Vol. 21, 1966; V. Ganapathi Rao and K. S. Hanumantha Rao, "The Incidence of the Corporate Income Tax in the Short Run: The Case of Indian Corporations", in *Public Finance*, Vol. 26, 1971.

12

Tax Evasion: Magnitude, Causes and Remedial Measures

Tax evasion exists in all countries, though in varying degrees. It is a serious problem in developing countries which are in the process of evolving their tax systems.

12.1 Meaning of Tax Evasion

Tax evasion is an illegal attempt to reduce the tax payable by deliberately under-reporting or not reporting taxable incomes or concealing one's true *state of affairs* from tax authorities. Tax evasion is a criminal offence and if detected is punishable by financial penalties or even by imprisonment or both.

12.1.1 Tax Evasion and Tax Avoidance: Tax avoidance means preventing or reducing one's tax liability through manipulations within the framework of existing tax legislation. Tax avoidance, as against tax evasion, is legally permissible and hence a legitimate aim of taxpayers.

Tax avoidance is resorted to through such devices as formation of holding companies to claim artificial deductions, constitution of trusts [1] and family partnerships, transfer of income earning assets to one's wife and children for fractioning income for tax purposes, investing in provident funds and life insurance policies, and manipulation of capital gains.

Since tax avoidance has a colour of legality about it, clever taxpayers do their best to avoid or keep down tax payments. This may force the government to raise tax rates, making the less clever assessees bear a disproportionate tax burden.

Tax laws in many countries incorporate anti-tax avoidance provisions under which certain incomes are included in an assessee's total income, though such incomes legally belong to other persons. For example, in India, Sections 60 to 65 of the Income Tax Act, 1961, deal with instances where an assessee may attempt to reduce his tax liability either by transferring his assets in favour of his family members or by arranging his sources of income in such a manner that tax incidence falls on others, whereas benefit of income, directly or indirectly, is derived by the assessee himself. Thus, income arising to the spouse, minor child, son's wife, son's minor child and certain other persons are clubbed with the assessee's income in certain circumstances. In this regard, the Indian income tax law deviates from the general principle that a person can be assessed in respect of his own income.

12.2. Devices Adopted to Evade Taxes

12.2.1 Income Tax: The following devices are generally employed to evade income tax:

1. Non-reporting/under-reporting of taxable income.
2. Maintaining multiple set of account books, fraudulent changes in account books, and keeping transactions out of account books.
3. Opening and operating bank accounts under assumed names.
4. Doing business in the name of dummies.
5. Over-reporting expenses.
6. Fragmenting income to reduce tax liability.
7. Under-invoicing sales and other transfer pricing manipulations.

Although evasion of tax is a common tendency among people belonging to different groups, opportunities for it vary according to the nature of income earned by taxpayers. In the case of income from salaries and interest from deposits, evasion is less likely because of proper recording and auditing of transactions, and deduction of tax at source. However, opportunities for tax evasion are very large in the case of self-employed in business and professions. Doctors, lawyers, architects, property dealers, individual contractors can evade taxes more easily than others. They can insist on their customers to pay them in cash or accept invoices which underestimate the payment.

12.2.2 Excise Duties: Excise evasion is generally resorted to by adopting, *inter alia*, following malpractices.

1. Incorrect accountal of goods.
2. Undervaluation of goods.
3. Flouting the conditions subject to which any goods may be exempted from duty.

12.2.3 Value-Added Tax: The proponents of VAT claim that evasion under it is difficult and minimal. The tax credit method ensures cross-checking of the records of taxpayers through invoices. Buyer firms insist on supplier firms to furnish invoices which help the former to claim tax credit. Since tax liability of a single taxpayer under VAT is only a fraction of the total amount of tax, the incentive for evasion is relatively weak. Even a successful evasion would mean less revenue loss as compared to the one suffered under a system of turnover tax on gross value (excise duty or sales tax).

Despite the self-policing nature of VAT, opportunities do exist under it for evasion and fraud. In fact, VAT provides opportunities for fraud (fictitious claims for refunds) which are not available under other forms of commodity taxation. The methods commonly applied to defraud tax authorities under VAT include, *inter alia,* the following.

1. Use of fake invoices to claim tax credit.
2. Tax credit claims on purchases for personal use.
3. Over-reporting of sales of zero-rated goods.
4. Secret deals between buyers and sellers as regards issuance of receipts.
5. Formation of fake companies which sell receipts to traders to enable them to claim tax credit on inputs.

In short, VAT is as susceptible to evasion and fraud as any other tax. An efficient tax machinery capable of cross-checking a large number of invoices through an elaborate computer system is a pre-requisite for the successful implementation of VAT. This is precisely what is lacking in an underdeveloped country.

12.2.4 Customs Duties: Evasion of customs duties takes place through following malpractices.

1. Invoice misclassification.
2. Manipulation of documents.
3. Suppression of quantities imported.

12.3. Causes of Tax Evasion

12.3.1 Level of Tax Rates: Among the host of causes of tax evasion, the level of tax rates is probably the most crucial. It is widely believed that higher the rate of tax, the greater is the tendency to evade taxes. High tax rates make tax evasion more tempting. Tax evaders readily take greater risks if they know that in the event of success the reward is high.

12.3.2 Attitude towards Government and its Laws: Tax evasion is more in countries where there is general apathy on the part of people towards the government and its laws. People will have less respect for tax laws if they perceive the tax system to be unfair in terms of level of taxation (tax-GDP ratio) and/or distribution of tax burden among various classes. Similarly, there can be a feeling among taxpayers that government is indulging in wasteful expenditure, e.g. digging the roads too often, spending excessively on government functionaries, permitting loan waivers, maintaining perpetually sick public undertakings, and granting unnecessary subsidies.

12.3.3 Lenient Penal Action: Lenient penal action in case violation of law is detected also encourages tax evasion. Tax evasion by politicians and bureaucrats sends wrong signals to the general public that non-compliance is acceptable. A regime of controls, licences, and shortages also breeds tax evasion and black money.

12.3.4 Nature of the Economy: The problem of tax evasion in underdeveloped countries is associated with the peculiar characteristics of their economies which, in most cases, are agriculture-based in the sense that a substantial part of national income originates from and the majority of the work force is engaged in agriculture. Moreover, there is widespread illiteracy, lack of accounting practices, limited monetisation and shortage of administrative resources.

12.4 Consequences of Tax Evasion

The effects of tax evasion on an economy are indeed disastrous.

1. Tax evasion cuts at the very root of the revenue potential of a tax system and therefore hinders the resource mobilisation efforts of a government. Lack of funds may distort implementation of development plans and force a government to resort to deficit financing in case public expenditure is inelastic.
2. Tax evasion may interfere with the declared economic policies of a government by distorting saving/investment patterns and availability of resources to various sectors of the economy. For instance, government may impose credit restrictions to discourage certain activities (e.g. speculation) but money saved through tax evasion may finance and encourage the same activities.
3. Evasion of tax seriously undermines the equity attribute of a tax system. Honest taxpayers, who are obliged to bear disproportionate tax burden, feel demoralised and tempted to join the tax evaders' camp.
4. Tax evasion leads to the creation of black money [2] which in turn is a menace to the economy in its own way. Tax evasion and black money encourage concentration of economic power in the hands of undesirable groups in the country.
5. Tax evasion eats into the time and energy of tax administration which is obliged to unravel the intricate manipulations of tax dodgers.
6. Tax evasion leads to degradation of social and moral standards. Social abuses like bribery, intimidation, blackmailing, tampering with official records, submitting fake documents etc. all go with tax evasion.

12.5 Measures to Curb Tax Evasion

The following methods may be adopted by governments to check tax evasion.

12.5.1 Lowering of Tax Rates: High tax rates increase premium on tax evasion which in turn generates black money. Contrarily, it can be expected that lowering of tax rates improves tax compliance and broadens the tax base.

12.5.2 Withholding Tax: This is a system of collecting income tax whereby money is periodically deducted by the employers, financial institutions, and others from wages of employees, returns on securities, and other payments. Thus, intermediaries (or third parties) do the job on behalf of the government as regards assessment of the taxable base and the collection of tax thereon.

Generally, a fixed percentage is withheld from the payment made and the same is deposited in government's account. At the time of filing the return of income, the taxpayer encloses withholding tax receipts and in case of overpayment he can claim refund of tax.

Tax withholding system (also called tax deduction at source or Pay-As-You-Earn) satisfies the canon of convenience both for the fiscal authorities and the taxpayers. It is beneficial for the government because it reduces the possibility of tax evasion, ensures prompt tax payment, and simplifies tax collection. It does not allow any lag between the time of receiving income and the time of tax payment. For the taxpayer, it is an instalment plan of taxation and hence convenient.

However, tax withholding involves additional paper work on the part of tax deductors. It also adds to the burden of taxpayers who have to obtain tax deduction certificates from deductors, fill additional tax forms, and wait for refunds.

12.5.3 Presumptive Tax: In every country, there are some soft-to-tax and hard-to-tax sources of income. Wages and salaries are properly recorded and therefore it is easy to assess and collect taxes on them through the Pay-As-You-Earn system. Similarly, income from securities paid through banks can easily be subjected to deduction at source.

Contrarily, the three hard-to-tax classes of the non-corporate sector are: (a) unincorporated commercial and industrial units, (b) self-employed professionals, and (c) rich peasantry. The problem of taxing the first two categories relates to accounting difficulties while in the case of third category, it is essentially the lack of political will. Non-reporting and under-reporting of income is quite sizeable in these sectors. The growing small business sector is a tax haven. It is very difficult to enforce a reliable system of book-keeping to assess earnings of this sector. Pragmatically, a system of lump sum taxation may be tried in place of taxation of profits.

Presumptive tax relates to the use of appropriate indicators of income, wealth etc. instead of the actual records of these tax bases. In the case of income tax, a presumptive tax is imposed on the basis of an estimated taxable income. Presumptive income is exogenously determined. The base for the presumptive income tax is fixed and does not depend on the behaviour of individual entrepreneurs. In essence, a presumptive income tax works like a lump sum tax and therefore does not impose marginal tax burden on actual income. Varying methods of presumptive taxation are in operation in Israel, Argentina, Chile, and Columbia. The French *forfait* system is a typical example of presumptive taxation. The chief advantage of presumptive taxation is its simplicity, both for the tax collectors and the taxpayers. It is, therefore, cost-effective for the administration. The simplicity attribute may also encourage tax compliance. Presumptive taxation particularly suits the developing countries with a large unorganised business sector consisting of small retail establishments, and self-employed professionals. It is easy to administer this tax which can become an effective source of revenue. It also promotes horizontal equity.

12.5.4 Tax Amnesties: A tax amnesty is an opportunity offered by a government to tax evaders to declare their past concealment of income, wealth etc., without fear of being prosecuted. Tax amnesty (or impunity) is granted only for the past in order to secure better compliance and thus higher tax yield in the present and future.

A tax amnesty brings the concealed money in the open, broadens the base of investment, and hence accelerates economic development.

However, tax amnesties set bad precedents and encourage tax evaders in the hope that they will be let off leniently for their past sins any time in the future. Practically, the same group of tax evaders takes advantage of tax amnesties announced by the government. The honest taxpayers are demoralised and the tax enforcement machinery also loses respect in the eyes of the common man.

12.5.5 Computerisation: Storage and exchange of information is an essential element of any scheme to control tax evasion. This is particularly so in dynamic economies where economic transactions are expanding fast. The use of computer facilitates storage and cross-checking of economic information. The assignment of Permanent Account Number to taxpayers becomes important in this context.

12.6 Various Estimates of Tax Evasion in India

Widespread tax evasion is a bane of the Indian tax system. The history of taxation law amendments in India is essentially a history of plugging loopholes, as and when discovered, to prevent leakages of revenue.

Soon after Independence in 1947, the Indian Income Tax Investigation Commission, 1948, investigated all matters relating to taxation of income, with particular reference to preventing evasion and avoidance. The Commission recommended several changes in the law to plug loopholes in the income tax system. It recommended, *inter alia*, that the law should be amended so as to allow speculative losses to be set off only against speculative gains.

Since early 1950s, various commissions/committees/individual scholars have made estimates of tax evasion in India, particularly evasion of income tax. The findings of these studies are summarised below chronologically.

12.6.1 Taxation Enquiry Commission (Chairman: John Matthai), 1953-54: TEC which dealt at length with the administration of income tax, found staggering levels of tax evasion. To quote, "It is observed from statistics in connection with the 'Disclosure Drive' that income as originally included in the returns sent to the income tax department by assessees who made disclosures was grossly understated, the difference between the income as originally returned and that disclosed later to the department being, on the average, as much as 600 per cent. Such other statistics as have been made available to us by the Central Board of Revenue also give evidence of the fact that evasion is prevalent on a considerable scale." [3] The Commission maintained that improvement and strengthening of the enforcement machinery was the only way to tackle evasion effectively.

12.6.2 Nicholas Kaldor: Nicholas Kaldor, a British economist, made the first systematic estimates of income tax evasion in India in the mid-1950s. He estimated income tax loss through tax evasion at Rs. 200 to Rs. 300 crore for the year 1953-54. [4] The estimates of Kaldor were based on certain tentative figures relating to national income provided to him by the Central Statistical Organisation. Kaldor made it clear in his report that his estimates were tentative and should be interpreted with caution.

12.6.3 Central Board of Revenue: Another study by the Central Board of Revenue for the same year (1953-54) recorded a much lower estimate of tax evasion at Rs. 20 to Rs. 30 crore, almost one-tenth of Kaldor's estimate. [5] One main reason for the wide divergence between the two estimates was the inclusion in Kaldor's estimate of what the Central Board of Revenue counted as avoidance rather than evasion. Kaldor himself had admitted while tendering oral evidence before Direct Taxes Administration Enquiry Committee, 1958-59, that his estimate represented the loss of tax not only through evasion but also through avoidance. [6] Therefore, it is generally agreed that the estimates of income tax evasion by Kaldor were on the high side.

12.6.4 Direct Taxes Enquiry Committee (Chairman: K.N. Wanchoo), 1971: DTEC considered, *inter alia,* the problem of tax evasion and established the income on which tax was evaded for 1968-69 at a figure of Rs. 1,400 crore. The amount of tax evasion for the same year was put at Rs. 470 crore. [7]

12.6.5 National Institute of Public Finance and Policy (NIPFP): NIPFP in a report estimated the ratio of tax-evaded income to GDP in the range of 3.7 per cent to 5.7 per cent in 1975-76, and 4.2 per cent to 8.6 per cent in 1980-81. [8]

12.6.6 Tax Reforms Committee (Chairman: Raja Chelliah)), 1991: According to TRC, "not more than 30-35 per cent of legally taxable income is being disclosed, on the average." [9] In this context it observed, "it would be fair to say that the income tax department which is in-charge of all the Central Government direct taxes is in shambles. It cannot complain of lack of manpower, but the majority of personnel is constituted by inspectors and clerks who are not adequately trained and are paid fairly low salaries." [10]

Apart from the foregoing estimates, some evidence of general nature also suggests widespread non-reporting and under-reporting of taxable income in India. In this connection, the Finance Minister in his 1997-98 budget speech observed, "It is inexplicable that in a country of over 900 million people, only 12 million people are assessed to income tax and what is worse, only about 12,000 assessees are in the tax bracket of income above Rs. 10 lakh." [11]

Evasion is not confined to income tax only, rather it is widely practised for other direct taxes also like wealth tax, estate duty (now abolished), and gift tax. The ridiculously low yield from these taxes is partly due to plethora of exemptions/concessions and also due to widespread evasion. In India, economic inequalities have been caused mainly by the inequitable ownership of wealth and the failure of the wealth tax to make a headway in lessening inequalities is indeed regrettable.

Estimation of evasion of indirect taxes in India has always remained a hard task even for the officially appointed committees. For example, the Central Excise (Self-Removal Procedure) Review Committee, 1973, made extensive studies of excise evasion, both sector-wise and commodity-wise. However, it could not quantify the total magnitude of evasion. It observed, "we have reached the conclusion that evasion is considerable and, in certain sectors, pervasive. This is an inference we have drawn from the totality of what we have seen, heard and investigated." [12]

12.7 Government's Policy to Curb Tax Evasion

The nexus between tax evasion and black money and its distortion of the redistributive role of tax policy was noted by India's Seventh Five Year Plan as follows, "With a sizeable proportion of income and wealth evading taxation, the redistributive impact of progressive taxation had been severely blunted. A reduction in the scale of black income generation would improve distribution of income and wealth after taxation. Besides, if the magnitude of tax evasion is significantly reduced, there would be a greater volume of tax revenue, and a greater volume of public expenditure benefiting the poorer section of the population would become possible." [13]

Direct Taxes Enquiry Committee, 1971, had suggested various measures to fight the evil of tax evasion. Some of the measures suggested were as follows.

1. Reduction in tax rates.
2. Minimisation of controls and licences.
3. Regulation of donations to political parties.
4. Creating confidence among small taxpayers.
5. Substitution of sales tax by excise duty.
6. Vigorous prosecution policy.
7. Compulsory maintenance of accounts.

To give effect to the recommendations made by the Committee, the Government enacted the Taxation Laws (Amendment) Act, 1975. This Act, *inter alia,* provided stringent punishment for tax evaders. In cases where tax evasion exceeded Rs. 1 lakh or prosecution was for the second or subsequent offence, the maximum punishment prescribed was seven years rigorous imprisonment. Also, the discretionary powers to courts to award monetary punishment as an alternative to imprisonment or to reduce the term of imprisonment less than the minimum period, was withdrawn.

Efforts have been made to curb tax evasion through lowering of tax rates, tax amnesties, penalties and prosecutions, advance payment and deduction at source, and presumptive tax.

12.7.1 Lowering of Tax Rates: The Report of the Direct Taxes Enquiry Committee (DTEC), 1971, was a milestone in the area of income tax rates. The Committee made a number of far-reaching suggestions for unearthing black money, preventing evasion and avoidance of taxes, and reducing arrears. One important recommendation of the Committee related to reduction in the rates of direct taxes which in its view were mainly responsible for tax evasion because they made tax evasion profitable and attractive. The rates of individual income tax were quite high till the year 1973-74. However, pursuant to the recommendations of the DTEC, the Government initiated a series of rate reductions in individual income tax. The rate of tax was reduced from 97.7 per cent in 1973-74 to 77 per cent in 1974-75, and further down to 66 per cent in 1976-77. It is noteworthy that DTEC had recommended a maximum marginal rate of 75 per cent. [14]

The downward trend in the rate of income tax was temporarily reversed during the brief Janata Government rule at the Centre. The top marginal rate of income tax was increased from 66 per cent in 1976-77 to 69 per cent in 1977-78, and further up to 72 per cent in 1979-80. However, the policy of low direct tax rates started by the Congress Government in 1974 and carried forward in 1976 was further reinforced after it came back to power at the Centre in 1980. After a series of revisions, the maximum marginal rate of individual income tax was 54 per cent (including employment surcharge of 8 per cent), applicable from the financial year 1990-91. Consequent upon the recommendations contained in the Interim Report of the Tax Reforms Committee, 1991, the marginal rate was fixed at 44.8 per cent (including surcharge) from the financial year 1992-93. The Finance Act, 1994 abolished the surcharge of 12 per cent and hence the maximum marginal rate of tax was 40 per cent from the financial year 1994-95. From the same year it was made applicable on incomes over Rs. 1,20,000. It may be recalled that the top marginal rate of income tax applied to incomes above Rs. 1 lakh from 1967-68 to 1993-94. The Rs. 1 lakh of 1967-68 was approximately equivalent to Rs. 5.5 lakh of 1993-94. This shows the laxity of the administration in adjusting tax brackets for inflation. It is noteworthy that Tax Reforms Committee had recommended 40 per cent maximum rate inclusive of surcharge for income exceeding Rs. 2 lakh.

The maximum marginal rate of personal income tax was further reduced from 40 per cent to 30 per cent in the 1997-98 budget. In another significant move, it was made applicable to incomes above Rs. 1,50,000.

Low tax rates are welcome provided they improve compliance and revenue yield. However, to expect that lowering of rates would improve compliance automatically is unrealistic because tax evasion occurs at all levels of income. As the Indian Direct Taxation Administration Enquiry Committee, 1958-59, observed, "While we cannot deny that the higher the rate of tax, the greater will be the temptation for evasion and avoidance, we feel that the tax rates by themselves are not to blame for the large extent of evasion in the country. Even if the rates of tax are reduced, evasion will still continue, because it exists at all levels of income." [15]

12.7.2 Tax Amnesties: In India, tax amnesties with varied characteristics have been offered from time to time to unearth black money. These amnesties provided taxpayers immunity from interest, penalty, investigation or prosecution in exchange for disclosures of incomes which did not pay tax.

In 1951, a voluntary disclosure scheme was announced under which penal provisions of tax laws were relaxed to persuade tax evaders to disclose their unaccounted incomes.

Under another scheme, announced in 1965, tax evaders were required to pay 60 per cent of the disclosed income by way of tax and allowed to bring into books of account the remaining 40 per cent.

Another scheme announced in 1975 provided for clubbing together of all black income irrespective of the years over which it was earned and treated as a block separately from other taxable income for the purpose of income tax liability. It provided for a concessional rate of tax ranging from 25 per cent to 60 per cent on income disclosed under the scheme.

In 1981, Government offered Special Bearer Bonds to the public. The Bonds were redeemable after 10 years (i.e. in 1991) and carried 2 per cent per annum simple rate of interest. The Bonds were marketable and the holders were not required to explain their origin. On their redemption, the holders were allowed to bring them into their books. The value of the Bonds and interest thereon were exempt from income tax and wealth tax till their redemption.

Three recent tax amnesties announced by the Government of India to unearth black money are explained below.

A. Voluntary Deposit Scheme, 1991: This scheme to mobilise unaccounted money was announced through the Voluntary Deposits (Immunities and Exemptions) Act, 1991. Under this scheme, any person could make a deposit with the National Housing Bank on or before January 31, 1992. Thereupon, 40 per cent of such deposit was deducted and set apart as a special levy for financing slum clearance and low cost housing for the poor. The balance of 60 per cent was credited to the depositor's account which he was allowed to withdraw in one or more instalments for any purpose specified by him. Persons who made deposits under this scheme were not required to disclose the sources of funds from which the deposits were made. Hence, the money deposited was completely immune from all sorts of inquiry and investigation.

B. Gold Bond Scheme, 1993: This scheme was introduced through the Gold Bonds (Immunities and Exemptions) Ordinance, 1993, promulgated by the President on January 31, 1993. The objective of the scheme was to mobilise idle gold reserves of the country to supplement official reserves and thereby strengthen the credit position of the country in the international market. The scheme allowed amnesty from the provisions of direct tax laws to induce persons to legitimise their unaccounted holding of gold.

The scheme remained open for subscription from March 15, 1993 to June 14, 1993. Subscription to the Gold Bonds was made in the form of gold only. The minimum limit for subscription was 500 grams of gold. There was no maximum limit. A subscriber was not required to disclose, for any purpose whatsoever, the nature and source of acquisition of the gold subscribed for the Gold Bonds, including the money with which the gold was acquired.

The Bonds will mature after 5 years from the date of issue and will be repaid in the form of gold. Besides, a lump sum interest of Rs. 40 per gram of gold for the period of 5 years is payable on maturity.

C. Voluntary Disclosure of Income Scheme, 1997: In his 1997-98 budget speech, the Finance Minister announced the introduction of a Voluntary

Disclosure Scheme to harness black money for productive purposes. The scheme was rechristened as Voluntary Disclosure of Income Scheme, 1997 by the Finance Minister while moving amendments to the Finance Bill in the Lok Sabha on May 7, 1997.

The Voluntary Disclosure of Income Scheme (VDIS), 1997 announced by the Central Board of Direct Taxes on June 18, 1997 has the following provisions.

1. The scheme will come into force from July 1, 1997. Any eligible person can make a disclosure of income on or after this date. The last date for making the disclosure is December 31, 1997. Thus, the scheme will last for six months.
2. A person may make a disclosure in respect of income chargeable to tax under the Indian Income Tax Act, 1961 for any assessment year.
3. The particulars furnished by a declarant shall be kept a secret. Nothing contained in any declaration shall be used against the declarant for the purpose of any proceedings relating to imposition of penalties or launching of prosecution under the Income Tax Act, 1961, Wealth Tax Act, 1957, Foreign Exchange Regulation Act, 1973 or the Companies Act, 1956.
4. The tax payable on the disclosed income in respect of any assessment year shall be at the rate of 35 per cent in the case of companies and 30 per cent in the case of other assessees including individuals.
5. The tax payable under the scheme must be paid before the filing of the declaration. In other words, the declaration must be accompanied by the proof of payment of tax. In case a person is not in a position to pay the tax before the filing of the declaration, he may do so within three months of the date of filing of the declaration. In such a case, a simple interest at the rate of 2 per cent shall be charged for every month or part of a month beginning from the date of filing of the declaration to the date of payment of the tax.
6. The declaration shall be made to the Commissioner of Income Tax in his area and shall be in a prescribed format. The declaration can be signed in the case of an individual by the individual himself. In the case of a Hindu Undivided Family, company, firm etc. the declaration can be signed and verified by persons specified in Section 65 of the Finance Act, 1997.
7. Where voluntarily disclosed income is represented by jewellery, the value of the jewellery or bullion shall be substantiated by a registered valuer's certificate. In case the jewellery declared is from a period before the financial year 1987-88, the value for purposes of declaration shall be taken to be value as on April 1, 1987.
8. The disclosure made in respect of any assessment year shall not affect the finality of any completed assessment.

9. The voluntarily disclosed income shall not be added to the total income of the declarant if the declarant credits such amount in his books of account and intimates the credit so made to the Assessing Officer.
10. The VDIS does not apply to the following categories of persons: (a) those on whom an 'order of detention' has been served under the Conservation of Foreign Exchange and Prevention of Smuggling Activities Act, 1974 in certain circumstances, (b) those punishable under the Narcotic Drugs and Psychotropic Substances Act, 1985, (c) those punishable under the Terrorists and Disruptive Activities (Prevention) Act, 1987, (d) those notified under Section 3 of the Special Court (trial of offences relating to transaction in securities) Act, 1992, (e) those on whom notices under Section 142 or 148 have been served.
11. A person is not eligible for the income disclosure benefit if that income is before or for a year when a search had been initiated under Section 132 or a requisition made under Section 132A. However, persons surveyed under Section 133A of the Income Tax Act are barred from making a declaration only for income in the year of the survey.
12. State Governments will get 77.5 per cent of the total resources secured under the scheme. The remaining portion, being share of the Central Government, will be used entirely to finance the Basic Minimum Services Programme and infrastructure needs.

At a press conference on January 3, 1998, Finance Minister P. Chidambaran announced that Voluntary Disclosure of Income Scheme netted Rs. 10,050 crore towards tax revenue. The total disclosure of black money in the six-month-long campaign was Rs. 33,000 crore and an estimated 4.6 lakh declarations were made under the VDIS.

12.7.3 Advance Tax Payment and Tax Deduction at Source: Though the regular assessment in respect of any income is made in a later assessment year, the tax on such income is payable by way of advance payment or deduction at source. Section 208 of the Act makes it obligatory to pay advance tax in every case where the advance tax payable is Rs. 5,000 or more. Similarly, there are provisions under various sections of the Act regarding tax deduction at source (TDS), e.g. deduction of tax from salaries (Section 192). Other incomes covered under the scheme of TDS include fees for professional or technical services, interest, rent from real estate, commission from insurance, sale of lottery tickets, and winnings from lotteries, crossword puzzles and horse racing.

In recent years, improvement in the percentage share of direct taxes (mainly income tax) has taken place due to widening of the tax base, presumptive taxation and broadening the scope of tax deduction at source (TDS). In this context, the

Ninth Five Year Plan (1997-2002) observed, "The share of TDS in gross collection of income tax increased from about 23 per cent in 1980-81 to about 37 per cent in 1989-90, but declined subsequently to about 31 per cent in 1994-95. One of the major loopholes which contributes to the decline in revenue from TDS relates to the branch-wise threshold of Rs. 10,000 for the purpose of deducting income tax at source from interest on time deposits with banks. Further, the provision for TDS does not apply to non-banking financial companies. Other deficiencies from which the TDS scheme suffers arise from lack of proper monitoring and scrutiny." [16]

12.7.4 Presumptive Tax: See section 14.7 of chapter 14 of this book.

12.7.5 PAN/GIR: In order to strengthen the efforts at enforcement, the Finance Minister in his 1998-99 budget made it obligatory for assessees to quote their Permanent Account Number (PAN) or General Index Register Number (GIR) mandatorily in respect of the following high value transactions: purchase and sale of immovable property; purchase and sale of motor vehicles; transactions in shares exceeding Rs. 10 lakh; opening of new bank accounts; fixed deposits of more than Rs. 50,000; applications for allotment of telephone connections; and payments to hotels exceeding Rs. 25,000.

12.7.6 Survey of Income Tax: Income tax authorities may conduct, from time to time, a shop to shop or house to house survey to rope in new assessees. Potential assessees are required to fill up a questionnaire in Form 45-D. Officials conducting the survey cannot seize any books of account, cash, or articles. If any person fails to comply with a notice under section 133B requiring the survey information in Form 45-D, he shall be liable to pay a penalty up to Rs. 1,000 [Sec. 272AA].

12.7.7 Summons, Search, and Seizure

A. Summons: Under section 131, an authorised income tax officer can issue summons when he has reasons to suspect that any income has been concealed by any person within his jurisdiction. Summons is issued to enforce attendance of any person for the purpose of examining him. The person concerned may be examined to verify the authenticity of various types of transactions, the following being the common ones.

1. Capital Contributions: Summons can be issued to owners of a business (i.e. proprietors, partners, and shareholders) to verify their capital contributions and sources of money thereof. Borrowed funds can be sources of money for capital contributions.

2. Business Transactions: An assessee makes claim in his return of income regarding purchases, sales, revenue expenditure, and capital outlays. To verify such claims, the assessing officer can issue summons to suppliers, buyers, and recipients of commissions, salaries, rent. etc.

3. Borrowing of Funds: An assessee may borrow funds from institutional and/or non-institutional sources for various purposes. Borrowings from non-institutional sources (e.g. private moneylenders, relatives, friends etc.) may need to be confirmed by income tax authorities. Hence, summons can be issued to persons who have lent money to explain sources of money lent.

4. Investment Transactions: Summons can be issued to any person who has made substantial investments in shares, securities, land, buildings, and costly consumer durables. The person so summoned is expected to explain with documentary evidence the sources of his funds. These sources may include borrowings, gifts received, property inherited, sale of jewellery etc. However, documentary evidence is necessary to prove these sources of money. It is advisable to reveal correct factual information which can be cross-verified.

B. Search and Seizure: To conduct search (popularly called raid) and seizure, an authorisation in the prescribed form is issued by the competent income tax authority under his signature and seal. Income tax officials are vested with considerable powers to carry out search operations. Thus, they can (a) enter and search any building, place or vehicle in occupation of the person being searched, (b) break the lock and examine any box, locker, almirah etc., (c) seize any books of account, other documents, money, bullion, jewellery etc. Books of account and other documents impounded cannot be retained beyond 180 days without obtaining approval of the Commissioner. However, the assessee can have copies made out of the original books impounded by the authorities [Sections 132, 132A].

12.7.8 Purchase of Immovable Property: The Income Tax Act imposes certain restrictions on the transfer of high value immovable properties. These restrictions are meant to ensure effective tax compliance and prevent generation of black money.

A. Income Tax Clearance for Properties: Under section 230A, a document of transfer of immovable property valued at above Rs. 5 lakh cannot be registered unless a certificate is obtained from Income Tax Department in respect of payment of tax liability of the transferor. An application for this purpose is to be made in Form No. 34A in duplicate to the assessing officer accompanied by a copy of the document which is to be registered. The certificate is granted/refused within 60 days of the receipt of the application.

B. Pre-emptive Acquisition of Properties: Transfer of any immovable property situated in certain big cities for consideration exceeding prescribed amounts is subject to compliance with certain requirements prescribed in section

269UC. The important specified areas with prescribed amounts are the following: Greater Mumbai (Rs. 75 lakh), Union Territory of Delhi (Rs. 50 lakh), Calcutta, Chennai, Bangalore, Ahmedabad, Pune (Rs. 25 lakh), Chandigarh, Jaipur, Nagpur (Rs. 20 lakh). Thus, it is compulsory for the transferor and the transferee to enter into an agreement in writing, at least four months before the intended date of transfer, and to submit a statement in duplicate in Form No. 37-I within 15 days from the agreement for transfer to the office of the appropriate income tax authority.

After receipt of the statement, the appropriate authority may make an order for the purchase of the immovable property by the Central Government, at the price specified in the agreement of transfer.

12.7.9 Penalties and Prosecutions

A. Penalties: Income Tax Act contains provisions under which penalties are imposed for various defaults committed by the taxpayers. The important provisions in this regard are summarised in Table 12.1.

Table 12.1: Select Penalty Provisions for Different Defaults under Income Tax Act, 1961

Section	Nature of default	Minimum penalty	Maximum penalty
271(1)(C)	Concealment of particulars of income	100 per cent of tax sought to be evaded	300 per cent of tax sought to be evaded
271A	Failure to keep or maintain books of account as required under section 44AA	Rs. 2,000	Rs. 1 lakh
71C	Failure to deduct tax as required under sections 192 to 196C	Amount of tax required to be deducted at source	----
271F	Failure to furnish return of income under section 139(1) i.e. persons owning immovable property, motor vehicle, telephone etc.	Rs. 500	----
272A(1)	Failure to apply for allotment of Permanent Account Number	Rs. 500	Rs. 10,000

B. Prosecutions: Income Tax Act contains provisions under which prosecution proceedings can be started for different offences committed by taxpayers. The important provisions in this regard are summarised in Table 12.2.

Table 12.2: Select Prosecution Provisions for Various Offences under Income Tax Act, 1961

Section	Nature of offence	Rigorous imprisonment	
		Minimum Period	Maximum Period
276 B	Failure to deposit tax deducted at source	3 months	7 years
276 C(2)	Wilful attempt to evade Tax	3 months	3 years
276 CC	Wilful failure to file return of income in time	6 months if tax evaded exceeds Rs. 1 lakh Otherwise 3 months	7 years if tax evaded exceeds Rs. 1 lakh Otherwise 3 years
277	Making a false statement in verification or delivering a false account	6 months if tax evaded exceeds Rs. 1 lakh otherwise 3 months	7 years if tax evaded exceeds Rs. 1 lakh otherwise 3 years

C. Penal Provisions: A Comment: There are quite a few Sections in the Income Tax Act which confer discretionary powers on income tax officers. Thus, Section 273(1) of the Act allows income tax officers to reduce or waive penalties for tax evasion if it is voluntarily disclosed before being discovered by the assessing officer. According to the Act, this can be done only once in the life time of a taxpayer.

However, in practice it is likely that the penalty is waived several times for the same taxpayer even when the disclosure criterion is not met. The possibility of misuse of Section 273 (1) cannot be ruled out.

Similarly, Section 273A(4) of the Act allows tax officers to reduce or waive penalty on grounds of genuine hardships.

Furthermore, Section 279 (2) of the Act allows out of court settlement with income tax authorities in case the tax evaded exceeds Rs. 50,000. This section leaves arbitrary powers with income tax officials.

12.8 Conclusion

To conclude, it is necessary to change the attitude of the people towards Government and its laws. In this connection, the Indian Tax Reforms Committee,

1991, observed, "...there is a widespread feeling among the electorate that there is considerable waste in government expenditure, that there is excess staff and that the tail to teeth ratio is unduly high. And with it all, it is generally felt that the public which pays the taxes gets poor service and members of the public are treated often not as masters who pay but as supplicants." [17] Moreover, salaried persons envy tax evasion opportunities available to self-employed professionals and retail traders, and are tempted to conceal their incomes from non-salary sources.

Notes

1. Generally, charitable trusts are not required to pay tax on donations received by them. Similarly, income tax laws allow charitable contributions as deductions from taxable income. Since marginal rates of tax are high at upper brackets of income, charitable contributions are less costly to wealthy people.

These provisions are sometimes misused in the sense that donors exercise considerable control in managing the affairs of trusts/institutions to which charitable contributions are made. Private or family interest in the management of charitable trusts leads to control in the use of what are essentially public funds. Family control over a charitable trust generally leads to promoting private interest, defeating in the process the essential purpose of the tax concession.

2. The term 'black money' stands for money earned by illegal means and kept secret and unaccounted for. It is widely used for smuggling activities, hoarding of scarce commodities (for the purpose of speculation, profiteering, and black marketing), bribing government officials, financing political activities, and ostentatious living. Secret business deals through black money in turn lead to tax evasion and a vicious circle is created in which one evil thrives on the other.

3. Government of India, Ministry of Finance, *Report of the Taxation Enquiry Commission* (Chairman, John Matthai), 1953-54, Vol. II, p. 189.

4. Nicholas Kaldor, *Indian Tax Reform - Report of a Survey* (Government of India, Ministry of Finance, 1956), p. 105.

5. Quoted by Government of India, Ministry of Finance, *Report of the Direct Taxes Administration Enquiry Committee* (Chairman: Mahavir Tyagi), 1958-59, p. 148.

6. *Ibid.*, p. 148.

7. Government of India, Ministry of Finance, *Final Report of Direct Taxes Enquiry Committee* (Chairman, Justice K. N. Wanchoo), December 1971, pp. 7-8.

8. Government of India, Ministry of Finance, *Aspects of the Black Economy in India*, March 1985, p. 161.

9. Government of India, Ministry of Finance, *Interim Report of the Tax Reforms Committee* (Chairman, Raja Chelliah), December 1991, p. 47.

10. *Ibid.*, p. 37.

11. Government of India, Ministry of Finance, *Budget 1997-98, Speech of the Finance Minister*, Part B, p. 25.

12. Government of India, Ministry of Finance, *Report of the Central Excise (Self-Removal Procedure) Review Committee* (Chairman, B. Venkatappiah), 1973, p. 65.

13. Government of India, Planning Commission, *The Seventh Five Year Plan, 1985-90*, Vol. I, p. 71.

14. *Final Report of Direct Taxes Enquiry Committee*, 1971, *op. cit.*, para 2.52.

15. *Report of the Direct Taxes Administration Enquiry Committee, op. cit.,* 1958-59, p. 149.

16. Government of India, Planning Commission, Ninth Five Year Plan (1997-2002), Vol. I, p. 168.

17. *Interim Report of the Tax Reforms Committee*, op. cit., December 1991, p. 44.

Section C: Central Taxes

This Section is devoted to trends in Central taxes in terms of tax-GDP ratio and relative roles of direct and indirect taxes. Individual Central taxes have been discussed in detail. The taxes covered are: income tax, wealth tax, Union excise duties, taxation of services, and customs duties.

13

Trends in Central Taxes

Central taxes account for about two-thirds of total tax collections in India. [1] The relative significance of various taxes in Central revenues has undergone major changes since Independence. Income tax and wealth tax are the direct taxes while excise levies and customs duties are the indirect taxes of the Central Government.

13.1 Central Taxes as Per Cent of GDP

In 1950-51, gross central taxes accounted for 4.08 per cent of GDP. With the widening and deepening of the tax net to raise resources for development projects, the percentage started increasing with every passing decade. It increased to 5.21 in 1960-61, to 7.02 in 1970-71 and stood at 9.17 in 1980-81. [2]

In 1990-91, when the process of economic reforms was initiated, gross central taxes accounted for 10.12 per cent of GDP. However, as a result of tax reforms introduced since then, this percentage started falling and it became as low as 8.20 in 2001-02. Stating the reasons for this fall of more than 2 percentage points, the Twelfth Finance Commission noted, "The impact of these reforms on direct and indirect taxes was diametrically opposite. While the direct taxes showed, even with the lower rates, a rising tax-GDP ratio, this ratio for the indirect taxes kept sliding down. The indirect taxes had a larger share in the total tax revenues of the centre and the fall in the indirect tax to GDP ratio could not be compensated by a rise in the direct taxes. As a result, the overall central tax-GDP ratio fell." [3]

Of late, however, recovery is noticeable in the tax-GDP ratio at the level of Central Government (Table 13.1).

13.2 Direct and Indirect Taxes

As in the case of combined (Centre and States) tax revenues, tax structure at the Central level also evolved around indirect taxes during the post-Independence period. The ratio between direct and indirect taxes in gross central taxes declined from 43.4:56.6 in 1950-51 to 32.6:67.4 in 1960-61, to 27.1:72.9 in 1970-71 and to 22.7:77.3 in 1980-81. [4] Resultantly, indirect taxes came to occupy a dominant place in Central finances.

In the wake of reforms initiated in the early 1990s, rates of both corporate and personal income tax were substantially reduced. Following better compliance, the decline in the relative share of direct taxes has been reversed. Direct taxes as a percentage of Centre's total tax collections rose from 19.2 per cent in 1990-91 (pre-reform period) to 34.7 per cent in 1997-98. The figure stood at 47.9 per cent in the 2005-06 budget (Table 13.2). In the 2007-08 budget, the ratio between direct and indirect taxes was estimated at 48.8:51.2 (Table 13.3).

Table 13.1: Gross Central Taxes as per cent of GDP: 1990-91 to 2005-06

(Rs. crore)

Year	Gross Central taxes*	Col. 2 as % of GDP
1	2	3
1990-91	57,577	10.12
1991-92	67,361	10.31
1992-93	74,636	9.97
1993-94	75,742	8.82
1994-95	92,297	9.11
1995-96	1,11,224	9.36
1996-97	1,29,762	9.48
1997-98	1,39,220	9.14
1998-99	1,43,797	8.26
1999-00	1,71,752	8.77
2000-01	1,88,603	8.95
2001-02	1,87,060	8.20
2002-03	2,15,905	8.81
2003-04	2,54,348	9.21
2004-05	3,06,020	9.80
2005-06	3,70,025	10.48

* Before transferring States' share in Central taxes.
2004-05 = Revised estimates; 2005-06 = Budget estimates.
Note: The ratios of GDP since 1950-51 are with reference to new series GDP (Base: 1993-94) at current market prices.
Source: Rearranged data from Government of India, Ministry of Finance, *Indian Public Finance Statistics*, 2005-2006, Tables 1.7 and 1.8.

13.3 Composition of Direct Taxes

13.3.1 Income Tax: In 1950-51, personal income tax accounted for almost one-third (32.7 per cent) of Central tax collections. However, the relative contribution declined over the years and was less than one-tenth (9.3 per cent) in 1990-91. After the tax reforms initiated since early 1990s, the share of personal income tax in gross tax revenues of the Central Government increased sharply. In the 2007-08 budget, it was estimated at 18.0 per cent (Table 13.3). In the case of corporation tax, the relative contribution was 9.9 per cent in 1950-51 while in 1990-91 it was 9.3 per cent. In the intervening period, however, moderate changes are noticeable in the proportionate share of corporation tax. As in the case of personal income tax, the proportionate share of corporation tax in Centre's gross tax revenues has increased sharply during the post-1991 period. In the 2007-08 budget, it was estimated at 30.7 per cent (Table 13.3).

Table 13.2: Gross Central Taxes, Breakdown between Direct and Indirect Taxes with Percentage Shares: 1990-91 to 2005-06

(Rs. crore)

Year	Gross Central taxes*(3+4)	Direct taxes	Indirect taxes	Col. 3 as % of Col. 2	Col. 4 as % of Col. 2
1	2	3	4	5	6
1990-91	57,577	11,030	46,547	19.2	80.8
1991-92	67,361	15,353	52,008	22.8	77.2
1992-93	74,636	18,140	56,496	24.3	75.7
1993-94	75,742	20,299	55,443	26.8	73.2
1994-95	92,297	26,973	65,324	29.2	70.8
1995-96	1,11,224	33,564	77,660	30.2	69.8
1996-97	1,29,762	38,898	90,864	30.0	70.0
1997-98	1,39,220	48,282	90,938	34.7	65.3
1998-99	1,43,797	46,601	97,196	32.4	67.6
1999-00	1,71,752	57,960	1,13,792	33.7	66.3
2000-01	1,88,603	68,305	1,20,298	36.2	63.8
2001-02	1,87,060	69,197	1,17,863	37.0	63.0
2002-03	2,15,905	83,363	1,32,542	38.6	61.4
2003-04	2,54,348	1,05,091	1,49,257	41.3	58.9
2004-05	3,06,020	1,34,197	1,71,824	43.8	56.2
2005-06	3,70,025	1,77,080	1,92,945	47.9	52.1

* Before transferring States' share in Central taxes.

2004-05 = Revised estimates; 2005-06 = Budget estimates.

Source: Rearranged data from Government of India, Ministry of Finance, *Indian Public Finance Statistics*, 2005-2006, Tables 1.7. Columns 5 and 6 calculations own.

It is noteworthy that both personal and corporate income taxes were rationalized as part of the package of economic reforms initiated in 1991. The

Table 13.3: Trends in the Level and Composition of Gross Tax Revenues* of the Central Government: Selected Years

(Rs. crore)

Central taxes	1950-51	1960-61	1970-71	1980-81	1990-91	2000-01	2007-08#
A+B Gross tax revenues	404 (100.0)	888 (100.0)	3,206 (100.0)	13,179 (100.0)	57,576 (100.0)	1,88,603 (100.0)	5,48,122 (100.0)
A. Direct taxes of which	174 (43.1)	290 (32.6)	870 (27.1)	3,004 (22.8)	11,025 (19.1)	68,306 (36.2)	2,67,490 (48.8)
1. Corporation	40 (9.9)	11 (12.5)	371 (11.6)	1,310 (9.9)	5,235 (9.3)	35,696 (18.9)	1,68,401 (30.7)
2. Personal income tax	132 (32.7)	166 (18.7)	473 (14.8)	1,506 (11.4)	5,371 (9.3)	31,764 (16.8)	98,774 (18.0)
3. Other taxes**	2 (0.5)	13 (1.5)	26 (0.8)	188 (1.4)	319 (0.5)	846 (0.5)	315 (0.1)
B. Indirect taxes of which	229 (56.7)	599 (67.5)	2,337 (72.9)	10,175 (77.2)	46,552 (80.9)	1,20,297 (63.8)	2,80,632 (51.2)
1. Customs duties	157 (38.9)	170 (19.1)	524 (16.3)	3,409 (25.8)	20,644 (35.8)	47,542 (25.2)	98,770 (18.0)
2. Union excise duties	68 (16.8)	414 (46.6)	1,759 (54.9)	6,500 (49.3)	24,514 (42.6)	68,526 (36.3)	1,30,220 (23.8)
3. Service tax	-	-	-	-	-	-	50,200 (9.2)
4. Other taxes***	4 (1.0)	15 (1.7)	54 (1.7)	266 (2.0)	1,394 (2.4)	4,229 (2.2)	1,442 (0.3)

* Before transferring States' share in Central taxes; # Budget estimates.

** These are wealth tax and some other taxes of minor revenue significance.

*** These are State excise duties, taxes on vehicles, sales tax, octroi, duties on electricity, stamp and registration, entertainment tax (all from Union Territories without legislature) and foreign travel tax.

Figures in parentheses are corresponding percentages of total tax collections.

Sources: Government of India, Ministry of Finance, *Explanatory Memorandum on the Budget of the Central Government* (various years); *Receipts Budget* (various years); and *Budget at a Glance*, 2007-08.

number of rate categories, as well as the marginal income tax rates, was substantially reduced.

Income Tax is discussed separately in chapter 14 of this book.

13.3.2 Wealth Tax: This so-called capital tax of the Central Government is without much revenue significance. Chapter 15 deals with it in some detail.

13.4 Composition of Indirect Taxes

13.4.1 Union Excise Duties: In the post-Independence period (1950-70), a major change in the Indian tax system pertained to the phenomenal rise in the relative revenue significance of Union excise duties. In 1950-51, excise revenue accounted for a modest 16.8 per cent of total Central tax collections: Rs. 68 crore out of Rs. 404 crore. Within a span of 20 years, the proportionate share shot up to 54.9 per cent in 1970-71. It declined to 49.3 per cent in 1980-81. In 1990-91 it was recorded at 42.6 per cent. In the 2007-08 budget, the contribution of excise duties in gross tax revenues of the Centre was estimated at 23.8 per cent (Table 13.3). The relative contribution of excise revenue has declined due to reduction in the average tax rates without a compensatory rise in the tax base, evasion, and litigation.

Union excise duties are examined in detail in chapter 16.

13.4.2 Service Tax: In view of the need for additional resources and the rising contribution of service sector to GDP, a modest effort was made in the 1994-95 budget when a 5 per cent tax was imposed on the services of telephones, non-life insurance, and stock brokers with effect from July 1, 1994. Since then the coverage of service tax has been extended to a host of other services and it is considered as the tax of the future. In the 2007-08 budget, the contribution of service tax in gross tax revenues of the Centre was estimated at 9.2 per cent (Table 13.3).

Service tax is discussed separately in chapter 17.

13.4.3 Customs Duties: During pre-Independence days and even during the early post-Independence period, customs duties formed the mainstay of Central tax revenues. However, the relative share of customs duties started declining from early 1950s in view of a protective trade policy and dwindling foreign exchange reserves. The share of customs revenue in Centre's total tax collections dropped from 38.9 per cent in 1950-51 to as low as 16.3 per cent in 1970-71. After that customs revenue maintained an upward swing, accounting for 35.8 per cent of Central taxes in the year 1990-91. This upward trend was attributable to a changed emphasis from physical to fiscal controls to regulate imports, a policy reiterated in the Long-Term Fiscal Policy of December 1985. However, during the post-liberalisation period, a sharp fall is noticeable in the relative share of customs duties in gross tax revenues of the Central Government. This is due to drastic reductions in the tariff rates across the rate categories including the peak rate in the wake of WTO commitments and to become globally competitive. In the 2007-08 budget the share of customs revenue was estimated at 18.0 per cent (Table 13.3).

Customs duties are discussed separately in chapter 18.

Notes

1. Tax collections (or gross tax revenues) of the Central Government are different from its net tax revenues because a part of the proceeds from taxes is transferred to State Governments under tax sharing arrangements of the Constitution.
2. See Table 2 in Part IX of this book.
3. *Report of the Twelfth Finance Commission* (2005-10), November 2004, p. 31.
4. See Table 2 in Part IX of this book.

14

Income Tax

Besides being the main source of direct tax revenue for the Government, income tax is an effective instrument to realise various socio-economic objectives of national policies. This chapter traces the evolution, explains the legal framework, and describes the present system of income tax in India.

14.1 History of Indian Income Tax

14.1.1 Income Tax Act, 1860: Consequent upon the financial difficulties created by the events of 1857, income tax was introduced in India for the first time by the British in the year 1860. [1] However, the imposition of income tax remained irregular till the year 1886 when a systematic legislation was enacted for its operation on a permanent basis. Since then the form of income tax has undergone a series of changes to meet the changing requirements of Government finances and economic policy.

The Act of 1860 was passed only for five years and therefore it lapsed in 1865. It was replaced in 1867 by a licence tax on professions and trades and the latter was converted into a certificate tax in the following year. The certificate tax was replaced in 1869 by a general income tax which after remaining in force for four years was abolished in 1873. In 1876, the Government imposed a licence tax on traders to create a famine fund to deal with the famine of 1876-78. This licence tax on traders remained in operation till 1886 when it was merged in the Income Tax Act of that year. Noting the haphazard nature of enactments, the Indian Taxation Enquiry Committee, 1924-25, remarked, "...the whole period (1860-1886) was one of continuous trial and error with different schemes of direct taxation, no less than 24 Acts being passed in 26 years." [2]

14.1.2 Income Tax Act, 1886: The Act of 1886 levied a tax on the income of residents as well as non-residents in India. The Act defined agricultural income and exempted it from tax liability in view of the already existing land revenue, a kind of direct tax. (In the 1860 legislation, agricultural income was also subject to taxation). The absolute exclusion of agricultural income from the purview of income tax law continued till the Government of India Act, 1935 made it a provincial (State) subject. This provision was retained in the Constitution of independent India.

The Act of 1886 exempted life insurance premiums paid by an assessee on policies on his own life or on that of his wife, a provision that has continued till now. Under another provision of the Act, a Hindu undivided family was treated as a distinct taxable entity, a position maintained by all subsequent Income Tax Acts.

The assessment and collection procedures of income tax in the early days of its operation were simple and somewhat arbitrary. As the Taxation Enquiry Commission, 1953-54 noted, "The Income Tax Act of 1886 laid an obligation only on companies to file every year statements of their net income and it was entirely within the discretion of the Collector to devise means for finding out other persons likely to have taxable income and to adopt the appropriate method of determining their income ... the procedure for assessment was summary, and the Collector could intimate the amount of income and tax determined by him to the assessee either through a list published in his office or through an individual notice." [3] In 1886-87, the total income assessed was Rs. 33 crore and the net collection from income tax was Rs. 1.37 crore. The Act of 1886 remained in force for 32 years, i.e. until 1918 and during this period a number of amendments were made in it including the introduction of the principle of graduation in income tax in 1916 and of super tax in 1917.

14.1.3 Income Tax Act, 1918: The Act of 1918 brought under charge also receipts of casual or non-recurring nature pertaining to business or profession. This was contrary to the generally accepted meaning of income that it should, *inter alia*, be received with some degree of regularity. The Act granted exemption to contributions to provident funds governed by the Provident Funds Act.

Although income tax in India has been a charge on net income since inception, it was in the Act of 1918 that specific provisions were inserted for the first time pertaining to business deductions for the purpose of computing net income. Prior to that, deductions were granted on the basis of executive orders. For example, there was no specific provision for depreciation allowance in the Act of 1886 but the Act of 1918 inserted in the statute itself the provision for depreciation allowance on the straight-line method.

The Act of 1918 remained in force for a short period and was replaced by a new Act (Act XI of 1922) in view of the reforms introduced by the Government of India Act, 1919.

14.1.4 Income Tax Act, 1922: The Act of 1922 provided for the first time the set off of loss from one source against income from other sources in the same year. An amendment of the Act in 1939 permitted carry forward of unabsorbed business losses for a period of six years with the restriction that carried forward loss could be set off only against the profits of the same business. Pursuant to a recommendation of the Income Tax Investigation Commission (1948), the income tax law was appropriately amended in 1953 to provide for the set off of speculative losses, even during the same year, only against speculative gains.

Under the Act of 1886, the paying officers had the obligation to deduct tax at source from the salaries of Government servants and employees of local bodies. However, the Act of 1922 extended to all employers the responsibility to deduct tax at source on salaries. Prior to 1922, there was no separate department for income tax administration. The assessment and collection of income tax was done by the land revenue officers as a subsidiary duty. It was only in 1922 that a separate Central Department was created to deal with income tax administration.

14.1.5 Recommendations of the Indian Taxation Enquiry Committee (Chairman: Charles Todhunter), 1924-25: The Government of India appointed this Committee under the chairmanship of Sir Charles Todhunter to examine in detail the entire field of taxation in India. Chapter IX of its report contained recommendations pertaining to income tax. The Committee rejected the idea of differentiation between earned and unearned income for income tax purpose.

A major recommendation of the Committee pertained to the distribution of income tax revenue between the Centre and the Provinces. Prior to 1919, income tax was a 'divided head' of revenue. However, the Montague-Chelmsford Reforms resulted in a complete separation of Central and Provincial finances, and income tax became a part of the Central revenues. The Todhunter Committee opined that in the event of any division of taxes between the Centre and the Provinces, the choice of income tax as the main balancing factor was inevitable. The Government of India Act, 1935, did assign to the Provinces a part of the net proceeds of income tax levied by the Centre.

14.1.6 Recommendations of the Income Tax Enquiry Committee, 1935: This Committee was appointed by the Government of India "to make an investigation of the Indian income tax system in all its aspects and to report upon both the incidence of the tax and the efficiency of its administration". Many amendments based on its recommendations became law in 1939. According to one such amendment, the then prevailing *step* rates system of income tax was changed to a *slab* rates system in 1939. Under the step system of rates, all persons in a particular income bracket bear the same effective rate on every rupee of their income. Under a slab system of rates, tax on each slab of income is calculated separately and then added up. Under another amendment, closely-held companies were required to distribute 60 per cent of their net of tax profits as dividend. The Income Tax (Amendment) Act, 1939, provided also for the taxation of profits of the business of mutual life insurance which had remained exempt from tax prior to 1939.

Another notable development in the evolution of income tax was the imposition of excess profit tax in 1940. It was levied on profits earned by businesses and professions between September 1, 1939 and March 31, 1946. A 'standard profit' was calculated for each accounting year falling within the above years. Standard profit was approximately equated with the profits earned in normal times, i.e. in the pre-War years. Companies started before 1936 had the following five options to choose from for determining standard profit: profits during 1935-36 or 1936-37 or average of the profits during 1935-36 and 1936-37 or 1936-37 and 1937-38 or 1937-38 and 1938-39. In the case of companies started after 1936, the 'capital standard' was used. Thus, a statutory 8 per cent of the capital invested was considered the standard rate of profit. Excess profit tax was levied at the rate of 50 per cent on the excess over the standard profits earned between September 1, 1939 and March 31, 1941. For the period between April 1, 1941 and March 31, 1946, the rate of excess profit tax was 66.66 per cent.

During the pre-Independence period, revenue-raising was the main purpose of income tax system. There were hardly any concessions/exemptions for savings, investments, industrial growth, and other desirable socio-economic objectives. Incentives for such activities started building up in the system soon after Independence. Thus, a provision introduced in 1949 exempted from tax new industrial undertakings for the first five years of their manufacturing operations.

Shortly after Independence, the Government appointed the Income Tax Investigation Commission (1947) under the chairmanship of Srinivas Varadachariar to (a) investigate and report on all matters relating to taxation of income, with particular reference to preventing evasion and avoidance, and (b) to investigate specific cases referred to the Commission by the Government. The Commission submitted its report in 1948 and recommended several changes in the law to plug loopholes in the income tax system. For example, it recommended that the law should be amended so as to allow speculative losses to be set off only against speculative gains. A number of Commission's recommendations were incorporated in the law by the Income Tax (Amendment) Act, 1953.

14.2 Constitutional Provisions and Legal Framework

14.2.1 Constitutional Provisions: Taxation of income in India may be classified into two broad categories: (a) taxation of non-agricultural income, a Central subject and (b) taxation of agricultural income, a matter for State legislation. The two relevant entries in List I (Union List) of the Seventh Schedule of the Constitution which empower the Parliament to levy income tax are: entry 82, "taxes on income other than agricultural income", and entry 85, "corporation tax". According to Article 366(6) of the Constitution "corporation tax means any tax on income, so far as that tax is payable by companies."

The States are empowered to make laws with respect to taxes on agricultural income vide entry 46 of List II (State List) of the Seventh Schedule of the Constitution. Therefore, agricultural income is exempt from Central income tax. However, from the assessment year 1974-75, agricultural income is taken into account to determine the rate of tax on non-agricultural income if agricultural income exceeds Rs. 5,000. Although the power to impose tax on agricultural income is vested in State Governments, in practice very few States have imposed this tax and wherever it is imposed the revenue is negligible.

Till recently, the proceeds from income tax were shareable with the States under Article 270 (1) of the Constitution. The Finance Commission recommended the formula for the distribution of income tax revenue between the Centre and the States and the distribution of States' share among the States themselves. Thus, income tax played an important role not only in Central finances but also in the finances of the State Governments.

The Constitution (Eightieth Amendment) Act, 2000 substituted a new Article for Article 270 under which States are now given a percentage share of all Central taxes and duties. However, the surcharge levied for purposes of the Union under Article 271 is excluded from the divisible pool.

14.3 Revenue Significance of Income Tax

Income tax is the only notable source of direct tax revenue in India. In 1950-51, personal income tax accounted for almost one-third (32.7 per cent) of Central tax collections. However, the relative contribution declined over the years and was less than one-tenth (9.3 per cent) in 1990-91 (Table 14.1). Lamenting the sharp decline in the relative revenue significance of personal income tax, the Tax Reforms Committee, 1991, observed, "It is a matter for concern that the share of taxes on income particularly personal income tax has registered a sharp decline over the years and despite efforts to raise more revenue from these taxes, no appreciable improvement seems to have come about." [4]

After the tax reforms initiated in 1991, the percentage share of personal income tax in total Central tax collections has increased. It was estimated at 18.0 per cent in the 2007-2008 budget (Table 14.1).

In the case of corporation tax, the relative contribution was 9.9 per cent in 1950-51 while in 1990-91 it was 9.3 per cent. In the intervening period, however, moderate changes are noticeable in the proportionate share of corporation tax. Again, after recent reforms the proportionate share of corporation tax has increased. It was estimated at 30.7 per cent in the 2007-2008 budget (Table 14.1).

Table 14.1: Trends in the Relative Significance of Income Tax in Gross Tax Revenues* of the Central Government: Selected Years

(Rs. crore)

Central taxes	1950-51	1960-61	1970-71	1980-81	1990-91	2000-01	2007-08#
A+B Gross tax revenues	404 (100.0)	888 (100.0)	3,206 (100.0)	13,179 (100.0)	57,576 (100.0)	1,88,603 (100.0)	5,48,122 (100.0)
A. Direct taxes of which	174 (43.1)	290 (32.6)	870 (27.1)	3,004 (22.8)	11,025 (19.1)	68,306 (36.2)	2,67,490 (48.8)
1. Corporation	40 (9.9)	11 (12.5)	371 (11.6)	1,310 (9.9)	5,235 (9.3)	35,696 (18.9)	1,68,401 (30.7)
2. Personal income tax	132 (32.7)	166 (18.7)	473 (14.8)	1,506 (11.4)	5,371 (9.3)	31,764 (16.8)	98,774 (18.0)
B. Indirect taxes	229 (56.7)	599 (67.5)	2,337 (72.9)	10,175 (77.2)	46,552 (80.9)	1,20,297 (63.8)	2,80,632 (51.2)

* Before transferring States' share in Central taxes; # Budget estimates.

Figures in parentheses are corresponding percentages of gross tax revenues.

Sources: Government of India, Ministry of Finance, *Explanatory Memorandum on the Budget of the Central Government* (various years); *Receipts Budget* (various years); and *Budget at a Glance*, 2007-08.

14.4 Income Tax Act, 1961: Main Provisions

The present law of income tax in India is governed by the Income Tax Act, 1961 (hereinafter called the Act), which is amended from time to time by the annual Finance Act and other legislations pertaining to direct taxes. The Act which came into force on April 1, 1962, replaced the Indian Income Tax Act, 1922, which had remained in operation for 40 years. Furthermore, a set of rules known as Income Tax Rules, 1962 have been framed for implementing the various provisions of the Act. [5] The law of income tax is stated here as applicable for the financial year 2007-2008 (i.e. assessment year 2008-2009).

14.4.1 Meaning of Income: Section 4 of the Act deals with the basis of charge of income tax. Thus, income tax is an annual tax on income charged on every person. It is levied on the *total income* of every assessee computed in accordance with the provisions of the Act. *Total income* means the income for which an assessee is chargeable to tax. [6] As in most other countries, income is exemplified rather than defined. The Act does not define the term *income*, but Section 2 (24) of the Act describes the various receipts as income which include, *inter alia*, the following: profits and gains, dividends, voluntary contributions received by a charitable trust, the value of any perquisite or profit in lieu of salary, any capital gains, any winnings from lotteries, crossword puzzles etc.

Apart from the aforesaid receipts, any other receipt is taxable under the Act if it comes within the general and natural connotation of the term *income*. Thus, the law brings under charge various types of income which may be classified as follows: (a) income received, (b) income deemed to be received (Sec. 7), e.g. annual accretion to the account of an employee participating in a recognised provident fund, dividend declared by the company but not yet received by the individual shareholders etc., (c) income accrued [Sec. 5(1)(b)], and (d) income deemed to have accrued (Sec. 9). Income is said to be received when it reaches the assessee. It is said to accrue or arise when the right to receive the income becomes vested in the assessee. In short, the description of the term *income* in Section 2 (24) is inclusive and not exclusive.

It is indeed very difficult to reduce the concept of income to a precise and unambiguous definition. Various forms of imputed and accrued incomes pose serious practical difficulties of measurement and guidance is sought from judicial pronouncements on the subject. The Taxation Enquiry Commission, 1953-54, opined, "It will be impracticable to reduce the principles evolved by judicial decisions in the leading cases on this subject (income) into an exhaustive and self-contained definition of income in our taxation Act. We are also of the opinion that perhaps more harm than good may result from including in the taxation Act a rigid definition of income. We think that guidance in this matter should continue to be drawn in the future as heretofore, from the extensive case law in the subject." [7]

14.4.2 Residential Status: Income which is subject to charge of tax varies according to the residential status of taxpayer. In the case of a person *resident* in India, all income derived from whatever source is within the scope of taxation. Thus, he is liable to pay tax in respect of his income received or deemed to be received by him in India, income accruing or deemed to accrue to him in India, and income accruing or arising to him outside India. In short, a resident is charged to income tax on his world income, subject to a double taxation relief in respect of foreign incomes taxed abroad. However, in the case of a *non-resident*, tax liability extends only to income which (a) is received or is deemed to be received in India by or on behalf of the non-resident or (b) accrues or arises, or is deemed to accrue or arise, to the non-resident in India. It is evident that income which accrues or arises outside India (i.e. foreign income) is beyond the scope of tax liability in India in the case of a non-resident. However, if he is a *resident but not ordinarily a resident*, his liability in respect of such income arises only if it is from a business controlled or a profession set up in India. There are elaborate rules for ascertaining the residential status of an assessee. These are given in Sections 5 and 6 of the Act.

14.4.3 Incomes Exempt from Tax: Sections 10 of the Act describes incomes that are completely or partially exempt from income tax, i.e. tax free incomes. These exclusions are meant to serve various socio-economic objectives through the medium of tax policy.

The following is a select list of types of income that are exempt from income tax either fully or up to specified limits under various clauses of Section 10 of the Income Tax Act, 1961.

1. Agricultural income [Sec. 10(1)].
2. Receipts by a member from a Hindu Undivided Family [Sec. 10(2)].
3. Partner's share in the profits of a firm [Sec. 10(2A)].
4. Certain income from interest received by non-residents [Sec. 10(4)].
5. Value of any leave travel concession or assistance received by the employee from the employer in connection with the former proceeding on leave to any place in India [Sec. 10(5)].
6. Remuneration received by employees of foreign missions, foreign enterprises, foreign philanthropic institutions [under various sub-clauses of Sec. 10(6)].
7. Salaries of a foreign government employee under co-operative technical assistance programme [Sec. 10(8)].
8. Income of a family member of a technical assistant/consultant/employee

[Sec. 10(9)].

9. Death-cum-retirement gratuity subject to a maximum of Rs. 3,50,000 with effect from 24.9.1997 [Sec. 10(10)].

10. Any payment in commutation of pension received by Government or semi-government employee. Payment in commutation of pension received by private sector employee is exempt subject to certain limits [Sec. 10(10A)].

11. Any payment received by an employee of Central/State Government as the cash equivalent of the leave salary in respect of the period of earned leave at his credit at the time of his retirement. In the case of other employees, the exemption is available subject to limits prescribed [Sec. 10(10AA)].

12. Any compensation received by a workman at the time of retrenchment or closure or transfer of undertaking subject to prescribed limits [Sec. 10(10B)].

13. Any payment received by an employee of a company at the time of his voluntary retirement [Sec. 10(10C)].

14. Any sum received under a life insurance policy, including any bonus allocated on such policy [Sec. 10(10D)].

15. Payment from provident fund [Secs. 10(11), (12)].

16. Payment from superannuation fund [Sec. 10(13)].

17. House rent allowance [Sec. 10(13A)].

18. Special allowance or benefit to employees [Sec. 10(14)].

19. Interest on certain securities [Sec. 10 (15)].

20. Scholarships granted to meet the cost of education [Sec. 10 (16)].

21. Daily allowance of Members of Parliament [Sec. 10 (17)].

22. Any amount received in connection with an award instituted by Central/State Government [Sec. 10 (17A)].

23. Income of a local authority (Sec. 10 (20); a scientific research association (Sec. 10 (21); a university [Sec. 10 (22)]; a hospital [Sec. 10 (22A)]; *Khadi* or Village Industries [Sec. 10 (23B)]; certain national funds [Sec. 10 (23C)]; mutual funds [Sec. 10 (23D)]; trade unions [Sec. 10 (24)]; provident funds [Sec. 10 (25)]; a member of scheduled tribe [Sec. 10 (26)]; a body for promoting interest of scheduled castes/tribes etc. [Sec. 10 (26B)]; a co-operative society for promoting interest of scheduled castes/tribes [Sec. 10 (27)].

24. Subsidy received from the Tea Board [Sec. 10 (30)].

25. Subsidy received from commodity boards [Sec. 10 (31)].

26. Income of minor child liable to be included in the income of his parent up to a maximum of Rs. 1,500 per minor child [Sec. 10 (32)].

14.4.4 Tax Holiday Schemes: These schemes are extensions of the provisions which exempt certain incomes from the purview of income tax.

A. Tax Holiday for Newly Established Industrial Undertakings in Free

Trade Zones, Electronic Hardware Technology Parks, or Software Technology Parks or Special Economic Zones: This scheme provides for a complete tax exemption in respect of the profits and gains of an industrial undertaking set up in any free trade zone, electronic hardware technology park, or software technology park or special economic zone as specified by the Central Government for the purpose of Section 10A. Complete tax exemption can be claimed for a period of 10 consecutive assessment years beginning from the first year of production. From the assessment year 2003-04, the amount of deduction is 90 per cent of export profits for the first ten consecutive assessment years.

This tax concession is available to all categories of taxpayers. The tax holiday is in lieu of all other tax concessions available in the Income Tax Act. Assessees availing this tax holiday scheme are not entitled to various benefits and deductions under various sections of the Act. However, the assessees have the option to choose either the complete tax holiday under section l0A or all other tax concessions available under the Act.

B. Tax Holiday for Newly Established 100 Per Cent Export-Oriented Undertakings: Under provisions of Section l0B, any profits and gains made by an assessee from a 100 per cent export-oriented undertaking are not included in the total income of the assessee. This benefit is available to the assessee in respect of 10 consecutive assessment years beginning with the initial assessment year in which the undertaking begins to manufacture or produce articles. From the assessment year 2003-04, the amount of deduction is 90 per cent. Assessees availing this tax holiday scheme are not entitled to other tax concessions available in the Act.

C. Tax Holiday for Exporters of Wood-based Handicraft Items: Under provisions of Section 10BA, any profits and gains derived by an undertaking from the export of wood-based handicraft items, manufactured without the use of imported raw materials, are deductible as per rules.

14.4.5 Heads of Income: Income tax is a composite tax on the aggregate of incomes from various sources. However, taxable income is first computed under different heads of income and then aggregated. From the aggregated amount certain deductions are made to arrive at taxable income. Section l4 of the Act prescribes five broad heads under which the income of an assessee is classified for purposes of computation of total income and the charge of income tax. These are: salaries, income from house property, profits and gains of business or profession, capital gains, and income from other sources. These five heads of income are mutually exclusive. If any income falls under one head, it cannot be considered under any other head.

The method of computing income and the permissible deductions differ with each head of income. The heads of income are intended to indicate the classes of income to which different rules of computation are applied. The aggregate of income under these heads is termed as *gross total income* which, when reduced by the deductions available under Sections 80C to 80U (also called Chapter VI-A deductions) gives total income on which the charge is applied. A brief explanation of the different rules governing the computation of taxable income under each of the above-mentioned heads is as follows.

A. Salaries: Those payments which are connected with employment are taxable under the head *salaries*. The existence of employer-employee relationship is essential for taxing income under this head. Under Section 17(1), salary is defined to include, *inter alia*, the following: (i) wages, (ii) any annuity or pension, (iii) any fees, commissions, bonus, (iv) any advance of salary, (v) any arrears of salary. It also includes perquisites, i.e. the value of any benefit or amenity provided by the employer like rent-free accommodation. However, Section 17 provides for exemption from tax in respect of perquisites in the form of medical facilities provided by the employer. Broadly speaking, whatever is received from the employer is salary.

The Act allows some relief in respect of salary paid in arrears or in advance in lump sum. The computation of relief is governed by Section 89(1) and Rule [21A(2)].

From the aggregate amount of salary, a standard deduction was allowed (sec. 16) till recently to account for the expenditure incidental to the employment of an assessee. [8] However, it was withdrawn by the Finance Act, 2005.

B. Income from House Property: The scope of income charged under this head is defined by Section 22 and the computation of income under this head is explained by Sections 23 to 27. Income tax is payable by an assessee on the annual value of property consisting of buildings and land appurtenant thereto of which he is the owner. The annual value of such property, called house property, is deemed to be the sum for which the property might reasonably be expected to let from year to year. The annual value is ascertained by taking into consideration all relevant facts such as rent received, terms of the lease, the municipal valuation, and rent paid for similar property in the locality. The concept of taxation under this head does not extend to properties used for the purpose of any business or profession pursued by the owner of the property because house property is regarded as any other business asset. One house used by the owner for his own residence is exempt from tax. Prior to the assessment year 1987-88, income from owner-occupied houses used to be assessed notionally subject to a maximum of 10 per cent of the total income. However, from that year onward, no income is imputed from owner-occupied houses due to valuation problems.

From the annual value of the house property, various deductions are allowed in computing the net annual value of a house property. Deduction is first made in respect of municipal taxes. Presently (financial year 2007-2008), a deduction of 30 per cent of annual value of house property is allowed for repairs etc. Similarly, deduction is allowed in respect of the current interest liability on money borrowed for the acquisition, construction, repair or renewal of the property.

As a result of various deductions, taxpayers in many cases showed negative income from house property which was then set off against income from other sources such as salaries, business or professional income. The Finance Act, 1992, provided that the loss from house property will not be allowed to be set off against income under any other head of income from the assessment year 1993-94. Further, the carry forward of losses of any year from house property will be allowed to be set off only against income from house property of subsequent years.

C. Profits and Gains of Business or Profession: This head of income is beset with complicated rules of computation, often leading to controversies and litigation. According to Section 2(13), business includes any trade, commerce, or manufacture or any adventure in the nature of a trade, commerce, or manufacture. A profession, under section 2(36), is an occupation requiring purely intellectual skill or manual skill such as that of a lawyer, accountant, engineer, surgeon, author etc. Section 28 defines various incomes which are chargeable to tax under the head profits and gains of business or profession. Sections 30 to 44D specify the method of computation of income under this head by describing the nature and amount of permissible and non-permissible deductions. Broadly speaking, all expenses that are wholly or exclusively laid out or expended for the purpose of business and that are not of capital nature are deductible.

Deductions Expressly Allowed. There is a long list of deductions expressly allowed while computing taxable income under this head. The important ones are listed below.

1. Rent, taxes, repairs and insurance for building (Sec. 30). In respect of premises owned by the assessee, no deduction is allowed. However, amount spent on current repairs is allowed. In respect of premises taken on rent, actual rent paid is admissible as deduction. Insurance premium against the risk of damage or destruction of the business premises is also allowable as business deduction.
2. Repairs and insurance of machinery, plant, and furniture (Sec. 31).
3. Depreciation allowance (Sec. 32). The Act provides for different rates of depreciation for different categories of assets. However, if the actual cost of any machinery or plant does not exceed Rs. 5,000, it is straight way deducted as

revenue expense in the year it is first put to use. Depreciation is not allowed in respect of any motor car manufactured outside India unless it is used in a business of running it on hire for tourists.

Where an asset is acquired during the previous year and is used for less than 182 days in that previous year, the depreciation allowable in respect of such asset is restricted to 50 per cent of the amount normally allowable.

Unabsorbed depreciation can be carried forward and claimed by the assessee in the following years against income from 'profits and gains of business or profession'. Any amount remaining still unabsorbed can be carried forward till it is finally set off.

4. Expenditure on Scientific Research (Sec. 35).

5. Expenditure on acquisition of patent rights and copyrights (Sec.35A).

6. Expenditure on know-how (Sec. 35AB).

7. Expenditure on eligible projects or schemes for promoting social and economic welfare (Sec. 35AC).

8. Payments to associations and institutions for carrying out rural development programmes (Sec. 35CCA).

9. Payment to associations and institutions for carrying out programmes of conservation of natural resources (Sec. 35CCB).

10. Amortisation of preliminary expenses (Sec.35D). Certain preliminary expenses incurred before or after the commencement of business in connection with the extension of an industrial undertaking or setting up a new industrial unit qualify for amortisation. The amount is allowed against the profits of the assessee in ten equal instalments over a period of ten years. The aggregate amount of the qualifying expenditure should not exceed 2.5 per cent of the cost of project. Some of the heads of qualifying expenditure specified for the purpose are: expenditure in connection with preparation of a feasibility report, conducting a market survey, legal charges for drafting the memorandum and articles of association of the company, printing expenses of the memorandum and articles of associations, and expenses in connection with the public issue of shares.

11. Insurance premium [Sec. 36(1)(i)]. The amount of any premium paid in respect of insurance against risk of damage or destruction of stocks or stores used for the purpose of business is admissible as deduction.

12. Bonus or Commission to employees [Sec. 36(1)(ii)]. Bonus or Commission paid to an employee is allowable as deduction subject to certain conditions.

13. Interest on borrowed capital [Sec. 36(1)(iii)].

14. Employer's contribution to recognised provident fund and approved superannuation fund [Sec. 36(1)(iv)].

15. Contribution towards approved gratuity fund [Sec. 36(1)(v)].

16. Bad debts [Sec. 36(1)(vii)].

17. General deductions (Sec. 37). In order to claim deduction under this section, the expenditure should not be of the nature described under Sections 30 to 36. A variety of expenses are allowed under the residuary Section 37 and it is not possible to draw an exhaustive list. A few instances of such expenses are: entertainment expenditure, expenses on advertisements, travelling expenses, litigation expenses in protecting trade or business, commission paid to selling agents, salary and perquisites to employees, expenses incurred on the occasion of *diwali* and *mahurat* subject to the satisfaction of the income tax officer, and expenses on registration of trade marks.

Expenses Expressly Disallowed. The following expenses, *inter alia,* are expressly disallowed while computing taxable income under this head.

1. Expenditure on advertisement in any souvenir, brochure etc. of a political party [Sec. 37(2B)].

2. Any interest or salary payable outside India from which due tax has not been deducted at source; any tax calculated on the basis of profits or gains of business or profession [Sec. 40(a)].

3. Payment to partner [Sec. 40(b)].

D. Capital Gains: Under Section 45 of the Act, any profits or gains arising from the transfer of a capital asset are chargeable to tax under the head capital gains. Taxation of capital gains has been discussed below in this chapter separately.

E. Income from Other Sources: Income of every kind, which is not chargeable to tax under any of the other four heads and which is not to be excluded from the total income, is chargeable to tax under the residuary head *income from other sources*. Section 56 defines the scope of income chargeable under this head and Sections 57 and 58 lay down the basis of computation of such income. Some examples of incomes included under this head are: (i) dividends, (ii) winnings from lotteries, crossword puzzles, races including horse races, card games, gambling or betting, (iii) income from machinery, plant or furniture belonging to an assessee and let on hire, (iv) interest on bank deposits and loans, and (v) interest on securities issued by the Government; and interest on debentures and other securities issued by a local authority, a company, or a public sector corporation.

The following deductions are allowed under Section 57 in computing income chargeable to tax under this head: 1. In the case of dividends any reasonable sum paid by way of commissions etc. for the purpose of realising the dividend. 2. In the case of income from machinery, plant or furniture let on hire, current repairs, depreciation, and unabsorbed depreciation etc. 3. Any other expenditure (not being a capital expenditure) expended wholly and exclusively for the purpose of making or earning such income. In computing income from securities etc., a taxpayer may deduct (a) any reasonable sum expended by him for the purpose of realising such interest, and (b) any interest payable on moneys borrowed for the purpose of investment in securities by the assessee.

14.4.6 Clubbing of Income: To counteract practices of tax avoidance, the Act contains provisions under which income of other persons is included in an assessee's income. Sections 60 to 64 of the Act deal with instances where an assessee may attempt to reduce his tax liability either by transferring his assets in favour of his family members or by arranging his sources of income in such a manner that tax incidence falls on others whereas the benefit of income, directly or indirectly, is derived by the assessee himself. To counter such attempts, the Act incorporates provisions under which certain incomes are included in the assessee's total income, though such incomes legally belong to other persons. In other words, incomes arising to the spouse, minor child, son's wife, son's minor child and other persons are clubbed with the assessee's income in certain circumstances. In this respect, the Act deviates from the general principle that a person can be assessed in respect of his own income.

14.4.7 Set Off and Carry Forward of Losses: As already noted, income chargeable under the Act is computed under five different heads. The aggregation of *gross total income* is relatively easy if income under each head and from each source is positive. However, loss may be sustained in one or more sources under one or more heads of income. Therefore, in the computation of *gross total income* of an assessee, appropriate adjustments should be made of the losses suffered by him. Sections 70 to 80 of the Act deal with provisions concerning set off of losses and their carry forward. The following three steps may be followed to understand the procedure of set off and carry forward of losses: (a) Inter-source adjustment under the same head of income. (b) Inter-head adjustment in the same assessment year. Provisions of (b) are applied only if a loss cannot be set off, fully or partly, under (a). (c) Carry forward of loss. Provisions of (c) are applied only if a loss cannot be set off, fully or partly under (a) and (b).

The purpose of these provisions is to mitigate the disincentive effects of fluctuating income. Under a system of progressive income tax based on yearly assessment, a taxpayer whose income fluctuates from year to year will surrender a larger proportion of his income in tax than a taxpayer with the same average income more evenly distributed over the years. To prevent this violation of the principle of horizontal equity, some form of income averaging method is necessary. Set off and carry forward provisions are proxy for income averaging principle.

14.4.8 Deductions from Gross Total Income: Gross total income of an assessee is obtained by adding up incomes under different heads. While computing incomes under various heads, certain deductions are allowed, which are in the nature of expenses incurred in earning the specific incomes under different heads. These have already been discussed while dealing with various heads of income.

The Act provides certain special deductions under Chapter VI-A and these are intended to promote various national policy objectives like industrialisation of backward areas, encouragement to small-scale industries, export promotion, and helping an assessee in meeting certain essential expenditures. These deductions are made from the gross total income of an assessee and not from any particular head of income.

The aggregate amount of deductions allowable cannot exceed the gross total income. No such deduction is allowed against long-term capital gains. Thus, where the gross total income includes long-term capital gains, the gross total income is reduced by such long-term capital gains for the purpose of deductions. These deductions are allowed under various clauses of Section 80 of the Act (i.e. Sections 80CCC to 80U), and are arranged alphabetically. The following select list shows the deductions which are available to an individual assessee.

A. Deductions in Respect of Certain Payments: Deductions under this category relate to certain kinds of payments made by an assessee. These payments are not made in connection with earning of any income chargeable to tax. These are of the following types.

1. Deduction under section 80C is allowed for investment in PPF, LIC, annuity schemes, repayment of housing loan, tuition fee, subscription to eligible shares/infrastructure bonds etc. up to a maximum of Rs. 1 lakh. Further, aggregate deduction under section 80C, 80CCC (pension scheme of LIC) and 80CCD (Central Government pension scheme) shall not exceed Rs. 1 lakh.

2. Deduction in respect of contribution to LIC pension fund (Jeevan Suraksha) [Sec. 80CCC]. Deduction is allowed for the amount paid by the assessee during the previous year out of his taxable income to the annuity plan (Jeevan Suraksha) of LIC. The maximum amount of deduction is Rs. 10,000.

3. Deduction in respect of medical insurance premiums (Sec. 80D). Deduction is allowed up to a maximum of Rs. 15,000 in general and Rs. 20,000 for senior citizens in the case of an individual in respect of insurance on his health or on the health of spouse or dependent parents and children.

4. Deduction in respect of medical treatment of handicapped dependants (Sec. 80DD). Deduction is allowed to an individual for (a) the medical treatment of one

or more handicapped dependant and (b) amount deposited for the benefit of a handicapped dependant. The deduction allowable is Rs. 50,000 in aggregate for any of or both the purposes mentioned above.

5. Deduction in respect of certain medical treatment [Sec. 80DDB]. A maximum deduction of Rs. 40,000 in general and Rs. 60,000 for senior citizens is allowed in respect of expenditure for the treatment of specified diseases (AIDS, cancer etc.).

6. Deduction in respect of repayment of loan taken for higher education [Sec. 80E]. Any amount paid by the assessee by way of repayment of loan taken for the purpose of pursuing higher education.

7. Donations to the Prime Minister's National Relief Fund and certain other funds (Sec. 80G). A deduction of 100 per cent is allowed in respect of donations to (a) National Defence Fund, (b) the Prime Minister's National Relief Fund, (c) National Foundation for Communal Harmony, (d) An approved university or educational institution of national eminence, (e) The Government or any approved local authority, institution or association for promoting family planning, (f) Chief Minister's Relief Fund.

A deduction of 50 per cent of the qualifying amount donated is allowed for donations to (a) Jawaharlal Nehru Memorial Fund, (b) Prime Minister's Drought Relief Fund, (c) National Children's Fund, (d) Indira Gandhi Memorial Trust, (e) Rajiv Gandhi Foundation, (f) Any temple, mosque, gurudwara, church, or other place of worship which is of historic, archaeological or artistic importance, (g) Any fund or institution established in India for a charitable purpose as is referred to under Section 80G (5).

If the aggregate of donations made by the assessee exceeds 10 per cent of his taxable income, such excess does not qualify for deduction.

8. Donations for scientific research or rural development are deductible as per rules (Sec. 80GGA). This deduction is not applicable if the gross total income of the assessee includes the income chargeable under the head *profits and gains of business or profession.*

B. Deductions in Respect of Certain Incomes: Deductions are allowed, *inter alia*, in respect of the following kinds of income of an assessee.

1. Deduction in respect of profits and gains from industrial undertakings or enterprises engaged in infrastructure development etc. [Sec. 80-IA]. There are elaborate rules for claiming deduction under this section.

2. Deduction in respect of profits and gains from certain industrial undertakings other than infrastructure development undertakings [Sec. 80-IB]. There are elaborate rules for claiming deduction under this section.

3. Deductions in respect of profits and gains from certain undertakings or

enterprises in the States of Himachal Pradesh, Uttranchal, Sikkim and North-Eastern States [Sec. 80-IC]. There are elaborate rules for claiming deduction under this section.

4. 100 per cent deduction is allowed to co-operative societies in respect of profits attributable to certain specified activities (Sec. 80P).

5. Deduction in respect of disabled persons (Sec. 80U). A resident individual suffering from any disability is allowed a deduction of Rs. 50,000. In case of a person with severe disability, the amount of deduction is Rs. 75,000.

14.4.9 Rebates: Till recently, the Act provided for a rebate (or tax credit) on tax liability for investment in specified schemes (section 88), for senior citizens (section 88B), for women assessees (section 88C) and for small assessees. However, all these rebates were withdrawn by the Finance Act, 2005. [9]

14.4.10 Computation of Total Income: According to Section 2(45), the total income of an assessee means the income for which he is chargeable to tax on the basis of his residence. It is computed in the following manner:

1. Ascertain the residential status of the assessee and find out which income is chargeable in his hands. For a resident assessee, the whole of his world income is chargeable to tax while for a non-resident assessee, his Indian incomes only are taxable.
2. Compute such incomes under different heads of income after allowing deductions relevant to each head of income and total them up (an individual may earn income from all the heads but a company can earn income from all the heads except salaries).
3. Add others' incomes with the assessee's income wherever applicable (Sections 60 to 64).
4. Allow set off and carry forward of losses. The resultant figure is known as *gross total income* of the assessee.
5. From the *gross total income* make the deductions allowed by chapter VI-A on account of certain payments and in respect of certain incomes (sections 80C to 80U). The balance is called *total income* i.e. the base for charging income tax.
6. Compute tax liability on total income.
7. From the tax liability so determined, tax already paid to arrive at net tax liability. The procedure for computation of income and determination of tax liability is summarised in Table 14.2.

14.4.11 Units of Assessment: There are seven categories of persons (i.e. units of assessment or taxable entities) chargeable to tax under the Act. According to Section 2(31) the word *person* includes: (i) an individual, (ii) a Hindu undivided family, (iii) a company, (iv) a firm, (v) an association of persons or a body of individuals whether incorporated or not, (vi) a local authority, (vii) every artificial juridical person, not falling within any of the preceding categories. [10] However, individuals and companies are the two main taxpaying entities. Depending upon the residential status, companies are classified into *domestic* and *foreign* companies.

Table 14.2: Computation of Income and Determination of Tax Liability

1. Income from salary
2. Income from house property
3. Profits and gains of business/profession
4. Income from capital gains
   (a) Short-term capital gains
   (b) Long-term capital gains
5. Income from other sources

Aggregate of Incomes
[Total of 1+2+3+4+5]
Add: Others' incomes with the assessee's income wherever applicable.
Less: Adjustments for set off and carry forward of losses
Gross Total Income
Less: Deductions under chapter VI-A [Sections 80C to 80U]
Total Income (or taxable income)
Tax on long-term capital gains
Add: Tax on taxable income less long-term capital gains.
Total Tax
Less: Rebates/reliefs, if any
Net Tax
Add: Surcharge, if any
Total Tax Payable
Less: Tax deducted at source
Less: Advanced tax paid
Balance: Tax payable/refundable

14.4.12 Basic Exemption: A company is liable to income tax however small its income may be while a basic exemption is allowed to individual taxpayers. Basic exemption is allowed to permit a minimum standard of living or some level of income which does not reflect the taxpaying capacity of a person. For the financial year 2007-2008 (i.e. assessment year 2008-2009), the basic exemption limit is Rs. 1,10,000 (Rs. 1,45,000 in case of resident women below 65 years and Rs. 1,95,000 in case of resident senior citizens).

Table 14.3 records trends in the basic exemption limit for individual income taxpayers during the post-Independence period.

Table 14.3: Basic Exemption Limit for Individual Income Taxpayers 1947-48 to 2007-2008

Financial year	Basic exemption limit (Rs.)
1947-48	2,500
1948-49 to 1950-51	3,000
1951-52 and 1952-53	3,600
1953-54 to 1956-57	4,200
1957-58 to 1965-66	3,000
1966-67 to 1969-70	3,500
1970-71 to 1973-74	5,000
1974-75 and 1975-76	6,000
1976-77	8,000
1977-78 to 1979-80	10,000
1980-81	12,000
1981-82 to 1984-85	15,000
1985-86 to 1989-90	18,000
1990-91 and 1991-92	22,000
1992-93	28,000
1993-94	30,000
1994-95	35,000
1995-96 to 1997-98	40,000
1998-99 to 2004-2005	50,000
2005-06 and 2006-07	1,00,000
2007-08	1,10,000

Source: Government of India, *Budget Papers* (various years).

The exemption limit has generally been raised from time to time to make adjustments for inflation. Only once it was actually reduced from Rs. 4,200 to Rs. 3,000 in 1957-58. Proposing the reduction the Finance Minister remarked, "The minimum limit had been raised over the past few years mainly for administrative reasons. An income of Rs. 4,200, modest though it is in absolute terms, is quite a large multiple of the average level of incomes in the country. It is reasonable to expect that those with an income over Rs. 3,000 should also make their contribution, however small, to the public exchequer, and should come within the range of direct taxation." [11]

14.4.13 Rate Structure: Prior to 1916, income tax was levied at a flat rate of 5 *pies* in a rupee on all incomes above Rs. 2,000. With a rupee containing 192 *pies*, the rate of tax worked out to 2.6 per cent approximately. It was in 1916 that the income tax came to be levied at graduated scale and this principle has been followed since then. In 1945-46, the maximum rate of income tax was 57 pies in a rupee (29.7 per cent). In 1946-47, there was a steep rise in the maximum rate of income tax to 15.5 *annas* in a rupee (96.9 per cent). The Taxation Enquiry Commission, 1953-54, recommended 92 per cent rate of tax (including surcharge) on the highest slab of income.

The Report of the Direct Taxes Enquiry Committee (DTEC), 1971, was a milestone in the area of income tax rates. The Committee made a number of far-reaching suggestions for unearthing black money, preventing evasion and avoidance of taxes, and reducing arrears. One important recommendation of the Committee related to reduction in the rates of direct taxes which in its view were mainly responsible for tax evasion because they made tax evasion profitable and attractive. The rates of individual income tax were quite high till the year 1973-74. However, following the recommendations of the DTEC, the Government initiated a series of rate reductions in individual income tax.

The rate of tax was reduced from 97.7 per cent in 1973-74 to 77 per cent in 1974-75, and further down to 66 per cent in 1976-77. It is noteworthy that DTEC had recommended a maximum marginal rate of 75 per cent. [12]

The downward trend in the rate of income tax was temporarily reversed during the brief Janata Government rule at the Centre. The top marginal rate of income tax was increased from 66 per cent in 1976-77 to 69 per cent in 1977-78, and further up to 72 per cent in 1979-80. However, the policy of low direct tax rates started by the Congress Government in 1974 and carried forward in 1976 was further reinforced after it came back to power at the Centre in 1980. After a series of revisions, the maximum marginal rate of individual income tax was 54 per cent (including employment surcharge of 8 per cent), applicable from the financial year 1990-91. Consequent upon the recommendations contained in the Interim Report of the Tax Reforms Committee, 1991, the marginal rate was fixed at 44.8 per cent (including surcharge) from the financial year 1992-93. The Finance Act, 1994, abolished the surcharge of 12 per cent and hence the maximum marginal rate of tax was 40 per cent from the financial year 1994-95. From the same year it was made applicable on incomes over Rs. 1,20,000. It may be recalled that the top marginal rate of income tax applied to incomes above Rs.

1 lakh from 1967-68 to 1993-94. The Rs. 1 lakh of 1967-68 was approximately equivalent to Rs. 5.5 lakh of 1993-94. This shows the laxity of the administration in adjusting tax brackets for inflation. It is noteworthy that the Tax Reforms Committee had recommended 40 per cent maximum rate inclusive of surcharge for income exceeding Rs. 2 lakh.

Table 14.4 summarises the decline in the maximum marginal rate of income tax beginning with the year 1974-75.

Table 14.4: Trends in the Maximum Marginal Rate of Individual Income Tax: 1973-74 to 2007-2008 (per cent)

Financial Year	Top marginal rate	Surcharge, if any	Rate including surcharge
1973-74	85	15	97.7
1974-75 and 1975-76	70	10	77.0
1976-77	60	10	66.0
1977-78 and 1978-79	60	15	69.0
1979-80	60	20	72.0
1980-81 to 1982-83	60	10	66.0
1983-84	60	12.5	67.5
1984-85	55	12.5	61.9
1985-86 and 1986-87	50	Nil	50.0
1987-88 and 1988-89	50	5	52.5
1989-90	50	8	54.0
1990-91 and 1991-92	50	12	56.0
1992-93 and 1993-94	40	12	44.8
1994-95 to 1996-97	40	Nil	40.0
1997-98 and 1998-99	30	Nil	30.0
1999-00	30	10	33.0
2000-01	30	15	34.5
2001-02	30	2	30.6
2002-03	30	5	31.5
2003-04 and 2004-05	30	10	33.0
2005-06 to 2007-08	30	2.5	30.75

Note: The maximum marginal rate of individual income tax was applicable on income over Rs. 1,00,000 up to the year 1993-94. From 1994-95, it was applicable on income over Rs. 1,20,000. From the financial year 1997-98, it was applicable on income above Rs. 1,50,000. From the financial year 2005-06, it is applicable on income above Rs. 2,50,000.

Source: Government of India, *Budget Papers* (various years).

The maximum marginal rate of personal income tax was further reduced from 40 per cent to 30 per cent in the 1997-98 budget. In another significant move, it was made applicable to incomes above Rs. 1,50,000. After further revisions, the maximum rate (inclusive of surcharge) stood at 30.75 per cent for the financial year 2007-2008.

The philosophy of low tax rates presupposes improved tax compliance to control the growth of black money, and broadening of the tax base. It is argued that high tax rates increase premium on tax evasion which, in turn, generates black money. Low tax rates are welcome provided they improve compliance and revenue yield. However, to expect that lowering of rates would improve compliance automatically is unrealistic because tax evasion occurs at all levels of income.

Broadly speaking, the present system of income tax is *global* in nature in that it does not discriminate between different sources of income. Income from various sources is pooled together for determining tax liability. Elements of schedular system (under which different sources of income are taxed differently) exist insofar as agricultural income is excluded from the tax base, and long-term capital gains, though included in the definition of income, are given special concessions.

As already noted, income tax revenue originates mainly from two taxpaying entities, viz. companies, and individuals. Although the concept of taxable income and the procedure for its computation is the same, except for minor differences, for all taxable entities, the income tax rates vary among different entities. From the standpoint of differential tax treatment, the tax on companies (also referred to as corporation tax) and firms is essentially a proportional tax while the tax on non-corporate entities (also referred to as personal income tax) is basically a progressive income tax. The different constituents of the non-corporate entities, viz. individuals, Hindu undivided families etc., are subject to varying rates of income tax. Likewise, the rate of tax on corporate entities differs depending on whether a company is *domestic* or *foreign*. In general, a domestic company is taxed at a lower rate than a foreign company.

Prior to the enactment of the Finance Act, 1994, a distinction existed among domestic companies, viz. widely-held companies, and closely-held companies. Widely-held companies were subject to lower tax rates as compared to closely-held companies. Again, prior to the enactment of Finance Act, 1991, domestic companies were categorised into industrial and trading companies. The industrial companies were taxed at a lower rate than the non-industrial companies.

A. Surcharge: A notable feature of the rate structure is the imposition of surcharge on income tax wholly for the purpose of the Centre. Surcharge was levied in 1951 and continued uninterrupted when it was completely abolished in 1985. However, a drought surcharge was levied at the rate of 5 per cent in 1987 on incomes above Rs. 50,000 and the same was replaced by an employment surcharge of 8 per cent in 1989. It was increased to 12 per cent in December 1990. The Finance Act, 1994, abolished the surcharge from the financial year 1994-95. Surcharge was reimposed at the rate of 10 per cent from the financial year 1999-2000 and the same was increased to 15 per cent from the next year (i.e. financial year 2000-2001). For the financial year 2001-2002, surcharge was levied at the rate of 2 per cent to provide relief to quake hit areas of Gujarat. The present rate of surcharge is indicated in Table 14.5.

Rates of income tax are fixed by the annual Finance Act and not by the Income Tax Act. (In the case of other direct taxes, e.g. wealth tax, the rates are specified in a schedule to the Act imposing the tax). Rates of income tax applicable to various entities for the financial year 2007-2008 (i.e. assessment year 2008-2009) are given in Table 14.5.

Table 14.5: Rates of Income Tax for Various Entities: 2007-2008 (A.Y. 2008-2009)

Individuals (other than resident senior citizens and women below 65 years), Hindu undivided families, association of persons etc.		
Slab of income (Rs.)		Rate of income tax
From	To	
0	1,10,000	Nil
1,10,000	1,50,000	10 per cent of the amount exceeding Rs. 1,10,000
1,50,000	2,50,000	Rs. 4,000 plus 20 per cent of the amount exceeding Rs. 1,50,000
2,50,000 and above		Rs. 24,000 plus 30 per cent of the amount exceeding Rs. 2,50,000
Companies and partnership firms		
Domestic companies and partnership firms		30 per cent
Foreign companies		40 per cent

Persons having total income exceeding Rs. 10,00,000 are required to pay 2.5 per cent surcharge on total income tax payable. A surcharge at the rate of 10 per cent is payable by domestic companies and partnership firms with taxable income of above Rs. 1 crore. Rate of surcharge on foreign companies is 2.5 per cent. Education cess of 2 per cent is payable by all assessees. Secondary and Higher Education cess of 1 per cent is payable by all assessees.

14.4.14 Advance Payment of Tax: Though the regular assessment in respect of any income is made in a later assessment year, the tax on such income is payable by way of advance payment. Section 208 of the Act makes it obligatory to pay advance tax in every case where the advance tax payable is Rs. 5,000 or more. Furthermore, every income (including capital gains, winnings from lotteries, crossword puzzles etc.) is liable for payment of advance tax. Thus, all assessees are required to pay tax in advance on incomes which they expect to earn during the current financial year. For instance, for the financial year 2007-08 (i.e. assessment year 2008-09) advance tax is payable in instalments during the financial year 2007-08 itself. The advance tax so paid is adjusted when assessment takes place in 2008-09.

14.4.15 Tax Deduction at Source: There are provisions under various sections of the Act regarding tax deduction at source (TDS), e.g. deduction of tax from salaries (Sec. 192). Other incomes covered under the scheme of TDS include fees for professional/technical services, interest, dividends, rent from real estate, commission from insurance, sale of lottery tickets, winnings from lotteries, crossword puzzles and horse racing etc.

Persons responsible for making payments of such specified incomes are liable to deduct tax at source on such payments and deposit the same with the Government within the stipulated time. Select payments subject to tax deduction at source along with rates are given in Table 14.6.

14.5 Taxation of Companies

Companies have been treated as separate taxable units from the very beginning. In the 1886 Act, profits of a company were taxed at a flat rate. In 1916, companies with an income of less than Rs. 1,000 were exempted from paying income tax. The Act of 1918 inserted a new provision under which dividends received by a shareholder were included in his total income for the purpose of determining the rate of tax on his other income. The dividends as such continued to be exempt in the hands of the shareholders. Under the differentiation principle introduced in 1948, companies with a total income not exceeding Rs. 25,000 were required to pay income tax of only 2.5 *annas* in a rupee (15.5 per cent) as against 5 *annas* in a rupee (31.2 per cent) on other companies.

Prior to the year 1960-61, a company was deemed to have paid income tax on behalf of its shareholders on dividends declared out of income on which the company had paid income tax. Each shareholder was entitled for a tax credit against his income tax liability to the tune of the tax deemed to have been paid on his behalf by the company. The tax credit entitlement of a shareholder was determined on the basis of gross dividend income, instead of net dividend income, and the rate at which the tax deemed to have been paid by the company was the rate applicable to companies in that given year in which the dividend was declared or paid. If, for example, a shareholder received net dividend of Rs. 900 paid entirely out of the profits of a company, and the income tax rate (including surcharge) applicable to the company in that year was 40 per cent, the gross dividend was calculated by the formula G = N/(1-R), where G = gross dividend, N = net dividend, and R = income tax rate. For the above example G = 900/(1-0.4), or G = 1500. The difference between G and N, i.e. Rs. 600 was taken to be the tax payment made by the company on behalf of the shareholders.

Table 14.6: Select Payments Subject to Tax Deduction at Source under the Income Tax Act, 1961

Nature of income	Relevant Section of the Act	Rate of TDS (per cent)
Salaries	192	---
Payment of dividends (No TDS is deductible on dividends declared, distributed or paid on or after 1.6.1997 which have been subjected to additional income tax of 10% under Sec. 115-O)	194	20
Interest on time deposits with a banking company where the interest (payable by each branch) exceeds Rs. 5,000 per annum.	194A	10
Winnings from lotteries and crossword puzzles exceeding Rs. 5,000	194B	40
Winnings from horse races exceeding Rs. 2,500	194BB	40
Payments to contractors exceeding Rs. 20,000 for carrying out any work	194C	2
Commission to insurance agents exceeding Rs. 5,000	194D	10
Commission, remuneration or prize on lottery tickets exceeding Rs. 1,000	194G	10

However, the super tax paid by companies was assumed as paid by a company on its own behalf. Thus, there was an important distinction between income tax and super tax paid by companies, the former on behalf of shareholders and the latter on its own behalf. The super tax was often called the real corporation tax. The distinction was rendered irrelevant when beginning with the year 1960-61, a company was deemed to have paid income tax on its own behalf.

The scheme of tax credit to shareholders was discontinued with effect from the financial year 1960-61, making dividends received by shareholders subject to personal income tax.

14.5.1 Main Features of Company Taxation: These are the following.

1. Under the Indian income tax law, a company is regarded as a separate entity for the purpose of income tax. Till recently, dividends were taxed twice, first in the hands of the company, and second in the hands of the shareholders. This was an example of double taxation of a source of income, viz. dividends. Business community had often demanded that dividends should be totally exempted from tax and treated as an allowable expenditure in the hands of a company. Hence, from the financial year 1997-98, tax on dividends in the hands of the shareholder was abolished. Instead, a tax on distributed profits at the rate of 10 per cent on the amount so distributed was levied. In the 2002-03 budget, dividends on shares were again made taxable in the hands of the recipients (i.e. share holders). For the financial year 2007-08, the rate of dividend distribution tax is 15 per cent.
2. Corporate assessees pay tax on their total income which in the case of resident companies is the total world income and in the case of non-resident companies total Indian income.
3. The total income of a company is arrived at with reference to its profits shown in its profit and loss account. To such profits (or losses) are added those expenses which, though actually incurred by the company, are disallowed, partially or wholly, under the Act. From this total, the amount of tax concessions is deducted to arrive at the base for company taxation.
4. Prior to the assessment year 1984-85, the rate structure of company tax was progressive. However, from that year a flat rate is charged depending upon the domicile and nature of a company. This single rate formula provides strong inducement to companies to close their books showing a marginal loss. Such malpractices can be discouraged by introducing a two-tier rate structure, e.g. 25 per cent rate of tax for the initial slab of income and 40 per cent for the remaining income.
5. Under the income tax law, a parent (or a holding) company and its subsidiary company are separate legal entities and are, therefore, taxed separately. Thus, if a holding company receives dividends from its subsidiary, the former has to pay tax on such dividends. Taxation of inter-corporate earnings is designed to prevent concentration of economic power in the hands of corporate giants.

However, this provision is said to give rise to treble taxation of such dividends: first in the hands of the earning company, then in the hands of the receiving company, and finally in the hands of individual shareholders. The law provides certain concessions to facilitate inter-corporate investment. Thus, under section 80M of the Act any domestic company is allowed deduction of the amount of dividend received from another domestic company, subject to the maximum of the amount of dividend distributed by the recipient company.

6. Minimum Alternate Tax (MAT). Income tax laws throughout the world generally provide for a number of tax concessions. A profit-making clever company may arrange its affairs in such a manner that the cumulative effect of all tax concessions is to reduce its income declared in the tax return to zero. MAT is a device to keep a zero tax company within the tax net. In the 1996-97 budget, an effort was made to tackle the phenomenon of zero tax companies (having substantial book profits) by bringing them under MAT. Thus, where the total income of a company after availing all eligible deductions was less than 30 per cent of the book profit, the total income of such companies was deemed to be 30 per cent of the book profit and charged to tax accordingly. From the financial year 2000-2001, MAT was charged at 7.5 per cent of the *book profit* as determined under the Companies Act. In the 2006-07 budget, the rate was increased from 7.5 per cent to 10 per cent.

14.5.2 Compulsory Filing of Returns by Companies: According to sub-section (1) of section 139 of the Income Tax Act, every person, if his total income during the previous year exceeded the maximum amount which is not chargeable to income tax, is required to file a return of such income. It was observed that a number of companies which incurred losses were not filing returns on the plea that they had not earned any income. Therefore, the Finance Act, 2001 amended section 139(1) to provide that every company is required to file a return of income, even if it incurs a loss. The amendment became effective retrospectively from April 1, 2001.

14.6 Taxation of Partnership Firms

Prior to the assessment year 1993-94, taxation of partnership firms was rather cumbersome. For example, the method of taxation differed according to whether the firm was registered or not under the Income Tax Act. Following the recommendations contained in the Interim Report of the Tax Reforms Committee, 1991, the taxation of partnership firms was drastically modified through the Finance Act, 1992. The chief feature of these changes was to avoid double taxation of profits of firms. Thus, from the assessment year 1993-94 the scheme of taxation of firms and their partners is as follows.

1. A partnership firm is taxed as a separate entity. Like a company, it is liable to income tax however small its income may be. There is no distinction between registered and unregistered firms. Similarly, there is no distinction between firms carrying professions or business. The procedure for registration of firms has been abolished. A new procedure for the assessment of a firm as a firm has been prescribed in Section 184. In order to be assessed as a firm, the partnership should be evidenced by an instrument of partnership, specifying the individual shares of the partners and a copy of the same certified in writing by all the partners should be filed along with the first return of the firm.
2. The share of the partner in the income of the firm is not included in computing his total income, i.e. it is fully exempt from income tax [Sec. 10(2A)].
3. Any payment of salary, bonus, commission, remuneration etc. to any partner under the terms of the partnership deed is allowed as a deduction in the computation of the total income of the firm subject to certain restrictions. Thus, salary can be paid only to a working partner.
4. Interest paid by a firm to any partner is deductible from its income. However, 12 per cent per annum is the maximum rate at which interest can be allowed to a partner. Interest paid must be in accordance with the terms of the partnership deed [Sec. 40(b) (ii) and (iii)].
5. The maximum amount of payment (i.e. interest, salary, bonus etc.) to all the partners during the previous year should not exceed the following limits.

In the case of firms carrying on a profession, e.g. law, medicine, engineering, accountancy, technical consultancy etc. (Sec. 44AA).

- On the first Rs. 1 lakh of the book-profit: @ 90 per cent of the book-profit or Rs. 50,000, whichever is more.
- On the next Rs. 1 lakh of the book-profit: @ 60 per cent of the book-profit.
- On the balance of the book-profit: @ 40 per cent of the book-profit.

In the case of any other firm

- On the first Rs. 75,000 of the book-profit: @ 90 per cent of the book-profit or Rs. 50,000, whichever is more.
- On the next Rs. 75,000 of the book profit: @ 60 per cent of the book-profit.
- On the balance of the book-profit: @ 40 per cent of the book-profit.

6. Any interest, salary, bonus, remuneration etc. received by a partner from the firm is chargeable to tax under the head 'profits and gains of business or profession'. They are not taxable under the head 'salaries' and therefore standard deduction cannot be claimed in respect of such remuneration.

However, any expenditure incurred in order to earn such income can be claimed as a deduction from such income under Sections 32 to 37 of the Act. Thus, if a partner borrows money to make his capital contribution to the firm and he is paid interest on his capital contribution, the amount of interest paid by him on the borrowed money is allowed as a deduction from interest on capital.

7. Where the net result of computation of income of a firm is a loss, it may be carried forward in accordance with Section 72 to be set off against business income in the subsequent eight assessment years.
8. Since the firm is to be separately taxed, the clause in Section 64 relating to the clubbing of income arising to the spouse or minor child from the partnership by way of share is deleted. The income arising to the spouse by way of salary etc. however continues to be clubbed under Section 64.

14.7 Tax Treatment of Small Traders (Presumptive Tax)

In its Interim Report, submitted in December 1991, the Tax Reforms Committee examined the problems and possibilities of taxing the small business sector. The Committee suggested two new presumptive taxes on small businesses:

1. A fixed tax on businesses whose turnover was less than Rs. 5 lakh.
2. An estimated income scheme on small businesses with a turnover above Rs. 5 lakh but less than Rs. 25 lakh.

The schemes envisaged profit to be a certain percentage of turnover depending on the type of activity from which it was earned. The Government introduced the first scheme through the Finance Act, 1992, but deferred its decision to introduce the second scheme.

The presumptive tax system for persons engaged in retail trade with an annual turnover up to Rs. 5 lakh was introduced on an experimental basis. The scheme was in operation initially for two assessment years 1993-94 and 1994-95. It was continued after the expiry of these two years. The objective of the new simplified procedure for taxation was to widen the tax base by encouraging shopkeepers (including those engaged in vocations like tailoring, typewriting, photocopying, repair work etc.) and other small retail traders to pay taxes. The scheme had the following features: The scheme was optional and open to individuals not assessed to tax earlier and who had an income from the business of retail trade having an annual turnover up to Rs. 5 lakh. Persons opting for the scheme were deemed to have a turnover of Rs. 5 lakh and their total income was deemed to be Rs. 35,000 (Rs. 37,000 for A.Y. 1994-95) on which the tax worked out to Rs. 1,400 after allowing for the basic exemption of Rs. 28,000 (Rs. 30,000 for A.Y. 1994-95). A retail trader opting for the scheme had only to file the simplified statement (name, address, nature of business etc.) and pay a tax of Rs. 1,400 by 15th March of the financial year in which the income was earned. The scheme was optional to avoid objection on constitutional grounds. If presumptive tax results in a higher tax burden than the one on the basis of book profit, it can be said to violate Article 14 of the Constitution which guarantees equality before law. Thus, the taxpayer had the option to pay presumptive tax or ask for regular assessment of his income, whichever he thought was advantageous to him.

Unfortunately, the scheme of presumptive taxation did not gain popularity with small traders and self-employed entrepreneurs. In 1992-93, the first year of the operation of the scheme, 1,16,644 persons opted for the scheme and paid a total tax of Rs. 16.4 crore, as against the anticipated revenue collection of Rs. 140 crore. [13] This was by no means a significant addition to the existing 70 lakh individual assessees under the income tax net. The number of shopkeepers and other small traders was much higher. The scheme touched only the tip of the iceberg.

The Government introduced through the Finance Act, 1994 two new schemes for estimating the income from the business of civil construction and plying or hiring trucks. The Finance Act, 1994 introduced Sections 44AD and 44AE in the Income Tax Act to provide for a method of estimating income from these businesses. While the section for civil construction applied to all assessees whose gross receipts from the business did not exceed Rs. 40 lakh, the section for plying trucks applied to businessmen owning not more than 10 trucks. Under Section 44AD, the income from these businesses was estimated at 8 per cent of the gross receipts paid or payable to an assessee. Income of truck owners is assessed at Rs. 3,500 p.m. per heavy vehicle and at Rs. 3,150 p.m. per medium and light vehicle.

In the 1997-98 budget, the Finance Minister discontinued the presumptive scheme under Section 115K as it failed to yield the desired results. In its place, he introduced a new estimated income scheme for retail traders. The new scheme is applicable to persons engaged in the business of retail trade of any goods or merchandise having a total turnover of less than Rs. 40 lakh. The income of the trader will be estimated at 5 per cent of the total turnover. A trader with a turnover of less than Rs. 10 lakh is exempted given the present exemption limit of Rs. 50,000. Assessees who file a return showing an income less than 5 per cent of turnover are required to maintain books of account and get their accounts audited.

To deal with small commercial and industrial establishments, the French have followed the forfait system. The French forfait system has several features. Firstly, the taxable profit of a given business unit is agreed upon mutually between the tax authorities and the assessee. Secondly, the assessment remains valid for a limited number of years. Finally, the taxpayer is required to submit a set of simple facts to the authorities, namely the amount of his purchases and sales, the wage bill, the value of his inventory, and the number of employees. Alternatively, small businesses may be subject to a system of licence fee charged in accordance with some well-defined criteria such as the location of business and its size.

14.8 One-by-Six Criteria Scheme

With a view to widening the income tax net, the Finance Minister announced a new scheme in his 1997-98 budget speech. As per this scheme, a person was required to mandatorily file a return if he satisfied any two of the following four economic criteria: (a) occupation of immovable property exceeding a specified floor area whether by way of ownership, tenancy or otherwise, (b) ownership of a motor vehicle, (c) subscription to a telephone, (d) expenditure for himself or for any other person on travel to any foreign country. A new return form (Form No. 2C) was prescribed for the purpose. The Central Board of Direct Taxes notified urban agglomerations of the following 12 cities for implementing the new provisions under Section 139(1) of the Income Tax Act: Mumbai, Delhi, Calcutta, Chennai, Bangalore, Ahmedabad, Kanpur, Jaipur, Ludhiana, Hyderabad, Pune, and Chandigarh.

In the 1998-99 budget, two additional criteria, viz. holding a credit card and membership of expensive clubs were added to the scheme, taking the total parameters to six. Moreover, filing of return was made compulsory for individuals who fulfil even one of the six criteria. The revised version was labelled as *One-by-Six Scheme*. Furthermore, the scheme was extended to cover 23 more cities in India, taking the total coverage to 35 cities. In the 1999-2000 budget, the scheme was extended to 19 more cities having a population of more than 5 lakh.

Expressing satisfaction at the performance of the one-in-six scheme, the Finance Minister in his 2000-01 budget speech observed, "One of the major initiatives towards better tax compliance has been the introduction of the one-by-six scheme. This, along with other measures, has contributed substantially to increasing the number of taxpayers, which had languished at the level of just over a crore till 1996-97, but has now crossed the two crore mark, with the biggest boost coming over the last two years. The momentum generated by this and other measures to widen the tax base needs to be sustained." [14] He, therefore, extended the one-by-six scheme from the then existing 54 cities to an additional 79 cities in the country. With this, all the cities having a population of two lakh and more on the basis of the 1991 census now stand covered under the scheme.

In the 2001-02 budget, the scheme was extended to all urban areas in the country as defined by the 1991 census.

In the 2005-06 budget, cellular phones were removed from and expenditure exceeding Rs. 50,000 on electricity consumption in any previous year was added to the list of one-by-six criteria scheme.

14.9 Taxation of Capital Gains

A tax on capital gains was in operation in India for a short period in respect of capital gains which arose during the period April 1, 1946 to March 31, 1948. Following the recommendations of British economist Nicholas Kaldor, the tax was revived in 1956 and made applicable on capital gains arising on or after April 1, 1956. It is levied within the framework of Indian Income Tax Act, 1961. Section 14 of the Act prescribes five broad heads under which the income of an assessee is classified for purposes of computation of total income and the charge of income tax. These are: salaries, income from house property, profits and gains of business or profession, capital gains, and income from other sources. Sections 45 to 55A of the Act relate to the taxation of capital gains. Since capital gains are not annual accruals from a given source but represent appreciation in the market value of assets over a period of time, they are treated on a different footing. The preferential treatment is given to long-term capital gains only.

14.9.1 Meaning and Scope of Capital Gains Tax: According to Section 45 of the Act any profits or gains arising from the transfer of a capital asset are chargeable to tax under the head 'capital gains'. The term 'capital asset' means property of any kind, movable or immovable, held by an assessee but it does not include the following: stock-in-trade, consumable stores or raw materials held for the purpose of his business or profession, personal effects, i.e. movable property (clothes, motor car, furniture etc., but excluding jewellery) held for personal use, and agricultural land in India [Section 2(14)]. The gains on transfer of assets in relation to which there is no cost of acquisition like self-generated goodwill of a business are also liable to capital gains tax.

14.9.2 Transactions Regarded as *Transfer*: The act of transfer has special and extended meaning under the law [Section 2(47)]. Besides the sale of the asset or its exchange for another asset, it includes: relinquishment of the asset, extinguishment of any rights in the asset, compulsory acquisition of the asset under any law, conversion of the asset into stock-in-trade, handing over the possession of an immovable property in part performance of a contract for the transfer of that property, and transactions which have the effect of transferring, or enabling the enjoyment of any immovable property.

However, certain transactions, though falling within the foregoing meaning of transfer, are not regarded as transfers. These are: transfers under a gift, will, or an irrevocable trust, transfer of shares of the amalgamating company in consideration of allotment of shares in an Indian amalgamated company, and transfer of works of art, books, manuscripts etc., to the government, a university or any other notified museum or institution.

Prior to the assessment year 1988-89, distribution of assets on the dissolution of a firm, body of individuals or other association of persons was also not regarded as a transaction resulting in taxable capital gains. However, for and from the assessment year 1988-89 the position has changed and such transactions are now regarded as transfers resulting in taxable capital gains.

14.9.3 Year of Taxability: As regards the year of taxability, the basic rule is that capital gains are deemed to be income of the previous year in which the transfer giving rise to the gains takes place. Thus, the year of charge is the year in which the sale, exchange, relinquishment etc., takes place. In case of conversion of a capital asset into stock-in-trade, the gains are deemed to arise in the year in which such stock-in-trade is sold or otherwise transferred.

14.9.4 Short-term versus Long-term Capital Gains: The incidence of tax on capital gains depends upon whether such gains arise from the transfer of a short-term or a long-term capital asset. Under Section 2(42A), a short-term capital asset is one which is held by the assessee for less than 36 months from the date of its acquisition. (However, in order to improve the mobility of capital, equity shares, units of the Unit Trust of India and other mutual funds are treated as short-term capital assets if they are held for less than 12 months). If the asset is held for more than 36 months, it is regarded as a long-term capital asset.

Capital gains arising from the transfer of a short-term capital asset are taxable like an ordinary income in the case of all assessees. However, capital gains relating to long-term capital assets are taken as a separate block and get lenient tax treatment (flat rate of 20 per cent).

14.9.5 Computation of Short-term Capital Gains: Under Section 48, the procedure to compute capital gains involves the following steps: Firstly, the full value of consideration received or accruing as a result of the transfer is ascertained. If the transaction is in cash the full value of consideration is the cash payment received. In case the consideration for transfer is in the form of another asset, the fair market value of the asset received as consideration is ascertained. Also, the value of any debt settled by way of consideration is included in the full value of consideration. It is likely that the consideration is not paid in cash but by way of promise to pay after a period. In such cases the full value of consideration will be the present value of the amount to be paid at maturity discounted at the market rate.

Secondly, the following deductions are made from the full value of consideration: (a) cost of acquisition of the asset including cost of any improvements made to the asset, and (b) expenditure incurred in connection with the transfer of such asset such as brokerage paid for arranging the deal, legal expenses incurred for preparing transfer documents, cost of inserting advertisement in newspapers for sale of the asset, and commission paid to auctioneer. However, it is necessary that the expenditure should be incurred wholly and exclusively in connection with the transfer. The balance is the amount of short-term capital gain to be included in the gross total income of the assessee. After allowing deductions under chapter VI-A (Sections 80CCC to 80U), the total income is subject to tax and surcharge, if any, at the prescribed rates for different types of assessees. Rebate under Section 88 is available from the tax computed on the total income in respect of deposits/payments made in approved schemes.

14.9.6 Computation of Long-term Capital Gains: Following the recommendations contained in the Interim Report of the Tax Reforms Committee, 1991, the scheme of capital gains tax was drastically recast in the following manner by the Finance Act, 1992: (a) The cut-off date for valuation of assets acquired in earlier years was shifted from April 1, 1974 to April 1, 1981, (b) a system of indexation was introduced for the first time under which long-term capital gains are now computed by allowing the cost of acquisition and the cost of improvement of the asset to be adjusted for general inflation, (c) a new section 112 was inserted in the Income Tax Act to provide that long-term capital gains would be subject to a flat rate of income tax. The rate of tax is 20 per cent. Presently, concessionary treatment to long-term capital gains is given through inflation indexing, relatively low flat rate of tax, and a set of exemptions.

In fact, the assessee has two options as regards the computation of long-term capital gains: (a) calculate the difference between the cost of acquisition and the sale price and pay the tax on the same at a flat rate of 10 per cent or (b) adjust the cost of the asset sold for inflation and pay tax at the rate of 20 per cent.

A. Inflation Indexing: This new procedure to compute long-term capital gains effective from the assessment year 1993-94 is as follows. The full value of consideration received as a result of the transfer is ascertained. From the full value of consideration, the Indexed Cost of Acquisition (I.C.A.) and the Indexed Cost of Improvement (I.C.I.) are deducted. Also, from the full value of consideration the expenditure incurred in connection with such transfer is deducted. Indexed cost of acquisition is actual cost of acquisition multiplied by Cost Inflation Index (C.I.I.) for the year of transfer and divided by C.I.I. for the year of purchase. Thus,

$$\text{I.C.A.} = \frac{\text{Cost of acquisition x C.I.I. for the year of transfer}}{\text{C.I.I. for the year of acquisition}}$$

and

$$\text{I.C.I.} = \frac{\text{Cost of improvement x C.I.I. for the year of transfer}}{\text{C.I.I. for the year of improvement}}$$

With 1981-82 as the base year (i.e. 1981-82 = 100) the Central Government notifies each year the C.I.I. having regard to 75 per cent of average rise in consumer price index for urban non-manual employees. C.I.I. notified by the Government from time to time is given in Table 14.7. The cost of acquisition is adjusted with reference to the rate applicable for the relevant year. There is similar indexation of cost of improvement. The index factors are applied uniformly to all assets without making any distinction between shares, buildings, and machinery. The new procedure is related to the period of time for which the asset is held and takes into account the inflation that may have crept in over time.

Table 14.7: Cost Inflation Index

Financial Year	C.I.I.	Financial Year	C.I.I.
1981-82	100	1993-94	244
1982-83	100	1994-95	259
1983-84	116	1995-96	281
1984-85	125	1996-97	305
1985-86	133	1997-98	331
1986-87	140	1998-99	351
1987-88	150	1999-00	389
1988-89	161	2000-01	406
1989-90	172	2001-02	426
1990-91	182	2002-03	447
1991-92	199	2003-04	463
1992-93	223	2004-05	480

The cost of acquisition of an asset is the amount for which it was originally acquired by the assessee. However, where the capital asset became the property of the assessee before April 1, 1981, he has the option to substitute for the actual cost the fair market value of asset as on April 1, 1981. Furthermore, where the capital asset became the property of the assessee by succession, inheritance, or under a gift or a will etc., the cost of acquisition of the asset in the hands of the assessee is the cost for which the previous owner of the asset had acquired it. In case the asset was acquired by the previous owner prior to April 1, 1981, the assessee enjoys the option to substitute the fair market value of the asset as on April 1, 1981 for the cost of the asset to the previous owner. Any expenditure of a capital nature incurred by an assessee to increase the value of the asset is to be added to the cost of acquisition by way of cost of improvement.

Deductions under chapter VI-A (Sections 80C to 80U) are not available in respect of long-term capital gains. Prior to the assessment year 1993-94, income arising under the head capital *gains* was included in the gross total income of the assessee and after allowing deductions under chapter VI-A, the total income was subject to tax and surcharge at the rates in force. Rebate under Section 88 was available from the tax computed on the total income in respect of deposits/payments made in approved schemes and instruments. As already noted, the Finance Act, 1992 inserted a new section 112 in the Income Tax Act to provide that long-term capital gains will be subject to a flat rate of income tax. The rate of tax is 20 per cent. Hence, deductions under chapter VI-A and rebate under Section 88 were withdrawn in respect of long-term capital gains.

B. Certain Long-term Capital Gains Exempt from Tax: Exemptions available to an assessee with regard to certain long-term capital gains may be classified into the following two categories.

Category A: This category includes exemptions relating to capital gains which arise where an asset is transferred to acquire another asset of the same kind within the time specified for the purpose. Various cases for which exemptions are allowed are the following.

1. Capital gains arising from the transfer of a residential house enjoy exemption if the assessee has purchased a new residential house within a period of 1 year before the date of transfer or within 2 years after the date of transfer or has constructed a residential house property within a period of 3 years after the date of transfer (Sec. 54). The amount of exemption available is equal to the amount so utilised or the amount of capital gain, whichever is less.

2. Capital gains arising from the transfer of agricultural land are exempt from tax if the assessee has purchased another land for agricultural purposes within a period of 2 years from the date of such transfer (Sec. 54B).

3. Where an industrial undertaking is to be shifted as a result of compulsory acquisition of its land or buildings by the Government, the capital gain arising from the payment of compensation is exempt from tax if the assessee has purchased any other land or building forming part of industrial undertaking

within a period of 3 years from the date of acquisition (Sec. 54D).

4. Capital gains made from the transfer of machinery, plant, land, and building etc., forming part of an industrial undertaking are exempt where transfer is effected for the shifting of the industrial undertaking from an urban area to any other area, provided these are reinvested in approved relocation schemes within 1 year before or 3 years after the date of transfer (Sec. 54G). The amount of exemption is equal to the amount so utilised or the amount of capital gain, whichever is less. The purpose of this exemption is to encourage industries to shift out of congested urban areas to reduce pollution and other hazards.

For all the four cases mentioned above, exemption in respect of the entire amount of capital gain is allowed where the capital gain is less than or equal to the investment in the new asset. However, if the amount of the capital gain is more than the cost of the new asset, the difference between the amount of capital gain and the cost of the new asset is taxable. Again, for all the four cases mentioned above, if the new asset is transferred within 3 years of its acquisition, the capital gains exempted earlier become taxable. This is done by taking the cost of acquisition of the new asset as reduced by the amount of capital gain exempted earlier. In other words, if the newly acquired asset is transferred within 3 years, the capital gain arising therefrom, together with the amount of capital gain exempted earlier, become chargeable to tax. It may be noted that exemption regarding gains on the transfer of fixed assets of an industrial undertaking is available to all categories of assessees while exemptions of gains on the transfer of a residential house and agricultural lands are claimable by individuals only.

Category B: Exemption under this category is given on the basis of the nature of asset in which the net consideration for transfer is invested rather than by the type of asset transferred. Net consideration in respect of the transfer of a capital asset means the full value of the consideration after deduction of any expenditure incurred in connection with the transfer.

1. Capital gains on the transfer of a long-term capital asset other than a house property are tax-exempt if the net consideration for the transfer is invested in a residential house (Sec. 54F). This exemption is available to an individual assessee provided he does not own any residential house on the date of transfer of the original asset. The investment in residential house must be made in case of purchase within 1 year before or 2 years after the date of transfer and in case of construction within 3 years of such transfer.

Meanwhile, the amount of net consideration or the unutilised part of it must be kept in the Deposit Account like in other cases discussed above. If the cost of the newly acquired house is less than the net consideration in respect of the asset transferred, the exemption is allowed only in respect of part of the capital gain proportionate to ratio of the amount invested to the net consideration. In other words, the amount of exemption shall be equal to

$$\frac{\text{Capital gains} \times \text{Cost of new residential house}}{\text{Amount of net consideration}}$$

If the assessee transfers the newly acquired residential house within a period of three years of its purchase or construction, then the amount of capital gains arising from the transfer of the original asset which was not charged to tax, will be deemed to be the income from capital gains for the year in which the new asset is transferred. In addition to this, there is another circumstance when exemption granted may be withdrawn. This happens if the assessee within the time for acquiring new house (within 2 years of the transfer of original asset in case of purchase or within 3 years in case of construction) purchases or constructs another residential house in addition to the new house. In that case the capital gains earlier exempted from tax are charged to tax as income of the year in which that second house is purchased or constructed.

2. Long-term capital gains are exempt from tax if the whole of the *net consideration is invested*, within a period of six months from the date of transfer, in any of the specified bonds, debentures or shares of a public company or units of any mutual fund notified under section 10 (23D) of the Income Tax Act.

However, if only a part of net consideration is so invested, the amount of capital gains exempt shall be equal to

$$\frac{\text{Capital gains} \times \text{Cost of specified securities}}{\text{Amount of net consideration}}$$

If the specified securities are transferred within a period of 3 years from the date of their acquisition, the amount of capital gain claimed to be exempt shall be taxable as long-term capital gain for the year in which the securities are so transferred (Section 54EA).

3. Long-term capital gains are exempt from tax if the whole of the amount of such capital gains is invested within a period of six months from the date of transfer, in the long-term specified assets. If, however, only a part of the capital gain is invested in the long-term specified assets, the amount of capital gains exempt shall be equal to the amount so invested. If the long-term specified assets are transferred within a period of 7 years from the date of their acquisition, the amount of capital gains claimed to be exempt shall be taxable as long-term capital gain for the year in which the long-term specified assets are so transferred (Section 54EB).

14.9.7 Capital Gains Account Scheme, 1988: This scheme is applicable to all the five types of exemptions mentioned above under sections 54, 54B, 54D, 54F, and 54G. However, an assessee has to open a separate account under each section if he wishes to avail the benefit under more than one section. Under this scheme, if the amount of capital gain is not utilised by the assessee for purchase or construction of the new asset before the due date for furnishing the return of income for the relevant year, it must be deposited by him on or before the due date of furnishing the return of income, in the Deposit Account in any branch (except rural branch) of a public sector bank in accordance with Capital Gains Account Scheme, 1988. The amount utilised for acquiring the new asset together with the amount so deposited is deemed to be the amount utilised for acquiring the new asset. If the amount deposited is not utilised fully for purchase or construction of the new asset within the stipulated period, then the amount not so utilised is treated as the capital gain of the year in which the period specified for investment in new asset (3 years from the date of transfer of original asset) expires.

14.9.8 Set Off and Carry Forward of Capital Losses: A capital loss represents the amount by which the full value of consideration for the transfer of an asset falls short of the sum of cost of acquisition and improvement of that asset and the expenditure incurred in connection with the transfer of that asset.

From the assessment year 2003-04, the provisions are as follows:

1. Any short-term capital loss can be set off against any capital gain (both long-term and short-term) and against no other income.
2. Any long-term capital loss can be set off only against long-term capital gain and against no other income.
3. Any short-term capital loss can be carried forward to the next 8 assessment years and set off against capital gains (both short-term and long-term) in those years.
4. Any long-term capital loss can be carried forward to the next 8 assessment years and set off only against long-term capital gain in those years.

It is noteworthy that if there is loss under any head, it can be set off against income from long-term capital gain and the balance of long-term capital gain is subject to tax at the rate of 20 per cent.

14.9.9 A Critique: How has the scheme of inflation indexing worked? There is a widespread feeling that introduction of inflation indexing for capital gains has unnecessarily complicated the income tax law.

The argument in favour of inflation indexing is that capital gains resulting from inflation are illusory in real terms. To offset the inflationary rise in the value of an asset, it is rational to increase the acquisition cost by the rate of inflation in the period between acquisition and realisation. True, an inflation-proof tax system is more certain and equitable in an inflationary economy but this is an ideal situation for all sources of income and not only for capital gains alone.

Surprisingly, salary incomes which suffer the most due to inflation are left out and only capital gains are accorded the coveted treatment of inflation adjustment. Experience suggests that real estate prices move upward more quickly than the general index of prices while wage level adjustments not only lag but fall short of the rate of inflation.

The solution to the inflation problem lies in revision of exemptions and allowances for various types of income. Thus, the Finance Act, 1992, shifted the cut-off date for valuation of assets acquired in earlier years from April 1, 1974 to April 1, 1981. It means an assessee has the option of substituting the fair market value as on April 1, 1981 for the cost of acquisition where the asset had been acquired prior to that date. This concession itself offsets, though partially, the inflationary effect on capital gains.

Prior to the assessment year 1993-94, a basic exemption of Rs. 15,000 and a further deduction of 50/60 per cent depending on the category of asset was provided to individual assessees in computing long term capital gains. This concession gave relief, particularly to assessees in the lower income group. It also provided a kind of incentive for new entrants to the capital market. Revival of the basic exemption would make the capital gains tax more equitable.

The flat rate of 20 per cent for capital gains as compared to the maximum marginal rate of 30 per cent for other incomes in the case of individuals has reduced the effective progressivity of income tax besides producing differential tax liabilities at given levels of income, violating the principle of horizontal equity. Moreover, this differential will induce people to earn income in the form of capital gains (often speculative) rather than as business profits, dividends, or interest. The inducement will be stronger at higher income levels because of the high tax rates applicable thereon.

14.10 Recommendations of the Task Force on Direct Taxes (Chairman: Vijay Kelkar), 2002 Pertaining to Income Tax

At the time of presenting the first batch of supplementary demands for grants to Parliament in July 2002, the Finance Minister had proposed setting up of two task forces to recommend measures for simplification and rationalization of direct and indirect taxes. Accordingly, two task forces were set up in September 2002 under the chairmanship of Dr. Vijay Kelkar, Adviser to Minister of Finance and Company Affairs.

The Task Force on Direct Taxes presented its consultation paper to the Government on November 2, 2002. The discussion paper on indirect taxes was presented on November 25, 2002. These consultation papers were made public to facilitate an informed discussion on tax policy.

After taking in to account the response on the discussion papers, the Task Forces submitted their final reports to the Government in December 2002. These Task Forces have made important recommendations on toning up tax administration to put in place a system that is simple, effective and at par with international standards.

The main recommendations on direct taxes relate to raising of exemption limit of personal income tax, rationalization of exemptions, abolition of concessional treatment to long-term capital gains, and abolition of wealth tax. In respect of indirect taxes, the main recommendations relate to widening of the tax base, removal of exemptions, expansion in the coverage of service tax etc.

The Task Force on Direct Taxes was assigned the following Terms of Reference:

- Rationalisation and simplification of the direct taxes with a view to minimizing exemptions, removing anomalies and improving equity;
- Improvement in taxpayer services so as to reduce compliance cost, impart transparency and facilitate voluntary compliance,
- Redesigning procedures for strengthening enforcement so as to improve compliance of direct tax laws; and
- Any other matter related to the above points."

14.10.1 Personal Income Tax: The Task Force recommended a two rate schedule for personal income tax (Table 14.8).

Table 14.8: Rate Structure of Personal Income Tax Recommended by the Task Force on Direct Taxes

Income level	Tax rates
Below Rs. 1,00,000	Nil
Rs. 1,00,000 – 4,00,000	20 per cent of the income in excess of Rs. 1,00,000
Above Rs. 4,00,000	Rs. 60,000 plus 30 per cent of the income in excess of Rs. 4,00,000

Source: Government of India, Ministry of Finance and Company Affairs, *Report of the Task Force on Direct Taxes* (Chairman: Vijay Kelkar), December 2002, p. 71.

It recommended the abolition of surcharge on income tax. It was of the opinion that revenue gain from levy of surcharge is generally illusory since such a levy has the effect of increasing the marginal rate of tax, which adversely affects compliance.

It recommended that residents but not ordinarily residents must be subjected to tax on their global/world-wide income at par with residents. To do so, this unusual category of resident but not ordinarily resident taxpayers must be deleted. Most countries across the world provide for only two status: residents and non-residents.

It recommended that standard deduction under section 16(1) of the Income Tax Act should be eliminated. However, the exemption of conveyance allowance subject to a ceiling of Rs. 9,600 should be continued. This should serve as a reasonable deduction for employment related expenses.

As regards tax treatment of agricultural income, the Task Force recommended as follows:

- A tax rental arrangement should be designed whereby States should pass a resolution under Article 252 of the Constitution authorizing the Central Government to impose income tax on agricultural income. The taxes collected by the Centre would however be assigned to the States.
- Tax from agricultural income for the purpose of allocation between States will be the difference between the tax on total income (including agricultural income) and the tax on total income net of agricultural income.
- Where a taxpayer derives agricultural income from different States, the revenues attributable to a State will be in the ratio of the income derived from a particular State to the total agricultural income.
- A separate tax return form should be prescribed for taxpayers deriving income from agriculture.

It recommended the elimination of the tax incentives for savings under section 88, section 80L, section 10(15)(i), section 10(15)(iib), section 10(15)(iic), section 10(15)(iid), section 10(15)(iv)(h) and section 10(15)(iv)(i) of the Income Tax Act. It insisted that these benefits must be immediately withdrawn and not through a sunset clause

It recommended that the basic exemption limit for senior citizens should be Rs. 50,000 more than the exemption limit for the general class of individual taxpayers. To put it differently, the exemption limit for senior citizens should be Rs. 1,50,000 as against Rs. 1,00,000 for the general category of individual taxpayers. It further recommended that the exemption limit for senior citizens should be revised as and when the exemption limit for the general category of individual taxpayers is revised. Still further, it recommended that this benefit of higher exemption limit should also be extended to widows.

14.10.2 Corporate Tax: The Task Force on Direct Taxes made the following recommendations for the reform of corporate income tax:

1. Reduction in corporate tax rate from the existing levels of 36.75 per cent to

30 per cent for domestic companies and to 35 per cent for foreign companies.

2. Exemption of dividend from taxation in the hands of the shareholders. There will also be no tax on distribution of dividends by a company.
3. Exemption of long-term capital gains on listed equity.
4. Elimination of Minimum Alternate Tax under section 115JB.
5. Removal of the distinction between unabsorbed depreciation and unabsorbed business loss.
6. Removal of the following deductions under section 10 and Chapter VIA of the Income Tax Act with immediate effect and not by a sunset clause:

- Elimination of section 10A and 10B of the Income Tax Act for all taxpayers other than those engaged in manufacturing computer software.
- In the case of taxpayers engaged in manufacturing computer software, the Government of India must take immediate steps to negotiate with foreign governments to enter into a comprehensive totalisation agreement leading to a single point incidence of taxes.
- Section 80 IA in respect of profit and gains from industrial undertakings engaged in infrastructure development or telecommunication service or development of industrial park or special economic zones or generation, transmission or distribution of power.
- Section 80IB in respect of profits and gains from certain industrial undertakings other than infrastructure development undertakings (this includes backward areas also).
- Section 80JJA in respect of profits and gains from business of collecting and processing of biodegradable wastes.
- Section 80 JJAA in respect of employment of new workman.
- Section 80M in respect of inter-corporate dividends.
- The phase out programme in respect of sections 80HHB, 80HHBA, 80HHC, 80HHD, 80HHE, 80HHF, 80-O, 80R, 80RR and 80RRA will continue.

7. Depreciation rates for the purposes of depreciation allowance under section 32 should be reduced to 15 per cent for the general category of plant and machinery and to appropriate lower rates for other categories of block of assets.
8. Elimination of section 33AB relating to tea development allowance.
9. Elimination of section 33AC relating to reserve for shipping business.
10. Elimination of section 33B relating to rehabilitation allowance.
11. Elimination of section 35 relating to scientific research.
12. Elimination of section 35AC relating to expenditure on eligible projects.
13. Elimination of section 35CCA relating to expenditure by way of payment to

associations and institutions for carrying out rural development programmes.

14. Elimination of section 36(1)(iii) in respect of interest on borrowed capital.
15. The provision for bad and doubtful debts allowable under section 36(1)(viia) of the Income Tax Act will henceforth be restricted to the amount of provision debited to profit and loss account as audited subject to the maximum amount of provisioning permitted under the prudential guidelines issued by the Reserve Bank of India.

14.10.3 Capital Gains: The Task Force on Direct Taxes recommended that concessional treatment of long-term capital gains through a reduced scheduler rate of tax must be abolished. In other words, the long-term capital gains would be aggregated with other incomes and subjected to taxation at the normal rates.

14.11 Critical Evaluation of the Indian Income Tax System

14.11.1 Unstable Law: There is considerable instability in the income tax law of India, owing mainly to introduction, withdrawal, and reintroduction of exemptions and concessions for various purposes. According to one estimate, there were 3,300 amendments to the Income Tax Act during 1961-90. [15] As the Direct Tax Laws Committee remarked, "The instability of our tax laws is another of their worst features. The laws are riddled with uncertainties and statutory amendments are as unpredictable as they are frequent. Surely, after more than half a century of the working of income tax Acts of 1922, and 1961, it should be possible to have an enduring tax system." [16] Frequent amendments have led to uncertainty and confusion among taxpayers and tax collectors.

14.11.2 Multitude of Exemptions/Concessions: It is quite common in tax laws to incorporate provisions which exclude certain items and deduct others from the tax base. These tax preferences are referred to as *tax expenditures* in the literature and often resemble the more notorious term *tax loopholes*. As in other countries, exclusions, deductions, and rebates are integral part of the Indian income tax system designed to promote a variety of socially desirable activities. However, their wide amplitude has adversely affected revenue yield. These concessions, each with a rationale of its own, have the combined effect of eroding the tax base and impairing the progressivity of the tax system. The supposedly high statutory rates of income tax turn out to be illusory in view of the various exemptions/concessions which lower the effective rates of taxation significantly.

The plethora of exemptions/concessions has led to complexities in the income tax law, obscuring its evaluation, particularly from equity angle. Exemptions and concessions are often the result of persistent representations and pressure tactics by vested interests rather than any economic justification.

Income tax concessions are subsidy payments and need to be devised carefully. For example, there is no fundamental difference between outright subsidy payment to a newly established export-oriented undertaking and a tax holiday for it under Section 10B of the Income Tax Act, 1961. Indeed, outright subsidy payments attract public attention more readily than tax concessions which lie scattered in the cobwebs of ever-changing tax laws. For a simple and efficient income tax system, exemptions and concessions should be kept to the minimum and used selectively for very genuine purposes. A review of the whole gamut of exemptions and concessions is called for to streamline revenue and administration. Measures other than income tax concessions should also be considered to encourage activities which deserve governmental support.

14.11.3 Earned versus Unearned Incomes: Another serious lacuna in the present system of personal income tax is the non-discriminatory treatment of earned and other forms of income for tax purposes. Income of an assessee from various sources is pooled together for the purpose of computation of taxable income and tax liability determination. This so-called *global principle* of income tax does not differentiate between different sources of income.

Earned income (or employment income) is derived from actual work or service performed and includes wages, salaries, and income from professions. Unearned income (or capital income) is derived from investments, rents etc.

The Indian Taxation Enquiry Committee, 1924-25 examined, for the first time, the desirability of differentiation between earned and unearned incomes for the purpose of income tax. The Committee, however, rejected the idea, maintaining that it was premature in the context of the Indian conditions. It was in 1945 that a distinction between earned and unearned incomes was introduced when assessees were allowed to exclude from their earned incomes a fixed proportion subject to a maximum limit.

The Taxation Enquiry Commission (TEC), 1953-54, made several recommendations regarding income tax, some of which dealt with the broad structure of taxation while others related to maters of detail like inclusion and exclusion of certain categories of income from taxation, grant of concessions to promote objectives of economic policy and so on. A notable recommendation of the TEC pertained to the withdrawal of the concession relating to earned income beyond a certain level of income which it suggested should be Rs. 24,000. Agreeing with this recommendation that earned income relief should not be allowed on higher brackets of income, the Government, as a first step, reduced the allowance in the 1955-56 budget by stages on incomes in excess of Rs. 25,000, the concession ceasing when the level of Rs. 45,000 was reached. Under the recast scheme, an allowance of 20 per cent subject to a maximum of Rs. 4,000 was granted to earned incomes not exceeding Rs. 25,000. For incomes in excess of this amount the allowance of Rs. 4,000 was reduced at the rate of 20 per cent of the excess over Rs. 25,000 so that for an earned income of Rs. 45,000 the allowance was reduced to nil. From 1957-58, the relief was given in the form of a lower surcharge on earned income than on unearned income. The surcharge was fixed at 5 per cent of the tax on earned incomes up to Rs. 1 lakh and 10 per cent on incomes in excess of that sum while for unearned incomes a uniform surcharge of 20 per cent was imposed. However, the distinction between earned and unearned incomes introduced in 1945 under which the earned income was treated leniently was completely abolished from April 1, 1968. This decision was widely criticised as a retrograde fiscal measure.

The present law of income tax does recognise and tax different sources of income differently, though to a limited extent. Thus, long-term capital gains enjoy special concessions under the income tax law. The Finance Act, 1992, introduced inflation indexation of the cost of acquisition of assets for computing long-term capital gains. Moreover, a flat rate tax of 20 per cent was fixed on long-term capital gains arising to individuals and HUFs. It is ironical that preferential tax treatment denied to earned incomes is available to long-term capital gains which are purely accidental in nature and bear no relationship to efforts on the part of the recipient. Till 1990-91, the differentiation principle was followed in the case of company taxation when trading and investment companies were subject to a higher flat rate tax (50 per cent) than industrial and other companies (45 per cent).

If the distinction between earned and unearned incomes is to be revived, it may take the form of (a) reduction in the base of earned income (for example, exclusion from income of a fixed proportion subject to a maximum limit) and/or (b) lower rate structure for earned incomes.

Notes

1. For historical details of income tax in India, see 1. Government of India, *Report of the Indian Taxation Enquiry Committee* (President: Sir Charles Todhunter), 1924-25, chapter 9, pp. 189-91; 2. Government of India, *Income Tax Investigation Commission* (Chairman: Sir Srinivasa Varadachariar), 1947, pp. 1-4; 3. Government of India, Ministry of Finance, *Report of the Taxation Enquiry Commission* (Chairman: John Matthai), 1953-54, Vol. II, chapter 1.

2. *Report of the Indian Taxation Enquiry Committee*, 1924-25, *op. cit.* Vol. 1, para 259.

3. *Report of the Taxation Enquiry Commission,* 1953-54, op. cit., Vol. II, chapter 1, p. 16.

4. Government of India, Ministry of Finance, *Interim Report of the Tax Reforms Committee* (Chairman, Raja Chelliah), 1991, p. 20.

5. Ordinarily, the legislature enacts a bare Act and makes provision in the Act itself for details to be taken care of by the executive authority created for administration of the Act. Thus, rules and regulations concerning direct tax laws are framed by the Central Board of Direct Taxes and are referred to as delegated, subordinate or administrative law. It is noteworthy that rules

made under an Act have the same force as sections of the Act itself. However, they must be within the powers given to the rule-making authority. In case of any conflict, the Act overrides the rules framed under it.

6. In the terminology of Section 3 of the Act, the year during which the income is received or otherwise earned is called the *previous year* (i.e. the income year). It is a period of twelve months starting from April 1 of every year and ending on March 31 of the next year, being also the financial year of the Government of India. The year immediately succeeding the previous year and in which the income so earned is assessed to tax is called, under Section 2(9), the *assessment year* (i.e. the tax year). For example, income for the period from April 1, 2006 to March 31, 2007 (i.e. 2006-07) is income of the previous year relevant for the assessment year 2007-08. An assessee means a person by whom any tax or other sum of money is payable under the Act.

7. Government of India, Ministry of Finance, Report of the Taxation Enquiry Commission, 1953-54, op. cit, Vol. II, chapter 3, p. 41.

8. Prior to the assessment year 1975-76, the computation of income under the head salaries allowed deduction of expenditure from gross salary income incurred by a taxpayer on purchase of books and for maintenance of conveyance for employment purposes. The deduction was allowed to the taxpayer only on production of proof of having incurred such expenditure. The procedure was obviously cumbersome for the salaried persons and to simplify it the Finance Act of 1974 substituted it with a standard deduction for all types of expenditure incurred towards employment. The maximum amount of deduction allowed for this purpose was fixed at Rs. 3,500. According to the provisions of the Income Tax Act, standard deduction was granted, 'in respect of deduction incidental to the employment of the assessee'. However, this clause was deleted by an amendment introduced by the Finance (No. 2) Act, 1980. Consequently, standard deduction is now claimable by an employee regardless of the fact whether or not any expenditure incidental to employment has actually been incurred. For example, a pensioner is eligible to claim it although he does not incur, under normal circumstances, any expenditure to collect his pension. Even a person who is in receipt of family pension can claim this deduction. Family pension is included under the head 'income from other sources' and this deduction is available under Section 57 (iia). Thus, standard deduction, originally envisaged as a device to arrive at an assessee's net salary income, has virtually become a blanket deduction against salary income. It shows how tax designing is subject to pressures and influences.

Standard deduction was raised from Rs. 3,500 to Rs. 5,000 in 1981, Rs. 6,000 in 1983, Rs. 10,000 in 1986, Rs. 12,000 in 1988, and Rs. 15,000 in 1993. Thus, salaried employees were entitled to a standard deduction at the rate of 33.3 per cent of salary income or Rs. 15,000 whichever was less. However, in 1996 standard deduction was raised from Rs. 15,000 to Rs. 18,000 for salaried employees having an income up to Rs. 60,000.

As a special consideration for women, the Finance Act, 1992 provided for a higher standard deduction of Rs. 15,000 (as against the general Rs. 12,000) in respect of working women having total income up to Rs. 75,000. When the general standard deduction was increased from Rs. 12,000 to Rs. 15,000 by the Finance Act, 1993, a corresponding increase from Rs. 15,000 to Rs. 18,000 was made in the case of women.

In the 1997-98 budget, a uniform standard deduction of Rs. 20,000 was introduced for all salaried taxpayers. In the 1998-99 budget, the ceiling of standard deduction was raised from Rs. 20,000 to Rs. 25,000 in the case of salary earners having income up to Rs. 1 lakh. For salary earners having income between Rs. 1 lakh and Rs. 5 lakh, the existing position (i.e. Rs. 20,000) remained unchanged. However, entitlement to standard deduction was discontinued for salary earners having income above Rs. 5 lakh. In the 2001-02 budget, standard deduction was raised to Rs. 30,000 for taxpayers earning up to Rs. 1.5 lakh, and Rs. 25,000 for those earning between 1.5 lakh and 3 lakh. The limit of Rs. 20,000 was retained for taxpayers earning between 3 lakh and 5 lakh. Denial of standard deduction to salary earners having income above Rs. 5 lakh continued. Standard deduction was completely withdrawn for all categories of salary earners by the Finance Act, 2005.

9. Till March 31, 1990, incentives to promote savings and investments were based entirely on deductions from gross total income. When a deduction is made from income, an assessee gets tax relief at the highest marginal rate of tax applicable to him. Apparently, this system confers higher amount of tax benefit to a person with higher income compared to a person with lower income. To do away with this iniquitous system, the Finance Act, 1990, introduced a new scheme of tax rebate for individuals and HUFs on gross amount of savings. The new scheme covered under Section 88 provided for a rebate (or tax credit) on tax liability to the extent of 20 per cent of the sums invested in National Savings Certificates, provident funds, life insurance policies etc. The maximum amount eligible for rebate was Rs. 50,000 generally and Rs. 70,000 in the case of authors, playwrights, artists, musicians, actors, and sportsmen, thereby permitting a maximum rebate of Rs. 10,000 and Rs. 14,000 respectively.

Under this new scheme with uniform tax rebate, all taxpayers derive the same amount of tax benefit on a given amount of savings irrespective of their levels of income. It also led to simplification in tax deduction at source by the employers. It is a good example of how equity and simplicity criteria can be combined in the tax system.

The Finance Act, 1992, increased the maximum amount eligible for rebate for general category of investors from Rs. 50,000 to Rs. 60,000 (or the ceiling of tax rebate was increased from Rs. 10,000 to Rs. 12,000). It extended also the scope of Section 88 by including under it the National Savings Scheme (formerly under section 80 CCA), and the Equity-Linked Savings Scheme (formerly under section 80 CCB). Within the overall ceiling of Rs. 60,000, a sub-ceiling of Rs. 10,000 was fixed in respect of investments in the Equity-Linked Savings Scheme in order to ensure continued viability of other saving schemes contained in Section 88.

Again, by the Finance Act, 1992, the scheme of tax credit under Section 88 was further liberalised in the case of authors, playwrights etc. to compensate them for the fluctuating nature of their income. As against the 20 per cent tax rebate allowed normally, it was raised to 25 per cent in their case. Also, the ceiling of the maximum rebate in their case was raised from Rs. 14,000 to Rs. 17,500. With a view to allowing this concession only to those persons having a significant portion of their income from the above mentioned professions, the enhanced rebate is allowed only to such persons whose income from their professions as authors, playwrights etc. is at least 25 per cent of their total income.

Furthermore, the Finance Act, 1992, inserted a new Section 88B to provide for a special tax relief in the form of an additional rebate of 10 per cent from the tax payable by resident individuals who had attained the age of 65 years and had a gross total income not exceeding Rs. 50,000. This special relief was designed to help senior citizens meet the increased expenses in their old age. The Finance Act, 1993, raised the tax rebate to 20 per cent and further increased the income limit from Rs. 50,000 to Rs. 75,000. In 1994, the tax rebate admissible was raised from 20 per cent to 40 per cent and the benefit made available to senior citizens having an income up to Rs. 1,00,000. In 1996, the income limit was raised from Rs. 1,00,000 to Rs. 1,20,000. It is noteworthy that this rebate was admissible before computing any rebate under Section 88. By the Finance Act, 1997, the rate of rebate available to senior citizens was increased to 100 per cent from the existing 40 per cent subject to a limit of Rs. 10,000. Furthermore, the Finance Act, 1997 allowed tax rebate under section 88 on infrastructure bonds up to 6the value of Rs. 70,000. The scheme of rebate was modified a number of times after that and was finally withdrawn by the Finance Act, 2005.

10. Units of Assessment under Income Tax Act

An Individual: An individual means only a natural person, i.e. a human being. An individual is taxed separately, though he may belong to any of the other units subject to tax.

A Hindu Undivided Family (HUF): HUF in India is a joint family recognised for all purposes, including taxation, as a separate and distinct legal unit. It is ordinarily headed by *Karta* who is either the father or some other senior member of the family. HUF consists of all persons lineally descended from a common ancestor and includes their wives and unmarried daughters.

The HUF enjoys a higher exemption limit for income tax purposes than for individuals. This is justified on the ground that the liabilities of HUF, in terms of the total membership of the HUF consisting of earners and their dependents, are, in general, larger than that of the individual income-earners. For income tax purposes HUF must satisfy two conditions: (a) that the family possesses common property and (b) that there is a Hindu coparcenary.

A Company: Under section 2(17), a company means (i) any Indian company, or (ii) any body corporate incorporated under the laws of a foreign country, or (iii) any institution, association or a body which was assessed as a company for any assessment year up to and including the assessment year 1970-71 and (iv) any institution, association or a body which is declared by the Central Board of Direct Taxes to be a company for purposes of the income tax. Thus, the definition of the term 'company' under the Act is much wider than in the Companies Act, 1956.

Under section 2(26) an Indian company means (i) a company formed and registered in India under the Companies Act, 1956, (ii) a corporation established by or under a Central, State or Provincial Act, (iii) any institution, association or a body which is declared by the Central Board of Direct Taxes to be an Indian Company. It is notable that in the foregoing cases, a company, corporation, institution, association or body will be treated as an Indian company only if its registered office is in India.

Domestic company is defined as an Indian company or any other company which in respect of its income liable to tax under the Act, has made prescribed arrangements for the declaration and payment of dividends within India. It has to meet the following three requirements before it could be called a domestic company: (a) The share register of the company for all shareholders should be regularly maintained at its principal place of business in India, (b) the general meeting for passing of accounts and for declaring dividends should be held only at a place within India, and (c) the dividends declared, if any, should be payable only within India to all shareholders.

Foreign company means a company which is not a domestic company.

Widely-held companies are companies in which the public are substantially interested [sec.2 (18)]. The following types of companies are deemed to be widely-held companies: (i) A company owned by the Government or the Reserve Bank of India or in which not less than 40 per cent of the shares are held by Government or the Reserve Bank of India or a corporation owned by that Bank; or (ii) a company registered under section 25 of the Companies Act, 1956, viz. companies for promotion of commerce, art, culture etc. and prohibiting the payment of any dividends to its members; (iii) a company having no share capital and it is declared by the Central Board of Direct Taxes to be a company in which the public are substantially interested; or (iv) a company which carries on, as its principal business, the business of acceptance of deposits from its members and which is declared by the Central Government to be a *Nidhi* or a mutual benefit society; or (v) a company which is not a private company and its equity shares are listed in a recognised stock exchange in India; or (vi) a company which is not a private company and its shares carrying 50 per cent of voting power have been allotted unconditionally to, or acquired unconditionally by (a) the Government or (b) a statutory corporation.

A company in which the public are not substantially interested is deemed to be a closely-held company (or private company).

An industrial company is a company which is mainly engaged in the business of generation or distribution of electricity or any other form of power or in the construction of ships or in the manufacture or processing of goods or in mining. A consultancy service company is an Indian company whose business consists wholly in the provision of technical know-how. An investment, company is one whose gross total income consists mainly of income chargeable under the heads 'income from house property', 'capital gains', and 'income from other sources'. Similarly, a trading company is one whose business consists mainly of dealing in goods or merchandise manufactured, produced or processed by a person other than that company.

A Firm: Persons who have entered into partnership with one another are individually called partners and collectively a firm. A firm is a taxable entity separate and distinct from its partners. For the purpose of assessment, a firm may be registered or unregistered. A registered firm means a firm registered under sections 184 and 185 of the Act, and an unregistered firm means a firm which is not a registered firm. A registered firm gets the benefit of lower rates of tax than those which would otherwise apply to the income of a firm.

An Association of Persons or Body of Individuals: An association of persons may be an association of individuals, firms, Hindu Undivided Families or companies. It means, for income tax purposes, an association in which two or more persons join in a common purpose to produce income, profits or gains.

Local Authority: Local authority means a municipal committee, district board etc. and is a separate unit of assessment.

Every Artificial Juridical Person: It is a residuary classification covering deities and other artificial juridical persons like statutory corporations. It does not cover taxable units falling within any of the preceding classifications.

Under section 2(19), a co-operative society means a society registered under the Co-operative Societies Act of 1912 or under any State law for the registration of co-operative societies. Such societies get favourable treatment under the Income-Tax Act in view of Government's policy to encourage co-operative activities.

11. Government of India, Ministry of Finance, *Speeches of Union Finance Ministers, 1947-48 to 1984-85*, p. 155.

12. Government of India, Ministry of Finance, *Final Report of Direct Taxes Enquiry Committee* (Chairman: Justice K. N. Wanchoo) December 1971, para 2.52.

13. Government of India, *Economic Survey*, 1993-94, p. 26.

14. 6. Government of India, Ministry of Finance, Budget 2000-2001, *Speech of the Finance Minister, Part B*, p. 36.

15. N. A. Palkhivala and B.A. Palkhivala, *The Law and Practice of Income Tax* (Bombay: N.M. Tripathi Private Ltd., 1990), Vol. I, p. 9.

16. Government of India, Ministry of Finance, *Final Report of Direct Tax Laws Committee* (Chairman: C.C. Chokshi), 1978, para 1-0, 10.

15

Wealth Tax

Following the recommendations of Professor Nicholas Kaldor, an 'integrated direct tax system' was introduced in India in the mid-1950s. Kaldor, a British economist, was invited by the Government of India in 1956 to examine the Indian tax system in the light of the revenue requirements of the Second Five Year Plan launched in the same year. Kaldor's review of Indian taxation was restricted to personal and business taxation and was widely debated. It may be recalled that an extensive review of the Indian tax system had already been undertaken by the Indian Taxation Enquiry Commission, 1953-54.

In 1957 and 1958, three new taxes were introduced, viz. wealth tax, expenditure tax, and gift tax. Estate duty was already in operation since 1953. The basic philosophy underlying the introduction of the system of integrated direct taxes was to prevent evasion and avoidance of direct taxes and thereby to reduce inequalities of income and wealth. However, the yield from wealth tax, expenditure tax, gift tax, and estate duty has never been of much significance in the Central tax structure. The meagre revenue collection from these taxes ultimately led to their abolition. Gift tax, estate duty and expenditure tax were abolished in 1998, 1985 and 1966 respectively. (See Appendices 10, 11 and 12 in Part VIII of this book for provisions of these taxes at the time of their abolition).

15.1 Rationale for Wealth Tax

Wealth tax is advocated on both benefit and ability-to-pay considerations. Protection of life and property has traditionally been the primary function of the government, and to perform it considerable cost is incurred on the law enforcement machinery and the judicial administration. The main beneficiaries of these services are people with fabulous wealth who as a rule should contribute towards the expenses on such services. Pavement sleepers hardly need the services of the state as a protector of property. Another dimension of the benefit argument is that public services like roads, street lighting, community centres, public parks etc. increase the value of real estates, conferring unearned benefits on the owners of such estates. It can, therefore, be argued that property owners should pay for these services.

In terms of ability-to-pay, possession of property is a measure of economic well-being and therefore of taxable capacity, quite apart from the income earned from that property. A tax on capital itself may seem undesirable when capital income is subject to income tax (as is generally the case). However, the coverage of capital income under the income tax is usually incomplete in view of liberal exemptions, tax avoidance, and evasion. Moreover, an income tax system does not include non-earning assets. Therefore, taxation of wealth is essentially a supplement to taxation of income. Hence, taxation of wealth is justified on equity criterion. It may be argued that wealth tax is unjust in cases where property does not yield money income directly. In this context Professor Kaldor has opined, "If a property does not yield money income, it must either yield an equivalent psychic income to the owner or it must be held in the expectation of a certain appreciation in value which makes it at least as attractive to the holder as other property on which a current money return is obtained." [1]

Yet another argument for taxation of wealth is social control over the most unjust and dangerous form of economic inequality. To quote Musgraves, "Alternatively, the taxation of wealth may be approached not as a matter of charging for benefits received or ability-to-pay, but as a form of social control. The social consequences of inequality in the distribution of wealth, as is easily seen, differ from those in the distribution of consumption, so that society may wish to deal with them separately. For this purpose, a progressive tax on wealth, rather than on income, is the proper instrument." [2] Situations may arise when certain taxpayers have taxable wealth but very low current incomes. One way to resolve this problem is to exempt from wealth tax liability all those taxpayers whose annual income from all sources does not exceed a specified limit.

In spite of being a potentially important source of revenue and economic control, the administration of wealth tax is difficult, particularly in developing countries. Imposition of wealth tax requires the preparation of an annual balance sheet of assets and liabilities of the taxpayer. For an honest exercise of this sort, an assessee should first declare, truthfully, all taxable assets with their proper current value. He must also make a genuine claim for deductible debts. Honesty of the sort required is an exception rather than the rule. Thus, tax officials for most of their part are busy detecting taxable assets, grappling with undervaluation of properties and verifying claims of deductible debts. Some of these problems (e.g. valuation of assets) are encountered also in connection with estate duty, capital gains tax, and local property tax. Valuation of assets for purposes of one tax is generally used as a basis for computing tax liability under another tax. However, the continuous rise in prices (leading to appreciation of real estates), the underdeveloped nature of money markets (causing difficulty in the valuation of shares), and the ingenuity of tax evaders leave the tax authorities groping in the dark without much success.

15.2 Wealth Tax Act, 1957: Main Provisions

An annual tax on net wealth was introduced in India with the enactment of the Wealth Tax Act, 1957, which came into force from April 1 of that year. The rationale behind the imposition of wealth tax lies essentially in furthering the equity objective of tax policy. Since ownership of wealth is the main source of economic inequalities in India, a tax on wealth is intended to reduce its concentration in a few hands to promote vertical equity.

Wealth Tax Act, 1957 (hereinafter called the Act), is amended from time to time by the annual Finance Act and other legislations pertaining to direct taxes. The law of wealth tax is stated here as applicable for the assessment year 1997-98. A set of Wealth Tax Rules also exists to enforce the provisions of the Act.

15.2.1 Persons Chargeable to Wealth Tax: Section 3 of the Act is the charging section. It provides for the levy of wealth tax for every assessment year in respect of net wealth, as on the valuation date, of individuals, Hindu undivided families, and all companies having net wealth exceeding Rs. 15 lakh. Wealth tax on companies was discontinued from the assessment year 1960-61. The Finance Act, 1983, however, revived the levy of wealth tax on closely-held companies from the assessment year 1984-85. The Finance Act, 1992, extended the scope of wealth tax to all companies.

15.2.2 Net Wealth and Residential Status: The wealth tax liability is affected by residence and citizenship of the assessee. In the case of an individual, the incidence of the tax depends upon his residential status and nationality. Thus, for an Indian citizen who is also 'resident' in India, the net wealth includes wealth in India as well as wealth outside India, but the foreign wealth is chargeable to wealth tax at half the average rate. However, if an Indian citizen is 'not ordinarily' resident, or is 'non-resident', the foreign wealth is completely exempt. In the case of an individual who is not a citizen of India, only his wealth in India is taxable. Furthermore, if the foreign national happens to be a non-resident, the wealth tax payable by him on his Indian wealth is reduced by 50 per cent thereof (Section 6 of the Act). For the purpose of wealth tax, residential status is the same which an individual enjoys under the Income Tax Act.

15.2.3 Meaning of Net Wealth: Wealth tax in India is a levy made with reference to the net wealth which, as defined in Section 2(m) of the Act, broadly corresponds to the excess of assets over liabilities. It means provision is made for the deduction of debts from the assets owned by the assessee on the valuation date. All debts owned by the assessee, which have been incurred in relation to assets chargeable to tax, are deductible. As in the case of income tax, wealth tax is charged on a global basis, i.e. all pieces of wealth are pooled together and a flat rate tax is applied. In other words, all components of wealth tax are treated alike for the purpose of the tax.

Unlike income tax and gift tax, there is no previous year for wealth tax. Wealth tax is imposed on net wealth possessed by an assessee on the valuation date and the value of his assets is determined as on that date. Valuation date means the last day of the previous year, i.e. March 31 [Sec. 2(q)]. For example, for the assessment year 1998-99, the valuation date will be March 31, 1998. Valuation of assets, for determining the net wealth of a taxpayer, is an important and difficult subject under the wealth tax law. Valuation is easy in the case of quoted shares and for assets like cash and bank balances. However, serious problems arise in most other cases partly because the value of assets changes from year to year. Under the Act, the value of an asset has been defined (Section 7) as the price it would fetch if sold in the open market on the valuation date. A wealth tax officer is empowered to make the estimate of market value subject to the various rules made in this regard. Since the tax is imposed on net wealth which represents the excess of assets over debts, it is necessary to understand the concepts of 'assets' and 'debts' as used in the Act.

15.2.4 Meaning of Assets: The term 'assets' has been described in Section 2(e) of the Act. The definition of 'assets' was drastically narrowed by the Finance Act, 1992. It means: (a) a guest house, (b) a residential house, (c) a farmhouse situated within 25 kilometres from the local municipal limits, (d) motor cars, (e) jewellery, bullion etc., (f) yachts, boats, and aircrafts, (g) urban land (of certain description), and (h) cash in hand in excess of Rs. 50,000.

It is noteworthy that the term 'assets' does not include, *inter alia,* (a) a house meant exclusively for residential purposes and allotted to a whole-time employee, (b) residential house, jewellery, bullion, motor cars used as stock-in-trade, and (c) yachts, boats, and aircrafts used for commercial purposes. In other words, assets held as stock-in-trade are not taxable.

From the assessment year 1997-98, commercial properties other than those occupied by the assessee for the purpose of any business or profession carried on by him have also been included in the term 'assets' and are consequently taxable.

15.2.5 Deemed Assets: As already noted, wealth tax is chargeable on the net wealth of an assessee. Ordinarily speaking, this would mean assets belonging to the assessee form part of his net wealth. However, the Act provides for the inclusion of certain assets in the net wealth of an individual though such assets do not legally belong to the individual on the valuation date. In other words, such assets are deemed to belong to the taxpayer. These provisions correspond to those contained in Section 64 of the Income Tax Act, 1961, which deals with the clubbing of income. The purpose of these provisions in both the cases is to check tax avoidance by the assessees. The following assets, *inter alia,* are included as belonging to the assessee while computing his net wealth (Section 4).

1. Assets held by the spouse of an individual where such assets have been transferred by the individual without adequate consideration.
2. Assets held by a minor child, not being a married daughter, of such individual. However, assets acquired by a minor child out of his income derived from manual work etc. are not included in the net wealth of his parent.
3. Assets held by a person to whom such assets have been transferred by the individual without adequate consideration for the immediate or deferred benefits of such individual, his or her spouse.
4. Assets held by a person to whom such assets have been transferred by an individual under a revocable transfer.
5. Assets held by an individual's son's wife to whom such assets have been transferred by such individual without adequate consideration.
6. Assets held by any person to whom such assets have been transferred by an individual for the benefit of his son's wife.
7. If an individual throws his self-acquired property into the common stock of the Hindu undivided family of which he is a member, the said property is included in his net wealth.
8. An individual, being a partner in a firm, may gift some money by crediting the amount in the account of the donee and by debiting his own account in the account books of the firm. In such cases, if the physical possession of the money is not given to the donee and the same continues to be invested in the business, and the gift is made only by making entries in the books of account without actually delivering the money to the donee, the value of such gift is included in the net wealth of the individual making the gift.

15.2.6 Assets Exempt from Wealth Tax: Section 5 of the Act provides for exemption of certain assets from the charge of wealth tax. Prior to the assessment year 1993-94, the list of exempted assets was quite lengthy and served to explain leakages in the base of wealth tax. The exempted assets were broadly divided into two categories: (a) assets which were totally exempt and therefore left out totally in computing the net wealth, and (b) assets which enjoyed only partial exemption. In the case of partial exemption, a ceiling was prescribed and the value of the assets in excess of the prescribed limit was included in the net wealth of the assessee for wealth tax purposes.

The Finance Act, 1992, drastically pruned the list of taxable assets for the purpose of wealth tax. Correspondingly, the list of exemptions/ deductions allowable under Section 5 was also restricted. Thus, from the assessment year 1993-94, only the following assets are exempt from being included in the net wealth of an assessee:

1. Any property held by any assessee under trust for any public purpose of charitable or religious nature in India.
2. Interest of an assessee in the property of any Hindu undivided family of which he is a member. It may be noted that Hindu undivided family itself is liable to wealth tax.
3. Any one building in the occupation of an ex-ruler which is declared by the Government as his official residence.
4. Recognised heirloom jewellery of an ex-ruler. 5. Value of assets brought by persons of Indian origin.

15.2.7 Basic Exemption and Rate of Tax: Wealth tax liability is computed by applying the rate schedule to net wealth (i.e. taxable wealth). The rates of wealth tax are given in Schedule 1 of the Act. From the assessment year 1993-94, wealth tax is charged at the flat rate of 1 per cent in the case of all assessees having taxable wealth exceeding Rs. 15 lakh.

15.3 Critical Comments

15.3.1 Shrinkage of Base: Prior to the enactment of the Finance Act, 1992, the term 'assets' as described in Section 2(e) included property of every description, movable and immovable, such as cash, bank balances, shares, jewellery, and other assets. The term 'assets' was of widest import and sufficiently comprehensive.

However, consequent upon the recommendations contained in the Interim Report of the Tax Reforms Committee, 1991, [3] the various provisions of the wealth tax law were drastically restructured by the Finance Act, 1992. The Committee had recommended that in order to encourage the taxpayers to invest in productive assets such as shares, securities, bonds, bank deposits, mutual funds etc., these financial assets should be exempted from wealth tax. Wealth tax should be levied on individuals, Hindu undivided families, and all companies only in respect of non-productive assets such as residential houses, jewellery, bullion, motor cars, yachts, and aircrafts which are not used for commercial purposes. Hence, as already noted, the definition of the term 'assets' was significantly narrowed from the assessment year 1993-94. In short, the basis of taxation was shifted from wealth to unproductive assets. Following pressure that a residential house is a universal necessity and should not be subjected to tax, the Finance Act, 1993, exempted the value of one house from the levy of wealth tax.

15.3.2 Lowering of Top Marginal Rate: The maximum marginal rate of wealth tax, applicable to net wealth above Rs. 15 lakh, was quite high at 8 per cent till the year 1975-76. It was drastically reduced to 2.5 per cent the following year (1976-77). In a reversal of policy of low rates, it was increased to 3.5 per cent in 1977-78, and further up to 5 per cent in 1979-80. In 1985-86, it was again lowered to 2 per cent and made applicable to net wealth over Rs. 20 lakh.

The Tax Reforms Committee, 1991, suggested that wealth tax should be charged at the flat rate of 1 per cent with a basic exemption of Rs. 15 lakh instead of the then existing Rs. 5 lakh. These recommendations were accepted and incorporated in the Finance Act, 1992. The trends in the maximum marginal rate of wealth tax beginning with the year 1973-74 are given in Table 15.1.

Table 15.1: Trends in the Maximum Marginal Rate of Wealth Tax in India

Financial year	Top rate of wealth tax (per cent)	Applicable to net wealth
1973-74 to 1975-76	8.0	Over Rs. 15 lakh
1976-77	2.5	Over Rs. 15 lakh
1977-78 and 1978-79	3.5	Over Rs. 15 lakh
1979-80 to 1984-85	5.0	Over Rs. 15 lakh
1985-86 to 1991-92	2.0	Over Rs. 20 lakh
1992-93 to 2007-08	Flat rate of 1 per cent on wealth exceeding Rs. 15 lakh	

Sources: Government of India, *Finance Acts* (various years).

Thus, following the recommendations of the Tax Reforms Committee, 1991, the scope of wealth tax, both in terms of base and rate, was drastically reduced. Presently, wealth tax has only decorative value for the statute book. In view of the maegre revenue and problems of administration and compliance, the Task Force on Direct Taxes (Chairman: Vijay Kelkar) recommended the abolition of wealth tax.

Notes

1. Nicholas Kaldor, *Indian Tax Reform - Report of a Survey* (Government of India, Ministry of Finance), 1956, p. 22.
2. Richard A. Musgrave and Peggy B. Musgrave, *Public Finance in Theory and Practice* (McGraw-Hill, International Student Edition, 1980), p. 472.
3. Government of India, Ministry of Finance, *Interim Report of the Tax Reforms Committee* (Chairman, Raja Chelliah), December, 1991, chapter 7.

16

Union Excise Duties

In India, the history of excise taxation in its modern form can be traced back to the year 1894 when excise duty at the rate of 5 per cent was imposed on yarn above twenty counts. Since then, the Indian excise system, which represents the single largest source of tax revenue for the government, has undergone various changes. This research document describes and critically examines various aspects of excise duties, viz. historical evolution, constitutional provisions, revenue significance, commodity coverage, tariff structure, introduction of MODVAT and CENVAT, and the scheme of exemptions and concessions.

16.1 Pre-Independence History of Excise Duties

Prior to Independence in 1947, excise taxation in India was selective in terms of commodity coverage and modest from revenue angle. Excise duties were not important as a source of revenue due to the narrow production base of the Indian economy. The relative share of Central excises in total tax revenue of the Government was 4.7 per cent and 4.4 per cent in 1920-21 and 1925-26 respectively. The policy of *discriminating protection* followed from the mid-1920s did give some impetus to domestic industry and the share of excise revenue increased to 8.8 per cent in 1931-32. At the start of the Second World War, the contribution of excise revenue was 10.7 per cent (Table 16.1).

Table 16.1: Pre-Independence Trends in the Relative Share of Excise Duties in Total Tax Revenue of the Central Government: Selected Years

(Rs. crore)

Year	Total tax revenue	Central excise revenue	Col. 3 as per cent of Col. 2
1	2	3	4
1920-21	60.85	2.85	4.7
1925-26	72.86	3.21	4.4
1931-32	75.62	6.19	8.2
1938-39	81.37	8.72	10.7

Source: Government of India, Ministry of Finance, *Report of the Taxation Enquiry Commission* 1953-54, Vol. II, p. 258, Table 3 (excerpted).

The selected commodities on which excise duties were imposed included cotton textiles, salt, motor spirit, and kerosene. A commodity-wise history of excise taxation is as follows:

16.1.1 Cotton Textiles: Cotton textile mills were first built in India in the 1850s. By 1896 their number had risen to 167 and by 1923 to 323. Following pressure from Britain, an excise duty of 5 per cent, corresponding to the duty imposed on imported goods, was imposed in 1894 on Indian yarn above twenty counts. It was in the nature of a countervailing duty on domestic yarn and hence on cloth which competed with imported goods from Lancashire. In 1896, excise duty on yarn was changed to duty on cloth at a reduced rate of 3.5 per cent. Simultaneously, import duty was reduced to the same level as the excise duty. The policy of equal duties on imported and domestically produced goods continued till 1917. It was from this year that the period of differential duties started with the raising of the import duty on cloth to 7.5 per cent. It was further raised to 11 per cent in 1921. The domestic producers thus enjoyed protection to the extent of 7.5 per cent on cloth. The Indian Fiscal Commission, 1921-22 examined in detail the question of protection to domestic industries and recommended that the Tariff Board should consider the rate of import duty necessary for the protection of the domestic industry. When duty is imposed on local production, the import duty should be enhanced by a like amount. Following its recommendations, the Government adopted what came to be called the policy of 'discriminating protection' under which tariff protection was granted to selected industries against foreign competition. The industries which benefited from the policy of discriminating protection included, *inter alia*, iron and steel, cement, textiles, sugar, paper, matches, and jute.

16.1.2 Salt: Excise on salt was another important source of revenue for the Government during pre-Independence days. The commodity was preferred for taxation because of its inelastic demand and also because it is used in small quantity by all strata of society. Even a low rate of duty on this essential commodity yields some revenue for the exchequer without anybody feeling the pinch. However, the duty was opposed on the ground that it falls on an absolute necessity of life. Since salt is necessary for human existence, duty on it is in the nature of a poll tax. Even the poorest of the poor are made to contribute to state exchequer.

The Indian Taxation Enquiry Committee, 1924-25, examined in detail the pros and cons of salt duty. It opined, "It may be concluded that, if it is desirable to impose any tax on the mass of the community at all, there is much to be said for the continuance of the salt tax. The present rate of duty is appropriate and causes no serious hardship." [1] Excise duty on salt remained a major source of revenue till Independence. Abolition of salt duty was chosen by Mahatma Gandhi to spearhead his non-co-operation movement against the British rulers. The duty on salt was abolished with the achievement of Independence in 1947.

16.1.3 Petroleum Products: Excise duty at the rate of 6 *annas* (Rs. 0.37) per Imperial Gallon (4.55 litres) was imposed on motor spirit in 1917. The purpose of this levy was to restrict consumption of petrol to conserve supplies for war needs. Kerosene was another petroleum item placed on the tariff list in 1922. The rate of duty was one *anna* (Rs. 0.06) per Imperial Gallon. The duty on motor spirit was mainly a tax on transport while the burden of kerosene duty fell chiefly on almost all classes of the population. For the next 34 years (i.e. until 1956) there was no addition to the list of petroleum products subject to excise tariff. It may be mentioned here that before Independence, the Indian oil industry was characterised by small-scale, localised operations under foreign firms. The Assam Oil Company (a subsidiary of Burmah Oil Company) produced about half a million tonnes of crude oil in Assam. A small refinery of the company at Digboi processed this crude. With the Digboi refinery producing about 7 per cent of the total consumption of petroleum products in India, the remainder was imported and marketed by various foreign oil companies operating in India, the chief among them being Burmah Oil, and Stanvac.

16.1.4 Tobacco: Taxation of tobacco and tobacco products in India was suggested, for the first time, by the Indian Taxation Enquiry Committee, 1924-25. It observed, "The absence of any internal taxation on tobacco is a feature which distinguishes the fiscal system of India from that of almost every other civilised country in the world. The considerations which have led in other countries to the selection of tobacco as one of the principal subjects for consumption taxation apply with equal force to India. It is a typical instance of a conventional luxury whose use goes down to the poorest classes, and it is an article the consumption of which can be varied greatly both in quality and quantity according to the means of the consumer." [2] Following the recommendations of the Committee, the taxation of tobacco was examined on various occasions, but the administrative difficulties involved in implementing such a levy prevented its imposition. Moreover, taxation of tobacco was a State subject before the enactment of the Government of India Act, 1935. After this enactment, the power to impose tobacco excise was vested in the Central Government.

Excise on unmanufactured tobacco was levied for the first time with effect from April 1, 1943 with a view to mobilising additional resources to meet the requirements of the Second World War. The levy was imposed under the Tobacco (Excise Duty) Act, 1943 which was subsequently merged with the consolidated Central Excises and Salt Act, 1944. The revenue realised from tobacco in the first year of the excise, viz. 1943-44 was Rs. 9.65 crore.

The rates of duty levied on unmanufactured tobacco in 1943 were designed on a progressive scale depending upon the intended use of the commodity. In addition to this, a graduated duty on the basis of value slabs was imposed on the higher grades of the manufactured cigars and cheroots. The tobacco tariff was extended in 1948 when an excise duty was imposed on cigarettes on the same pattern as the tariff for cigars and cheroots, namely value slabs for fixation of rates. Duty on unmanufactured tobacco brought the excise machinery into contact with a large number of growers and licensees and thus led to tariff complexities and administrative difficulties.

16.1.5 Other Products: Excise duty on silver was imposed in 1930. To quote, "It was in 1934 that the first step in the rationalisation of excise levies was made and their coverage extended. Excise duties were imposed mainly as a revenue measure on sugar, matches, steel ingots and mechanical lighters. Sugar and matches production had made rapid strides under heavy protection in the years following the First World War and the stage had been reached when they could be taxed." [3] Duties were imposed on tyres in 1941 and on vegetable products and tobacco in 1943, mainly to meet the exigencies of war finances. The year 1944 saw excise duties being imposed on coffee, tea, and betel nut. Cigarettes came within the excise net in 1948. Prior to 1944, excise duties were levied under separate enactments for different goods. For example, tobacco levies were imposed under the Tobacco (Excise Duty) Act, 1943. About 16 such separate laws were in force till 1944. However, in that year the various enactments were consolidated into the Central Excises and Salt Act and the Central Excise Rules, 1944.

According to Lakdawala and Nambiar, "In the early stages of its evolution, the Indian excise system has had a basic purpose and philosophy behind its development. The main objective was either to restrict internal consumption of such commodities whose supply was scarce or to make good the loss of revenue resulting from the shrinkage of revenue from protective customs duties on imports of parallel commodities. The initial imposition of duties on items such as motor spirit and kerosene belonged to the first category while the subsequent levies on items such as tyres, textiles and cigarettes belonged to the second category." [4]

16.1.6 Rules of Excise Taxation: This brief description of pre-Independence developments in the excise system may be concluded by quoting the five golden rules of excise taxation enunciated by the Indian Fiscal Commission, 1921-22, which with necessary modifications, seem to be relevant to this day.

"1. Excise duties should ordinarily be confined to industries which are concentrated in large factories or small areas.

2. They may properly be imposed for the purpose of checking the consumption of injurious articles and especially on luxuries coming under this category.

3. Otherwise they should be imposed for revenue purpose only.

4. While permissible on commodities of general consumption, they should not press too heavily on poorer classes.

5. When an industry requires protection, any further necessary taxation on its products may, if the other conditions are fulfilled, take the form of excise duty *plus* an additional import duty. The latter should fully countervail the former and may be pitched at a higher price." [5]

16.2 Constitutional Provisions

By virtue of powers vested in it under entry 84 of List I (Union List) in the Seventh Schedule of the Constitution, the Central Government is authorised to impose, "duties of excise on tobacco and other goods manufactured or produced in India except (a) alcoholic liquors for human consumption, (b) opium, Indian-hemp and other narcotic drugs and narcotics, but including medicinal and toilet preparations containing alcohol or any substance included in sub-paragraph (b) of this entry". Excise duties on liquor and other narcotics are imposed by the State Governments under provisions of entry 51 of List II (State List) in the Seventh Schedule. Duties of excise on medicinal and toilet preparations containing alcohol are levied by the Centre under Article 268 but they are collected and appropriated by the States within which they are leviable. These are levied by the Centre to ensure uniformity in their rate throughout the country.

Apart from allocating taxation powers, the Constitution also provides for the sharing of certain taxes between the Centre and the States. Prior to the Constitution (Eightieth Amendment) Act, 2000, excise duties belonged to the category of taxes which *may* be divided between the Centre and the States (Article 272) and the subject matter of this division fell within the purview of the Finance Commission [Article 280 (3)(a)]. The sharing of excise duties was permissive and therefore the States did not enjoy a constitutional right to claim a share out of the revenues from Central excises. However, successive Finance Commissions took the view that permissive sharing, contemplated under Article 272 was not only justified but even necessary in view of the growing financial needs of the States. Therefore, ever since April 1, 1952, the States got a share of the proceeds of Central excises. The Tenth Finance Commission fixed this share at 47.5 per cent for the quinquennium 1995-2000. However, the Constitution (Eightieth Amendment) Act, 2000 substituted a new Article for Article 270 under which States are now given a percentage share of all Central taxes and duties. However, the surcharge levied for purposes of the Union under Article 271 is excluded from the divisible pool. Moreover, Article 272 of the Constitution was omitted by the same amendment.

16.3 Various Types of Excise Duties

In accordance with the provisions of the Constitution, various types of excise duties and cesses are imposed by the Union Government on commodities covered by the Central Excise Act, 1944 and other Acts. The important duties currently in operation are the following.

16.3.1 Basic Excise Duty: Levied under Section 3 of the Central Excise Act, 1944, this is the main duty commonly known as basic excise duty. This duty may be fixed with reference to the value, weight, volume, unit, length or area of the excisable goods. These details are given in the Schedule of the Central Excise Tariff Act, 1985.

16.3.2 Additional Duties in Lieu of Sales Tax: These duties are imposed under the Additional Duties of Excise (Goods of Special Importance) Act, 1957, which provides for the levy and collection of additional duties on sugar, tobacco, cotton fabrics, rayon or artificial silk fabrics and woollen fabrics produced or manufactured in India. These duties are in addition to the duties payable under the Central Excises and Salt Act, 1944, and replace, by agreement with State Governments, the sales tax levied by them on these commodities. The net proceeds from additional excise duties are distributable among the States in accordance with the principles of distribution formulated and the recommendations made by the Finance Commissions from time to time.

16.3.3 Cesses: These are levied under separate enactments on certain commodities and the revenue is earmarked for specific purposes. For example, handloom cess is levied on fabrics to raise funds for developing *khadi* and other handloom industries and for promoting the sale of *khadi* and other handloom cloth. Cesses are also levied under various Acts on tea, jute, indigenous crude oil, paper, sugar, *bidis*, automobiles, vegetable oils, and television sets.

The Central Excise Act, 1944, is the main enactment under which duties are levied on different commodities. Under Section 37 of this Act, a set of rules known as the Central Excise Rules, 1944, has been framed to implement the provisions of the Act. Another set of rules under the same section deals exclusively with the valuation of the excisable commodities and is known as Central Excise (Valuation) Rules, 1975. The Act and the Rules are amended from time to time. Broadly speaking, the Act embodies substantive law, and the Rules contain both substantive law and procedural matters.

Although the Central Government is empowered to levy duties on agricultural products also, it has refrained to do so in view of the administrative difficulties involved. Therefore, the excise system has remained confined mostly to the products of the industrial sector with the notable exceptions of tea and coffee.

16.4 Different Procedures to Collect Excises

Central excise duties are assessed and collected through a vast network of offices scattered all over the country. There are various procedures to assess and collect excise duties.

16.4.1 Physical Control System: This procedure, based on personal verification of production by excise officers, was the chief procedure to realise excise duties till it was replaced by a new system called self-removal procedure from June 1, 1968. Under the physical control method, excise control was exercised by the officers of the Excise Department who were posted at the factory to keep watch over the operations in the various departments of the factory to prevent illegal disposal of the manufactured articles. The physical control procedure was based on personal verification of production, storage, and clearance of excisable goods.

The manufacturers, however, were unhappy with this direct interference in the manufacturing process. Therefore, ever since Independence they had been demanding abolition of the physical control scheme and its replacement by a system based on audited accounts. The Taxation Enquiry Commission, 1953-54, favoured the retention of the physical control system. It observed, "It seems to us reasonable for the Government to ensure that for the period intervening between production and clearance the goods should be kept in a proper place and under adequate supervision. The procedure followed in India in this regard is also practically the same as that obtaining elsewhere. Physical supervision is considered to be necessary in such cases in almost every country." [6]. The organised sector, however, continued to build up pressure for the replacement of the physical control system and ultimately the self-removal procedure was introduced with effect from June 1, 1968. A few commodities are still subject to the physical control system including sugar, chewing tobacco, and matches.

16.4.2 Self-Removal Procedure (SRP): Under this liberal system, introduced in place of the physical control system, an assessee is allowed to take clearances on his own assessment of the duty liability without prior permission of physical checks by excise officers. This procedure is applicable to most of the commodities under the excise net. An assessee is, however, required to get his classification list approved by the excise authorities before effecting any removal. In the classification list the assessee details the description of the goods produced so that they may be categorised in terms of the rate of duty applicable to them. In case of *ad valorem* duties, the assessee is further required to submit a price list showing the prices charged along with discounts and deductions, if any. In essence, the SRP is a record-based system of duty collection relying on mutual trust and belief. Unfortunately, heavy evasion of excise duty has taken place under this scheme. Excise evasion under this liberal scheme is generally resorted to by following such malpractices as incorrect accounting of goods, undervaluation of goods, and flouting the conditions subject to which any goods may be exempted from duty.

16.4.3 Compounded Levy Scheme: This is another procedure for the benefit of small-scale sector and for administrative convenience. Levying of excise duties on small-scale sector has always remained a major problem of the Indian excise system. In many cases, small-scale sector accounts for a significant portion of the output of an industry and it becomes necessary to subject it to excise taxation. However, the procedures adopted for collection of excise from big firms have often been found expensive and time-consuming when applied to small firms. This has necessitated the adoption of special procedures suitable for small-scale sector. Under the compounded levy scheme introduced in 1954, a lump sum payment is made on the basis of some installations, e.g. the number of looms in case of textile units. Once the compounded levy has been paid, the producer becomes free from all excise formalities except to maintain a record of looms in operation. The scheme is applicable at present to small units producing *khandasari* and cotton fabrics produced on powerlooms. This system affords considerable advantages to the small producers insofar as they are saved from the cumbersome normal excise procedures and also by the fact that the fiscal burden under compounded levy is generally lower than the burden under normal procedures.

16.5 New Excise Tariff Nomenclature

The year 1986 was a landmark in the evolution of excise taxation in India. In that year a new internationally accepted harmonised system of commodity classification was introduced in place of the then existing antiquated system introduced by the British. The history of excise tariff classification dates back to the year 1944 when the Central Excises and Salt Act was passed, consolidating separate enactments for different goods. This Act of 1944 covered 11 tariff items which were arranged in alphabetical order.

In 1960, the tariff items, the number of which had soared to 30, were rearranged in accordance with the sections of the Standard International Trade Classification (SITC). By 1986, the excise tariff schedule covered 137 tariff items and if account is taken of the sub-items, the number was well over 355 main classifications. The description of tariff commodities was based on the definitions of the Indian Standard Institution, and the descriptions and explanatory notes of the Customs Co-operation Council Nomenclature (CCCN). The domestic trade parlance was also relied upon.

On September 22, 1984, the Government set up a Technical Study Group to undertake a comprehensive review of the then existing tariff nomenclature. The Group drafted a comprehensive and elaborate tariff nomenclature broadly patterned on Harmonised System Nomenclature (HSN), fully corresponding up to 2-digit level (i.e. Chapter level) in respect of 82 of the effective 96 chapters in the HSN. It also suggested that the new tariff should be provided for by a separate Act to be called the Central Excise Tariff Act in place of the then existing system of tariff being governed by the First Schedule of the Central Excises and Salt Act, 1944.

The recommendation of the Technical Study Group as regards the new tariff nomenclature was accepted by the Government and a new Central Excise Tariff Act, 1985, was passed for the purpose. The excise tariff based on the internationally accepted harmonised commodity description and coding system came into effect from February 28, 1986, ushering a new era in excise taxation. The Schedule of the Central Excise Tariff Act, 1985, describes the excisable commodities and the rate of duty leviable on them. The new tariff is spread over 91 chapters and covers around 700 four-digit headings and 1,400 six-digit headings.

16.6 Administration of Excise Taxation

There is an elaborate administrative machinery for the collection of excise duties. At the apex level is the Central Board of Excise and Customs which is a statutory Board forming part of the Department of Revenue in the Ministry of Finance. The Board, consisting of a chairman and five members, is responsible for the proper collection of customs and Central excise duties, and framing and implementation of related fiscal policies under the control and direction of the Union Finance Minister.

At the field level, under the Central Board of Excise and Customs there are 34 Commissionerates of Central excise entrusted with the task of collecting Central excise duties. Each of the Commissionerates is headed by a Commissioner of Central Excise who is aided by a number of Additional Commissioners and Deputy Commissioners. A group of Commissionerates is headed by a Chief Commissioner.

For administrative convenience, each Commissionerate is divided into a number of divisions, each such division headed by an Assistant Commissioner. A division is further sub-divided into a number of ranges. Each range is headed by a Superintendent of Central Excise who in turn is assisted by a number of Inspectors.

In fact, the range is the basic unit in the administrative set up responsible for the proper assessment of Central excise duties and generation of the statistical information relating to revenue collection. The range is the primary unit which is in contact with the assessees and tries to ensure that the laws and procedures are properly followed by the production units.

To ensure that the goods are properly classified, assessable value correctly determined, and the duties correctly paid, each Commissionerate has an internal audit wing which is headed by an Additional Commissioner directly responsible to the Commissioner of Central Excise. The internal audit is in addition to the statutory audit conducted by the Comptroller and Auditor-General of India.

Each Commissionerate has an anti-evasion wing headed by an Additional Commissioner directly responsible to the Commissioner of Central Excise. The anti-evasion wing makes checks on the basis of intelligence and information to ensure that proper duties are paid and there is no evasion of duties or leakage of revenue. In some Commissionerates, there is a separate Commissioner to look after the judicial and adjudication work. There are Commissioners who attend to appeals against orders passed by officers lower in rank to them.

Moreover, a number of supportive organisations under the Central Board of Excise and Customs undertake work of a specialised nature. Thus, there is the Directorate of Inspection headed by a Chief Commissioner which undertakes the inspection of Central excise formations. The Directorate of Anti-Evasion has the responsibility to ensure all-India co-ordination of anti-evasion work. The National Academy of Customs, Excise and Narcotics is entrusted with the task of training officers. The Directorate of Publicity and Public Relations is responsible for printing and publicity. The Directorate of Statistics and Intelligence is responsible for compiling and updating statistical information.

16.7 Revenue Significance

In the post-Independence period, the relative share of excise duties in Central Government's tax collections has increased precipitously. In 1950-51, excise duties accounted for a modest 16.8 per cent of the total Central tax collections: Rs. 68 crore out of Rs. 404 crore. Within a span of 20 years, the proportionate share shot up to 54.9 per cent in 1970-71. It declined to 49.3 per cent in 1980-81 and further down to 42.6 per cent in 1990-91. It was estimated at 23.8 per cent in the 2007-2008 budget (Table 16.2). A Government document noted the following

Table 16.2: Trends in the Relative Significance of Union Excise Duties in Gross Tax Revenues* of the Central Government: Selected Years

(Rs. crore)

Central taxes	1950-51	1960-61	1970-71	1980-81	1990-91	2000-01	2007-08#
A+B Gross tax revenues	404 (100.0)	888 (100.0)	3,206 (100.0)	13,179 (100.0)	57,576 (100.0)	1,88,603 (100.0)	5,48,122 (100.0)
A. Direct taxes	174 (43.1)	290 (32.6)	870 (27.1)	3,004 (22.8)	11,025 (19.1)	68,306 (36.2)	2,67,490 (48.8)
B. Indirect taxes of which	229 (56.7)	599 (67.5)	2,337 (72.9)	10,175 (77.2)	46,552 (80.9)	1,20,297 (63.8)	2,80,632 (51.2)
2. Union excise duties	68 (16.8)	414 (46.6)	1,759 (54.9)	6,500 (49.3)	24,514 (42.6)	68,526 (36.3)	1,30,220 (23.8)

* Before transferring States' share in Central taxes; # Budget estimates.

Figures in parentheses are corresponding percentages of gross tax revenues.

Sources: Government of India, Ministry of Finance, *Explanatory Memorandum on the Budget of the Central Government* (various years); *Receipts Budget* (various years); and *Budget at a Glance*, 2007-08.

reasons for this downward trend, "The buoyancy of excise has suffered because of a variety of factors including numerous exemptions and concessions which have given rise to substantial administrative and legal complexities. Recent years have witnessed an unprecedented increase in litigation." [7]

Although excise duties are imposed on a large number of commodities, a substantial proportion of revenue is derived from a limited number of items. These high revenue yielding commodities include iron and steel, motor spirit, tyres and tubes, cigarettes, cement, plastics and refined diesel oil. It is noteworthy that many of the high revenue yielding items are commodities of mass consumption and therefore the burden of excise duties falls on all sections of society.

16.8 Commodity Coverage

As already noted, excise taxation in India was fairly selective in terms of commodity coverage during the pre-Independence period. However, the need for resources required for planned economic development made it necessary to rely on excise taxation for additional funds. This was particularly so in view of the extremely narrow base for direct taxation and the dwindling relative revenue significance of customs duties owing to euphoria for import restrictions and substitution. The scope for extension of excise coverage improved considerably as development efforts were intensified for the production of industrial goods that enjoyed a relatively large and stable domestic market.

The Taxation Enquiry Commission (TEC), 1953-54, after having studied the then existing excise system, made important recommendations in terms of commodity coverage. It recommended the extension of excise coverage to sewing machines, vegetable oils, woollen textiles, biscuits, paper, dry batteries, electric lamps, aerated waters, electric fans, glass and glassware, paints and varnishes, and ceramics. In the opinion of the TEC these industries had developed sufficiently as a result of protection and it was necessary to impose excises on them to raise the much needed revenue for financing development programmes.

Consequent upon the recommendations of the TEC, the history of excise taxation in India since 1954 is one of increasing commodity coverage. Cement, footwear, rayon or artificial silk fabrics, and soap were added to the excise system in 1954. In 1955, excise duties were imposed on paints and varnishes, paper, woollen fabrics, electric batteries, electric light bulbs, and electric fans. In 1956, the excise net was extended to vegetable non-essential oils, rayon or synthetic fibres and yarn, and motor cars.

With the start of production of diesel oil and other fuel oils at the new refineries in Bombay, excise duty was imposed on a variety of petroleum products for the first time in 1956. These included refined diesel oil, diesel oil, and furnace oil. In 1959, excise duties were imposed on asphalt, bitumen, and tar.

The early 1960s witnessed another big expansion in the coverage of excise taxation in India. In 1960, eleven additional goods were subjected to excise duties including aluminium, pig iron, silk fabrics, and motor vehicles. In 1962, the number of additional products brought under the excise system was sixteen and included, *inter alia*, soda ash, caustic soda, cosmetics and toilet preparations, glass and glassware, copper and copper alloys etc. In 1962, ten more products including gases, rubber products, plywood, jute manufactures, and iron and steel products were covered under the excise net.

In 1968, duties were imposed on radio-parts, steel furniture, leather cloth, and chocolates. The biggest expansion was witnessed in 1971 when 25 additional products including linoleum, ready-made garments, vacuum flasks, and pressure cookers were brought under the excise net. The process of covering more and more items under the excise system reached its pinnacle when Tariff Item No. 68 was introduced in 1975. Tariff Item No. 68 was a catch-all item which encompassed all goods not elsewhere specified in the excise tariff. This residual tariff item was abolished with the introduction of a harmonised system of commodity classification introduced from February 28, 1986. The large assortment of commodities under this head got scattered under proper heads in the new nomenclature of excise tariff.

The Tax Reforms Committee, 1991, identified many items which are currently outside the excise net but which could be considered for levying excise duty. Some of the identified items are: butter and cheese, skimmed milk powder, spices, fertilisers, feature films, wood pulp, umbrellas, bicycles, toys and sports goods, buttons, and vacuum flasks.

16.9 Excise Tariff Structure

Once the commodities for excise taxation are identified, the next step is to formulate a tariff structure for various commodities. The nature of excise tariff and the issues related to its rationalisation are now described.

16.9.1 Statutory versus Effective Rates: Rates of excise duty approved by the Parliament are termed as statutory or tariff rates. However, the Government enjoys the power to exempt, by notification, any excisable goods from the whole or any part of duty leviable on such goods. In exercise of this power, the Government determines and notifies from time to time the effective rates of duty. The rationale for granting such powers to the executive is that during the period intervening two consecutive budgets, necessary adjustments might be made to regulate exports, consumption, and prices of different commodities. However, the delegation of this power to the executive has led to frequent changes in excise rates, creating an unsettling atmosphere for trade and industry and problems for the administration.

Moreover, since the notifications are technically not rules, there is no obligation to place them on the table of the House. Consequently, the Parliament does not always have the information on the variations made in the rates approved by it. The determination of the operative or effective rates of duty by executive decisions leads to abridgement of Parliamentary control over the excise system. Duty changes should be discussed and legislated in sessions of Parliament which are held regularly at short intervals.

Under the Central Excise Tariff Act, 1985, the Government is empowered to enhance the rates of duty specified in the Schedule of the Act through notifications. The increase of duty is subject to certain limits and such powers are exercised only in emergent circumstances. The notifications bringing into force such increases are subject to approval by the Parliament. The said limits are: (a) in case where the rate of duty immediately before the issue of notification is nil, a rate of duty not exceeding 50 per cent *ad valorem* may be specified, and (b) in any other case, the increase in the rate of duty shall not be more than twice the rate of duty in force immediately before the issue of notification.

16.9.2 Specific versus *Ad Valorem* Duties [8]: In the early days of the excise system of independent India, the emphasis was on specific rates due to administrative reasons. However, the emphasis shifted to *ad valorem* rates when the economy started experiencing frequent spells of inflation. The 1970s saw a big shift from specific rates of duty to *ad valorem* rates. While introducing the change in the 1969-70 budget, the Finance Minister observed, "...*ad valorem* duties are more rational than specific duties whose incidence declines during periods of rising prices and increases when prices fall. *Ad valorem* duties can also act as a spur to reduction in costs and prices." [9] He converted the then existing specific rates into *ad valorem* rates on cement, vegetable products, electric fans, lighting tubes and bulbs, soaps, soda, and sodium silicate. The change of duties on paper and cotton fabrics into *ad valorem* tax was effected in 1976 and on paints, varnishes, radios, and tape recorders in 1977.

However, beginning with the 1980s, the tendency to shift to *ad valorem* rates was not only halted but reversed in view of an unprecedented spurt in litigation which mainly pertained to disputes over classification and valuation of goods for purposes of excise levies. As a measure to combat tax avoidance and evasion, the basis of duty was changed from *ad valorem* to *ad valorem*-cum-specific rate or specific rate on a number of commodities. Important commodities where the shift took place (with year of change given in brackets) were: flat glass, aluminium metal (1982), paper, aerated waters, motor cars, cigarettes, sugar (1983), paper boards, tyres for buses and trucks (1984), gases, tubes and flaps of tyres, and colour television sets (1985).

The Technical Study Group on Central Excise Tariff, 1985, made estimates of the relative revenue significance of various forms of excise duty. The share of specific duties (including the specific component of *ad valorem*-cum-specific duties) was estimated at Rs. 8242.91 crore or 66.7 per cent of the total estimated excise revenue of Rs. 12361.35 crore for the year 1985-86. The rest of the revenue was attributable to *ad valorem* duties. Broadly speaking, specific duties accounted for two-thirds of the revenue and the *ad valorem* duties for the remaining one-third. [10]

The balance further tilted in favour of specific duties as the policy of conversion from *ad valorem* rates to specific rates continued right up to 1990-91. In this connection, the Tax Reforms Committee, 1991, observed, "As a result of this gradual shift to more and more specific rates over the years, the share of revenue from specific-rated items has increased from a level of about 46 per cent of the total revenue in 1981-82 to 65 per cent in 1986-87 and has currently (presumably 1990-91) reached a level of about 70 per cent." [11] The Committee examined the advantages and disadvantages of *ad valorem* and specific rates of duty and concluded, "the advantages of having *ad valorem* duties far outweigh the administrative benefits derived by switching over to specific duties. In a system of comprehensive taxation with a wide coverage of Modvat, it would be necessary to have by and large only *ad valorem* duties in order to ensure a rational system of taxation." [12] Following the recommendations of the Committee, a modest switch over to *ad valorem* rates was made in the 1992-93 budget.

At present, important commodities which bear wholly specific rates of duty are cigarettes, coffee, tea, sugar, beverages, mineral fuels, mineral oils, silk, man-made staple fibres, and iron and steel. *Ad valorem* rates of duty predominate for commodities including organic chemicals, pharmaceutical products, leather, footwear, ceramic products, tools and implements, machinery and mechanical appliances, electrical machinery and equipment, and miscellaneous manufactured articles. A few commodities, viz. cotton fabrics, paper and paper boards, are subject to *ad valorem*-cum-specific rates of duty.

16.9.3 Multiplicity of Excise Tariff: The excise rate structure is provided by the Schedule of the Central Excise Tariff Act, 1985, which includes goods ranging from toys to nuclear reactors. The Schedule is divided into 20 sections covering 96 chapters. Goods falling under each chapter are divided and sub-divided into numerous headings and sub-headings. The statutory rate of duty applicable in respect of each item is shown against the appropriate commodity heading/sub-heading. These statutory rates are modified, if necessary, by Government notifications to determine effective rates of duty.

Prior to tax reforms initiated in 1991, excise taxation in India was an interesting example of the multitude of rates which were subject to frequent revisions. Numerous considerations contributed to the complexity of excise rates. The labyrinthine intricacies of the tariff often led to confusion and litigation amongst the taxpayers and revenue authorities.

Commodities such as sewing machines, water coolers, and bicycles, though on the tariff list, were completely exempt from the payment of duty. However, a host of other commodities were subject to a wide amplitude of excise rates. The rate of duty on necessities of life like food products (cheese, butter, vegetable oils), pharmaceutical products, and footwear ranged from 10 to 15 per cent *ad valorem*. Rates of excise duty on semi-luxuries like washing machines, tape recorders, refrigerators, and colour televisions ranged from 25 per cent to 40 per cent *ad valorem*. Luxury items like cosmetics and air-conditioners suffered a high rate of duty ranging from 100 to 110 per cent.

Most capital goods, classified under chapter 84 of excise tariff, were subject to duty ranging from 15 to 20 per cent *ad* valorem. Some important items under this category were machine tools, cranes, agricultural machinery, textile machinery, printing machinery, calculating machines, automatic data processing machines, and other office machines.

Tobacco items were, and continue to be, conspicuous by high rates of duty. Successive upward revision of excise duty on cigarettes has all along remained a notable feature of tobacco tariff in India. Upward revision of excise duty on cigarettes is almost an annual feature. No surprise that the commodity has earned such nicknames as *annual hardy, old faithful* etc. In the 1997-98 budget, excise duty on various categories of cigarettes was increased ranging from Rs. 20 to Rs. 70 per thousand.

Broadly speaking, necessities of life were either exempt or paid a low rate of duty, semi-luxuries were moderately taxed, and luxuries and tobacco products stood out distinctly as high-rated tariff items. Capital goods were subject to a relatively low rate of duty.

16.9.4 Committee on Rationalisation and Simplification of the Tax Structure (Chairman: S. Bhoothalingam), 1968: In 1968, the Government of India appointed Mr. S. Bhoothalingam to examine the structure of direct and indirect taxes in India. In his report he recommended, *inter alia*, a general excise duty at the rate of 10 per cent *ad valorem* on all manufactured products. [13] However, this recommendation was not accepted by the Government.

16.9.5 Indirect Taxation Enquiry Committee (Chairman: L.K. Jha), 1978: The problem of multiplicity of rates was also considered by the Indirect Taxation Enquiry Committee, 1978 which recommended a set of four excise rates. The Committee observed, "Instead of a pattern of which some product groups are very heavily taxed while others have remained either totally exempt or have been taxed at very low rates, the attempt should be to tax all consumer products, including those now falling under Tariff Item No. 68, at rates of 10, 20, 30 or 40 per cent (cumulative), though some exceptional products may need to be taxed at lower or higher rates on special consideration." [14]

By suggesting a 10 to 40 per cent range, the Committee virtually favoured a ceiling on excise rates. The Government disfavoured any drastic regrouping of the then existing rates. In his 1979-80 budget speech the Finance Minister observed, "A major restructuring of the excise tariff has to be ruled out in view of the need for resources and on other pragmatic considerations. Also, there is reason to apprehend that a major departure from the present pattern of excise taxation may upset the balance between different sectors of production." [15]

16.9.6 Technical Study Group on Excise Tariff (Chairman: J. Dutta), 1985: The Technical Study Group on Central Excise Tariff, 1985, also favoured a drastic reduction in the number of duty rates to simply duty collection and compliance. The group recommended a band of five duty rates: middle rate, two rates below it and two above. Besides this, it also suggested a *zero rate* category. The middle rate (M) was defined to represent overall average incidence of excise duties. The two rates below this middle rate (L1 and L2) were suggested for adoption for inputs and important items of real mass consumption. The two rates in the upper scale (H1 and H2) could be applied to a few inputs, consumer durables and items consumed largely by the rich. The *zero rate* was recommended for products which deserve exceptional treatment on economic or social or administrative considerations.

The Group attempted only a broad and vague exercise of rate levels in terms of middle, below the middle, and above the middle rates of duty without specifying, even on a tentative basis, the duty rates in numerical terms. By leaving the actual fixation of rates to fiscal authorities, the Group left the exercise wide open.

The Finance Minister announced, in his 1997-98 budget speech, three new rates of excise duty, namely 8 per cent, 13 per cent and 18 per cent. He was of the view that eventually the excise rate should gravitate towards a mean rate of 18 per cent.

16.9.7 Triple Rate Excise Structure: Multiple rates of commodity taxes have long been considered a weakness of the indirect tax system of India.

Admitting the problems created by the multiplicity of rates, the Finance Minister in his 1999-2000 budget speech observed, "The multiple rates of indirect tax are generally recognised to be a major source of misclassification, tax evasion and avoidance and cumbersome litigation. The multiplicity also encourages inefficient allocation of resources. Over a 100 countries in the world now enjoy the benefits of a Value Added Tax (VAT) with very small number of rates in each case." [16]

Thus, in a landmark move, the Finance Minister announced in his 1999-2000 budget a triple rate excise structure. In other words, the then existing 11 major ad valorem rates were reduced to 3, viz. a central rate of 16 per cent, a merit rate of 8 per cent and a demerit rate of 24 per cent. This was done by (a) merging the existing rates of 5 per cent, 10 per cent and 12 per cent into the existing 8 per cent rate, (b) creating a new rate of 16 per cent by merging the existing 13 per cent, 15 per cent and 18 per cent rates into it and (c) fixing a new rate of 24 per cent in substitution of the existing rate of 25 per cent. The initiative of the Finance Minister to rationalise the rate structure of excise system was widely appreciated.

16.9.8 Task Force on Indirect Taxes (Chairman: Vijay Kelkar), 2002: The Task Force on Indirect Taxes recommended the following excise duty structure (Table 16.3).

Table 16.3: Central Excise Duty Structure Recommended by the Task Force on Indirect Taxes

0 per cent	For life-saving drugs and equipments, security items, food items, necessities and the like, and agricultural products.
6 per cent	For processed food products and matches.
14 per cent	Standard rate for all items not mentioned against other rates.
20 per cent	For motor vehicles, air-conditioners and aerated water.
Separate rates for tobacco products and their substitutes (like pan masala)	

Source: Government of India, Ministry of Finance and Company Affairs, *Report of the Task Force on Indirect Taxes*, December 2002, p. 181.

As regards duty exemption for the small scale sector, the Task Force on Indirect Taxes recommended

- Duty exemption should be extended to only small units with a turnover of Rs. 50 lakh.
- Duty exemption limit for the larger SSI units should be gradually brought down to Rs. 50 lakh as per the following time frame: from Rs. 100 lakh to Rs.

75 lakh by the year 2004-05 and from Rs. 75 lakh to Rs. 50 lakh by the year 2005-06.

16.10 Excises on Inputs

One perennial problem of the Indian excise system has been the taxation of inputs (raw materials, components, and other intermediates) and the resulting cascading effect on the prices of final products. Prior to the Second Five Year Plan (1956-61), excise coverage was limited to consumer goods with the notable exception of steel ingots. However, the need for additional resources for successive Plans necessitated extension of the excise net to capital goods and raw materials. Various inputs like internal combustion engines, aluminium, cotton yarn, woollen yarn, fertilisers, chemicals, were, and continue to be, within the excise ambit. The disadvantages of input excises are well-known. [17] However, levies on inputs form an integral part of the excise system in India for reasons of sheer administrative convenience.

16.10.1 Pre-MODVAT Arrangements: Prior to the introduction of MODVAT in 1986, there were provisions in the Central Excises and Salt Rules, 1944, under which certain inputs were exempted from taxation to minimise the cumulative effect of excise levies. Thus, Rule 56-A of the said Rules, introduced in 1962, allowed the manufacturers of certain notified finished excisable goods to bring excise-paid components (for example compressors for refrigerators) to take credit for the said duty in the Proforma Credit Account to get adjustment of duty on the final excisable good.

The Indirect Taxation Enquiry Committee, 1978, which made an in-depth study of the cascading effect of input excises, recommended a wider extension of Rule 56-A to products falling under different tariff items. The same Committee recommended also the introduction of Value Added Tax (VAT) at the manufacturing stage, called MANVAT, to tackle the problem of cascading effect of excise taxation.

The Long Term Fiscal Policy (December 1985) also envisaged the extension of the Proforma Credit Scheme and observed, "The basic approach will be to move towards an extension of the present system of proforma credit to all excisable commodities with the exception of a few like petroleum, tobacco, and textile products. This programme would amount to a modified system of VAT or MODVAT for short. The programme will be implemented in a phased manner over a period of years, taking due account of the revenue implications, the need to revise administrative procedures and the lessons from experience gained in the early stages of the reform." [18] In pursuance of the proposal made in the Long Term Fiscal Policy Statement, the Government introduced a modified system of value added tax or MODVAT with effect from March 1, 1986.

16.10.2 MODVAT Scheme: The features and advantages of MODVAT scheme are explained below.

A. Features: MODVAT scheme provides for instant and complete reimbursement of excise duty and additional duty of customs (countervailing duty) paid on the components and raw materials when used in the manufacture of the final products. Articles which are not used as inputs in the manufacturing process are not eligible for credit under this scheme.

Initially, the MODVAT scheme covered 38 chapters of the schedule to the Central Excise Tariff Act, 1985. These chapters pertained to the products of chemical and allied industries, paints and packaging materials, plastics, glass and glassware, rubber products, base metals and articles of base metals, machinery and mechanical appliances including electrical equipment, motor vehicles, and certain miscellaneous manufactured products. The scheme was extended to all the remaining chapters (except those relating to textiles, tobacco, and the petroleum sector) in 1987. The extension covered food products, mineral products, leather and travel goods, footwear, paper and paper-board, wood and cork products, asbestos cement products, and precious metals. As long as the inputs and the final products are covered by the specified chapters, credit of duty on inputs is available. In 1994, MODVAT scheme was extended to tobacco, fibres, yarn and fabrics, and petroleum products (excluding motor spirit and high speed diesel oil) used as input. The features of the MODVAT scheme are as follows.

1. The credit under MODVAT is available to a manufacturer of a final product only if the final product is dutiable. Where the final product manufactured by a manufacturer is exempt from excise duty then no credit of the duty paid on the inputs is available. Credit is allowed only after the evidence of payment of duty has been received by the Department.

2. Where the same input is used for different finished products, some of which are not dutiable, the credit of duty is allowed only for that part attributable to inputs which are used for the manufacture of dutiable finished products.

3. The credit of the duty paid on the inputs under the MODVAT scheme may be utilised for payment of duty on the final products in which the inputs are used.

4. Under the MODVAT scheme, credit of duty is not restricted to raw materials and components only but covers all specified inputs which are used in the manufacture of final products.

5. Machines, plant, equipments, apparatus, tools or appliances used in the manufacture of the final products are not covered by the term 'inputs' for the purpose of MODVAT benefits.

6. Under the MODVAT scheme, inputs may be either procured from outside

or manufactured within the factory. In either case, the duty credit would be available to the extent of duty actually paid.

The Government had made it clear in its Long Term Fiscal Policy that the proposed MODVAT scheme was to be broadly revenue-neutral. Thus, along with the introduction of MODVAT which considerably reduced the cost of final products, the rates of duty on final products were suitably revised upwards by the Finance Act, 1986, to retain the collection of excise duties at the earlier level. This was justified on grounds of resource mobilisation for the Plans.

B. Advantages: MODVAT scheme is claimed to have the following advantages:

1. It aims at making excise levies transparent so that the effective rate of taxation on a particular commodity can be known. This information will be helpful in undertaking meaningful studies of excise incidence. The results of these studies may be used to control excise burden on different commodities to ensure the desired degree of progressivity in the excise levies.

2. It seeks to avoid cascading effects associated with a traditional turnover tax. In particular, it will work as a cost-saving device through the availability of instant credit of the duties paid on the inputs and the consequent reduction of the interest costs.

3. MODVAT scheme will improve the competitive strength of the small-scale sector by allowing credit of duty which may be in excess of the duty actually paid on the inputs made by the small-scale units.

4. MODVAT scheme is claimed to encourage indigenisation because full set off is available when indigenous inputs are used. However, no credit of basic and auxiliary customs duties is permissible on imported materials and components. Although MODVAT scheme provides for set off of countervailing duty [19], this element of import duty is not very significant in comparison with other elements of import duty viz. basic and auxiliary duties. As the scope of MODVAT is widened, the process of indigenisation would gather momentum.

5. MODVAT scheme is designed to encourage exports by making them more competitive in the international market. Since MODVAT allows set off through different stages of production, the final duty becomes clear on final goods which can be exported without payment of duty under bond. The payment of duty drawback will be swifter in view of the transparency of excise duty.

6. It is claimed that MODVAT will check excise evasion because credit of input duty cannot be claimed unless actual production is declared to the excise authorities.

7. MODVAT scheme will also help reduce the number of disputes, arising on account of classifications requiring lower or higher rates of duty, because the

duty element on a large number of components will become irrelevant for manufacturers in view of set off. Previously, a selective set off triggered disputes as regards the eligibility of an input for set off. The introduction of Harmonised System Nomenclature will further reduce the scope for ambiguities.

Some experts feel that MODVAT is old wine in a new bottle because the facility under it is practically the same as was and is still available under Rule 56-A. In other words, MODVAT scheme is only an extension and liberalisation of the proforma credit facility in operation for the last three decades. Though some degree of similarity does exist, the two schemes cannot be termed identical. Rule 56-A scheme was restrictive and had several procedural formalities, e.g. a manufacturer had to intimate the Excise Department about the arrival of input materials for verification by the excise officials. Moreover, it was applicable on a commodity-to-commodity basis and involved discretion in taking decisions. MODVAT scheme is more comprehensive and rule-based and therefore curtails the discretionary powers of the Excise Department. MODVAT credit on inputs can be availed on the basis of a duplicate copy of the invoice.

The Tax Reforms Committee, 1991, examined, *inter alia,* the scope of extending the MODVAT scheme and observed, "there is no alternative to gradually transforming the present excise tax system, consisting of two parts, namely (a) Modvat and (b) excise on gross value basis with no set off for some sectors, into a genuine VAT at the manufacturing level. Manufacturing and such a VAT should include also the 'manufacture' of services although some services may be exempted on practical considerations." [20]

16.10.3 Introduction of CENVAT: In his 1999-2000 budget, the Finance Minister had introduced three ad valorem rates of basic excise duty, namely 8 per cent, 16 per cent and 24 per cent. Furthering the reform of excise taxation, the 2000-01 budget introduced a single rate Central Value Added Tax (CENVAT) by converging the three ad valorem rates to a single rate of 16 per cent. The 8 per cent excise rate was abolished and most of the items under it were moved to 16 per cent rate. Similarly, items that were mainly in the nature of raw materials or intermediates were moved from the 24 per cent rate to 16 per cent CENVAT.

However, in addition to the 16 per cent CENVAT rate, three rates of special excise, viz. 8 per cent, 16 per cent, and 24 per cent were introduced. While the CENVAT rate is modvatable, the special excise duties are not, i.e. users cannot avail of MODVAT credit of these duties. Some of the commodities on which special excise duties apply include white cement, glazed tiles, cosmetics, air conditioners, aerated water and chewing tobacco. Since these commodities are not in the nature of inputs therefore they are not modvatable.

MODVAT scheme (rechristened as CENVAT scheme) was further expanded and rationalised in the sense that now all inputs (excepting high speed diesel oil and petrol) and all capital goods are included in the eligible list of MODVAT scheme. However, the availability of MODVAT credit on capital goods is spread over a period of two years.

Underlining the significance of CENVAT, the Finance Minister observed that it would eliminate disputes pertaining to classification of goods and remove uncertainties in the minds of producers. He hoped that the establishment of CENVAT would encourage the State Governments to implement their agreed programme for converting their sales tax into VAT by April 1, 2001.

It is noteworthy that under the Constitution, the Central Government is empowered to impose excise duty on goods produced or manufactured. It has no power to carry forward the tax up to the retail stage. Thus, CENVAT is a kind of VAT at the manufacturing stage. In any case, it has paved the way for a national VAT.

16.10.4 Further Simplification: In his 2001-02 budget, the Finance Minister reduced the three rates of special excise duty to a single rate of 16 per cent. In other words, the 8 per cent and 24 per cent rates of special excise duty were abolished. Some of the items which bear 16 per cent basic rate of CENVAT plus 16 per cent special duty (32 per cent total duty) include aerated soft drinks, soft drink concentrates and motor cars).

Following these measures, about 80 per cent of the revenue in respect of ad valorem duties comes from the single rate of 16 per cent and about 17 per cent from the combined rate of 32 per cent. [21] Feeling satisfied after completing the task of excise rate rationalisation, the Finance Minister remarked, "...in the matter of rates of duties of excise, I have almost achieved the ultimate with only one basic rate of CENVAT and one rate of special excise duty." [22] Undoubtedly, the Government has provided a stable excise system to create confidence among the entrepreneurs, particularly the prospective ones, so that they may plan their investment and production without the Damocles sword of excise changes hanging over their heads.

16.11 Exemptions and Concessions

16.11.1 Rationale: As in other countries, exemptions and concessions are an integral part of the Indian excise system. Excise preferences and reliefs are given to promote a wide spectrum of socio-economic objectives. If judiciously used, such tax preferences can become an effective tool of economic change on desired lines. The rationale for excise preferences is as follows.

1. Exemptions and concessions are necessary to ensure progressivity in the structure of commodity taxation.

2. Excise preferences are justified to induce entrepreneurs to undertake activities which they would otherwise shirk, e.g. adopting labour-intensive techniques of production. Concessions are designed to promote enterprises deemed *vital* by society though it is controversial as to which activities are *vital* and require governmental support.
3. Exemptions/concessions provide the desired flexibility to the tax system to deal with changing market situation. They are used as a corrective mechanism to stabilise demand, production, and profits of different industries. Due to continuous diversification of the economy and inflation, markets for various commodities have not remained stable in India after Independence. Because of the changing market conditions, the levels of profit in different industries have also been fluctuating and on balance have shown a rising trend. Excise rates, it may be argued, should be modified upward to mop up excess profits and downward to boost sluggish demand for idle-capacity industries.
4. Exemptions may be granted on administrative considerations. The duty on unmanufactured tobacco was abolished in 1979 mainly on account of the administrative difficulty of assessing and collecting duty from a large number of growers, and curers. Similarly, exemption of smaller of the small industries is also due to administrative problems. Agricultural products are also exempt owing to the same reason.

16.11.2 Problems Created by Concessions: The desirability of excise preferences is to be viewed against problems created by them.

1. Excise concessions narrow the tax base and therefore shrink governmental revenues.
2. Excise concessions interfere with the designing of the excise system and lead to complexities in the excise law which in turn may lead to tax evasion and litigation.
3. They also obscure the evaluation of excise system, particularly from equity angle.
4. Excise concession to a particular industry may lead to a chain reaction, i.e. similar demands by other industries, causing unsettling effects on producers, consumers, and the administration. Exemptions/concessions are often the result of persistent representations and pressure tactics by industry and trade than any economic justification.
5. It is not always possible to segregate the effects of duty reduction on production, costs, prices, and consumption because duty concessions operate in conjunction with other non-tax policy measures to affect the production process.

16.11.3 General Exemptions: There are various general exemptions which purport to serve a wide variety of socio-economic objectives. Thus, goods of the following description are exempt from the whole of the duty of excise leviable thereon.

1. All excisable goods, produced in a technical, educational and research institute during the course of imparting technical training of an academic or vocational nature.
2. All excisable goods donated for the welfare of defence personnel.
3. All excisable goods donated to the National Defence Fund or to the Ministry of Defence.
4. Excisable goods, supplied as stores for consumption on board a vessel of the Indian navy.
5. All excisable goods sent abroad as exhibits in any international trade fair or exhibition.

Apart from these general exemptions, excise tariff is extensively used to serve a host of other objectives including export promotion, industrial development, and mopping up a part of high profits earned by certain industries. Excise exemptions and concessions are particularly important in promoting labour-intensive technology and small-scale industries. Central excise law contains provisions the sole objective of which is employment generation. Products of a number of industries are exempt from excise duty if they are manufactured without the aid of power. Duty differentials have been used to discourage mechanisation in certain industries.

Similarly, concessions are available to the handloom sector of the textile industry. Processed *khadi* cloth woven on handloom wholly from hand spun cotton yarn or in admixture with similar silk and/or woollen yarn enjoys full exemption since 1969. Cotton fabrics manufactured on handlooms and processed by a factory owned by a registered handloom co-operative society enjoy full exemption from duty.

The Expert Committee on Tax Measures to Promote Employment, 1980, made estimates of the annual cost of protecting or subsidising employment through concessions in excise duties. It found that the annual cost of protecting or subsidising employment through concessions in excise duties was Rs. 523 per full-time worker in the handloom industry, Rs. 881 in *khandasari*, and Rs. 2,669 in the cottage sector of the match industry. [23]

16.11.4 Concessions to Small Industries: In line with Government's policy of encouraging small-scale industries, a wide range of concessions and exemptions from excise duty is available to small producers to enable them to stand in competition with large-scale manufacturers. Also, relatively simple and concessional procedures are followed for the assessment and collection of excises from the small-scale sector. As a part of the Comprehensive Policy Package on SSI and Tiny Sector announced by the Prime Minister on August 30, 2000, the excise exemption limit for SSI was raised from Rs. 50 lakh to Rs. 1 crore with effect from September 1, 2000.

16.11.5 Misuse of Concessions: Though preferential treatment to small units and labour-intensive methods of production is desirable, the misuse of these concessions has created doubts as regards the ultimate beneficiaries of such facilities. Concerned about the misuse of excise concessions, the Finance Minister in his 2001-2002 budget speech announced the withdrawal of exemption on certain items and observed, "Products of SSI are exempt from excise duty up to RS. one crore. This exemption is intended to provide fiscal support to the genuinely small producers. I propose to withdraw this exemption in respect of the following items, in which misuse of the exemption is more than likely:

- cotton yarn
- ball or roller bearings
- Arms and ammunition for private use." [24]

It has now been well-established that certain products, particularly footwear, domestic electrical appliances, electronic goods, and wires and cables are purchased on a fairly large scale by established concerns from the exempted sector and marketed in the brand names of such concerns. However, under the present scheme introduced in 1986, a small-scale manufacturer of excisable goods is allowed to clear his goods with the brand name of another manufacturer and is eligible for exemption for such clearances. It is clear that small producers depend heavily on private marketing organisations to sell their products and this dependence needs to be reduced by strengthening and building up co-operatives and other officially sponsored marketing organisations to market the products of small sector. This seems to be one way out of the existing dilemma.

Notes

1. Government of India, *Report of the Indian Taxation Enquiry Committee* (President: Sir Charles Todhunter), 1924-25, Vol. I, para 168.

2. *Ibid.*, para 155.

3. Government of India, Ministry of Finance, *Report of the Central Excise Reorganisation Committee* (Chairman: A.K. Chanda), 1963, p. 4.

4. D. T. Lakdawala and K.V. Nambiar, *Commodity Taxation in India* (Ahmedabad: Sardar Patel Institute of Economic and Social Research), 1972, p. 41.

5. Government of India, *Report of the Indian Fiscal Commission* (Chairman: Ibrahim Rahimatoola), 1921-22, p. 87.

6. Government of India, Ministry of Finance, *Report of the Taxation Enquiry Commission,* (Chairman: John Matthai), 1953-54, Vol. II, p. 323.

7. Government of India, *Long Term Fiscal Policy*, 1985, p.25.

8. Excises are levied in specific and/or *ad valorem* forms. A specific or volumetric duty represents a fixed amount of tax on a unit of the physical quantity of the product. This type of duty is generally preferred for commodities the classifications and sub-classifications of which are not numerous, i.e. the commodity is standardised, e.g. sugar. Specific duties are easy to apply and have the political and psychological advantages of obscuring the actual ratio of the tax to the selling price. They are, however, price-neutral, i.e. price changes, if any, in the product do not affect the revenue yield. Specific duties are quality-neutral also unless differential rates are prescribed with reference to the quality of the product.

Ad valorem duties are imposed as a fixed percentage of the price of the product taxed. They are preferred when a commodity has many classifications and sub-classifications, e.g. textiles. *Ad valorem* duties are responsive to price changes and thus help maintain the proportion of taxes in national income. The main problem in applying *ad valorem* rates is the determination of the tax base, i.e. valuation of production.

9. Government of India, Ministry of Finance, *Speeches of Union Finance Ministers, 1947-48 to 1984-85*, p. 313.

10. Government of India, Ministry of Finance, *Report of the Technical Study Group on Central Excise Tariff*, Part I, 1985, Table 6, p. 7.

11. Government of India, Ministry of Finance, *Interim Report of the Tax Reforms Committee* (Chairman: Raja Chelliah), 1991, p. 113.

12. *Ibid.*, p.114.

13. Government of India, Ministry of Finance, *Final Report on Rationalisation and Simplification of Tax Structure* (Chairman: S. Bhoothalingam), 1968, p. 8.

14. Government of India, Ministry of Finance, *Report of the Indirect Taxation Enquiry Committee* (Chairman: L.K. Jha), Part II, 1978, p. 174.

15. *Speeches of Union Finance Ministers, op. cit.*, p. 459.

16. Government of India, Ministry of Finance, *Budget Speech of the Finance Minister*, 1999-2000, Part B, p. 21.

17. Excises on inputs enhance costs and profits and therefore increase the prices of goods much more than the amount of excise collected. The cost of production increases because producers and middlemen require larger amounts of working capital to maintain the necessary stocks of inputs. Prices of finished products tend to reflect taxes imposed on inputs used. If the middlemen apply fixed percentage mark ups to purchase prices as their profit and if the purchase prices include taxes, the mark ups will be applicable to the tax component of the purchase price as well. In other words, increase in the price of the manufactures is in excess of the excise revenue accruing from input taxes.

Further still, excises on inputs may promote vertical integration in an industry, a trend which is harmful to the growth of small-scale sector. Lastly, input excises impose an inequitable burden on different economic classes by not discriminating between essential and non-essential uses of a product. For example, an excise on aluminium hits indiscriminately the use of the product for decoration purpose as well as for making utensils (generally used by the poor).

Notwithstanding the various disadvantages of input excises, governments in many countries impose duties on inputs due to administrative convenience. Many items of inputs are the end-product of one manufacturer but merely a component for another (e.g. tyres and tubes) and are also used as replacement items. Exemption of such items will be discrimination in favour of replacement consumption and certain commodities (say motor cars) may be sold with avoidable components and accessories stripped off. Moreover, provisions can be made in tax laws to minimise the cascading effects of input excises.

18. *Long Term Fiscal Policy, op. cit.*, p.38.

19. It is an element of import duty equivalent to excise duty on domestically produced goods.

20. Government of India, Ministry of Finance, *Final Report of the Tax Reforms Committee* (Chairman: Raja Chelliah), Part I, 1992, p.36.

21. Government of India, Ministry of Finance, *Budget Speech of the Finance Minister, 2001-2002, Part B*, p. 26.

22. Government of India, *Long Term Fiscal Policy*, 1985, p. 38

23. Government of India, Ministry of Finance, *Report of the Expert Committee on Tax Measures to Promote Employment* (Chairman: V.M. Dandekar), 1980, pp. 91, 113, and 117.

24. Government of India, Ministry of Finance, *Budget Speech of the Finance Minister, 2001-2002, Part B*, p. 27.

17

Taxation of Services

Service sector is very wide in its range. It includes, *inter alia*, health care, education, social security, leasing, entertainment, credit rating agencies, telecommunications, transport, publicity and advertising, insurance, banking, legal and financial services.

17.1 Justification for Taxing Services

From equity point of view, services should be taxed in the same way as goods. Taxation of goods and exclusion of services distorts the relative prices of goods vis-à-vis services, encouraging artificially the demand for services. In the process, the allocation of resources is also distorted. If tax is imposed on goods and not on services, a relatively high rate of tax would be required on goods to generate a given amount of revenue. If tax is imposed both on goods and services, a moderate tax rate can yield the given revenue. Administratively, taxation of both goods and services is desirable because it would reduce disputes pertaining to distinction between goods and services.

Like goods, services can also be classified into two broad categories: essential services (e.g. health and education) and luxury services (e.g. entertainment and tourism). The rationale for exemption/lenient tax treatment of essential services is the same as for essential goods. Similarly, luxury services should be taxed at a high rate like luxury goods.

17.2 Constitutional Provisions

A scrutiny of List II (State List) in the Seventh Schedule of the Constitution of India shows that State Governments are empowered to tax entertainment and professional services (entries 16 and 18 of List II). The Central Government had no specific powers to tax services when it introduced service tax on select services in 1994. It was done under its residual powers of taxation vide entry 97 of List I (Union List in the Seventh Schedule). The collection of service tax was entrusted to the excise department.

However, the Constitution (Eighty-eighth Amendment) Act, 2003 put service tax in the Union List by inserting entry 92C in that List. Furthermore, service tax was put under Article 268A of the Constitution which specifies that the principles of collection and appropriation of taxes on services will be determined by

Parliament. In other words, revenue from service tax is outside the purview of the Finance Commission.

17.3 Growth of Service Sector in India

The composition of GDP in India has undergone significant changes since 1980, and particularly after the launching of economic reforms in early 1990s. The relative share of agriculture in GDP which stood at 38.1 per cent in 1980-81, declined to 30.9 per cent in 1990-91, 26.8 per cent in 1998-99 and was recorded at 19.7 per cent for the year 2005-06. Conversely, the share of services increased from 41.0 per cent in 1980-81 to 43.7 per cent in 1990-91 and 60.9 per cent in 2005-06. The share of industry in GDP moved up from 20.9 per cent in 1980-81 to 28.4 per cent in 1990-91 but then declined gradually to stand at 19.5 per cent in 2005-06 (Table 17.1).

Table 17.1: Changes in Inter-sectoral Composition of GDP in India: Selected Years (per cent)

Year	Share in GDP		
	Agriculture	Industry	Services
1980-81	38.1	20.9	41.0
1984-85	35.9	22.9	41.1
1990-91	30.9	28.4	43.7
1995-96	26.0	26.7	47.0
1996-97	28.0	22.0	49.9
1997-98	26.4	22.3	51.2
1998-99	26.8	22.0	51.2
2001-02	24.4	19.3	56.3
2002-03	21.9	19.9	58.3
2003-04	22.2	19.5	58.3
2004-05	20.8	19.5	59.7
2005-06*	19.7	19.5	60.9

*Advance estimates.

Source: Reserve Bank of India, *Report on Currency and Finance*, 1998-99, p. V-6; *Report on Currency and Finance*, 2004-05, p.6.

The compositional shift in favour of the service sector, brought about by the rapid expansion of the service sector, is in line with the development experience of a number of countries. It is well-known that as an economy develops, the shares of industrial and service sectors in GDP increase at the cost of the agricultural sector.

The need to tax service sector is well recognised by the Government. To quote, "The tax revenue from the agricultural sector being negligible, the industrial sector continues to constitute the only principal tax base though it has suffered a reduction in the share of GDP over the period. Despite the fact that the services sector has shown substantial buoyancy, its contribution to the exchequer is not significant in relation to its sizeable share in GDP. Thus, in order to impart buoyancy to the revenue receipts and to provide consistency and equity in the tax structure via-a-via the composition of income, it is imperative to bring a major part of the services sector under the tax net." [2]

Although the contribution of service sector to GDP has increased over the years, the tax system has remained confined mainly to commodity production. In this connection, the Finance Minister observed in his 1994-95 budget speech, "There is no sound reason for exempting services from taxation when goods are taxed and many countries treat goods and services alike for tax purpose." [3] The Tax Reforms Committee (TRC) [Chairman: Raja Chelliah], 1991 also recommended imposition of tax on certain select services, viz. advertising, non-life insurance and telephone services and services of stock brokers.

17.4 Present Structure of Service Tax

In view of the need for additional resources, rising contribution of service sector to GDP and the recommendations of TRC, a modest effort was made in the 1994-95 budget when a 5 per cent tax was imposed on telephone and non-life insurance services and services of stock brokers with effect from July 1, 1994. The coverage of service tax was extended to advertising, courier and radio paging services from November 1, 1996.

In his 1997-98 budget speech, the Finance Minister maintained that services are products as much as manufactured goods and hence both must bear taxes. With these considerations in view he extended the service tax to the services provided by the following: transporters of goods by road, consulting engineers, custom house, steamer and clearing and forwarding agents, air travel agents, tour operators and car rental agencies, outdoor caterers, *pandal* contractors and *mandap* keepers, and manpower recruitment agencies.

In the 1998-99 budget, service tax on the transportation of goods by road, outdoor caterers, and *pandal* contractors was abolished. However, its net was extended to services provided by architects, interior decorators, management consultants, chartered accountants, cost accountants, company secretaries, private security services, real estate agents and real estate consultants, market research agencies, credit rating agencies, underwriting agencies, and slaughter houses using mechanised means for large animals.

Acknowledging the potential of service tax, the Finance Minister in his 2000-2001 budget speech announced the setting up of an Expert Group to go into all its aspects and make suitable recommendations. The net of service tax was greatly expanded when the following 15 services were added to the list of taxable services in the 2001-02 budget.

1. Specified banking and financial services.
2. Authorised service stations for servicing of vehicles including two wheelers.
3. Port services.
4. Broadcasting services.
5. Photographic services.
6. Convention services.
7. Sound recording services.
8. Scientific and technical consulting services.
9. Telex services.
10. Telegraph services.
11. Facsimile services.
12. Online information and data base retrieval services.
13. Video tape production services.
14. Services auxiliary to insurance.
15. Services provided to lease circuit line holders.

In his 2004-05 budget speech, the Finance Minister announced the inclusion of some more services under the service tax ambit. These were the following.

1. Business exhibition services.
2. Airport services.
3. Services provided by transport booking agents.
4. Transport of goods by air.
5. Survey and exploration services.
6. Opinion poll services.
7. Intellectual property services other than copyright.
8. Brokers of forward contracts.
9. *Pandal* and *shamiana* contractors.
10. Outdoor caterers.
11. Independent TV/radio programme producers.
12. Construction services in respect of commercial or industrial constructions.
13. Life insurance services to the extent of the risk premium.

In the 2005-06 Budget, the following 9 items were added to the list of taxable services.

1. Transport of goods through pipeline or other conduit.
2. Site preparation and clearance, excavation, earth moving and demolition services, other than those provided to agriculture, irrigation and watershed development.
3. Dredging services of rivers, ports, harbours, backwaters and estuaries.
4. Survey and map making other than by Government Departments.
5. Cleaning services other than in relation to agriculture, horticulture, animal husbandry or dairying.
6. Membership of clubs or associations.
7. Packaging services.
8. Mailing list compilation and mailing.
9. Construction of residential complexes having more than twelve residential units of apartments together with common areas and other appurtenances.

The 2005-06 Budget also expanded the scope of certain existing services in the following manner.

1. Commercial or industrial construction service to include renovation of such building or civil structure, post construction completion and finishing services for such building or civil structure, construction, repair, alteration, renovation or restoration of pipeline or conduits.
2. Erection, commissioning or installation services to include specified installation services.
3. Maintenance or repair services to include maintenance or management of immovable properties, maintenance or repair including reconditioning or restoration undertaken as part of any contract or agreement.
4. Broadcasting services to include charges recovered by broadcasting agencies from multi-system operator and provision of direct to home signals to the customers.
5. Sound recording to include recording of sound on any media and includes post-production services such as sound mixing or re-mixing.
6. Video-tape production to include recording of any programme, event or function on any media and includes post production services.
7. Taxable services provided by authorised service station to include reconditioning or restoration of motor-cars, two wheeled and light motor vehicles.
8. Beauty parlour services to include all services provided by beauty parlours.
9. manpower recruitment service to include supply of manpower, temporary or otherwise.

10. franchisee service to cover all agreements by which, the franchisor grants representational rights to franchise to sell or manufacture goods or provide services identified with the franchisor.
11. business auxiliary service to include production or processing of goods for or on behalf of the client.
12. outdoor catering service to include catering from a place or premises provided, by way of tenancy or otherwise by the person receiving such services.

The Budget for 2006-07 added the following new services under the service tax net.

1. Service provided by a Registrar to an issue.
2. Service provided by Share Transfer Agent.
3. Automated Teller Machine operations, maintenance or management.
4. Service provided by recovery agent.
5. Sale of space or time for advertisement, other than in print media.
6. Sponsorship services provided to anybody, corporate or firm, other than sponsorship of sports events.
7. Transport of passengers, other than economy class passengers, embarking on international journey by air.
8. Transport of goods in containers by rail by any person, other than Government railway.
9. Business support services.
10. Auctioneers' service, other than auction of property under directions or orders of a court of law or auction by the Central Government.
11. Public relation service.
12. Ship management service.
13. Internet telephony service.
14. Transport of persons by cruise ship.
15. Credit card, debit card, charge card or other payment card related services.

In the 2007-08 Budget, service tax net was extended to the following services.

1. Services outsourced for mining of mineral, oil or gas;
2. Renting of immovable property for use in commerce or business; however, residential properties, vacant land used for agriculture and similar purposes, land for sports, entertainment and parking purposes, and immovable property for educational or religious purposes will be excluded;
3. Development and supply of content for use in telecom and advertising purposes;
4. Asset management services provided by individuals; and
5. Design services.

Keeping in view the social objectives of state policy, the Government of India has refrained from taxing services in the field of health and education. [4] Table 17.2 records the growth in revenue from service tax in India.

Table 17.2: Growth of Service Tax in India (Rs. crore)

Year	Number of services	Number of assesses	Tax rate (per cent)	Revenue (Rs. crore)
1994-95	3	3,943	5	407
1995-96	3	4,866	5	862
1996-97	6	13,982	5	1,059
1997-98	15	45,991	5	1,586
1998-99	26	1,07,479	5	1,957
1999-00	26	1,15,495	5	2,128
2000-01	26	1,22,326	5	2,613
2001-02	41	1,87,577	5	3,302
2002-03	52	2,32,048	5	4,122
2003-04	60	4,03,856	8	7,891
2004-05	75	7,40,267	10	14,200
2005-06	84	8,05,591	10	23,055
2006-07	99	---	12	38,169*
2007-08	104	---	12	50,200#

* Revised estimates; # Budget estimates.

Sources: Government of India, *Economic Survey*, 2006-07, p. 29, Table 2.4; Government of India, Budget Papers, *Budget at a Glance,* 2007-2008.

17.5 Conclusion

The Indian tax system has traditionally relied on commodity taxation for generating revenue for the Central and State Governments. The two major commodity taxes of the Central Government are excise duties and customs duties while at the level of the States, sales tax is the main commodity tax, accounting for about two-thirds of States' own tax revenue.

The extension of excise duties to more and more commodities of the industrial/manufacturing sector has now reached a saturation point. However, the service sector remained outside the tax net till 1994. This pattern of tax structure development in India was contrary to the experience of most other countries where taxation of commodities and services grew hand in hand.

Presently, service tax is levied on as diverse services as credit rating on the one hand and mechanised slaughter houses on the other. It is clear that service sector in India constitutes a tax base with vast potential which has not been exploited as yet.

To quote in conclusion, "Central Service tax reform and extension must be designed to integrate it with the CENVAT by the end of the 10th Plan, keeping in mind the ultimate objective of a National VAT. All services, particularly modern production services such as transport, communication and financial services, under the tax authority of the centre should be subject to the same basic CENVAT rate. Similarly the tax paid on any services used as input into the production of excisable services or goods should be given set-off. Any comprehensive Service Tax law must keep these objectives in view." [5]

Notes

1. Concurrent taxation powers are a characteristic feature of a federal set up like the United States, Canada, and Australia. Most tax fields in these countries are jointly occupied by the federal and provincial governments. The overlapping taxation powers have often caused frictions not only between the federal and provincial governments but also among the provinces *inter se.* Tax problems owing to joint occupancy of tax fields are solved through tax rental and tax sharing negotiations and agreements.

2. Reserve Bank of India, *Report on Currency and Finance*, 1998-99, p. V-6.

3. Government of India, Ministry of Finance, *Budget Speech of the Finance Minister, 1994-95, Part B*, p. 24.

4. In the case of excise and sales tax also, commodities such as medicines and books are either exempt or taxed at very low rates.

5. D.K. Srivastava, *Issues in Indian Public Finance* (New Century Publications: New Delhi), 2005, p. 78.

18

Customs Duties

Having consolidated political power after the disturbances of 1857, the British Indian Government introduced in 1859 a uniform all-India customs tariff which replaced separate provincial rates of duty. Since then, customs tariff, which presently accounts for a quarter of Central Government tax collections, has been subjected to a series of changes to act as a policy instrument to generate revenue, protect the domestic industry, conserve and ration foreign exchange and frame general international trade policy. This chapter describes and critically examines Indian customs tariff in its various aspects, viz. historical evolution, constitutional provisions, trends in revenue, and import and export tariff policy.

18.1 Introduction

Customs duties are probably the most ancient form of taxation. They are as old as international trade itself. Just as domestic production flows provide the base for excise taxation so also international trade flows are the basis for customs duties. Customs duties are payable on goods exported from or imported into a country. Import duties are usually levied with *ad valorem* rates and their base is determined by the domestic value of the imported goods calculated at the official exchange rate. Similarly, export duties are imposed on export values expressed in domestic currency. Customs duties are imposed to raise revenue for the government. Apart from the revenue function, import duties provide a protective barrier for domestic industries. Other measures to protect indigenous industries from foreign competition include import licensing, import quotas, and outright import ban.

18.2 Pre-Independence History of Customs Duties

Prior to 1857, the regulation of customs duties in India was haphazard and lacked all-India uniformity due to unstable political and economic conditions. Rates of import duty, though not uniform, were relatively low, ranging from 3 to 5 per cent *ad valorem* on raw materials and manufactured articles. These rates were doubled in the case of goods imported from countries other than Britain.

18.2.1 Period 1859 to 1894: Under the uniform all-India tariff, introduced by the British in 1859, almost everything imported into India was assessed at 10 per cent of its value for purposes of customs duty. Some important articles, viz.

tobacco, beer, wines, and spirits were taxed at 20 per cent. Likewise, nearly all exports from India paid 3 per cent rate of duty. High rates of customs duty soon proved counter-productive and by mid-1860s a process of lowering import tariff had started. Moreover, the country was also showing signs of recovery from the trauma of 1857. Import duties were reduced to 7.5 per cent in 1864 and further down to 5 per cent in 1875. Import duties were abolished in 1882, except those on arms and liquors. For all practical purposes, the import of goods into India was free until 1894. According to K. T. Shah, "...from 1875 to 1900, the Indian customs policy became the subject of a violent controversy between doctrinaire free traders and passionate protectionists; and in consequence there were frequent changes. The ruling caste, taking their cue from the prominent British statesmen, adopted an attitude of uncompromising freedom in trade, irrespective of India's economic or financial interests. The Indian public opinion of the day, such as it was, was gradually driven by the sheer intolerance of the rulers in their second-hand exposition of the free trade principles, to an attitude of equally unyielding protectionism." [1]

Broadly speaking, from mid-1870s the Government of India was well on the path of establishing freedom of trade. Even in the case of exports, exemptions from duty were granted freely and in 1875 the only commodities which were still subject to export duties were rice, indigo, and lac.

18.2.2 Period 1894 to 1919: The euphoria for free trade which dominated Government's policy between 1875 and 1890 gave way to economic realism with the beginning of 1890s. The loss of revenue from the abolition of import duties was felt to be adversely affecting Central finances. Hence, in a reversal of tariff policy, a general import duty of 5 per cent was reimposed in 1894. A notable exception to this rate was the duty free import of railway materials and machinery. Similarly, a low duty of 1 per cent was imposed on iron and steel. There were a few commodities, viz. arms, liquors, and tobacco which were subject to a comparatively high rate of duty. This arrangement continued till the outbreak of the First World War.

The outbreak of the War led to an urgent need for additional revenues and customs duties came in handy for the Government. The general rate of import duty was raised from 5 per cent to 7.5 per cent in 1916. In the same year, an export duty was imposed on jute. A duty on raw hides and skins at 5 per cent *ad valorem* was imposed in 1919.

Export duties formed an important part of the customs tariff soon after the events of 1857. They were gradually abolished and between 1880 and 1916, rice was the only item subject to export duty. The financial difficulties created by the First World War led to their revival. Jute and tea were brought under the export duty net in 1916, and hides and skins in 1919. Justifying the export duty on rice, the Indian Taxation Enquiry Committee, 1924-25, observed, "Though rice is not a monopoly of India, the export duty has been in operation for many years without any bad effects. Its justification lies in special circumstances. The only countries which export appreciable quantities of rice are India, Siam (now Thailand), and Indo-China. The Indian share of the trade varies between one-third and one-half. As each of these countries levies an export duty, the Indian duty does not handicap the producer and its remission would in fact put an equivalent amount of money into the hands of the producers and the middlemen." [2] Export duty on tea was justified on similar grounds because India's principal competitor Ceylon (now Sri Lanka) also imposed export duty on tea.

18.2.3 Inter-War Period: The general rate of import duty was raised from 7.5 per cent to 11 per cent in 1921, and further up to 15 per cent in 1922. A new category of *luxury goods* (such as motor cars, silk goods, and watches) was introduced in 1921 for which a 20 per cent rate was prescribed and the same was increased to 30 per cent in the following year. Although, the successive upward revisions in import tariff were made for additional revenue, they did provide the much-needed protection to the domestic industry.

In 1921, the Indian Fiscal Commission was appointed to examine the tariff policy of the Government of India. It submitted its report in 1922 with the following main recommendations:

- That the Government of India should adopt a policy of protection to be applied with discrimination along the lines indicated in this report.
- That discrimination be exercised in the selection of industries for protection, and in the degree of protection afforded, so as to make the inevitable burden on the community as light as is consistent with the due development of industries.
- That the Tariff Board in dealing with claims for protection should satisfy itself

1. That the industry possesses natural advantages,
2. That without the help of protection it is not likely to develop at all, or not so rapidly as is desirable, and
3. That it will eventually be able to face world competition without protection.

- That raw materials and machinery be ordinarily admitted free of duty and that semi-manufactured goods used in Indian industries be taxed as lightly as possible.

- That industries essential for purposes of national defence and for the development of which conditions in India are not unfavourable be adequately protected, if necessary.
- That no export duties be ordinarily imposed except for purely revenue purposes and then only at very low rates; but that when it is considered necessary to restrict the export of foodgrains, the restriction be effected by temporary export duties and not by prohibition. [3]

The recommendations of the Fiscal Commission were debated in the Legislative Assembly in February 1923 and a resolution was passed accepting in principle the need to tailor India's tariff policy for encouraging Indian industries. As suggested by the Fiscal Commission, a Tariff Board was set up which investigated the claims of a number of industries for protective duties. Following the recommendations of the Tariff Board, the Government adopted what came to be called the policy of *discriminatory protection* under which tariff protection was granted to select industries against foreign competition. The industries which benefited from the policy of discriminating protection included, *inter alia,* iron and steel, cement, textiles, sugar, paper, matches, and jute.

An adverse consequence of the high rates of customs duty during and after the First World War was the encouragement to smuggling. The Indian Taxation Enquiry Committee, 1924-25, examined the smuggling problem at length and observed, "...while the present high tariff offers great temptations to the smuggler, there is a lack of cohesion in the preventive arrangements, which certainly offer many facilities for his operations. It is not desirable to recite instances of the way in which advantage has been taken of these facilities, but it may be said that, though there is no evidence that any considerable percentage of the customs revenue is lost through smuggling, it is clear that there is a loss amounting at least to several lakhs a year." [4]

The economic depression of early 1930s resulted in heavy deficits in the finances of the Central Government. The general rate of import tariff was raised to 25 per cent as a part of additional taxation efforts introduced under the Indian Finance Act, 1931.

During the inter-War period, customs duties remained the single largest source of Central revenues. In 1921-22, they accounted for 39.5 per cent or two-fifths of the Central revenues. By 1938-39, their share had gone up to almost one-half, 48.9 per cent to be exact. At the end of the Second World War, i.e. in 1944-45, their contribution was as low as 11.9 per cent: Rs. 39.77 crore out of a total revenue of Rs. 334.40 crore (Table 18.1).

Table 18.1: Pre-Independence Trends in the Relative Share of Customs Duties in Total Revenues of the Central Government

(Rs. crore)

Year	Total Central revenues	Customs	Col. 3 as per cent of col. 2
1	2	3	4
1921-22	80.00	31.61	39.5
1936-37	81.45	38.11	46.8
1938-39	82.90	40.51	48.9
1944-45	334.40	39.77	11.9

Figures for 1921-22 and 1936-37 are inclusive of those for Burma. Figures for 1938-38 and 1944-45 relate to undivided India.

Source: Government of India, Ministry of Finance, *Report of the Taxation Enquiry Commission,* 1953-54, Vol. I, p. 23, Table 5 (excerpted).

18.2.4 Second World War: In the Finance Act of 1942, an overall surcharge of one-fifth on all duties was imposed. It continued from year to year till 1951 when it was increased to one-fourth in the wake of Korean boom. In 1944, the rate of surcharge on certain items, viz. potable spirits, cigars, cigarettes, and tobacco was increased from one-fifth to one-half. During the War, an export duty at 3 per cent was imposed on cotton cloth and yarn but the same was converted into an export cess in 1945.

Another important wartime development was the introduction of import control (quotas) to ensure that available foreign exchange and shipping space were utilised for essential imports. The policy of import control continued during the post-war period to meet conditions created by the partition of the country, particularly the import of massive quantities of foodgrains.

It is pertinent to note that during the pre-Independence period, maritime Princely States enjoyed the right to levy and retain sea customs duties at their own ports. However, the States were not allowed, through conventions with the British Indian Government, to levy such duties at rates lower than those charged at entry into British Indian ports. This arrangement ensured that there was no undue diversion of trade from British Indian ports to ports developed and maintained by the States. The maritime Princely States of British India with their major ports mentioned in parentheses were the following: Travancore State (Trivandrum, Quilon, Alleppey), Cochin State (Cochin), Bhavnagar State (Bhavnagar), Junagadh State (Verawal, Mangrol), Porbandar State (Porbandar), Baroda State (Okha), Nawanagar State (Bedi, Rozi), Morvi State (Navlakhi), and Cutch State (Mandvi, Kandla).

The authority of the Princely States in terms of sea customs and ports was well-recorded in the Report of the Indian States Enquiry Committee (Financial), 1932. It observed, "...the revenue they (Princely States) derive from these customs duties is substantial, elastic, and an important part of their total revenues, from which their State expenditure (including that on nation building activities) has to be met; that the appointment of staff by which they collect, and the manner in which they disburse, the revenue so realised from customs duties are entirely matters for their own decision; and, in particular, that they cannot be debarred from utilising that revenue in the maintenance and development of the ports at which the customs duties are levied." [5]

18.3 Legal Framework

The Constitution of India grants exclusive powers to the Central Government to impose duties of customs. By virtue of entry 83 of List I in the Seventh Schedule of the Constitution of India, the Central Government is empowered to impose 'duties of customs including export duties'.

During the British rule, various customs and tariff enactments were passed from time to time, the following two being the main: 1. The Sea Customs Act, 1878, and 2. The Tariff Act, 1934. After Independence, the Sea Customs Act and other allied enactments were repealed by a consolidating and amending legislation entitled the Customs Act, 1962. Similarly, the Act of 1934 was repealed by the Customs Tariff Act, 1975.

18.3.1 Various Types of Customs Duties: In accordance with the provisions of the Constitution, various types of customs duties are imposed by the Government under different Acts of Parliament. Following are the important customs duties levied on goods imported into or exported from India.

A. Basic Customs Duty: Under Section 12 of the Customs Act, 1962 (the main enactment), all goods imported into India are chargeable to a duty. The rates of this duty, popularly known as basic customs duty, are indicated in the First Schedule of the Customs Tariff Act, 1975. The duty may be a percentage of the value of the goods or at a specific rate. The Central Government has the power to reduce or exempt any goods from these duties.

B. Additional (Countervailing) Duty of Customs: Under Section 3(1) of the Customs Tariff Act, 1975, an additional duty on goods imported into the country is leviable. The rate of this duty, popularly known as countervailing duty, is equal to the excise duty on like articles if produced or manufactured in India. If the rate of this duty is on *ad valorem* basis, the value for this purpose will be the total of the value of the imported article and the customs duty on it (both basic and auxiliary). The underlying philosophy of a countervailing duty is to ensure that the protection provided by the import duty to domestic industry is not reduced. Till the early 1960s, countervailing duty was levied on a select basis on products which were considered to erode the margin of protection to the domestic industry on account of the excise duty. In course of time when the number of excisable goods increased, the selective use of countervailing duty was found to be inadequate and complicated. Therefore, the Indian Tariff Act, 1934, was amended in 1963 to insert a new Section 2A to provide for the levy of countervailing duty in all cases where excise duty was leviable on a similar indigenous commodity.

C. Export Duty: Under Section 12 of the Customs Act, 1962, goods exported from India are chargeable to an export duty. The items on which export duty is chargeable and the rate at which the duty is levied are given in the Second Schedule of the Customs Tariff Act, 1975. Under Section 8 of this Act, the Government enjoys emergency powers to increase the existing rate or to levy fresh export duty depending on the circumstances.

D. Cesses on Exports: Certain cesses are leviable on specified articles of export under various enactments of the Government of India. These cesses are collected as duties of customs and handed over to the agencies in-charge of the administration of the commodity concerned. Presently, cesses are imposed on exports of coffee, coir, lac, mica, tobacco (unmanufactured), oil cakes and meal, marine products, cashew kernels, black pepper, cardamom, iron ore, animal feed and turmeric.

18.4 New Customs Tariff Nomenclature

As in the case of excise duties, a major problem in the administration of customs duties pertains to disputes and delays relating to interpretation of definitions of dutiable goods. The enactment of the new Customs Tariff Act, 1975, was a landmark in the history of customs tariff in India. The revised nomenclature for customs tariff was recommended by the Tariff Revision Committee set up in 1964. Though the Government accepted the recommendations of the Committee, the Bill to implement the revised nomenclature could only be passed in 1975 and came into effect from August 2, 1976. The Act of 1975, which replaced the Indian Tariff Act, 1934, is based on the Customs Co-operation Council Nomenclature (originally known as Brussels Tariff Nomenclature). The First Schedule of the Act contains import tariff while the Second Schedule deals with export tariff. As a further measure to rationalise and modernise customs administration, the Parliament passed the Customs Tariff Amendment Act, 1985, to adopt the Harmonised Commodity Description and Coding System. The new commodity classification became operative from February 28, 1986. Similarly, India adopted the GATT Valuation Agreement

(Valuation Code) on August 16, 1988. The GATT Valuation Code lays down broad principles for valuation of goods for levy of customs duty.

18.5 Revenue Significance

The relative contribution of customs revenue in the total tax yield of the Central Government has shown fluctuations due to changes in the foreign exchange situation, domestic production levels, and trends in international trade. For example, in the late 1950s, several restrictions and bans were imposed on imports in view of the difficult foreign exchange position, resulting in fall in revenue from import duties.

During pre-Independence days and even during early post-Independence period, customs duties formed the mainstay of Central tax revenues. However, the relative share of customs duties started declining from early 1950s in view of protective trade policy and dwindling foreign exchange reserves. The share of customs revenue in Centre's total tax collections dropped from 38.9 per cent in 1950-51 to as low as 16.3 per cent in 1970-71. Since then, customs revenue has maintained an upward swing, accounting for 25.8 per cent in 1980-81, and 35.8 per cent in 1990-91 (Table 18.2). This upward trend was attributable to the changed emphasis from physical to fiscal controls to regulate imports. As the Long Term Fiscal Policy, 1985, maintained, "The basic thrust of customs tariff reforms will be to place increasing reliance on tariffs to regulate imports and progressively reduce the role of quantitative restrictions in this regard. The move in this direction should increase revenues, encourage less import-intensive forms of production, moderate the unjustifiably high protection granted by quantitative restrictions to certain industries and reduce the delays and uncertainties associated with the administration of import licensing." [6]

Of late, there has been a decline in the relative importance of customs as a source of revenue. In the 2007-2008 budget, the share of customs revenue in the total Central tax collections was estimated at 18.0 per cent (Table 18.2). This reversal of trend is due to opening up of the economy and the policy of progressively reducing import duties.

Customs revenue is mainly composed of import duties levied on a wide range of commodities. In the budget estimates for 2007-2008, import duties account for Rs. 54,660 crore (99.7 per cent) of total customs revenue of Rs. 54,822 crore (Table 18.3). Apart from revenue function, import duties act as policy instrument to provide protection to domestic industry, conserve and ration scarce foreign exchange, and frame general international trade policy.

Table 18.2: Trends in the Relative Significance of Customs Duties in Gross Tax Revenues* of the Central Government: Selected Years

(Rs. crore)

Central taxes	1950-51	1960-61	1970-71	1980-81	1990-91	2000-01	2007-08#
A+B Gross tax revenues	404 (100.0)	888 (100.0)	3,206 (100.0)	13,179 (100.0)	57,576 (100.0)	1,88,603 (100.0)	5,48,122 (100.0)
A. Direct taxes	174 (43.1)	290 (32.6)	870 (27.1)	3,004 (22.8)	11,025 (19.1)	68,306 (36.2)	2,67,490 (48.8)
B. Indirect taxes of which	229 (56.7)	599 (67.5)	2,337 (72.9)	10,175 (77.2)	46,552 (80.9)	1,20,297 (63.8)	2,80,632 (51.2)
1. Customs duties	157 (38.9)	170 (19.1)	524 (16.3)	3,409 (25.8)	20,644 (35.8)	47,542 (25.2)	98,770 (18.0)

* Before transferring States' share in Central taxes; # Budget estimates.

Figures in parentheses are corresponding percentages of gross tax revenues.

Sources: Government of India, Ministry of Finance, *Explanatory Memorandum on the Budget of the Central Government* (various years); *Receipts Budget* (various years); and *Budget at a Glance*, 2007-08.

Table 18.3: Trends in the Relative Shares of Import and Export Duties in Total Customs Duties: Selected Years

(Rs. crore)

Year	Customs duties	Import duties	Export duties	As per cent	
				Col.3 of Col. 2	Col. 4 of Col. 2
1	2	3	4	5	6
1950-51	157	110	47	70.1	29.9
1955-56	166	128	38	77.1	22.9
1960-61	170	156	14	91.8	8.2
1965-66	539	537	2	99.6	0.4
1970-71	524	461	63	88.0	12.0
1975-76	1,419	1,336	83	94.1	5.9
1980-81	3,409	3,292	117	96.6	3.4
1985-86	9,526	9,443	83	99.1	0.9
1990-91	20,568	20,532	36	99.8	0.2
1995-96	35,757	35,647	110	99.7	0.3
2000-01	47,542	47,400	142	99.7	0.3
2006-07#	81,800	81,015	795	99.1	0.9
2007-08*	98,770	94,620	4,150	95.8	4.2

Revised estimates; * Budget estimates.

Sources: Government of India, Ministry of Finance, *Explanatory Memorandum on the Budget of the Central Government;* and *Receipts Budget* (various years).

Like excise levies, the revenue from import duties is also concentrated in a select few commodities including petroleum oils and crude, electrical machinery, organic chemicals, project imports, plastics etc. These are the items which form the bulk of India's imports and hence customs revenue.

18.6 Import Tariff Policy

18.6.1 Early Post-Independence Period: Soon after Independence, the Government decided to follow a restrictive import policy, particularly in view of the rapid depletion of sterling balances. In his very first budget (1947-48) of independent India, the Finance Minister outlined the salient features of this restrictive policy as follows, "Broadly speaking, that policy consists of dividing imports into three categories: free, restricted, and prohibited. Imports of food, capital goods, the raw material of industry and certain essential consumer goods are free and no exchange restrictions are placed upon their imports. Consumer goods which are not absolutely essential are licensed on a quota basis, while others which in the context of the economy of this country must be regarded as totally unessential and luxury imports have been altogether prohibited." [7]

During the early post-Independence period, customs policy remained in turmoil owing to a series of domestic and international happenings. India's commitments under the General Agreement on Tariffs and Trade (GATT) were given effect to in 1948, the rupee was devalued in September 1949, and the Korean War broke out in 1950. Being a signatory to GATT, India could not raise, above a certain level, import duties on a wide variety of goods, but enjoyed reciprocal concessions from its trade partners. Imports of articles which enjoyed concessions under GATT constituted 19 per cent of the value of total imports while the value of exports which received concessions was 79.6 per cent of our total exports in 1952-53. The concessions obtained included items like mica, cashewnut, and various jute goods. The concessions granted pertained mainly to consumer goods and machinery. Since the actual rates of import duty on machinery, which formed the bulk of imports, were already low than the rates fixed by the Agreement, the effective concessions were chiefly on consumer goods. Although the Fiscal Commission, 1949-50, supported India's adherence to GATT in view of the need for international co-operation, the country later on felt the need to withdraw from GATT 'bindings' when the domestic production base was strengthened and diversified. Following re-negotiations in 1971 and 1973, a host of items 'bound' under GATT were freed to provide protection to domestic industries.

After the outbreak of the Korean War, important changes were introduced in the tariff structure under the Finance Act, 1951. The general surcharge of one-fifth on import duties (levied in 1942) was increased to one-fourth. The rate of surcharge on liquors which was fixed at 100 per cent in 1948 was raised to 155 per cent.

In pursuance of its general policy of gradually replacing quantitative restrictions by higher import duties, the Government raised import duties on a number of items including articles made of paper, cutlery etc., in the 1955-56 budget. Simultaneously, import quotas were liberalised. The already high level of import duties, particularly on luxury articles, did not leave much scope for raising additional revenue from this source, a fact lamented by the Finance Minister in his 1957-58 budget (final) speech.

18.6.2 Customs Reorganisation Committee (Chairman: F.C. Badhwar), 1957-58: In January 1957, the Government of India appointed the Customs Reorganisation Committee under the chairmanship of F.C. Badhwar. The Committee was asked "to conduct a comprehensive enquiry into customs procedures and organisation and to make recommendations for their improvement." The Committee found that a major cause of disputes and delays in the clearance of imported goods was the faulty and inadequate classification system for determining customs tariff. It observed, "The complexity of the Customs Tariff will be evident from the fact that the whole range of goods constituting the country's foreign trade are grouped under 576 tariff items only as compared with 4850 classification heads in the 'Statistical Indian Trade Classification' which has recently been adopted for purposes of recording the country's trade statistics. Whilst the range and variety of imported goods have been continuously expanding in the post-war period, there has been little or no corresponding revision or elaboration of the customs tariff schedule." [8]

The Committee was also critical of too many rates of duty. It commented, "we should similarly point out the existence in the Indian Customs Tariff of too wide a range of *ad valorem* rates of duty which must inevitably add to the difficulties in the day to day application of the tariff, particularly when tariff descriptions carrying different rates could apply to the same article. Almost all multiples of 5 up to 100 are to be found in these rates." [9].

The Committee recommended, *inter alia*, (a) thorough revision of the Customs Tariff by aligning it closely with the Import Trade Control Licensing Schedule, and (b) removal of anomalies in rates of duty for similar categories of goods.

The worsening foreign exchange crisis reached its climax when in 1965 foreign exchange reserves touched the critically low level of less than Rs. 100 crore. Moreover, the Customs Reorganisation Committee, 1957-58, had criticised the multiplicity of tariff rates. Consequently, a drastic rationalisation of the import duty structure was undertaken in 1965, resulting in the introduction of a set of three rates of import duty: 40 per cent on basic raw materials, 60 per cent on semi-processed and intermediate goods, and 100 per cent on finished consumer goods. The Committee on Rationalisation and Simplification of Tax Structure, 1968, also favoured few rates of import tariff. It opined, "Except for a few 'luxury' items like watches, jewellery, alcoholic beverages and perfumes, there is need only for three or four rates of duty." [10]. In spite of the rationalisation exercise of 1965, duty changes were made frequently depending upon the emerging situation. The three rates of import duty were scaled down following devaluation of the rupee in June 1966 to prevent the cost of imports going up to the full extent of the devaluation. However, in view of the difficult balance of payments position, the rates of import duty were gradually restored in due course to pre-devaluation levels. Rationalisation of import tariff was again attempted in 1971 when the following four rates of import duty were introduced: 30 per cent, 40 per cent, 60 per cent, and 100 per cent.

18.6.3 Indirect Taxation Enquiry Committee (Chairman: L.K. Jha), 1978: The Indirect Taxation Enquiry Committee, 1978, examined at length the structure of import duties and recommended its rationalisation on the following lines, "(a) a levy adequate to give the degree of protection deemed necessary for particular products, (b) a revenue element, which would generally be the countervailing duty, being equal to the excise duty leviable on the same or similar domestic product, and (c) a regulator element which will be used on such factors as reinforcing import restrictions, preventing excess profits on account of scarcity of products in domestic market, and generally to regulate imports from the angle of conserving foreign exchange." [11]

18.6.4 Long-Term Fiscal Policy, 1985: The need for import tariff rationalisation was underlined in the Long Term Fiscal Policy (LTFP), 1985, also. The official document noted that the prevailing tariff rates were high and the tariff system was very complicated. Therefore, it stressed the need to reduce the rates and simplify the system. For carrying out these reforms, the LTFP distinguished between the following broad categories of imports:

1. Capital goods.
2. Raw materials.
3. Other intermediate goods including components.
4. Essential consumer goods like foodgrains, edible oils, and life saving drugs.
5. Non-essential consumer goods.

Understandably, essential goods were preferred to either remain exempt or bear low rates of import duties while non-essential items were singled out to either remain banned or subjected to high import tariff. Regarding the first three categories of goods the LTFP observed, "Ideally, in the long-run, there is a strong case for subjecting all capital goods, raw materials, components and other intermediate products to the same rate of nominal tariff. This system, if it could be implemented, would have several important advantages. First, the substitution of the present multiplicity of nominal tariff rates by a single rate would constitute an enormous simplification for both trade and industry as well as for the customs administration. Second, this would vastly reduce incentives for misclassification of imports to evade taxes. Third, a single nominal rate of import duty would assure a uniform rate of effective protection (that is, protection of value added) at different stages of production of intermediate and capital goods. This would encourage the economy to specialise in those activities in which it has competitive strength." [12]

However, the LTFP cautioned that a major deviation from the present pattern of import tariff is not immediately feasible. Domestic industries have grown under different levels of protection and are in different stages of maturity. The rationalisation of import tariff has to be phased over a long period providing some differentials in import tariff short of a uniform system of duties.

Consequent upon the rationalisation of import tariff on capital goods by the Finance Act, 1987, the rate of import duty on general machinery was reduced to 85 per cent *ad valorem*. Import duty on components for machinery was fixed at 15 per cent below the applicable rate on complete machines. This differential, in line with the recommendations of the LTFP, was intended to encourage the domestic production of capital machines instead of their total imports. Imports of capital goods for certain preferred sectors were allowed at relatively low rates of duty. For example, duty on equipment for fertiliser plants was 15 per cent *ad valorem* and on machines, equipment, and tools for gem and jewellery 25 per cent *ad valorem*. Electronics industry emerged as a preferred sector for fiscal incentives. The Finance Act, 1988, fixed a uniform concessional import duty of 60 per cent *ad valorem* in respect of 280 items of machinery for the electronics sector. By the same Act, the duty on moulds, tools, and dies required by the electronics industry was reduced from 60 per cent to 30 per cent *ad valorem* with the underlying purpose of indigenisation and development of electronics and computers.

In short, guidelines suggested by the LTFP for reform of import tariff were never implemented comprehensively. In a half-hearted manner, some rationalisation of rates was effected in the case of components of capital goods, drug intermediates, and electronic goods.

In mid-1991 when the new Government assumed office at the Centre, it began the process of reducing import duties. The Finance Act (No. 2), 1991, reduced the *ad valorem* rate of basic plus auxiliary duties of customs to a maximum of 150 per cent where it was more than that. Thus, tariff peaks above 150 per cent were eliminated with the exceptions of duty on imported alcoholic beverages and passenger baggage. The then prevailing rates of import duty on capital goods for general projects and machinery were reduced from 85 per cent to 80 per cent. The rate of duty on their components was also reduced by 5 percentage points from the existing level of 65 per cent.

18.6.5 Tax Reforms Committee (Chairman: Raja Chelliah), 1991: Reform of the customs tariff was high on the agenda of the Tax Reforms Committee constituted by the Government in August 1991. Its terms of reference enjoined it to examine and make recommendations, *inter alia*, on "simplification and rationalisation of customs tariffs with a view to reducing the multiplicity and dispersion of rates and to eliminate exemptions which have become unnecessary; (and) reducing the level of tariff rates, keeping in view the need for mobilising resources to facilitate fiscal adjustment and the objective of promoting international competitiveness." [13]

In its Interim Report submitted to the Government in December 1991, the Committee suggested the following as elements of the programme of import tariff reform, "(a) reduction of the general level of tariff, (b) reduction of the spread or dispersion of tariff rates, (c) simplification of the tariff system, (d) rationalisation of tariff rates, along with the abolition of numerous exemptions and concessions, and (e) abolition of the practice of making changes in effective rates through notifications." [14]. Stressing the need for time-bound action, the Committee observed, "By 1995-96, the average tariff rate should be brought down to about 50 per cent and the peak rate to about 80 per cent. In the years 1996-97 to 1998-99, tariff rates should be reduced further to bring down the average rate to around 25 per cent and the maximum rate to 50 per cent by 1998-99." [15]

18.7 Post-liberalisation Reduction and Rationalisation of Import Tariff

Following the recommendations of the Tax Reforms Committee, 1991, the Finance Act, 1992, lowered the peak level of import duties to 110 per cent with the exception of passenger baggage and alcoholic beverages. With a view to reduce the cost of new investment, the duty on project imports was lowered from 80 per cent to 55 per cent and in the case of electronic industry to 50 per cent. A deeper reduction to 30 per cent was granted for capital goods for projects of coal mining and crude petroleum refining. For power projects, a uniform duty of 30 per cent was fixed.

The underlying philosophy of reduction in tariffs was to promote competitiveness in the Indian industry. There was a feeling in Government circles that high tariff rates had the effect of creating a high cost industrial structure.

The Finance Act, 1993, made a significant simplification in the import tariff by merging auxiliary duty with basic duty, and also by reducing the maximum rate of import duty from 110 per cent to 85 per cent. The peak rate of import duty was further reduced from 85 per cent to 65 per cent by the Finance Act, 1994.

Continuing the process of reducing the high level of protection to domestic industry is continuing so as to foster competition and promote efficiency. The peak rate of import duty was reduced from 65 per cent to 50 per cent in 1995, and further down to 40 per cent in the 1997-98 budget.

A special customs duty of 2 per cent was imposed in the 1996-97 budget and a further special customs duty of 3 per cent was imposed on certain items in 1997-98. In other words, special customs duty of 5 per cent was in force for a period valid till 31.3.1999. However, the Finance Minister announced in his 1999-2000 budget speech the discontinuance of the 5 per cent special customs duty with effect from 28.2.1999.

In another significant move, the Finance Minister reduced the then existing 7 major ad valorem rates of customs duty to the following 5 basic rates.

- 5 per cent (the existing one)
- 15 per cent (by substituting the existing 10 per cent rate)
- 25 per cent (by merging the 20 per cent and 25 per cent rates)
- 35 per cent (by merging the 30 per cent and 35 per cent rates)
- 40 per cent (the existing one)

However, in another move the Finance Minister imposed a uniform surcharge of 10 per cent on all commodities excluding the following categories.

- Crude oil and petroleum products.
- Items attracting 40 per cent rate of basic duty.
- Certain GATT-bound items.
- Gold and silver.

In other words, the imposition of surcharge raised the basic rate by 10 per cent. For example, basic rate of 5 per cent became 5.5 per cent and 15 per cent became 16.5 per cent.

Still further, the Finance Minister reduced the peak rate of basic customs duty from 40 per cent to 35 per cent in his 2000-2001 budget, thereby reducing the total number of customs duty rates from 5 to 4, i.e. 35 per cent, 25 per cent, 15 per cent and 5 per cent. The surcharge of 10 per cent imposed in the 1999-2000 budget became applicable to new peak rate of 35 per cent. However, in the 2001-2002 budget, the surcharge of 10 per cent was discontinued, making the peak level of customs duty decline from 38.5 per cent to 35 per cent. As regards further reduction in the peak rate of duty, the Finance Minister observed, "I have already promised that our customs tariff would be brought down to East Asian levels. I will like to move progressively within three years to reduce the number of rates to the minimum with a peak rate of 20%." [16]

The Government reduced the peak customs duty from 30 per cent to 25 per cent in the 2003-04 budget.

18.7.1 Off-budget Package of Tax Concessions, January 2004: The Finance Minister Jaswant Singh announced on January 8, 2004 an off-budget package of tax concessions which mainly pertained to indirect taxes (excise and customs). The most notable of these was the reduction in the peak rate of import duty across the board (except for agricultural goods) from 25 per cent to 20 per cent. Simultaneously, he abolished the 4 per cent special additional customs duty

(SACD). Both these changes became effective from January 9, 2004. These measures considerably lowered the protection levels for the domestic industry. However, the two measures are expected to bring down input costs of the manufacturing sector, enabling it to make Indian products globally competitive.

It may be recalled that former Finance Minister Yashwant Sinha announced an 8 per cent SACD in 1998-99 and rolled it back to 4 per cent in the official amendments. SACD was meant to offset the burden of local taxes borne by the domestic industry.

In the 2005-06 Union budget, the peak rate of import duty on non-agricultural products was reduced from 20 per cent to 15 per cent. It was further reduced to 12.5 per cent and 10 per cent in the 2006-07 and 2007-08 budgets respectively.

18.8 Recent Thinking on Customs Tariff

18.8.1 Customs Tariff Report (Chairman: Arvind Virmani), 2002: This Report was submitted to the Government by the Inter-ministerial Group in January 2002. The Report made the following main recommendations to the Government.

- Introduction of a single customs duty (20 per cent) on all products by 2004-05. Tariff rates below 20 per cent on some products be brought to 20 per cent while peak tariff rate be brought down to 20 per cent. According to the Report, a single uniform import tariff implies that the effective protection for all producers is also equal to this single uniform tariff.
- Phasing out all exemptions, barring those on security considerations, by 2004-05.
- Removal of all anomalies in the levy of customs duty by reclassifying all goods and services into two broad categories, viz. producer goods and consumer goods instead of raw materials, components and parts, and final goods.

The Group made out a case for reducing import duties to a near-uniform basic rate of 10 per cent by the end of 2005-06 and 5 per cent by the end of 2011-12. The ASEAN free trade agreement proposes to bring down ASEAN rates to the 0-5 per cent range by 2010 even for highly sensitive agricultural goods.

It is noteworthy that producers seek a low import tariff on raw materials and intermediate goods, and high tariff on finished goods.

18.8.2 Import Duty Structure Recommended by Task Force on Indirect Taxes (Chairman: Vijay Kelkar), 2002: The Report of the Task Force on Indirect Taxes, 2002 (Chairman: Vijay Kelkar) laid down a broad approach to customs tariff reforms in India. It envisages a zero duty for essential items, 10 per cent duty for raw materials, inputs and intermediate goods and 20 per cent for final goods by 2004-05. Following introduction of States' Value Added Tax (VAT), these duties are proposed to be further reduced to 5 per cent for basic raw materials, 8 per cent for intermediate goods, 10 per cent for finished goods and 20 per cent for consumer durables by 2006-07. However, in order to reap efficiency gains from further opening up of the economy, systemic changes in customs procedures and trade facilitation based on modern best practices, which rely on self compliance, may be necessary.

As regards customs exemptions, the Task Force recommended removal of all exemptions except in case of:

- Life-saving goods.
- Goods of security and strategic interest.
- Goods for relief and charitable purposes.
- International obligations including contracts.

The Task Force recommended the following pattern of import duty (Table 18.4).

Table 18.4: Import Duty Structure Recommended by the Task Force on Indirect Taxes

0 per cent	For items like life-saving drugs and equipments, sovereign imports (defence and security related goods) and imports by RBI.
For other goods by 2004-05	10 per cent for raw materials, inputs and intermediate goods. 20 per cent for consumer durables.
By 2006-07	5 per cent for basic raw materials like coal, ores and concentrates, xylenes etc. 8 per cent for intermediate goods which will be used for future manufacture (capital goods, basic chemicals, metals etc.) 10 per cent for finished goods other than consumer durables. 20 per cent for consumer durables.

Source: Government of India, Ministry of Finance and Company Affairs, *Report of the Task Force on Indirect Taxes*, December 2002, p. 169.

To recapitulate, prior to tax reforms initiated in 1991, import tariff had a variety of rates for different items, and even for the same item depending on its end use. Such a cumbersome system led to legal disputes pertaining to import classifications and encouraged corruption in the administration of customs tariff.

Radical reforms have been introduced in the import tariff since 1991. These reforms were necessary because the customs tariff had become, over the years, very complicated in terms of multiple rates, innumerable exemptions, excessive controls, and elaborate procedures. These infirmities of the customs tariff often led to delays, harassment, corruption, and litigation. Moreover, rationalisation and simplification of the customs duties was needed to move towards a market economy, freedom of trade, and opening up the Indian economy to the outside world. The country has moved towards moderate rates of taxation with a view to improve compliance and reduce litigation.

18.9 Export Tariff Policy

Export duties can become an important source of revenue when a country enjoys monopoly or near-monopoly in certain products in the international market. In the early 1950s, India had foreign market dominance in commodities such as jute, tea, and textiles. Hence, export duties fetched sizeable revenues. As this dominance grew weaker over the years, the rates of export duty had to be reduced.

The devaluation of rupee, along with the sterling, against the dollar in September 1949, and the Korean boom considerably increased the demand for India's exports. The comparatively strong position in respect of certain commodities in the world market led to wide profit margins, encouraging the Government to impose or enhance export duty on a number of items including jute manufactures, cotton textiles, and black pepper. Apart from raising revenue, export duties also served to stabilise domestic prices. However, the need to promote India's exports led to a gradual scaling down of export duties. Following the devaluation of the rupee in 1966, export duties were reimposed on a number of goods including jute manufactures, tea, raw cotton, groundnuts, hides and skins, and mineral ores. The objective was to mop up a part of the windfall gain accruing to the exporters as a result of devaluation. However, they had to be withdrawn in course of time to ensure competitiveness of our exports in the world market. Exports are encouraged, in certain cases through subsidies, to narrow the ever-widening deficit in the balance of payments.

Although at present the share of export duties in customs revenue is negligible (0.5 per cent), it was not always so. In the early 1950s, export duties formed a significant proportion of customs revenue, though this situation could not be maintained for long. The yield from export duties reached a peak figure when it formed 29.9 per cent of total customs revenue in 1950-51. By 1960-61, export duty revenue had been reduced to 8.2 per cent of total customs revenue. Another upsurge in the relative share of export duties is observed in 1970-71 when they formed 12.0 per cent of customs revenue. Since then, their revenue importance has continuously decreased and in fact they have virtually disappeared (Table 18.3).

Despite the fact that export duties have lost their importance from revenue angle, they have not been completely dispensed with. Occasions do arise when there is considerable disparity between the domestic and international prices of certain goods enjoying a comparatively stronger position in the export market, and levying of export duties may be justified to mop up a part of the profits of the exporters. At present, export duties are levied on a few commodities such as coffee, mica, black pepper, hides and skins and leather. Export duty on an item is levied after considering such factors as domestic production and likely exportable surpluses, demand for the item in the foreign markets, changes in exchange rates, and the prices prevailing in the international market. It is noteworthy that the Government can impose/enhance export duties without prior approval of the Parliament because such duties do not fall on the Indian consumers.

Notes

1. K. T. Shah, *Sixty Years of Indian Finance* (London: P. S. King and Son Ltd., 1927), pp. 282-83.
2. Government of India, *Report of the Indian Taxation Enquiry Committee* (President: Sir Charles Todhunter), 1924-25, Vol. I, para 157.
3. Government of India, *Report of the Indian Fiscal Commission* (Chairman: Ibrahim Rahimatoola), 1921-22, pp. XV and XVI.
4. *Report of the Indian Taxation Enquiry Committee, 1924-25, op. cit.*, para 152.
5. Government of India, *Report of the Indian States Enquiry Committee* (Financial), 1932 (Chairman: J.C.C. Davidson), para 240.
6. Government of India, *Long Term Fiscal Policy,* 1985, p. 40.
7. Government of India, Ministry of Finance, *Speeches of Union Finance Ministers: 1947-48 to 1984-85*, p. 8.
8. Government of India, *Report of the Customs Reorganisation Committee,* (Chairman: F.C. Budhwar), 1957-58, p. 12.
9. *Ibid*., p. 13.
10. Government of India, *Final Report on Rationalisation and Simplification of Tax Structure,* (Chairman: S. Bhoothalingam), 1968, p. 14.
11. Government of India, Ministry of Finance, *Report of the Indirect Taxation Enquiry Committee,* (Chairman: L. K. Jha), Part II, 1978, p. 139.
12. *Long Term Fiscal Policy,* op. cit., p. 41.
13. Government of India, Ministry of Finance, *Interim Report of the Tax Reforms Committee,* (Chairman: Raja Chelliah), December 1991, p. l.
14. *Ibid.*, p. 97.
15. *Ibid.*, pp. 143-44.
16. Government of India, Ministry of Finance, *Budget Speech of the Finance Minister, 2001-2002, Part B*, p. 31.

Section D: State Taxes

This Section explains the various direct and indirect taxes levied by the State Governments in India. Two individual taxes of the State Governments, viz. taxation of agricultural income, and sales tax have been discussed in detail.

19

Trends in State Taxes

From a modest amount of Rs. 222 crore in 1950-51, revenue from States' taxes has grown consistently over the years and was estimated at Rs. 1,85,891 crore in the 2004-05 budgets of the State Governments. The relative significance of State taxes has changed over the years since Independence in 1947. Land revenue, which contributed 22.1 per cent to State taxes in 1950-51, has almost disappeared. In the 2005-06 budgets of the State Governments, the share of land revenue was estimated at 1.1 per cent. Conversely, sales tax, which contributed 26.1 per cent to State taxes in 1950-51, has become the mainstay of State finances. In the 2005-06 budgets of the State Governments, the share of sales tax in State taxes was estimated at 57.0 per cent (Table 19.3). Apart from sales taxes, other important state level taxes are state excise duties, motor vehicle tax, stamp duties and registration fees, entertainment tax, and electricity duties.

19.1 State Taxes as Per Cent of GDP

In 1950-51, state taxes accounted for 2.23 per cent of GDP. This percentage started increasing with every passing decade with the growth of tax bases allocated to the states under the Constitution. The percentage increased to 2.65 in 1960-61, to 3.38 in 1970-71 and to 4.64 in 1980-81. [1]

On the eve of initiation of economic reforms, state taxes accounted for 5.30 per cent of GDP in 1990-91. The percentage fell to a low of 5.12 in 1998-99, owing to tax competition among the States. Of late, the percentage has improved and was estimated at 6.11 in the 2005-06 budgets of the State Governments (Table 19.1). This improvement is chiefly attributed to agreement among the States to implement floor rates of sales tax and to reduce and rationalize various exemptions and concessions.

19.2 Direct and Indirect Taxes

States' own tax revenue has increasingly relied upon indirect taxes during the post-Independence period. The ratio between direct and indirect taxes at the State level dropped from 24.8:75.2 in 1950-51 to 24.2:75.8 in 1960-61, to 9.0:91.0 in 1970-71 and further down to 4.1:95.9 in 1980-81. [2]

Table 19.1: States' Own Taxes as Per Cent of GDP: 1990-91 to 2005-06

(Rs. crore)

Year	States' own taxes	Col. 2 as % of GDP
1	2	3
1990-91	30,145	5.30
1991-92	35,837	5.49
1992-93	39,530	5.28
1993-94	46,219	5.38
1994-95	55,552	5.49
1995-96	64,034	5.39
1996-97	71,294	5.21
1997-98	81,439	5.35
1998-99	89,220	5.12
1999-00	1,02,831	5.25
2000-01	1,16,717	5.54
2001-02	1,27,475	5.59
2002-03	1,40,372	5.73
2003-04	1,59,736	5.79
2004-05	1,87,996	6.02
2005-06	2,15,601	6.11

2004-05 = Revised estimates; 2005-06 = Budget estimates.

Note: The ratios of GDP since 1950-51 are with reference to new series GDP (Base: 1993-94) at current market prices.

Source: Rearranged data from Government of India, Ministry of Finance, *Indian Public Finance Statistics*, 2005-2006, Tables 1.7 and 1.8.

During the post-reforms period, the ratio between direct and indirect taxes worsened further. It declined from 4.1:95.9 in 1990-91 to 2.3:97.7 in 2005-06 (Table 19.2). Presently, there is no direct tax of revenue significance at the level of States. This highly unbalanced tax structure is a cause for concern.

19.2.1 Composition of Direct Taxes: There is no direct tax which can claim a prominent place in the tax systems of the States.

A. Land Revenue: Land revenue (entry 45 in List II in the Seventh Schedule of the Constitution) which formed the bulwark of States' tax revenue during the pre-Independence period and even in the early post-Independence years has declined in importance over the years (Table 19.3). In some States, land revenue has been abolished altogether.

B. Agricultural Income Tax: Agricultural income tax (entry 46 of List II in the Seventh Schedule of the Constitution) which could have been an important source of revenue for the States has remained negligible till date. It is discussed separately in Chapter 20.

Table 19.2: States' Own Taxes, Breakdown between Direct and Indirect Taxes with Percentage Shares: 1990-91 to 2005-06

(Rs. crore)

Year	States' own taxes (3+4)	Direct taxes	Indirect taxes	Col. 3 as % of Col. 2	Col. 4 as % of Col. 2
1	2	3	4	5	6
1990-91	30,145	1,230	28,915	4.1	95.9
1991-92	35,837	1,304	34,533	3.6	96.4
1992-93	39,530	1,247	38,283	3.2	96.8
1993-94	46,219	1,414	44,805	3.1	96.9
1994-95	55,552	1,905	53,647	3.4	96.6
1995-96	64,034	2,213	61,822	3.5	96.5
1996-97	71,294	2,163	69,131	3.0	97.0
1997-98	81,439	2,256	79,183	2.8	97.2
1998-99	89,220	2,518	86,702	2.8	97.2
1999-00	1,02,831	1,904	99,927	2.8	97.2
2000-01	1,16,717	3,457	1,13,260	2.9	97.1
2001-02	1,27,475	2,911	1,23,564	3.1	96.9
2002-03	1,40,372	4,002	1,36,370	2.8	97.2
2003-04	1,59,736	4,455	1,55,281	2.8	97.2
2004-05	1,87,996	4,820	1,83,176	2.6	97.4
2005-06	2,15,601	5,054	2.10,547	2.3	97.7

2004-05 = Revised estimates; 2005-06 = Budget estimates.

Source: Rearranged data from Government of India, Ministry of Finance, *Indian Public Finance Statistics*, 2005-2006, Tables 1.7. Columns 5 and 6 calculations own.

C. Professions Tax: A tax on professions (entry 60 of List II in the Seventh Schedule of the Constitution) is levied as a fixed amount per person per year on professions. It is a kind of licence fee to practice a profession. The tax is levied irrespective of the income derived by a person from the profession practiced by him. The scope of this tax is spelt out in Article 276, the clause (2) of which fixes the amount payable by a person on account of this tax. Presently, the total amount payable in respect of any one person to the State by way of such tax is not to exceed Rs. 2,500 per annum.

19.2.2 Composition of Indirect Taxes:

A. Sales Tax: An outstanding development in the sphere of State finances since Independence has been the precipitous growth in the relative revenue significance of sales tax levied under entry 54 of List II in the Seventh Schedule of the Constitution. It has grown considerably in depth and coverage, and forms the mainstay of States' tax revenue. It is levied not only on consumer goods but also on raw materials and capital goods. In 1950-51, the relative share of sales tax was 26.1 per cent: Rs. 58 crore out of a total collection of Rs. 222 crore from States' taxes. In the budget estimates for 2005-06, this share stood at 57.0 per cent (Table 19.3).

Prior to tax reforms initiated in early 1990s, sales tax was characterised by a multiplicity of tax rate and exemptions, lack of uniformity across States, large number of exemptions and concessions, and differing procedures for tax collection. In mid-1990s, most states had agreed to phase out the incentive related exemptions and implement floor rates of sales tax. As part of the nation wide efforts to redesign commodity taxation and the implementation of CENVAT at the level of the Centre, many States have modified their sales tax regimes to launch a state level VAT under the scheme prepared by the Empowered Committee for this purpose.

Sales tax is examined separately in Chapter 21.

B. State Excises: Under entry 51 of List II in the Seventh Schedule of the Constitution, the States are empowered to levy, "duties of excise on ... (a) alcoholic liquors for human consumption; (b) opium, Indian hemp and other narcotic drugs and narcotics; but not including medicinal and toilet preparations containing alcohol or any substance included in sub-paragraph (b) of this entry". The revenues accrue to the states in the form of licence duties from the vendors as well as the tax, which can be specific or ad valorem.

After sales tax, State excise duties (on liquors and other narcotics) are the most important source of States' own tax revenues. Though second in importance, their relative revenue significance has declined over the years from 21.6 per cent in 1950-51 to 11.7 per cent in 2005-06 (B.E) [Table 19.3]. This has happened mainly because of the policy of prohibition adopted in some States from time to time. However, it is difficult to totally prohibit the consumption of alcohol in the states. Attempts at full prohibition lead to illegal production and export of the tax base to the neighboring states.

It is noteworthy that while in Western countries the main objective of duties on intoxicants is revenue collection, in India the overriding consideration in imposing these duties is to discourage consumption of intoxicants as a matter of public policy. Since demand for alcoholic beverages is generally price-inelastic,

Table 19.3: Trends in the Level and Composition of Revenue from States' Own Taxes: Selected Years

(Rs. crore)

State taxes	1950-51	1960-61	1970-71	1980-81	1990-91	2000-01	2005-06#
A+B Revenue from States' taxes	222 (100.0)	455 (100.0)	1,546 (100.0)	6,665 (100.0)	30,145 (100.0)	1,16,717 (100.0)	2,15,601 (100.0)
A. Direct taxes of which	55 (24.8)	110 (24.2)	140 (9.0)	271 (4.1)	1,230 (4.1)	3,457 (3.0)	5,054 (2.3)
1. Land revenue	49 (22.1)	97 (21.3)	113 (7.3)	145 (2.2)	607 (2.0)	1,377 (1.2)	2,297 (1.1)
2. Agricultural income tax	3 (1.3)	10 (2.2)	10 (0.6)	46 (0.7)	169 (0.6)	76 (0.0)	55 (0.0)
3. Other taxes*	3 (1.3)	3 (0.6)	17 (1.1)	80 (1.2)	454 (1.5)	2,004 (1.7)	2,688 (1.2)
B. Indirect taxes of which	167 (75.2)	345 (75.8)	1,406 (91.0)	6,394 (95.9)	28,915 (95.9)	1,13,260 (97.0)	2,10,557 (97.7)
1. Sales tax	58 (26.1)	158 (34.7)	755 (48.8)	3,887 (58.3)	16,476 (54.6)	68,386 (58.6)	1,22,796 (57.0)
2. State excises	48 (21.6)	53 (11.6)	194 (12.5)	824 (12.4)	4,798 (15.9)	15,825 (13.6)	25,168 (11.7)
3. Taxes on vehicles	7 (3.2)	33 (7.2)	104 (6.7)	415 (6.2)	1,535 (5.1)	6,506 (5.6)	12,713 (5.9)
4. Stamps and registration fees	26 (11.7)	43 (9.4)	122 (7.9)	425 (6.4)	2,089 (6.9)	9,343 (8.0)	22,031 (10.2)
5. Other taxes**	28 (12.6)	58 (12.7)	231 (14.9)	843 (12.6)	4,017 (13.3)	13,200 (11.3)	27,849 (12.9)

#Budget estimates.

*Profession tax, surcharge on cash crops and urban immovable property tax.

**Taxes on passengers and goods, electricity duty, entertainment tax and cess on sugarcane etc.

Figures in parentheses indicate corresponding percentages of the total revenue from States' own taxes.

Sources: Reserve Bank of India, *Report on Currency and Finance,* Vol. II, (various years); and Government of India, Ministry of Finance, *Indian Public Finance Statistics*, 2005-2006, Tables 1.7 and 3.2.

this tax provides a case for keeping high tax rates for controlling the level of consumption. In fact, high tax rates yield both high revenues and greater control on consumption.

C. Taxes on Motor Vehicles: Under entry 57 of List II in the Seventh Schedule, State Governments enjoy the power to levy taxes on vehicles suitable for use on roads. These are levied for registration, permits, driving licences etc. and are based on the type of vehicle (truck, bus, car, scooter etc.). In the 2005-06 budgets, taxes on vehicles accounted for 5.9 per cent of tax revenue from States' own taxes (Table 19.3). In most states a compounded system of motor vehicle tax exists, where a one time levy is paid for the life of the vehicle. This arrangement has saved the taxpayers from the hassle of interacting with the tax department every year.

D. Entertainment Tax: Under entry 62 of List II in the Seventh Schedule of the Constitution, States are empowered to levy taxes on entertainment. Such taxes are levied on the price charged for admission to any place of entertainment such as a circus, cinema, theatre, exhibition, variety show, etc. The bulk of revenue from this tax is provided by the cinema shows. Though the tax is collected from the exhibitors, the ultimate burden is borne by the cinegoers. According to Tenth Five Year Plan (2002-07), "The tax rates in the entertainment industry are among the highest in the world. Though some State Governments are waiving entertainment tax on multiplex theatres for periods ranging from three to ten years, on the whole tax on film theatres continues to be high. Lowering of these rates will not only benefit the entertainment industry, which has an annual turnover of Rs. 400 crore, but will also promote real estate development in the form of theatres in cities, towns and even villages." [3]

In recent times, entertainment tax has lost its importance due to proliferation of means of home-based entertainments.

E. Stamp Duty and Registration Fees: Under entry 63 of List II in the Seventh Schedule of the Constitution, Stamp duty is levied on the registration of property or other conveyances. In the 2005-06 budgets of the State Governments, the share of stamp duty and registration fees in revenue from own taxes of the States was estimated at 10.2 per cent (Table19.3).

Till recently, the stamp duty rates were quite high in most states and the procedures for evaluating the conveyances were also complicated. In this context, the Tenth Five Year Plan (2002-07) remarked, "Stamp duty needs to be paid on all documents which are registered and the rate varies from state to state. With stamp duty rates of 13 per cent in Delhi, 14.5 per cent in Uttar Pradesh and 12.5 per cent in Haryana, India has perhaps one of the highest levels of stamp duty. Some states even have double stamp incidence, first on land and then on its development. In contrast the maximum rate levied in most developed markets whether in Singapore or Europe is in the range of 1-2 per cent. Even the National Housing and Habitat Policy, 1998, recommended a stamp duty rate of 2-3 per cent. Most of the methods to avoid registration are basically to avoid payment of high stamp duty.

Another fall out of high stamp duty rates is the understatement of the proceeds of a sale. This is also linked to payment of income tax and capital gains tax. When registration has not been effected, a transfer is not deemed to have taken place and hence capital gains tax can be totally avoided. Thus, the present provisions in various laws and their poor implementation have led to a situation where there is considerable financial loss to the exchequer on account of understatement of sale proceeds, non-registration and consequent non-payment of stamp duty and avoidance of capital gains tax." [4]

Of late, states have undertaken reforms by reducing the duty rates and streamlining procedures for evaluation of property. After the reduction of rates, the general experience has been revenue-augmenting due to improved compliance of law.

F. Electricity Duty: Under entry 53 of List II in the Seventh Schedule of the Constitution, the electricity duty is charged to consumers along with the electricity consumption rates. The rates are meant for the providers of electricity (electricity boards) while the electricity duty is meant for the state treasury.

G. Octroi: Octroi, an important source of revenue for local bodies, is a tax on the entry of goods into a local area from other areas for the purpose of consumption or sale. It is mentioned in entry 52 of List II (State List) in the Seventh Schedule. Industry and trade circles have criticised the continuation of octroi and termed it as a retarding factor in the growth of business and commerce in the country. By obstructing the free movement of vehicles carrying goods, the levy of octroi causes delays and thus hampers industrial progress. Therefore, it is suggested that octroi should be replaced by some other form of taxation, e.g. surcharge on sales tax. Unfortunately, State Governments are not favourably disposed to these suggestions and prefer to continue with the controversial levy.

H. Land and Buildings: Under entry 49 of List II in the Seventh Schedule of the Constitution, States are empowered to impose taxes on land and buildings, popularly known as property tax or house tax. State Governments generally assign this tax to municipal bodies.

Property tax is charged by the municipal authorities for the upkeep of basic civic services in the city. Generally, the property tax is levied on the basis of reasonable rent at which the property might be let from year to year. The reasonable rent can be actual rent if it is found to be fair and reasonable. In the case of un-let properties, the rental value is to be estimated on the basis of letting rates in the locality.

19.3 Local Finance

The Constitution does not reserve any taxes for the local bodies. Since local government is a State subject (entry 5 of List II), State Governments may assign any of the taxes in the State List, wholly or partially, to urban local bodies. Taxes usually assigned to local bodies are property taxes, octroi and taxes on professions. Property tax (house tax) is an important source of revenue for local bodies.

Assigning taxes enables State Governments to exercise a degree of supervision and control over the affairs of city corporations, municipalities, district boards, and other local bodies. These local bodies provide certain public services like basic health and education, construction and maintenance of local roads, sanitation, street lighting, and parks. Local governments also receive grants-in-aid from State Governments and earn non-tax revenue from enterprises operated by them.

Local Finance is discussed separately in Part VII of this book.

Notes

1. See Table 5 in Part X of this book.
2. See Table 5 in Part X of this book.
3. Government of India, Planning Commission, *Tenth Five Year Plan* (2002-07), Vol. II, p. 835.
4. Ibid., pp. 833-834.

20

Taxation of Agricultural Income

When income tax was introduced in India in 1860, agricultural income was also subject to taxation. However, the Income Tax Act, 1886, defined agricultural income and exempted it from the purview of income tax law and this arrangement continued till the enactment of the Government of India Act, 1935. The Act of 1935, segregated agricultural and non-agricultural incomes and provided, for the first time, a separate provincial levy on agricultural incomes.

20.1 Constitutional Provisions

The Constitution retained the distinction between the two types of income and allocated the power to tax agricultural incomes to the States. [1] Entry 82 of List I (Union List) in the Seventh Schedule of the Constitution empowers the Parliament to levy 'taxes on income other than agricultural income.' The State Governments enjoy exclusive powers to make laws with respect to taxes on agricultural incomes vide entry 46 of List II (State List) in the Seventh Schedule. Although exempt from Central income tax, agricultural incomes are taken into account for the limited purpose of determining the rate of tax on non-agricultural incomes in certain cases from the assessment year 1974-75.

Presently, about half a dozen States levy agricultural income tax, in three of them it is confined to plantation crops, and in all cases the revenue is meagre. The share of this tax in the total revenue from States' taxes is negligible (Table 20.1). Thus, agricultural income tax, which could have been a dependable source of revenue for the States, has remained largely untapped so far. Moreover, land revenue which formed the mainstay of States' tax revenue during pre-Independence years and even in the early post-Independence period, has receded into insignificance over the years (Table 20.1).

20.2 Committee on Taxation of Agricultural Wealth and Income (Chairman: K.N. Raj), 1972

The Taxation Enquiry Commission, 1953-54, had suggested the taxation of agricultural income by all States on equity considerations. A more comprehensive examination of the question of direct taxation of agriculture was undertaken by the Committee on Taxation of Agricultural Wealth and Income. [2] Appointed in February 1972 by the Government of India, the Committee was required, under

Table 20.1: Trends in the Relative Shares of Land Revenue and Agricultural Income Tax in States' Own Taxes: Selected Years

(Rs. crore)

State taxes	1950-51	1960-61	1970-71	1980-81	1990-91	2000-01	2005-06#
A+B Revenue from States' own taxes	222 (100.0)	455 (100.0)	1,546 (100.0)	6,665 (100.0)	30,145 (100.0)	1,16,717 (100.0)	2,15,601 (100.0)
A. Direct taxes of which	55 (24.8)	110 (24.2)	140 (9.0)	271 (4.1)	1,230 (4.1)	3,457 (3.0)	5,054 (2.3)
1. Land revenue	49 (22.1)	97 (21.3)	113 (7.3)	145 (2.2)	607 (2.0)	1,377 (1.2)	2,297 (1.1)
2. Agricultural income tax	3 (1.3)	10 (2.2)	10 (0.6)	46 (0.7)	169 (0.6)	76 (0.0)	55 (0.0)
3. Other taxes*	3 (1.3)	3 (0.6)	17 (1.1)	80 (1.2)	454 (1.5)	2,004 (1.7)	2,688 (1.2)
B. Indirect taxes of which	167 (75.2)	345 (75.8)	1,406 (91.0)	6,394 (95.9)	28,915 (95.9)	1,13,260 (97.0)	2,10,557 (97.7)

#Budget estimates.

*Profession tax, surcharge on cash crops and urban immovable property tax.

Figures in parentheses indicate corresponding percentages of the total revenue from States' own taxes.

Sources: Reserve Bank of India, *Report on Currency and Finance,* Vol. II, (various years); and Government of India, Ministry of Finance, *Indian Public Finance Statistics*, 2005-2006, Tables 1.7 and 3.2.

the terms of reference, to suggest methods by which direct taxation of agricultural wealth and income could be used more effectively for raising additional resources for development. It was further asked to recommend specifically ways and means by which taxation of agricultural wealth and income could be used to reduce economic disparities and promote more efficient utilisation of the available land and labour resources. The Committee submitted its report in October 1972.

The Committee disfavoured, on practical considerations, a full-scale coverage of agricultural incomes under the Central income tax. However, it suggested partial integration of agricultural incomes with non-agricultural incomes for the limited purpose of determining the rates of taxation. It also maintained that the additional revenue realised as a result of the partial integration of agricultural with non-agricultural income in the above manner, should go entirely to the State of origin of the agricultural income so aggregated. Consequently, from the assessment year 1974-75, Central income tax takes into account the income of an assessee from agriculture for the limited purpose of determining the rate of tax on non-agricultural incomes in certain cases.

Although averse to the idea of full integration of agricultural and non-agricultural incomes for income tax purposes, the Committee favoured the possibility, with certain cautions, of integrated taxation of agricultural and non-agricultural wealth. While the power to tax agricultural income belongs exclusively to the States, there is no constitutional impediment to an integrated taxation of agricultural and non-agricultural wealth by the Centre.

As its main recommendation, the Committee suggested the imposition of Agricultural Holding Tax (AHT) which in its view would secure for the States an additional revenue from well-off sections of agriculturists with much less harassment of the assessees than is likely if Central income tax is extended to the farm sector. The Committee accepted the view that the incidence of direct taxation should broadly be the same on comparable income and wealth groups irrespective of the sources and the forms in which wealth is held. In devising a system of direct taxation of agriculture, it is necessary to ensure progressivity, a principle that has not governed the land revenue. The Committee emphasised that for purposes of direct taxation, the family should be the basic unit of assessment so as to prevent large-scale avoidance.

For a rational system of direct taxation of agriculture, the Committee laid down the following criteria: 1. It should take account of the difference in productivity of land depending upon the particular crops grown in a region. 2. Its incidence should be uniform in different parts of the country. 3. It should reflect changes in productivity and prices over a period of time. 4. It should be possible to build into the tax an element of progression. As for differences in productivity of land, the Committee pinpointed the following factors: (a) soil-climatic differences, (b) conditions of water supply, and (c) crops grown.

Taking into account various factors which cause variations in the productivity of land, the Committee recommended a scheme of Agricultural Holding Tax (AHT) with the following salient features.

1. The country should be divided into a sufficiently large number of soil-climatically homogenous districts/tracts so that differences having any significant influence on productivity are taken into account.
2. For each such district/tract norms of output of different crops per hectare for each year should be worked out on the basis of estimates of yield for the previous 10 years and these should be valued at the relevant average harvest prices of the preceding three years.
3. From the value of the gross output of the crops arrived at in the above manner, allowance should be made for the paid out costs of cultivation (40 to 50 per cent of the value of gross output) and also for depreciation of assets.
4. The norms arrived at in the above manner would form the rateable value of a hectare of land growing different crops in different districts/ tracts.
5. To provide for the costs of development, the Committee suggested granting of development allowance to all agricultural holdings at the rate of 20 per cent of the rateable value subject to a maximum of Rs. 1,000.
6. To determine the actual tax liability under AHT, the Committee devised a simple formula to be applied to the rateable value of the holdings minus the development allowance. If the rateable value of a holding (minus the development allowance) is 'X' thousand rupees, the AHT should form X/2 per cent of this amount. For example, if the rateable value of a holding is Rs. 10,000, the AHT would be 9/2 or 4.5 per cent of Rs. 9,000 (i.e. Rs. 10,000 minus Rs. 1,000 deductible as development allowance) which is equal to Rs. 405.
7. As the incidence of AHT decreases progressively on small holdings, the Committee favoured the application of the formula to rateable value up to Rs. 600. For holdings of rateable value below Rs. 600, the AHT may be fixed at a flat rate of Re. 1 per holding.

Although the recommendations of the Committee were widely welcomed, it is unfortunate that the State Governments have generally remained lukewarm in taxing agriculture directly. Exemption of agricultural income from taxation deprives the States of a potential source of revenue. Emphasising the need for taxing agricultural sector, the Sixth Five Year Plan noted, "Direct taxes on agriculture at present constitute less than 1 per cent of the total agricultural income. Land revenue, which is the principal direct tax on agriculture, is generally a flat rate levy and, consequently, regressive in character. Fixation of minimum support and procurement prices for major agricultural crops and provision of various inputs such as fertilisers, irrigation, and electricity at subsidised or concessional rates have helped raise agricultural incomes particularly of large farmers. It is, therefore, necessary to consider measures for raising additional resources from the agricultural sector and introducing a measure of progressivity in agricultural taxation." [3]

The near absence of direct taxation of the agricultural sector is partly due to the preponderance of big landlords and other vested interests in State legislatures. It shows how the rural rich have effectively resisted additional tax burden upon themselves. The absence or inadequacy of tax on agricultural incomes is an example of the insufficient use of taxation powers allotted to the States. Moreover, the exclusion of agricultural incomes from the income tax base provides opportunities for tax evasion by camouflaging taxable income and black money as gains from agriculture. It is not uncommon among the urban elite to own agricultural farms on the outskirts of metropolitan cities for the sole purpose of diverting their high non-agricultural incomes from a taxable zone to a tax haven. The unequal tax treatment of similar incomes, though from different sources, violates the principle of horizontal equity.

20.2.1 Views of the State Governments: The States, on their part, have highlighted serious problems in the assessment of agricultural incomes. These include shrinkage of the tax base due to the ceiling on holdings, widely dispersed potential assessees, fluctuations in production due to uncertain weather conditions, and lack of accounting practices in the agricultural sector. Although disinterested in levying tax on agricultural incomes, States have also expressed themselves against any move to transfer the tax to the Union List. More interestingly, the Centre too is not enthusiastic to adopt the tax as was made clear in the Long Term Fiscal Policy, "It is often stated that exclusion of agricultural income is a major shortcoming of the personal income tax base in India and constitutes an important explanation for the weak revenue raising capacity of the personal income tax. Taxing agricultural income presents many conceptual and administrative problems. Land revenue and taxation of agricultural income are State subjects under the Constitution. The Centre has no intention of seeking any change in this position." [4] For proper assessment of agricultural incomes, some knowledge of local conditions is required and so the primary responsibility of administering agricultural income tax should preferably be left to the States. Therefore, the taxation of agricultural incomes continues to remain a doubly neglected child of the Indian tax system.

It is well-known that since Independence, agriculture has remained the focus of developmental efforts in terms of irrigation facilities, availability of better quality seeds, subsidised fertilisers and electricity, credit and marketing facilities, and support prices for the main crops. The success of green revolution in many parts of the country is reflected in the increased productivity per hectare of various crops, and in the total production of foodgrains. It is also a known fact that the benefits of green revolution are unevenly distributed, creating an affluent elite group in rural areas. It is this class which must pay its due to the national exchequer, and revenue so raised may be earmarked for ameliorating the economic conditions of the downtrodden in villages. The States must exercise their constitutional power and tax the upper income agriculturists.

20.3 Tax Reforms Committee (Chairman: Raja Chelliah), 1991

The Tax Reforms Committee, 1991, recommended that agricultural income above Rs. 25,000 accruing to non-agriculturist assessees should be brought under the tax net. To quote, "the provisions for the taxation of agricultural income by the Central Government that we have recommended would not affect those agriculturists who (a) have agricultural income not exceeding Rs. 25,000 per year; or (b) have non-agricultural income not exceeding Rs. 28,000. This means that agriculturists who have only agricultural income or who have also non-agricultural income but have agricultural income not exceeding Rs. 25,000 will be left out. Thus, the tax will fall mainly on the larger non-agricultural assessees whose agricultural incomes exceed Rs. 25,000." [5] The Committee suggested that the tax proceeds attributable to the agricultural component of income should be distributed in their entirety among the States on the basis of origin.

In terms of the recommendations of the Committee, a person having agricultural income say of Rs. 26,000 and non-agricultural income of Rs. 36,000 (above the then existing exemption limit of Rs. 35,000) pays tax on both the incomes while another person having agricultural income of say Rs. 3 lakh (or even more) and non-agricultural income of Rs. 34,000 has no tax liability on any of his income. Such an arrangement will hardly stand the test of equity. True, the entire tax yield attributable to the agricultural component of income is to be distributed among the States on the basis of origin, there is the need for obtaining the consent of State Governments for making a Central provision for such a tax. It can be a lengthy and uncertain process.

20.4 Task Force on Direct Taxes (Chairman: Vijay Kelkar), 2002

The Task Force on Direct Taxes (Chairman: Vijay Kelkar) suggested the taxation of agricultural income in its report presented to the Government. [6] It recommended a tax rental arrangement between the Centre and the States (under Article 252 of the Constitution) authorising the Centre to impose a tax on agricultural incomes, the proceeds of which will be assigned to the States. The main argument for the proposal is the shifting of non-agricultural income to agricultural income by some unscrupulous assessees.

20.4.1 Critical Comments: The proposal needs to be examined from the following three different, though related, angles: economic logic, administrative feasibility, and political expediency. The case for taxing agricultural income is weak on all the three counts.

From the economic viewpoint, agriculture in India, for most farmers, is not a business as is the case in the United States, Canada, Australia, New Zealand and some other developed Western countries. It is essentially subsistence farming for the large majority of Indian farmers. This is borne out by the niggardly land-man ratio (0.33 hectare) and the utterly small average size of farms (1.6 hectares). With land availability remaining the same, the two ratios are expected to fall further in view of the increasing population. There is hardly any surplus for the tax collector.

Also, agriculture is gradually losing its shine as the leading sector of the Indian economy. A quarter of a century ago, it contributed around 50 per cent to India's national income. Presently, the figure stands at 27 per cent. Hence, agriculture is a receding economic activity, at least in relative terms. Conversely, the services sector has emerged as the dominant field of activity, accounting for 47 per cent share in national income. Tax collectors would do well if they concentrate on sunrise rather than sunset sectors.

The Kelkar Committee has taken the view that tax exemption of agricultural income violates the principle of horizontal equity (equal treatment of equals). This view is based on the erroneous assumption that incomes from various sources are alike. In fact, the amount of toil and suffering associated with an earning differs from case to case. Thus, it would be imprudent to treat alike Rs. 1 lakh earned by a property dealer in one transaction and Rs. 1 lakh earned by a farmer through year-long exertion and uncertainty. Income tax laws of various countries recognise this fact and accordingly treat different sources of income differently for tax purposes (called the schedular system of taxation). For example, in the United States the law distinguishes between earned and unearned incomes to provide tax credit (rebate) to earned income. Even in India, the distinction between earned and unearned incomes, introduced in 1945, continued for a long time before it was abolished from April 1, 1968. The present law of income tax does recognise and tax different sources of income differently, though to a limited extent. Thus, long-term capital gains enjoy special concessions including inflation indexing and a flat rate tax of 20 per cent. Till 1990-91, the differentiation principle was followed in the case of company taxation when trading and investment companies were subject to a higher flat rate tax (50 per cent) than industrial and other companies (45 per cent).

It is true, as pointed out by the Kelkar Committee, that some dishonest assessees do report their non-agricultural income as agricultural income to evade taxation. However, this is by no means a general practice and it would be unwise to punish the Indian farming community at large for the misdeeds of a few tax dodgers. Moreover, if such cases of fraud come to the notice of assessing officers, the culprits can be proceeded against under the existing anti-evasion laws. Showing non-agricultural income as agricultural income is simply a case of wrong-reporting of income and should be dealt with in the same manner as non-reporting and under-reporting of income.

Still further, Government concessions to the agricultural sector (fertiliser subsidy, minimum support price) are under review for possible reduction/withdrawal in the near future. To burden the agricultural sector with additional taxation at this juncture would be a retrograde step.

Administratively, taxing agricultural income is nothing short of a nightmare for tax authorities. There are serious conceptual and administrative problems in the assessment of agricultural incomes. These include widely dispersed potential assessees, fluctuations in production due to uncertain weather conditions, and lack of accounting practices in the agricultural sector. Furthermore, for proper assessment of agricultural incomes, some knowledge of local conditions is required and in the absence of it, the Central Government staff would be hard-pressed to administer agricultural income tax.

Taxing agricultural income is also politically inexpedient. The Kelkar Committee is not the first to recommend taxation of agricultural income. As far back as 1972, the Committee on Taxation of Agricultural Wealth and Income (Chairman: K.N. Raj) had also suggested direct taxation of agricultural income. More recently, the Tax Reforms Committee, 1991 (Chairman: Raja Chelliah) also favoured partial integration of agricultural income with non-agricultural income. However, these recommendations were never implemented.

The tax rental arrangement recommended by the Kelkar Committee is presumably based on the experience of the existing tax rental arrangement pertaining to additional excise duties on textiles, tobacco and sugar in lieu of sales tax. This arrangement was made way back in 1957 when the political climate of the country was far different from what it is presently. During the first two decades of Independence (1947-67), the Congress party ruled, with some exceptions, both at the Centre and in the States. This political homogeneity facilitated taxation agreements between the two tiers of the Government including the agreement reached in 1957. Since 1967, the politics of confrontation pursued by different political parties ruling at the Centre and in the States has hindered the rationalisation and harmonisation of India's tax system. Non-implementation of the recommendations of the Expert Committee on Replacement of Sales Tax by Additional Excise Duty, 1983 (Chairman: Kamlapati Tripathi) is a case in point. This Committee had recommended the replacement of sales tax by additional excise duty on *vanaspati*, drugs and medicines, cement, paper and paper board, and petroleum products.

Taxation of agricultural income is a State subject under the Constitution. Given the existing political equations, it is highly unlikely that the States would agree to surrender this right to the Centre.

Notes

1. For a historical account of agricultural income tax in India, see Government of India, Ministry of Finance, *Report of the Taxation Enquiry Commission* (Chairman: John Matthai), 1953-54, Vol. III, Chapter 3.

2. Government of India, Ministry of Finance, *Report of the Committee on Taxation of Agricultural Wealth and Income* (Chairman: K. N. Raj), 1972.

3. Government of India, Planning Commission, *Sixth Five Year Plan*, p. 77.

4. Government of India, *Long-Term Fiscal Policy*, December 1985, p. 35.

5. Government of India, Ministry of Finance, *Report of the Tax Reforms Committee* (Chairman: Raja Chelliah), Part I, 1992, p. 26.

6. Government of India, Ministry of Finance and Company Affairs, *Report of the Task Force on Direct Taxes* (Chairman: Vijay Kelkar), December 2002.

21

Sales Tax

In India, sales tax in its modern form was levied for the first time by the Government of Central Provinces (now Madhya Pradesh) in 1938. Since then, the levy has proved an outstanding development in the sphere of State finances. It has grown considerably in depth and coverage, and forms the mainstay of States' tax revenue. It is levied not only on consumer goods but also on raw materials and capital goods. In 1950-51, the relative share of sales tax was 26.1 per cent: Rs. 58 crore out of a total collection of Rs. 222 crore from States' taxes. Recording a precipitous growth in relative revenue significance, sales tax was estimated to contribute 55.5 per cent to States' own tax revenues in the 2004-05 budgets of the State Governments (Table 21.1).

21.1 Different Forms of Sales Tax

Sales tax is normally an *ad valorem* levy imposed on the seller with reference to the transaction of sale. On the basis of the stage of collection, sales tax is classified into (a) multi-point sales tax, and (b) single-point sales tax.

21.1.1 Multi-point Sales Tax: As a multi-point levy, sales tax may be applied at two or more stages of production and distribution and becomes akin to a turnover tax applicable at each transaction of purchase and sale. Multi-stage sales tax is politically expedient. A given amount of revenue can be raised at a lower rate of taxation which also reduces the temptation for tax evasion.

The chief demerit of multi-point sales tax is its encouragement to vertical integration of production and distribution processes. Thus, it discriminates against non-integrated firms. Producers of finished products prefer to produce their own materials and components, and this tendency harms the interest of independent suppliers, particularly small ones. Furthermore, multi-point sales tax discriminates against those goods, and their consumers, which have to pass through numerous transactions. In view of these disadvantages, John Due has opined, "On administrative as well as economic and equity grounds the objections to the multi-stage form are so great as to suggest its complete rejection, regardless of circumstances." [1]

21.1.2 Single-point Sales Tax: A single-point sales tax applies to one stage, either at the manufacturing, or the wholesale, or the retail level. At the manufacturing level, sales tax applies to the sale by manufacturer of finished

Table 21.1: Trends in the Relative Share of Sales Tax in States' Own Taxes: Selected Years

(Rs. crore)

State taxes	1950-51	1960-61	1970-71	1980-81	1990-91	2000-01	2005-06#
A+B Revenue from States' own taxes	222 (100.0)	455 (100.0)	1,546 (100.0)	6,665 (100.0)	30,145 (100.0)	1,16,717 (100.0)	2,15,601 (100.0)
A. Direct taxes	55 (24.8)	110 (24.2)	140 (9.0)	271 (4.1)	1,230 (4.1)	3,457 (3.0)	5,054 (2.3)
B. Indirect taxes of which	167 (75.2)	345 (75.8)	1,406 (91.0)	6,394 (95.9)	28,915 (95.9)	1,13,260 (97.0)	2,10,557 (97.7)
Sales tax	58 (26.1)	158 (34.7)	755 (48.8)	3,887 (58.3)	16,476 (54.6)	68,386 (58.6)	1,22,796 (57.0)

#Budget estimates.

Figures in parentheses indicate corresponding percentages of the total revenue from States' own taxes.

Sources: Reserve Bank of India, *Report on Currency and Finance,* Vol. II, (various years); and Government of India, Ministry of Finance, *Indian Public Finance Statistics*, 2005-2006, Tables 1.7 and 3.2.

product and is similar to excise duty. At the wholesale level, the tax applies to the last wholesale transaction, i.e. purchase by retailer. The retail sales tax applies to the final sale which means sale to the consumer.

The main advantage of single-point sales tax is that it does not discriminate against non-integrated firms as does multi-point sales tax. It, thus, discourages vertical integration and promotes horizontal integration. As regards the stage of its imposition, the retail stage is considered the most satisfactory due to the following reasons.

1. Sales tax at the retail stage is collected when final sale to the consumer takes place. Thus, it avoids what economists call the cascading or pyramiding effect of a tax. The contention is that middlemen apply fixed percentage mark ups to purchase prices and if the purchase price include taxes (as is the case if sales tax is imposed at manufacturer's, or wholesaler's level), the mark ups will be applicable to the tax component of the purchase prices as well, a situation which must be avoided in the interest of the consumers.
2. A given revenue can be realised by applying a lower tax rate at the retail stage as compared to other stages because the margins of all middlemen are included at the final stage of sale, meaning thereby the enlargement of the tax base at the retail stage.
3. The desired change in the ratio of tax to consumer expenditure can be achieved more effectively in case of retail-stage sales tax. This will be difficult at 'other stages' because the margins of dealers on various goods, besides being applied to the tax component of the purchase prices, may differ significantly.
4. Sales tax at the retail stage can be shown separately from the price and thus made known to the purchaser, increasing tax consciousness among the taxpayers.
5. Expected changes in the rates of retail sales tax do not lead to changes in inventory position of the firms. Anticipated changes in the rates of sales tax at 'other stages' may influence inventory decisions of the firms causing dislocation in trade circles.

However, retail-stage sales tax has its own problems, the chief being the large number of taxpayers in the form of small shopkeepers and scattered retail outlets. In developing countries, the problem of tax administration is more acute in view of widespread illiteracy, lack of monetisation, and poor accounting practices. From administrative viewpoint, this form of taxation is costlier and cumbersome, offering ample scope for tax evasion and corruption.

Sales tax at manufacturing or wholesale stage is administratively preferable because the number of taxpayers is small and readily identifiable. However, the problem of 'cascading' will reappear. In fact, the farther we move from the retail level, the more serious the problem of 'cascading' becomes. In short, the problem boils down to a trade off between economic rationale and administrative efficiency. The relative weightage to competing objectives depends on political judgement and the economic circumstances under which the sales tax system has to operate.

21.2 Pre-Constitution Developments

Entry 48 of List II in the Seventh Schedule of the Government of India Act, 1935, vested in the Provinces the power to levy 'taxes on the sale of goods and on advertisements'.

The Government of the Central Provinces (now Madhya Pradesh) was the first to take advantage of this provision when it levied a retail sales tax on motor spirit and lubricants in 1938. This so-called 'petrol tax' was a selective sales tax imposed through the Central Provinces and Berar Sales of Motor Spirit and Lubrication Taxation Act, 1938.

In 1939, Madras levied a general multi-point sales tax through the Madras General Sales Tax Act, 1939. The tax levied at the rate of half per cent was ostensibly meant to compensate the loss of revenue resulting from the policy of prohibition.

21.2.1 Initial Legal Hurdles: Since its very inception, sales tax has been a controversial levy embroiled in legal wranglings. Thus, soon after its enactment, the Central Provinces Act referred above was challenged by the Central Government as unconstitutional. It may be recalled that entry 45 of List II in Seventh Schedule of the Government of India Act, 1935 had given the Central Government the power to levy excise on tobacco and other goods manufactured or produced in India. Hence, the Central Government maintained that sales tax on motor spirit and lubricants by Central Provinces was *ultra vires* because the power to levy excise on such products belonged to it (Central Government). Deciding in favour of the Provincial Government, the Federal Court observed that such taxes were in no way connected with the production or manufacture of goods, but were imposed on their sale.

In another legal battle, the Central Government contested the Madras General Sales Tax Act, 1939 referred to above. Being a multi-point sales tax, it covered sales by manufacturers also which was challenged by the Central Government. Once again, the Federal Court decided in favour of the Provincial Government and held that it had the power to tax sales of every kind, including sales by a manufacturer or producer.

The above two judicial pronouncements made it clear that the Provinces were competent to tax sales of any commodity and at any stage. In other words, a clear-cut distinction was drawn between the two, excise to be a tax on the act of production or manufacture, and the sales tax to be a levy on the act of sale.

Initial legal squabblings over, sales tax gained rapid popularity among the Provinces with the beginning of 1940s. Bengal adopted a single-point general sales tax levied at retail level in 1941. In the same year, Punjab introduced a general sales tax broadly based on the multi-point model of Madras. A general sales tax on the lines of single-point system of Bengal was introduced by Bihar in 1944 and by Bombay in 1946. Other Provinces followed suit and by 1948, all of them were operating sales tax in one form or the other with the notable exception of Jammu and Kashmir. This State was the last to introduce sales tax in 1962.

21.2.2 Beggar-my-neighbour Policies: There was no provision in the Government of India Act, 1935, to restrict or prohibit the Provinces from levying sales tax on inter-State transactions. In other words, the Act did not require the Provinces to levy sales tax only on those transactions which exclusively took place in their respective territories.

Taking advantage of this loophole in the Act, almost all the Provincial legislatures enacted sales tax laws which enabled them to tax goods exported from one State to another. These practices led to multiple taxation of the same transaction by different Provinces. As one scholar remarked, "Perhaps, the most important problem relating to sales taxation in the pre-Constitution period was the taxation of inter-State sales. All the Provinces, with the exception of West Bengal, were collecting sales tax on goods being sent to other Provinces and were, in effect, indulging in 'beggar-my-neighbour policies." [2]

In order to sort out these problems and to ensure all-India co-ordination, the Government of India convened a conference of the Finance Ministers of States in October, 1948. At this conference, attempts were made to achieve some degree of uniformity in the taxation of inter-State sales. However, these attempts failed in view of the widespread disagreement among the States. In particular, States which produced important raw materials/ manufactured goods were opposed to changes that would result in the exclusion of inter-State trade from the purview of their sales tax laws. In short, the system of sales tax during the pre-Constitution period was arbitrary and bereft of national considerations.

21.3 Constitution of India and the Provisions for the Regulation of Taxation of Inter-State Sales

The problems relating to taxation of inter-State sales were considered by the Drafting Committee of the Constituent Assembly. It proposed incorporation of provisions in the Constitution restricting the powers of the State Governments in respect of the levy of sales tax in the course of foreign trade, inter-State trade, and on essential commodities. In spite of opposition from some States, these provisions were finally incorporated in the Constitution as Article 286 (described below).

Under entry 54 of List II (State List) in the Seventh Schedule of the Constitution, the States were given the power to levy "a tax on sales or purchases of goods other than newspapers". This provision was quite similar to entry 48 of List II in the Seventh Schedule of the Government of India Act, 1935. However, under the Constitution, the States' power to levy sales tax was subject to a number of restrictions. These restrictions on the sale or purchase of goods as mentioned in Article 286 of the Constitution were the following.

1. No law of a State shall impose a tax on the sale or purchase of goods where such sale or purchase takes place: (a) outside the State, or (b) in the course of import of goods into, or export of goods out of, the territory of India.
2. Except in so far as the Parliament may by law otherwise provide, no law of a State shall impose a tax on the sale or purchase of any goods where such sale or purchase takes place in the course of inter-State trade or commerce.
3. No law made by the legislature of a State imposing a tax on the sale or purchase of any such goods as have been declared by Parliament by law to be essential for the life of the community, shall have effect unless it has been reserved for the consideration of the President and has received his assent.

In simple words, the States were prevented from taxing the following transactions: 1. Sales or purchases in the course of foreign trade. 2. Sales of goods delivered in another State for consumption purpose. 3. Sales in the course of inter-State trade and commerce. Furthermore, the power of States to levy the tax on commodities declared to be 'essential' by the Parliament was made subject to the prior approval of the President.

21.3.1 Consequences of Constitutional Restrictions on Sales Tax: The first restriction resulted in considerable loss of revenue to States, which were levying sales tax on exports. The main losers in this category were Bombay, Bihar, Madhya Pradesh, Orissa, and Assam. Nevertheless, this was the least controversial provision of Article 286.

The second and third restrictions, the benefits of which applied equally to registered dealers, unregistered dealers, and consumers, led to large scale evasion and avoidance of tax and hence loss of revenue to the States in general. As the Taxation Enquiry Commission, 1953-54, observed, "Traders in one State started to sell direct to unregistered dealers and consumers in another. Similarly, consumers of valuable commodities tried to get these from dealers in another State rather than buy the articles from their local dealers. The practice grew for sales of goods within a State itself to be shown in the books of accounts as having been made to fictitious dealers outside the State and the goods having then been resold by those dealers to consumers within the State. For valuable commodities like motor vehicles, jewellery, watches, etc. this practice became very common. On transactions that could be shown to be in the course of inter-State trade, the 'exporting' State was prohibited under Article 286 from levying the sales tax; and if the goods delivered as a result of these transactions were shown to be received by individual consumers or unregistered dealers neither could any tax be levied on them by the 'importing' State. Thus, many of these transactions escaped sales tax altogether." [3]

The loss of revenue was more for States with single-point system as compared to States having multi-point sales taxation. This was so because the restriction was not applicable to sales in the State prior to the last point of sale for export to another State.

The constitutional restrictions led to uneconomic diversion of trade and production centres. The problems which the constitutional provisions sought to solve got further compounded *albeit* with a different nature. To quote, "The constitutional restrictions on sales taxation greatly increased the scope for evasion. While the problem before the Constitution had been multiple taxation (by different States) on the same act of inter-State sale, the problem after the Constitution was that inter-State sales frequently escaped taxation altogether." [4]

21.3.2 Essential Goods Act, 1952: As already noted, in addition to the above restrictions, Article 286 also prevented the States from levying tax on sales or purchases of goods declared by the Parliament to be essential for the life of the community, except with the previous assent of the President. For this purpose, the Parliament enacted the Essential Goods (Declaration and Regulation of Tax on Sale or Purchase) Act, 1952, and various commodities were declared as essential including cereals and pulses, fresh and dried fruits, fresh milk, meat, fish, salt, hides and skins, iron and steel, coal, fertilisers, petroleum products, and books.

As to the desirable purpose of the Act, the Taxation Enquiry Commission, 1953-54, noted, "It is obvious that the object of restricting the power of the states to levy a tax on the sale or purchase of 'essential goods' is to achieve some degree of uniformity in the tax burden on those goods, and not necessarily or in all cases to eliminate altogether the sales tax on such goods. When the Bombay Government sought the assent of the President to tax some of the 'essential goods' under their new multi-point tax system, the assent was given on condition that the tax burden on these goods should not in any event exceed the previous tax burden under the single-point system. This seems to indicate that the policy underlying the restriction is one of freezing the existing tax levied on these goods and of ensuring that new proposals to tax them are confined within reasonable limits." [5]

In spite of its desirable objectives, the enactment of the Essential Goods Act, 1952, led to various problems and criticism from some State Governments. Since the legislation was not retrospective, the States which had been levying sales tax on 'essential goods' prior to the passage of the Essential Goods Act, continued to levy the tax. However, those States which sought to levy the tax after the passage of the Act had to obtain the consent of the President. This evoked sharp resentment among the State Governments.

The resentment among the States was further fuelled by the fact that the Central Government itself was levying relatively high rates of excise/customs duties on some of the so-called 'essential goods'.

21.4 Constitution (Sixth Amendment) Act, 1956

In view of the problems arising from constitutional restrictions on the taxation of inter-State sales, the Taxation Enquiry Commission, 1953-54, recommended as follows, "In essence, the sales tax must continue to be a State tax. However, power and responsibility of the State must end and that of the Union begin when the sales tax of one State impinges administratively and fiscally on the consumers of another State. Inter-State sales tax should be the concern of the Union." [6]

Consequently, the Constitution was amended by the Sixth Amendment Act of 1956. Under this Amendment, the Parliament was empowered to impose 'taxes on the sale or purchase of goods other than newspapers, where such sale or purchase takes place in the course of inter-State trade or commerce'. This new provision in the Constitution was made by inserting entry 92A in List I (Union List) in the Seventh Schedule. Simultaneously, entry 54 in List II (State List) was made subject to the provisions of the new entry 92A of List I. Also, Article 269 of the Constitution was amended which added a new clause (1)(g) which permitted taxes on the sale or purchase of goods in the course of inter-State trade to be levied and collected by the Government of India but assigned to the States. [7] Again, clauses (2) and (3) of Article 286 of the unamended Constitution were substituted by new clauses to make it read as follows.

(1) No law of a State shall impose or authorise the imposition of a tax on the sale or purchase of goods where such sale or purchase takes place (a) outside the State, or (b) in the course of import of goods into or export of goods out of the territory of India.

(2) Parliament may by law formulate principles for determining when a sale or purchase of goods takes place in any of the ways mentioned in clause (1).

(3) Any law of a State shall in so far as it imposes or authorises the

imposition of a tax on the sale or purchase of goods declared by Parliament by law to be of special importance in inter-State trade or commerce, be subject to such restrictions and conditions in regard to the system of levy, rates and other incidents of the tax as Parliament may by law specify.

The new Article 286(2) gave Parliament the powers to define a sale outside a State. The new Article 286(3) is different from the old 286(3) in the following respect: In the old provision, Parliament had the authority to restrict State taxation of commodities declared by Parliament to be 'essential for the life of the community'. In the new provision, Parliament is empowered to restrict State taxation of goods declared to be of special importance in inter-State trade only. [8]

21.5 Central Sales Tax (CST) Act, 1956

Consequent upon the Constitution (Sixth Amendment) Act, 1956, the Central Sales Tax (CST) Act was passed in 1956. The following three main objectives of the CST Act were stated in the Preamble: 1. To formulate principles for determining when a sale or purchase of goods takes place in the course of inter-State trade or in the course of import into or export from India. 2. To provide for the levy, collection, and distribution of taxes on sale of goods in the course of inter-State trade or commerce. 3. To declare certain goods to be of special importance in inter-State trade and specify the restrictions to which State laws imposing taxes on the sale and purchase of such goods of special importance shall be subject.

21.5.1 Main Provisions of CST Act: The regulations contained in the CST Act provide, *inter alia*, for a degree of uniformity by prescribing a maximum rate of sales tax on certain goods considered important for the whole country. According to Section 3 of the CST Act, a sale or purchase of goods is deemed to take place in the course of inter-State trade if it (a) occasions the movement of goods from one State to another, or (b) is effected by a transfer of documents of title to the goods during their movement from one State to another.

Section 14 of the Act declares certain goods to be of special importance in inter-State trade and commerce. These are: coal, cereals, cotton, cotton yarn, cotton fabrics, crude oil, hides and skins, iron and steel, jute, oilseeds, pulses, rayon and artificial silk fabrics, sugar, tobacco, woollen fabrics. The list of 'declared goods' originally covered by the Act in 1956 was expanded twice, once in 1957 to include textiles, sugar, and tobacco, and again in 1976 to include cereals (like wheat, paddy, rice etc.), crude oil, and pulses.

Section 15 of the Act lays down the rate structure. The rates are different depending upon the classes of goods and the status of the person to whom the goods are sold. Thus, goods are either 'declared goods' (goods of special importance) or 'non-declared goods' while a person may be a registered or a non-registered dealer. Based on these classifications, the rates of sales tax are prescribed by the Central Government though the tax is administered (i.e. assessed, collected and appropriated) by the State Governments by virtue of the powers delegated to them by the Central Government under Article 258(1) of Constitution.

The maximum prescribed rate of sales tax on 'declared goods' inside a State is 4 per cent of the sale price and is not leviable at more than one stage. [9] Thus, although sales tax on intrastate sales is levied by the States, taxation of intrastate sales of 'declared goods' (goods of special importance) is subject to certain restrictions in terms of the nature of the levy (not to be levied at more than one stage) and the rate of tax (not more than 4 per cent).

In the case of inter-State sale of such goods to registered dealers, the rate of tax is the same as applicable to the sale of such goods inside the exporting State. In respect of sale of 'declared goods' to non-registered dealers (including consumers) the CST is chargeable at twice the rate applicable to the same goods inside the State, i.e. 8 per cent. Where 'non-declared' goods are sold in the course of inter-State trade to a registered dealer, the ceiling rate is 4 per cent [10] or the rate applicable to internal sales of the concerned goods, whichever is lower. [11] However, on inter-State sale of non-declared goods to non-registered dealers, the rate of CST is l0 per cent or the rate applicable to the sale of such goods inside the exporting State, whichever is higher. [12]

The Act further specifies that when a sales tax has been levied inside a State on any declared goods and such goods are sold in the course of inter-State trade, the tax so levied shall be refunded. Provision also exists that goods which are generally and unconditionally exempt from the sales tax within a State will also be exempt from CST in the course of inter-State trade.

21.5.2 Working of CST Act: It is clear as to why some kind of Central control is necessary on sales tax for larger national interest. Had Punjab, and Haryana been free to levy sales tax on foodgrains at will, the people of food deficit States would have suffered. Similarly, uncontrolled imposition of sales tax by West Bengal, and Bihar on iron and steel, and coal would have impeded the growth of engineering industry in Gujarat and Maharashtra.

CST Act authorises a State to tax residents of other States. Lest this power should be misused to export undue tax burden to the other States, the original scheme devised in 1956 kept the rate of CST low at 1 per cent ensuring some reasonable revenue for the exporting States. However, over the years the rate of CST has been raised by stages to 4 per cent. This trend has benefited industrially advanced States (like Maharashtra, Gujarat, Tamil Nadu, and West Bengal) at the cost of industrially backward States. Since manufactures are the main items of inter-State trade, the developed States are able to export a part of their taxation to other States. In effect, it amounts to transfer of financial resources from poorer States to well off States, much against the declared objective of regional balanced development and equitable distribution of resources among the States. Moreover, the high rate of CST hinders the free flow of trade and commerce within the country.

It may be suggested that the rate of CST should be reduced to the original level of 1 per cent to safeguard the interests of poorer States. Furthermore, the Central Government should declare some more inputs as goods of special importance in inter-State trade to restrict the power of the States to tax such goods. However, these suggestions have met with stiff resistance from most State Governments. At the New Delhi Conference of Chief Ministers held on September 16-17, 1980, there was a unanimous opinion that the rate of CST should not be brought down from 4 per cent to 1 per cent. However, it was agreed to constitute a panel of Chief Ministers to consider, *inter alia*, additions to the list of 'declared goods'. The Conference also expressed unanimity over the need for uniform sales tax laws in the country because various variants of the sales tax pose problems for the collecting authorities as well as for the taxpayers. The Chief Ministers' Conference decided to request the Law Commission to undertake, on a high priority basis, the drafting of a model sales tax law for consideration by the States.

21.6 Additional Duties of Excise (Goods of Special Importance) Act, 1957

Another landmark in the evolution of sales tax in India was the year 1956 when, following a voluntary agreement between the Centre and the States at a meeting of the National Development Council (NDC) held in December, 1956, it was decided to replace sales tax on textiles, tobacco, and sugar by additional duties of excise and to distribute revenues derived therefrom among the States. The agreement provided also that the share accruing to each State shall not in any case be less than the revenue realised from the levy of sales tax on these goods for the financial year 1956-57 in that State. The Council's decision was implemented through the Additional Duties of Excise (Goods of Special Importance) Act, 1957, the First Schedule of which prescribed the rates of additional duties of excise and the Second Schedule the scheme of distribution of the net proceeds among the States.

The Act does not debar States from the levy of sales tax on the specified commodities, but it does provide that if in any year any State levies and collects a tax on the sale or purchase of such commodities, no sum shall be paid to that State in that year by way of share out of the net proceeds of the additional duties of excise, unless the Central Government by special order decides otherwise. The commodities covered under the scheme (textiles, tobacco, and sugar) were declared goods of special importance in inter-State trade so that no State could find it worthwhile to opt out of the voluntary agreement not to impose sales tax on these goods. [13] The revenue derived from additional duties of excise, levied and collected by the Centre, is distributed among the States in accordance with the formula prescribed by the Finance Commission. The Fourth Finance Commission described it as a *tax rental arrangement.* [14]

21.6.1 Rationale of the Scheme: The scheme of additional duties of excise in lieu of sales tax has the following advantages: 1. It minimises tax evasion by levying the tax at first point and saving industry, trade, and consumers from administrative complexities involved in the collection and payment of sales tax. 2. It helps in maintaining uniformity in the prices of widely consumed goods throughout the country. 3. Such an arrangement contributes to the development of an integrated market by facilitating movement of goods across State borders. 4. Rationalisation of commodity taxation at the national level becomes easy. 5. Cost of collection is reduced.

21.6.2 Views of the State Governments: The scheme of additional duties of excise in lieu of sales tax has been in force for the last 40 years. While the business community has demanded extension of this scheme to other commodities, the States have generally remained disinclined in this regard. The distrust between the Centre and the States regarding the operation of this scheme by the Central Government is an irritant in Centre-State relations. States have argued that (a) sales tax is the only elastic source of revenue available to them and in view of its regional applicability it is also the only effective instrument for shaping their economic policies, (b) replacement of it by Central levy will encroach on their constitutional rights leading to erosion of their financial autonomy, (c) if taxes are levied and collected by a State itself then it is more conscious of its responsibilities towards the taxpayers. Subventions from the Centre may lead to reckless spending causing fiscal indiscipline.

As regards the working of the existing scheme, the dissatisfaction of State Governments is borne out of their belief that revenue potential of additional duties of excise has not been fully exploited by the Centre. Their complaint is that the growth of revenue from additional excise duties on textiles, sugar, and tobacco lags behind the growth in revenue from basic excise duties on the same commodities. The States complain that once sales tax on the three commodities was replaced by additional excise duties, the Centre did not feel the need for consultation with the States for reviewing the working of the scheme. They claim that the growth rate of their sales tax revenue is much higher than the growth rate of the yield from additional excise duties.

21.6.3 Decisions of the National Development Council (NDC): Following complaints from the States, the whole issue was reconsidered by the NDC in its meeting held on December 28, 1970. The Council decided to continue the scheme with the following conditions: (a) that the incidence of additional duties would be stepped up to 10.8 per cent of the value of clearances within a period of two or three years, (b) that a ratio of 2:1 between basic and additional excise duties would be achieved and maintained, (c) that specific duties would be converted into *ad valorem* duties except in regard to unmanufactured tobacco. It was also agreed that a Standing Review Committee consisting of representatives of the Central and State Governments with the Economic Adviser, Planning Commission, as convenor, would be set up and the same would meet at least once a year to review the working of the new arrangement and make such recommendations as may be necessary for its further improvement.

As a follow up action, specific duties were replaced by *ad valorem* rates and significant enhancements were made in additional excise duties in the Central budgets for the three consecutive years 1971-72 to 1973-74. The Standing Review Committee met for the first time in February 1981 and appointed a sub-committee which recommended that the incidence of 10.8 per cent should be achieved in three stages: 8.5 per cent by 1984-85; 9.75 per cent by 1987-88; and 10.8 per cent by 1989-90. The Ninth Finance Commission was informed by the Union Finance Ministry that the incidence achieved by the end of 1988-89 was 10.7 per cent. The Commission hoped that the committed level of 10.8 per cent would be actually achieved by the end of 1989-90. In a significant move, the Commission recommended that during its award period (1990-95), if in any year the incidence of additional excise duties falls short of the level of 10.8 per cent of the value of clearances, the shortfall should be made good by the Centre by providing an equivalent amount by way of grants-in-aid to be distributed among the States in the same manner as recommended for sharing the proceeds of additional excise duties. [15] As regards the ratio between basic excises and additional excises, the Centre fulfilled its obligations by achieving the stipulated 2:1 ratio by 1981-82.

21.6.4 Expert Committee on Replacement of Sales Tax by Additional Excise Duty (Chairman: Kamlapati Tripathi), 1983: As already noted, sales tax on textiles, tobacco, and sugar was replaced by additional duties of excise in 1957. The scheme of additional excise duties was proposed to be extended to some more commodities in 1980. At a conference of the Chief Ministers convened by the Centre on September 16-17 of that year, it was resolved to bring *vanaspati*, and life-saving drugs under additional excise duties in lieu of sales tax. It was also decided to constitute a committee of Chief Ministers to consider what other items could be added to the list for additional excise duties. However, the Non-Congress (I) States viz. Kerala, Tamil Nadu, Tripura, and West Bengal did not agree with the resolution passed at the Chief Ministers Conference.

The matter was further examined at another conference of Chief Ministers held in February 1981, which recommended the appointment of an expert committee by the Central Government to look into this matter. The expert committee under the Chairmanship of Mr. Kamlapati Tripathi submitted its report [16] in January 1983. It recommended the replacement of sales tax by additional excise duty on *vanaspati*, drugs and medicines, cement, paper and paper board, and petroleum products. The recommendations were considered in a conference of Chief Ministers held on November 2, 1983. However, the six Chief Ministers of the non-Congress (I) States, viz. Andhra Pradesh, Jammu and Kashmir, Karnataka, Tamil Nadu, Tripura, and West Bengal opposed the Centre's initiative to implement the recommendations. The recommendations of the Tripathi Committee were further discussed at a conference of Chief Ministers held in New Delhi on February 9-10, 1989. Unfortunately, no progress could be made in this regard and the matter is still hanging fire.

The opposition of non-Congress (I) States was based on the belief that implementation of the scheme would erode their revenue position. However, a close perusal of the recommendations of the Tripathi Committee suggests that it evolved elaborate formulae for protecting the financial interests of the States. In the case of three commodities, namely paper and paper board, *vanaspati*, and drugs and medicines, it suggested that the annual growth rate of the amount to be collected by way of additional excise duty in lieu of sales tax should be related to the future annual growth rate of sales tax revenue of all the States. For petroleum products and cement, which are substantially subject to administered prices, the Committee recommended and worked out linkages between the amount to be collected by way of additional excise duty from year to year and value of consumption on which normal sales tax would be leviable.

In spite of these safeguards, the apprehension of some States that their resource position would be adversely affected reflects their lack of confidence in the Centre in implementing the scheme sincerely. Thus, an important tax reform has become a casualty of the distrust between the Central and the State Governments. The scheme of additional excise duties in lieu of sales tax has merits of its own. In view of the safeguards provided by the Tripathi Committee and the Ninth Finance Commission, the scheme should not only be retained but extended to other commodities as well.

It is pertinent to mention here that during the first two decades of Independence (1947-67), the Congress party ruled, with some exceptions, both at the Centre and in the States. This political homogeneity facilitated taxation agreements between the two tiers of the Government, e.g. the agreement reached in 1957 regarding substitution of sales tax by excise duties on sugar, textiles, and tobacco. Since 1967, the politics of confrontation pursued by different political parties ruling at the Centre and in the States has hindered the process of rationalisation and harmonisation of commodity taxation. In fact, reform of commodity taxation is closely interwoven with the political process. Unfortunately, the political response to economic logic so far has neither been adequate nor helpful.

21.7 Constitution (Forty-sixth Amendment) Act, 1982 and Consignment Tax

Consequent upon the Sixth Amendment of the Constitution, the Central Sales Tax (CST) Act was passed in 1956. Section 14 of the Act declares certain goods to be of special importance in inter-State trade while section 15 of the Act lays down the rate structure.

However, the CST Act left out of its ambit the consignments (or despatches or stock-transfers) from a company to its branch located in a different State. Since no sale is involved, it is called in-house transaction by a company. The loophole has come in handy for unscrupulous parties to evade sales tax by showing virtual sales as consignments from one State to another. By this method, the payment of CST is avoided. Only local sales tax becomes payable. Therefore, through the Constitution (Forty-sixth Amendment) Act, 1982, the Parliament was empowered to levy `taxes on the consignment of goods (whether the consignment is to the person making it or to any other person), where such consignment takes place in the course of inter-State trade or commerce.' This was done by inserting entry 92B in List I of the Seventh Schedule and simultaneously amending Article 269 by inserting sub-clause 269(1)(h). Consignment tax is a levy on inter-State transfer of goods.

Ever since, the States have been pressing the Centre to levy the tax, the net proceeds of which are entirely assignable to States under Article 269. The proposed tax is intended to check avoidance of CST. The Commission on Centre-State Relations, 1988, also impressed upon the Government to "bring in suitable legislation in this regard without further loss of time." [17]

21.7.1 Issues Related to Consignment Tax: Though the necessary legislation is still to be enacted, industrial and commercial circles have expressed grave concern about the deleterious effects of the impending levy. Trade circles maintain that consignments become necessary in view of seasonal fluctuations in the demand for goods as well as frequent transport bottlenecks. Commercial practices like 'branch transfer' or 'transfer on consignment basis' also help manufacturer-supplier to reduce avoidable costs of holding high levels of inventory.

What will be the impact of consignment tax on prices? What should be the rate of tax? Who shall have the exemption powers? How will it affect the location of industries? How will the proceeds of this tax be shared among the States? These are some of the issues to be sorted out.

The impact of the consignment tax on prices will depend on the rate of the new levy and the commodities covered under its ambit. Since the new levy will be in addition to CST leviable at 4 per cent, it is bound to push up prices. To minimise the inflationary potential, the rate of the new levy may preferably be fixed at a low level of 1 per cent. It may be recalled that in 1956 when the CST Act was passed the rate was fixed at 1 per cent. However, over the years the rate of CST has been raised by stages to the present level of 4 per cent. Thus, the rate of proposed consignment tax should be low and pegged to that level through constitutional provisions to avoid frequent hikes as in the case of CST.

Furthermore, to lessen the adverse impact on prices, it is necessary to grant exemptions to items of mass consumption. To achieve this, it would be desirable that the power to grant exemptions from the proposed levy be concurrently enjoyed by the Centre and the States. The concurrent power of exemption would enable the Centre to ensure uniformity of taxation of goods of national importance, particularly those which are subject to the scheme of administered prices.

The levy of consignment tax may encourage lopsided industrial development of the country. Producers in States which are self-sufficient with respect to raw materials and the market for goods manufactured out of them will remain unaffected by the consignment tax. Conversely, the entrepreneurs in States which import raw materials from other States and also market their manufactures in other States will be doubly taxed, once on the raw materials and then on the manufactured goods. Under such circumstances, prospective entrepreneurs would be tempted to opt for self-sufficient States to enjoy price advantage on the final product, negating in the process the national policy of regional balanced development.

As regards the sharing of tax proceeds, it is apparent that producer-States like Maharashtra, and Gujarat would like the proceeds to accrue to the respective States in full. Contrarily, the backward States would prefer to see a higher proportion of the proceeds distributed among the States through the Finance

Commission. At a conference of the Chief Ministers held in February 1989, it was agreed that 50 per cent of the proceeds of the consignment tax would be retained by the collecting States and the remaining 50 per cent would flow into a divisible pool from which the amount would be distributed among the States in accordance with the formula devised by the Finance Commission. At the same Conference, the Government announced its decision to introduce a Bill in this regard in the monsoon session of Parliament of that year. Since then nothing has been heard about this legislation.

Sales tax system has already played havoc with internal freedom of industry and trade. Enjoying their constitutional right, different State Governments levy sales tax on a wide range of commodities at different rates with different procedures and rules for its collection. In a scenario like this, the introduction of consignment tax will further confound the existing confusion about commodity taxation at the State level. The imposition of consignment tax would discourage free movement of goods from one State to another. Restricting movement of goods across State borders through tax practices runs counter to the needs of a growing and diversifying economy. Moreover, in view of the current experiment with MODVAT at the Central level to save industry of the cumulative effects of excise duty, the introduction of consignment tax would hinder the process of rationalisation of commodity taxation. Ideally, imposition of consignment tax should be avoided. In case it is unavoidable, a cautious approach is necessary keeping in view the national interest.

21.8 Present Nature of Sales Tax

Under the Constitution, the right to levy sales tax belongs to the State Governments. Each State is, therefore, empowered to collect tax on the sale of goods within its territory according to the rules framed by it. Thus, different State Governments levy sales tax on a wide range of commodities at different rates with diverse procedures and rules for its collection. The Central Government also enters the field in so far as it prescribes the ceiling rate of sales tax on goods in inter-State trade. In the case of three important commodities, viz. textiles, sugar, and tobacco, additional duties of excise are imposed in lieu of sales tax, the proceeds of which are distributed among the States.

Different States have adopted different variants of the sales tax due to a number of reasons including administrative convenience, ad hoc measures to increase tax revenues, and to attract enterprise in their respective areas. Sales tax in a State may take the form of a single point, double-point and/or multi-point levy. However, single-point is the main type of sales tax imposed on most commodities in all States. In most States a significant part of sales tax revenue originates from first-point levy, i.e. at the manufacturer's level. Some States also levy surcharges on sales tax as an ad hoc measures to augment their resources.

The rate structure of sales tax is further complicated in view of different lists of exemptions/concessions, numerous nominal rate categories, and different administrative procedures in each of the States. These variations have caused disparities in the effective rate of sales tax on similar commodities in different States. Agricultural commodities like cereals and pulses are either exempt or bear low rate of sales tax ranging from 2 to 3 per cent. For most commodities, the rate of single-point levy varies between 4 to 8 per cent. However, in the case of luxury items like motor cars, refrigerators, and VCRs, the rate may go up to even 15 per cent in some States. The rate of multi-point levy hovers around 4 per cent.

21.9 Problems Created by Sales Tax

Perhaps no other tax impinges on so large a number of interests as sales tax. Firstly, it hurts the consumers who ultimately bear its burden. Next, there are the dealers from whom it is collected, and in many cases the producers also come in its ambit in case it is levied at the manufacturer's level. Then there are the State Governments, always anxious to extend its scope and retain their hold on it. Furthermore, the Central Government decides the rate of sales tax on goods of special importance in inter-State trade. Consequently, the operation of sales tax creates a host of problems which may be summarised as follows.

1. Sales tax is a levy on commodities which, in most cases, are also subject to excise duties. As excise duty and sales tax are levied by different layers of Government, it becomes difficult to determine judiciously the impact of these levies on production, investment, and the consumers. No attempt to rationalise commodity tax system can succeed if the Centre and 25 States act independently without co-ordination among themselves.

2. A closely related problem is the taxation of inputs and capital goods, by the Central and State Governments, through excise duties and sales tax respectively. Apart from generating cascading effect, sales taxation of inputs benefits the comparatively richer States at the cost of poorer States. To quote, "The (sales) taxation of inputs also means that its burden falls on consumers outside the State. While procedures exist for refund of excise duties on a product when it is exported outside the country, the sales tax paid on inputs is not rebated. In consequence, the more developed States which have attained high levels of agricultural or industrial production are able to derive additional resources, by taxing consumers in other States, while the resource mobilisation capacity of the less developed States, which have to depend on most of their needs being met by imports from other States, is weakened." [18] This reverse flow of funds is

further strengthened by the frequent hikes in the rate of Central sales tax.

Originally at 1 per cent, the Central sales tax rate has steadily increased to 4 per cent, thereby imposing undue burden on the importing States and defeating, in the process, the very objective of Central Sales Tax Act of 1956.

To tackle the problem of cascading effect associated with the taxation of intermediate goods, recent reforms at the Central level provide instant credit of excise duty paid on inputs under the MODVAT scheme. Although State laws do provide relief through exemptions in regards to sales tax when inputs are sold to manufacturers, such concessions are limited and lack uniformity. This lacuna in the sales tax system has hindered reform of indirect tax system in India.

3. In order to attract trade and industry to their respective areas, some States have been indulging in a kind of 'rate war' (competitive reductions in sales tax rates). It is true that some States lack infrastructural facilities and to compensate for that sales tax concessions come handy to attract industries, but this shortcut erodes the resource-base of the States, so vital for the development of infrastructure which alone guarantees their speedy development on permanent footing.

Differential rates of sales tax on the same set of commodities in different States often lead to uneconomic diversion of trade as well as production centres. It is not uncommon for people of one State making purchases in other States to avoid or reduce sales tax liability. Apparently, purchases from lower tax States to those where rates are higher are beneficial so long as the cost of transporting goods is lower than the tax differential. Purchase of truck chassis in Daman (a Union Territory levying a low rate of 3 per cent) by the residents of a far off State of Jammu and Kashmir is a popular case in point. Similarly, rate differentials may cause flight of capital and enterprise from high to low tax rate States thereby distorting natural selection of production centres based on geographical advantages, leading to unnecessary transportation of raw materials and finished goods and hence cost escalations. Such a misallocation of resources undermines economic efficiency and thereby retards developmental efforts.

4. Sales tax has another disadvantage in that it discourages horizontal integration and on the contrary encourages vertical integration in industries. Firms try to produce their own components in order to avoid sales tax. This tendency harms the growth of ancillary units which are mainly in the small-scale sector.

5. Different types of sales tax (multi-point, double-point, and single point) with varying procedures and rules in different States cause difficulties for the traders, particularly small ones, leading to harassment, corruption, and litigation.

21.10 Alternative Remedies

To deal with the foregoing weaknesses of the sales tax system, experts have put forward various suggestions.

21.10.1 Sales Tax as Central Levy: It is argued that through a constitutional amendment, the levy of sales tax can also be made a Central subject and thereafter a rationalised system of indirect taxation of domestic production and consumption can be administered by the Centre. This is a drastic suggestion which has not found favour with statesmen. The Taxation Enquiry Commission (TEC), 1953-54, was quite categorical in rejecting this suggestion. Emphasising the impracticability of centralisation of sales tax the Commission observed, "On account of its yield and flexibility, sales tax has come to occupy a large and indispensable place in the State financial systems. Centralisation of the tax must be ruled out. Difficulties which confront the tax administrations vary considerably in character and composition from State to State and taken together present a large and almost bewildering variety of problems." [19]

The views of the TEC appear to be still valid considering the present fiscal arrangements and political equations. Thus, a constitutional amendment to make sales tax a Central subject has to be ruled out.

21.10.2 Complete Substitution of Sales Tax by Excise Duty: It is suggested, particularly by the business community, that in place of sales tax corresponding enhancements should be made in Central excises the proceeds of which could be earmarked for distribution among the States. This will facilitate rationalisation of commodity taxation and also reduce the cost of collection apart from saving the business community from harassment from the differing sales tax practices of the various States.

Is a complete substitution of sales tax by excise duties possible? Unfortunately not. Like sales tax, excise duties cannot become universal in scope because of administrative reasons. For instance, the Centre has the legal power to impose excises on agricultural products but it has refrained from doing so. Similarly, small and tiny units of the industrial sector are left out because of administrative reasons.

However, what is small for excise duty may be large for the purpose of sales tax. The Indirect Taxation Enquiry Committee, 1977, estimated that nearly Rs. 500 crore of sales tax was being collected on goods not subject to excise duties such as agricultural products, articles of jewellery which for administrative or other reasons cannot be reached by excises. It concluded, "The consequence of a simple abolition of sales tax from the angle of resource mobilisation would be a substantial loss of revenue to compensate for which something like a 50 per cent increase in excise duties on the average would be necessary, given the present base of excise taxation." [20]

Since excise duties are of all-India nature, they cannot take into account regional variations in the levels of income and patterns of consumption. However, different rates of sales tax in individual States permit consideration of regional factors. Moreover, if sales tax is levied at the retail stage, the value base of the tax is large and even low rates of tax can yield sufficient revenues. The cumulative effect is also absent.

21.10.3 Partial Substitution of Sales Tax by Excise Duty: The approach towards substitution of sales tax by excise duties has to be selective. Some arrangements already exist in this regard in the form of additional duties of excise in lieu of sales tax on three important commodities namely textiles, tobacco, and sugar. The extension of this arrangement to certain other commodities as recommended by Tripathi Committee has already been discussed in section 21.6.4 of this chapter.

21.10.4 Minimum Rate Agreement among States: As already noted, some States have been indulging in a sort of `rate-war' to attract trade and industry to their respective regions. To avoid this unhealthy competition, the Chief Ministers agreed, at their conference in New Delhi on February 9-l0, 1989, that all the States would adopt the minimum floor level rates as recommended by the Committee of Sales Tax Commissioners in its report of 1984 in respect of 29 identified items. The follow up action is yet to take place. Even at the regional level, the response is not encouraging. The Chief Secretaries of northern States (Punjab, Haryana, Himachal Pradesh, Rajasthan, Delhi, and Uttar Pradesh) had recommended in May 1994 that there should not only be a uniform rate of sales tax but the slabs of this tax be reduced in these States. The recommendation is still to be implemented. The lack of concern on the part of States to harmonise their sales tax systems is apparent.

21.10.5 Single-Point VAT: To deal with the cascading effects of a traditional turnover tax, some experts have suggested a single-point VAT at the Central level to replace both excise duties and sales taxes. Since sales tax is the most important source of tax revenue for the States, such a drastic suggestion, which will leave the States at the mercy of the Centre, is difficult to implement. Replacement of existing system of excises, sales taxation, and octroi by a comprehensive VAT would require amendment of the Constitution by a two-thirds majority in Parliament and its approval by more than half of the States. A comprehensive VAT at the national level has to be ruled out on economic as well as political considerations.

Switch over to VAT has to be an independent exercise by the Central Government and 25 State Governments. In this connection the Tax Reforms

Committee, 1991, observed, "As regards sales tax, the Committee is of the view that this tax could be converted into a form of State VAT within the manufacturing sector. There may be no need for levying sales tax at more than two rates since the distributional and other non-revenue objectives could be left to be performed by the Central taxes which apply uniformly throughout the country." [21] Even this dual VAT system is difficult to achieve because it is highly unlikely that the 25 States will move in tandem to ensure smooth transition to a uniform system of VAT in place of their differing practices of sales tax. Thus, the problem of co-ordination is not only between the Centre and the States but also among the States themselves.

The introduction and extension of MODVAT scheme at the Central level is a step in the right direction to reform excise taxation. Unfortunately, similar reforms have not been introduced at the level of States. The State Finance Ministers' Conference held in New Delhi on May 27, 1994 failed to arrive at a consensus on the replacement of indirect taxes at the State level by a value added tax. The matter was deferred indefinitely by appointing a ten-member Committee of State Finance Ministers to go into this and related questions.

21.10.6 Agreement of November 1999: At a conference of Chief Ministers and Finance Ministers of the States in New Delhi on November 16, 1999, States and Union Territories decided to put an end to all sales tax-based incentives to industry and enforce floor rates of sales tax with effect from January 1, 2000. They also decided to move over to the simple, transparent and efficient regime of Value Added Tax (VAT) with effect from April 1, 2001.

The agreement to impose a set of minimum rates (floor rates) of sales tax on all commodities will ensure sales tax uniformity throughout the country. Four general floor rates of zero per cent, 4 per cent, 8 per cent and 12 per cent and two special floor rates of 1 per cent and 20 per cent were agreed upon.

Essential commodities such as foodgrains, raw meat, eggs, milk and plain water will be subject to the zero rate. There will be a minimum sales tax rate of 4 per cent on commodities such as edible oils, vanaspati, processed vegetables, kerosene, bicycles, chemicals and fertilisers. Products like electricals, tyres and tubes, butter and ghee, blades and razors, drugs and medicines, cooking gas, tea and coffee, biscuits and computers will attract a floor rate of 8 per cent. Television sets, VCRs, air-conditioners, diesel, paints, telephone equipment and carpets will attract the highest floor rate of 12 per cent.

The 1 per cent special floor rate will apply to bullion, gold and silver while the 20 per cent special floor rate will cover petrol, liquor, rectified spirit and narcotics.

It was also decided at the Conference that a standing committee of State

Finance Ministers will be constituted to oversee the preparations for the switch over to VAT and to review the progress of the implementation of sales tax floor rates in the interim.

The decision to implement these sweeping tax reforms came about after the Union Finance Minister gave an assurance to make good any consequential revenue loss the States may suffer.

The prolonged tax war among the States had strained the finances of several States. The race among the States to lure industries by offering competitive concessions in sales tax is expected to come to an end. If implemented sincerely, these tax reforms at the level of States will go a long way in creating conducive climate for the growth of country's economy, industry and trade.

However, some fiscal experts feel that the floor rates of sales tax fixed are too high and hence unrealistic. Since the floor rates are already high, there is hardly any scope for individual States to determine effective rates above the floor level depending on expectations of growth of industry and trade in each state. Moreover, the high floor rates are contrary to the post-liberalisation policy of low tax rates to ensure better tax compliance. It is also being felt in some quarters that uniformity in tax rates is not necessarily a desirable objective to pursue. In many federations (e.g. USA), state governments compete with each other to attract industry and trade to their respective areas.

21.10.7 Empowered Committee of State Finance Ministers (Chairman: Asim Kumar Dasgupta), 2001: At a Conference of Chief Ministers and Finance Ministers of various States held on July 5, 2001 in New Delhi, the report of the Empowered Committee of State Finance Ministers on VAT, headed by West Bengal Finance Minister Asim Kumar Dasgupta, was accepted and adopted for the introduction of VAT with effect from April 1, 2002. The VAT design recommended by the Committee had the following elements.

1. The VAT system will eliminate the cascading burden of taxation by setting off the tax paid on inputs against that on output.
2. It will reduce distortions in the economy caused by double taxation.
3. It will end market fragmentation with a uniform regime of taxation followed in all the States.
4. There will be one category of tax-exempted commodities for all the States.
5. There will be two VAT rates: a uniform 4 per cent for all States on goods of basic necessities and a uniform floor rate of 10 per cent for other commodities (except a few items such as bullion and liquar).
6. A uniform set of procedures for VAT assessment will also be followed by all the States, including the use of Permanent Account Number (PAN) as a common business identifier.

7. The States which do not implement 100 per cent uniform floor rates of sales tax by July-end 2001 should be penalised by discontinuing Central Government assistance.
8. The Centre has undertaken to make good any revenue loss to States on their switch over to VAT. A committee of State Finance Secretaries would evolve clear and measurable criteria for judging revenue loss, if any, due to the introduction of VAT. It will also recommend the manner and quantum of compensation.

As many as 12 States have agreed to implement VAT by April 1, 2002.

However, the road to the Indian common market seems to be dotted with hurdles. Many fear that VAT, as worked out by the Empowered Committee of the State Finance Ministers, would make the Indian market place chaotic and confusing. There are many issues which must be resolved to smoothen the transition to the modern and efficient system of VAT.

1. The uniform floor rate of 10 per cent does not ensure that States would not charge various higher rates on the same commodity. There should be a cap rate of tax.
2. It is not sure whether the classification of goods into the zero rate VAT and the 4 per cent VAT would be done on a scientific basis.
3. It is not clear what treatment would be given to inter-State trade. The biggest concern of industry and trade is the non-eligibility for set-off of CST paid on inputs sourced from across the State border.
4. The fate of exemptions/concessions being enjoyed by various industries under the sales tax system is uncertain when switch over to VAT takes place. By its very nature, VAT cannot be successfully implemented if there are too many exemptions and concessions.
5. A few States have not yet fully implemented even the uniform floor rates of sales tax.
6. From the Government side also, the promised amendment to the Central Sales Tax Act is still to be carried out. Moreover, it is not clear whether changes in CST would coincide with the transition to VAT or not. To reduce distortions, the business circles would like the CST (levied at 4 per cent) to be abolished in one go rather than phased out.

The benefits of VAT at the State level can be achieved fully only when all the States comply with the recommendations of the Empowered Committee. If all the States move towards a uniform VAT system, it would be an example of cooperative federalism. The introduction of VAT in place of the existing sales tax system would make the common market dream a reality.

21.10.8 Agreement of January 23, 2002: At the Conference of State Finance

Ministers held on January 23, 2002 a final decision was taken that all States and Union Territories would introduce VAT from April 2003. This position was reiterated by all States at the Conference of State Chief Ministers held on October 18, 2002. Empowered Committee of State Finance Ministers endorsed the suggestion that every State Legislation on VAT should have a minimum set of common features. Accordingly, a model VAT Bill was circulated to all the States. Introduction of VAT is expected to increase revenue buoyancy, as the coverage expands to value addition at all stages of production and distribution chain.

Again, at a meeting of the Finance Ministers of all States/Union Territories on January 17, 2003, States and Union Territories again reiterated their firm commitment to introduce VAT from April 1, 2003. It was decided that the VAT legislations of all States and UTs would have common provisions in respect of all important matters and that a simple VAT legislation with maximum convergence would be implemented. It was also agreed that along with the introduction of VAT, the origin based Central Sales Tax would be phased out. It was also agreed that the Additional Duties of Excise (Goods of Special Importance) Act would be suitably amended to empower States to levy sales tax/VAT on sugar, textiles and tobacco with a ceiling rate of 4 per cent. This would be done without affecting the existing levy of Additional Duties of Excise on these items by the Union Government

In view of the apprehensions expressed by a large number of States about possible revenue losses in the initial years of introduction of VAT, an assurance was given to the States that the Government of India would compensate the States to the extent of 100 per cent of revenue loss in the first year (2002-03), 75 per cent of the loss in the second year (2003-04) and 50 per cent of the loss in the third year (2005-06).

The Empowered Committee of State Finance Ministers agreed upon the following sequence of steps to ensure introduction of VAT in place of retail sales tax system in States.

1. Passing of VAT legislation and framing of rules and regulations.
2. Computerisation of dealers who will fall within the ambit of VAT.
3. Training of tax officials, traders and consumer associations.
4. Publicity for consumers.
5. Implementation of VAT, assigning VAT identification numbers to tax payers.
6. Implementing transitional measures for introduction of VAT.

21.10.9 Task Force on Indirect Taxes (Chairman: Vijay Kelkar), 2002: The Task Force on Indirect Taxes, unanimously acknowledged that VAT is a major reform in the indirect tax system of India. For a smooth and speedy implementation of VAT at the level of Centre and States, it made the following recommendations.

1. A publicity awareness programme should be started jointly by the Central and State Governments and the former should extend financial support for this, if required. Since State VAT is expected to be implemented from 1.4.2003 it is also necessary that the publicity awareness programme should be implemented at the earliest.
2. An attempt should be made towards uniformity of all State legislations, procedures and documentation relating to VAT.
3. The issue of compensation, if it arises, must be primarily tackled through mutually acceptable mechanism of additional resource mobilization through service tax and not through budgetary support.
4. With the introduction of VAT, all other local taxes be discontinued.
5. Whereas additional duty of excise may continue for textiles up to 2005, it may continue even thereafter for cigarettes which should not be subjected to VAT.
6. The VAT scheme should provide for grant of credit of duty by the importing State for the duty paid in the exporting State, in the course of inter-State movement of goods.

For the stability and continuity of VAT, the possibility of a VAT Council or a permanent suitable alternative, vested with adequate powers to take steps against discriminatory taxes and practices and eliminate barriers to free flow of trade and commerce across the country, should be explored

21.10.10 Agreement of June 2004: At a meeting of the State Finance Ministers with the Union Finance Minister on June 18, 2004, it was decided that all States will introduce a uniform VAT from April 1, 2005. The proposed VAT will replace the taxes levied by different States like sales tax and octroi. Coinciding with the introduction of VAT, the Central Government will bring down the Central Sales Tax (CST) rate from 4 per cent to 2 per cent. The CST will be phased out in 2006-07. It was also decided that traders with an annual turnover up to Rs. 5 lakh will be exempt from VAT. This decision was aimed at ending traders' opposition to VAT. It may be recalled that States have missed at least five deadlines for the introduction of VAT, mainly due to resistance from trading community.

21.10.11 Salient Features of the State-level VAT Design: VAT is essentially a federal or central tax, while in India it is aimed at replacing State as well as Central sales taxes. Its effective implementation depends almost entirely on the co-operation of the State Governments. In an ideal situation, VAT is supposed to be a tax to end all taxes. Many countries that have adopted VAT do not levy excise duty, entry tax or luxury tax. However, State Governments in

India are demanding the right to retain and, in fact, widen the tax net by levying a range of taxes, including entry tax. This would defeat the basic purpose of the imposition of VAT, namely unifying and harmonizing the complex commodity tax structure in the country.

A VAT regime is theoretically meant for a unified market in which the VAT levied can always be set off against taxes already paid, irrespective of the state-wise location of the manufacturing or trading entities. In India, these inter-state adjustments are proving to be difficult to implement in view of the existing constitutional provisions regarding distribution of taxation powers between the Centre and the States. It needs, however, to be emphasised that the States must think in terms of economic development of the country as a whole and encourage the free flow of trade and commerce in the economy. A national approach is necessary to harmonise and rationalise the existing system of commodity taxation.

In view of the above constraints and also to provide some flexibility to the States, the Empowered Committee, through its deliberations over the years, finalised a design of VAT to be adopted by the States. The model design seeks to retain the essential features of VAT, while at the same time, providing a measure of flexibility to the States, to enable them to meet their local requirements. The main features of the VAT design finalised by the Empowered Committee are the following:

1. Rates of VAT on various commodities shall be uniform for all the States/UTs. There are 2 basic rates of 4 per cent and 12.5 per cent, besides an exempt category and a special rate of 1 per cent for a few selected items. The items of basic necessities have been put in the zero-rate bracket or the exempted schedule. Gold, silver and precious stones have been put in the 1 per cent schedule. There is also a category with 20 per cent floor rate of tax, but the commodities listed in this schedule are not eligible for input tax rebate/set off. This category covers items like motor spirit (petrol), diesel, aviation turbine fuel, and liquor.
2. Model VAT design makes provision for eliminating the multiplicity of taxes. In fact, all the State taxes on purchase or sale of goods (excluding entry tax in lieu of octroi) are required to be subsumed in VAT.
3. Provision has been made for allowing input tax credit, which is the basic feature of VAT. However, since the VAT being implemented is intra-State VAT only and does not cover inter-State sale transactions, input tax credit will not be available on inter-State purchases.
4. There are provisions to make the system more business-friendly. For instance, there is provision for self-assessment by the dealers. Similarly, there is

provision of a threshold limit for registration of dealers in terms of annual turnover of Rs. 5 lakh. Dealers with turnover lower than this threshold limit are not required to obtain registration under VAT and are exempt from payment of VAT. There is also provision for composition of tax liability up to annual turnover limit of Rs. 50 lakh.

5. Regarding the industrial incentives, the States have been allowed to continue with the existing incentives, without breaking the VAT chain. However, no fresh sales tax/VAT-based incentives are permitted.
6. Exports will be zero-rated, with credit given for all taxes on inputs/purchases related to such exports.

21.10.12 Progress of VAT Implementation: According to *Economic Survey,* 2006-07, "VAT has been introduced by 30 States/UTs so far. Tamil Nadu has implemented VAT from January 1, 2007. The union territory of Puducherry has communicated its decision to implement VAT from April 1, 2007. Uttar Pradesh has not yet taken any decision in this regard. Since Sales Tax/VAT is a State subject, the Central Government has played the role of a facilitator. A compensation formula has also been finalised in consultation with the States, for providing compensation, during 2005-06, 2006-07 and 2007-08, for any losses on account of introduction of VAT and compensation is being released according to this formula. Technical and financial support has also been provided to the States for VAT computerization, publicity and awareness and other related aspects. [22]

Broadly speaking, the experience of implementing VAT has been quite encouraging. The new system has been received well by all the stakeholders, and the transition has been quite smooth with the Empowered Committee constantly reviewing the progress of implementation. The EC has advised the States to constantly interact with trade and industry to remove their apprehensions, if any, and to ensure that the benefits of VAT due to input tax credit and reduction in tax rates (wherever applicable) are passed on to the consumers. The EC is also persuading the remaining States/UTs to implement VAT at the earliest.

21.10.13 Towards National Goods and Services Tax (GST): The strategy of the Government in respect of indirect taxes is to continue the tariff reform process towards mean ASEAN levels of customs tariff, convergence towards CENVAT rate for excise duty, widening of service tax base and phased move towards a fully integrated goods and services tax by April 1, 2010. In his 2006-07 budget speech, the Union Finance Minister observed, "It is my sense that there is a large consensus that the country should move towards a national level Goods and Services Tax (GST) that should be shared between the Centre and the States. I propose that we set April 1, 2010 as the date for introducing GST. World over, goods and services attract the same rate of tax. That is the foundation of a GST.

People must get used to the idea of a GST." [23]

In pursuance of the above policy, the Union Cabinet decided on February 22, 2007 to reduce Central sales tax (CST) by one percentage point from April 1, 2007. By reducing CST by one percentage point every year, the Government intends to phase out CST completely by the year 2010-11 to enable it to implement the uniform goods and services tax regime. The move is designed for the success of value added tax to facilitate the process of developing a national common market. In other words, the objective is to ensure that the Centre and all the States have a uniform rate of tax on goods and services. It is clear that the CST, being an origin-based and non-rebatable tax, is inconsistent with the concept of VAT and needs to be phased out.

The Centre will compensate the States for the loss of revenue arising from the phasing out of CST.

Notes

1. John F. Due, *The Problems of Tax Administration in Latin America* (Baltimore: The John Hopkins Press, 1959), p. 417.

2. Walter Mahler, *Sales and Excise Taxation in India* (New Delhi: Orient Longman Ltd., 1970), p. 151.

3. Government of India, Ministry of Finance, *Report of the Taxation Enquiry Commission, 1953-54* (Chairman: John Matthai), Vol. III, p. 26.

4. Walter Mahler, *op. cit.*, p. 154.

5. *Report of the Taxation Enquiry Commission,* 1953-54, Vol. III, *op. cit.*, p. 30.

6. *Ibid.*, p. 519.

7. Under Article 258(1), the Union has the power to delegate to any State Government any of its executive functions (including the power to assess and collect sales tax on inter-State trade). Thus, the power to levy and collect sales tax on inter-State trade belongs to the Centre [Article 269(1)(g)] though it has delegated the power to collect it to the States.

8. Clause (3) of Article 286 was further amended by the Constitution (Forty-sixth Amendment) Act, 1982. In its present form it is as follows.

Any law of a State shall in so far as it imposes, or authorises the imposition of

(a) a tax on the sale or purchase of goods declared by Parliament by law to be of special importance in inter-State trade or commerce; or

(b) a tax on the sale or purchase of goods, being a tax of the nature referred to in sub-clause (b), sub-clause (c) or sub-clause (d) of clause (29-A) of Article 366, be subject to such restrictions and conditions in regard to the system of levy, rates and other incidents of the tax as Parliament may by law specify.

9. In 1956, when the Central Sales Tax Act was passed the rate was fixed at 1 per cent. Subsequently, it was raised to 2 per cent, 3 per cent, and 4 per cent in 1958, 1966, and 1975 respectively.

10. Originally, the rate was fixed at 1 per cent in 1956. It was raised to 2 per cent, 3 per cent, and 4 per cent in 1963, 1966, and 1975 respectively.

11. It means the States are free to fix the rate of sales tax on the internal sales of non-declared goods but there is a ceiling rate of 4 per cent on the sale of such goods in inter-State trade. For

example, if the rate of sales tax on internal sale is 6 per cent, it will be 4 per cent for inter-State trade, being lower of the two.

12. In other words, the rate of CST is a minimum of 10 per cent. For example, if general sales tax is charged at the rate of 5 per cent on the sale of colour television in a State, the rate of CST on the same will be 10 per cent, being higher of the two rates. In 1956, the minimum rate was fixed at 7 per cent but was raised to 10 per cent by the Central Sales Tax (Amendment) Act, 1963.

13. Internal as well as inter-State sales tax on goods of special importance is governed by the Central Sales Tax Act, 1956. The present rate of CST is 4 per cent.

14. India's federal system of government creates a dual polity based on divided governmental functions and taxation powers. Taxation laws of the Central Government extend to the whole of the country while those of State Governments are applicable within their respective jurisdictions. A tax belonging to the States may be imposed with a varying base and/or rate in different States. Even the procedures and rules for its collection may differ from State to State. The lack of uniformity in the imposition of State tax laws can cause difficulties for traders and consumers and thus hinder inter-State trade. To overcome these problems, arrangements could be made to transfer from the States, the legal right to levy the tax, to the Centre with the proviso that revenue collected will be assigned to the States. This is known as 'tax rental arrangement'.

15. *Second Report of the Ninth Finance Commission,* December 1989, p. 34.

16. Government of India, Ministry of Finance, *Report of the Expert Committee on Replacement of Sales Tax by Additional Excise Duty* (Chairman: Kamlapati Tripathi), January 1983.

17. Government of India, *Report of the Commission on Centre-State Relations* (Chairman: Justice R.S. Sarkaria), 1988, Part I, p. 293.

18. Government of India, Ministry of Finance, *Report of the Indirect Taxation Enquiry Committee* (Chairman: L.K. Jha), 1977, Part I, p. 50.

19. *Report of the Taxation Enquiry Commission,* 1953-54, Vol. III, *op. cit.*, p. 519.

20. *Report of the Indirect Taxation Enquiry Committee,* 1977, Part I, *op. cit.*, p. 49.

21. Government of India, Ministry of Finance, *Tax Reforms Committee - Final Report*, Part I (Chairman: Raja Chelliah), August 1992, p. 174.

22. Government of India, *Economic Survey,* 2006-07, p. 46.

23. Government of India, Ministry of Finance, *Budget Speech of the Finance Minister,* 2006-07, Part B, p. 26.

17. Government of India, Report of the Taxation [illegible] on [illegible] State [illegible] (Chairman: [illegible]) 1958, Part [illegible], p. [illegible]

22. Government of India, [illegible] ... [illegible] p. 148.

Section E: International Aspects of Indian Taxation

This Section defines international double taxation, explains how it occurs and examines various methods through which double taxation of this kind is mitigated/eliminated, focusing on the role of double tax treaties. It also explains the devices used by international business entities to avoid/evade taxes. It then describes the provisions relating to taxation of non-residents in India. The aspects covered are: test of residence, residential status and tax liability, law on double tax relief, tax concessions for non-residents, and assessment and collection of tax from non-residents.

22

International Aspects of Indian Taxation (Double Taxation)

Business and investment operations of individuals and companies are becoming increasingly international in scope in the wake of current wave of globalisation and openness sweeping across the countries of the world. Tax systems of different countries differ in terms of types of taxes, definition of income and expenses, exemptions and concessions, rates and collection procedures. Varying tax practices of different countries complicate decision-making by multinational enterprises as to what is most profitable on an international basis. The study of international taxation becomes relevant in this context.

22.1 What is Double Taxation?

Double taxation (or tax duplication) occurs when the same base (e.g. income) is assessed twice, either by the same tax jurisdiction or by two competing tax jurisdictions, either at different levels of government in a country or at the same level of government in different countries. All the three versions of double taxation are described below.

22.1.1 Double Taxation by the Same Tax Jurisdiction: A common example of this kind of double taxation is the taxation of corporate earnings, first in the form of corporate income tax, and then in the form of personal income tax on dividends distributed to shareholders. Tax laws usually contain provisions which mitigate or even eliminate tax duplication of this kind. Under one method, a shareholder is granted credit against his tax liability on overall income for the tax paid by the company on distributed profits. The credit may be granted on full or partial basis (say 50 per cent) on account of company tax on distributed profits.

22.1.2 Double Taxation by Competing Tax Jurisdictions at Different Levels of Government in a Country: Double taxation of this type arises when different levels of government impose taxes on the same base, e.g. taxation of income by Federal and State Governments in USA, and Canada. This kind of double taxation arises due to joint occupancy of tax fields. [1]

22.1.3 Double Taxation by Competing Tax Jurisdictions at Same Level of Government in Different Countries: This kind of double taxation is also called *international double taxation* or *territorial multiple taxation.* In this case, two sovereign countries claim jurisdiction in taxing the same base, usually income.

22.2 International Double Taxation

International double taxation occurs when a taxpayer is resident in one country but has a source of income situated in another country so that tax is imposed by both the countries on the same income. Thus, international double taxation arises due to overlapping of two tax claims of two or more countries. OECD has defined international double taxation as "the imposition of comparable taxes in two (or more) states on the same taxpayer in respect of the same subject matter for identical periods." [2]

In most cases, individuals work in countries where they live and companies invest in countries in which they are resident. However, world economies are becoming increasingly international and flow of labour and capital from one country to another is common. Multinationals operate in a number of countries, and individual investors possess internationally diversified investment portfolios. Thus, companies and individuals receive foreign income in the form of profits, dividends and royalties. When a person undertakes cross-border activities or maintains connections in two or more countries, he is likely to encounter the tax laws of another country. That encounter influences the way in which the person is taxed in his home country. This is how the tax systems of different countries get linked with each other.

Like international law, there is no such thing as international taxation. Taxes are not international because they are not levied at an international level by any supranational authority. Taxes are levied by central, state and local governments. International taxation (or more appropriately international tax law) includes all those rules which affect the taxation of a person and which are different from the rules that would apply if all his activities and connections were in a single country. These rules include the laws, regulations, juridical pronouncements and practices of different countries. They are meant to minimise/eliminate international tax duplication so that international flow of labour and capital is not unduly obstructed.

22.3 Assignment Rules of Foreign Income

Two fundamental assignment rules govern the right of nations to impose taxes on foreign income: (a) the source rule or the territoriality rule and (b) the residence or domicile rule.

22.3.1 Source Rule: The source rule holds that income ought to be taxed in the country in which it originates irrespective of whether the income accrues to a resident or a non-resident assessee. The claim for tax jurisdiction is made on the ground that source country allows non-residents to use its infrastructure and other inputs for production purposes and therefore it can legitimately take a bite into their earnings.

22.3.2 Residence Rule: According to the residence rule, the power to tax foreign income should belong to the country in which the taxpayer resides. The claim of the residence (or home) country rests on the ground that the source (or host) country utilises and benefits from manpower and other resources trained and perfected by the home country. The tests of residence including nationality of individual assessees are complex and vary from country to country. Similarly, different countries follow different rules to define a domestic/foreign company.

22.4 Methods to Alleviate International Double Taxation

The problem of international tax duplication can be avoided if all the countries follow either the source or the residence rule. In practice, most countries exercise source and residence rules concurrently. If a country observes only the residence rule, then it surrenders tax claim on incomes which originate within its political jurisdiction and accrue to non-residents. A country would normally not go for this option which favours the foreigners vis-à-vis its own citizens. In most cases, countries tax their residents on their world income, and the non-residents on their incomes originating within their borders. International tax duplication arises when the country of residence extends the tax net to the world income of a taxpayer and the host country follows the source rule. Double taxation of this kind discourages international movement of factors of production.

Various methods may be followed by concerned countries to reduce or even eliminate double taxation of foreign-source income of their residents.

22.4.1 Exemption Method: A country may voluntarily and unilaterally sacrifice its tax claim on the foreign income of its residents. In other words, foreign income of residents is exempt from taxation in the home country. For example, there is no further tax on repatriated profits in countries such as France, and Germany.

22.4.2 Foreign Tax Credit: The home country permits deduction of taxes paid by the residents in the host country (on dividends, royalties etc.) from the tax on world-wide income due in the home country. The foreign tax credit is a mechanism provided unilaterally by a number of countries to alleviate the effect of double taxation. The object is to reduce tax on foreign-source income to the extent that income has already been taxed in the foreign jurisdiction. Under the tax credit system, the taxpayer pays the higher of the two taxes. If the foreign tax is the same or higher than the domestic tax, then the tax credit reduces the domestic tax liability on the foreign income to nil.

A foreign tax credit system was introduced in Australia on July 1, 1987. Under this system, the foreign-source income of residents is taxed at normal rates in Australia, with a credit granted for the foreign taxes paid. Other important countries which operate a tax credit mechanism as a means of eliminating double taxation are USA, UK, Canada, and Japan.

A. Tax Sparing Credit: Developing countries often give tax incentives, e.g. tax holiday to encourage foreign investments. Many developed countries provide, in their double tax treaties with developing countries, for a tax sparing credit. Under tax sparing, the investor is deemed to have paid the tax foregone in the country of source (say, India) so that the investor's country of residence (say, USA) grants a tax credit for the tax not charged by the source country. In other words, the residence country treats the income remitted as if it had been fully taxed and had not benefited from the tax incentives (of the host country). This ensures that the full benefit of the tax incentive goes to the investor and is not simply transferred to the residence country's treasury.

22.4.3 Bilateral Tax Treaties: International double taxation is also avoided through bilateral tax treaties (or double tax treaties). A double tax treaty is a convention or an agreement among countries for the avoidance of double taxation of income and capital and bringing uniformity in the allocation of taxation rights in cross-border situations. It is essentially a bargain between two treaty countries as regards the division of tax revenue between them in respect of income falling to be taxed in both jurisdictions. Since treaty negotiations involve bargaining, each side seeks concessions from the other and it is not necessary that strict *quid pro quo* is achieved in the end.

Apart from relieving double taxation, a double tax treaty aids commercial relations between treaty partners. It creates an environment of fiscal certainty which encourages trade and investment between countries. It provides rules for resolving problems of dual residence or dual source of income, defines the different forms of taxable income, and determines the taxing rights of the two treaty countries. An important provision of all double tax treaties is the machinery for administrative co-operation between the tax authorities of treaty partners.

The advantages and disadvantages of a double tax treaty depend on the flow of trade and investment between treaty partners. If these flows are in balance, which is a rarity, the benefits and costs would be truly reciprocal. Where the flows of trade and investment are unbalanced, the advantages of the treaty may be weighed more in favour of one treaty partner than the other, though the provisions of the treaty may be expressed in reciprocal terms. This is generally the case regarding tax treaties between developed and underdeveloped countries where flows of trade and investment are one-sided.

Most tax treaties are bilateral. Some international organisations have done commendable work in the development and harmonisation of bilateral double tax conventions. Model tax treaties drawn up by these organisations have helped to harmonise national approaches to double tax relief. They have facilitated the negotiation of tax treaties by eliminating the need for elaborate analysis and protracted discussion of every issue involved in each treaty.

In 1963, OECD published a Draft Double Taxation Convention. In 1977, it issued a Model Double Taxation Convention based on the experience of OECD member states since 1963. The OECD Model gives the primary right of taxation to the state of residence. It operates largely in favour of the developed capital exporting countries, and to the consequent detriment of underdeveloped countries which are net importers of foreign investment.

In 1966, OECD issued a draft convention on estates and inheritances. In 1982, it published a revised version of the same which included gifts also. The OECD conventions have been widely accepted among OECD member states and other developed countries.

The United Nations adopted a resolution in 1967 to constitute a group of experts on tax treaties between developed and developing countries. Special problems arise where a double tax treaty is concluded between developed and developing countries. Based on the report of the group of experts, the United Nations issued in 1979 a Manual for tax treaty negotiators. In 1980, it issued its Model Double Taxation Convention Between Developed and Developing Countries.

The basic difference between the United Nations model and the OECD model is that the former predominantly gives the source country the right to tax income while the latter grants the country of residence the right to tax income. The United Nations model is generally used when one of the countries is a developing one. This is so because normally investments flow from a developed country to a developing country which *ipso facto* means that incomes flow from developing to developed countries, i.e. developing countries are the source of income.

22.4.4 Multilateral Tax Treaties: Multilateral double tax treaties, though considered at different times in various contexts, have not gained acceptance for being complex. It is difficult to understand and apply a multilateral treaty than a bilateral one. Moreover, a multilateral convention is less flexible in terms of amendment, revision, or termination.

Though multilateral approach is not generally followed, there are, at least, three notable multilateral double income tax agreements. 1. Andean Pact. This agreement among the member states of Andean Group (Bolivia, Chile, Columbia, Ecuador, Peru, and Venezuela) is based on the principle of giving the state of source the exclusive right of taxation. 2. Comecon Conventions. There are two multilateral agreements for the avoidance of double taxation among 8 of the 10 member states of Comecon (Bulgaria, Czechoslovakia, erstwhile GDR, Hungary, Mongolia, Poland, Romania, erstwhile U.S.S.R, Cuba, and Vietnam). The last two are not signatories to the multilateral agreements. 3. Nordic Countries. A multilateral treaty covering tax on income and capital exists among Nordic countries (Denmark, Finland, Iceland, Norway, and Sweden).

22.5 International Tax Avoidance and Evasion

While it is true that international business operations are exposed to the risk of being subject to double taxation, it cannot be gainsaid that such activities provide opportunities for tax avoidance/evasion. Following are the devices generally applied for the purpose.

22.5.1 Transfer Pricing: It refers to the price attached to transactions between the divisions (e.g. branches or subsidiaries) of a company. Transfer pricing is usually considered in a global context, particularly in relation to cross-frontier transactions within a multinational company.

Determination of transfer price has significance in relation to such matters as taxation, exchange restrictions, and currency fluctuations. The incentive for transfer price manipulations is provided by varying rates of taxation in countries where a multinational company operates. Thus, where goods are being transferred from a company in a low tax country to a subsidiary company in a high tax country, there is a clear tax incentive if a high transfer price is ensured to maximise profit within the low tax country.

Similarly, sales of a multinational group may be routed through a specially formed tax haven distribution company. The tax haven company purchases goods from affiliated companies at the lowest possible prices and sells to independent purchasers at the full market price, ensuring that most or all of the profit from the transaction is earned in the tax haven.

Due to the inherent difficulties in determining a fair or market price for inter-company transactions, a multinational company has always the option to fix artificial transfer prices.

A. Arm's Length Price: It refers to market price that would have been negotiated by unrelated parties engaged in the same or similar transactions under the same or similar conditions. Arm's length standard is used to prevent the use of transfer pricing technique for tax avoidance. Many countries exercise their right to adjust reported transfer prices to conform to an arm's length criterion. Implementing the arm's length principle is a difficult task for tax authorities.

22.5.2 Tax Havens: The expression is used to describe any country or locality which levies very low taxes, or none at all, on foreigners.

Tax havens can be broadly classified into three categories based on the degree of tax concessions.

1. Where there is no tax at all, e.g. Bahamas, Bermuda, and Cayman Islands.
2. Where only a low rate of tax is imposed, e.g. British Virgin Islands, Hong Kong, Isle of Man.
3. Where the tax system favours particular activities or entities, e.g. Luxembourg, Panama, and Switzerland.

Tax havens are used in a number of ways to avoid/evade high taxes of non-tax haven countries. The commonest device is to use a tax haven only as a conduit for transactions the real economic impact of which is located elsewhere. Thus, international transactions between two high tax rate countries may be channelled through a tax haven company so that any resulting profit is realised in the tax haven with a consequent minimisation of tax.

22.5.3 Tax Treaty Shopping: It is a situation where a person resident in a third country seeks to obtain benefits of a double tax treaty between two other countries. A double tax treaty confers substantial benefits on the residents of treaty countries. Let us suppose that Mr. Wilson, resident in country A, wants to invest in country B. Assuming that there is no double tax treaty between country A and country B, any income received by Mr. Wilson will be subject to full rates of taxation in country B. In such a situation, Mr. Wilson may find it advantageous to channel his investment to country B through a company in country C because country C has double tax treaties with countries A and B. For example, Mauritius is a popular treaty shopping haven for many foreign companies for channelling investments into India because of favourable tax treaty provisions.

To prevent the misuse of tax treaties through tax treaty shopping, many countries take care to include anti-treaty abuse provisions in these agreements. For example, there is a specific clause in the double tax treaty between India and USA under which benefits of the treaty are available only to genuine residents of either country. In other words, the treaty restricts the use of USA as a treaty shopping centre for investments in India.

22.6 Taxation of Non-residents in India

Income which is subject to charge of tax varies according to the residential status of a taxpayer. In the case of a person *resident* in India, all income derived from whatever source is within the scope of taxation. However, in the case of a *non-resident,* the tax liability extends only to income which (a) is received or is deemed to be received in India by or on behalf of the non-resident and (b) accrues or arises, or is deemed to accrue or arise, to the non-resident in India. It is evident that income which accrues or arises outside India (i.e. foreign income) is beyond the scope of tax liability in India in the case of a non-resident.

Since the scope of income chargeable to tax in India is dependent upon the residential status of the taxpayer, it is important to understand the terms resident and non-resident which have a technical meaning under the law.

22.6.1 Rules to Determine Residential Status: Section 6 of the Act lays down the test of residence for different taxable entities. Here, the residential status of the two major taxable entities, viz. individuals and companies is discussed.

The residential status of an assessee may not remain the same in each income year. An assessee who is resident during one year may be a non-resident in the next year. Moreover, the residence of an assessee has nothing to do with his domicile or nationality. Also, residential status of an assessee is the same for all sources of income.

Assessees are either (1) resident in India or (2) non-resident in India. Resident individuals are further divided into two categories, namely (a) resident and ordinarily resident and (b) resident but not ordinarily resident. A company is simply either a resident or a non-resident.

A. Residential Status of an Individual: An individual is said to be resident in India in any previous year if he satisfies any of the following two *basic conditions*: (1) He was in India in the previous year for a period of 182 days or more; or (2) he was in India for a period of 365 days or more during the four years preceding the previous year and 60 days or more during the previous year (182 days or more in the case of an Indian citizen or a person of Indian origin coming on a visit to India or in case of an Indian citizen going abroad as a member of the crew of an Indian ship or for employment). [3] Although these conditions require the personal presence of the assessee in India, his stay in India for a particular number of days in different cases need not be continuous in a previous year.

As already noted, a resident individual may either be an ordinarily resident or not ordinarily resident in India. A resident individual is treated as resident and ordinarily resident in India if he satisfies the following *additional conditions*: (a) he has been resident in India in at least 9 out of 10 previous years preceding the relevant previous year and (b) he has been in India for a period of 730 days or more during 7 years preceding the relevant previous year. In other words, an individual becomes resident and ordinarily resident in India if he satisfies *at least one of the two basic conditions* and *both of the additional conditions*. An individual who satisfies at least one of the two basic conditions but does not satisfy both the additional conditions is treated as a resident but not ordinarily resident in India.

An individual is non-resident in India if he satisfies neither of the two basic conditions. In the case of non-resident individuals, the additional conditions are not relevant.

Thus, an individual assessee may be: 1. Resident and ordinarily resident. 2. Resident but not ordinarily resident. 3. Non-resident.

B. Residential Status of a Company: An Indian company (i.e. a company registered under the Companies Act, 1956) is always resident in India. A foreign company is treated as resident in India only if control and management [4] of its affairs is situated wholly in India during the previous year. A foreign company is non-resident if control and management of its affairs is either wholly or partly situated out of India during the previous year.

22.6.2 Relationship between Residential Status and Tax Incidence

Incidence of tax on an assessee depends on his residential status. Under section 5 of the Act, the tax liability of different classes of assessees on the basis of their residence is as follows.

A. Resident: An assessee who is resident and ordinarily resident in India is assessed to tax in respect of income (i) received or deemed to be received in India in the previous year by him or on his behalf, (ii) which accrues or arises or is deemed to accrue or arise to him in India during such year, and (iii) which accrues or arises to him outside India during such year.

B. Not Ordinarily Resident: An assessee who is a resident but not ordinarily a resident is assessed to tax in respect of income (i) received or deemed to be received in India in the previous year by him or on his behalf, (ii) which accrues or arises or is deemed to accrue or arise to him in India during such year, and (iii) which accrues or arises to him outside India during such year and is derived from a business controlled in or a profession set up in India. It means income accrued outside India from a business controlled from outside India or a profession set up outside India is not chargeable to tax in the case of resident but not ordinarily resident class of assessees. For a resident and ordinarily resident assessee, income accruing in any part of the world is chargeable to tax.

C. **Non-resident:** Non-resident assessee is chargeable to tax in respect of income (i) received or is deemed to be received in India during the previous year by or on behalf of such person, and (ii) which accrues or arises or is deemed to accrue or arise to him in India during such year.

The incidence of income tax on various categories of assessees according to their residential status is summarised in Table 22.1. It is evident that income received or deemed to be received in India or income accruing or deemed to accrue in India are taxable in the case of all assessees, irrespective of their residential status.

Table 22.1: Tax Liability of Different Types of Income on the Basis of Residential Status in India

Type of Income	Residential Status of the Assessee		
	Resident and ordinarily resident	Resident but not ordinarily resident	Non-Resident
1. Income received or deemed to be received in India	Taxable	Taxable	Taxable
2. Income accruing or arising or deemed to accrue or arise in India	Taxable	Taxable	Taxable
3. Income earned and received outside India from a business controlled in or a profession set up in India	Taxable	Taxable	Non-Taxable
4. Income earned and received outside India from a business controlled from outside India or a profession set up outside India	Taxable	Non-Taxable	Non-Taxable

The aforesaid provisions of the Act point out that tax incidence is the highest in the case of a resident and ordinarily resident taxpayer. It is lower for resident but not ordinarily resident assessees, and lowest in the case of non-residents.

22.7 Indian Law on Double Tax Relief

As in most other countries, India gives unilateral as well as treaty relief in respect of foreign taxes suffered by Indian residents on their foreign income. Sections 90 and 91 of the Act deal with relief from international double taxation.

Section 90 of the Act gives relief bilaterally through tax treaties. It provides, *inter alia*, that a treaty may be entered into (a) for grant of relief in respect of income which is taxed in both the countries, (b) for the avoidance of double taxation on income, (c) for exchange of information for the prevention of evasion or avoidance of income tax and (d) for the recovery of income tax.

Broadly speaking, India's tax treaties contain two alternatives: 1. Income which arises in the territory of one of the contracting States is not taxed by the other contracting State (exclusion method). 2. Income is taxed in both the countries in accordance with their respective tax laws but the country of the residence of the taxpayer allows him a credit against the tax charged thereon in the country of the source of such income (tax credit method). Where any such agreement for avoidance of double taxation exists, the provisions of the Act apply to the extent they are more beneficial to the assessee.

Section 91 grants unilateral relief from double taxation to the residents in respect of foreign tax paid abroad. It is noteworthy that Section 91 comes into force only when relief is not available under Section 90. Following are the requirements of Section 91: (a) the assessee should be a resident of India in the previous year, (b) such income should not be deemed to accrue in India under the provisions of the Act, (c) the income should be taxed in both the countries and there is no double tax treaty with that country and (d) the assessee should have in fact paid the tax in such foreign country either by deduction or otherwise.

Thus, if an Indian resident proves that tax has been paid in respect of his income which accrued or arose to him in the countries with which India has no agreement for double taxation relief, he is entitled to a deduction from the Indian income tax payable by him.

22.8 Tax Incentives for Non-resident Indians

Over the last five decades, a good number of Indians have found career opportunities in the developed West and oil exporting Arab countries. Most of them have adopted foreign countries as their permanent homes. Although settled abroad, many of them continue to have their roots in India so that they may return to their homeland should the circumstances so demand.

Considering the number of Indians abroad, their relative sound financial status and their desire to make investments in their country of origin, the income tax law contains special incentives to attract non-resident investments into India. The purpose of these incentives/concessions is to establish useful and strong links between Indians abroad and their homeland. In fact, the inflow of funds from non-residents has emerged, in recent years, as a strategic tool of development policy with the following objectives in view: (a) to augment foreign exchange resources for strengthening economic base of the country, (b) to tide over the chronic deficits in the balance of payments, (c) to raise the overall level of investments in the economy, (d) to induct modern technology into India and (e) to provide an emotional shot to non-residents to plan and maintain their financial links with the home country.

The Act provides a large number of tax concessions to non-residents, the important ones being the following.

1. Exemption from tax of any income from interest on such securities as the Central Government may specify [Sec. 10(4)(i)].

2. Exemption from tax of interest on money in non-resident (external) account [Sec. 10(4)(ii)].

3. Income from interest on specified savings certificates, received by a non-resident, being a citizen of India or a person of Indian origin, is exempt from income tax provided such certificates are subscribed to in convertible foreign exchange remitted from outside India [Sec. 10(4B)].

4. Income of a consultant under a technical assistance grant agreement is exempt from tax [Sec. 10(8A)].

5. Income in connection with any technical assistance programme is exempt from tax [Sec. 10(8B)].

6. Interest on Non-resident (Non-repatriable) Rupee Deposit Scheme is exempt from tax [Sec. 10 (15)(i)].

7. Interest payable by a scheduled bank on deposits in foreign currency is exempt from tax [Sec. 10(15)(iv)(f)].

8. Interest on bonds for non-resident Indians is exempt from tax [Sec. 10(15)(iid)].

9. Income in respect of foreigners such as passage money, remuneration to officials of embassies is exempt from tax [Sec. 10(6)].

22.9 Assessment and Collection of Tax from Non-residents

Notwithstanding the various concessions/exemptions given to non-residents under the income tax law, a stringent and pervasive system of assessment and collection of tax is followed. For example, the conditions laid down for the test of residence are not diluted and no relief is granted even if the stay of an assessee in India exceeds or falls short of the prescribed limits just by one day.

The income of a non-resident assessee is assessed for tax purposes either directly or indirectly (i.e. through his agent). The agent can either be a duly constituted agent or a person who can be treated as an agent. If there is no duly constituted agent, the tax authorities are empowered to treat any of the following class of persons as the agent of a non-resident.

1. A person employed by or on behalf of the non-resident.
2. A person having a business connection with the non-resident.
3. A person from whom the non-resident is in receipt of any income either directly or indirectly.
4. A person who is trustee of the non-resident.

5. A person who has acquired any capital asset from a non-resident if that asset is situated in India.

It is noteworthy that any of the persons mentioned above and treated as agent should be in India at the time of assessment, though he need not necessarily be a resident in India. In other words, even a non-resident may be an agent for a non-resident assessee.

Still further, an agent may be a person who does not belong to any of the above-mentioned five categories. In short, any person may be treated as an agent of a non-resident if he has some connection with the income sought to be assessed. Under the law there are elaborate guidelines concerning the appointment and liabilities of a duly constituted agent.

1. The agent is chargeable as a representative assessee of the non-resident for the incomes which are received or deemed to be received and accrue or are deemed to accrue in India.
2. The agent should have some connection with the income sought to be assessed in his hands even though the income belongs to the non-resident.
3. The agent is assessable for such incomes only as may belong to the non-residents and not to the residents.
4. The agent is assessed in the same manner and to the same extent as the non-resident himself would have been.
5. No one would be treated as an agent unless there is a liability to income tax on the non-resident.
6. The liability of the agent is personal and not conditional upon his having in hand any funds of the profit of the non-resident.

A person who is treated as an agent of a non-resident is given an opportunity of being heard before he is treated as such. And if he is treated as the agent of a non-resident, he enjoys the right to deduct from the payments to the non-resident an amount equal to the tax estimated to be paid on the profits made by the non-resident in India.

The problem of tax recovery from the non-resident becomes more serious where there is no agent who can be made liable by the tax authorities for the purpose. To deal with such situations, the income tax law has devised the following two methods:

1. Deduction of tax at source.
2. Recovery of tax from assets.

Under the law, any income from salaries, interest on securities and dividends is subject to deduction of tax at source. The person responsible for paying such incomes is required to deduct income tax at source at the prescribed rates and deposit the same with the Government within the prescribed time limit.

Deduction of tax at source is made on all such sums payable to a non-resident which are chargeable to income tax. Such sums may also include payments other than salaries, interest on securities and dividends [Sec. 195].

In case where there is no agent from whom the tax, payable by a non-resident, may be recovered or if it has not been deducted at source, the tax authorities are empowered to recover the tax from any assets of the non-resident which are in India or which may come to India any time later. Under the law there is no time limit for the recovery of a tax through this method.

The income tax law deals specifically with the assessment and collection of tax (i) on profits of non-residents from shipping business and (ii) on persons leaving India for good.

Cases may arise where non-residents are engaged in shipping business in India as the owners or charterers of ships without employing an agent from whom the tax on profits of such business can be recovered. To meet such cases the law provides that where a ship carries passengers or other items, 7.5 per cent of the amount paid or payable in this respect to the owner or the charterer shall be deemed to be his income accruing in India for such carriage [Sec. 44B]. It is immaterial whether such an amount is paid or is payable in or out of India. Before leaving any port in India, the master of the ship has to prepare and furnish to the tax authorities a return of the full amount paid or payable to the owner or charterer of the ship in respect of the carriage of passengers or other items at that port since the last arrival of the ship there. This means the master of the ship is required to furnish a full account of carriage charges of the passengers etc. booked at the Indian port. On receipt of the return, the income tax officer has to assess the income and determine the amount of tax payable at the rates applicable to non-resident assessees. The master of the ship may be exempted from furnishing such a return if the income tax officer is satisfied that the former has made satisfactory arrangement of furnishing the return and payment of tax through some other person acting on his behalf. As a cross-checking, port clearance is not granted to the ship until the collector of customs is satisfied that the tax assessable has been duly paid or that satisfactory arrangement for its payment has been made. Thus, cross-checking through inter-departmental co-operation is an important device to collect taxes from non-residents.

Another interesting provision of the income tax law pertains to the assessment and collection of tax from a person, resident or non-resident, who in the opinion of tax authorities, may leave India during the current assessment year for good [Sec. 230]. In such a case the total income of that individual for the period from the expiry of the previous year up to the probable date of his departure from India is chargeable to tax in the same assessment year. [5] Where the income of such an individual cannot be determined properly, the income tax officer is authorised to estimate the same as per his own judgement without prejudice to the assessee. Individuals falling under this provision of the income tax law are required to obtain a tax clearance certificate from the foreign section of income tax office before leaving India.

Notes

1. It relates to concurrent taxation powers enjoyed by different tiers of government in a federal polity. Concurrent taxation powers are a characteristic feature of fiscal federalism in USA, Canada, and Australia. Most tax fields in these countries are jointly occupied by the federal and provincial governments. Thus, personal income tax, corporation tax, general sales tax, and consumption tax (excise duty) are levied by the Federal as well as Provincial Governments in Canada. The only notable exception is the customs duties which belong exclusively to the Federal Government.

The overlapping taxation powers often cause friction not only between the federal and provincial governments but also among the provinces *inter se* as regards the sharing of a tax base. The problem is solved through tax rental and tax sharing negotiations and agreements.

In India, the Central and the State Governments have no concurrent powers of taxation. Taxes with inter-state base and those in the case of which all-India uniformity in rates is needed to facilitate industry and trade are vested in the Central Government. Taxes which are location-specific and relate to subjects of local consumption are with the States. The absence of joint occupancy of tax fields has successfully minimised double taxation, duplicate tax administration, and tax rivalry between the Centre and the States, and among the States themselves.

2. OECD, *Model Double Taxation Convention of Income and Capital*, 1977, p. 7.

3. The term non-resident Indians refers to individuals, being citizens of India or persons of Indian origin, who are not residents in India. A person is said to be of Indian origin if he, or either of his parents, or any of his grandparents, was born in undivided India.

4. The expression *control and management* means the direction, management and control and the directing power of its affairs are situated at a place where the directors' meetings are held and not at a place where shareholders' meetings are held.

5. Understandably, this is a departure from the general practice that the income of the previous year is to be assessed in the assessment year immediately following.

Part IV: Public Expenditure

This Part of the book deals with public expenditure in India. It provides theoretical insights into issues involved in public expenditure policies and explains the structure of Central Government expenditure. It specially focuses on subsidies which form a significant part of the non-Plan expenditure of the Government.

Chapter 23: Public Expenditure: Theoretical Overview
Chapter 24: Public Expenditure in India: Structure and Policies
Chapter 25: Subsidies in India: System and Current Issues

23

Public Expenditure: Theoretical Overview

Public expenditure is an important instrument of the economic policy of a government. The size and pattern of public spending has great relevance in the growth process and in the reduction of economic disparities. The pressure on public expenditure is particularly great in developing countries because of growing population and the consequent need for medical, educational, housing and employment facilities. In the emerging developing economies of Asia and Africa, people are aspiring for a better standard of living after centuries of subjugation. Public expenditure is an effective policy instrument in this context.

23.1 Determinants of Public Expenditure

The level and composition of public spending in a country is determined by a host of diverse factors.

23.1.1 Political Determinants: The ideological character of the ruling party influences decisions regarding public expenditure. Thus, a socialist government will ordinarily spend more on social welfare activities than a conservative government. The proportion of national income spent on public services depends not only on national income per head but also on how backward or progressive are the rulers of the state. Political biases and rigidities also influence the occurrence of wars and internal disturbances. These disturbances in turn influence governmental expenditure on defence and law and order machinery.

Changes in political structure alter the demand for public goods and hence affect expenditure levels. In general, a change from authoritarian to representative government strengthens the demand for collective goods. Democratisation of a government through the broadening of voting rights leads to enhanced public spending on the maintenance of democratic institutions and holding of elections. The extension of electoral franchise increases public spending as politicians try to woo the new voters. Under a system of universal suffrage it is almost imperative to increase public spending on those items which benefit the majority poor. Maintenance of diplomatic relations and membership of international bodies have further enhanced state expenses. To this list may be added the expenditure on cold war among nations, particularly among superpowers.

23.1.2 Economic Determinants: Various theories of economic development suggest that capital formation is of crucial importance in the early stages of development. Any scheme of national economic development calls for the creation of infrastructural facilities such as roads, bridges, training centres, power stations, harbours, communications, improved agricultural techniques, irrigation facilities etc. These areas of activity require long-term investment of enormous amounts. Private investors either lack resources or are unwilling to risk their capital for longer periods. These investments, the benefits of which are largely external, should preferably be undertaken by the government. In the early stages of development, the scope for private capital and entrepreneurial talent is limited. Therefore, government's initiative to provide economic and social overheads becomes necessary.

Economic development leads to diversification and complexity in the economy. These tendencies generate economic disequilibria such as unemployment, trade cycles, monopolistic tendencies and exploitation of labour. A new set of public services of remedial nature becomes necessary. The emergence of large joint stock companies necessitates the services of regulatory agencies (e.g. Monopolies and Restrictive Trade Practices Commission in India).

Left to itself, the free play of market forces may not produce an income distribution which is in tune with the currently acceptable goals of socio-economic policies of the government. Through fiscal means a government may intervene to give desired directions to the pattern of income distribution among various economic classes in the economy. Through transfer payments and subsidies in kind, a government can help the economically depressed sections of society. Political philosophy of the 20th century (e.g. the concept of welfare state) has contributed significantly to increase in state activities and hence in public expenditure.

Technological changes are yet another determinant of public spending. Modern warfare is a case in point. Even poor countries are competing with each other to possess costly weapons of military combat. Huge public expenditure programmes for atomic research, satellite communications, space technology are no longer limited to developed countries or for peaceful purposes.

23.1.3 Social Determinants: Industrialisation generates its own ill-effects on social life. It leads to congestion, pollution, insanitation and problems of law and order. Increase in public expenditure is inevitable to offset these social diseconomies created by industrialisation and urbanisation. Similarly, economic risks of unemployment, industrial accident and retirement associated with modern system of production call for social insurance against them. Government has to interfere to make such provisions.

Demographic factors also influence the level of public expenditure. Population growth necessitates more educational, medical and housing facilities. Changes in the rate of growth of population bring about changes in the age composition of population. Thus, the proportion of school going children in total population is an important determinant of educational expenditure of a government.

From the foregoing discussion, it is evident that there is no single and simple determinant of public spending. According to Richard Bird, "The level of government expenditure is, therefore, it appears, set in any country at any point in time, not in accordance with some sweeping law of historical development (Wagner), nor in obedience to the displacement caused by exogenous socio-economic crises (Peacock-Wiseman), nor yet as the result of the unrestrained actions of power-hungry bureaucrats (Parkinson). Though influences in all these directions may play some role, they are never the only and seldom the crucial determinants of government spending. Many other items also enter in: the rate of growth of population and its age structure; the nature of productivity differentials; the personal interests of influential groups both within and outside the political sphere; the character of political and social institutions - to name but a few." [1]

23.2 Wagner's Law of Increasing State Activity

In 1883, a German economist Adolph Wagner (1835-1917) propounded his famous *law of ever increasing state activity*. He based his conclusions on an extensive survey of public expenditure records of several countries in the 19th century. Although he did not make it clear as to what he precisely meant by increasing state activity, it is generally believed that he was referring to growth in public expenditure as a percentage of national income.

Wagner put forward three reasons for the operation of his law.

1. He believed that an expansion would come about with respect to the administrative and protective functions of the state. This would require substitution of public for private activity. As a result of industrialisation there would be greater division of labour, communications and legal complexities. All this would increase the regulatory and protective activities of the government.
2. The pressure for social progress was thought to be another reason for the expansion of state activities. He anticipated considerable expansion of cultural and welfare expenditure, particularly with respect to education and the redistribution of income.
3. Changes in technology and the large amount of investment required in many economic activities would create private monopolies. The state would be

required to offset the effects of these monopolies in the interest of economic efficiency. In certain cases as, for example, railways, only state could finance the scale of investment required.

Wagner's law of expanding state expenditure has received extensive comments from economists the world over. Various empirical studies have given conflicting evidence regarding the validity of Wagner's law. Frederic Pryor in his study of government expenditures has concluded that neither highly developed nor highly underdeveloped countries fit Wagner's generalisations. According to Pryor the law appears to be supported for countries in the process of transition from a rural agricultural economy to an urban industrial one. [2] American public finance expert Richard Musgrave, on the other hand, has supported Wagner's law in his study of public expenditures of Germany, USA and UK. [3]

Though the evidence on Wagner's formulation remains puzzling, one drawback of his analysis is definite, viz. his neglect of war expenditure. It has specially been noted by economists that Wagner took no particular note of the effects of wars on public expenditure. Probably in tune with the 19th century optimism he anticipated fewer wars in the future than in the past. However, he was proved grossly wrong by the events of the subsequent years. Unfortunately, major international conflicts have dominated lives and patterns of public expenditure in the 20th century. Any theory of public expenditure which ignores wars and their effects must be termed incomplete in its scope. Thus, while Wagner's law may appear to hold good in aggregate terms, serious doubts arise regarding its validity if studied in disaggregated form.

23.3 Peacock-Wiseman Hypothesis

In their study of public expenditure trends in the British economy for the period 1890-1955, Alan T. Peacock and Jack Wiseman confirmed the operation of Wagner's Law but they provided a rather complicated and controversial explanation for it. [4]

Behaving like private individuals, governments spend more as they get more. There is automatic increase in tax yield due to enlargement of the tax base in the wake of economic development. The pressure for new spending is always there and if revenues are available the government will seldom hesitate to spend them. It might become cautious if financing of new spending requires raising of tax rates or imposition of new taxes.

23.3.1 Displacement Effect: Apart from this natural growth of expenditure in line with revenues, occasions may arise to finance a war. New taxes are imposed and rates of existing taxes are revised. It has been observed that the tax system does not return to its pre-war position after the war is over. With tax arrangements made during a war being continued after the war, the growth trend of revenues and expenditures is moved upward permanently. Peacock and Wiseman called this movement the *displacement effect.*

The displacement hypothesis states that government spending grows over time not at a constant rate but rather stepwise. The movement from one step to another generally coincides with a war. Such disturbances create a displacement effect, shifting public revenues and expenditures to new plateau.

23.3.2 Inspection Effect: There are two aspects of the displacement effect. Firstly, in times of crisis, people accept methods of raising revenues formerly thought intolerable. The acceptance of new tax levels remains when the disturbance has disappeared. *It is harder to get the saddle on the horse than to keep it there.*

Secondly, social upheavals impose new and continuing responsibilities on governments such as payment of war pensions, reparation payments, rehabilitation of war victims etc. Wars often force the attention of government and people to problems of which they were formerly less conscious. There is, thus, what Peacock and Wiseman call an *inspection effect*. Their hypothesis is not limited to wars but includes the effects of other social upheavals like depressions.

Peacock-Wiseman hypothesis has been subjected to rigorous statistical scrutiny by economists, particularly by S.P. Gupta, and the existence of displacement effect has been confirmed in a number of countries. [5]

23.4 Requirements of a Good Public Expenditure Policy

It is difficult to formulate a universally acceptable set of public expenditure principles. This is so because of differing nature of world economies, their socio-economic objectives and political set-ups. Still, economists have tried, from time to time, to provide general guidelines for public authorities in-charge of spending public funds. These guidelines are as follows:

23.4.1 Principle of Maximum Social Benefit: Public expenditure should be so incurred that its benefit to society is the maximum. In economic theory, the law of equi-marginal utility states that an individual should so distribute his expenditure on various commodities that the marginal utilities of all these expenditures are equal. If he does this, he will maximise his satisfaction from out of his fixed income which he can spend on various commodities available in the market. This Marshallian principle of consumer equilibrium for individuals is sought to be extended to the behaviour of governments. As Dalton opined, "A public authority, not being a person except in a legal sense, cannot estimate the marginal utilities of its various expenditures as an individual can. But the general principle, on which statesmen should attempt to act, is the same. The marginal utility to the community of all forms of public expenditure should be equal and the distribution of a given total of expenditure between different objects is thus theoretically determined." [6] In other words, government expenditure in different fields should be carried just so far, that the advantage to the community of a further small increase in any field is just offset by the disadvantage of a corresponding small increase in taxation.

Clearly, the principle of maximum benefit as enunciated above has limited practical significance in view of the difficulty of quantifying the benefits which society receives from various forms of government spending. It is difficult to state exactly (or even approximately) what amount of benefit the people get from defence services or from maintenance of relations with foreign countries. Moreover, in practice, expenditure decisions are influenced by a host of non-economic factors like pressures from politicians, organised interests and external disturbances. Similarly, certain public expenditures are based on legal contracts (like salaries and interest payments) which cannot be varied at short notice. All these realities of practical life make the operation of maximum benefit principle difficult. To quote Dalton again, "But the difficulty is inherent in the subject, and cannot legitimately be avoided by substituting a wrong principle for a right one, in order to arrive more easily at practical conclusions." [7]

Recent advances in economic analysis have also affected public expenditure procedures. The cost-benefit approach, which can be viewed as an alternative to maximum benefit principle, is increasingly being applied to evaluate public expenditure programmes. Under this approach, intended public schemes are subjected to social cost and social benefit analysis in order to determine their social usefulness. However, the application of social cost-benefit analysis is restricted to certain types of public spending. The analysis defies application on a significant portion of public expenditure like that on national defence, law and order and maintenance of international relations.

23.4.2 Principle of Economy: A good public expenditure system is one which avoids extravagance and corruption. This is the meaning of the term economy used here. It does not connote reduction in government spending because strong pressures exist for the expansion rather than curtailment of governmental welfare activities.

Granted that public expenditure should be incurred wherever necessary, it must be determined rationally within a framework of a series of arrangements and procedures. The first such arrangement is the government budget which should be comprehensive in scope and prepared and approved in advance of the operations to be conducted under it. The execution of budgetary provisions (on the expenditure side) should be clearly defined, i.e. who shall have the authority to supervise and control programmes contemplated in it. Similarly, there should be arrangements for a proper system of accounts and auditing.

Economy in public spending is all the more necessary in underdeveloped countries because they lack investible resources. Any wastage of the scarce resources by public authorities will undermine development efforts in the country. Lavish and wasteful spending will shake public confidence in government's ability to provide collective goods efficiently. It is, therefore, desirable that public expenditure in various areas should be carried to what is just necessary. Schemes of expenditure should be formulated, sanctioned and executed in time so that wastages arising out of delays are avoided. The practice of zero-base budgeting is relevant in this regard. [8]

23.4.3 Principle of Sanction: A good public expenditure system is that which prohibits spending of public funds without proper authorisation and for purposes other than sanctioned. The objective of this canon is to avoid wasteful expenditure and check misappropriation of public funds. In democratic societies, the sanctioning authority is the legislature. For example, in India each grant by Parliament or a State Legislature is regarded as a distinct service and the sum voted on a particular grant is appropriated to that service. Thus, money voted under one grant cannot be appropriated to another without legislative sanction. However, it is legal to reappropriate money from one major head to another or from one minor head to another within the same grant. This gives a certain amount of flexibility in adjusting expenditure of a ministry/department.

Another aspect of the sanction principle is the rule of lapse. Public funds are sanctioned by the legislature for a financial year. Any unspent balance lapses and is not available for utilisation in the following year. Such unspent balances have to be surrendered by the spending departments to the finance ministry. Depending upon the nature of public activity, exceptions are sometimes made to this rule. Thus, the rule of lapse may not apply to long-term irrigation projects and the money may be sanctioned specifically for a period of years.

23.4.4 Principle of Surplus: Though obsolete, the canon of surplus postulates that government should raise enough revenue to meet its expenditure and leave some surplus. Stated differently, it means that state should avoid budgetary deficit. This principle is a legacy of the thinking of classical economists.

Modern fiscal experts recognise the compensatory role of public expenditure in stabilising economic activities in the economy. The great depression of 1930s exposed the hollowness of classical ideas in this regard. Keynesian ideas on public work programmes and deficit financing still hold good in dealing with business cycles in the capitalist world. Whether a government should have surplus or deficit in its budget depends upon the economic environments under which budgetary decisions are taken. Surplus budget, instead of being a virtue, may prove politically inexpedient because people may interpret it as placing unwanted money in government hands as a result of unnecessary taxes.

23.5 Effects of Public Expenditure

The effects of public expenditure may be discussed under three categories: effects on production, distribution and stabilisation.

23.5.1 On Production: Most theories of economic development stress that an increasing proportion of additions to national income should be devoted to capital formation. Since the marginal propensity to consume of households in poor countries is high, it is necessary to transfer a part of additions to national income to government treasury. If these transferred resources, which otherwise would have been used for private consumption, are put to productive uses, the development process can be speeded up.

Public use of resources may influence production either directly or indirectly. The numerous industrial and commercial enterprises of the Central and State Governments in India contribute to production directly. These enterprises are engaged in producing goods and services which require huge investment over long periods of time or are commercially unattractive to private investors or require secrecy of operations in national interest.

Indirectly, public expenditure, by providing social and economic overheads, induces private investment and risk. Some examples of these overheads or infrastructural facilities are: means of transport and communications, banking and insurance services, educational and training centres and research and development institutions. These services provide congenial environment for private enterprise. Government may also encourage private initiative in these areas through soft loans, grants and subsidies.

The public provision of free or subsidised medical, recreational, educational and housing facilities enhances people's ability and desire to work more. The availability of these facilities leaves a margin in the family budget, enhancing the ability and desire to save more. If ability and desire to save more increases, the ability and desire to invest more also increases. A significant part of public expenditure is devoted to national defence and internal security. Both these services ensure conducive atmosphere for private enterprise.

23.5.2 On Distribution: The political and economic thinking of the 20th century has stressed the establishment of welfare societies within democratic framework. Left to itself, the market mechanism may not produce that distribution of income and wealth which is desired by society. Due to imperfections of the market and other malpractices by the owners of the means of production, economic inequalities may increase. If no corrective measures are taken, this may lead to social tensions. Public expenditure is a powerful and democratic method to realise distributive justice.

The provision of beneficial public services constitutes an addition to the real income of the citizens. Free/subsidised medical, educational and transport facilities, and slum improvement schemes are examples of positive additions to the real income of beneficiaries. Pensions, annuities, scholarships and unemployment allowances directly add to the money incomes of the receivers. The pattern of public expenditure should be such that its effect on reducing economic inequalities is the strongest.

It is important that benefits intended for the poor should preferably be given in kind rather than cash grants. Aid given in kind, e.g. medicines, books, clothes etc. cannot be turned into cash and diverted for other purposes. However, money given for a particular purpose may not be used to that end.

23.5.3 On Stabilisation: Fluctuations in the level of economic activities are inherent in market economies. These fluctuations, called business cycles or trade cycles, cause changes in prices, production and employment of resources. Such fluctuations, which hinder the smooth functioning of an economy, are caused by variations in the aggregate demand. Since government demand for goods and services is a significant component of aggregate demand, public expenditure can act as a stabilising mechanism to control business cycles.

Government consumption and investment should be stepped up during depression. A depression occurs when aggregate demand falls short of the installed productive capacity in the economy. Some of the factors of production are rendered unemployed and income levels decrease. This further leads to deficiency of demand and sagging prices. Public investment, through the multiplier effect, generates incomes and demand to boost the economy. This policy of compensatory finance helps to put the economy back on the rails.

Conversely, public expenditure, particularly for consumption purposes, should be curtailed or at least strictly controlled during inflation. Thus, by manipulating the level of its own expenditure, a government can control business cycles. In other words, public expenditure policy is a potent anti-cyclical weapon. However, the potency of this weapon is determined by two factors:

1. How well-organised and interrelated is the economic system?
2. What is the adjustment capacity of the economy?

The first factor implies that the economy should be responsive to public expenditure measures and in a position to transmit them to various sectors of the economy. The second condition stipulates unutilised capacity during times of depression. These conditions limit the effectiveness of public expenditure as an anti-cyclical instrument in underdeveloped countries which are characterised by lack of monetisation, small-scale production, and a vast rural sector. Changes in one part of the economy are not transmitted to other sectors sufficiently and quickly. These countries also suffer from technical and institutional rigidities. These special features limit the role of expenditure policy as a stabilisation tool in these countries.

Notes

1. Richard M. Bird, *The Growth of Government Spending in Canada* (Toronto: Canadian Tax Foundation, 1970), p. 138.
2. Frederic L. Pryor, *Public Expenditure in Communist and Capitalist Nations* (London: George Allen and Unwin, 1968), pp. 51-52.
3. Richard A. Musgrave, *Fiscal Systems* (New Haven: Yale University Press, 1969), p. 92.
4. Alan T. Peacock and Jack Wiseman, *The Growth of Public Expenditure in the United Kingdom* (London: George Allen and Unwin, 1967), p. XXXIV.
5. For details, see S. P. Gupta, "Public Expenditure and Economic Growth: A Time-Series Analysis", *Public Finance*, XXII (1967).
6. Hugh Dalton, *Principles of Public Finance*, p. 14.
7. *Ibid*, p. 7.
8. Under ZBB, each item of expenditure is challenged for its very existence in every budget cycle and no base or minimum expenditure level is presumed for any activity. Zero-base budgeting means the past is cut off, the present is regarded as a clean slate and all departments have to start from a scratch (hence zero-base). It is also called sunset budgeting, meaning that the sun would set on each governmental activity after a specified period. Before the sunset date, each department would be required to present ZBB, indicating achievements of its activities and what would result if the activities were not renewed.

24

Public Expenditure in India: Structure and Policies

Central and State Governments in India spend massive amounts on developmental, welfare and administrative activities. At the time of Independence in 1947, public expenditure formed around 10 per cent of national income. Presently, this figure hovers around one-quarter of national income (Table 24.1).

Table 24.1: Combined Expenditure of the Centre and the States (Revenue and Capital) in India

(Rs. crore)

	1990-91	1995-96	2000-01	2005-06*
GDP at market prices (current prices)	5,68,674	11,88,012	21,07,661	35,31,451
Total expenditure	1,52,601	2,87,496	5,44,832	9,47,069
Total expenditure as per cent of GDP	26.8	24.2	25.9	26.8

*Budget estimates.

Source: Government of India, Ministry of Finance, *Indian Public Finance Statistics*, 2004-2005 and 2005-2006, Table 1.9 (excerpted).

24.1 Classification of Public Expenditure in India

Public expenditure in India has various classifications which are important because they (a) explain the interrelationship between the government sector and the rest of the economy and (b) reveal the relative size of different governmental activities in the economy.

While certain classifications are the outcome of constitutional requirements, others are meant to facilitate understanding of the significance of governmental transactions. Thus, under Articles 112 and 202 of the Constitution, Central and State Governments are required respectively to present their expenditure estimates under the categories of revenue expenditure and capital expenditure.

To this classification is added a further classification, viz. Plan and non-Plan expenditure. Plan expenditure by tradition includes only new expenditure (both capital and revenue) on Plan projects undertaken during a Plan period. Furthermore, convention has it that new expenditure only under developmental heads can be included in the Plan. Thus, construction of a new jail house, though capital expenditure, does not qualify to be Plan expenditure.

24.1.1 Structure of Revenue Expenditure: Revenue expenditure relates to the normal running of Government departments and various services, interest charges on debt incurred by the Government, and grants given to State Governments and other parties. Broadly speaking, all those expenditures of the Government which do not result in the creation of physical or financial assets may be treated as revenue expenditures.

Budget documents classify total revenue expenditure into revenue non-plan and revenue plan expenditure. Revenue plan expenditure pertains to Central Plan and Central assistance for State and Union Territory Plans. However, the more important revenue non-plan expenditure covers a wide variety of general, social and economic services of the Government. The three major items of revenue non-plan expenditure are (a) interest payments, (b) defence and (c) subsidies (for details, see section 4.1 in chapter 4 of this book).

24.1.2 Structure of Capital Expenditure: Those expenditures of the Government which lead to the creation of physical or financial assets or reduction in recurring financial liabilities fall under the category of capital expenditure. Such expenditures pertain to payments on acquisition of assets like land, buildings, machinery, equipment, as also investment in shares, and loans and advances given to State Governments, public sector enterprises and other parties. Capital disbursements are of two kinds: those spent directly (capital outlays) and those spent indirectly by extending loans and advances.

Budget documents categorise total capital expenditure into capital non-plan and capital plan expenditure. Capital plan capital expenditure relates to Central Plan and Central assistance for State and Union Territory Plans. Capital non-plan expenditure covers various general, social and economic services provided by the Government (for details, see section 4.2 in chapter 4 of this book).

24.2 Factors Responsible for Increase in Public Expenditure

Public expenditure at the Central as well as at the level of State Governments has registered sharp rise since Independence. The reasons for increase in public activities and hence public expenditure are many and of diverse nature. The main items (interest payments, defence and subsidies) have already been discussed. Apart from these, many other factors have contributed to the growth of public expenditure in India.

The concept of economic planning has made Indian government an active partner in the growth process. The Industrial Policy Resolutions of 1948 and 1956 ensured state participation in the development efforts in a big way. Ever since the launching of the First Five Year Plan in 1951, every successive Plan has entailed more and more investment in the public sector. Five Year Plans are aimed to achieve such objectives as removal of poverty and unemployment, self-sufficiency, balanced regional development, provision of educational and medical facilities, and overall development of various sectors of the economy. The expansion of public sector through new units and nationalisation of existing units involved huge expenditure on the part of public authorities.

The cost of civil administration has gone up considerably due to revision of pay scales, fringe benefits and liberalised schemes of pensions and other retirement benefits. Administrative set up has expanded to implement various regulatory measures, particularly in respect of labour and industry, and also to run the democratic institutions. Preventive and corrective measures are needed on the part of public authorities to deal with business cycles, monopolistic tendencies, hoarding and profiteering.

The rapid growth of population is also responsible for increase in public expenditure. The massive size of population has led to urbanisation, congestion, pollution, and sporadic outbreak of epidemics. Even the provision for basic amenities of life requires investment of huge resources. Public expenditure has increased to meet the cost of various schemes aimed at improving the conditions of scheduled castes, scheduled tribes and other weaker sections of society.

The frequent occurrence of natural calamities has also strained public funds. Floods, droughts and epidemics hit one or the other part of the country and public spending on relief and rehabilitation has often upset budgetary calculations.

24.3 Public Expenditure Policy

At present and in the near future, public expenditure policy has to deal with the scrutiny and pruning of non-Plan expenditure of Central and State Governments. In this connection, the Eighth Five Year Plan (1992-97) observed, "With suitable deregulation of industry and trade and a movement away from detailed and discretionary *microplanning* of the economy, many of the supervisory and regulatory functions of the Government should be minimised. This would help a great deal in containing the growth of Government's administrative expenditure in the future." [1]

To quote RBI, "The combined expenditure of Centre and State Governments as a ratio to GDP declined from 28.8 per cent in 1990-91 to 25.1 per cent in 1996-97. However, the trend reversed and the expenditure to GDP ratio once again began to follow an upward movement after 1996-97 and reached 29.5 per cent in 2001-02. Furthermore, the efforts to augment investment expenditure by cutting consumption expenditure did not materialise. This was due to the fact that at both the national and sub-national levels of Government, expenditure correction was brought about mainly through cut in capital expenditure." [2]

Successive Central budgets in the 1990s contemplated a host of measures to curb growth in expenditure and to bring about structural changes in the composition of expenditure. These measures included the following.

1. Subjecting all ongoing schemes to zero-based budgeting.
2. Assessment of manpower requirements of Government departments.
3. Review of all subsidies.
4. Review of budgetary support to autonomous institutions and PSUs.

Apart from these reforms aimed at fiscal consolidation, a number of institutional measures were taken during the 1990s. Public sector restructuring and disinvestments were undertaken with a view to increase the efficiency of the Public Sector Undertakings (PSUs) as also to provide additional resources to the Government. The Ahluwalia Committee Report on Fiscal Transparency (2001) underscored the need for improvements in budgetary practices, which prepared the ground for the enactment of the Fiscal Responsibility and Budget Management (FRBM) Act, 2003. The Act requires the Central Government to take appropriate measures to reduce the fiscal deficit and revenue deficit, so as to eliminate the latter by 2007-08 and thereafter build up an adequate revenue surplus. The target date for this has since been modified to 31st March, 2009 through the Finance Act, 2004. In terms of the Rules made under the Act, the fiscal deficit is required to be reduced to 3 per cent of GDP by 31st March, 2009.

Also, the Central Government has brought about pension reforms by introducing a new pension scheme meant for new entrants to government service.

The issue of expenditure control is vast and complicated. To identify non-essential expenditure and to suggest economy in essential expenditure, a full-fledged expenditure commission needs to be set up. It may be recalled that a Commission on Public Expenditure, the first in independent India, was set up by a resolution of the Government of India on May 29, 1979 but it was wound up on January 31, 1980 before it could submit its report.

While in the field of taxation various Commissions/Committees have reported at the Central and State levels from time to time, there has been no official exercise to study the various aspects of public expenditure in India. This neglect not only indicates the lop-sided study of public finances in India but also undermines the importance of expenditure policy as a tool of general economic policy.

Expressing his concern for the high rate of growth of non-developmental expenditure, the Finance Minister observed in his 1999-2000 budget speech, "The most effective and lasting solution to this problem is to begin the process of downsizing Government. We are making an immediate beginning by abolishing four Secretary-level posts through a process of merger and rationalisation of Central Government departments. This will take effect on April 1, 1999. To carry this process forward in a systematic way towards reducing the role and the administrative structure of the Government, we will constitute an Expenditure Reforms Commission headed by an eminent and experienced person." [3]

Fulfilling the promise, the Government, though belatedly, announced the setting up of an expenditure reforms commission on February 29, 2000. The Commission, headed by the former finance secretary K. P. Geethakrishnan, was set up to find solution to the process of downsizing of government in a systematic manner so that the role and administrative structure of the government could be reduced.

More specifically, the lack of information on the incidence of public expenditure has hindered the evaluation of the redistributive role of fiscal policy over the years. In the absence of this information, a broad idea of the benefits of public expenditure is sometimes gained from certain anti-poverty programmes launched by the Government at the national level. The important among these programmes are: Integrated Rural Development Programme (IRDP), the National Rural Employment Programme (NREP), and the Rural Landless Employment Guarantee Programme (RLEGP). An evaluation of these programmes may be used as a proxy for formal studies of Government expenditure incidence.

The traditional apathy towards public expenditure studies is probably due to the belief that the level and structure of government expenditure is determined politically and hence beyond the scope of economists' investigation.

In the context of social justice, public expenditure can become a powerful weapon if it is used to benefit the poor masses. This can be done by taking up schemes which improve the productivity and earning capacity of the poor. As the problems of unemployment and poverty are more acute in rural areas, the focus of expenditure programmes has to shift away from metropolitan cities to villages. Among the rural people, the landless and the bonded labourers must get priority in receiving benefits from schemes of land clearance and distribution, credit facilities, rural housing and employment opportunities. Subsidies represent a sizeable and growing item of non-plan expenditure. Subsidies, on food and fertilisers, are primarily meant to help poor households in urban and rural areas. However, under the present system even the well-off sections of society are also beneficiaries of subsidised items. Application of some economic criterion is necessary to rationalise and regulate the benefits of subsidies without jeopardising the interest of weaker sections.

24.4 Restructuring of Government Expenditure Suggested by the Eleventh Finance Commission

The Eleventh Finance Commission examined at length the pattern of public expenditure at the level of Central and State Governments and made a number of suggestions to rationalise it in order to control budgetary deficits. It observed, "Alongside revenue augmentation, restructuring of public finances will require structural changes on the expenditure side as well. While the thrust should be on compression, the composition of expenditure would need to be restructured in favour of priority sectors like elementary education, primary health care, water supply, sanitation, roads and bridges and other infrastructure. Items that would require a tight rein are salary and pensions, interest payments and subsidies. There has to be a radical change in the method of financing the plan expenditure as well.

Salaries: Wages and salaries have been growing primarily because of periodic revisions carried out on the recommendations of the Pay Commissions of the Centre, and the States falling in line, without due regard to the capacity of individual States to pay. The burden of pay revision is compounded by releases of DA twice a year by the Centre which has an effect on the States too. While it is the prerogative of the States to decide the size of their government, the total wage bill cannot be allowed to rise beyond a certain proportion of revenue receipts which represent the capacity to pay. In this background, we recommend the following:

- As full neutralisation for the increase in the prices has been given to all categories of employees there is no need to appoint any new Pay Commission as a matter of routine and at intervals of ten years. A new Pay Commission should be appointed only when warranted by special circumstances.
- As the recommendation of the Central Pay Commission have an impact on the States, the terms of reference of the Pay Commission should be settled in consultation with the States. Similarly, the decision on the recommendations of the Pay Commission should be taken in consultation with the States.
- It is noticed that the size of establishment is disproportionately large in relation to the requirements of administration in several States. In implementing the Pay Commission recommendations the Central Government has been in some respects more generous than what the recommendations of the Pay Commission implied. Some States have gone even beyond those levels resulting in the rise of emoluments of the employees beyond what is warranted by their capacity to pay.
- Salaries and other allowances should bear a relationship with the revenue expenditure of the Central and the States and the ratio should be such so as to

leave adequate funds for maintenance and development expenditure. It is suggested that an Expert Committee may be appointed to determine the present relationship between salaries and other allowances with the revenue expenditure of the Centre and the States to suggest the relationship which would be attempted.

- The capacity of the Centre/States to pay salaries from their own resources should be one of the main criteria for determining the pay and allowances of the employees.

Pensions: Pensions have been the fastest growing item of the States' budgets in recent years. At the rate at which pensions are growing, liability for pension payments is going to cast a very heavy burden on the budgets in the coming years. Several factors have contributed to the growth of pensions. One has been the generous rise in the pensions recommended by the Fifth Pay Commission and, two the recent judicial pronouncement directing that no distinction should be made between people retiring at different points of time and all pensioners should be treated alike in the matter of their pension rights. Another factor has been the addition of the liability on account of pensions payable to retired employees of aided institutions and local bodies to the government's pension bill. The increasing longevity of people, though welcome, has also meant growing pension liability of governments. What causes concern is the fact that pensions are paid by governments on pay as you go basis i.e. there is no corpus or fund which could take care of the pension liabilities. Consideration needs to be given to evolving a system under which pensions do not become an unsustainable burden on the State exchequer. A large amount of pension burden is on account of retired defence employees. A suitable scheme to absorb the retirees from the armed forces in other government departments can help to contain the growth of defence pensions.

Interest Payment: Interest as a proportion of the revenue receipts of the States has increased sharply over the years, particularly during the last 10 years. The scheme of deficit reduction outlined in our restructuring plan, should help to check the debt growth of the States and thereby the growth of interest payments. From the supplementary memorandum on small savings received from the Ministry of Finance, it appears that the Centre may offer the State governments an option of pre-payment or rescheduling of past loans attributable to small savings. The guiding principle would be incentive based maturity reduction. Thus a loan of 25 years' duration could be rescheduled to 15 years' loan with lower interest rates.

Subsidies: Subsidies are provided by governments implicitly as well as explicitly. While the Centre's budget provides estimates of explicit subsidies in the State budgets, the outgo on account of subsidies is scattered under several heads. Subsidies, no doubt, have their uses as these help to alleviate the poverty of the low income segments of the population by providing access to essential goods and services free or at affordable prices. However, subsidies are apt to be misused and often go to the benefit of the non-poor." [4]

24.5 Restructuring of Government Expenditure Suggested by the Twelfth Finance Commission

After examining in detail the structure of expenditure at the levels of Central and State Governments, the Twelfth Finance Commission recommended its restructuring on the following lines, "In restructuring expenditures, there is need to make reference to the basic objectives of government intervention in economic activities, as also to the basic objectives for assignment of responsibilities as between central and sub-national governments. It is also important to relate government expenditures to outcomes in terms of the quality, reach, and impact of government services. This would be facilitated if governments focus more on their primary responsibilities rather than spreading resources thinly in many areas where the private sector can provide the necessary services. The primary role of government is to provide public goods like defence, law and order, and general administration. This represents one kind of market failure. The role of governments extends to merit goods and services with large positive externalities like education and health. The services should be assigned to the central government if the scope of public goods is nation-wide like defence. The services get assigned to state governments if the scope of the public good is limited to regions or if externalities are more local in character like the health services. Admittedly there may be many examples of benefit spillovers, some of which can be internalized to the state level decision makers by a suitable scheme of grants. There is a felt need to examine whether the central government is not partaking in many responsibilities that legitimately belong to the domain of the states. Governments at both levels have also stepped into the provision of many private goods, which adversely affects the quantum and quality of service in regard to public and merit goods. Two key elements of restructuring government expenditures relate to augmentation of capital expenditure relative to GDP, focused on infrastructure and a reduction of central government's expenditures on subjects listed as state responsibilities." [5]

24.6 Conclusion

Expenditure reforms in the context of liberalisation have two aspects (a) consolidation so as to reduce the quantum of expenditure and (b) restructuring with a view to changing the composition of government expenditure, i.e. shift towards growth-inducing expenditure on infrastructure and human resource development and reduction in unwarranted subsidies.

A successful expenditure control policy should include the following: (a) subjecting all ongoing schemes to zero-based budgeting, (b) assessment of manpower requirements of government departments, (c) review of all subsidies, (d) introducing cost-based user charges wherever possible, (e) review of budgetary support to autonomous institutions, and (f) greater commercialisation of the operations of public sector enterprises.

Notes

1. Government of India, Planning Commission, *Eighth Five Year Plan* (1992-97) Vol. I, p. 93.
2. Reserve Bank of India, *Report on Currency and Finance, 2001-02*, p. IV-15.
3. Government of India, Budget Papers 1999-2000, *Speech of Minister of Finance*, Part A, pp. 16-17).
4. Report of the Eleventh Finance Commission, June 2000, pp. 29-31.
5. Report of the Twelfth Finance Commission, November 2004, pp. 78-79.

25

Subsidies in India: System and Current Issues

25.1 Provision for Public Goods

The government is big and important in our times. We depend on the government to protect ourselves against external aggression, internal disorders, pollution, epidemics, social injustice, exploitation, unemployment and poverty. Furthermore, government is expected to (a) provide educational, medical and housing facilities, (b) build roads, bridges and communication networks, (c) ensure personal freedom and enforcement of contracts and (d) maintain our democratic institutions and cordial relations with foreign countries.

Though the list is not exhaustive, it does provide an idea of the amplitude of the multifarious activities of modern governments.

25.1.1 Market for Private Goods: Market mechanism operates almost successfully in the case of private goods. The two chief characteristics of private goods are (a) benefits derived are internalised and (b) consumption is rival.

In other words, market for private goods functions on the basis of exclusion principle. According to this principle, he who pays the price gets the commodity, and he who does not pay the price is denied the same. The principle applies in the case of private goods like food, furniture, houses, cycles, and hundreds of other marketable goods. As we see in our daily life, the nature of these goods is such that the exclusion principle can be readily applied. When A pays the price, he is handed over the shirt but B is refused the same if he fails to make the payment. This is so because benefits derived are internalised and consumption is rival.

25.1.2 Limitations of Market Mechanism: Left to itself, market mechanism cannot perform all economic functions optimally. The premise that market mechanism leads to efficient use of resources, i.e. it produces in the cheapest way what consumers want the most, is based on the following assumptions:

1. There is perfect competition in the factor market as well as in the commodity market.
2. Individuals can be excluded from consuming goods if they do not pay for them.

These conditions are rarely fulfilled in practice. Monopolistic and oligopolistic tendencies replace competitive forces to rob capitalism of its virtues. To quote, "In reality, various difficulties arise. Markets may be imperfectly competitive, production may be subject to decreasing cost, consumers may lack sufficient information or be misled by advertising, and so forth. For these reasons, market mechanism is not as ideal a provider of private goods as it might be." [1]

State intervention becomes necessary to curb such tendencies to protect consumers' interests. Even if it is assumed that competition is assured in the factor and commodity markets, still certain goods, because of their peculiar production and consumption characteristics, cannot be provided through market mechanism. In view of the problem of externalities, certain services (like defence, and street lighting) have to be provided through the public sector. This leads us to the discussion of public or social goods.

25.1.3 Public (or Social) Goods [2]: According to Richard Musgrave, "Social goods are goods the consumption of which is non-rival. That is, they are goods where A's partaking of the consumption benefits does not reduce the benefits derived by all others." [3] Two appropriate examples of non-rival consumption are: (a) defence services and (b) internal security.

Market mechanism fails in the case of public goods. The production and consumption characteristics of social goods are such that they cannot be provided through the market economy.

It would be inefficient to apply exclusion principle in the case of above two services. Efficient resource use requires that price should equal marginal cost. Since the marginal cost in this case is zero, the additional consumer should be admitted even if he pays zero price. It is noteworthy that exclusion, even if desired, is not possible in the above mentioned two cases.

In short, market may fail due to non-rival consumption or due to non-excludability or both of these reasons.

25.2 Nature and Role of Subsidies

25.2.1 What is a Subsidy? A subsidy is a grant of money from an outside third party to either the buyer or the seller of a commodity. Subsidies allow a buyer to procure a commodity/service at a lower price than would otherwise have been necessary. Similarly, a business firm will not stay in operation unless revenue is sufficient enough to cover cost plus some return on investment. If revenue from buyers is insufficient, a subsidy from an outside agency may keep the firm in operation.

The effect of a subsidy is opposite of the effect of a tax. A cash subsidy is the opposite of a direct tax while a subsidised commodity is the opposite of a taxed commodity. Hence, subsidies are sometimes called negative taxation.

25.2.2 Are Tax Concessions Subsidies? These are provisions in tax laws which encourage individuals and corporations to undertake activities desired by the government. Almost all tax systems incorporate provisions which exclude certain items and deduct others from the tax base. These provisions may take the form of exemptions, deductions, allowances, and tax credits. Tax incentives (or tax preferences) reduce the amount of tax which would otherwise be payable by a taxable entity. These tax preferences are referred to as tax incentives. Broadly speaking, items which erode the normally accepted base of a tax may be treated as tax incentives.

Tax incentives, an integral part of tax systems the world over, are designed to promote a wide spectrum of socio-economic objectives. If judiciously used, they can become an effective tool of economic change on desired lines.

Tax incentives involve sacrifice of tax revenue and hence need to be devised carefully. The revenue foregone is similar to a subsidy or a grant to a taxable entity and hence akin to government expenditure. For example, there is no fundamental difference between an outright subsidy payment to a new industrial undertaking set up in a backward area and foregoing tax revenue on account of tax concession to it. However, outright subsidy payments attract public attention more readily than tax concessions (hidden subsidies) which lie scattered in the cobwebs of frequently changing tax laws. Thus, activities which deserve budgetary support should preferably be encouraged through expenditure programmes rather than the nebulous medium of tax incentives. The alternatives to tax incentives are: direct subsidies, government loans at subsidised interest rates, and foreign exchange facilities.

However, when support through tax concessions becomes necessary, their economic effects should be properly evaluated, i.e. whether the cost in terms of revenue foregone is justified by the likely benefits. In other words, a tax incentive should be appraised in the same way as any other item of public expenditure. The loss of revenue must be estimated on net basis because some increase in revenue may be attributable to stepped up economic activities due to tax favour. To what extent the intended positive effects (increased savings, investments, production etc.) of tax concessions are realised and to what degree they offset the negative effects (loss of revenue, equity distortions), are complex questions requiring rigorous empirical analysis.

25.2.3 Subsidies in National Income Calculation: The value of goods and services produced in a country are ordinarily measured at prices at which these are traded in the market. When we buy a tube of toothpaste the price we pay includes an element of tax like excise duty or sales tax (indirect taxes). Thus, the payment we make does not go wholly to the people who produce the goods. A part of the payment goes to the government in the form of taxes. This payment to government does not reflect the true cost of producing the goods concerned.

Contrarily, when the government pays subsidies (say to handloom weavers) the money incomes of factors exceed the market value of their output. Valuation of goods at market prices violates the basic principle that the value of goods produced is equal to the sum of the money income received by the factors of production.

In order to get a total of national income which corresponds to the income payments actually received by factors of production, we must subtract the total of indirect taxes from and add the value of subsidies to national income measured at market prices. Hence,

National income at factor cost = National income at market prices − Indirect taxes + Subsidies

25.2.4 Targeting of Subsidies: Subsidies may be categorised in terms of the target in view.

A. Subsidies for a Product: Such subsidies are used to promote a product in various ways as, for example, product development including research for quality improvement, sales promotion, product storage and export

B. Subsidies to a Person: Subsidies targeted to a person are specific subsidies. These are provided to a person under special circumstances. Thus, monetary assistance received by widows, handicapped and other needy persons from the social welfare departments of governments falls under this category.

C. Subsidies to a Group of Persons: These are provided to a group or category of persons such as landless labourers, freedom fighters and displaced persons.

D. Subsidies for a Region: To ensure regional balanced development, governments generally provide extra funds for special problem regions of a country. These regions may include desert lands, drought prone areas, hilly terrains and tribal areas.

25.2.5 Classification of Subsidies (in order of preference): Subsidies are financed either from tax or non-tax revenue, or result in a deficit. Since some subsidies are less justifiable than others, it is important to categorise services in terms of their desirability vis-à-vis subsidisation.

Subsidies are generally classified into the following three categories (a) public goods, (b) merit goods and (c) non-merit goods.

A. Public Goods: The best examples of public goods are defence, internal security and general administration. These services are characterised by non-rivalry and non-excludability in consumption. Such services are available to all citizens and cannot be priced. Hence, they are not included in the calculation of subsidies.

B. Merit Goods: These goods encompass a large variety of services like anti-pollution measures, malaria eradication programme, primary education and health, roads and bridges, scientific research, flood control, and soil and water conservation. The social benefits resulting from these services are much greater than the sum of private benefits to individual consumers. This is so because these services contain elements of *externality* beneficial to the society as a whole. Subsidies on these services are justified because of availability of benefits in the form of externality.

C. Non-merit Goods: These include, *inter alia*, food, fertilisers, higher education. The element of externality is either absent or limited. Social and equity objectives are generally the ground for subsidising these services. Considerable controversy exists about such subsidies.

25.2.6 Role of Subsidies: Subsidies play a vital role in the economy of a country. A country has various resources which are to be gainfully deployed for the benefit of the population of the whole country. Subsidies are provided to ensure equitable utilization of the resources for the people. The developed, developing and underdeveloped countries have different kinds of subsidies. Developed countries provide subsidies to their population for improving standard of living, the underdeveloped countries provide subsidies for meeting bare minimum needs of the vast majority of population.

Subsidies are the converse of indirect taxes and are specific to goods and services. Subsidies are different from transfer payments, which are straight income supplements to individuals, who are normally the poor and the vulnerable.

25.2.7 Effects of Subsidies: Subsidies generate various types of effects on the functioning of an economy.

A. Positive Effects of Subsidies: Providing minimum consumption entitlement to the poor by subsidizing the items consumed by them is an extremely important welfare dimension of fiscal policy. Subsidies can correct for the under-consumption of goods with positive externalities. With the social benefits of a particular service or commodity exceeding the aggregate of private benefits to individual consumers, market solutions result in under-consumption and subsidies can make the necessary correction. However, the benefits can be maximised only when the subsidies are transparent, well targeted, and suitably designed for effective implementation without any leakages.

B. Negative Effects of Subsidies: Subsidies can generate negative effects also. Once received, people become dependent on the subsidies. Hence, subsidies are sometimes termed as sweet poison. Misuse of subsidies for political purpose is known worldwide. Subsidies support one industry at the expense of the other. When a person is given subsidy benefit, it imposes burden on some other person in the country. Subsidies interfere in the free working of the economy in the following ways.

1. Through subsidies, free money circulates in the economy without increase in actual income/production.
2. Subsidies make the beneficiaries lethargic.
3. Subsidies lead to misallocation of resources.
4. Malpractices have often been noticed in the administration of subsidies.
5. Subsidies are often misused by politicians.

25.2.8 Measures for Effective Utilisation of Subsidies: Operational inefficiency in the case of provision of any public good or service leads to higher cost of production and greater subsidies. There is a wedge between subsidies that are actually received by the users of the service and subsidies that are borne by the Government. Several types of inefficiencies may accompany the public provision of services. Apart from direct costs like overstaffing, poor maintenance of assets, procedural delays, and delays in taking critical decisions, there are systemic inefficiencies.

Subsidies can prove effective to achieve the desired goals if they have the following components:

1. The focus should be on physical achievements and not on financial disbursements.
2. The effects of subsidies should be monitorable and measurable in terms of quality or quantity.
3. Subsidies should be given as a one-time help or for a short period. Subsidies on continuing basis should be avoided.
4. The parameters fixed for the subsidy should be transparent.
5. Subsidies should be cost-effective. Most of the assistance should reach the intended beneficiary and very small amount should be spent on administrative arrangements.
6. Subsidies should be properly targeted, i.e. benefit should go to the really deserving.
7. Timing of subsidies should be made proper. For example, free seed distribution should be just before sowing.

25.3 Subsidies in India

Subsidies represent a sizable item of the Centre's non-Plan revenue expenditure. In the 2007-08 Union budget, they accounted for Rs. 54,330 crore (14.2 per cent) out of a total revenue non-plan expenditure of Rs. 3,83,546 crore. Food and fertilisers are the two main items subsidised by the Government through budgetary support.

25.3.1 Vadilal Dagli Committee (1979): The Government of India constituted a committee in February 1978 under the chairmanship of Vadilal Dagli. The Committee submitted its report in May 1979.

The Committee was set up to evaluate and review the whole gamut of controls and subsidies and make suitable recommendations. It was asked to examine the following matters.

1. The manner in which subsidies had actually operated and whether or not the objectives sought to be achieved had actually been achieved.
2. In what manner was the system of controls connected to the system of subsidisation in the national economy?
3. Are such subsidies justifiable and will it be possible to moderate or eliminate the system of subsidisation by suitable modification in the system of controls?

The Committee noted with concern the substantial growth in the magnitude and diversity of subsidies. It identified three types of subsidies (a) direct subsidies given from the budget, (b) cross subsidies without any budgetary implications where one set of consumers subsidise the other and (c) covert subsidies where the cost of a subsidy is borne by the budget but not shown as such.

On the basis of its findings, it made the following recommendations.

1. The costs and recipients of benefits of all subsidies should be reviewed periodically, say once every three years.
2. Subsidies should in general be given only to sustain tiny units, decentralised production, or to support the consumption of the weaker sections of population.
3. Where necessary, clear-cut, overt subsidies should be given in lieu of indirect subsidies as, for example, losses of PSUs arising out of a deliberate policy decision of the Government to keep prices below the cost of production in the interest of keeping down the general price level.
4. Budget of the Central Government should be restructured in terms of the above criteria.

25.3.2 Post-liberalisation Thinking on Subsidies: Of late, drastic changes have occurred in Government's policy towards subsidies. The crux of this policy is to roll back subsidies and thus curb the growth of non-Plan expenditure. Another dimension of the present policy is to restrict the availability of subsidised items to vulnerable sections of society.

Three reasons account for the increase in the Central Government subsidies in recent years.

1. Moving the petroleum sector to a transparent system of budgetary subsidies and delay in the announced phasing out of the subsidies on PDS kerosene and domestic LPG.

2. Increase in explicit budgetary subsidies on food and fertilizer.
3. Increase in input costs unaccompanied by any improvement in recovery rates resulting in escalation of implicit subsidies on a variety of economic and social services.

The economic reforms programme initiated in 1991 aimed at, among other things, reducing fiscal imbalances and improving allocative efficiency by minimizing the distortions in relative prices arising from budgetary and fiscal imprudence. Containing and targeting subsidies constituted an important element of reforms. Containment and targeting of subsidies can serve the following objectives (a) remove economic distortions, thereby improving economic efficiency and growth, (b) achieve redistributive objective and (c) reduce budgetary burden and release precious resources.

As per the human Development Report, 2004 of the UNDP, India has been placed at a rank of 127th position out of 177 countries. The report measures the life expectancy, undoubtedly related to the quality and quantity of the food we consume (which in turn is impacted by the medical care that follows), educational attainment and the adjusted real income. All these measures reflect very poorly in the case of India. Out of all this food is the first thing. Hence there is a strong case for India to provide the subsidies to those poor people.

Government showed its seriousness about targeting subsidies at the poor and the truly needy in the budget speech for 2006-07. Extensive discussions with stakeholders on three major subsidies, namely, food, fertilizer and petroleum were held for the purpose. Views of the general public were also sought. Working groups/committees have gone into the question of fertilizer and petroleum subsidies. The latest committee formed in this regard is C. Rangarajan Committee. Government is trying to evolve a consensus on the issue of subsidies. However the Government has pledged that all subsidies will be targeted sharply at the poor and the truly needy the small and marginal farmers, farm labour and urban poor.

25.4 Food Subsidy

25.4.1 Components of Food and Nutritional Security: Foodgrains occupy an important place in the family budget of a large section of the population in India. Hence, a certain minimum supply of foodgrains at reasonable prices constitutes the rock-bottom of Government's economic policy. To ensure minimum health and efficiency standards, the prices of foodgrains must be held stable at levels within the reach of the poorer sections of the community.

Food Security is one of the major components of social security. It consists of ensuring (a) that food is available at all times, (b) that all persons have means of and access to it, (c) that it is nutritionally adequate in terms of quantity, quality and variety, and (d) that it is acceptable within the given culture. There are three elements in the above definition: availability, access and suitability.

In recent years, nutrition has been considered as part of food security, and is therefore, referred to as Food and Nutrition Security.

25.4.2 Purpose of Food Subsidy: The objectives of a sound agricultural price policy are two-fold (a) to ensure fair prices for the produce of the farmers, and (b) to ensure adequate and regular supply of agricultural commodities to the consumers at reasonable prices.

Food subsidies in India comprise subsidies to farmers through support prices and purchase operations of the Food Corporation of India (FCI), consumer subsidies through the public distribution system (PDS), and subsidies to FCI to cover all its costs. Food subsidies are mainly on account of paddy and wheat. The rapid increase in food subsidy in recent years is attributable to what is called the 'economic costs' of foodgrains, which include the minimum support prices paid to farmers in the procurement process.

Government notifies the FCI about the purchase prices of the relevant foodgrains that it has to observe for the coming agricultural marketing season. These prices, known as minimum support prices (MSP) are based on the recommendations of the Commission on Agricultural Costs and Prices (CACP). In practice, the notified purchase prices have been consistently higher than the MSP recommended by the CACP in recent years.

The Food Corporation of India procures foodgrains from the market at prices (support prices) fixed by the Government. To these prices are added the handling costs (transportation, storage etc.) to arrive at the economic cost of procuring foodgrains. The procured foodgrains are then released to the public through the public distribution system. The issue price of foodgrains is less than the economic cost to the Government. The difference between the two is reimbursed to the Food Corporation of India as subsidy. The major determinants of food subsidy are (a) cost of procurement, (b) storage and distribution, (c) foodgrain stocks and (d) issue price of cereals.

The main benefits of food subsidies are the resultant food security provided to the citizens, particularly the poor at affordable prices, and incentives to the farmers to keep foodgrains production at a comfortable level. A key aspect of the system is the Central Issue Price (CIP) and its relativity to the non-PDS price faced by those who either do not get the benefit of the PDS, or cannot meet their entire demand from the PDS.

India is not unique in providing either producer subsidies or consumer subsidies in the foodgrains sector. Several countries, including the developed ones, provide subsidies in the area of agriculture and allied operations at levels that are fairly high compared to that in India. In some developed countries, such subsidies which are mainly for the producers, are several times higher than that in India.

25.4.3 Components of Food Subsidy: Producers and consumers and within this group the vulnerable sections of the society are the major beneficiaries of food subsidy. The subsidy incurred on the supply of foodgrains through the PDS at below FCI's economic cost constitutes the consumer subsidy while the producer subsidy is the direct offshoot of the price support based procurement operations of the government. The producer subsidy together with the cost of maintaining the buffer stock accounts for the cost of buffer stock operations. The consumer subsidy together with the buffer carrying cost constitutes the food subsidy.

The FCI issues foodgrains to the State Governments at a uniform Central Issue Price (CIP) which is considerably lower than the economic cost incurred by the Central Government by way of procurement, storage, transport and distribution. The difference between the economic cost and the CIP is called the consumer subsidy. Since the FCI maintains a large buffer stock of foodgrains, it entails a substantial carrying cost. The consumer subsidy and the carrying cost together add up to the total food subsidy which is borne by the Central Government. It is an important item of the non-Plan revenue expenditure of the Government as shown in its annual budget.

25.4.4 Minimum Support Prices: An important element of the agricultural price policy of the Government of India is the announcement every year of minimum support prices for major commodities. The co-operative societies and government agencies have helped the farmers to escape the exploitative practices of the private traders.

A. Historical Perspective: As a result of the partition of India in 1947, the balance between foodgrains availability and population was disturbed, leading to food shortages in new India. Therefore, the First Five Year Plan (1951-56) was mainly devoted to agricultural development. The recurring scarcities and shortages of essential food items forced the Government to adopt an elaborate system of public procurement and distribution of foodgrains. For this purpose, the Food Corporation of India (FCI) was established in 1965, and a price support system for major agricultural crops was introduced. In spite of certain drawbacks, the system worked reasonably well till the late 1970s. Since then, production of foodgrains in the country has kept pace with the requirements of the population, owing mainly to the spread of new technology among farmers.

The price support policy of the Government is directed at providing insurance to agricultural producers against any sharp fall in farm prices. The minimum guaranteed prices are fixed to set a floor below which market prices cannot fall. Till the mid 1970s, government announced two types of administered prices (a) minimum support prices (MSPs) and (b) procurement prices.

The MSPs served as the floor prices and were fixed by the Government in the nature of a long-term guarantee for investment decisions of producers, with the assurance that prices of their commodities would not be allowed to fall below the level fixed by the government, even in the case of a bumper crop.

Procurement prices were the prices of kharif and rabi cereals at which the grain was to be domestically procured by public agencies (like the FCI) for release through PDS. It was announced soon after harvest began. Normally procurement price was lower than the open market price and higher than the MSP.

This policy of two official prices being announced continued with some variation up to 1973-74, in the case of paddy. In the case of wheat it was discontinued in 1969 and then revived in 1974-75 for one year only. Since there were too many demands for stepping up the MSP, in 1975-76, the present system was evolved in which only one set of prices was announced for paddy (and other kharif crops) and wheat being procured for buffer stock operations.

B. Methodology for Cost Calculation: The minimum support prices for major agricultural products are announced each year after taking into account the recommendations of the Commission for Agricultural Costs and Prices (CACP). The CACP, while recommending prices takes into account all important factors including cost of production, changes in input prices, input/output price parity, trends in market prices, inter-crop parity, demand and supply situation, parity between prices paid and prices received by farmers etc. Among these multiple factors that go into the formulation of support price policy, the cost of production is the most significant. Thus, for making the support price policy functionally meaningful, the minimum guaranteed prices ought to cover at least the reasonable cost of production in a normal agricultural season obtained from efficient farming.

The CACP analyses the cost of production data for various States in respect of various commodities in consultation with the states. After a meeting of the State Chief Ministers, the MPS/procurement prices are declared. With costs of production for the same crops varying between regions and also across farms within the same region and for different producers, the level of costs that could be accepted as a norm poses enormous difficulties.

In fixing the support prices, CACP relies on the cost concept which covers all items of expenses of cultivation including in that the imputed value of inputs owned by farmers such as rental value of owned land and interest on fixed capital. Some of the important cost concepts used by CACP are the C2 and C3 costs.

C2 cost includes all actual expenses in cash and kind incurred in production by actual owner plus rent paid for leased land plus imputed value of family labour plus interest on value of owned capital assets (excluding land) plus rental value of owned land (net of land revenue).

C3 Cost means Cost C2 + 10 percent of cost C2 to account for managerial remuneration to the farmer.

Costs of production are calculated both on per quintal and per hectare basis. Since cost variations are large over states, CACP recommends that MSP should be considered on the basis of C2 cost. However, increases in MSP have been so substantial in case of paddy and wheat that in most of the States MSPs are way above not only the C2 cost but the C3 cost as well. For instance, weighted average of C3 costs of eight wheat growing states is presently only Rs. 532 per quintal while the weighted average of C2 cost is Rs. 483 per quintal as against which CACP recommended MSP is Rs. 620 per quintal. The producer subsidy at C2 cost is therefore Rs. 137 per quintal (MSP minus C2 cost) and Rs. 88 per quintal at C3 cost (MSP minus C3 cost).

Trends in the MSP of wheat and paddy in recent years are given in Table 25.1

Table 25.1: Minimum Support/Procurement Price of Wheat and Paddy in Recent Years (Rs./quintal)

Crop Year	Wheat		Paddy (Common)	
	MSP	Per cent change	MSP	Per cent change
1997-98	510	7.4	415	9.2
1998-99	550	7.8	440	6.0
1999-00	580	5.5	490	11.4
2000-01	610	5.2	510	4.1
2001-02	620	1.6	530	3.9
2002-03	620	-	530	-
2003-04	630	1.6	550	3.8
2004-05	640	1.6	560	1.8
2005-06	650	1.6	570	1.8
2006-07	750	15.4	580	1.8

Source: Government of India, *Economic Survey*, 2006-07, p. 103, Table 5.19.

Realising the importance of inter-sectoral terms of trade [4], the Government of India modified the terms of reference for the Commission for Agricultural Costs and Prices (CACP). Consequently, the CACP has been regularly taking into account the terms of trade ever since 1980 while recommending support /procurement prices for agricultural commodities.

In the meantime, Government constituted a Task Force in March 1993 (Chairman: A.S. Kahlon) to suggest methodology for constructing an index of terms of trade between agricultural and non-agricultural sectors. The Government of India now computes the terms of trade between the two sectors on the basis of the methodology recommended by the Task Force. [5]

C. Economic Cost of Foodgrains to Food Corporation of India (FCI): The economic cost of foodgrains to FCI is of strategic importance, as it influences not only the food subsidy bill but also the country's competitiveness in international markets for foodgrains. The FCI is reimbursed the difference between the economic cost of foodgrains and the issue price. The economic cost of foodgrains to FCI has been on the rise over the years. The increase in the MSPs of rice and wheat, high State-level levies, which account for almost 50 per cent of the procurement incidentals for foodgrains, and the rising trend in distribution costs have contributed to the increase in the economic costs of foodgrains over the years.

Fixing the MSP at a level equal to C2 cost (all cost in cash and kind, including the imputed cost of family labour) of the least cost State would help in containing the rising trend in economic cost of foodgrains. The major procurement States, viz. Punjab, Haryana and Andhra Pradesh have been imposing State taxes and levies of over 10 per cent ad valorem on the procurement of foodgrains, thereby inflating the economic cost. There is scope for rationalisation of these State levies. More decentalised procurement will help in containing the increase in the distribution and hence economic costs.

The 2004-05 (BE) projected a reduction in economic cost of wheat from Rs 952.51 per quintal in 2003-04 to Rs 924.82 per quintal and a marginal increase in the economic cost of rice from Rs 1,253.04 per quintal in 2003-04 to 1,262.51 per quintal in view of decline in distribution cost of both wheat and rice in 2004-05.

25.4.5 Buffer Stock Operations: Excessive fluctuations in agricultural prices generate harmful effects both for the producers and the consumers. The beneficiaries of unstable prices are the middlemen and the speculators. It is for these reasons that Government undertakes buffer stocks operations, i.e. making purchases when there is glut of produce in the market and releasing stocks during period of scarcity.

Periodically, an official committee is set up to recommend the volume of minimum buffer stocks to be maintained at the beginning of each quarter for the purpose of food security. This quantum, together with the amount needed to run the PDS, constitutes the minimum operational stocks of the FCI. However, the purchases of the FCI are open-ended in that it has to accept all the grains that are sold to it at the declared purchase price, and this sometimes results in mounting stocks well beyond the buffer stock norms.

Foodstocks reached a peak of 63 million tonnes in July 2002, more than two-and-a-half times the norm of 24 million tonnes. By April 2004, the stocks were down to 20 million tonnes, still higher than the norm of 16 million tonnes for April. The reduction of the stocks, however, was not brought about by increased PDS off-take. PDS off-take at 20-22 million tonnes was less than the allocation in the last two years.

The rising MSPs for rice and wheat induce the farmers to cultivate these two crops more than other crops. Increased production of rice and wheat leads to their higher procurement by official agencies which, in turn, results in large accumulation of Government food stocks. On the other hand, the off-take of foodgrains through PDS is relatively low due to the following reasons.

1. Narrow price differential between the open market price and the price at which foodgrains are made available through the PDS.
2. Altered consumption pattern of the population (towards milk, eggs and meat as against cereals) owing to improved income levels.
3. Lacklustre export performance of agricultural products.

The off-take from the PDS appears to be poor especially in some States like Bihar. It could be due to the fact that the economic cost has been going up, the prices at which foodgrains are supplied to people below the poverty line are also going up, and have become unaffordable to the poor in the category. It could also be due to the poor quality of the foodgrains supplied through the PDS. Besides, the quantities supplied at subsidised prices are not adequate for the sustenance of the whole family, and people have to supplement them by purchase from the open market. Thus, the implementation of the PDS does not seem to be serving the purpose of making foodgrains available to people at affordable prices.

Large stocks of foodgrains raise the subsidy bill through increased handling and carrying costs along with the losses. Besides, withdrawing such large quantities from the market also results in rising open market prices of foodgrains, neutralising much of the consumer benefits that the subsidy provides.

To run the excessive stocks down, Government took special measures during 2001-02 which continued through 2002-03, such as release of foodgrains from the FCI at concessional rates for exports, offloading of the old and low quality foodgrains through tender sale and reduction in the APL issue price to bring back APL population to the PDS fold, to dispose of the excess stock of foodgrains. These measures helped in reducing the excess stock of foodgrains with the FCI. Further, the Government also adopted the policy of restraint in the announcement of the MSPs of wheat and rice, as part of its strategy to remove market distortions, and to restore the role of private trade in the grain market, thereby easing the pressure of procurement on the FCI. Some success has been achieved in this respect, because the market prices of rice and wheat, which remained below the MSP in different parts of the country during 2001-02 and 2002-03 recovered to prevail at a level higher than the MSP during 2003-04 and, 2004-05. All these helped in tackling the problem of excess stock of foodgrains with the FCI and the declining trend in stock levels, which started in 2003-04, continued through 2004-05.

25.4.6 Public Distribution System (PDS): PDS is the cornerstone of Government's price policy and food security system in India. It ensures availability of certain essential commodities (sugar, kerosene, rice and wheat) at affordable prices, especially for the poor. Through its agency the Food Corporation of India (FCI), the Government procures and stocks foodgrains which are released every month for distribution through the PDS network across the country. These commodities are distributed to the public through a network of Fair Price Shops (FPS).

A well-targeted and properly functioning PDS is an important constituent of the strategy for poverty alleviation. PDS is operated under the joint responsibility of the Central and State Governments. The Central Government takes the responsibility for procurement, storage, transportation and bulk allocation of foodgrains, at subsidized prices. The responsibility of distribution to consumers including target groups through a network of 4,63,000 fair price shops rests with the State Governments.

A. Targeted Approach: Government from time to time fixes the central issue prices (CIP) of rice and wheat, which together with transportation and retailers' margins, determines the prices at which consumers receive their entitlements at the fair price outlet in the PDS system. A common strategy to reduce the burden of food subsidy, without affecting the interests of the poor, is to build in specific features that target the poor.

Outlining its policy on food subsidy, the Ninth Five Year Plan (1997-2002) observed, "Self-sufficiency in foodgrains for the country as a whole does not necessarily imply food and nutrition security for all. Making food available through the PDS at affordable prices has been a key element of our food security system. However, untargeted PDS has resulted in a steady rise of budgetary food subsidy. During the Ninth Plan subsidised foodgrains is proposed to be targeted only to people below the poverty line so as to ensure that budgetary subsidies reach the needy and become sustainable." [6]

Since June 1997, the uniform CIP system has been replaced by a targeted PDS (or TPDS), to provide greater subsidies to the poor. Consumers below the poverty line (BPL) pay a lower price and receive a higher quantum of foodgrains than those above the poverty line (APL). Despite this, there are indications that there are both inclusion and exclusion errors. Besides, there are wide disparities in PDS penetration in different States.

TPDS follows a two tier subsidised pricing structure for families Below Poverty Line (BPL) and for those Above Poverty Line (APL). BPL population receives rice and wheat at a much lower price (hence highly subsidised) whereas APL population is supplied at a price which is much higher and closer to the economic cost. The identification of the poor under the scheme is done by the States.

Criticising the present system of differential PDS pricing, Mid-term Appraisal of Tenth Five Year Plan (June 2005), observed, "The present system of differential PDS pricing, with very low prices for BPL consumers, is a highly inefficient way of serving the equity objective. There are heavy leakages of as much as 55 per cent according to a recent Planning Commission study. The system also distorts incentives for grain producers in non-surplus areas where FCI procurement is poor or non-existent, because it depresses grain prices below the MSP. With the Food for Work Programme in place and the expansion of Mid-Day Meals and the universalisation of Integrated Child Development Services (ICDS), there is a strong case for moving to uniform PDS pricing. In other words, the PDS, should not be viewed as a poverty reducing instrument as much as an instrument for protecting the common man (including the poor) by stabilising issue prices at a level which may imply only a limited subsidy but which insulates the consumer from sudden increases in prices due to scarcity. The procurement side of the operation should continue to aim at stabilising MSP reasonably above costs of production. Procurement support should also be extended to cover the entire country." [7]

25.4.7 Food Subsidy Bill: The food subsidy bill has increased from year to year in recent times (Table 25.2). Though pruning of the existing subsidy level is imperative and could be done by reducing operational inefficiency, the interests of the poor also have to be safeguarded. The surplus stocks of foodgrains with the government provide a vital resource for providing income support to the poor and the vulnerable. Better targeting of subsidies is now beginning to be visible. But it has been found that PDS has failed in large parts of the country, and that it needs to be restructured to be an effective tool of food security. To quote, "The primary motivation for reform originates in the size of the food subsidy bill, even as a proportion of GDP. With escalating economic cost and poor targeting, the food subsidy bill has reached a level that is a significant proportion of the total government expenditure. Further, it also restrains the process of crop diversification." [8]

Table 25.2: Growth of Food Subsidies in India in Recent Years

(Rs. crore)

Year	Food subsidy	As per cent of GDP#
1999-00	9,435	0.48
2000-01	12,060	0.57
2001-02	17,499	0.77
2002-03	24,176	0.99
2003-04	25,160	0.91
2004-05	25,800	0.83
2005-06*	23,200	0.66
2006-07**	24,200	---

New series based on 1999-00.

* Revised estimates; ** Budget estimates.

Source: Government of India, *Economic Survey,* 2006-07, p. 105, Table 5.22.

Inefficiencies in the FCI are also responsible for the subsidy bill. Since all costs of FCI are automatically reimbursed, there is little incentive to raise efficiency and reduce costs.

25.4.8 Critical Assessment of Food Subsidies in India: Main areas of controversy regarding food subsidies are as follows.

A. Assessment of Minimum Support Prices (MSPs): MSPs lay the floor for the market price of foodgrains, especially the two dominant foodgrains: rice and wheat. With sharp increases in MSP every year despite surpluses having replaced shortages, the MSP has become the maximum selling price instead of being the floor price. This coupled with the system of open-ended procurement has made FCI the buyer of the first resort resulting in huge accumulation of surplus public stocks of foodgrains, leading to much higher commitments for government subsidy. FCI has thus become the main buyer, stockiest and seller in the domestic market. It is also the main exporter.

1. Negative Fallouts of MSPs Policy: A careful of food subsidies in India leads to the conclusion that a large part of the recent problems arise from the relatively high MSPs. In recent years, with the MSPs announced by the

Government at levels higher than those recommended by the CACP, procurement has been high and off-take low, resulting in an inevitable build-up of stocks and a bloated food subsidy bill. The macro implications of burgeoning food stocks are manifold but the following two are more important. Firstly, higher procurement, along with additional storage and maintenance costs, means higher food subsidy which increases deficit on the already strained revenue account of the Central Government. Secondly, since food stocks are financed by preferential food credit, they have monetary implications as well. Higher demand for food credit can give rise to possible crowding-out effects on other sectors. In view of the present high level of food security, there is need to focus on the distributional aspects of foodgrains rather than encouraging unsustainable levels of cereal production and procurement through the MSP.

The other negative fallouts of the declared MSPs may be summarised as follows.

1. Since the issue price and the purchase price are linked, higher purchase prices result in higher issue prices. Further, with a large part of the marketed surplus in FCI warehouses, the lower supply exerts an upward pressure on prices in the open market. Everyone, except those farmers with marketable surpluses of foodgrains, is affected adversely.
2. High MSP combined with open-ended purchases by FCI has almost eliminated private wholesale trade and storage with lower incidental and storage costs in foodgrains.
3. Exclusive attention to wheat and rice has distorted the cropping pattern of farmers in favor of these two foodgrains alone.
4. Higher water and fertilizer intensity of these two crops has had adverse environmental impacts.
5. Concentration of FCI purchases in just two foodgrains and in few States has facilitated tax exportation by some of these States. Although necessities like foodgrains are normally kept outside the tax net, Punjab and Haryana have imposed taxes such as mandi fees on the purchases of foodgrains. With FCI paying such taxes, the tax gets exported to consumers in other States.
6. High statutory levies (including mandi charges, cesses and fees to commission agents) on grain purchase, not only discourage private trade but also increase FCI's cost, thus putting a pressure on the food subsidy bill. The levies imposed by the State Governments (ad valorem) differ from State to State and are highest in case of Punjab, Haryana and Andhra Pradesh. The High Level Committee on Long Term Grain Policy recommended that government may, for open-ended procurement, in future announce a gross price, inclusive of MSP and a uniform 4 per cent allowance for State taxes as

the price that its agencies would be allowed to pay. It would be better for the centre and states to agree on a ceiling on statutory levies, and announce MSPs which farmers could actually expect to receive net of all compulsory levies.

7. Shortage of storage space has pushed up costs through wastage and deterioration of stocks.
8. High carrying cost is a subsidy benefiting neither the consumers nor the producers.
9. There are severe regional imbalances in the operation of the entire food subsidy scheme, as FCI's purchase operations are mainly confined to five areas, viz. Punjab, Haryana, Western Uttar Pradesh, Andhra Pradesh and Chhattisgarh. The implication for the present policy of purchase is that farmers of only a few States get the entire farmers' subsidy. A large percentage of these farmers are not even poor.

2. Realistic MSPs: It is of paramount importance to set more realistic MSPs, particularly with respect to wheat. To conform to its true nature, the MSP should correspond to the CACP-determined C2 cost, which includes all cash costs and imputed cost of family labor. Since these estimates may vary across regions, a simple average of these costs should be used as the uniform MSP.

3. Open-ended versus Close-ended Purchase Operations: The purchase operations should not be open-ended. Before every sowing season, procurement targets should be fixed on the basis of norms and a margin of error of about 10 per cent. FCI should suspend purchase operations once targets are achieved. The FCI should have the flexibility of adding to these target quantities in specific markets only in case overall procurements fall short of the target in other markets. A system of price insurance, similar to the Farm Income Insurance Programme introduced recently on a pilot basis, may be developed. The scheme should be self-financing and without any subsidy obligation. This can operate in conjunction with the purchase operations to benefit those farmers who miss out on the opportunity of selling their surplus at the support price because of the close-ended purchase operations.

4. Decentralised Procurement Operations: The decentralised procurement scheme of the Government of India is in operation since 1997. Under this scheme, the designated States procure, store and also issue foodgrains as per allotments indicated by the Central Government under TPDS. The difference between the economic cost of the State Governments and the Central Issue Price is passed on to the State Governments as subsidy. The decentralised system of procurement, apart from helping to cover more farmers under the MSP of the Central Government, has the merit of economising the transport and administrative costs involved in procurement and distribution operations. Further, it helps in minimising the dependence of State Governments on the FCI for PDS requirements and reducing the complaints about quality, as consuming States themselves are the custodians of the procured foodgrains.

However, the scheme has evoked limited response from the State Governments. Out of the State Agencies' share of nearly 58 percent of total rice and 80 percent of total wheat procured by the FCI, only 33 percent rice and 13 percent wheat are contributed by the States with decentralised procurement. At present, the State Governments of West Bengal, Madhya Pradesh, Uttar Pradesh, Chhattisgarh, Uttaranchal and Tamil Nadu are implementing this scheme in a limited way. The States of Assam and Nagaland and the Union Territory of Andaman & Nicobar Islands have also evinced interest in the scheme.

The concerns of the State Governments broadly relate to financing of operations (RBI valuation norms for stocks of foodgrains) and reimbursement of expenses and release of subsidy by the Central Government (fixation of economic cost of foodgrains of State Governments and delays in the release of the subsidy). The concerns relating to the reimbursement of expenses and release of subsidy have been largely addressed through a process of consultation of the stakeholders concerned. On the request of the States, the issues relating to valuation norms have been taken up with the RBI.

To quote, "In the short run, decentralization of procurement may not be a practical option. However, it should be pursued as a long-run objective to usher in greater efficiency in the purchase and distribution operations, and to distribute the benefits of the price support operations more evenly across the country. A useful approach can be to work out the details of the scheme and announce it as soon as possible, allowing States to join in at the time of their choice. Once the farmers of non-participating States appreciate the benefits of their States joining in, the political process should ensure participation of a growing number of States. Eventually, the FCI should act only as a coordinating agency in the matter of procurement with important parameters like procurement prices and aggregate stock requirements provided by the Government of India. In the meantime, the FCI should include a greater number of States in their price-support operations. Further, the tendency for tax exportation needs to be curbed, by appropriate legislation, if necessary. Since it is easy to identify the States that indulge in this practice, it should also be possible to work out differential purchase prices for individual States based on the basic price and maximum allowed tax on the price. [9]

5. Normative versus Actual Unit Costs: In order to enforce efficiency, the reimbursement of costs to FCI should be based on normative unit costs and actual quantity involved, instead of reimbursement on actual basis. If some of the functions of the FCI can be carried out by others, it would help to trim the unwieldy size of the FCI. For example, actual delivery of grain may be postponed at the time of purchase, and a small mark-up on the purchase price may be allowed for this purpose. This will reduce the burden of storage on FCI. Active participation by private traders can also relieve the burden on FCI, but necessary institutional changes, including a revision of the concerned laws, are pre-requisites. The responsibility for losses will have to be put squarely on the personnel above a given level, with general cuts in staff payments and perquisites. To balance this, costs reduced below norm-based ones may be retained and distributed among the staff as annual bonus or any other mechanism deemed fit.

B. Assessment of Public Distribution System (PDS): PDS is recognised as a permanent feature of the strategy to control prices, reduce fluctuations and achieve an equitable distribution of essential goods. An efficient public distribution system requires a nexus between production, procurement, transportation, storage, and distribution of the selected commodities.

The working of the PDS is periodically reviewed in consultation with the State Governments and corrective measures are taken from time to time to improve the supply of various essential commodities to the consumers.

The main challenges in this regard are to improve PDS penetration and reduce leakages. The former is the responsibility of the State governments, and barring moral suasion, the Centre can do little under the present system.

1. Food Coupons: One possibility is to introduce food coupons, which was proposed as a possibility in the Union Budget 2004-05. This method has been tried in several other countries, with mixed results. There is need for caution in its introduction because of unforeseen difficulties in administering it at the massive scale that characterises PDS. Only the additional subsidy given to the poor can be tried first, while continuing with the exclusive PDS outlets. At present, the additional subsidy for BPL families over and above that for APL is Rs. 195 per quintal on wheat and Rs. 265 per quintal on rice. BPL cardholders can be given coupons worth Rs. 1.95 per kg. of entitlement of wheat and Rs. 2.65 per kg. of their entitlement of rice. The poor would then pay to the PDS outlet the same price as the APL families, but partly with coupons and partly with cash. For the PDS outlet, there will be only one price, but it will be entitled to exchange the coupons collected for cash. Gradually the system could be extended to any foodgrains seller even outside the fair price shops.

2. Self-targeting: The PDS in its present form has no self-targeting characteristics, except perhaps for the poor quality of the grains distributed driving away the non-poor. Self-targeting can be brought in by subsidizing coarse grains consumed generally by the poor alone. Two other measures, which may encourage self-targeting are (a) locating of PDS shops in areas where the poor live, and (b) allowing/restricting PDS grain purchases on a weekly basis rather than monthly basis. Often the very poor cannot afford purchase of monthly requirements in one go. On the other hand, restricting bulk purchases will discourage the not-so-needy from PDS outlets.

3. Need for Eligibility Criterion: The basic purpose of food subsidy is to help the weaker sections of population to obtain cereals at reasonable prices. Presently, every citizen of India, irrespective of his economic circumstances, is entitled to draw subsidised items (cereals, sugar, kerosene) from fair price shops. This is also true in case of subsidised educational and medical facilities. There is hardly any justification for this non-discriminatory treatment of every section of society and some eligibility criterion based on income needs to be fixed. If the cut-off income level is kept low, it will exclude a large section of deserving population. A high cut-off level will have marginal effect. The administrative and enforcement costs of implementing such measures should also be borne in mind. To begin with, income tax assessees may be excluded from the purview of subsidised cereals, sugar, and kerosene. A national consensus is required for norms to exclude the non-poor.

C. Recommendations of the High Level Committee on Long Term Grain Policy, 2002: The Department of Food and Public Distribution had constituted a High Level Committee on November 16, 2000 for formulating a long term Grain Policy for the country. The Committee submitted its final report on July 31, 2002. Some of the recommendations made by the Committee for Long Term Grain management are listed below.

1. Quality norms should be strictly adhered to while procuring foodgrains for PDS distribution.
2. Payments as statutory levies to state governments by FCI are essentially transfers from the centre to the state governments. These should be taken care of separately between the Centre and the states without involving the FCI.
3. MSP for paddy should be fixed only for a single grade.
4. APL price should be reduced to 80 percent of the economic cost and BPL price to 50 percent of the economic cost excluding statutory levies. This would also help improve the viability of the fair price shops in the distribution network.
5. Once the current high stocks are reduced, the resultant savings could be used for employment schemes, for which there was a strong felt need and which could be used to develop rural infrastructure.

6. The existing Antyodaya scheme of food support could also be expanded to become a food security system for the entire destitute population.
7. A system of universal PDS be introduced with uniform CIP, one each for rice and wheat respectively, for all consumers in all parts of the country.
8. The Central Government should announce its MSP policy before the sowing season on recommendations of the Commission for Agricultural Costs and Prices (CACP).
9. The CACP should be made an empowered statutory body.
10. In recommending MSPs which should apply only to Fair Average Quality grain, the CACP should go strictly on the basis of C2 cost of production (i.e. all costs including imputed costs of family labour, owned capital and rental on land) in more efficient regions.
11. While the Centre has to continue to take the primary responsibility for procurement, as production is dispersed procurement should also become more dispersed and this process can definitely save costs of transportation and meet consumer needs more adequately.
12. All compulsory levy orders on rice millers under the Essential Commodities Act (ECA) should be removed with immediate effect.
13. A different problem likely to arise as a result of lower MSPs is that there will be a probability for market prices to exceed MSP and, therefore, quantities offered for sale at MSP may fall short of PDS and buffer stocks requirements. In situations where market conditions are such that MSP purchases fall short of PDS requirements. Government would need to make purchases on the basis of best terms. This may include imports, open market purchases from secondary markets or through open tender purchases or purchase from farmers at a market determined price above MSP.
14. Crop diversification is very important at the current stage of India's agricultural development, given the changing dietary patterns. There is need for special packages for diversification.
15. There should be an automatic and transparent policy of variable tariffs on both agricultural imports and exports linked to the deviation of spot international prices from their long run trends. This is required for stabilisation of prices in an open economy.
16. Barriers to private trade, economic as well as legal, should be eased.
17. FCI has performed its role in its core functions reasonably well and should continue to do so keeping in mind that there has to be a work culture of total quality management.

18. It is desirable that that the FCI's role be confined to procurement of the major cereals for the PDS and that price support operations in coarse cereals be handled by State agencies.

25.4.9 Conclusion: The policy of providing price support by raising the MSP continuously though making the terms of trade for agriculture favourable, has not only distorted domestic market prices but has also eroded our export competitiveness. While developed economies continue to protect their exports through export subsidies, Indian rice (except perhaps basmati rice) and wheat are not export competitive. An exporting country cannot have its grain prices greatly mis-aligned with free-on-board export prices. But, with MSPs of foodgrains ruling at the existing high and being totally mis-aligned with the costs of production as also free market prices, India is no longer competitive internationally.

Strong corrective steps aligning the minimum support prices with the cost of production of foodgrains are called for. Perhaps, the only solution we have at hand is to freeze the current MSP until such time it becomes equal to C2 cost or until annual procurement settles down to earlier levels of 24-30 million tonnes.

Similarly, future trading, particularly in foodgrains, should be promoted first so that dependence on MSP mechanism for price stabilisation could be avoided.

To quote, "any subsidy restructuring has to address the issue of food subsidy. For foodgrains, support prices should be kept at the C2 level recommended by the CACP. To contain operational costs, reimbursement of expenses to the FCI should be based on normative unit costs and actual quantities involved. With respect to PDS, the system of dual prices encourages leakages. A uniform price policy with a system of food coupons for the BPL families needs serious consideration. The system may be implemented in phases." [10]

25.5 Fertiliser Subsidy

25.5.1 Manures and Fertilisers: An Introduction: Manures and fertilisers play the same part in relation to the soil as food in relation to the body. Just as a well-nourished body is capable of the maximum effort, a well nourished soil will have the best fertility.

The quality of the soil varies greatly in a country of the size of India. It is generally known that Indian soils are deficient in organic matter, nitrogen and phosphates.

Organic matter, nitrogen, phosphorus and potash are the chief constituents which must be supplied to the soil. Nitrogen is of the first importance in crop production. The soil has a mechanism by which it absorbs nitrogen from the atmosphere and makes it available to living beings in the form of grain and fodder; men and cattle derive energy from the consumption of these and the nitrogen taken from the soil is returned to it in the form of organic manures like farmyard manure, green manure, oilcakes, composts of various kinds, bone-meal and various types of chemical fertilizers, thus completing the nitrogen cycle.

Next in importance is phosphate. Plants absorb phosphates from the soil which are returned to it through animal and human excreta and through decayed plants and their ashes and the bones of dead animals.

Indian soils, while deficient in nitrogen and phosphates, are generally rich in potash. Lack of potash does not, therefore, present a serious problem at present but it is one that should be watched.

Manures may be classified into two categories (a) organic manures and (b) inorganic manures. Organic manures may further be sub-divided into (a) bulky organic manures and (b) concentrated organic manures.

Bulky organic manures include farmyard manure, compost manure, night soil and green manure, while concentrated manures are oil cakes, bone meal, dried blood, horns and hoofs etc. Tropical soils often lack humus. The addition of bulky organic manures like farmyard manure, which is a by-product in farming by bullocks, helps the soil by increasing its water holding capacity, improving soil aeration, and by changing the plant nutrients through slow decomposition into forms readily available to plants. There are other advantages in the use of organic manures, namely (a) steadiness in yield over a period of time, (b) benefit to the succeeding crops by their residual effects and (c) ability to withstand unfavourable weather conditions.

In the case of inorganic or synthetic fertilisers, the most important nitrogenous ones are ammonium sulphate, ammonium nitrate, calcium nitrate, ammonium phosphate and urea. The important phosphatic fertilizers are super phosphate, rock phosphate, and ammonium phosphate.

25.5.2 Fertiliser Consumption in India: The consumption of fertilizers has been steadily increasing in India over the years. However, a great deal of variability is observed in fertiliser consumption among the States. Amongst States in the plains, per hectare consumption is highest in Punjab, Haryana, Andhra Pradesh and Tamil Nadu. It is lowest in Madhya Pradesh and Rajasthan. Earlier, *Kharif* crops accounted for nearly one-third of the total fertiliser consumption, whereas the *rabi* crops accounted for a much larger share. This has now changed. Consumption is more evenly spread between the two sowing seasons, reflecting perhaps more assured water availability in *kharif* season at all-India level.

Use of fertilisers is necessary to improve yield of various crops. The objective of providing fertilizers to farmers at affordable prices, while also ensuring adequate return on investment to the producing units, has been the corner stone of the fertilizer pricing policy of the government.

25.5.3 How is Fertiliser Subsidy Given? In order to control the fluctuations in fertilizer prices, the Government of India regulates the fertilizer market through the Retention Price Scheme (RPS). The RPS was first introduced for nitrogenous fertilizers in November 1977, and extended to complex fertilizers in February 1979.

The RPS is essentially a cost-plus approach with some norms for capacity utilization and conversion coefficients. The plant specific retention prices (RP) are revised every quarter so that price increases in plant inputs can be taken into account. The retail price of fertilizers is fixed and is uniform throughout the country. The difference between the retention price (adjusted for freight and dealer's margin) and the price at which the fertilizers are provided to the farmer is paid back to the manufacturer as subsidy. Transportation costs are also compensated on the basis of equated freight computed on a normative basis.

The relative benefit-incidence of the substantial fertilizer subsidy on the farmers and the fertilizer industry has been a matter of some research. The difference between the hypothetical farm-gate price of imported fertilizers and the actual price paid by the farmers on fertilizer under the RPS, multiplied by the quantity consumed, may be taken as the fertilizer subsidy accruing to the farmers. The balance of the total subsidy on fertilizer after deducting the portion of subsidy accruing to farmers may be taken as the share of subsidy to the fertilizer industry.

Since the selling prices of fertilizers are less than the cost of production, the difference between the selling price and the cost of production as assessed by the Government is borne as subsidy on urea.

25.5.4 Reform and Rationalisation of Fertiliser Subsidies: The issue price of fertilisers is revised from time to time. In the 1991-92 budget, the issue price of fertilisers was increased by 40 per cent on an average. Later on, it was reduced by 10 per cent to make it 30 per cent with effect from August 14, 1991. However, the small and marginal farmers were exempted from the price increase. In spite of this substantial increase in the issue price, subsidy on fertilisers is an important item of non-plan expenditure. While it is desirable that small and marginal farmers should continue to enjoy the benefits of subsidised fertilisers, it is questionable if such benefits should continue to be extended to big farmers as well.

Consequent to decontrol of phosphatic and potassic fertilizers on August 25, 1992, the prices of these fertilizers rose sharply resulting in a sharp fall in their consumption. A separate subsidy scheme (called concession scheme) was then introduced to stimulate the consumption of these fertilizers. The price concession (subsidy) on these fertilizers has been substantially increased in recent years.

It was only in the aftermath of the economic crisis of 1991 that a serious attempt was made to reform RPS to rationalize the fertilizer subsidies. Government decontrolled the import of complex fertilizers such as di-ammonium phosphate (DAP) and muriate of potash (MOP) in 1992, and extended a flat-rate concession on these fertilizers. But, urea imports continued to be restricted and canalized. Thus, flat-rate concessions are provided on imported and indigenous fertilizers, while urea is subsidized under the RPS.

A. Hanumantha Rao Committee, 1997: Government constituted a high-powered committee to review the existing RPS and suggest a new pricing policy for urea under the chairmanship of C. H. Hanumantha Rao in January 1997. The committee recommended a Normative Referral Price (NRP) system in place of the RPS.

B. Expenditure Reforms Commission (ERC), 2000: ERC, in its report submitted in 2000, suggested phasing out of the unit-wise RPS in stages over a period of six years and its replacement with the group-concession scheme.

The new urea pricing policy for the industry suggested by the ERC came into effect from April 1, 2003. The new scheme is to be implemented in three stages: the first from April 1, 2003 to March 31, 2004; the second from April 1, 2004 to March 31, 2006. The modalities of the third stage will be decided after a review of the first two stages. The Group Retention Pricing (GRP) recommended by the ERC, which had also been recommended by several other committees in the past, was implemented with some modification with effect from April 1, 2003. The second stage with revised norms is currently under implementation.

25.5.5 Phasing out of Fertiliser Subsidy: Implications: It is being increasingly felt that the RPS has resulted in certain aberrations over the years. RPS has led to the adoption of a cost plus approach in reimbursing cost of production to the fertiliser units. This approach generates no compulsion for producers to improve their efficiency.

The Ninth Five Year Plan also criticised the present system of subsidies when it observed, "It, therefore, becomes essential that the Government gradually shifts its expenditure patterns away from providing non-transparent and non-targeted subsidies. Unfortunately, the beneficiaries of the present system of subsidies are much more organised and politically more vocal than the vast majority of our common citizens who silently suffer the lack of even the basic amenities of a decent and healthy existence." [11]

With more than a third of the total fertilizer subsidy benefitting the fertilizer industry, an obvious question to ask is the impact of phasing out of the fertilizer subsidy on the output of foodgrains. The ERC estimated that an increase in the farm-gate price of urea to import-parity price without an increase in the procurement price of foodgrains would lead to a fall in foodgrains production of about 13.5 million tonnes.

This estimate of ERC has been questioned on several grounds. To quote, "Any estimate of the adverse impact of phasing out fertilizer subsidy on foodgrains production is based on the condition that other things remain the same. However, they are unlikely to remain unchanged. First, fertilizer use and application is more dependent on technological and non-price factors than on price or agro-economic variables. These factors include irrigation facilities, cropping pattern, spread of high yielding varieties (HYVs), effective fertilizer distribution and availability of credit. Irrigation is a critical factor determining the use of fertilizers, and has a very significant impact on foodgrains production. Enhancing irrigation would therefore help minimize loss of output from decontrol of fertilizer prices. A reduction in subsidy effected through an increase in urea prices may not translate into lower production through declines in fertilizer use, particularly if the non-price factors are made conducive to fertilizer use. Public investment in irrigation is an effective instrument to promote the use of fertilizers.

Second, rationalization of the urea price subsidy would have a significant salutary impact on balanced application of N (nitrogen), P (phosphate) and K (potash). The role of balanced nutrients cannot be overemphasized. It is possible that the increase in foodgrain production due to a favourable mix of fertilizer nutrients could well be in excess of any reduction in foodgrain production because of an increase in urea prices.

Third, since the procurement prices are cost-based, it is possible that an increase in procurement prices would also partially offset the negative impact of fertilizer price increase on foodgrains production. With high foodgrains stock with government procurement agencies in recent years, instead of further increases in procurement prices to offset any possible urea price increase, an alternative could be to distribute fertilizers to targeted cultivator households alone (small and marginal) in the form of tradable coupons." [12]

25.5.6 Conclusion: The Finance Commissions have emphasised, from time to time, the need to curtail fertiliser subsidy. The Seventh Finance Commission assumed a progressive decrease in fertiliser subsidy and its complete elimination by 1983-84. The Eighth Finance Commission regretted that the stipulations of the previous Commission did not materialise. The Ninth Finance Commission also felt that further growth in fertiliser subsidy should be severely restricted.

Rationalisation of fertilizer subsidy primarily revolves around rationalization of pricing of urea, the only fertilizer under the RPS. The impact of any rationalization will depend upon two important factors (a) efficiency of domestic fertilizer industry and the domestic cost of production and (b) the international price of urea.

An important reason for the high cost of domestic production is the dominance of naphtha or fuel-oil/low-sulphur heavy stock as feedstock, which is more costly than natural gas. With raw material and power and fuel constituting around 64 per cent of sales revenue of the domestic fertilizer industry, there is need to switch to cheaper options like liquefied natural gas for cost-efficiency.

For bridging the gap between the demand and supply of urea in the medium term, Government is in the process of formulating a policy for new units and expansion of existing urea units, de-bottlenecking leading to higher capacity, and conversion of existing costlier feedstock units to gas-based units. The proposed policy for new units and expansion of existing urea projects will encourage private investment in urea plants. Equally important is the firming up of policy for conversion of existing non-gas based urea units of natural gas (NG)/Liquified Natural Gas (LNG), which are clean, efficient and cost-effective source of energy. While at present natural gas based plants account for more than 60 per cent of urea capacity, balance capacity is based on naphtha, fuel oil and LSHS as feedstock. Switchover from non-gas based urea units to NG/LNG will result in savings in the subsidy on account of reduced cost of feedstock.

To quote, "In the case of fertilizer, both farmers and fertilizer industry have been subsidized. There is a need for policy measures to reduce subsidy to both the groups. Fertilizer subsidies should be done away with in their present form. Urea imports should be de-canalized and a flat rate subsidy system may be introduced with two different rates of subsidy for domestic producers and importers in the short run, and a single rate in the medium term. Further, given the problem of domestic availability of natural gas, which is the cheapest feedstock, the option of setting up fertilizer plants in countries where natural gas is available in plenty may be considered. The fertilizer produced there can be shared between the host country and India as per the agreement reached. Another reason for the mounting burden of fertilizer subsidy is the lack of a mechanism to increase the farm-gate price of urea at regular intervals. A system that provides for such a periodic increase is required." [13]

25.6 Petroleum Subsidy

Prior to April 2002, prices of motor spirit, high speed diesel, kerosene for public distribution system (PDS) and domestic liquified petroleum gas (LPG) were decided by the Government and administered through the Oil Coordination Committee (OCC), and there was an elaborate system of cross-subsidisation of PDS kerosene and domestic LPG through higher prices of motor spirit. The net result from cross-subsidization of products by petroleum companies, predominantly public sector companies both in the upstream and downstream sectors, constituted the so-called oil-pool surplus or deficit. These balances were carried on the books of the state-owned oil companies, and occasionally settled by Government intervention. Thus, subsidisation in the oil sector was in the nature of a quasi-fiscal operation.

In November 1997, Government set a timetable for a phased transition from an administered price regime to a market-determined system with continued subsidization of PDS kerosene and LPG, but on a gradually reducing scale. Subsidies on kerosene and LPG for household use were to be phased down over time to smaller price subsidies of 33.3 per cent and 15 per cent, respectively, by end-March 2002. As part of the energy sector reforms, the prices of many petroleum products, for example, naphtha, furnace oil, low-sulphur heavy stock (LSHS), light diesel oil (LDO) and bitumen, have been liberalized since April, 1998. One important achievement was the linking of high speed diesel prices to international prices and an elimination of subsidy since September 1997 for some time. However, LPG and kerosene, consumed mainly by the domestic sector, continue to be heavily subsidized.

The phased reduction in subsidies has fallen behind schedule. In March 2002, Government decided that the subsidy on domestic LPG and PDS kerosene would be provided on a specified flat-rate basis from the Consolidated Fund from April 1, 2002. In this situation, Government reimburses the firms for the cost of the subsidy, which is carried as a line item in the budget and called the petroleum subsidy.

25.6.1 Calculation of Petroleum Prices: Retail selling prices of motor spirit and high speed diesel for the consumers are calculated by taking into account the following factors.

1. Basic price at refinery level on import parity basis.
2. Freight up to depots.
3. Marketing cost and margin.
4. State-specific irrecoverable levies.
5. Excise duty.
6. Delivery charges from depot to retail pump outlet.
7. Sales tax and other local levies.
8. Dealers' commission.

The basic selling prices of motor spirit and high speed diesel are uniform at all refinery locations throughout the country. As per the existing arrangement between the oil marketing companies and refineries, the element at (1) is revised on a fortnightly basis in line with movements in international prices. The marketing costs and margins, dealers' commission, and delivery charges within free delivery zones are also uniform. The prices at various locations vary depending upon the distance from the refinery, rate of sales tax and other local levies.

Although the oil marketing companies were granted freedom to fix retail selling prices of motor spirit and high speed diesel on a fortnightly basis, in practice, this arrangement has not appeared to have worked in quite a transparent manner. For example, there was no revision of motor spirit and high speed diesel prices between January 1, 2004 and June 16, 2004, while the prices of crude and petroleum products in international markets increased rapidly.

In order to mitigate the hardship of oil companies, Government worked out a new methodology with effect from August 1, 2004 allowing the oil marketing companies limited freedom to revise the prices of motor spirit and high speed diesel within a price band. Oil companies are permitted to adjust prices on their own within a band of ± 10 per cent of the mean of rolling average import-parity price including cost of freight of the previous 12 months and last quarter. When prices move beyond this band, the oil marketing companies have to approach the government to modulate the excise duty rates.

25.6.2 LPG and Kerosene Subsidies: LPG subsidy benefits largely the higher expenditure groups in the urban areas, and may be regressive. With regard to kerosene, on a per capita basis, the urban areas receive a larger subsidy. The limited availability of subsidized kerosene in rural areas biases its use in favour of lighting rather than cooking. Moreover, the kerosene subsidy in rural areas is regressive as higher expenditure groups receive more subsidized kerosene than lower expenditure groups. Kerosene subsidy is prone to mis-utilisation with about half the subsidized kerosene supplies diverted and never reaching the intended groups. These arguments suggest that the LPG and kerosene subsidies are ineffective in serving the desired objectives. Therefore, the removal of LPG subsidy in a gradual manner, or at least a substantial reduction in the subsidy element, may be recommended. A more cautious approach may be justified in the reduction of kerosene subsidies since about a half of the rural households use kerosene primarily to light their homes.

Generally, it is assumed that clean fuels like kerosene, that are relatively environment-friendly compared to fuel wood, are not used as they are not affordable because of high prices and low purchasing power of the poor households. However, it is not affordability, but non-availability that may be restricting the use of clean fuels by poor rural households. Thus, the approach that may be sustainable in the long run for the purposes of expanding access and improving the quality of service is to create an open and competitive market with clearly defined and well-enforced rules and regulations for all participants.

Cash transfer to the poor to compensate for the reduction or elimination of subsidy does not appear to be a suitable strategy for inducing a shift toward hydrocarbons for use as cooking fuels. The urban poor and all rural households may use more wood with enhanced incomes from a modest cash transfer. An alternate approach may be to channel all sales of kerosene through the retail markets, and encourage small distributors of fuels. Coupons may be issued only to poor ration card holders with entitlement to purchase kerosene from a retailer at the subsidised price. This would discourage direct diversion of subsidised kerosene to other sectors.

To conclude, the domestic LPG and PDS kerosene subsidies seem to be ineffective in serving the desired objectives. Therefore, the domestic LPG subsidy may be gradually reduced or at least substantially restricted to people outside the purview of income tax. However, a more cautious approach is needed as regards reduction of subsidy on kerosene.

Notes

1. Richard Musgrave and Peggy Musgrave, *Public Finance in Theory and Practice* (New York: McGraw-Hill Book Company, 1985), p. 48.

2. The terms public goods and social goods are used interchangeably here. For niceties of the distinction between the two, see *ibid*, pp. 50-51.

3. *Ibid*, p. 49.

4. Terms of trade between the agricultural and non-agricultural sectors is a subject of controversy among agricultural economists in India. Terms of trade are defined as the ratio of agricultural prices to non-agricultural prices. There are two schools of thought. According to one, terms of trade have moved in favour of the agricultural sector with the result that the development of the industrial sector has slowed down. Hence, it is contended that agricultural prices should be lowered to give a boost to industries.

Contrarily, many hold the view that terms of trade have moved against the farm sector and therefore higher agricultural prices are needed to induce the farmers to produce more. The debate is inconclusive because the results of various studies are conflicting due to different methodologies and assumptions adopted by the researchers.

5. For more details on the index of terms of trade between the agricultural and non-agricultural sectors, see Reserve Bank of India, *Report on Currency and Finance*, 1998-99, pp. III-4 and 5.

6. Government of India, Planning Commission, *Ninth Five Year Plan* (1997-2002), Vol. II, p. 2.

7. Government of India, Planning Commission, *Mid-term Appraisal of Tenth Five Year Plan*, June 2005, pp.6-7.

8. Government of India, Ministry of Finance, *Central Government Subsidies in India*, December 2004, p. 9.

9. Ibid., p. 13.

10. Ibid., p. 21.

11. Government of India, Planning Commission, *Ninth Five Year Plan* (1997-2002), Preface.

12. Government of India, Ministry of Finance, *Central Government Subsidies in India*, December 2004, p. 17.

13. Ibid., p. 21.

Part V: Public Debt

The Government of India borrows heavily both internally and externally. Internal borrowings of the Government are chiefly meant to meet budgetary deficit. External borrowings are meant to meet deficit in the balance of payments.

The main sources of internal borrowings are: individuals, commercial banks, financial institutions and the Reserve Bank of India (RBI). Borrowings from the RBI are through ways and means advances (WMA). The major sources of external borrowings are the international agencies like the IMF and the World Bank, foreign governments, and foreign private sources.

26

Public Debt in India: Sources and Restructuring

Public debt is a method by which governments obtain money. Public debts are incurred through public loans. A loan may be either voluntary or compulsory. A government may raise loans either internally or externally. Clearly, external loans are voluntary in nature. Public loans may be for short, medium or long period. Short-term loans are also known as *floating debt*. Long term loans are also called *funded debt*. Debt requirements of a government may be classified on the basis of purpose also. A government may resort to borrowings for productive or unproductive purposes.

Public borrowings involve problems of debt management which is clearly related to monetary policy. The payment of interest on and the repayment of principal of public debt (debt servicing) form part of public expenditure. Public debts, unlike taxes, leave behind liabilities for future generations.

26.1 Rationale for Government Borrowings

Long-term borrowings by a government are justified when the benefits of a capital project undertaken by it are likely to be reaped over a long period of time, i.e. by more than one generation of taxpayers. The financing of such projects should place the repayment burden on the present as well as future generations. If long-term capital projects are financed out of current revenues and/or short-term borrowings, the future generations would enjoy free riding. Thus, it is both fair and efficient that projects with long-term benefits are financed through long-term borrowings.

Access to long-term borrowings by a lower level government though desirable is hindered by a variety of factors. Generally, central government imposes restrictions on the borrowing powers of the state governments which, in turn, impose restrictions on the borrowing powers of the local bodies under them. Since borrowings by the lower level government are guaranteed, in most case, by the higher level government, the latter has a right to impose such restrictions. These restrictions apply to (a) the type of debt, (b) amount of debt, (c) term of the debt, (d) rate of debt, and (e) use of debt funds. Approval of the higher level government, often cumbersome, is needed before the debt is floated.

Moreover, capital markets in underdeveloped countries are not fully developed. As in the developed West, bond markets cannot be successfully introduced in the absence of institutional set up in place. Besides, the track record of state/local governments as borrowers is rather poor. Till they establish their credit worthiness, and financial intermediaries come of age, borrowings by lower level governments in underdeveloped countries are not likely to dominate their finances.

26.2 Constitutional Provisions Pertaining to Public Borrowings in India

Under Article 292 the executive power of the Centre extends to borrowing, either within or outside India, upon the security of the Consolidated Fund of India, within such limits, if any, as may from time to time be fixed by Parliament. However, the borrowing power of a State (Article 293) is subject to a number of restrictions: (i) it cannot borrow outside India; (ii) it can borrow within the territory of India subject to the following conditions (a) limitations as may be imposed by the State Legislature, (b) consent of the Union Government to raise fresh loan if the Union has guaranteed an outstanding loan of the State, (c) consent of the Union to raise fresh loan if a Union loan to the State remains outstanding. Since all the States are in debt to the Centre, they have to obtain Centre's permission for raising loans. These restrictions are meant to avoid uncontrolled borrowings by the States and thus to prevent the possibility of any State becoming defaulter or insolvent.

There is a feeling in some quarters that the Constitution has unduly restricted the borrowing powers of the States. The Commission on Centre-State Relations, 1988 had suggested that a distinction should be made between short-term loans (under one year) and medium and long-term loans. It recommended that the Centre should give its consent freely to States for borrowing from banks and other financial institutions for periods less than one year under clause (4) of Article 293.

The suggestion that a thorough examination of the States indebtedness should be undertaken by a National Debt Commission as 'one-shot operation' did not find favour with the Commission which believed that in the fast changing situation, the results from such an operation will soon be outdated. The problem of States indebtedness is serious and remedial measures are called for in this regard. Any delay in this matter would only compound the difficulties of the States, particularly highly indebted States.

26.3 Instruments of Government Borrowings in India

The Government of India borrows heavily both internally and externally. Internal borrowings of the Government are chiefly meant to meet budgetary deficit. External borrowings are meant to meet deficit in the balance of payments.

The main sources of internal borrowings are: individuals, commercial banks, financial institutions and the Reserve Bank of India. Borrowings from the RBI are through ways and means advances (WMA).

Another important instrument of Government borrowing is the Statutory Liquidity Ratio (SLR). Under this system, commercial banks and other financial institutions are required to invest prescribed proportions of their assets/liabilities in Government securities. The Committee on Financial Reforms (Chairman: M. Narasimham), 1991 had suggested the gradual lowering of this ratio to 25 per cent. Government also raises loans from the general public through regular floatation of securities and bonds like Kisan Vikas Patras and various other small saving schemes.

The major sources of external borrowings are the international agencies like the IMF and the World Bank, foreign governments, and foreign private sources. Short-term borrowings from abroad are mainly used to meet balance of payments requirements. Long-term foreign borrowings are needed to finance development projects under the Five Year Plans.

26.4 States' Indebtedness

The mounting debt and debt-servicing liabilities of the States have attracted considerable attention in recent years. The non-Plan revenue gap of the States is looked after by the Finance Commission while the Planning Commission takes care of the Plan gap, both on revenue and capital accounts. Thus, the deficit in non-Plan capital account of the States which mainly concerns repayment of Central loans has remained neglected.

Another reason for the high and growing indebtedness of the States is the composition of Central assistance for Plans given under the Gadgil Formula. The existing pattern of assistance has a loan-grant ratio of 70:30. The States are generally unhappy with this arrangement made way back in 1969. The large loan component of Plan assistance has proved very burdensome for the States over the years. [1] The findings of the Commission on Centre-State Relations, 1988, regarding the composition of Plan assistance are noteworthy. "For the State Plan as a whole, the actual pattern of Central assistance during the Sixth Plan works out to be 40 per cent grant and 60 per cent loan. Central assistance for the Centrally Sponsored and Central Sector Schemes has a high grant component (92.3 per cent in the Sixth Plan period). In the totality of Plan transfers during this period, the proportion of grant was 56.1 per cent and of loan 43.9 per cent. This is a significant fact which should be kept in view in any discussion on the pattern of Central assistance, both from the viewpoint of States repayment liability and

Union Government's ability to transfer more capital resources to the States." [2] In the context of grant-loan components of Plan assistance, it is important to bear in mind that Centre itself raises a significant part of its total resources through borrowings.

The problem of States indebtedness is not new though it has aggravated in recent years. Debt-related relief to the States may be provided in various forms, viz. write-offs, rescheduling of the loans with a view to shifting the timing of repayments, consolidation of past loans on common terms, and reduction of interest rate.

The Second Finance commission was asked to examine this problem and make suitable recommendations to reduce States debt burden. The Commission recommended, *inter alia*, the postponement of repayments but it did not help to tackle the problem on a long-term basis. The matter was again referred to the Fourth Finance Commission which expressed its inability to make a thorough investigation of the problem and suggest lasting solutions in a short period of time at its disposal.

At the time of appointment of the Fifth Finance Commission, the problem of States unauthorised overdrafts had become quite serious. The Central Government asked this Commission to examine the issue and suggest measures to discourage the States from resorting to unauthorised overdrafts. The Commission came down severely on the States and recommended that the Central Government should repay the amount of States unauthorised overdrafts to the Reserve Bank of India by adjusting that amount against the grants payable to the concerned States. The Commission further recommended that even after such repayments through grant adjustment, if the States continue to over borrow unauthorisedly from the Reserve Bank of India, the Central Government should invoke constitutional provisions to assume administrative responsibility on account of the financial breakdown of the concerned States. The Government accepted the first recommendation in principle and rejected the second one.

The matter again came up in the terms of reference of the Sixth Finance Commission. It was asked to estimate the non-Plan capital gaps in the States budget and recommend the extent of revision of terms of repayment of outstanding Central loans to the States so as to reduce such gaps. The Commission recommended moratorium on the repayment of certain Central loans and writing off a few old loans of small amount. The Eighth and the Ninth Finance Commissions recommended debt reliefs of Rs. 2,285 crore (for the period 1984-89) and Rs. 494 crore (for the period 1990-95) respectively.

The Tenth Finance Commission noted the following disturbing features of the debt profile of States and its management, "(i) diversion of borrowed funds for meeting revenue expenditure, (ii) use of loans in unproductive enterprises, or enterprises which are potentially productive but are beset by poor performance, and currently yielding low or even negative returns, (iii) non-provision for depreciation or amortisation funds in respect of government owned assets, leading to repayments out of fresh borrowing." [3]

The Commission considered debt relief measures keeping in view the following objectives, "(i) that the quantum of relief is limited; (ii) that priority is given to States under severe fiscal strain; and (iii) that incentives are given for better fiscal management." [4] Its scheme for debt relief had two parts, "(i) a scheme for general debt relief for all States linked to fiscal performance, and (ii) specific relief for States with high fiscal stress, special category States, and States with debt problems warranting special attention." [5] The Commission estimated the quantum of relief on account of special debt relief schemes at Rs. 701 crore. The quantum of relief with respect to the incentive scheme suggested by it could not be estimated as it depended on the future performance of the States.

There is a feeling in some quarters that the Constitution has unduly restricted the borrowing powers of the States. Under Article 292 the executive power of the Centre extends to borrowing, either within or outside India, upon the security of the Consolidated Fund of India, within such limits, if any, as may from time to time be fixed by Parliament. However, the borrowing power of a State (Article 293) is subject to a number of restrictions: (i) it cannot borrow outside India; (ii) it can borrow within the territory of India subject to the following conditions (a) limitations as may be imposed by the State Legislature, (b) consent of the Union Government to raise fresh loan if the Union has guaranteed an outstanding loan of the State, (c) consent of the Union to raise fresh loan if a Union loan to the State remains outstanding. Since all the States are in debt to the Centre, they have to obtain Centre's permission for raising loans. These restrictions are meant to avoid uncontrolled borrowings by the States and thus to prevent the possibility of any State becoming defaulter or insolvent.

The Commission on Centre-State Relations, 1988 had suggested that a distinction should be made between short-term loans (under one year) and medium and long-term loans. It recommended that the Centre should give its consent freely to States for borrowing from banks and other financial institutions for periods less than one year under clause (4) of Article 293. The suggestion that a thorough examination of the States indebtedness should be undertaken by a National Debt Commission as 'one-shot operation' did not find favour with the Commission which believed that in the fast changing situation, the results from such an operation will soon be outdated. The problem of States indebtedness is serious and remedial measures are called for in this regard. Any delay in this matter would only compound the difficulties of the States, particularly highly indebted States.

26.5 Recent Trends in Central Government Liabilities

India's internal and external debt has reached alarming proportions. The country is virtually caught in a debt trap. Moreover, the budgets of Central and State Governments are showing huge deficits of chronic nature. The fiscal policy has failed to contain budgetary deficits with the result that deficit financing has to be resorted to on a large scale. Had the debt servicing burden been contained, there could have been larger amount of resources spared for sectors such as health, education, social welfare and other productive sectors of the economy.

As a proportion of GDP, outstanding liabilities of the Central Government (including external debt at historical exchange rate) stood at 59.9 per cent in 2001-02 and were estimated at 60.3 per cent in the 2006-07 budget (Table 26.1).

26.6 Debt Restructuring Suggested by the Twelfth Finance Commission

In its Report submitted to the Government in November 2004, the Twelfth Finance Commission made the following points concerning debt restructuring:

- "In 2002-03, the central government brought out a debt-swap scheme to facilitate the state governments to swap their high cost debt owed to government of India with additional market borrowings and a part of current small saving transfers…The central government has used the receipts under the debt-swap scheme to repay its liabilities to the National Small Savings Fund (NSSF). This has the effect of bringing down centre's overall debt as well as its effective interest rate.
- The central government should phase out its intermediation in borrowing by the states. Where necessary, this should be managed through a public account. However, there is a need to determine borrowing limits for each state taking into account borrowing from all sources including small savings and states public accounts and reserve funds. The prescribed borrowing limit on states' aggregate fiscal deficit in our restructuring plan is 3 per cent. In their case also, revenue deficits should be brought to zero by 2008-09. Once stabilized, these deficit rules should be taken to apply over the medium term with some changes to take into account the cyclical pattern.
- Our suggested debt restructuring programme for the states will have two components: a consolidation of all state debt to the centre outstanding at the end of 2004-05 at an interest rate of 7.5 per cent to be repaid in 20 years, and a debt relief scheme linked to achievement in reducing revenue deficits. We are proposing that as a precondition for availing the benefit of the scheme, all

Table 26.1: Recent Trends in Outstanding Liabilities of the Central Government

(end-March) (Rs. crore)

	2001-02	2002-03	2003-04	2004-05	2005-06#	2006-07*
1. Internal liabilities	1294862	1499589	1690554	1933544	2126995	2396846
(a) Internal debt	913061	1020688	1141706	1275971	1355943	1522030
(b) Other internal liabilities	381801	478901	548848	657573	771052	874816
2. External debt (outstanding)$	71546	59612	46124	60878	68392	76716
Total outstanding liabilities (1+2)	1366408	1559201	1736678	1994422	2195387	2473562
As per cent of GDP						
1. Internal liabilities	56.8	61.0	61.1	61.8	59.6	58.5
(a) Internal debt	40.0	41.5	41.3	40.8	38.8	37.1
(b) Other internal liabilities	16.7	19.5	19.8	21.0	21.6	21.3
2. External debt (outstanding)$	3.1	2.4	1.7	1.9	1.9	1.9
Total outstanding liabilities (1+2)	59.9	63.4	62.8	63.8	61.5	60.3

#Revised estimates; *Budget estimates.

$External debt figures represent borrowings by the Central Government from external sources and are based on historical rates of exchange.

Source: Government of India, *Economic Survey*, 2006-07, p. 34, Table 2.6 (excerpted).

states should enact a fiscal responsibility legislation, that provides for eliminating revenue deficit in the respective states no later than 2008-09, incorporates annual targets for reduction of fiscal and revenue deficits, and presents to the respective legislatures a consolidated growth and fiscal strategy statement along with their budgets. As the states are increasingly exposed to the markets for borrowing, their fiscal positions would be increasingly assessed by the markets. They may be forced to pay higher than average interest rates to cover additional risk if the public finances are not evaluated to be robust by the assessment of the market. We are relying therefore on two mechanisms for fiscal correction: self evaluation under the Fiscal Responsibility Act and exposure to market. These in our view may prove to be effective instruments of fiscal discipline without compromising the autonomy of the states." [6]

Notes

1. Article 293(2) empowers the Union Government to make loans to the States and it has been doing so ever since the commencement of the Constitution. These loans are largely given for implementing Five year Plans.

2. Government of India, *Report of the Commission on Centre-State Relations* (Chairman: Justice R. S. Sarkaria), Part I, 1988, pp. 306-307.

3. *Report of the Tenth Finance Commission*, December 1994, p. 55.

4. *Ibid.*, p. 56.

5. *Ibid.*, p. 57.

6. *Report of the Twelfth Finance Commission*, November 2004, pp. 83-84.

Part VI: Centre-State Financial Relations in India

This Part provides a detailed description and analysis of the evolution of Centre-State financial relations in India during the post-Independence period and examines the existing arrangements for intergovernmental financial transfers. It also explains the role of the Finance Commission and the Planning Commission in effecting these transfers, particularly the principles followed by these agencies to reduce vertical and horizontal imbalances in the availability of resources to various tiers of government in India.

27

Centre-State Financial Relations: Theoretical Settings

To begin with, the principal theoretical issues involved in financial relations between different layers of the government in a federal set up are examined.

27.1 Essential Features of a Federal Polity

According to the traditional classification followed by political scientists, constitutions are either unitary or federal.

A federation means a union of several states brought about by the instrument of a treaty or agreement. The modern concept of federalism is associated with the establishment of American federation in 1787. Since there is no agreed definition of a federal state, the model of the United States is often taken as the reference point.

Federalism is a dynamic and not a static concept. It can best be understood in terms of its essential features. The consensus of opinion is that a federal system involves the following essential features. The consensus of opinion is that a federal system involves the following essential characteristics.

27.1.1 Dual Government: In a unitary state, there is only one Government, namely the national government. However, in a federal state, there are two layers of government: the union government and the state governments. A component state has no right to secede from the federation. This distinguishes a federation from a confederation.

27.1.2 Distribution of Powers: A federal state involves a division of authority between the federal government and the states. The method of distribution may not be alike in different federal constitutions.

27.1.3 Supremacy of the Constitution: A federal state derives it existence from the constitution. Every power (executive, legislative, or judicial) whether it belongs to the Union or to the State is subordinate to and controlled by the constitution.

27.1.4 Authority of Courts: As already noted, the legal supremacy of the constitution is essential to the existence of a federal system. There should be no violation of the provisions of the constitution by any tier of government. This is secured by vesting in the courts a final power to interpret the constitution.

27.1.5 Doctrine of Harmonious Construction: Harmonious construction means that different entries in different lists are so interpreted that a conflict between them is avoided. It must be accepted that the Constitution does not want to create conflict and make any entry nugatory. Hence, whenever there appears to be a conflict between two entries in the two different lists, the two entries should be so interpreted that each of them is given effect. For this purpose, the scope and meaning of one may be restricted so as to give meaning to the other.

27.1.6 Doctrine of Pith and Substance: In a federal set up, the central and the state governments should keep themselves within the respective domain assigned to them. In other words, no government should trespass into the legislative powers reserved for the other. A law made by a government which encroaches upon the field assigned to the other government is invalid. However, before a law is declared invalid, the courts should apply the rule of pith and substance.

The rule of pith and substance means that a law enacted by a legislature which is competent to enact it shall not become invalid merely because it incidentally touches a matter outside the competence of that legislature. It often happens that a legislation intending to deal with a subject in one list touches also upon a subject in another list. Blind adherence to a strict interpretation would result in a large number of statutes being declared invalid. Thus, where such overlapping occurs, it is asked what in 'pith and substance' is the effect of the enactment in question and in which list is the true character to be found.

27.1.7 Rule of Repugnancy: Repugnancy or inconsistency between two pieces of legislation means that conflicting results are produced when both the laws are applied to the same facts. Repugnancy between two legal provisions can arise in a number of ways.

A. Tests of Repugnancy

1. An obvious case of repugnancy arises when one statute says 'do it' and the other statute says 'do not do it'. In such a case there is clear and direct inconsistency between the two Acts and the situation is absolutely irreconcilable.
2. Even if there is no apparent conflict between the two statutes, yet there may be repugnancy because both cover the same field. For example, when a statute describes an offence already created by another statute, and imposes a different punishment, repugnancy arises between the two.
3. When two statutes pertain to the same subject mater, but when Parliament intends to make its enactment a complete code and cover the whole field. In such a case, the State law whether passed before or after would be overruled on the ground of repugnancy.

27.2 Nature of Indian Federalism

The very first Article of the Constitution defines India as a Union of States. Though the word federation has been deliberately avoided in the Indian Constitution, the fiscal structure created under it is essentially federal in nature.

The political system introduced by India's constitution possesses all the essentials of a federal polity.

India's constitution is the supreme organic law of our land. Both the Centre and State Governments derive their authority from the constitution. The States are not allowed to secede from the union.

There is a division of legislative, administrative and financial powers between the Union and the State Governments. These are elaborated in lists I, II and III of the Seventh Schedule of the constitution. List I (Union List) describes the functions and powers of the Union Government. List II (State List) mentions the functions and powers of the State Governments. List III (Concurrent List) describes the subject matter on which both the Union and the State Governments can legislate.

The Supreme Court stands at the head of our judiciary to guard this distribution of powers and to invalidate any action which violates the limitations imposed by the Constitution.

According to Article 254 of the Constitution of India, if any provision of a State law is repugnant to any provision of a Central law, then the Central law shall prevail and the law made by the State shall be void to the extent of repugnancy.

The most common application of Article 254 arises when both the Central and State Governments enact legislation on the same matter contained in List III (Concurrent List) of the Seventh Schedule of the Constitution. In such a situation, if there is repugnancy then Central law prevails over the State law.

It is, of course, true that the Indian constitution has a strong Central bias. The financial powers of the Central Government are overwhelming. According to some scholars the constitution of India is neither purely federal nor purely unitary but is a combination of both. India's constitution is sometimes described as federal in times of peace and unitary in times of war.

27.3 Federal Polity: A Mixed Blessing

A federal set up creates a multiple polity based on divided functions and powers among central, state and local governments. Fiscal federalism deals with financial arrangements and their working in a federal polity. Federal system of government is a mixed blessing. It has the advantage of economic integration which promotes industrial and defence capabilities of a nation. Simultaneously, decentralised decision-making meets the politico-economic aspirations of the people at the sub-national level.

Decentralisation of political and administrative powers is a virtue because it institutionalises the participation of those affected by local decisions. Following are the main advantages of decentralisation in a democratic set up.

1. Decentralisation of governmental functions allows better matching of public goods supply to local needs, tastes and preferences and hence increases social welfare.
2. State/local governments are more responsive and accountable to people than national government. Linkages between the decision to spend and that to raise resources improve fiscal discipline.
3. Mobilisation of resources at the state/local level reduces dependence and strain on the finances of national government.

However, a country cannot reap fully the economies of scale if provision for public goods is decentralised.

27.4 Problems of Multi-level Finance

27.4.1 Functional Responsibilities: Devolution of funds follows devolution of functions. The financing pattern of a government can be examined and decided only in the light of functions assigned to it. In fact, two factors determine the level of expenditure of a government: (a) its functional jurisdiction and (b) the standard at which its different functions are to be performed.

According to the theory of fiscal federalism, functions which involve national interest, economies of scale, lumpy investments, and substantial spatial externalities (spill overs) should be left to the national government. Defence services are a case in point. Functions the benefits of which largely confine to regional jurisdictions and which are subject to heterogeneous preferences should be assigned to the state governments. Sanitation, street lightning, fire safety are services the benefits of which are localised and hence should be assigned to and performed by local governments (e.g. municipalities). In short, expenditure and service responsibilities should be assigned according to the benefit area of each service.

27.4.2 Vertical and Horizontal Fiscal Imbalances: Although a federal system provides for divided governmental functions and powers, imbalances often (rather invariably) arise between functional responsibilities and financial resources at different layers of the government. This is so because revenue-raising capacities and revenue needs of various federating units are different. This is a characteristic feature of all federations, particularly of those whose economies are more dynamic. Even in older federations (like the United States, and Canada) financial conflicts persist between the national and sub-national governments and their once-for-all solution is unachievable.

The mismatch between functions and financial powers occurs partly because of changing responsibilities of different tiers of government and partly due to the dominant position of the national government in regard to taxation powers, which is often by design. Therefore, vertical imbalance of resources and expenditure responsibilities emerges between different levels of the government, calling for transfer of resources from the centre to the states. This is the familiar problem of federal finance.

Financial imbalances at the vertical level (centre versus states), and at the horizontal level (among the states) are sought to be removed/reduced through constitutional arrangements, and in some countries through political bargaining as well.

27.5 Financing Pattern

27.5.1 Taxes: Tax revenue is generally the main source of financing public expenditure at different levels of the government. In most democratic countries, taxation powers of central, state and local governments are mentioned in the constitution itself. Taxation powers of the government at different levels may be mutually exclusive or overlapping. For example, most tax fields in Canada are jointly occupied by the federal and provincial governments. Personal income tax, corporation income tax, general sales tax, and consumption taxes (excise duties) are levied by the federal as well as provincial governments in that country. Customs duties which belong exclusively to the federal government are the only notable exception. The joint occupancy of tax fields has often caused friction not only between the federal and provincial governments but also among the provinces themselves. Mark Krasnick, a Canadian fiscal expert, observed, "The fact that both the federal government and the provinces occupy the lucrative income and commodity tax fields implies that in addition to any competition or conflict that may exist among the provinces, competition also exists between the federal government and the provinces. This conflict concerns the manner in which the tax capacity of a particular tax base is shared between the two levels; or, to use the common jargon, the way in which tax room is apportioned." [1]

In India, the centre and the states have no concurrent powers of taxation. Taxes with inter-state base and those in the case of which all-India uniformity in rates is desirable, to facilitate industry and trade, are vested in the central government. Taxes which are location-specific and relate to subjects of local consumption are with the states. Broadly speaking, taxes on production are levied by the centre and taxes on sale and purchase by the state governments. The absence of joint occupancy of tax fields has successfully minimised double taxation, tax rivalry between the centre and the states, and duplicate tax administration.

A. Assignment of Taxes: Assignment of a tax means transfer of taxation power from a higher level to a lower level of government. Taxation power includes the following: the right to levy the tax, collect the tax, and appropriate the proceeds from the tax. Thus, there can be three interpretations of assignment of a tax. In the first case, the higher level government may levy and collect a tax but handover the entire proceeds to a lower level government. Taxes levied by the Government of India under Article 269 of the Constitution are a case in point. [2] Secondly, the higher level government may levy a tax but allow the lower level government to collect it and retain fully the proceeds therefrom. Taxes levied by the Government of India under Article 268 of the Constitution fall under this category. [3] Finally, the higher level government may transfer a tax to a lower level government lock, stock and barrel, a situation which defines assignment of a tax in its strictest sense.

Assignment of taxes should not be unconditional. Along with the determination of tax domain for a state, the central government ought to prescribe conditions so that the underlying purpose of assignment is adequately served. Thus, it should be obligatory on the part of a state to levy the tax assigned to it. Not only this, the state should not have powers to alter the basic structure of the assigned tax. The state may enjoy flexibility in fixing the tax rates within a minimum and maximum range prescribed by the central government. Tax exemptions/concessions should be minimum because a state is not expected to serve national objectives through its tax policy. As at other levels, tax default through disputes should be discouraged by requiring full payments prior to disputing an assessment.

27.5.2 Transfers: Transfers (tax sharing and grants) are used to correct vertical fiscal imbalances. However, before such transfers are effected, it should be ensured that taxes, duties, and levies assigned to the lower level government are being optimally tapped. Thus, tax effort, if not a pre-condition, should at least form part of the formula for transfers.

A. Need for Transfers: The need for transfers arises because the own revenues of a lower level government are generally insufficient to meet the expenditure required for providing services allotted to it. Very often central government retains with it elastic revenue sources such as income tax, excise levies, and customs duties. Contrarily, inelastic sources of revenue (such as sales tax, excise on liquor, and motor vehicle tax) are allotted to state governments. The gap between 'own resources' and expenditure needs indicates the degree of dependence of state governments on the central government.

The theory of fiscal federalism justifies intergovernmental transfers on the following grounds.

1. **Fiscal Gap Correction:** Fiscal gap occurs when there is a mismatch between the expenditure needs and revenue means of a state. Fiscal capacity and fiscal needs differ because geographical and climatic conditions are more favourable in some areas as compared to others. Hence, the access to revenue base varies from region to region. Similarly, per unit cost of services (e.g. supply of drinking water) varies depending upon the nature of terrain, and density of population. Sometimes fiscal gap may occur due to inappropriate assignment of revenue sources and functional responsibilities.
2. **Minimum Standard of Services:** Transfers from the centre to the states may be needed to upgrade the existing level of services to ensure a common minimum standard across regions. For example, the central government may provide grants to states to ensure a national standard in the provision of some public services (say 70 litres of drinking water per person per day).
3. **Inter-jurisdictional Spill Overs:** Spill overs (or spatial externalities) occur where the benefits of a locally provided service spread to persons who are not legally required to contribute to costs of the service. Services the benefits of which generally spill over to neighbouring jurisdictions include public transport, subsidised educational and medical facilities, anti-pollution measures, parks and recreational facilities. Inter-governmental grants are a major and often the most practical way of correcting for spill over effects.
4. **Performance of Agency Functions:** Central government may use the services of state governments to implement certain schemes of national importance, e.g. disease control, preserving ecological balance, propagation of research and improved technology. Funds (often in the form of grants) are provided to state governments to perform such agency functions.

B. Forms of Transfers: Transfers from the higher level to a lower level of government are made in the form of (a) tax sharing, (b) grants and (c) loans. The first two items generally account for the bulk of transfers on the revenue account.

1. **Tax Sharing:** Formula-based tax sharing is a predictable source of revenue and the state governments automatically gain from the buoyancy of the shared central taxes. There are two types of tax sharing mechanism. Under the first method (called global sharing), the whole of the central tax revenue forms a pool for sharing with the state governments. A certain percentage of the total tax revenue of the centre is allocated to the state governments. The second method (called scheduler or itemised sharing) involves sharing of revenue from individual central taxes. Tax sharing may take the form of a fixed

amount or a fixed proportion of tax revenue. Central government should share at least one buoyant tax (e.g. income tax) with state governments.

2. **Grants:** Grants have the advantage of being targeted towards fiscally disadvantaged states to reduce horizontal fiscal imbalances. They can also be made conditional regarding their utilisation. Grants are given mainly for the purpose of equalisation, though they are often given to promote the objectives and priorities of the central government. It is noteworthy that while a state cannot be denied a part of a shared central tax even if it has no demonstrated financial need, grants are given upon genuine financial needs of a state. It is possible that even before tax devolution from the centre, some high-income states have surplus in their revenue account.

Keeping in mind the criteria of fiscal equity and efficiency, three types of grants may be given by the central government to states.

- General purpose (or unconditional) grants are given to offset fiscal disadvantages arising from lower taxable capacity and/or higher unit cost of the services provided (due to bad terrain etc.). Such equalising grants have to be general and their basic purpose is to enable different states to come up to a minimum standard of services provided.
- Specific purpose (or conditional) grants are tied to the achievement of specific objectives. They may be with or without matching requirements. They are used to ensure minimum levels of specified public services to be provided by state governments. Such grants are justified also where services have spill over effects. Thus, afforestation, slum improvement and literacy drives create benefits not only to local residents but also to community as a whole. Such schemes should preferably be financed through grants from the centre to the states.
- The incentive grants are given for the purpose of encouraging states to streamline their operations. These grants should depend on the measures taken by the states to strengthen their financial position.

3. **Loans:** Financial resources from the higher level of government to lower level of government also flow in the form of loans. These loans are generally given for capital projects

C. Principles of Transfers: The designing of a sound system of transfers is of vital importance in the context of financial discipline and promotion of local initiatives. Central government may keep in mind the following broad principles so that amount transferred is equitably distributed among the states.

1. The scheme of transfers should be based on well-defined objective criteria so that financially weak states are adequately assisted. These may include size of

population, level of economic development, availability of infrastructure, and minimum service standards.

2. The system of transfers should be so designed that states are not discouraged to mobilise resources on their own. Contrarily, the system should contain in-built mechanism to promote internal mobilisation of resources and their judicious management. For this purpose, the following additional criteria may be adopted and given due weightage: tax effort, adoption of sound financial management, innovations in the provision of public services, and economy in expenditure.
3. The amount and frequency of transfers should be reasonably predictable. They should be pre-determined rather than being open-ended. Transparency, through explicit and identifiable budget entries, should also be ensured.

27.5.3 Borrowings: See section 26.1 of chapter 26 of this book.

27.6 Earmarking of Revenue

Earmarking is a fiscal practice under which revenue from one or more sources is pooled into a separate independent fund which is used to finance a pre-determined public service.

The purpose of earmarking is to ensure stable funding for important public activities. Another objective of earmarking is to introduce market prices into the budgetary process. In this context, earmarked taxes represent market prices charged indirectly for rendering public services.

27.6.1 Conditions for Successful Earmarking: For successful earmarking, the following conditions need to be satisfied.

A. Expenditure Specificity: Expenditure to be financed through earmarked revenue should be well-defined and specific, i.e. the taxpayers should be able to identify its obvious benefits.

B. Tight Linkage: The linkage between earmarked revenue (e.g. motor vehicle tax) and pre-determined expenditure (e.g. construction of a flyover) should be tight. If the amount earmarked is substantially less than the amount spent on the designated function, earmarking will be less effective.

C. Strong Benefit Linkage: There should be a close correspondence between the tax levied and the benefit received. Preferably, the tax should take the form of a direct user charge, e.g. a toll.

Traditionally, financing of expenditure on construction and maintenance of municipal roads and bridges from out of tolls, motor vehicle taxes, and fuel taxes has been considered an activity with strong economic rationale for earmarking. Similarly, airport tax is levied to meet expenditure on airport maintenance. The principle of earmarking could be applied to such municipal services as water supply and sewage disposal through water and sewer charges, using the base for property tax. However, earmarking should not be applied indiscriminately because too many funds created under it would be difficult to manage.

Notes

1. Mark Krasnick, *Fiscal Federalism* (Toronto: University of Toronto Press, 1986), p. 6.

2. These taxes are: (a) taxes on the sale or purchase of goods other than newspapers, where such sale or purchase takes place in the course of inter-State trade or commerce, and (b) taxes on the consignment of goods where such consignment takes place in the course of inter-State trade or commerce. These taxes correspond to entries 92A and 92B in the Union List in the Seventh Schedule of the Constitution. It is noteworthy that out of these two taxes only one is being levied at present, viz. inter-State sales tax (entry 92A).

3. These are duties of excise on medicinal and toilet preparations containing alcohol, and stamp duties, and correspond respectively to entries 84, and 91 of the Union List with corresponding qualification of entry 51 of the State List in the Seventh Schedule of the Constitution.

28

Centre-State Financial Relations: Pre-Independence Developments

Pre-1947 arrangements for intergovernmental financial transfers and their bearing on the making of the Constitution of India are examined below.

Although it is desirable to look back at the historical developments of a subject to understand its current features, the situation is different in the present case. The political and economic scene in India is greatly different today from what existed during British rule. Before 1947, India was a dependency of the United Kingdom and consisted of British India, and the Princely States. It encompassed the entire area which now forms the four countries of India, Pakistan, Burma, and Bangladesh. The Princely States enjoyed internal financial autonomy and therefore did not form part of the public finances. They had separate budgets and separate sources of revenue. Neither there was any plan of economic development nor was there any attempt to build a welfare society.

Presently, India is an independent country and it includes the former Princely States but excludes the other three countries mentioned above. Due to changed circumstances there is a lack of continuity and comparability. Therefore, only a sketchy account of the developments in fiscal federalism during pre-Independence period is provided.

The present fiscal structure of India is the result of a gradual evolution over the last 135 years. A look back at the pre-1947 developments in fiscal federalism is necessary to understand influences on the framing of the Constitution of independent India, and the present position and trends in Centre-State relations.

After the events of 1857, the British Crown assumed sovereignty over India from East India Company in 1858. The British had realised that governance of so vast and diverse a country of sub-continental size through centralisation of all power was difficult and some degree of decentralisation of authority to Provinces (or States) was necessary. [1] Prior to 1871, the administration of the country was rigidly centralised, characterised by absolute imperial control over Provincial revenues and expenditures. Provinces were entirely dependent on annual cash assignments from the Centre for the maintenance of their administration.

28.1 Mayo Scheme, 1870

The first beginning towards decentralisation of finances was made when the resolution of Lord Mayo was issued on December 14, 1870. The Mayo resolution explained the scheme by which the Government of India envisaged enlargement of the powers and responsibilities of the Provinces. Thus, services like jails, police, education, medical, roads and civil works were transferred to the administrative control of the Provinces and to meet their costs, the departmental receipts under these heads were also assigned to them. This was done to encourage their interest in collections as well as to induce economy in expenditure. This arrangement came to be known as 'Provincial Financial Settlements'. However, due to the inadequacy of these new heads of revenue, the existing system of fixed grants from Central revenues also continued. To quote, "The system of decentralisation was welcomed by the Provinces, because friction with the Central Government was thereby obviated and much useless correspondence avoided. But it did not give adequate resources to the Provinces nor provide conditions for the progressive administration of the services transferred to them. The only consideration which really weighed with the Government of India was that of administrative convenience." [2]

Satisfied with the Mayo scheme, the Government decided to carry it further and the next step towards decentralisation was taken in 1877 when subjects like land revenue, and general administration were transferred to the Provinces. The Mayo settlements were subject to revision annually but from 1882, they were made on quinquennial basis. Over the period 1882 to 1904, these settlements gave rise to the system of 'divided heads of revenue' under which Provinces were given a share in certain growing sources of revenue like irrigation charges, excise duties, and stamp duties. Even this arrangement did not provide sufficient revenue to the Provinces and the system of fixed cash assignments had to be continued. In 1904, the settlements were made quasi-permanent and in 1911 began the period of permanent settlements. As the Indian Taxation Enquiry Committee (1924-25) observed, "The intention of the Government in adopting this change was on the one hand to give more elasticity to the settlements and more freedom to Local Governments in working them, and, on the other hand, to protect the general taxpayer of India against possible mismanagement in any particular province, and to put an end to the frequent and undesirable controversies over the adequacy of the existing settlements." [3]

28.2 Government of India Act, 1919

The next landmark in the history of Centre-State financial relations was the Montague-Chelmsford Report on Constitutional Reforms which led to the passing of the Government of India Act, 1919. The Act sought to secure for the Provinces a greater degree of financial independence by abolishing the 'divided heads' and effecting a complete separation between the Central and Provincial heads of revenue. Thus, revenue heads like income tax, non-alcoholic excises including salt, customs, currency and mint, and contributions from railways, and post and telegraph came to the share of Central Government while relatively inelastic sources of revenue like land revenue, alcoholic excises, irrigation charges, judicial stamps, forest receipts, and registration fee were assigned to the Provinces. These arrangements enabled the Provinces to run their administration with the help of revenue raised by themselves. The Provincial budgets were separated from that of the Government of India and each Province presented its own budget and levied taxes assigned to it. With revenue heads distributed on these lines, it was estimated in the Report that there would remain a large deficit in the Government of India budget. It was, therefore, proposed in the Report that the Provinces should make contributions to the Central budget.

28.3 Meston Settlement, 1920

To advise on the amounts of Provincial contributions the Financial Relations Committee was appointed under the chairmanship of Lord Meston which reported in March 1920.

The Committee proposed, *inter alia*, a scheme of initial contributions and of standard contributions to be attained over a period of seven years. The initial contributions were calculated on the basis of the increased spending power of each Province resulting from the new scheme of the separation of the sources of revenue. The standard contributions were computed on the basis of the relative taxable capacity of the Provinces and other economic factors. However, the latter never came into operation. From the very beginning, the scheme of 'Provincial contributions' came in for sharp criticism from various quarters, particularly from the Provinces themselves. The trends in the Central and Provincial budgets in the early 1920s vindicated the stand of critics and the demand for abolition of contributions grew still more persistent with the result that contributions were abolished from 1928-29. Provincial contributions under the Meston Settlement during the 1920s provide, perhaps, the only example of transfer of funds from the Provinces to the Centre in the long history of fiscal federalism in India.

There were some important lessons to be learnt from the Reforms of 1919. According to the Fourth Finance Commission, "The failure of the system of a rigid division between the Central and Provincial heads of revenue introduced by the Government of India Act of 1919 could not be prevented by the Meston award and the ultimate result was unsatisfactory both to the Centre and to the Units. The experience of the nineteen-twenties led, however, to the emergence of the idea that the authority most suited for discharging a particular governmental function need not necessarily be the authority most suited to raise the financial resources required to discharge the function. The taxes on income had already been recognised before 1919 as a balancing factor and it continued to be recognised as such after 1935. But it also came to be recognised that other taxes could appropriately be levied and collected by the Central Government and distributed, wholly or partly, to the Provinces or States. The Government of India Act of 1935 recognised this principle and the Constitution adopted in 1950 made clear provisions (on these lines)." [4] However, the framework of fiscal federalism set up in 1919 remained unaltered, by and large, till the Government of India Act, 1935 came into operation.

28.4 Indian Taxation Enquiry Committee (President: Charles Todhunter), 1924-25

In the meantime, the Indian Taxation Enquiry Committee (President: Sir Charles Todhunter),1924-25 examined, *inter alia*, the division of sources of revenue between the Centre and the Provinces. It recommended that the excise duty on country-made foreign liquor, excise on opium, and general stamps should be transferred to the Centre. The recommendation regarding said excises on liquor and opium was rejected by the Government in view of administrative difficulties involved. Similarly, owing to stiff opposition from the Provinces, the proposal to centralise general stamps was dropped and only duties on documents of commercial nature were transferred to the Central Government. The proposal of the Committee to give the provinces a small share of the receipts of the corporation tax was also rejected by the Government.

28.5 Government of India Act, 1935

The Government of India Act, 1935 was a watershed in the evolution of Centre-State financial relation. To quote, "While under all the previous Government of India Acts, the Government of India was unitary, the Act of 1935 prescribed a federation, taking the Provinces and the Indian States as Units. But it was optional for the Indian States to join the federation; and since the Rulers of the Indian States never gave their consent, the Federation envisaged by the Act of 1935 never came into being." [5] Nevertheless, the Act was a step towards consolidation and enhancement of Provincial autonomy in matters of resources and functions. It laid the foundations for the structure of Centre-State relations as incorporated in the present Constitution of India. The Act divided taxation heads into the following three broad categories.

1. Taxes levied by and meant exclusively for the Central Government.
2. Taxes levied by and meant exclusively for Provincial Governments.

3. Taxes levied by the Centre but shared with the Provinces or completely assigned to them.

The Act also provided for grants-in-aid from the Centre to the Provinces in need of assistance.

The main provisions of the Act of 1935 relating to the subject under study were as follows.

1. Agricultural income tax was included in the list of Provincial subjects.
2. Provision was made under Section 138 of the Act for the assignment to Provinces of a percentage of the net proceeds of taxes on income other than agricultural income.
3. Section 140 of the Act provided that duties on salt, Central duties of excise, and export duties, while levied and collected by the Centre would, if an Act of Central legislature so provided, be assigned wholly or in part to the Provinces.
4. Under Section 142 provision was made for the payment of grants-in-aid of the revenues of such Provinces as might be in need of assistance.
5. The Act also provided for the levy by Central legislation of duties in respect of succession to property other than agricultural land, stamp duties, terminal taxes on goods and passengers carried by railway or air and taxes on railway fares and freights, and for the distribution of net proceeds to the Provinces.

28.6 Indian Financial Enquiry Report, 1936

Fiscal arrangements of the Act of 1935 left several questions to be decided and Sir Otto Niemeyer was appointed to make recommendations on matters which had to be determined by the Government. His main recommendations as contained in the Indian Financial Enquiry Report 1936 were the following.

1. That 50 per cent of the net proceeds of income tax should be assigned to the Provinces.
2. That the share of jute-growing Provinces in the jute export duty be raised by 12.5 per cent to 62.5 per cent of the net proceeds of the duty.
3. The outstanding debts (to the Centre) of Bengal, Bihar, Assam, North-West Frontier Province, and Orissa, contracted prior to April 1, 1936 be cancelled, and the outstanding debt of the Central Provinces be reduced.
4. Annual grants of different amounts were also recommended for United Provinces, Assam, North-West Frontier Province, Orissa, and Sind.

The recommendations of Sir Otto Niemeyer were accepted by the Government and embodied in the Government of India (Distribution of Revenues) Order, 1936. This Order, subject to a change made in 1940 in the wake of World War II, continued to regulate the allocation of resources between the Centre and the Provinces until the partition of the country in 1947.

28.7 Financial Adjustments after the Partition

The partition of the country gave rise to new problems of financial adjustments. Though the scheme of distribution of both income tax and jute export duty, as suggested by Sir Otto Niemeyer, were retained, the shares of the divided Provinces of Bengal, and Punjab were reduced in proportion to population while the shares of Sind, and North-West Frontier Province were pooled for distribution so far as income tax was concerned. Regarding jute export duty, the Provincial share was reduced from 62.5 per cent to 20 per cent, roughly in proportion to the jute growing area which went to the share of Pakistan.

At the time of the drafting of the new Constitution, the financial provisions in the Draft Constitution were referred to an Expert Committee headed by Mr. N.R. Sarkar. Its main recommendations were as follows.

1. The whole of income tax, including corporation tax, should be shared between the Centre and the Units in the ratio of 40:60.
2. The existing arrangements for the sharing of the net proceeds of jute export duty with the Provinces should be terminated.
3. Provincial Governments should be given some share of Central excise duties so as to impart a better balance to their revenue structure.
4. That a Finance Commission should be set up to deal with matters connected with the division of revenues between the Centre and the States and the States *inter se*.

28.8 Deshmukh Award

Since a Finance Commission could not be appointed immediately after the commencement of the Constitution, the States' share of income tax and the payment of grants-in-aid had to be regulated by the Order of the President during the intervening period. Also, some of the States were not happy with the arrangements regarding the allocation of income tax and the jute export duty made by the Government immediately after the partition. It was, therefore, decided to refer these matters to an impartial authority for reconsideration. Accordingly, Mr. C.D. Deshmukh was requested to enquire into and decide these matters. Deshmukh enquiry confined itself to the reallocation of the percentages released as a result of the partition from the share of the divided Provinces and the Provinces wholly included in Pakistan.

Table 28.1 records the percentage distribution among the States of their share of income tax before the partition, immediately after the partition, and under the Deshmukh award. The Deshmukh award came into operation from April 1, 1950 and remained in force till March 31, 1952.

Table 28.1: Percentage Distribution among the States of Their Share of Income Tax

Province	Pre-partition share	Share under Government of India allocation	Share under Deshmukh award
Madras	15	18	0.5
Bombay	20	21	21.0
West Bengal	20*	12	13.5
Uttar Pradesh	15	19	18.0
Punjab	8*	5	5.5
Bihar	10	13	12.5
Madhya Pradesh	5	6	6.0
Assam	2*	3	3.0
Orissa	2	3	3.0

* relates to the undivided Provinces

Source: *Report of the Finance Commission, 1952*, p. 25.

Notes

1. It may be noted that Princely States enjoyed internal financial autonomy and therefore did not form part of the structure of public finances of British India. They had separate budgets and separate sources of revenue. After Independence, the former Princely States were integrated into the fiscal and financial system of the country.

2. Gyan Chand, *The Essentials of Federal Finance: A Contribution to the Problem of Financial Re-adjustment in India* (Humphrey Milford, Oxford University Press, 1930), p. 42.

3. Government of India, *Report of the Indian Taxation Enquiry Committee*, 1924-25, Vol. I (President: Sir Charles Todhunter), p. 372.

4. *Report of the Fourth Finance Commission*, 1965, pp. 6-7.

5. Durga Das Basu, *Introduction to the Constitution of India* (New Delhi: Prentice-Hall of India Pvt. Ltd., 1987), p. 9.

29

Financial Relations under the Constitution

This chapter explains the complex nature of constitutional provisions pertaining to Centre-State financial relations in India. It also examines the role of the Finance Commission and the Planning Commission in effecting financial transfers from the Centre to the States.

29.1 Constitutional Provisions Pertaining to Taxes (See chapter 7 of this book.)

29.2 Centralisation of Revenues and the Need for Transfers

Constitutional provisions regarding taxation and borrowing powers of the Centre and the States, place the former in a commanding position. Not only the major sources of tax revenue belong to the Centre, its borrowing (internal and external) powers are also unlimited. Moreover, the Central Government enjoys the exclusive right to print currency. Budget estimates for the year 2005-06 showed total tax collections at the all-India level at Rs. 5,85,626 crore of which Central taxes (gross) accounted for Rs. 3,70,025 crore (63.2 per cent). The remaining Rs. 2,15,601 crore (36.8 per cent) was shown the share of all the States put together. In the case of non-tax revenue of Rs. 1,13,146 crore at the all-India level for the same year, the shares of Centre and the States were Rs. 78,266 crore (69.2 per cent) and Rs. 34,880 crore (30.8 per cent) respectively. Similarly, total revenue collections (tax plus non-tax) at the all-India level were projected at Rs. 6,98,772 crore with shares of the Centre and the States standing at Rs. 4,48,291 crore (64.2 per cent) and Rs. 2,50,481 crore (35.8 per cent) respectively (Table 29.1). These figures show the degree of centralisation of revenues, size of the vertical fiscal gap and hence the need to transfer resources from the Centre to the States.

29.3 Mechanism of Central Transfers to the States

Though the Constitution creates a dual polity based on divided governmental powers and functions, this division is not watertight. As the Administrative Reforms Commission, 1968, observed, "Exact correspondence of resources and functions is not possible to secure in any federal situation but in India the balance is tilted rather heavily in favour of the Centre and the outstanding feature of the financial relationship between the Centre and the States consequently is that the former is always the giver and the latter the receivers. The favourable position given to the Centre in regard to financial resources reflects the strong-centre theme running through the Constitution and many feel that this has been an important factor in keeping the country united." [1]

Table 29.1: Centralisation of Tax and Non-tax Revenues in India, 2005-06*

(Rs. crore)

Total Tax Collections (All-India)	5,85,626 (100.0)
Centre's Tax Collections (before Transferring States' Share)	3,70,025 (63.2)
States' Tax Collections	2,15,601 (36.8)
Total Non-tax Revenue (All-India)	1,13,146 (100.0)
Centre's Non-tax Revenue	78,266 (69.2)
States' Non-tax Revenue	34,880 (30.8)
Total Revenue (All-India)	6,98,772 (100.0)
Total Revenue Raised by the Centre	4,48,291 (64.2)
Total Revenue Raised by the States	2,50,481 (35.8)

*Budget estimates.

Figures in parentheses indicate percentages of the respective totals.

Source: Rearranged data from Government of India, Ministry of Finance, *Indian Public Finance Statistics*, 2005-2006, Tables 1.7, 2.2 and 3.2.

Emergence of imbalances between functional responsibilities and financial resources of different tiers of government is a characteristic feature of all federations, particularly of those whose economies are more dynamic. Even in older federations (like the United States, and Canada), financial conflicts between the national and sub-national governments persist and their once-for-all solution is difficult to find. The mismatch between functions and taxation powers occurs partly because of changing responsibilities of governments at different levels and partly because of the dominant position of federal government in regard to taxation powers, which is often by design. Therefore, vertical imbalances in terms of resources and expenditure responsibilities emerge between different levels of government calling for transfer of resources from the Centre to the States. This is the familiar problem of federal finance.

Thus, intergovernmental transfers are an inherent part of a multi-level fiscal system. Such transfers are justified on horizontal equity considerations.

Recognising the fact that the financial resources of the States may prove inadequate for undertaking welfare, maintenance, and development activities, the framers of India's Constitution did make elaborate, *albeit* complex, arrangements relating to flow of funds from the Centre to the States. The disequilibrium between proliferating functional responsibilities of the States and their own resources is corrected by Central transfers effected through three main channels.

1. Statutory transfers through the Finance Commission.
2. Plan transfers through the Planning Commission.
3. Discretionary transfers for Centrally Sponsored Schemes, relief from natural calamities, and relief and rehabilitation of displaced persons.

Apart from these direct transfers, resources also flow to the States indirectly through the following channels.

1. Establishment/expansion of Central public sector enterprises.
2. Subsidised lending by banking and financial institutions.
3. Subsidised borrowing by the States from the Central Government and the banking system.

These may be called invisible transfers or subterranean transfers

29.4 Transfer of Resources through the Finance Commission

Transfers routed through the Finance Commission pertain to sharing of certain Central taxes, and grants-in-aid of revenues of the States. In other words, although the taxation powers allocated to the Centre and the States are mutually exclusive yet all the taxes and duties levied by the Centre are not meant entirely for the Centre. In fact, revenues from certain taxes and duties leviable by the Centre are totally assigned to or shared with the States to supplement the revenues of the States in accordance with their needs.

The architects of the Constitution probably realised that even with a share in the proceeds of divisible taxes, some States might still need financial assistance. Accordingly, they made provision for annual grants-in-aid of revenues under Article 275(1) to such States as may be in need of assistance. Also, the Centre is required to give grants-in-aid to the States for the welfare of Scheduled Tribes and for raising the level of administration in Scheduled Areas and separately for Assam. These provisions which set apart a portion of Central revenues for the benefit of States indicate flexibility of India's Constitution in terms of distribution of financial resources between the Centre and the States.

Although the Constitution provides for Central transfers, it neither indicates the share of the States in the divisible taxes nor prescribes any principles for the distribution of States' share among the States themselves. Framers of the Constitution consciously avoided permanent formulae in this regard in view of expected changes in the spheres of taxation and public expenditure. Thus, the precise manner of sharing taxes and the actual determination of grants is left to the deliberations of the Finance Commission which is appointed by the President (under Article 280) every quinquennium, or earlier if necessary. [2] The Finance Commission, consisting of a chairman and four members, recommends to the President, *inter alia*, the principles of distribution between the Union and the States of the proceeds of taxes and the allocation among the States of the shares of such proceeds. The recommendations of Finance Commissions are based on a detailed assessment of the financial position of the Central and State Governments. For this purpose, the Commissions visit the State Capitals and hold discussions with government leaders and officials. Discussions are also held with public finance experts and studies are commissioned on specific topics.

Under Article 281 of the Constitution, the report of the Finance Commission, together with the Explanatory Memorandum on the action taken on the recommendations of the Commission, is laid on the Table of the House by the Government. Though the President is not bound to accept the recommendations of the Finance Commission, they are generally accepted in view of the quasi-judicial nature of the Commission. [3] By and large, the Finance Commissions have worked independently and some of them, particularly the recent ones, have been quite assertive. Award of a Finance Commission generates considerable interest in issues pertaining to financial relations between the Centre and the States. Twelve Finance Commissions have reported since the commencement of the Constitution. The years of establishment, years of reporting, periods of award, and the names of Chairmen of various Finance Commissions are given in Table 29.2.

Finance Commission is a unique feature of the Indian Constitution having no parallel in the existing federal constitutions of the world. As the Commission on Centre-State Relations, 1988 observed, "Unlike the Commonwealth Grants Commission of Australia, the Indian Finance Commission is a Constitutional body and the objectivity in its role has been facilitated by keeping it outside the Union executive. Compared with its Australian counterpart, the Indian Finance Commission has a greater scope inasmuch as it recommends sharing of tax proceeds also, besides the grants-in-aid, and advises on other matters referred to it in the interest of sound finance. The absence of clear Constitutional provisions for revenue sharing created many problems in other federations and they had to evolve a variety of arrangements to overcome them. For example, in Canada, tax-rental arrangements were resorted to. In Australia, the Australian Commonwealth Grants Commission was set up to consider allocation of grants among the claimant States. Specific purpose grants, with strict enforcement conditions, came into existence in countries like USA." [4]

Table 29.2: Chronology of Finance Commissions in India

Finance Commission	Year of establishment	Year of reporting	Period of award	Name of the chairman
First	November 1951	December 1952	1952-57	K.C. Neogy
Second	June 1956	September 1957	1957-62	K. Santhanam
Third	December 1960	December 1961	1962-66	A.K. Chanda
Fourth	May 1964	August 1965	1966-69	P.V. Rajamannar
Fifth	February 1968	July 1969	1969-74	Mahavir Tyagi
Sixth	June 1972	October 1973	1974-79	K. Brahmananda Reddy
Seventh	June 1977	October 1978	1979-84	J.M. Shelat
Eighth	June 1982	April 1984	1984-89	Y.B. Chavan
Ninth	June 1987	July 1988 December 1989	1989-90 1990-95	N.K. P. Salve
Tenth	June 1992	November 1994	1995-00	K.C. Pant
Eleventh	July 1998	July 2000	2000-05	A.M. Khusro
Twelfth	November 2002	November 2004	2005-10	C. Rangarajan

Source: *Finance Commission Reports.*

The Australian Commonwealth Grants Commission recommends special purpose grants to the claimant States, but the general grants are determined largely on the basis of negotiations at the political level. In India, the Finance Commission has replaced political bargaining by objective criteria in regard to devolution of resources, ensuring at the same time flexibility in revenue-sharing.

What is a Finance Commission expected to achieve? Its first task is to evolve a scheme of transfer of financial resources from the Centre to the States so as to ensure financial equilibrium at the two levels of Government during the period of its award. Secondly, it is to design formulae to allocate resources so transferred among the States.

The task of the Finance Commission consists of the following.

1. Forecasting resources and expenditure of the Central Government to determine the volume of resources to be transferred to the States during the ensuing five years.
2. Forecasting own current revenues of the States and non-Plan current expenditures.

3. Devising formula for distribution of States' share among the States themselves.
4. Filling the post-devolution projected gaps with grants between the non-Plan current expenditures and current revenues.

The task of a Finance Commission is by no means easy as it has to judge the conflicting claims, needs, and resources of the Centre and the States and evolve a scheme of transfers which would balance the needs and resources of the two layers of the Government.

Broadly speaking, the procedure adopted by the Finance Commission to fulfil its duties is as follows: On the basis of the trends in the finances of Central and State Governments, it prepares estimates of revenue and expenditure for the period of its award. It then decides the total amount of transfers from the Centre to the States so as to maintain the desired equilibrium in the finances of the two tiers of the Government. Thereafter, the total amount of transfers is broken down into devolution and grants-in-aid among the States. Transfer of resources from the Centre to the States is designed to correct vertical imbalances while the distribution of resources among the States (with wide differentials in fiscal capabilities and needs) aims at correcting horizontal imbalances.

Should Central transfers to the States through the Finance Commission be examined in their totality or item-wise? For a better understanding of the nature and role of these transfers, it is necessary to examine them from both angles. The total approach is significant to understand adjustments in vertical financial imbalances while item-wise approach reveals adjustments in horizontal financial imbalances. It is noteworthy that various items included in the aggregate transfers are not alike and therefore have different importance for different States.

29.4.1 From Itemised Sharing to Global Sharing: The most important development in the field of Centre-State financial relations pertains to the new system of sharing Central taxes with the State Governments.

Prior to Constitution (Eightieth Amendment) Act, 2000, income tax and Union excise duties were the only taxes shared with the States, apart from the grants given in lieu of passenger tax, and the collections from additional excise duty in lieu of sales tax sugar, tobacco and textiles. Taxes on income and Union excise duties were shared with States under Article 270 and 272 respectively. The aforesaid amendment altered the pattern of sharing of Central taxes between the Centre and the States significantly. It substituted a new Article for Article 270 and omitted the old Article 272. The new Article 270 provides for the sharing of the net proceeds of all Union taxes and duties with the States. However, the surcharge levied for purposes of the Union under Article 271 is excluded from the divisible pool.

Eleventh Finance Commission was the first to make recommendations in accordance with the new provisions of the Constitution.

29.5 Transfer of Resources through the Planning Commission

Article 282 provides that the Centre or a State may make grants for any public purpose. These grants which are given at the discretion of the Government are different from the grants made under Article 275. With the establishment of the Planning Commission in 1950, the Central Government invoked Article 282 for making grants to the States for plan purposes. The Planning Commission, which for all practical purposes is a political body, makes an assessment of the existing resources of the individual States and the country as a whole and sets objectives in various fields and formulates plans for economic development in the light of requirements of each State. Ever since the launching of the First Five Year Plan, these grants have occupied an important place in Central financial transfers to the States. It is noteworthy that under Article 293, the Central Government may grant loans to the States or give guarantees in respect of loans raised by them. The permissive nature of this provision is obvious.

Grants given under Article 282 are a subject matter of controversy. These grants were intended by the Constitution makers to meet unforeseeable emergencies (like droughts, famines, and other natural calamities) and were not envisaged as part of normal Centre-State financial relations. Thus, Central grants to States to help settle persons displaced as a result of the partition of the country was a typical example of the purpose contemplated by Article 282. These grants, meant for emergency purposes, were kept outside the purview of the Finance Commission which otherwise was entrusted with all the major questions of Centre-State financial relations.

Some experts feel that the Planning Commission is an unintended channel for transferring resources to the States because the founding fathers envisaged a pre-eminent role for the Finance Commission in dealing with problems of fiscal federalism. They never anticipated the rise of the Planning Commission and the National Development Council with enormous powers in the matter of allocation of resources to the State Governments. In view of the dominant role of the Planning Commission, the effectiveness of the Finance Commission has been circumscribed, its role being restricted to non-Plan expenditure of State budgets. Therefore, it is often suggested that for healthy intergovernmental financial relations, the Finance Commission should decide grants-in-aid to each State under Article 282 of the Constitution. The Planning Commission should assist the Finance Commission by drawing up a priority list of projects, their costs, locational feasibility and other technical matters. If this is to happen, the task of the Finance Commission will become still more difficult and the oft-repeated suggestion that Finance Commission should be transformed from a quinquennial to a permanent body, will gain strength. Such a permanent arrangement will ensure continuity in the work of the Finance Commission and make mid-term readjustments in its recommendations possible.

29.5.1 Gadgil Formula: What is the basis for allocating Central assistance for State Plans? During the first three Five Year Plans and the three Annual Plans thereafter, the distribution of Central assistance was not based on any clear-cut principles, giving the Planning Commission considerable discretion in allocating funds. In view of demand from the States for the adoption of a well-defined formula, the entire issue was discussed on the eve of the formulation of the Fourth Five Year Plan (1969-1974). The deliberations resulted in the adoption of a formula which later became known as the Gadgil Formula (named after the then Deputy Chairman of the Planning Commission, Shri D. R. Gadgil). The formula, approved by the NDC, was as follows.

1. Requirements of Special Category States should first be met out of the total pool of Central assistance.
2. The balance of assistance should be distributed among the remaining 14 States on the basis of the following criteria:

- 60 per cent on the basis of population,
- 10 per cent on the basis of per capita State income of those States the per capita income of which is below the national level,
- 10 per cent on the basis of tax effort, determined on the basis of individual State's per capita tax receipts as percentage of the State's per capita income,
- 10 per cent on the basis of major irrigation and power projects which were to continue during the Fourth Plan and
- 10 per cent for special problems of individual States (Table 29.3).

Central Plan assistance during the Fourth and the Fifth Plans was distributed in accordance with the provisions of the Gadgil formula. The adoption of Gadgil formula reduced the scope of discretion of the Planning Commission and instead introduced objectivity and transparency in the allocation of Plan assistance to the States.

Gadgil formula was modified on the eve of the formulation of the Sixth Plan to make it more progressive for the benefit of economically backward States. The modified formula, approved by the NDC in 1980, and applied for the Sixth and the Seventh Plans, was different from the original formula in following respects.

The 10 per cent weightage given to ongoing irrigation and power projects in the original formula was dropped. The weightage to per capita income below the national average (backwardness factor) was increased from 10 per cent to 20 per cent (Table 29.3).

Table 29.3: Original, Modified, and Revised Gadgil Formula for Central Plan Assistance to States

Weight (per cent)

S. No.	Criterion	Original formula (Fourth and Fifth Plans)	Modified formula (Sixth and Seventh Plans)	Revised formula (Eight and subsequent Plans)
1.	Population	60	60	60
2.	Per capita income below the national average (deviation)	10	20	25*
3.	Per capita tax effort	10	10	--
4.	Outlay on continuing irrigation and power projects	10	--	--
5.	Performance	--	--	7.5
6.	Special problems	10	10	7.5
	Total	100	100	100

*5 per cent was allocated to all the States on distance method.
Sources: *Report of the Commission on Centre-State Relations*, Part I, 1988, p. 277, and decisions of the National Development Council reported in the Press.

The tug-of-war among the States for Central assistance continued as each State suggested a formula which best suited its interests. This led to further modifications in the Gadgil Formula. The Revised Gadgil Formula, meant for the Eighth Plan, was discussed and approved by the NDC at its meeting held on December 23-24, 1991. It had the following components (Table 29.3).

1. The weightage assigned to population factor was retained at 60 per cent.
2. The weightage given to per capita income factor was increased from 20 per cent to 25 per cent. Out of this 25 per cent, 20 per cent was allocated to States whose per capita income was below the national level. The remaining 5 per cent was allocated to all the States on the distance method.
3. The earlier tax effort factor with 10 per cent weightage was discarded.
4. A new factor called *performance* was introduced with 7.5 per cent weightage. It consisted of tax effort, fiscal management, national priorities including population, literacy, female welfare programmes, and land reforms.
5. The weightage given to special problems was reduced from 10 per cent to 7.5

per cent. The element of discretion associated with funds earmarked for special problems was considerably reduced with the identification of the following seven special problem areas in the Revised Formula: coastal areas, special environment issues, flood and drought prone areas, exceptionally sparse or thickly populated areas, special financial difficulties for achieving minimum reasonable Plan size, desert problems, and slums in urban areas.

29.5.2 Nature of Plan Transfers: Plan transfers by the Planning Commission are made under a set of clearly laid out objective criteria approved by the National Development Council and are subject to review by it. Therefore, it would be wrong to call Plan transfers as discretionary, as is believed by some experts. Even in the case of *other transfers* (for natural calamities etc.) there are standardised procedures as recommended by the Seventh and the Eighth Finance Commissions. It is, of course, true that though Plan assistance to States is formula-based, the total amount of such assistance to be transferred to the States each year is determined by the Centre.

As regards the nature of Plan transfers, the Commission on Centre-State Relations, 1988, observed, "The Plan and other transfers which are labelled *discretionary* do not amount to subversion of the Constitutional scheme. They cannot be considered either unreasonable or discretionary in a literal sense as their allocation follows predetermined criteria, or is tied to meet the specific requirements of the States. The large magnitude of Plan transfers should not pose any controversy in this regard as the framers of the Constitution could not anticipate the extent of development resource-needs under the Plans of the States. The significant growth of Central assistance to States for planned development is, indeed, a natural response to such needs. The crux of the matter is that the States' participation in the planning process should be such that the Plan transfers are treated by them as part of a commonly agreed programme for the deployment of the nation's resources." [5] The Commission further observed that the controversy regarding statutory versus discretionary transfers was more theoretical than realistic in nature.

29.6 Centrally Sponsored Schemes

A contentious issue related to Plan assistance pertains to Centrally Sponsored Schemes. In view of their national importance, these schemes are launched by the Centre and implemented by the State Governments with Central assistance. The Central Ministries concerned propose and formulate these schemes which are approved by the Planning Commission. The States execute these schemes under the technical guidance and supervision of the Centre which also issues guidelines regarding the contents, coverage, expenditure pattern, and staffing of such schemes. The assistance given for these schemes on a matching basis is over and above the assistance given for State Plans and the provision for it is made in the budgets of the Central Ministries. For example, in the agricultural sector, these schemes pertain to propagation of research and improved technology, disease control, preserving ecological balance, support to specific crops like pulses, cotton, jute etc.

The States are generally unhappy with their inadequate involvement in the formulation of Centrally sponsored schemes which mainly pertain to subjects included in the State List. Sponsoring of these schemes by the Centre is also considered an intrusion into subjects reserved for States. In this connection, the Administrative Reforms Commission opined, "The intrusion is not, technically, unconstitutional for it is protected by Article 282 but it is a question whether, with the help of financial carrot such intrusion is desirable and conducive to the growth of healthy federal relationship." [6]

The States have also complained against Centrally sponsored schemes on the ground that the system of matching grants involved in the schemes favours the richer States because they are better placed to provide matching funds to avail Central assistance. Such schemes induce the States to divert their limited resources to areas which may occupy low priority in the investment scheme of a State. As regards the magnitude of Centrally sponsored schemes, the Ninth Finance Commission observed, "Centrally sponsored schemes have grown in volume and number over the years. As of April 1985, the schemes under implementation were as many as 262. The outlay of Rs. 18,000 crore approximately of these schemes accounted for about 80 per cent of Central assistance provided for the State Plans during the Seventh Five Year Plan. This has happened despite States' objection to their proliferation and the decision of NDC in 1979 to roll them back to the level of 1/6th of the Central assistance for States' Plans by hacking away schemes costing a total of Rs. 2,000 crore. More recently, the NDC after considering the Ramamurti Committee Report in November 1985 had set up a Committee headed by the then Union Minister for Human Resources Development to go into this matter. This Committee had in turn constituted a group of officials whose recommendations favour retention of most of the schemes." [7]

The confrontation between the Centre and the States on this issue was considerably reduced when at the December 23-24, 1991 meeting of the NDC it was decided to transfer 113 sponsored schemes to the States along with the allocations being made for these schemes.

Government's policy regarding Centrally sponsored schemes was made clear in the 1996-97 budget speech of the Finance Minister, "...it is our desire that most

Centrally-sponsored schemes should be transferred to the control of the State Governments. In the meantime, States will be given greater flexibility in the implementation of these programmes. Provisions available under all other schemes will be pooled and the basic entitlement ratio will be worked out for each State. The States will be free to select for implementation, within their annual entitlement, such schemes that are more suited to their needs." [8]

29.7 Size and Pattern of Central Transfers

Regarding the magnitude of Central transfers to the States, it is natural to expect claims and counter claims by the two levels of the Government. The States have often complained that resources allocated to them are inadequate to enable them to discharge their responsibilities. They complain against widening gap between their own resources and needs, a trend indicating their increasing dependence on the Centre for resources. They assert that their resources should be commensurate with their obligations and responsibilities. Similarly, the Centre also feels constrained at the widening gap between its resources and needs, as reflected in the budgetary deficits. Since the early 1980s, the Centre has been running considerable deficit on its revenue account. Its commitments towards defence, subsidies, and interest payments claim a major chunk of its resources and there is little hope of any respite on these accounts in the near future.

Table 29.4 shows the magnitude and the composition of financial resources transferred from the Centre to the State in the 2007-08 budget.

Table 29.4: Financial Resources Transferred from the Centre to the States: Budget 2007-08

(Rs. crore)

1.	States' share of taxes and duties	1,42,450
2.	Non-Plan grants and loans	38,498
3.	Central assistance for State Plans	46,609
4.	Assistance for Central and Centrally sponsored schemes	21,880
5.	Gross resources transferred (1+2+3+4)	2,49,437
6.	Less: recovery of loans and advances	593
7.	Net resources transferred (5-6)	2,48,844

Source: Government of India, Ministry of Finance, *Budget at a Glance*, 2007-08, p. 17.

To conclude, the Central Government raises the major part of combined resources and a significant part of that is transferred to the States to ensure vertical equity in the distribution of resources. Centralisation of revenues and adjustments thereafter is a characteristic feature of most federations of the world. Hence, to view Central transfers to the States as indicative of the latter's dependence on the former is erroneous because a significant part of the transfers takes place under constitutional provisions and in accordance with predetermined formulas. To the question whether the Centre has been making adequate transfers to the States, the Commission on Centre-State Relations, 1988 opined, "The Union Government is thus already transferring substantial resources to the States. Under the present circumstances, there is need to pay attention to structural change in transfers for which there is apparently greater economy." [9]

Notes

1. Administrative Reforms Commission, *Report of the Study Team on Centre-State Relationships*, Vol. I, 1968, p. 15.

2. Since the President is guided in all his decisions by the advice of the Central Council of Ministers (Article 74), the appointment of the Finance Commission and the determination of its terms of reference becomes the prerogative of the Central Government for all practical purposes. This prerogative of the Centre is often criticised because the Centre itself is a party to the *dispute* between the Centre and the States regarding sharing of financial resources, and the role of the Finance Commission is that of an arbiter.

3. Article 280(3) requires the Finance Commission to make recommendations to the President who is to lay the same under Article 281 before each House of Parliament. It is nowhere laid down in the Constitution that recommendations of the Commission shall be binding upon the Government of India. They are, therefore, non-justiciable. However, to safeguard the interests of the States in the Union taxes which are divisible, the Constitution provides (Article 274) that no bill or amendment which (i) varies the rate of tax in which the States are interested; (ii) affects the principles on which moneys are distributable or (iii) imposes any surcharge on any such tax for the purpose of the Union, shall be introduced or moved in the Parliament except on the recommendation of the President.

The Centre has generally accepted the major recommendations of the Finance Commissions though there are some instances of partial acceptance of such recommendations. For example, the Centre did not accept the entire set of recommendations of the Eighth Finance Commission relating to the first year (1984-85) of the five year period covered by it. The Centre held the view that by the time the report was submitted (April 30, 1984), the Central and the State budgets had been passed and it was late to reopen the estimates. However, it was widely felt that this decision of the Government was in violation of the spirit of Article 280 of the Constitution.

4. *Report of the Commission on Centre-State Relations*, 1988, op. cit., p. 254.

5. *Report of the Commission on Centre-State Relations*, Part I, 1988, op. cit., p. 279.

6. Administrative Reforms Commission, *Report of the Study Team on Centre-State Relationships*, Vol. I, 1968, op. cit., p. 122.

7. *First Report of the Ninth Finance Commission*, 1988, p. 24.

8. Government of India, *Budget papers 1996-97: Speech of the Finance Minister*, Part I, p. 16.

9. *Report of the Commission on Centre-State Relations*, Part I, 1988, op. cit., p. 281.

30

Sharing of Revenue from Income Tax and Excise Duties Prior to the Recommendations of the Eleventh Finance Commission

The Constitution (Eightieth Amendment) Act, 2000 substituted a new Article for Article 270 under which States are now given a percentage share of all Central taxes and duties. This has already been explained in section 3.3.1 of Chapter 3 of this book. Prior to this arrangement, proceeds from certain individual taxes were shared with the States. Thus, income tax was levied and collected by the Centre but the proceeds were shared mandatorily with the States. Similarly, excise duties were levied and collected by the Centre but their proceeds were shared permissively with the States. The recommendations of the first ten Finance Commissions regarding sharing of income tax revenue and excise revenue between the Centre and the States are summarised below.

30.1 Sharing of Income Tax Revenue

By virtue of entry 82 of List I of the Seventh Schedule of the Constitution, the Central Government is empowered to levy 'taxes on income other than agricultural income'. Before the Eightieth Amendment of the Constitution, these were compulsorily shareable between the Centre and the States under Article 270(1) of the Constitution. However, the proceeds attributable to Union Territories, taxes payable in respect of Union emoluments, and corporation tax were kept out of the divisible pool in accordance with the provisions contained in clauses (2), (3) and (4) of Article 270. Similarly, surcharge levied for purposes of the Union under Article 271 was also excluded from the divisible pool. The Finance Commission was required to make recommendations on the following matters pertaining to income tax.

1. Determination of the percentage of net proceeds of income tax to be assigned to the States,
2. Formula for the allocation of States' share among the States, and
3. Determination of the net proceeds attributable to Union Territories.

30.1.1 Determination of States' Share: The share of the States in the net proceeds of income tax increased gradually ever since the recommendations of the First Finance Commission which fixed it at 55 per cent. The Second, the

Third, and the Fourth Finance Commissions enlarged the share to 60 per cent, 66.66 per cent, and 75 per cent respectively. The Third and the Fourth Finance Commissions recommended the increase in the States' share to make good the loss sustained by the States on account of non-inclusion of corporation tax in the divisible pool beginning 1959. The Fifth Finance Commission did not recommend any further increase in the States' share. The Sixth Finance Commission raised the States' share from 75 per cent to 80 per cent which was further increased to 85 per cent by the Seventh Finance Commission, making the Central Government virtually a collecting agency on behalf of the State Governments. The Eighth and the Ninth Finance Commissions retained it at 85 per cent. The Tenth Finance Commission reduced the share of States in the net proceeds of income tax from 85 per cent to 77.5 per cent. Table 30.1 summarises the recommendations of various Finance Commissions regarding the distribution of income tax revenue between the Centre and the States and the principles followed for the distribution of States' share among themselves.

Table 30.1: Recommendations of Various Finance Commissions Regarding Distribution of Income Tax Revenue between the Centre and the States

		Bases of distribution among the states (per cent)		
Finance Commission and period of award	States' share in income tax (per cent)	Population	Contribution	Other factors
First (1952-57)	55.0	80.0	20	--
Second (1957-62)	60.0	90.0	10	--
Third (1962-66)	66.0	80.0	20	--
Fourth (1966-69)	75.0	80.0	20	--
Fifth (1969-74)	75.0	90.0	10	--
Sixth (1974-79)	80.0	90.0	10	--
Seventh (1979-84)	85.0	90.0	10	--
Eighth (1984-89)	85.0	22.5	10	67.5
Ninth (1990-95)*	85.0	22.5	10	67.5
Tenth(1995-2000)	77.5	20.0	--	80.0

* A separate report was submitted for the year 1989-90.
Sources: *Reports of Finance Commissions*.

In reducing the share of the States in the net proceeds of income tax, the

Tenth Finance Commission was guided by the following two considerations, " (i) that the authority that levies and administers the tax should have a significant and tangible interest in its yield and (ii) that any change in the share on this account should not materially affect the level of overall devolution to the States. In other words, any downward revision in the share of States in the net proceeds of income tax should be mirrored in a revenue equivalent increase in their share in the net proceeds of Union excise duties." [1] The Commission did recommend enlargement in the share of States in excise duties from 45 per cent to 47.5 per cent.

30.1.2 Distribution of States' Share Inter Se: Prior to the recommendations of the Eighth Finance Commission, population was the dominant factor in the distribution scheme. The weightage given to the population factor varied between 80 per cent and 90 per cent and that for the *contribution factor* between 10 per cent and 20 per cent.

Although the Eighth and the Ninth Finance Commissions retained the share of States in the proceeds of income tax at 85 per cent, they changed the formula for the distribution of States' share *inter se* drastically. The Eighth Finance Commission recommended the following formula.

1. 10 per cent of the net proceeds of income tax to be distributed among the States on the basis of assessment of income tax.
2. 90 per cent of the net proceeds to be distributed among the States on the following criteria:

- 25 per cent on the basis of population in 1971,
- 25 per cent on the basis of inverse of per capita income of the State multiplied by 1971 population, and
- 50 per cent on the basis of distance of per capita income of the State from the highest per capita income State (i.e. Punjab) multiplied by the 1971 population of the concerned State.

The formula of the Ninth Finance Commission was as follows.

1. 10 per cent on the basis of contribution.
2. 45 per cent on the basis of distance of per capita income of a State from that of the State with the highest per capita income multiplied by the 1971 population.
3. 22.5 per cent on the basis of the population of the State in 1971.
4. 11.25 per cent on the basis of a composite index of backwardness compiled by the Commission.
5. 11.25 per cent on the basis of the inverse of per capita income multiplied by the population of the State in 1971. [2]

The Tenth Finance Commission adopted the following indices for determining the *inter se* shares of the States in the shareable proceeds of income tax.

1. 20 per cent on the basis of population in 1971.
2. 60 per cent on the basis of distance of per capita income. [3]
3. 5 per cent on the basis of *area adjusted* formula. [4]
4. 5 per cent on the basis of index of infrastructure, and
5. 10 per cent on the basis of tax effort.

The prominent weight given to the *distance factor* by the Eighth, the Ninth, and the Tenth Finance Commissions tilted the devolution scheme in favour of backward States and therefore was generally welcomed.

30.1.3 Controversies over Distribution of Income Tax Revenue: Major controversies between the Centre and the States regarding distribution of revenue from income tax were the following.

A. Corporation Tax: By virtue of entry 85 of List I read with Article 270(4)(a), the receipts from corporation tax belong exclusively to the Central Government. Consequent upon the simplification in the scheme of company taxation in 1959, the income tax paid by companies was reclassified as corporation tax. As an offshoot of this definitional change, company taxation ceased to be mandatorily shareable with the States as per provision of Article 270.

Ever since, States had been pressing for the inclusion of corporation tax in the divisible pool, particularly in view of its buoyant revenue. In the face of explicit Constitutional provision precluding revenue from corporation tax being shareable with the States, the Finance Commissions had gradually increased the share of States in the truncated divisible pool. The Centre had opposed the inclusion of corporation tax in the divisible pool on the ground that the disadvantage to the States due to definitional change in 1959 had been made good by Finance Commissions by enhancing their share in income tax which went up to 85 per cent and remained there till the recommendations of the Tenth Finance Commission. Taking note of this situation, the Commission on Centre-State Relations, 1988, observed, "It is a fundamental principle of taxation that the taxing authority should have interest in its proceeds. In order to maintain this principle and giving a more meaningful choice to the Union among fiscal alternatives, it is necessary to enlarge the base of devolution to the States but with a lower percentage share in individual taxes. This can be done by bringing into the divisible pool a major Union tax but still keeping a sizeable revenue source for exclusive utilisation by the Union." [5]

Therefore, the Commission recommended that the net proceeds of corporation tax could be made permissibly shareable with the States through an appropriate amendment of the Constitution. Simultaneously, it made it clear that in the event of inclusion of corporation tax in the divisible pool, necessary adjustments will have to be made by suitably lowering shares of the States in income tax and Central excise duties. Some State Governments also argued on these lines. For example, the Government of Maharashtra suggested to the Ninth Finance Commission that the share of the States in income tax could be reduced to 75 per cent provided 20 per cent of the receipts from corporation tax were assigned to the States. The Ninth Finance Commission, however, refused to examine the question of corporation tax because it was not referred to it by the President.

B. Surcharge on Income Tax: The Constitution provides under Article 271 for the levy of a surcharge on income tax wholly for the purpose of the Centre. Surcharge was levied in 1951 and continued uninterrupted (*albeit* with different nomenclatures like special surcharge, additional surcharge etc.) when it was withdrawn in 1985 following the recommendations of the Eighth Finance Commission. However, surcharge on income tax was reintroduced in 1987 for drought purposes and the same was replaced by an employment surcharge in 1989. Surcharge was abolished by the Finance Act, 1994. It was reimposed subsequently.

In fact, surcharge on income tax has remained almost a regular source of revenue for the Centre much against the spirit of the Constitutional provision. States have all along pleaded before successive Finance Commissions for the inclusion of surcharge in the divisible pool. The Commission on Centre-State Relations, 1988, was firmly of the view that surcharge on income tax should not be levied by the Central Government except for a specified purpose and for a strictly limited period only. The Eighth and the Ninth Finance Commissions opined that a surcharge continued indefinitely could be regarded an additional income tax and, therefore, shareable with the States. The Tenth Finance Commission emphasised that the surcharge on income tax should not be levied except to meet emergent requirements for a limited period. Thus, although the explicit Constitutional provision favours the Centre, the levy of surcharge remains an irritant in Centre-State relations till date.

C. Miscellaneous Receipts: Another point of controversy pertained to the receipts from penalties and interest recoveries under the head miscellaneous receipts. The Eighth Finance Commission was of the view that such receipts should form part of the divisible pool of income tax. Unfortunately, the Centre did not accept this recommendation, maintaining that interest and penalties, though payable under the Income Tax Act, are distinct from income tax. The

Ninth Finance Commission disagreed with this view of the Centre and cited several judgements of the Supreme Court to prove that there was no essential difference between tax and penalties related to it. The Tenth Finance Commission also opined that receipts on account of interest recoveries and penalties form part of the divisible pool and should be shared with the States. It recommended that this should be done with effect from April 1, 1995.

In most European countries fines and penalties associated with a tax are part of the receipts from that tax. According to OECD, "Receipts from fines and penalties paid for infringement of regulations identified as relating to a particular tax and interest on payments overdue in respect of a particular tax are recorded together with receipts from that tax." [6] The stand taken by the Central Government in this regard is untenable.

D. Cost of Collection: Apportionment of the cost of collection between income tax and corporation tax was another contentious issue between the Centre and the States. The cost of collection was deducted from the proceeds of income tax while working out the share of States. On the suggestion of Eighth Finance Commission, an expert committee was set up in 1985 which apportioned the cost of collection in the ratio of 1:7 between corporation tax and non-corporation income tax.

Following the observations made by the Ninth Finance Commission in its First Report, the Government of India constituted another expert Committee in 1989 to examine the allocation of the cost of collection between income tax and corporation tax. The Committee, which included representatives of the State Governments, made a detailed study in this regard and fixed the ratio at 1:6.5 which was accepted and used by the Tenth Finance Commission.

30.2 Sharing of Excise Revenue

Excise duties, levied by the Centre under entry 84 of List I in the Seventh Schedule of the Constitution, occupied a predominant place in the overall transfer of resources from the Centre to the States. These duties belonged to the category of taxes which may be divided between the Centre and the States (Article 272) and the subject-matter of this division fell within the purview of the Finance Commission [Article 280(3)(a)].

30.2.1 Nature of Revenue Sharing: The sharing of excise duties was permissive and therefore different from the compulsory assignment to the States of the whole proceeds of taxes under Article 269 and compulsory sharing of the proceeds of income tax under Article 270. Hence, the States did not enjoy a constitutional right to claim a share out of the revenues from Central excises. It was for the Parliament to decide whether the States should at all be given such a share and in taking this decision it may consider recommendations of the Finance Commission made in this regard. This permissive provision in the Constitution aimed at providing additional resources to the States in the event of necessity to augment transfers which could be effected under other provisions of the Constitution.

Successive Finance Commissions had taken the view that permissive sharing, contemplated under Article 272, was not only justified but even necessary in view of the growing financial needs of the States for developmental and other essential services. Therefore, ever since April 1, 1952, the States had been getting a share in the proceeds of Central excises. In fact, successive Finance Commissions had increasingly relied upon excise duties in their schemes of revenue transfers with the result that these duties found an important place in the revenue accruals of the State Governments.

30.2.2 Determination of States' Share: Understandably, there was near unanimity among the States to press for a higher proportion of excise revenue for distribution among themselves. This was thought necessary to impart viability and to introduce elasticity to finances of the States. However, Finance Commissions paying due regard to requirements of the States on the one hand and needs of the Centre on the other evolved their own sharing schemes considering the overall transfer of resources from the Centre to the States.

The sharing of excise revenue between the Centre and the States started on a rather low profile with the award of the First Finance Commission which recommended distribution of 40 per cent of excise revenue from three commodities (tobacco, matches, and vegetable products) among the States in proportion to their population. In making this recommendation, the Commission was guided by its desire to widen the field of divisible taxes so that a balanced scheme of distribution could be evolved for the benefit of the States. The division of excise revenue, however, was restricted to the above three commodities because the Commission thought it inadvisable to divide too many excises to begin with, particularly in view of the relatively small yield from some of the items. As regards the selection of excises for division, the Commission preferred commodities (a) which were of common and widespread consumption, (b) which yielded a sizeable sum of revenue for distribution, and (c) which possessed reasonable stability of yield. The selected commodities, namely tobacco, matches, and vegetable products were found to be the most suitable for the purpose.

Following the award of the First Finance Commission, a number of States urged upon the Second Finance Commission to bring all excise duties under the distribution scheme. Such a sweeping suggestion did not find favour with that

Commission which striking a note of compromise, preferred to widen the range by increasing the number of items to be shared from three to eight. These were: tobacco, matches, vegetable products, sugar, coffee, tea, paper, and vegetable non-essential oils. The Commission, however, decreased the share of States in distributable duties from 40 per cent to 25 per cent keeping in view the sum it proposed to transfer to the States from Central excises in its overall scheme of devolution. However, the reduction in the share was more than made good by the widening of the coverage of divisible duties and each State received a larger sum from this source than before.

States again pleaded before the Third Finance Commission for inclusion of all excisable commodities in the distributable pool. In support of this demand the States argued that the expanding coverage of Central excises and their increasing incidence had adversely affected the revenue potential of sales tax. Accepting this demand of the States in principle the Commission observed, "The viability of the States could best be secured by a larger devolution of the Union excise duties and this should be effected by providing for the participation of the States, by conventions, in the proceeds of all Union excises. It would give a great deal of psychological satisfaction to the States and dissipate any suspicion that the Union is pursuing a policy of excessive centralisation of resources." [7] However, the Commission considering its own scheme of transfers, recommended for distribution among the States 20 per cent of the excise revenue from commodities which each yielded in 1960-61 revenue of Rs. 50 lakh or more. The number of such commodities was 35.

In their representations to the Fourth Finance Commission, the States again argued for a share out of the proceeds of excise duties on all commodities including the commodities which might be brought under the excise net during the quinquennium relevant for the Commission's award. Accepting the States' view, the Commission recommended the sharing of the proceeds of all excise duties between the Centre and the States in the ratio of 80:20. The Fifth and the Sixth Finance Commissions merely carried forward the recommendations of the Fourth Finance Commission in this regard.

The Seventh Finance Commission drastically increased the share of States in excise duties from 20 per cent to 40 per cent, making them the most important shareable tax between the Centre and the States. In doing so, the Commission was guided by the objective of leaving as many of the less affluent States as possible with a surplus on revenue account. It preferred bulk of fiscal transfers by way of tax shares than grants-in-aid. The Eighth Finance Commission further enhanced the share of States in excise duties to 45 per cent, out of which 5 per cent was set aside for distribution among those States which continued to have deficits even after the devolution of taxes and loans as recommended by it. The Ninth Finance Commission retained the share of States at 45 per cent but used 5 per cent and 7.425 per cent from it for post-devolution deficits, in its First, and Second Reports respectively. In other words, the portion of the net proceeds of excise duties from which all States received a share was 40 per cent for the Eighth Finance Commission, it remained so in the one year (1989-90) report of the Ninth Finance Commission but it was reduced to 37.575 per cent in the Second Report of the same Commission for the period 1990-95.

The Tenth Finance Commission raised the share of States in the net proceeds of Union excise duties from 45 per cent to 47.5 per cent, keeping in view the decrease in the States' share of the net proceeds of income tax from 85 per cent to 77.5 per cent recommended by it. Out of 47.5 per cent, 7.5 per cent was kept apart for distribution among deficit States.

From the foregoing account of the sharing of excise revenue between the Centre and the States, it is clear that in the wake of recommendations of the successive Finance Commissions, the States had come to claim an increasingly larger proportion of excise revenue over the years. The underlying philosophy in this respect was to enlarge States' share in a buoyant source of Central tax revenue. This development, however, had taken place contrary to what the framers of the Constitution had envisaged. As already noted, the permissive sharing of excise proceeds was intended to supplement, in the event of necessity, transfer of resources under other provisions of the Constitution. However, the supplementary source had become by far the biggest source of revenue transfer. This development was partly attributed to significant structural changes in the Indian tax system since Independence. For example, the expansion in the range of commodities subject to excise duties and the increasing incidence of such duties had considerably reduced the scope for sales tax levied by the States and it was therefore desirable that the States had a substantial interest in the proceeds of Central excises.

30.2.3 Distribution of States' Share Inter Se: The next task of the Finance Commission was to evolve principles for distribution of the States' share of excises as between different States. In this connection, it is interesting to note the observations of the Sixth Finance Commission, "While there was near unanimity among the States in demanding an increase in the share of Union excise duties, there were naturally wide divergences in their approach to the principles for determination of relative shares of the States in the divisible pool. Each State was inclined to put forward a formula that would favour it most." [8]

The First Finance Commission distributed the States' share of excise duties among the States on the basis of States' respective population. The Second

Finance Commission also preferred distribution largely on the basis of population. The Third Finance Commission, while agreeing to population being the major factor, also took into account other factors like the relative financial weakness of the States, disparity in the levels of development, percentage of scheduled castes and tribes, and population of backward classes. However, it did not specify either the exact manner of distribution or the weightage assigned to different indices of economic backwardness.

The Fourth Finance Commission accepted population as a general measure of the needs of States and distributed 80 per cent of the States' share on the basis of population. The remaining 20 per cent was distributed on the basis of social and economic backwardness of the States which was assessed on the basis of the following factors.

1. Per capita gross value of agriculture production.
2. Per capita value added by manufacture.
3. Percentage of workers (as defined in the Census) to the total population.
4. Percentage of enrolment in classes I to V to the population in age group 6-11.
5. Population per hospital bed.
6. Percentage of rural population to total population.
7. Percentage of population of scheduled castes and tribes to total population.

However, the Commission did not indicate the exact manner in which the above mentioned factors were combined.

The Fifth Finance Commission distributed 80 per cent of the States' share of excise duties on the basis of population and the remaining 20 per cent on the basis of socio-economic backwardness. Two-thirds of the 20 per cent was distributed among States whose per capita income was below the average per capita income of all States in proportion to the shortfall of the States' per capita income from all States' average multiplied by population of the respective States. The remaining one-third of the 20 per cent was distributed according to an integrated index of backwardness on the basis of the following six criteria.

1. Population of the scheduled tribes.
2. Number of factory workers per lakh of population.
3. Net irrigated area per cultivator.
4. Length of railway and surfaced roads per 100 sq. km.
5. Ratio of the number of school going children as compared to those of school going age.
6. Number of hospital beds per 1,000 population.

The Sixth Finance Commission, after having considered the long list of indicators of backwardness suggested by the States concluded, "Even a cursory look at the list would show that most of the indicators put forward by the States refer either to characteristics that are themselves the causes of low per capita income or to characteristics that are direct or indirect consequences of low per capita income." [9] Therefore, it adopted per capita income as the sole criterion in assessing the relative economic position of the States. This approach of the Commission was partly the result of the difficulty it felt in assigning weightage among different indicators of economic backwardness. The Commission distributed 75 per cent of the States' share of excise duties on the basis of population and the remaining 25 per cent on the basis of economic backwardness. The distribution of weightage for backwardness was recommended in relation to the 'distance' of a State's per capita income from that of the State with the highest per capita income multiplied by the population of the State concerned in 1971. Thus, the Sixth Finance Commission rejected the approach of the Fifth Finance Commission which had classified the States into two categories, rich and poor: States with per capita income above the national average being regarded rich, and those below the average as poor. According to the Sixth Finance Commission, this approach of its predecessor had affected most adversely those States whose per capita income was just above the dividing line.

The Seventh Finance Commission evolved its own overall indicators of backwardness, viz. per capita income and the proportion of people below the poverty line, in preference to partial indicators like level of schooling, health services, population of scheduled castes and tribes, and road mileage as adopted by previous Commissions. It determined the shares of States in the divisible pool of excises by giving equal weights (i.e. 25 per cent each) to the following four factors.

1. Population.
2. Inverse of per capita State Domestic Product (SDP).
3. Percentage of the poor in each State. [10]
4. A revenue equalisation formula evolved by the Commission. [11]

Thus, the Seventh Finance Commission not only significantly enhanced the share of States in excise proceeds but also drastically changed the principles of allocation of excise revenue among the States.

The Eighth Finance Commission was guided by the following three overriding considerations while deciding the criteria for allocating shares of excise duty among the States.

1. That the formula should be progressive in the sense that it should allocate a larger share to those States which have relatively lower per capita incomes or which are otherwise backward and financially weak.
2. The formula should be simple.
3. Firm and reliable data should be available for applying the formula.

Based on these considerations, the Commission recommended the distribution of States' share (45 per cent) among the States in the following manner.

(a) 40 per cent on the following bases (or the same formula as recommended by it for the distribution of 90 per cent of the States' share in income tax),

- one-fourth (i.e. 25 per cent) on the basis of 1971 population,
- one-fourth (i.e. 25 per cent) on the basis of the inverse of per capita income of the State multiplied by 1971 population,
- the remaining 50 per cent on the basis of distance of per capita income of the State from that of the State with the highest per capita income (i.e. Punjab).

(b) The remaining 5 per cent was set aside for distribution among the States which had deficits after taking into account their shares from the devolution of all taxes and duties.

The Ninth Finance Commission retained the share of States in excise duties at 45 per cent and recommended its distribution among the States in the following manner.

(a) 37.575 per cent on the following bases:

1. 29.94 per cent on the basis of 1971 population.
2. 14.97 per cent on the basis of Income Adjusted Total Population.
3. 14.97 per cent on the basis of the index of backwardness.
4. 40.12 per cent on the basis of distance of per capita income of a State from that of the State having the highest per capita income (i.e. Punjab).

(b) The remaining 7.425 per cent was distributed among the States with deficits, after taking into account their shares from various taxes and duties. [12]

The Tenth Finance Commission recommended the distribution of States' share (47.5 per cent) among the States in the following manner.

(a) 40 per cent on the following bases (or the same formula as recommended by it for the distribution of States' share in income tax).

1. 20 per cent on the basis of population in 1971.
2. 60 per cent on the basis of distance of per capita income.
3. 5 per cent on the basis of *area adjusted* formula.
4. 5 per cent on the basis of index of infrastructure.
5. 10 per cent on the basis of tax effort.

(b) The remaining 7.5 per cent of the net proceeds of excise duties was distributed among the deficit States in accordance with the shares specified by the Commission.

Table 30.2 summarises the recommendations of successive Finance Commissions regarding the distribution of excise revenue between the Centre and the States and the bases for allocating the States' share *inter se*.

Table 30.2: Recommendations of Various Finance Commissions Regarding Distribution of Central Excise Revenue between the Centre and the States

		Bases of distribution among the states (per cent)		
Finance Commission and period of award	Coverage (number of commodities)	States' share in excise revenue (per cent)	Population	Other factors
First (1952-57)	3	40	100	--
Second (1957-62)	8	25	90	10
Third (1962-66)	35	20	Major factor	Weightage not stated
Fourth (1966-69)	All	20	80	20
Fifth (1969-74)	All	20	80	20
Sixth (1974-79)	All	20	75	25
Seventh (1979-84)	All	40	25	75
Eighth (1984-89)	All	45	25	75
Ninth (1990-95)*	All	45	29.94	70.06
Tenth(1995-2000)	All	47.5	20	80

* A separate report was submitted for the year 1989-90.
Sources: *Reports of Finance Commissions.*

30.2.4 Varying Emphasis on Criteria Adopted: The foregoing account of the principles adopted by Finance Commissions to distribute States' share of excise duties among the States brings out the following points.

1. The proposal for devising the distribution scheme on the basis of consumption of excisable goods did not find favour with the Finance Commissions. The argument of some of the States that consumption of excisable goods reflected the *contribution* that each State made to the total excise proceeds was rejected because the purpose of sharing excise duties was not to return to the States what was collected from them.
2. Distribution in proportion to sales tax collections, justified on the ground that the levy of excise duties limited the scope for mobilisation of resources by the States in the form of sales tax, was also disfavoured by the Finance Commissions. However, this argument of the States was taken care of in the overall sharing of excise revenue between the Centre and the States.
3. The Finance Commissions generally accepted population as a criterion for determining the share of each State in excise revenue. Population was

assigned predominant weightage, ranging between 80 to 100 per cent, by the first six Finance Commissions. However, the Seventh, the Eighth, the Ninth, and the Tenth Finance Commissions gave more weightage to backwardness factor in their distribution schemes. Population as a criterion was supported on the ground that it represented the needs of the States and proceeds of excises should be so distributed among the States that each got according to its needs. It was further argued that in the case of some commodities, population was a rough index of total consumption and therefore the proposal for devising the distribution scheme on the basis of consumption of excisable goods was partly taken care of. The undue emphasis on population criterion as a measure of general needs of the States by earlier Finance Commissions was somewhat unjustified. In India, States differ widely in respect of per capita income, geographical area, nature of the terrain, and population distribution over the area. Thus, it is not always that the populous States are poor or that the less populous States are rich. Under these circumstances, population may be taken as one of the determinants of the needs of a State but it cannot be considered an adequate measure of that need.

4. Beginning with the Third Finance Commission, relative economic backwardness was also accepted as a legitimate criterion in the distribution scheme. For this purpose, different Finance Commissions evolved their own indicators for measuring relative economic backwardness. The richer States had often argued against the adoption of backwardness as a criterion on the ground that excise duties should be related exclusively to non-discriminatory criteria such as population or consumption and that any special help to the backward States should be rendered through the mechanism of grants-in-aid under Article 275 of the Constitution. This view was rejected by the Finance Commissions.
5. Adoption of the backwardness criterion, though laudable, was assigned relatively low weightage (20 to 25 per cent) by the Third, the Fourth, the Fifth, and the Sixth Finance Commissions and therefore did not serve the needs of the backward States adequately. Thus, there was not only a late realisation of the need to adopt backwardness criterion but the weightage assigned to it was also low. However, the Seventh, the Eighth, the Ninth, and the Tenth Finance Commissions gave predominant weightage to the backwardness factor though indices of backwardness were obtained rather haphazardly and to some extent arbitrarily.

30.2.5 Areas of Controversy: Distribution of excise revenue between the Centre and the States was beset with controversies some of which were the following.

A. Special Duties of Excise: Special duties were in the form of surcharges on basic duties and were levied on certain goods for the first time in 1963 in the wake of Chinese aggression. These were earmarked exclusively for the Centre and were not shareable with the States. States had all along contended that proceeds of special excises should also be shared with them. While the Constitution specifically mentioned in Article 271 that surcharges on income taxes were exclusively for the use of the Centre, there was no such provision for surcharges on excise duties. Their sharing was disallowed only in the Finance Acts and could always be reviewed by the Parliament, particularly in the light of the recommendations of Finance Commissions in this regard.

The Fourth Finance Commission had taken the view that it was open to it to suggest that proceeds of special duties of excise should also be made shareable with the States. However, on practical considerations, it did not favour bringing the proceeds of special duties of excise within the sharing scheme. The Commission, however, suggested that the recourse to special excises by the Central Government should be an exception rather than the rule.

The Fifth Finance Commission found no justification to exclude special duties of excise from the divisible pool and recommended their inclusion in the scheme of sharing of excise revenue from 1972-73 onwards. As a consequence, special duties of excise got merged with basic duties from April 1, 1972.

In the meantime, the Central Government devised another method to augment excise revenue exclusively for its own purpose. It had introduced regulatory duties of excise in 1961 for the purpose of empowering the Executive to vary rates of duties on any item within certain limits.

This provision had remained dormant till 1970-71 in the sense that revenue from regulatory duties was either nil or negligible during all these years and therefore it did not attract the attention of either the States or the Finance Commissions. The situation, however, changed significantly when in the wake of large influx of refugees from Bangladesh and conflict with Pakistan, the Central Government imposed in 1971 regulatory duties of excise on such items as steel, iron and steel products, copper, zinc, and aluminium. Furthermore, the regulatory duties were replaced by auxiliary duties (i.e. special duties) under the Finance Act, 1973 and it was specifically laid down in the Act that the auxiliary duties were for the purposes of the Centre, meaning thereby that proceeds there from were not to be shared with the States.

The States resented this arrangement, apprehending that continuance of auxiliary duties as a separate entity may encourage the Centre to raise additional revenue increasingly through auxiliary duties rather than the shareable basic duties. Upholding the States' view, the Sixth Finance Commission recommended the merger of revenue from auxiliary duties in the divisible pool. Consequently, auxiliary duties of excise, wherever applicable, were merged with the basic duties under the Finance Act of 1977. To forestall any future ambiguity as regards division of revenue from special duties of excise between the Centre and the States, the Seventh Finance Commission categorically stated that revenue from excise duties, whether they were designated special or regulatory or by any other name, should also be included in the divisible pool. The Eighth and the Ninth Finance Commissions endorsed this view and recommended that the divisible pool should include all excise duties including special excise duties but excluding earmarked cesses and duties collected under the Additional Duties of Excise (Textiles and Textile Articles) Act, 1978.

B. Earmarked Cesses: States also insisted for the inclusion of earmarked cesses and the additional excise duties under the Act of 1978 in the divisible pool. These were cesses on commodities which were not subject to excise duty like iron ore, and coal. Then there were items which were subject to regular excise duties along with cesses like tea, sugar, and paper. Additional excise duties on textiles were also a kind of earmarked levy meant to finance controlled cloth and *Janata* cloth schemes. Like surcharge on income tax, cesses had also become permanent feature of excise taxation, and since they reduced the scope for regular excise duties, the States wanted their merger in the divisible pool. The Eighth and the Ninth Finance Commissions examined the question of the inclusion of cesses in the divisible pool but were content to observe that their number should be kept to the minimum.

The Tenth Finance Commission was more forthright in its views on this issue. It observed, "As regards the inclusion of revenues from the cesses in the divisible pool, it may be mentioned that a cess is levied on a specified commodity and is governed by a special Act of Parliament with the stipulation that it should be utilised for the development of the specific industry, the products of which bear the cess. The proceeds of such cesses cannot, therefore, be shared with the States." [13]

C. Administered Prices: Another contentious issue pertained to frequent hikes in administered prices by the Centre. The States desired that the Centre should raise resources by increasing excise duties instead of administered prices so that they could share the resources so raised. The Eighth Finance Commission distinguished between hike in administered prices to meet the increase in cost of production and for raising revenue. If revenue raising was the objective, then excise duties should be preferred. This view was endorsed by the Ninth Finance Commission.

Notes

1. *Report of the Tenth Finance Commission*, December 1994, pp. 21-22.

2. The use of 1971 census data was considered appropriate because some States fared better in implementing the family planning programme between 1971 and 1981. Adoption of the 1981 census figures would have been detrimental to the interest of the States which are promoting this desirable national objective.

3. According to the Tenth Finance Commission, "the respective 'distances' are multiplied by the population of the States, and the share of a State is obtained by dividing the product by the sum of such products for all the States. This procedure of multiplying an index by respective populations and deriving shares according to such products has been called scaling" (*Report of the Tenth Finance Commission*, 1994, p. 23).

4. Although the Tenth Finance Commission used area as a factor, it made certain adjustments at the upper and lower ends. Thus, it ensured that no State received a share higher than 10 per cent at the upper end and no State received a share less than 2 per cent at the lower end.

5. Government of India, *Report of the Commission on Centre-State Relations* (Chairman: Justice R.S. Sarkaria) Part I, 1988, p. 274.

6. Organisation for Economic Co-operation and Development, *Revenue Statistics of OECD Countries: 1965-85* (Paris, 1988), p. 38.

7. *Report of the Finance Commission, 1961,* p. 21.

8. *Report of the Finance Commission, 1973,* p. 15.

9. *Ibid.*, p. 16.

10. The Commission used the per capita State Domestic Product in a comparable series at State current prices by adopting the annual average for the triennial 1973-76. The poverty percentage in each State was taken as the proportion of people below an augmented poverty line in the State to the aggregate poor population in all the States. The augmented poverty line was the minimum per capita consumption expenditure level for 1970-71 on the well-known Dandekar-Rath criterion plus the State budget expenditure per capita on selected public services in that year.

11. For the revenue equalisation principle, the per capita revenue potential of each State with reference to the average per capita SDP for the triennial 1973-76 was computed. The per capita average of each State's own tax and non-tax revenue for 1975-76 and 1976-77 were regressed on the average per capita income of the States to derive the estimated values of per capita revenue of each State. The distance of the per capita revenue thus estimated for each State from the maximum estimated per capita revenue among all the States (i.e. Punjab) was multiplied by the estimated population of the State as on March 1, 1976. The percentage of the product of the distance of the per capita revenue so estimated from that of Punjab and the population for each State in the total of these products for all the States gave the share of each State in the component of the divisible pool based on revenue equalisation formula. The adoption of this formula was recognition of the fact that States which are less favourably placed with regard to their resource potential are helped to take steps for the betterment of the people living in those States.

12. To put it differently, the 45 per cent share of the States was distributed among the States on the following bases: (i) 25 per cent on the basis of 1971 population. (ii) 12.5 per cent on the basis of Income Adjusted Total Population. (iii) 12.5 per cent on the basis of the index of backwardness. (iv) 33.5 per cent on the basis of distance of per capita income of a State from that of the State having the highest per capita income (i.e. Punjab). (v) The remaining 16.5 per cent was distributed among the States with deficits, after taking into account their shares from various taxes and duties.

The weights given in the text were derived by multiplying the weights given above by a factor of (100/83.5).

13. *Report of the Tenth Finance Commission*, December 1994, p. 22.

31

Additional Duties of Excise in Lieu of Sales Tax

Following a voluntary agreement between the Centre and the States at a meeting of the National Development Council (NDC) held in December, 1956, it was decided to replace sales tax on textiles, tobacco, and sugar by additional duties of excise and to distribute revenues derived there from among the States. The agreement provided also that the share accruing to each State shall not in any case be less than the revenue realised from the levy of sales tax on these goods for the financial year 1956-57 in that State. The Council's decision was implemented through the Additional Duties of Excise (Goods of Special Importance) Act, 1957, the First Schedule of which prescribed the rates of additional duties of excise and the Second Schedule the scheme of distribution of the net proceeds among the States.

The Act does not debar States from the levy of sales tax on the specified commodities, but it does provide that if in any year any State levies and collects a tax on the sale or purchase of such commodities, no sum shall be paid to that State in that year by way of share out of the net proceeds of the additional duties of excise, unless the Central Government by special order decides otherwise. The commodities covered under the scheme (textiles, tobacco, and sugar) were declared goods of special importance in inter-State trade so that no State could find it worthwhile to opt out of the voluntary agreement not to impose sales tax on these goods. [1] The revenue derived from additional duties of excise, levied and collected by the Centre, is distributed among the States in accordance with the formula prescribed by the Finance Commission. The Fourth Finance Commission described it as a tax rental arrangement. [2]

31.1 Rationale of the Scheme

The scheme of additional duties of excise in lieu of sales tax has the following advantages.

1. It minimises tax evasion by levying the tax at first point and saving industry, trade, and consumers from administrative complexities involved in the collection and payment of sales tax.
2. It helps in maintaining uniformity in the prices of widely consumed goods throughout the country.

3. Such an arrangement contributes to the development of an integrated market by facilitating movement of goods across State borders.
4. Rationalisation of commodity taxation at the national level becomes easy.
5. Cost of collection is reduced.

31.2 Views of the State Governments

The scheme of additional duties of excise in lieu of sales tax has been in force since 1957. While the business community has demanded extension of this scheme to other commodities, the States have generally remained disinclined in this regard. The distrust between the Centre and the States regarding the operation of this scheme by the Central Government is an irritant in Centre-State relations. States have argued on the following lines.

1. Sales tax is the only elastic source of revenue available to them and in view of its regional applicability it is also the only effective instrument for shaping their economic policies.
2. Replacement of it by Central levy will encroach on their constitutional rights leading to erosion of their financial autonomy.
3. If taxes are levied and collected by a State itself then it is more conscious of its responsibilities towards the taxpayers. Subventions from the Centre may lead to reckless spending causing fiscal indiscipline.

As regards the working of the existing scheme, the dissatisfaction of State Governments is borne out of their belief that revenue potential of additional duties of excise has not been fully exploited by the Centre. Their complaint is that the growth of revenue from additional excise duties on textiles, sugar, and tobacco lags behind the growth in revenue from basic excise duties on the same commodities. The States complain that once sales tax on the three commodities was replaced by additional excise duties, the Centre did not feel the need for consultation with the States for reviewing the working of the scheme. They claim that the growth rate of their sales tax revenue is much higher than the growth rate of the yield from additional excise duties.

31.3 Decisions of the National Development Council

Following complaints from the States, the whole issue was reconsidered by the National Development Council in its meeting held on December 28, 1970. The Council decided to continue the scheme with the following conditions: (a) that the incidence of additional duties would be stepped up to 10.8 per cent of the value of clearances within a period of two or three years, (b) that a ratio of 2:1 between basic and additional excise duties would be achieved and maintained, (c) that specific duties would be converted into ad valorem duties except in regard to unmanufactured tobacco. It was also agreed that a Standing Review Committee consisting of representatives of the Central and State Governments with the Economic Adviser, Planning Commission, as convenor, would be set up and the same would meet at least once a year to review the working of the new arrangement and make such recommendations as may be necessary for its further improvement.

As a follow up action, specific duties were replaced by ad valorem rates and significant enhancements were made in additional excise duties in the Central budgets for the three consecutive years 1971-72 to 1973-74. The Standing Review Committee met for the first time in February 1981 and appointed a sub-committee which recommended that the incidence of 10.8 per cent should be achieved in three stages: 8.5 per cent by 1984-85; 9.75 per cent by 1987-88; and 10.8 per cent by 1989-90. The Ninth Finance Commission was informed by the Union Finance Ministry that the incidence achieved by the end of 1988-89 was 10.7 per cent. The Commission hoped that the committed level of 10.8 per cent would be actually achieved by the end of 1989-90. In a significant move, the Commission recommended that during its award period (1990-95), if in any year the incidence of additional excise duties falls short of the level of 10.8 per cent of the value of clearances, the shortfall should be made good by the Centre by providing an equivalent amount by way of grants-in-aid to be distributed among the States in the same manner as recommended for sharing the proceeds of additional excise duties. [3] As regards the ratio between basic excises and additional excises, the Centre fulfilled its obligations by achieving the stipulated 2:1 ratio by 1981-82.

31.4 Role of the Finance Commission

The Finance Commission comes in the picture for the purpose of determining the principles of distribution of the net proceeds of additional duties of excise among the States.

31.4.1 Guaranteed Amount: The first issue before the Finance Commission is to determine the yield in 1956-57 from sales tax on the commodities subject to additional excise duties for the purpose of guaranteeing to the States concerned the amount so determined. The Second Finance Commission, which was the first to deal with this problem, adopted elaborate procedures for working out estimates of yield (i.e. the guaranteed amount for the year 1956-57). These were primarily based on consumption estimates and figures of collection of sales tax obtained from each State for the years 1954-55 to 1956-57. The later Finance Commissions did not consider it feasible, in view of the lapse of time, to reassess the likely yield in 1956-57 of sales tax to redetermine the guaranteed amount and therefore accepted the Second Finance Commission's estimates with adjustments whenever necessary. [4]

31.4.2 Procedure for Guaranteed Amount: The second issue for consideration by the Finance Commission is whether the guaranteed amounts should first be set apart from the net proceeds and the balance then distributed among the States or to distribute the entire net proceeds on appropriate principles subject to the overriding proviso that no State should get less than the guaranteed amount. The Second, the Third, the Fourth, and the Fifth Finance Commissions preferred the first alternative thinking that unless the guaranteed amounts were first set apart and the balance alone distributed among the States, there was the risk of the share of some States falling below the guaranteed amount. However, the Sixth and the subsequent Finance Commissions did not feel the need to set apart the guaranteed amount as there was no risk of the share of any State falling short of the guaranteed amount. In adopting the second alternative, i.e. distributing the entire net proceeds on some appropriate principles, the Sixth and the Seventh Finance Commissions were guided by an underlying philosophy to help the weaker States. To the question whether the guaranteed amount should first be set apart, the Seventh Finance Commission remarked, "If that were done, there is no doubt that some States would receive, in the period covered by our Report, shares slightly larger than the shares they would receive if the guaranteed amounts were not so set apart. While it is true that under the NDC resolution earlier agreed to, a State is entitled to have a share which should not be less than the guaranteed amount, the agreement does not assure to any State any extra benefit what it would receive were the guaranteed amount first set apart." [5]

Thus, taking a technical view of the matter, the Seventh Finance Commission applied the principle of distribution to the entire net proceeds from additional excise duties. The Eighth Finance Commission endorsed this view and followed suit.

31.4.3 Basis of Distribution: The third issue relates to the determination of the basis for the distribution of additional excise duties among the States. The assurances of the guaranteed amounts in the original agreement were an indication of the logic that in the distribution of the net proceeds the principle of compensation was to be followed. In other words, each State should be enabled to get almost the same amount as it would have got had sales taxes on these commodities been in operation with the same order of incidence as the additional excise duties. This view, which has generally been accepted by the Finance Commissions, precludes other considerations like needs of a State, relative backwardness etc. which are relevant in relation to allocation of other Central taxes.

For proper implementation of the compensation principle, it is widely recognised that State-wise figures of consumption of commodities on which additional excise duties are levied accord the best reflection of the potential loss of revenue sustained by States' surrender of authority to levy sales tax on them. However, Finance Commissions have differed in adopting methods to assess relative levels of consumption of these commodities in different States. The divergence of opinion on this account has been mainly due to paucity of reliable data on State-wise consumption of these commodities. Thus, the Second Finance Commission recommended the distribution of additional excise duties on the basis of the then available consumption figures with population as a correctional factor. The Third Finance Commission distributed the collections in excess of the guaranteed amounts partly on the basis of the percentage increase in the collection of sales tax in each State since 1957-58 and partly on the basis of population. It did not, however, indicate the relative weightage given to these factors. The Fourth Finance Commission felt that figures of collection of all sales taxes in a State were a more direct indicator of the contribution made by each State to the divisible surplus than population. Abandoning the population factor altogether, it recommended the distribution of the balance over the total of guaranteed amounts on the basis of the proportion of sales tax revenue realised in each State to the total sales tax collections in all the States taken together. The Fifth Finance Commission reverted back to the Third Finance Commission's formula and recommended distribution of additional excise duties giving equal weightage to both sales tax collections and population.

The Sixth Finance Commission rejected sales tax collections outright as a possible indirect indicator of the level of consumption of textiles, sugar, and tobacco in different States. It observed, "sales tax is applicable to a wide range of commodities comprising luxuries, semi-luxuries, raw materials, intermediate goods and the like. Sales tax revenue derived from these commodities may be a measure of the tax effort of the State Government but it does not provide even an indirect clue to the levels of consumption of textiles, sugar, and tobacco on which additional excise duties are being levied in lieu of sales tax." [6]

Alternatively, the Sixth Finance Commission preferred data of State Domestic Product as indicator of the likely consumption of these commodities in view of the close relationship between income and consumption. However, with regard to coarser varieties of cloth, the Commission felt that the consumption was more likely to depend on population (the commodity being a necessity) than on State Domestic Product. With such considerations in mind, the Commission recommended the distribution of the entire net proceeds of additional duties of excise on the basis of population, State Domestic Product at State current prices, and production in the ratio of 70:20:10.

The Seventh Finance Commission examined in detail the available statistics of State-wise consumption of the commodities to which additional excise duties are applicable. In particular, it studied the suitability of household consumer expenditure data of the National Sample Survey (NSS) for adoption as a measure of the consumption of these articles in each State. However, in view of the various limitations of NSS data, [7] the Commission did not find it proper to use these data for estimating the consumption in each State of the articles subject to additional excise duties.

Departing from the approach of the earlier Finance Commissions, the Seventh Finance Commission adopted different formulae for distribution of additional excise duties on different commodities. In the case of sugar, it recommended the distribution of the net proceeds of additional duties among the States in proportion to the despatches of sugar to each of the States averaged for three years ending with 1976-77. Statistics of despatches of sugar to each State, obtained from the Department of Food of the Government of India, were taken as a fair approximation of consumption of sugar in each State. In the case of textiles and tobacco, the average per capita State Domestic Product of each State for the 3 years ending 1975-76 was multiplied by the population of the State according to 1971 census and the percentage shares of this product of each State in the corresponding all-States' total figure were worked out. It is pertinent to note that the Seventh Finance Commission made a specific suggestion to the Central Government regarding collection of suitable statistics for reliable estimates of consumption of these articles in each State for the benefit of future Finance Commissions.

The Eighth Finance Commission also could not obtain reliable estimates of consumption of these commodities. It, therefore, recommended the distribution of additional duties of excise on all the three commodities (sugar, textiles, and tobacco) by giving equal weightage to State Domestic Product and population.

The Ninth Finance Commission maintained that since sales tax itself is a tax on consumption therefore the shares of various States in additional duties of excise should correspond to their shares in the consumption of these commodities. It observed, "The fact that the proceeds of Additional Excise Duties are distributed only in pursuance of a tax rental arrangement between the Centre and the States (which has its origin in the National Development Council meeting in 1956) would clearly imply that this distribution cannot be treated as devolution or grant-in-aid in the sense that these terms are normally understood. The terms of reference would, therefore, not bind us to use the 1971 population for computing the States' share of Additional Excise Duties. But for the tax rental arrangement, the States would have been collecting sales tax on the current consumption of the relevant commodities. Since population is being used only as a proxy for consumption along with SDP, we consider it as only logical that any criterion which links the shares of the States nearest to the consumption of the relevant items in the individual States should be preferred." [8]

31.5 Expert Committee on Replacement of Sales Tax by Additional Excise Duty (Chairman: Kamlapati Tripathi), 1983 (see section 21.6.4 of chapter 21 of this book).

Notes

1. Internal as well as inter-State sales tax on goods of special importance is governed by the Central Sales Tax Act, 1956. The present rate of CST is 4 per cent.

2. India's federal system of government creates a dual polity based on divided governmental functions and taxation powers. Taxation laws of the Central Government extend to the whole of the country while those of State Governments are applicable within their respective jurisdictions. A tax belonging to the States may be imposed with a varying base and/or rate in different States. Even the procedures and rules for its collection may differ from State to State. The lack of uniformity in the imposition of State tax laws can cause difficulties for traders and consumers and thus hinder inter-State trade. To overcome these problems, arrangements could be made to transfer from the States, the legal right to levy the tax, to the Centre with the proviso that revenue collected will be assigned to the States. This is known as 'tax rental arrangement'.

3. *Second Report of the Ninth Finance Commission,* December 1989, p. 34.

4. For example, the Third Finance Commission had to make adjustments in view of the bifurcation of Bombay State into Maharashtra, and Gujarat.

5. *Report of the Seventh Finance Commission*, 1978, p. 59.

6. *Report of the Sixth Finance Commission*, 1973, p. 20.

7. For example, NSS data related to the year 1972-73 and was considered outdated for the Commission's period of award (1979-84). While NSS data covered only household expenditure, the Commission was interested in non-household consumption as well.

8. *Report of the Ninth Finance Commission,* 1989, p. 20.

32

Grant in Lieu of Railway Passenger Fare Tax

Prior to Constitution (Eightieth Amendment) Act, 2000, Article 269(1) included tax on railway passenger fare. Article 269(2) clarified that the proceeds were to be assigned to the States within which the tax was levied. The Finance Commission was required to formulate principles for distribution of the proceeds among the States.

A tax on railway passenger fares was levied for the first time in 1957. Following the recommendation of the Railway Convention Committee (1960) of the Parliament, the tax was repealed and merged in the basic fares from April 1, 1961. It may be recalled that the Railway Board had pleaded before the Committee that the tax had reduced the scope for raising passenger fares. Obviously, the States were unhappy on being deprived of a potentially elastic source of revenue. To compensate the States for the loss of revenue, the Government decided to pay annually a sum of Rs. 12.50 crore for distribution among the States during the five year period 1961-62 to 1965-66. In pursuance of the recommendations of the Railway Convention Committee (1965), the amount of this grant was raised to Rs. 16.25 crore per annum from 1966-67.

In the wake of Bangladesh crisis, the tax on railway passenger fares was revived in 1971 and later again repealed on March 31, 1973. With the consent of the States, the proceeds of the tax were transferred to the Centre to meet the expenditure on Bangladesh refugees. However, the grant of Rs. 16.25 crore continued to be paid uninterrupted and unchanged till it was raised to Rs. 23.12 crore by the Railway Convention Committee (1980) and it remained at that level during the period 1980-81 to 1983-84. The same Committee also suggested that future increase in the quantum of grant could be considered on the basis of the recommendations of the Eighth Finance Commission which drastically increased the amount of grant from Rs. 23.12 crore to Rs. 95 crore per annum during the period of its award (1984-89), though the terms of reference did not require it to make any such recommendation. The new amount of grant (Rs. 95 crore) was calculated on the basis of the total non-suburban passenger earnings in 1981-82 and the fact that the tax, when in operation, constituted roughly 10.7 per cent of the total fare structure. The Commission on Centre-State Relations, 1988, suggested a periodical review and suitable adjustments of such lump sum grant on the recommendations of the Finance Commission.

Going beyond its terms of reference, the Ninth Finance Commission also examined the question of the quantum of grant. Some States pleaded before it that the grant should be 10.7 per cent of the non-suburban railway passenger earnings in each of the years of its award (1990-95). After having examined the railway finances, the Commission concluded that calculation of the grant at 10.7 per cent would put too much burden on the railways, jeopardising its modernisation plans. According to the Railway Board, calculation of grant at 10.7 per cent would have meant a commitment of Rs. 232 crore in 1988-89. [1] Striking a note of balance, the Ninth Finance Commission fixed the grant at a lump sum amount of Rs. 150 crore per annum for each year of the period 1990-95.

The Tenth Finance Commission recommended Rs. 380 crore (being the said 10.7 per cent) as grant in lieu of railway passenger fare to be paid to the States annually during the period of its award (1995-2000).

The other task of the Finance Commission was to formulate principles for the distribution of this grant among the States. The Second Finance Commission, which was the first to deal with this question, adopted actual passenger travel on the railways within each State as the basis for which it considered route length as the proxy. This formula was endorsed and continued by the subsequent Finance Commissions up to the Sixth. It was the Seventh Finance Commission which changed the formula and distributed the grant in proportion to the non-suburban passenger earnings from traffic originating in each State. The Eighth, the Ninth, and the Tenth Finance Commissions followed suit.

Note

1. *First Report of the Ninth Finance Commission*, 1988, p. 40.

33

Grants-in-aid

Even after the transfer to the States of a share of divisible taxes, the resources of some of the States may remain inadequate to meet their needs. Therefore, the Constitution provides for grants-in-aid by the Centre to such States as are in need of assistance. Two types of grants are provided by the Centre to the States: the first under Article 275 which are routed through the Finance Commission, and the Second under Article 282 which have traditionally been determined by the Planning Commission.

Article 280 (3)(b) requires the Finance Commission to make recommendations as to the principles which should govern the grants-in-aid of the revenues of the States under Article 275(1). The First Finance Commission laid down the following guidelines for the allotment of these grants: Firstly, in determining the eligibility of a State for grants-in-aid, its budgetary needs would be an important criterion. In studying the budgetary needs of a State, receipts from shared Central taxes would be taken into account, adjustments would be made for unusual or non-recurring items of revenue and expenditure and due allowance would be made for failure to maximise tax effort or to economise expenditure. Secondly, grants-in-aid should help equalise the standards of basic social services in the various States. Thirdly, grants-in-aid may be given to promote any beneficent service of primary importance in regard to which it is in national interest to assist the less advanced States to get forward. Despite these guidelines, the Finance Commissions have distributed these grants, by and large, on the basis of budgetary needs of the States, i.e. to cover non-Plan gap on revenue account variously described as *budgetary gap*, *financial need*, *revenue gap*, *fiscal needs* etc.

The first eight Finance Commissions confined themselves to the non-Plan revenue accounts of the States. They determined the grants equal to deficit of each State so that the non-Plan revenue accounts of all the States were balanced or left with a surplus every year. This was called the *gap-filling approach* (or more appropriately *net gap filling approach*) meaning that the deficits on non-Plan revenue account which remained after tax devolution were covered through grants. The *gap-filling approach* adopted by successive Finance Commissions was to some extent attributable to the terms of reference issued to them. The main disadvantage of the *gap filling approach* was that it encouraged wasteful expenditure and discouraged revenue efforts on the part of State Governments.

The shortcomings of the *gap-filling approach* led the Centre to ask the Ninth Finance Commission to adopt a normative approach to make the States more revenue conscious. This Commission broke new grounds in at least two areas. As is well-known, this Commission assessed revenue receipts of the States normatively and also applied certain norms to assess expenditures. Therefore, it recommended grants to fill the *normative gaps* as opposed to traditional *budgetary needs*. Secondly, it dealt with the total revenue account (i.e. including Plan revenue account) and worked to eliminate deficits in the revenue account as a whole. [1]

Reverting back to the *gap-filling approach*, the Tenth Finance Commission recommended grants-in-aid equal to the amount of residual deficits, emerging after taking into account the transfers pertaining to taxes and duties, for each of the years during 1995-96 to 1999-2000. Hence, no State has a post-devolution deficit on the non-Plan revenue account in the terminal year. The total amount of grants on account of non-Plan revenue deficit for the period 1995-2000 was Rs. 7,582 crore.

It is noteworthy that while a State cannot be denied a part of a shared Central tax even if it has no demonstrated financial need, grants are given upon genuine financial needs of the States. It is possible that even before tax devolution from the Centre, some high-income States have a surplus in their non-Plan revenue account. The Seventh Finance Commission identified Punjab, Haryana, Gujarat, Tamil Nadu, and Karnataka as such States. Thus, grants-in-aid along with shared taxes serve as a levelling up force to promote regional balanced development. From this, it may also be inferred that States as a whole are not affected whether transfers are made by one means (shareable taxes) or another (grants). It is the total amount transferred which is important for them. However, the sources of transfer become important when it comes to individual States because the formulae applied for various transfers are different. It is not possible to adopt a single formula for all transfers in view of the differing nature of taxes, duties, and grants.

Note

1. In India, budgets of the Central and State Governments are divided into revenue budget and capital budget under provisions of Articles 112 and 202 of the Constitution respectively. After the commencement of the Five Year Plans, the revenue budgets of the Governments came to be sub-divided into Plan and non-Plan budgets, particularly on the expenditure side. Traditionally, Plan side is considered by the Planning Commission and the non-Plan side by the Finance Commission. However, implementation of Plan projects has led to new expenditures on non-Plan revenue account. Moreover, the Constitution in no way restricts the Finance

Commission's jurisdiction to only non-Plan side of the budget. This constitutional position was confirmed when the Government in its terms of reference asked the Ninth Finance Commission that Plan and non-Plan sides of the revenue accounts should be considered together in assessing receipts and expenditures of the Centre and the States or to assess the total revenues and total revenue expenditures of the Central and State Governments without making a distinction between Plan and non-Plan. The consideration of the Plan component of the revenue budget by the Ninth Finance Commission was a major departure from the past practice and in a way also an encroachment on the territory of the Planning Commission. It marked a turning point in the controversy regarding the role and authority of the Finance Commission versus the Planning Commission or the scope of Article 275 versus Article 282. For details of the controversy regarding the scope of Article 275, see *Second Report of the Ninth Finance Commission*, 1989, p. 28.

34

Issues in Centre-State Financial Relations

Since the commencement of the Constitution in 1950, various problems and conflicts have arisen in Centre-State financial relations in India. Such problems are endemic of all federal governments in the world.

34.1 Inter-regional Inequalities and Transfers

Regional imbalances may be natural due to unequal distribution of natural resources and/or man-made in the sense of neglect of some regions and preference for others for investment and infrastructural facilities. Since different provinces are not equally endowed with resources, they have dissimilar industrial bases. As a result, the well-endowed provinces have a higher per capita income and hence a sound revenue base for their governments than the less-endowed provinces.

In India, apart from uneven distribution of geographical advantages, historical factors have also contributed to regional inequities. The British rulers developed only those regions which possessed facilities for manufacturing and trading activities. Thus, in the pre-1947 period almost all industrial and commercial activities remained confined to major cities, viz. Bombay (in Maharashtra), Calcutta (in West Bengal), and Madras (in Tamil Nadu).

Federalism is not only a unifying but also a levelling up force. Considerable economic inequalities exist among different States of India and their reduction is an argument in favour of centralisation of resources.

Depending upon the availability of data, a number of indicators can be used to describe inter-State economic disparities in a federation. The most representative of these indicators is the per capita income in different States. Wide disparities exist in the per capita income of various States in India. Various policy instruments have been used to mitigate inter-State economic disparities, including the transfer of resources from the Centre to the States, particularly to financially weaker States.

34.2 Indebtedness of States (see section 26.4 of chapter 26 of this book)

34.3 Central Inroads into State Subjects

Although the division of taxation powers between the Centre and the States is clear-cut, it is not so in the case of economic activities. A number of economic functions fall in the Concurrent List and those which belong to State List are subject, in many cases, to the provisions of the Union List. As these situations are described below, it will be noticed that they are partly the result of the original scheme of the Constitution and partly attributable to the amendments of the Constitution after it became operative in 1950. Although each such amendment has a logic of its own, they can be said to have encroached upon States' sphere of legislation if considered collectively (Table 34.1).

Agriculture as such figures in the State List (Entry 14) but certain aspects of agriculture fall in the Concurrent List/Union List. Thus, fisheries belong to the State List (Entry 21) but fishing and fisheries beyond territorial waters belong to the Union List (Entry 57). The enlargement of Entry 33 in the Concurrent List through the Constitution (Third Amendment) Act, 1954 made agriculture virtually a concurrent subject. It reads as follows: "Trade and Commerce in, and the production, supply and distribution of: (a) the products of any industry where the control of such industry by the Union is declared by Parliament by law to be expedient in the public interest, and imported goods of the same kind as such products; (b) foodstuffs, including edible oilseeds and oils; (c) cattle fodder, including oilcakes and other concentrates; (d) raw cotton, whether ginned or unginned and cotton seeds; and (e) raw jute." Thus, trade, commerce, production, supply and distribution of foodstuffs including edible oils and oil seeds are covered by the Concurrent List.

Similarly, animal husbandry and veterinary training are State subjects (Entry 15) but prevention of cruelty to animals is a concurrent subject (Entry 17). Forestry and protection of wild animals and birds originally belonged to the State List (Entries 18 and 20). However, they were transferred to the Concurrent List (Entries 17A and 17B) through the Constitution (Forty-second Amendment) Act, 1976.

Also included in the Concurrent List are other economic activities such as economic and social planning, population control and family planning, commercial and industrial monopolies, trade unions, social security, and price control (Entries 20, 20A, 21, 22, 23 and 34 respectively).

Water and power development is another important area of State activity subject to the Central control. Water supplies, irrigation and canals, drainage and embankments, water storage and water power belong to the State List (Entry 17) but these are subject to the provisions of Union List (Entry 56) which deals with the regulation and development of inter-State rivers and river valleys. Since electricity belongs to Concurrent List (Entry 38), the Centre's concurrent jurisdiction on water power is automatic.

Table 34.1: Constitutional Amendments Affecting Division of Financial/Economic Powers between the Centre and the States

Name of the Act	Date of Commencement	Nature of the Amendment
Constitution (Third Amendment) Act 1954	22.2.1955	Entry 33 of Concurrent List of the Seventh Schedule was enlarged by transferring the contents of Article 369. Parliament was enabled to have concurrent jurisdiction to legislate on trade, commerce, production, supply, and distribution of foodstuffs, raw cotton, raw jute etc.
Constitution (Sixth Amendment) Act 1956	11. 9. 1956	Articles 269 and 286, and Entry 54 of State list of the Seventh Schedule amended. Entry 92A inserted in the Union List of the same schedule. Parliament was empowered to impose sales tax on inter-State trade.
Constitution (Seventh Amendment) Act 1956	1. 11. 1956	Entry 24 of State List of the Seventh Schedule pertaining to industries was made subject to entries 7 and 52 of the Union List of the same schedule. Entry 7 relates to industries considered necessary for defence while entry 52 covers industries the control of which is considered expedient in public interest. Before the amendment entry 24 was subject only to the provisions of entry 52.
Constitution (Forty Second Amendment) Act, 1976	Different provisions came into force on different dates commencing from 3.1.1977	Forests, and protection of wild animals and birds originally belonging to State List were transferred to Concurrent List. Population control and family planning were inserted in the Concurrent List as entry 20A. States power to levy tax on advertisements broadcast by radio or television was precluded in entry 55 of State List in addition to the already existing exception in that entry of tax on 'advertisements published in newspapers'.
Constitution (Forty Sixth Amendment) Act, 1982	2. 2. 1998	Parliament was empowered to levy taxes on the consignment of goods in inter-State trade. Entry 92B was inserted in the Union List of the 7th Schedule for the purpose and simultaneously sub-clause 269(1)(h) was inserted in Article 269.

Sources: Compiled from (1) Government of India, Ministry of Law, Justice and Company Affais, *The Constitution of India*; (2) *Report of the Commission on Centre-State Relations*, Part I, 1988, pp. 93-96; and (3) Durga Das Basu, *Introduction to the Constitution of India* (New Delhi: Prentice Hall of India Pvt. Ltd., 1987), pp. 403-12.

Regulation of mines and mineral development belongs to State List (Entry 23) subject to certain provisions of the Union List. Thus, mineral resources necessary for the production of atomic energy (List 1, Entry 6) belong to the Centre and so also oil fields and mineral oil resources, petroleum and petroleum products, and other dangerously inflammable liquids and substances (Entry 53). Similarly, Central Government is empowered to regulate mines and mineral development to the extent to which it is in public interest to do so (Entry 54). Moreover, the regulation of labour and safety in mines and oil fields is also a Central subject (Entry 55).

In the field of transport, roads, bridges, ferries, and other means of communication (not specified in List I), municipal tramways, ropeways, inland waterways and traffic thereon and vehicles other than mechanically propelled vehicles belong to the State List (Entry 13). However, this is subject to certain provisions in the Union List and the Concurrent List. Thus, national highways, and national waterways (List I, Entries 23 and 24 respectively) belong to the Central Government. Similarly, the Centre has concurrent jurisdiction over ports other than major ports, and shipping and navigation on inland waterways (List III, Entries 31 and 32 respectively). It may be noted that Centre enjoys exclusive powers in major areas of transport and communications. The following fields are included in the Union List: Railways, maritime shipping and navigation, major ports, airways, and posts and telegraphs (entries 22, 25, 27, 29 and 31 respectively).

The all important sphere of industries falls within the purview of Sate List (Entry 24) but through the Constitution (Seventh Amendment) Act, 1956, this field was made subject to Entries 7 and 52 of the Union List. Before this amendment entry 24 of State List was subject only to the provisions of Entry 52 of Union List. Entry 7 covers industries considered necessary for the purpose of defence or for the prosecution of war. Entry 52 covers industries the control of which by the Centre is considered expedient in public interest. Besides this, the Centre also enjoys concurrent jurisdiction (List III, Entry 33) in many matters related to industries. The main legislation used by the Centre to exercise its right under entry 52 is the Industrial (Development and Regulation) Act, 1951, the first schedule of which includes industries brought under the Central control in public interest. Almost all important industries in the country are included in this schedule. Added to this control is the Central ownership of a vast public sector comprising industrial, financial and commercial enterprises. However, in view of the liberalisation and privatisation moves of the Government since 1991, the Central authority in the industrial sphere is likely to get weakened in the years to come and it is unlikely that the States would insist for powers being relinquished by the Centre. Still, it cannot be gainsaid that Centre's inroads into State subjects have caused stresses and strains in the relations between the two-tiers of the Government.

34.4 Constitution (Forty-sixth Amendment) Act, 1982 and the Consignment Tax (see section 21.7 of chapter 21 of this book).

34.5 Financial Autonomy for States

Although the proponents are vague in defining greater financial autonomy for the States, it should, *inter alia*, include transfer of additional taxation heads from the Centre to the States. If such a transfer is to take place, the main beneficiaries would be the richer States who have adequate bases to collect tax revenues. What will a poor State like Orissa or Bihar do with more taxation powers in view of the already low standard of living of their people? The solution lies more in the speedy development of the backward States which will increase tax collections automatically with existing taxation powers.

Another question is whether the States have adequately used the taxation powers already available to them? Taxation of agricultural incomes is a State subject but unfortunately this source has not been tapped by the States. Presently, about half a dozen States levy agricultural income tax, in three of them it is confined to plantation crops, and in all the cases the revenue is meagre. The share of this tax in the total revenue from States' own taxes has remained negligible, just around 1 per cent. Similarly, land revenue which was the principal direct tax of the States at the time of Independence has been given up partially or fully by most of the States.

Moreover, any weakening of the financial strength of the Central Government will adversely affect the economic viability of weaker States and Special Category States. The backward States have often argued for a financially strong Centre to ensure their own speedy development. After all, Centre's duties are not confined to defence and external affairs only but extend also to correct regional imbalances. Thus, the system of Centre-State financial relations is a tug-of-war not only between the Centre and the States but also among the States themselves.

Is there a need to make changes in the existing arrangements relating to division of taxation powers between the Centre and the States? In this connection, the Commission on Centre-State Relations, 1988, observed, "Generally, the States have stated that there is no need to make any changes in the division of the areas of taxation envisaged in the Constitution. In fact, one State has pointed out that any transfer of taxation fields now with the Union to the States would make the rich States richer and the poor States poorer. The Union Ministry of Finance also holds that the present system has a sound rational basis and may not require any alteration." [1] A pragmatic approach based on national outlook is required to remove irritants in Centre-State financial relations.

34.6 Towards Co-operative Federalism

According to the Ninth Five Year Plan (1997-2002), "The essence of a co-operative federalism is that the Centre and the State Governments should be guided by the broader national concerns of using the available resources for the benefit of the people. Co-operative federalism encourages the Government at different levels to take advantage of a large national market, diverse and rich natural resources and the potential of human capabilities in all parts of the country and from all sections of the society for building a prosperous nation. Co-operative federalism makes it possible to raise all the available resources by the Government at different levels in a co-ordinated way and channel them for use for the common good of the people. This requires a harmonious relationship and co-operative spirit between the Centre and the States and among the States themselves. While a healthy competition among the States for evolving efficient and socially desirable policies and programmes is welcome, any competition which nullifies each other's advantages in development and erodes the resource base of the States should be avoided. Co-operative federalism is intended to ensure a minimum bundle of basic services and a nationally acceptable level of living for all the people of the country." [2]

Notes

1. Government of India, *Report of the Commission on Centre-State Relations* (Chairman: Justice R.S. Sarkaria), 1988, Part I, p. 255.
2. Government of India, Planning Commission, *Ninth Five Year Plan* (1997-2002), Vol. I, p. 241.

Part VII: State-Local Financial Relations in India

This Part describes the functional responsibilities and sources of revenue of local bodies, explains the present constitutional arrangements relating to state-local financial relations in India, and examines the role of various statutory bodies in this regard.

35

State-Local Financial Relations in India

This chapter describes the functional responsibilities and sources of revenue of local bodies, explains the present constitutional arrangements relating to State-Local fiscal relations in India, and examines the role of various statutory bodies in this regard.

Rapid urbanisation has increased the functional responsibilities of municipalities in India. To meet the scale and challenge of urbanisation, municipal governments are always looking for additional funds from various sources.

Since a significant part of national income originates in urban areas, efforts must be made to maintain and enhance urban productivity which, in turn, depends on the level and quality of urban infrastructure. The demand for urban infrastructure services has increased, and is likely to accelerate further, due to rising personal incomes, rapid growth of population, and general increase in economic activities. Inability of municipal governments to meet the rising demand would adversely affect growth prospects of the economy.

35.1 Functions of Local Bodies

Functional responsibilities of local bodies vary from country to country and within a country. Still some common patterns are discernible. Broadly speaking, the functions of a local body (e.g. a municipality) can be divided into the following three categories.

35.1.1 Essential Civic Functions: The main function of a municipality is to provide and maintain core (or essential) civic services. These include: refuse collection, street lighting, water supply, sewage disposal, fire protection, abattoirs, and primary health services. These are services for which decision-making rests with the municipalities.

35.1.2 Regulatory Functions: These functions pertain to regulation of industry, trade and construction activities. Municipalities issue licences, permits and levy fees of various kinds, and also impose fines for violation of rules and regulations. Charges for regulatory functions should be so fixed as to cover at least the cost of administration and surveillance. If these services are subsidised it would put strain on resources.

35.1.3 Agency Functions: These are functions (e.g. protection of environment) which are funded out of State revenues by specific transfers.

35.2 Financing of Local Bodies

In the public finance literature, the following general rules are mentioned as regards the financing of local bodies.

1. Where the benefits of a local public service are measurable and accrue to readily identifiable individuals/households within a jurisdiction, user charges are the most appropriate method of financing the service.
2. Local public services which are services to general public in the sense that identification of beneficiaries and measurement of benefits to individuals /households is difficult, should be financed by taxes on local residents. Such services include traffic control, street lighting, security, and general administration.
3. Services the benefits of which spill over to neighbouring jurisdictions should be financed by intergovernmental transfers. These services include health, education, anti-pollution measures, and other social welfare activities.
4. Long-term borrowings are the appropriate source to finance capital projects with long-term gains.

Higher level governments generally assign certain taxes to local bodies to augment their resources. Tax literature suggests the following principles regarding assignment of taxes to local bodies.

1. Municipal governments should be assigned those taxes that are leviable on bases which are 'immobile' or 'location-specific' and those whose burden cannot be exported outside the municipal jurisdiction. Property tax is a case in point.
2. Local tax base should be easily identifiable and its incidence transparent.
3. Tax yield should be stable, predictable, and buoyant.
4. Rate schedule of the tax should possess a reasonable degree of progressivity.
5. The tax should be easy to administer.

Based on the foregoing considerations, the following taxes are generally assigned to local bodies: (a) property tax, (b) entertainment tax, (c) tax on professions, (d) tax on advertisements and (e) Octroi/tolls.

35.3 Constitutional Provisions

Entry 5 of List II (State List) of the Seventh Schedule to the Constitution of India refers to local bodies as institutions created by State Governments. Furthermore, the Directive Principles of the Constitution (Article 40) requires the strengthening of the units of local self-government in the States, particularly *panchayati raj* Institutions. However, little was done in this regard during the first three decades of Independence. As a result, these institutions could not function effectively because of (a) inadequate devolution of functions and financial powers (b) failure to hold regular elections and prolonged supersession and (c) lack of participation from weaker sections of society. Consequently, local bodies in many States had become weak and ineffective as units of self-government in our democratic set up. It was only in 1991 that Bills were introduced in the Parliament to amend the Constitution for providing constitutional status to the *panchayats* and municipalities.

35.4 Decentralisation Initiative, 1992

The Seventy-third and Seventy-fourth Amendment Bills relating to *panchayats* and municipalities respectively were introduced in the Parliament in September 1991 to provide constitutional remedy for the inadequacies plaguing these bodies which were unable to perform effectively as vibrant democratic units of self-government. The Bills were referred to two joint bodies of Parliament and after necessary revision were reintroduced in July 1992, and passed by Parliament in December 1992. Both the Bills were ratified by the required number of States [Article 368(ii)] and the President gave his assent in April 1993. The Seventy-third Amendment Act relating to *panchayats* came into force from April 24, 1993. The Seventy-fourth Amendment Act relating to municipalities came into force from June 1, 1993. The changes made by the Seventy-third and Seventy-fourth Amendment Acts to the Constitution were of historical importance and are summarised in Table 35.1.

The passage of the Constitution (Seventy-third Amendment) Act, 1992 marked a watershed in the history of modern India. With this amendment, a uniform structure of *panchayats* emerged throughout the country.

Article 243 G read with Eleventh Schedule of the Constitution explicitly requires the States to devolve powers and authority on *panchayats* which may be necessary to enable them to function as institutions of self-government. The Eleventh Schedule of the Constitution is reproduced in Table 35.2.

Similarly, the passage of the Constitution (Seventy-fourth Amendment) Act, 1992 was a landmark in the history of municipal administration in India. Article 243W read with Twelfth Schedule of the Constitution provides the illustrative list for the devolution of functions to the municipalities. The Twelfth Schedule of the Constitution is reproduced in Table 35.3. Many States have amended their municipal laws to ensure conformity with the new constitutional provisions.

In short, *panchayats* and municipalities are now constitutional bodies forming third tier to the federal polity of India. India's decentralisation initiative in the form of Seventy-third and Seventy-fourth Amendments poses challenges and offers opportunities.

Table 35.1: Seventy-third and Seventy-fourth Constitutional Amendment Acts

Act	Date on which came into force	Amendments made
Constitution (Seventy-third Amendment) Act 1992	24. 4. 1993	A new Part IX relating to Panchayats was inserted. In clause (3) of Article 280, sub-clause (bb) was inserted which provides for measures to supplement the resources of the Panchayats. Eleventh Schedule added to the Constitution which provides an illustrative list for the devolution of functions to Panchayats.
Constitution (Seventy-fourth Amendment) Act, 1992	1. 6. 1993	A new Part IXA relating to Municipalities was inserted. In clause (3) of Article 280, sub-clause (c) was relettered as sub-clause (d) and before sub-clause (d) as so relettered, sub-clause (c) was inserted which provides for measures to supplement the resources of the Municipalities. Twelfth Schedule added to the Constitution which provides an illustrative list for the devolution of functions to Municipalities.

Source: Government of India, Ministry of Law, Justice and Company Affairs, *The Constitution of India (Supplement to the Third Edition)*, 1994.

35.5 Constitution (Seventy-fourth Amendment) Act, 1992

Through this amendment a new Part IX-A relating to municipalities was incorporated in the Constitution to provide for, *inter alia,* the constitution of three types of municipalities, viz. *Nagar Panchayat* for a transitional area, i.e. an area in transition from a rural to urban area [1]; Municipal Council for smaller urban area, and Municipal Corporation for larger urban area (Article 243 Q).

Table 35.2: Eleventh Schedule of the Constitution (Article 243 G)

1.	Agriculture, including agricultural extension.
2.	Land improvement, implementation of land reforms, land consolidation and soil conservation.
3.	Minor irrigation, water management and watershed development.
4.	Animal husbandry, dairying and poultry.
5.	Fisheries.
6.	Social forestry and farm forestry.
7.	Minor forest produce.
8.	Small-scale industries, including food processing industries.
9.	Khadi, village and cottage industries.
10.	Rural housing.
11.	Drinking water
12.	Fuel and fodder.
13.	Roads, culverts, bridges, ferries, waterways and other means of communication.
14.	Rural electrification, including distribution of electricity.
15.	Non-conventional energy sources.
16.	Poverty alleviation programmes.
17.	Education, including primary and secondary schools.
18.	Technical training and vocational education.
19.	Adult and non-formal education.
20.	Libraries.
21.	Cultural activities.
22.	Markets and fairs.
23.	Health and sanitation, including hospitals, primary health centres and dispensaries.
24.	Family welfare.
25.	Women and child development.
26.	Social welfare, including welfare of the handicapped and mentally retarded.
27.	Welfare of the weaker sections, and in particular, of the Scheduled Castes and the Scheduled Tribes.
28.	Public distribution system.
29.	Maintenance of community assets.

Table 35.3: Twelfth Schedule of the Constitution (Article 243 W)

1.	Urban planning including town planning.
2.	Regulation of land-use and construction of buildings.
3.	Planning for economic and social development.
4.	Roads and bridges.
5.	Water supply for domestic, industrial and commercial purposes.
6.	Public health, sanitation conservancy and solid waste management.
7.	Fire services.
8.	Urban forestry, protection of the environment and promotion of ecological aspects.
9.	Safeguarding the interests of weaker sections of society, including the handicapped and mentally retarded.
10.	Slum improvement and upgradation.
11.	Urban poverty alleviation.
12.	Provision of urban amenities and facilities such as parks, gardens, play-grounds.
13.	Promotion of cultural, educational and aesthetic aspects.
14.	Burials and burial grounds; cremations, cremation grounds and electric crematoriums.
15.	Cattle ponds; prevention of cruelty to animals.
16.	Vital statistics including registration of births and deaths.
17.	Public amenities including street lighting, parking lots, bus stops and public conveniences.
18.	Regulation of slaughter houses and tanneries.

The Constitution (Seventy-fourth Amendment) Act, 1992 conferred constitutional status to the structure and mandate of municipalities so as to enable them to function as vibrant democratic and self-governing institutions at the grassroots level. The objectives of the Seventy-fourth Amendment include decentralisation of power and popular participation in the planning, management, and delivery of civic services. The salient features of the Seventy-fourth Amendment are the following.

35.5.1 Salient Features:

1. It provides a framework for the assignment of appropriate governmental functions to municipalities through the Twelfth Schedule of the Constitution read with Article 243 W. The Twelfth Schedule defines the functional domain of municipalities. Many of the functions included in this Schedule have

distributional and developmental attributes.

The Twelfth Schedule generally contains traditional functions of municipalities. However, some non-traditional functions are also discernible from the list. These are: (a) protection of the environment and promotion of ecological aspects, (b) safeguarding the interests of weaker sections of society including the handicapped and mentally retarded, (c) urban poverty alleviation, and (d) promotion of cultural and aesthetic aspects.

2. States are statutorily required to constitute a finance commission (Article 243-I and 243-Y), once in every five years, to recommend to their legislatures measures to improve municipal finances including (i) assignment of taxes, duties, tolls, and fees, (ii) sharing of state taxes, and (iii) provision of grants-in-aid.

3. The Finance Commission constituted by the Government of India is obligated to recommend measures to augment the Consolidated Fund of State Governments to supplement the resources of the municipalities on the basis of the recommendations made by the State Finance Commissions [Article 280(3)(c)].

4. It is mandatory to constitute in every State at the district level a District Planning Committee to consolidate and prepare development plan for the district as a whole (Article 243 ZD). Similarly, it is mandatory to constitute in every metropolitan area a Metropolitan Planning Committee to prepare a development plan for the metropolitan area as a whole (Article 243 ZE).

5. It mandates that a municipality if dissolved by a State Government, must be reconstituted within six months [Article 243 U(3)]. This is meant to ensure the continuity of civic affairs by 'elected' representatives of the people.

6. It ensures reservation of seats for women and other disadvantaged categories (Article 243 T).

The situation existing before and after the Seventy-fourth amendment is summarised in Table 35.4.

35.5.2 New Status of Municipalities: The Seventy-fourth amendment was made with the intention to make municipalities self-governing units. Are they so?

In the federal polity of India, local bodies are institutions created by the State Governments (entry 5 of List II of the Seventh Schedule). They enjoy only those powers and responsibilities which are assigned to them. Twelfth schedule of the Constitution lists the functions and responsibilities that may be transferred to municipalities. The permissive nature of Seventy-fourth Amendment is clear and the State Governments enjoy full discretion as regards the transfer of functions to municipalities.

No doubt, municipalities have acquired constitutional status after the said Amendment, they are completely dependent on respective State Governments in terms of self-governance.

Table 35.4: Status of Municipalities in India

Before the 74th Amendment	After the 74th Amendment
No all-India framework for devolution of functions	12th Schedule read with Article 243 W of the Constitution provides guidepoints for assignment of functions to municipalities.
High degree of arbitrariness in the system of fiscal transfers from the State Governments to municipalities. No periodic assessment of financial needs of municipalities	State Finance Commission (SFC) to be constituted statutorily in every State every Fifth year (Article 243-I and 243-Y) to review the financial position of municipalities and suggest measures to improve the same.
No role for the National Finance Commission as regards the finances of urban local bodies.	National Finance Commission is required to augment the Consolidated Fund of State Governments to supplement the resources of the municipalities on the basis of the recommendations made by the SFCs [Article 280(3)(c)].
Absence of constitutional bodies to prepare development plans for local areas.	Mandatory constitution of District Planning Committees (Article 243ZD) and Metropolitan Planning Committees (Article 243ZE) for consolidation and preparation of development plans.
Failure to hold regular elections and prolonged supersessions.	A municipality if dissolved by a State Government must be reconstituted within six months [Article 243 U(3)].
Lack of participation from weaker sections of society	Reservation of seats for women and other disadvantaged categories (Article 243 T).

35.5.3 Desirability and Feasibility of Uniformity in Municipal Functions: A careful reading of the Twelfth Schedule shows that many of the functions listed in it found place in the Municipal Acts of various States even before the enactment of the conformity legislations by them. Hence, the Twelfth Schedule has been generally accepted as a guiding list of municipal functions.

Should there be all-India uniformity in delegating functions and financial powers to local bodies? There is a weak case for all-India uniformity as regards functional domain of local bodies. State Governments and their local bodies have diverse economic and social conditions. It is by no means rational to expect uniformity in the functions and powers of the Greater Bombay Municipal Corporation and the municipality of a small township of a backward State. Similarly, it is debatable if local bodies should have uniform taxation powers.

Though it will be useful to prepare a reference list regarding functions (Eleventh and Twelfth Schedules), assigned taxes, shareable taxes, user charges, fees etc., all-India uniformity in these matters would be too much to expect.

Feasibility of all-India uniformity as regards the functional jurisdiction of municipalities is poor in view of the permissive nature of Seventy-fourth Amendment. It is highly unlikely that the 25 States of India would make uniform transfer of functions and financial powers to their respective municipalities. All-India uniformity in the functions of municipalities has to be ruled out in view of inter-State disparities.

Even at the level of a State, uniformity is not desirable in view of diverse city conditions and intra-State disparities. This fact has been recognised by the Constitution while providing for the constitution of three types of municipal bodies: Nagar Panchayats, Municipal Councils, and Municipal Corporations (Article 243 Q). However, it does not distinguish between the functional domains of the three types of municipal bodies. The determination of the functions of municipalities of different sizes is left to the wisdom of the State Governments.

However, there exists a case for uniformity of functions among similar municipalities in a State. If a State chooses to allocate dissimilar functions and powers to similar municipalities (say Municipal Councils), there can be genuine resentment among the municipalities discriminated against. It is here that objective criteria based on population size, geographical area, or constitutional categorisation (Article 243 Q) are needed to prevent misuse of political authority.

The Constitution should provide, at least, a list of minimum functions to be transferred to municipalities of various types by the State Governments.

35.5.4 Role of State Finance Commissions: The State Finance Commission is set up under Article 243-I read with Article 243-Y of the Constitution. It is required to review the financial position of the municipalities and make recommendations as to

(a) the principles which should govern –

i. the distribution between the State and the Municipalities of the net proceeds of taxes, duties, tolls and fees leviable by the State, which may be divided between them, and the allocations between the Municipalities of their respective shares of such proceeds.

ii. the determination of the taxes, duties, tolls and fees which may be assigned to, or appropriated by, the Municipalities.

iii. the grants-in-aid to Municipalities from the Consolidated Fund of the State.

(b) the measures needed to improve the financial position of the Municipalities.

(c) any other matter referred to the Finance Commission in the interest of sound finance of the Municipalities.

As required under the Constitution, all State Governments have set up Finance Commissions. These State Finance Commissions (SFCs) are expected to strengthen local bodies so that they may function as democratic units for the socio-economic development of urban and rural areas of our country.

The task of the First Finance Commission of a State was difficult and arduous in the absence of precedence and it was expected to make suo moto all such studies in areas which never existed before. Nevertheless, the work of the First Finance Commission was crucial because it paved the way for subsequent commissions. The following observations may be made in this regard.

1. The new Constitutional arrangement (Seventy-fourth Amendment) implies that the whole range of a State's tax revenue is open to sharing with municipalities. SFCs are expected to evolve principles of tax assignment, tax sharing, and grants to municipalities with a view to mitigate their weak financial position. They are also required to evolve criteria with regard to adequacy and objectivity of grants.
2. Sharing of State tax revenue with municipalities depends wholly on the discretion of State Government.
3. In determining devolution of funds, the SFCs would do well to keep in mind, *inter alia*, the following factors.

(a) Resource position of the State.

(b) Normative deficits of municipalities. Any system which underestimates the gap between revenue and expenditure should be discouraged.

(c) The degree of dependence of municipalities for funds on the State Government.

(d) Capacity of a municipality to utilise devolved resources.

(e) A State Finance Commission may consider introduction of a system of incentives and disincentives into the entire governmental grants on objective lines. Municipalities which are able to raise resources through levy of user charges and benefit taxes should be considered for incentive grants from the State Government.

A. Determination and Filling of Budgetary Gaps: A State Finance Commission has to determine the budgetary gaps of municipalities for the period of its award. Thereafter, it has to devise formulae for filling the gaps so determined.

Determination of the Budgetary Gaps: Two approaches may be followed for this purpose: (a) trend growth rate and (b) normative approach.

Under the first approach, average annual growth rate in a variable during a reference period (say 1994-95 through 2003-04) is worked out and the same is projected for a future period (say 2004-05 through 2008-2009). It is assumed that past behaviour of the variable will be repeated in future. Thus, 'actuals' or 'accounts' of revenue and expenditure of a government may be used to compute the average annual growth rate of the two aggregates over a stated period. Applying the computed average to a future period, one can work out estimated revenue, expenditure and budgetary gap for any future year.

Under the second method, revenue of a government is assessed normatively and certain norms are applied to assess expenditure. In other words, 'needs' and 'capacities' of different governments are assessed normatively and such normative assessments are used to meet budgetary gaps of the governments. More specifically, fiscal performance of a government is judged on the basis of *what ought to be* rather than *what it actually is.*

In the context of the work of a State Finance Commission, normative approach should apply to both the State Government and municipalities and that the assessment of revenue and expenditure should be done in a manner so as to maintain incentives for greater revenue efforts and economy in spending.

Filling the Gap: Once budgetary gaps of municipalities are determined, the next task of a State Finance Commission is to devise formulae for filling these gaps. For this purpose, it has to work out a judicious mix of a tax devolution and grants.

It is noteworthy that the term 'gap-filling' in the context of State-municipal fiscal relations has a different connotation than at the national level.

At the national level, even after the transfer to the States of a share of divisible taxes, the resources of some of the States may remain inadequate to meet their needs. Thus, a Finance Commission determines the grants equal to deficit of each State so that the non-Plan revenue accounts of the States are balanced or left with a surplus every year. In other words, deficits of non-Plan revenue account which remain after tax devolution are covered through grants.

This is called the gap-filling approach (or more appropriately net gap-filling approach).

It is possible that even before tax devolution from the Centre, some high-income States have surplus in their non-Plan revenue account. Thus, while a State cannot be denied a part of a shared Central tax even if it has no demonstrated financial need, grants are given upon genuine financial needs of the States.

However, the working of a State Finance Commission is different. Like the National Finance Commission, it is not bound by any constitutional restrictions regarding the type of taxes to be shared with municipalities. In fact, the whole field of State taxation is open to it for determining tax devolution. In other words, tax devolution and grants are to be used simultaneously to cover the budgetary gaps of municipalities. In this case, gap-filling means how to cover the projected budgetary gaps of municipalities through a judicious mix of tax devolution and grants with due regard to the underlying principles of the two methods to effect transfers from a higher to a lower level government.

35.6 Municipal Commercial Borrowings

Plan allocations of Central and State Governments are the chief source of financing capital projects of municipal governments. Other sources of finance include (a) internal resources of municipalities, (b) institutional resources (HUDCO etc.), and (c) multilateral agencies.

The scope for additional funds from Central and State Governments is limited in view of the pressing need to reduce fiscal deficit. Similarly, institutional finances at low cost are unlikely to be available in the wake of financial sector reforms. Under such circumstances, municipal authorities should be permitted access to the capital market to mobilise additional resources. Recent expansion and modernisation of capital market in India suggests that inflow of capital into equity and debt market is quite high if attractive rate of return is offered.

35.6.1 Rationale for Municipal Commercial Borrowings: It is both fair and efficient that projects with long-term benefits are financed through long-term borrowings. If long-term capital projects are financed out of current revenues and/or short-term borrowings, the future generations would enjoy free-riding. Since the benefits of a capital project are reaped over a long period of time, i.e. by more than one generation of tax payers, the financing of such projects should place the repayment burden on the present as well as future generations.

35.6.2 Limitations: Municipal access to capital market, though desirable, is hindered by a variety of factors which may be classified into two categories: (a) restrictions imposed by the higher level government, and (b) other constraints.

The Constitution of India imposes various types of restrictions on the borrowing powers of the State Governments which, in turn, impose restrictions on the borrowing powers of the municipalities under them. Since borrowings by the lower level government are guaranteed, in most cases, by the higher level government, the latter has a right to impose such restrictions. These restrictions apply to (a) type of debt, (b) amount of debt, (c) term of the debt, and (d) use of debt funds. Approval of the higher level government, which is often cumbersome, is needed before the debt is floated.

Thus, no municipal authority can borrow without an explicit sanction of its State Government. When the loan amount exceeds Rs. 25 lakh or the repayment period is over 30 years, local borrowings need Central approval under the provisions of the Local Authorities Loan Act, 1914 (a Central Legislation).

Among the 'other constraints', the more important are the following: Low credit worthiness of municipalities, their poor tract record as borrowers, and lack of trustworthy financial intermediaries.

Despite the foregoing hurdles, some municipalities in India have successfully tapped the bond market.

35.6.3 Factors Determining Success of Municipal Bonds: To attract a share of capital market for municipalities, the following conditions need to be satisfied.

1. Urban infrastructure projects should be commercially viable.
2. Municipal bonds are rated by some recognised credit rating institution. This will help build confidence of investors in the bond issue as well as help in its subsequent trading on the secondary market.
3. Such bonds should carry tax concessions.
4. Revenues accruing to the municipal entity are sufficiently elastic.
5. Security behind the debt taken by the municipal entity is sound.
6. Municipal entity makes provision for the creation of debt-servicing funds and the legal procedures for seeking recourse in the event of default.
7. Municipal entity is competent to pledge revenues for debt-servicing and extend collateral in terms of commercial property, plant and machinery and other assets.

35.7 Privatisation of Municipal Services

The scope for privatisation of some municipal services in order to reduce costs is a moot question.

Municipalities alone cannot handle huge infrastructural projects like water supply, sewage disposal, and urban transport. Involvement of central, state, and private sector is required to meet the scale of investment needed in these areas. Similarly, greater participation of private sector is desirable in the provision of civic services, particularly those the consumption of which can be attributed to individuals/households. There are many types of arrangement in respect of public-private partnership depending on situation. However, care should be taken not to dilute current social commitments while embarking on public-private partnership.

The historical and ideological resistance to private sector participation persists in most places. Consequently, few local bodies have tried out private sector participation in civic services on any significant scale. Wherever it has happened, the experiment has remained limited to disposal of solid wastes, and maintenance of parks.

The disenchantment with utility enterprises of municipalities is not conceptual but borne out of their inefficient and sometimes corrupt management. The merits of privatisation are seen in terms of improvement in efficiency and reduction in the budgetary burden of state-owned enterprises.

Though the need for private sector participation is widely felt, it is not openly expressed. Very rarely political parties have spoken publicly against the public sector. Contrarily, there is a stiff opposition by political parties to any move to undermine the importance of public sector. The strong unions of public sector enterprises come in handy for politicians to prevent the erosion of state and municipal activities.

35.8 Tenth Finance Commission on Local Bodies

The Tenth Finance Commission did not have any mandate, in its terms of reference, to make recommendations for the local bodies. However, the 73rd and 74th Constitutional amendments had become effective before the Commission had finalised its report and, therefore, it took the view that in terms of the sub-clauses (bb) and (c) of the article 280(3), it was obliged to make recommendations regarding measures needed to augment the Consolidated Fund of the States for supplementation of the resources of the panchayats and the municipalities. The Commission analysed the scope of such duty cast on it and made the following observations:

1. The need for augmentation of the Consolidated Fund of the States should first be ascertained and only thereafter the measures for such augmentation be recommended.
2. Such measures need not necessarily involve transfer of resources from the Centre.
3. Once the SFCs complete their task, the Finance Commission becomes duly bound to assess and build into the expenditure stream of the States the funding requirements for supplementing the resources of the panchayats and the municipalities. Measures needed for augmentation of the Consolidated

Funds of the States may be determined accordingly.

4. The responsibility for sharing and assigning taxes and providing grants to the local bodies rests with the States and does not stand transferred to the Centre.
5. The transfer of duties and functions listed in the Eleventh and Twelfth Schedules of the Constitution would also involve concomitant transfer of staff and resources. Transfers of duties and functions to the local bodies should, therefore, not entail any extra financial burden.

Since the recommendations of the State Finance Commissions were not available to the Tenth Finance Commission, the latter was in doubt whether it could recommend measures for augmenting State resources for the purpose of supplementing the resources of panchayats and municipalities. To resolve the dilemma, it decided to make ad hoc provision of specific grants to States in the following manner.

1. An ad hoc provision of Rs. 100 per capita of rural population in each State to be distributed amongst panchayats over and above their due by way of their share of the assigned taxes, duties, tolls, fees etc.
2. A provision of Rs. 1,000 crore for the five year period (1995-2000) covered by its recommendations for urban local bodies.

While making these provisions for grants to panchayats/municipalities, the Commission made it clear that this need not necessarily be a precedent for future Commissions.

35.9 Eleventh Finance Commission on Local Bodies

EFC was the first to be required by the President, in terms of the 73rd and 74th Amendments to the Constitution, to recommend the measures needed to augment the Consolidated Fund of a State to supplement the resources of the panchayats and municipalities in the State on the basis of the recommendations of the State Finance Commissions.

The EFC recommended grants totalling Rs. 10,000 crore for local bodies during 2000-2005, to be utilised mainly for maintenance of civic services. Of this, Rs. 1,600 crore per annum is for rural local bodies and Rs. 400 crore per annum is for urban local bodies. EFC recommended that the amounts of Rs. 1,600 crore and Rs. 400 crore provided for the panchayats and municipalities respectively, for each of the five years (2000-05) be distributed among the States on the following criteria and weights.

1. Population 40 per cent.
2. Index of decentralisation 20 per cent.
3. Distance from highest per capita income 20 per cent.
4. Revenue effort 10 per cent.

5. Geographical area 10 per cent.

The grants given to local bodies are primarily meant for maintenance of civil services including primary health and family welfare, education as well as other public utility services. Details regarding inter-State distribution are given in Chapter VIII of the Report of the Commission.

It is noteworthy that while a State cannot be denied a part of share in Central taxes even if it has no demonstrated financial need, grants are given upon genuine financial needs of the States. It is possible that even before tax devolution from the Centre, some high-income States have a surplus in their non-Plan revenue account. The Seventh Finance Commission identified Punjab, Haryana, Gujarat, Tamil Nadu, and Karnataka as such States. Thus, grants-in-aid along with share in taxes serve as a levelling up force to promote regional balanced development. From this, it may also be inferred that States as a whole are not affected whether transfers are made by one means (share in Central taxes) or another (grants). It is the total amount transferred which is important for them. However, the sources of transfer become important when it comes to individual States because the formulae applied for various transfers are different. It is not possible to adopt a single formula for all transfers in view of the differing nature of taxes and grants.

35.10 Twelfth Finance Commission on Local Bodies

The Commission made the following recommendations regarding local bodies.

A total grant of Rs. 20,000 crore for the panchayati raj institutions and Rs. 5,000 crore for the urban local bodies may be given to the states for the period 2005-10.

The PRIs should be encouraged to take over the assets relating to water supply and sanitation and utilize the grants for repairs/rejuvenation as also the O&M costs. The PRIs should, however, recover at least 50 percent of the recurring costs in the form of user charges.

Out of the grants allocated for the panchayats, priority should be given to expenditure on the O&M costs of water supply and sanitation. This will facilitate panchayats to take over the schemes and operate them.

At least 50 per cent of the grants provided to each state for the urban local bodies should be earmarked for the scheme of solid waste management through public-private partnership. The municipalities should concentrate on collection, segregation and transportation of solid waste. The cost of these activities, whether carried out in house or out sourced, could be met from the grants.

Besides expenditure on the O&M costs of water supply and sanitation in rural areas and on the schemes of solid waste management in urban areas, PRIs and

ULBs should, out of the grants allocated, give high priority to expenditure on creation of data base and maintenance of accounts through the use of modern technology and management systems, wherever possible. Some of the modern methods like GIS (Geographic Information Systems) for mapping of properties in urban areas and computerization for switching over to a modern system of financial management would go a long way in creating strong local governments, fulfilling the spirit of the 73rd and 74th Constitutional amendments.

The states may assess the requirement of each local body on the basis of the principles stated by us and earmark funds accordingly out of the total allocation re-commended by us.

Grants have not been recommended separately for the normal and the excluded areas under the fifth and sixth schedule of the Constitution. The states having such areas may distribute the grants recommended by us to all local bodies, including those in the excluded areas, in a fair and just manner.

The central government should not impose any condition other than those prescribed by us, for release or utilization of these grants, which are largely in the nature of a correction of vertical imbalance between the centre and the states.

The normal practice of insisting on the utilization of amounts already released before further releases are considered, may continue and the grants may be released to a state only after it certifies that the previous releases have been passed on to the local bodies. The amounts due to the states in the first year of our award period i.e. 2005-06 may be released without such an insistence.

State governments should not take more than 15 days in transferring the grants to local bodies after these are released by the central government. The centre should take a serious view of any undue delay on the part of the state.

The central government should take note of our views on the issues, while formulating or revising various policy measures. In particular, action may be taken to raise the ceiling on profession tax.

The state should adopt the best practices to improve the resources of the panchayats.

The suggestions made by us in respect of state finance commissions should be acted upon with a view to strengthening the institution of SFCs, so that it may play an effective role in the system of fiscal transfers to the third tier of government.

Note

1. Here, 'a transitional area', 'a smaller urban area', or 'a larger urban area' means such area as the Governor may specify by public notification having regard to the population of the area, the density of the population, the revenue generated for local administration, the percentage of employment in non-agricultural activities and such other factors.

Part VIII: Appendices

Appendix 1

Main Recommendations of the Task Force on Direct Taxes (Chairman: Vijay Kelkar), 2002

At the time of presenting the first batch of supplementary demands for grants to Parliament in July 2002, the Finance Minister had proposed setting up of two task forces to recommend measures for simplification and rationalization of direct and indirect taxes. Accordingly, two task forces were set up in September 2002 under the chairmanship of Vijay Kelkar, Adviser to Minister of Finance and Company Affairs.

The Task Force on Direct Taxes presented its consultation paper to the Government on November 2, 2002. The discussion paper on indirect taxes was presented on November 25, 2002. These consultation papers were made public to facilitate an informed discussion on tax policy.

After taking in to account the response on the discussion papers, the Task Forces submitted their final reports to the Government in December 2002. These Task Forces have made important recommendations on toning up tax administration to put in place a system that is simple, effective and at par with international standards.

The main recommendations on direct taxes relate to raising of exemption limit of personal income tax, rationalization of exemptions, abolition of concessional treatment to long-term capital gains, and abolition of wealth tax. In respect of indirect taxes, the main recommendations relate to widening of the tax base, removal of exemptions, expansion in the coverage of service tax etc.

The Task Force on Direct Taxes was assigned the following Terms of Reference.

1. Rationalisation and simplification of the direct taxes with a view to minimizing exemptions, removing anomalies and improving equity;
2. Improvement in taxpayer services so as to reduce compliance cost, impart transparency and facilitate voluntary compliance,
3. Redesigning procedures for strengthening enforcement so as to improve compliance of direct tax laws; and
4. Any other matter related to the above points.

Personal Income Tax: The Task Force recommended a two rate schedule for personal income tax.

Rate Structure of Personal Income Tax Recommended by the Task Force on Direct Taxes

Income level	Tax rate
Below Rs. 1,00,000	Nil
Rs. 1,00,000 – 4,00,000	20 per cent of the income in excess of Rs. 1,00,000
Above Rs. 4,00,000	Rs. 60,000 plus 30 per cent of the income in excess of Rs. 4,00,000

Source: Government of India, Ministry of Finance and Company Affairs, *Report of the Task Force on Direct Taxes* (Chairman: Vijay Kelkar), December 2002, p. 71.

It recommended the abolition of surcharge on income tax. It was of the opinion that revenue gain from levy of surcharge is generally illusory since such a levy has the effect of increasing the marginal rate of tax, which adversely affects compliance.

It recommended that residents but not ordinarily residents must be subjected to tax on their global/world-wide income at par with residents. To do so, this unusual category of resident but not ordinarily resident taxpayers must be deleted. Most countries across the world provide for only two status: residents and non-residents.

It recommended that standard deduction under section 16(1) of the Income Tax Act should be eliminated. However, the exemption of conveyance allowance subject to a ceiling of Rs. 9,600 should be continued. This should serve as a reasonable deduction for employment related expenses.

As regards tax treatment of agricultural income, the Task Force recommended as follows:

1. A tax rental arrangement should be designed whereby States should pass a resolution under Article 252 of the Constitution authorizing the Central Government to impose income tax on agricultural income. The taxes collected by the Centre would however be assigned to the States.
2. Tax from agricultural income for the purpose of allocation between States will be the difference between the tax on total income (including agricultural income) and the tax on total income net of agricultural income.
3. Where a taxpayer derives agricultural income from different States, the revenues attributable to a State will be in the ratio of the income derived from a particular State to the total agricultural income.
4. A separate tax return form should be prescribed for taxpayers deriving income from agriculture.

It recommended the elimination of the tax incentives for savings under section 88, section 80L, section 10(15)(i), section 10(15)(iib), section 10(15)(iic), section 10(15)(iid), section 10(15)(iv)(h) and section 10(15)(iv)(i) of the Income Tax Act. It insisted that these benefits must be immediately withdrawn and not through a sunset clause

It recommended that the basic exemption limit for senior citizens should be Rs. 50,000 more than the exemption limit for the general class of individual taxpayers. To put it differently, the exemption limit for senior citizens should be Rs. 1,50,000 as against Rs. 1,00,000 for the general category of individual taxpayers. It further recommended that the exemption limit for senior citizens should be revised as and when the exemption limit for the general category of individual taxpayers is revised. Still further, it recommended that this benefit of higher exemption limit should also be extended to widows.

Corporate Tax Reforms: The Task Force on Direct Taxes made the following recommendations for the reform of corporate income tax:

1. Reduction in corporate tax rate from the existing levels of 36.75 per cent to 30 per cent for domestic companies and to 35 per cent for foreign companies.
2. Exemption of dividend from taxation in the hands of the shareholders. There will also be no tax on distribution of dividends by a company.
3. Exemption of long-term capital gains on listed equity.
4. Elimination of Minimum Alternate Tax under section 115JB.
5. Removal of the distinction between unabsorbed depreciation and unabsorbed business loss.
6. Removal of the following deductions under section 10 and Chapter VIA of the Income Tax Act with immediate effect and not by a sunset clause:

- Elimination of section 10A and 10B of the Income Tax Act for all taxpayers other than those engaged in manufacturing computer software.
- In the case of taxpayers engaged in manufacturing computer software, the Government of India must take immediate steps to negotiate with foreign governments to enter into a comprehensive totalisation agreement leading to a single point incidence of taxes.
- Section 80 IA in respect of profit and gains from industrial undertakings engaged in infrastructure development or telecommunication service or development of industrial park or special economic zones or generation, transmission or distribution of power.
- Section 80IB in respect of profits and gains from certain industrial undertakings other than infrastructure development undertakings (this includes backward areas also).

- Section 80JJA in respect of profits and gains from business of collecting and processing of biodegradable wastes.
- Section 80 JJAA in respect of employment of new workman.
- Section 80M in respect of inter corporate dividends.
- The phase out programme in respect of sections 80HHB, 80HHBA, 80HHC, 80HHD, 80HHE, 80HHF, 80-O, 80R, 80RR and 80RRA will continue.

7. Depreciation rates for the purposes of depreciation allowance under section 32 should be reduced to 15 per cent for the general category of plant and machinery and to appropriate lower rates for other categories of block of assets.
8. Elimination of section 33AB relating to tea development allowance.
9. Elimination of section 33AC relating to reserve for shipping business.
10. Elimination of section 33B relating to rehabilitation allowance.
11. Elimination of section 35 relating to scientific research.
12. Elimination of section 35AC relating to expenditure on eligible projects.
13. Elimination of section 35CCA relating to expenditure by way of payment to associations and institutions for carrying out rural development programmes.
14. Elimination of section 36(1)(iii) in respect of interest on borrowed capital.
15. The provision for bad and doubtful debts allowable under section 36(1)(viia) of the Income Tax Act will henceforth be restricted to the amount of provision debited to profit and loss account as audited subject to the maximum amount of provisioning permitted under the prudential guidelines issued by the Reserve Bank of India.

Capital Gains: The Task Force on Direct Taxes recommended that concessional treatment of long-term capital gains through a reduced scheduler rate of tax must be abolished. In other words, the long-term capital gains would be aggregated with other incomes and subjected to taxation at the normal rates.

Wealth Tax: In view of the maegre revenue and problems of administration and compliance, the Task Force recommended the abolition of wealth tax.

Expenditure Tax: The present tax on expenditure in hotels is in the nature of a consumption tax. It was introduced as a separate tax in the absence of a tax on services. Since tax on services has since been introduced, it is only appropriate that this levy is merged with the service tax.

Appendix 2

Main Recommendations of the Task Force on Indirect Taxes (Chairman: Vijay Kelkar), 2002

Commenting on the present weaknesses of the indirect tax system, the Task Force on Indirect Taxes observed, "despite all what has been done, the indirect tax system in the country suffers from the following drawbacks:

1. Lack of confidence in the tax administration on account of too much discretion, absence of accountability and a pro-revenue bias in all matters, especially quasi-judicial.
2. Alienation from tax administration, which manifests into corrupt practices and low compliance.
3. Uncertainty about tax policy, administration and absence of time bound decision making all of which affects business decisions.
4. Complexities of laws and procedures on account of lack of codification which is exploited for private gain by the unscrupulous taxpayer and the tax collector.
5. Too many laws and procedures which create an environment of confusion and mistrust.
6. Too many conditions attached to each exemption and procedure, delay in decision making and increase in transaction costs.
7. Absence of transparency in tax planning.
8. Customer orientation is missing in the tax collectors who view all taxpayers with suspicion.

Customs Duties: At present, besides the basic customs duty, we have the following levies.

1. Additional duty of customs (or countervailing duty or CVD).
2. Special additional duty of customs (SAD).
3. Additional duty of customs on motor spirit.
4. Additional duty of customs on high speed diesel oil.
5. Export duty.
6. Cesses on exports.
7. Anti-dumping/safeguard duty.

As a policy, multiplicity of levies must be reduced. Accordingly, it is recommended that there should be only three types of duties, viz. basic customs duty, additional duty of customs (or countervailing duty) and anti-dumping (safeguard duties). All other duties should be removed.

Import Duty Structure Recommended by the Task Force on Indirect Taxes

0 per cent	For items like life-saving drugs and equipments, sovereign imports (defence and security related goods) and imports by RBI.
For other goods by 2004-05	10 per cent for raw materials, inputs and intermediate goods. 20 per cent for consumer durables.
By 2006-07	5 per cent for basic raw materials like coal, ores and concentrates, xylenes etc. 8 per cent for intermediate goods which will be used for future manufacture (capital goods, basic chemicals, metals etc.) 10 per cent for finished goods other than consumer durables. 20 per cent for consumer durables.

Source: Government of India, Ministry of Finance and Company Affairs, *Report of the Task Force on Indirect Taxes*, December 2002, p. 169.

As regards customs exemptions, the Task Force on Indirect Taxes recommended, "As a policy, all exemptions must be removed except in case of:
1. Life-saving goods.
2. Goods of security and strategic interest.
3. Goods for relief and charitable purposes.
4. International obligations including contracts."

Excise Duties: The Task Force on Indirect Taxes recommended the following excise duty structure.

Excise Duty Structure Recommended by the Task Force on Indirect Taxes

0 per cent	for life-saving drugs and equipments, security items, food items, necessities and the like, and agricultural products.
6 per cent	for processed food products and matches.
14 per cent	standard rate for all items not mentioned against other rates.
20 per cent	for motor vehicles, air-conditioners and aerated water.
Separate rates for tobacco products and their substitutes (like pan masala)	

Source: Government of India, Ministry of Finance and Company Affairs, *Report of the Task Force on Indirect Taxes*, December 2002, p. 181.

As regards duty exemption for the small scale sector, the Task Force on Indirect Taxes recommended

- Duty exemption should be extended to only small units with a turnover of Rs. 50 lakh.
- Duty exemption limit for the larger SSI units should be gradually brought down to Rs. 50 lakh as per the following time frame: from Rs. 100 lakh to Rs. 75 lakh by the year 2004-05 and from Rs. 75 lakh to Rs. 50 lakh by the year 2005-06.

Value Added Tax (VAT): The Task Force on Indirect Taxes unanimously acknowledged that VAT is a major reform in the indirect tax system of India. For a smooth and speedy implementation of VAT at the level of Centre and States, it made the following recommendations.

1. A publicity awareness programme should be started jointly by the Central and State Governments and the former should extend financial support for this, if required. Since State VAT is expected to be implemented from 1.4.2003 it is also necessary that the publicity awareness programme should be implemented at the earliest.
2. An attempt should be made towards uniformity of all State legislations, procedures and documentation relating to VAT.
3. The issue of compensation, if it arises, must be primarily tackled through mutually acceptable mechanism of additional resource mobilization through service tax and not through budgetary support.
4. With the introduction of VAT, all other local taxes be discontinued.
5. Whereas additional duty of excise may continue for textiles up to 2005, it may continue even thereafter for cigarettes which should not be subjected to VAT.
6. The VAT scheme should provide for grant of credit of duty by the importing State for the duty paid in the exporting State, in the course of inter-State movement of goods.
7. For the stability and continuity of VAT, the possibility of a VAT Council or a permanent suitable alternative, vested with adequate powers to take steps against discriminatory taxes and practices and eliminate barriers to free flow of trade and commerce across the country, should be explored.

Appendix 3

Main Recommendations of the Advisory Group on Tax Policy and Tax Administration for the Tenth Plan (Chairman: Parthasarathi Shome), 2001

The Planning Commission constituted an Advisory Group on Tax Policy and Tax Administration for the Tenth Plan in July 2000 to study tax policy and tax administration issues and make appropriate recommendations. The Group submitted its Final Report in May 2001. The Group recommended deletion of a number of exemptions and deductions which were considered redundant and not in tune with modern tax systems. Major recommendations of the Group for the Tenth Plan are as follows

Direct Taxes (income tax)

1. Maximum marginal rate of personal income tax be retained at 30 per cent
2. Tax incentives under sections 80CCC, 88, 80L, and 10(15) of the Income Tax Act be abolished, at least in phases.
3. Tax concessions under sections 80D, 80DD, 80DDB and 80E be given in the form of tax credit rather than as deduction from income.
4. Provisions under sections 80-1A and 80-1B relating to regional/industrial development be deleted.
5. Corporate tax rate should not exceed the maximum marginal rate of personal income tax.

Indirect Taxes

1. For Union excise, introduce two-rate structure of 16 per cent together with a higher rate.
2. SSI units below a turnover of Rs. 3 crore should pay a duty of 85-90 per cent of the normal rate if they opt for CENVAT credit.
3. The median tariff rate (import duty) should be brought down to 15 per cent in 2004-05.
4. Remove as many exemptions as possible.

Appendix 4

The Constitution (Eightieth Amendment) Act, 2000

[9th June, 2000]

BE it enacted by Parliament in the Fifty-first Year of the Republic of India as follows:-

1. This Act may be called the Constitution (Eightieth Amendment) Act, 2000.

2. In article 269 of the Constitution, for clauses (1) and (2), the following clauses shall be substituted, namely:-

'(1) Taxes on the sale or purchase of goods and taxes on the consignment of goods shall be levied and collected by the Government of India but shall be assigned and shall be deemed to have been assigned to the States on or after the 1st day of April, 1996 in the manner provided in clause (2).

Explanation – For the purposes of this clause, -

(a) the expression "taxes on the sale or purchase of goods" shall mean taxes on sale or purchase of goods other than newspapers, where such sale or purchase takes place in the course of inter-State trade or commerce;

(b) the expression "taxes on the consignment of goods" shall mean taxes on the consignment of goods (whether the consignment is to the person making it or to any other person), where such consignment takes place in the course of inter-State trade or Commerce.

(2) The net proceeds in any financial year of any such tax, except in so far as those proceeds represent proceeds attributable to Union territories, shall not form part of the Consolidated Fund of India, but shall be assigned to the States within which that tax is leviable in that year, and shall be distributed among those States in accordance with such principles of distribution as may be formulated by Parliament by law'.

3. For article 270 of the Constitution, the following article shall be substituted and shall be deemed to have been substituted with effect from the 1st day of April, 1996, namely:-

'270. (1) All taxes and duties referred to in the Union List, except the duties and taxes referred to in articles 268 and 269, respectively, surcharge on taxes and duties referred to in article 271 and any cess levied for specific purposes under any law made by parliament shall be levied and collected by the Government of India and shall be distributed between the Union and the States in the manner provided in clause (2).

(2) Such percentage, as may be prescribed, of the net proceeds of any such tax or duty in any financial year shall not form part of the Consolidated Fund of India, but shall be assigned to the States within which that tax or duty is leviable in that year, and shall be distributed among those States in such manner and fr0m such time as may be prescribed in the manner provided in clause (3).

(3) In this article, 'prescribed" means, –

(i) until a Finance Commission has been constituted, prescribed by the President by order, and

(ii) after a Finance Commission has been constituted, prescribed by the President by order after considering the recommendations of the Finance Commission.'

4. (1) Article 272 of the Constitution shall be omitted.

(2) Notwithstanding anything contained in sub-section (1), where any sum equivalent to the whole or any part of the net proceeds of the Union duties of excise including additional duties of excise which are levied and collected by the Government of India and which has been distributed as grants-in-aid to the States after the 1st day of April, 1996, but before the commencement of this Act, such sum shall be deemed to have been distributed in accordance with the provisions of article 270, as if article 272 had been omitted with effect from the 1st day of April, 1996.

(3) Any sum equivalent to the whole or any part of the net proceeds of any other tax or duty that has been distributed as grants-in-aid to the States after the 1st day of April 1996 but before the commencement of this Act shall be deemed to have been distributed in accordance with the provisions of article 270.

Appendix 5

Main Recommendations of the Twelfth Finance Commission

The Twelfth Finance Commission (TFC) was appointed on November 1, 2002 to make recommendations regarding the distribution between the Union and the States of net proceeds of shareable taxes, the principles which should govern the grants-in-aid of the revenues of States from the Consolidated Fund of India and the measures needed to augment the Consolidated Fund of a State to supplement the resources of local bodies in the State on the basis of the recommendations made by the Finance Commission of the State. The terms of reference mandated the Commission to review the state of the finances of the Union and the States and suggest a Plan by which the Governments, collectively and severally, restore budgetary balance, achieve macroeconomic stability and debt reduction along with equitable growth. Furthermore, the Commission was also asked to suggest corrective measures for debt sustainability and to review the Fiscal Reform Facility introduced by the Central Government.

The Commission submitted its report on November 30, 2004 covering the period 2005-10. The recommendations of the Commission include a plan for restructuring of public finances of the Centre and the States through improvement in revenue mobilization and bringing down debt levels, and through enactment of fiscal responsibility legislation by States. The Commission recommended debt relief to States linked to fiscal reforms, doing away with the present system of Central assistance to State plans in the form of grants and loans and transfer of external assistance to States on the same terms and conditions as attached to such assistance by external funding agencies.

The TFC raised the share of States in shareable Central taxes from 29.5 per cent to 30.5 per cent. Total transfers to States recommended by the TFC amount to Rs. 7,55,752 crore over the five year period 2005-10. Of this, transfers by way of share in Central taxes and grants-in-aid amount to Rs. 6,13,112 crore and Rs. 1,42,640 crore, respectively.

The total transfers recommended by the TFC are higher by 73.8 per cent over those recommended by the Eleventh Finance Commission (EFC). Within the total transfers, while the share in Central taxes is higher by 62.9 per cent, grants-in-aid recommended by the TFC are higher by 143.5 per cent over those recommended by the EFC.

Main Recommendations

Restructuring Public Finances

1. Centre and States to improve the combined tax-GDP ratio to 17.6 per cent by 2009-10.
2. Combined debt-GDP ratio, with external debt measured at historical exchange rates, to be brought down to 75 per cent by 2009-10.
3. Fiscal deficit to GDP targets for the Centre and States to be fixed at 3 per cent.
4. Revenue deficit of the Centre and States to be brought down to zero by 2008-09.
5. Interest payments relative to revenue receipts to be brought down to 28 per cent and 15 per cent in the case of the Centre and States, respectively.
6. States to follow a recruitment policy in a manner so that the total salary bill, relative to revenue expenditure, net of interest payments, does not exceed 35 per cent.
7. Each State to enact a fiscal responsibility legislation providing for elimination of revenue deficit by 2008-09 and reducing fiscal deficit to 3 per cent of State Domestic Product.
8. The system of on-lending to be brought to an end over time. The long term goal should be to bring down debt-GDP ratio to 28 per cent each for the Centre and the States.

Sharing of Union Tax Revenues

1. The share of States in the net proceeds of shareable Central taxes fixed at 30.5 per cent, treating additional excise duties in lieu of sales tax as part of the general pool of Central taxes. Share of States to come down to 29.5 per cent, when States are allowed to levy sales tax on sugar, textiles and tobacco.
2. In case of any legislation enacted in respect of service tax, after the notification of the eighty eighth amendment to the Constitution, revenue accruing to a State should not be less than the share that would accrue to it, had the entire service tax proceeds been part of the shareable pool.
3. The indicative amount of overall transfers to States to be fixed at 38 per cent of the Centre's gross revenue receipts.

Local Bodies

1. A grant of Rs. 20,000 crore for the Panchayati Raj institutions and Rs. 5,000 crore for urban local bodies to be given to States for the period 2005-10.
2. Priority to be given to expenditure on operation and maintenance (O&M) costs of water supply and sanitation, while utilizing the grants for the Panchayats. At least 50 per cent of the grants recommended for urban local bodies to be earmarked for the scheme of solid waste management through

public-private partnership.

Calamity Relief

1. The scheme of Calamity Relief Fund (CRF) to continue in its present form with contributions from the Centre and States in the ratio of 75:25. The size of the Fund worked out at Rs. 21,333 crore for the period 2005-10.
2. The outgo from the Fund to be replenished by way of collection of National Calamity Contingent Duty and levy of special surcharges.
3. The definition of natural calamity to include landslides, avalanches, cloud burst and pest attacks.
4. Provision for disaster preparedness and mitigation to be part of State Plans and not calamity relief.

Grants-in-aid to States

1. The present system of Central assistance for State Plans, comprising grant and loan components, to be done away with, and the Centre should confine itself to extending plan grants and leaving it to States to decide their borrowings.
2. Non-plan revenue deficit grant of Rs. 56,856 crore recommended to 15 States for the period 2005-10. Grants amounting to Rs. 10,172 crore recommended for the education sector to eight States. Grants amounting to Rs. 5,887 crore recommended for the health sector for seven States. Grants to education and health sectors are additionalities over and above the normal expenditure to be incurred by States.
3. A grant of Rs. 15,000 crore recommended for roads and bridges, which is in addition to the normal expenditure of States.
4. Grants recommended for maintenance of public buildings, forests, heritage conservation and specific needs of States are Rs. 500 crore, Rs. 1,000 crore, Rs. 625 crore, and Rs. 7,100 crore, respectively.

Fiscal Reform Facility

1. With the recommended scheme of debt relief in place, fiscal reform facility not to continue over the period 2005-10.

Debt Relief and Corrective Measures

1. Central loans to States contracted till March, 2004 and outstanding on March 31, 2005 amounting to Rs.1,28,795 crore to be consolidated and rescheduled for a fresh term of 20 years, and an interest rate of 7.5 per cent to be charged on them. This is subject to enactment of fiscal responsibility legislation by a State.
2. A debt write-off scheme linked to reduction of revenue deficit of States to be introduced. Under this scheme, repayments due from 2005-06 to 2009-10 on Central loans contracted up to March 31,2004 will be eligible for write off.

3. Central Government not to act as an intermediary for future lending to States, except in the case of weak States, which are unable to raise funds from the market.
4. External assistance to be transferred to States on the same terms and conditions as attached to such assistance by external funding agencies.
5. All the States to set up sinking funds for amortization of all loans.
6. States to set up guarantee redemption funds through earmarked guarantee fees.

Others

1. The Centre should share 'profit petroleum' from New Exploration and Licensing Policy (NELP) areas in the ratio of 50:50 with States where mineral oil and natural gas are produced. No sharing of profits in respect of nomination fields and non-NELP blocks.
2. Every State to set up a high level committee to monitor the utilization of grants recommended by the TFC.
3. Centre to gradually move towards accrual basis of accounting.

Appendix 6

Eleventh Finance Commission: New Task and Main Recommendations

---

New Task

Finance Commission is constituted under Article 280 of the Constitution. Clause (3) of Article 280 lays down the following mandatory terms of reference for it.

"(a) the distribution between the Union and the States of the net proceeds of taxes which are to be or may be divided between them ... and the allocation between the States of the respective shares of such proceeds;

(b) the principles which should govern the grants-in-aid of the revenues of the States out of the Consolidated Fund of India."

By the Seventy-third and Seventy-fourth amendments to the Constitution, two new sub-clauses (bb) and (c) were introduced in clause (3) of Article 280. These sub-clauses make it obligatory upon the Finance Commission to make recommendations as to "the measures needed to augment the Consolidated Fund of a State to supplement the resources of the panchayats/municipalities in the State on the basis of the recommendations made by the Finance Commission of the State".

Thus, as per the amended clause (3) of Article 280, the Eleventh Finance Commission was duty bound to assess the resources required to be transferred from the Consolidated Fund of India to the State Government for passing on to the municipalities. This assessment has to be based on the recommendations of State Finance Commissions (SFCs) which enjoys complete freedom in this regard.

Hitherto, there were two primary functions of a Finance Commission: (a) to evolve a scheme of transfer of financial resources from the Centre to the States so as to ensure financial equilibrium at the two levels of Government during the period of its award, and (b) to design formulae to allocate resources so transferred among the States. Transfer of resources from the Centre to the States was designed to correct vertical imbalances while the distribution of resources among the States aimed at correcting horizontal imbalances in the availability of resources.

Now that it had to consider the needs of local bodies also, the Finance Commission had to ensure vertical equity in the distribution of resources not only between the Centre and the Sates but also between the States and the local bodies. By making the Finance Commission responsible for ensuring equitable distribution of resources at three levels instead of two, the Constitutional amendments distracted it from its traditional primary task of ensuring vertical fiscal equity as between the Centre and the States, and horizontal fiscal equity as among the States.

It is also well-known that while the States are unanimous in demanding an increase in their share of the divisible pool of Central taxes, their approach to the principles for determination of relative shares of the States differs widely. In their memoranda to the Finance Commission, the States suggest a variety of conflicting criteria for the distribution of States' share inter se. Each State suggests a formula which it considers will benefit it and most, the richer States emphasising the 'collection factor' and the poorer States the backwardness factor.

The Finance Commission had to consider not only the memoranda of the State Governments but also the Reports of SFCs, which in turn are based on the financial assessments of hundreds of municipalities and thousands of panchayats, it will have to perform a Herculean task to do justice to the work assigned to it. Generally, a Finance Commission takes one and a half years to complete its work. Now with the added burden of supplementing the resources of panchayats/municipalities, it will need more time. The old debate that Finance Commission should be converted from a quinquennial to a permanent body like the Planning Commission assumes relevance in this context.

Through greater devolution a Finance Commission may augment the Consolidated Fund of a State but how does it ensure supplementing the resources of the panchayats/municipalities. The Eleventh Finance Commission will have to make arrangements to operationalise enhanced transfer of resources from the States to the local bodies. Recommendations of the Commission in this regard will determine the efficacy of the Seventy-third and Seventy-fourth amendments.

A State Finance Commission has the power to decide the amount of assistance which may be needed from the Centre to supplement the resources of the municipalities of a State. It is plausible that a State Government may slacken its efforts to tap the potential available at its own level or the municipal level to contain expenditure and/or raise resources and instead put the burden on the national exchequer. If this happens, the National Finance Commission would find itself in the cobwebs of conflicting and exaggerated claims of not only Central and State Governments but also of thousands of municipalities through the SFCs.

It may be recalled that since the recommendations of the State Finance Commissions were not available to the Tenth Finance Commission, the latter was in doubt whether it could recommend measures for augmenting State resources for the purpose of supplementing the resources of panchayats and municipalities. To resolve the dilemma, it decided to make ad hoc provision of specific grants to States.

The Eleventh Finance Commission, which will be the first to deal with the provisions of the Seventy-third and Seventy-fourth amendments on a full-fledged basis, will have an enormous responsibility of assessing the financial needs of local bodies and recommending the scale of assistance to be given to them.

Main Recommendations

The Eleventh Finance Commission (EFC) was constituted by the President on July 3, 1998 with A.M. Khusro as Chairman. It was asked to give recommendations on specified aspects of Centre-State fiscal relations during the five years period commencing from April 1, 2000. The EFC submitted its Report on July 7, 2000. [1]

Recommendations of the EFC relating to (a) devolution of taxes and duties to the States, (b) grants-in-aid under Article 275 of the Constitution, (c) financing of relief expenditure and (d) debt relief to the States are summarised below:

Devolution of Central Taxes/Duties to the States: Prior to Constitution (Eightieth Amendment) Act, 2000 [2], income tax and Union excise duties were the only taxes shared with the States, apart from the grants given in lieu of passenger tax, and the collections from additional excise duty in lieu of sales tax sugar, tobacco and textiles. Taxes on income and Union excise duties were shared with States under Article 270 and 272 respectively. This amendment altered the pattern of sharing of Central taxes between the Centre and the States significantly. It substituted a new Article for Article 270 and omitted the old Article 272. The new Article 270 provides for the sharing of the net proceeds of all Union taxes and duties with the States.

Under Article 270 of the Constitution, the Finance Commission is required to recommend such percentage of the net proceeds of all Central taxes and duties (except Union surcharge, cess levied for specific purposes and the duties and taxes referred to in Articles 268 and 269) that may be assigned to the States within which that tax or duty is leviable. [3] It is further required to recommend the manner in which the States' share may be distributed among the States.

A. Share of States (Vertical Devolution): Under Article 280 (3)(a), the EFC was required to determine, first, the aggregate share of the States in all Union taxes and duties. This task required a comprehensive view of (a) expenditure needs of the Centre, (b) aggregate resources of the Centre, (c) aggregate requirements of States on revenue account and (d) resources of the States from their own sources.

On the basis of the analysis and assessment of the budgetary requirements of the Centre and the States, the EFC fixed the share of States at 28 per cent of the net proceeds of shareable Central taxes/duties for distribution amongst all such States where the Central tax/duty is leviable for each of the five years starting from April 1, 2000. Consequently, the recommendations made for the sharing of income tax and Union excise duties in the Interim Report got modified. In addition, 1.5 per cent of the net proceeds of shareable Central taxes/duties in a year was recommended for distribution amongst such States which do not levy sales tax on sugar, tobacco and textiles during that year, [4] thus totalling 28 + 1.5 = 29.5 per cent of the net proceeds of all Union taxes and duties. The distribution of this 1.5 per cent among the States is to be done in the same manner as the distribution of 28 per cent of the net proceeds. It was further recommended that if any State levies and collects sales tax on sugar, textile and tobacco, it will not be entitled to any share from this 1.5 per cent.

As regards States' views on the new scheme of devolution, the EFC observed, "In their memoranda, States are in unison in asking for the changeover to the alternative scheme of devolution and for giving up the present system of tax sharing of revenues from specified taxes, viz. income tax and Union excise duties. Many have, however, asked for a higher share in the pool of Central taxes as compared to the 29 per cent share that was recommended by the Tenth Finance Commission." [5]

B. Distribution of States' Share Inter Se (Horizontal Distribution): While States are almost unanimous in demanding an increase in the share of Union taxes, there are naturally wide divergences in their approach to the principles for determination of relative shares of the States in the divisible pool. Each State suggests a formula which it considers will benefit it the most, the richer States emphasising the *collection factor* and the poorer States the *backwardness factor*. The various criteria, often conflicting, suggested by the States to the Finance Commission include population, consumption, collection of revenue, economic backwardness, relative financial weakness, sales tax collections, and percentage of scheduled castes and scheduled tribes. Not surprisingly, relatively industrialised States like Gujarat, and Maharashtra argue in favour of collection factor because bulk of the tax revenue originates there. Poorer States like Uttar Pradesh, Orissa, and Bihar want significant weightage for backwardness criterion while Madhya Pradesh and Rajasthan prefer high weightage for geographical area. Therefore, it will not be wrong to say that fiscal federalism in India is a tug-of-war not only between the Centre and the States but also among the States themselves.

The EFC recommended percentage share of each State (in the share of all

States) and indicated the criteria adopted in arriving at those percentage shares.

The EFC claimed that the basic emphasis in their approach was to evolve a suitable structure of incentives in all mechanism of fiscal transfers. It may be recalled that the Tenth Finance Commission (TFC) had made a beginning in this direction by utilising an index of tax effort made by the States. Carrying forward the scheme of incentives, the EFC observed, "we feel that given the present fiscal situation of the States and the need for restructuring, as also the reference in our TOR for better fiscal management, further incentives need to be provided for fiscal discipline, and that this may be integrated in the principles of devolution. Accordingly, we are suggesting the use of an index of fiscal discipline." [6] Keeping all these requirements in mind, the EFC suggested six criteria with relative weights for determining the inter se shares of the States (Table below). There were three main considerations before the EFC in the selection of criteria: (a) resource deficiency of States, (b) higher cost of providing services and (c) fiscal discipline.

Criteria and Relative Weights for Determining Inter Se Shares of States

S. No.	Criteria	Relative weight (per cent)
1.	Population	10.0
2.	Income (distance method)	62.5
3.	Area	7.5
4.	Index of infrastructure	7.5
5.	Tax effort	5.0
6.	Fiscal discipline	7.5

Note: State-wise data on these criteria are given in Annexures VI.2 to VI.7 of the Report of the Commission.

Source: *Report of the Eleventh Finance Commission*, June 2000, p. 58.

Based on the criteria and their relative weights as given in table above, the percentage shares of different States in the net proceeds of all shareable Union taxes and duties (except the expenditure tax and service tax) were worked out in each of the financial years from 2000-01 to 2004-05. [7]

The percentage share of each State in the 29.5 per cent of the net proceeds of shareable Central taxes varies as per the fixed formula suggested by the EFC. The EFC distributed weights on the basis of six criteria: population, distance, area, index of infrastructure, tax effort and fiscal discipline. 72.5 per cent of the weights are accounted for by population and distance factors. It may be recalled that the TFC used only the first five criteria. The criterion of fiscal discipline was used by the EFC for the first time.

At the same time, the weightage given to each of these criteria was also altered. For instance, the weightage given to poverty or income was increased from 60 per cent in the devolution formula used by the TFC to 62 per cent in the EFC. Weights for area and index of infrastructure development were increased as compared to those assigned five years ago by its predecessor, the TFC. Weightage for tax effort was halved. In other words, EFC opted for large weights for distributive factors like *distance* but small weights for fiscal efficiency parameters.

Under the EFC dispensation, poorer States got a bigger share of Central taxes while richer States with better infrastructure, administrative and fiscal apparatus got less as compared to TFC formula. The biggest losers were Gujarat, Maharashtra, Haryana, Andhra Pradesh, Punjab and Tamil Nadu. This happened because the EFC altered the weights given to different criteria in the devolution formula used to determine the inter se distribution.

The recommendations of the EFC were severely criticised by the Chief Ministers of relatively developed States, particularly Andhra Pradesh and Maharashtra. It was argued that by reducing the percentage share of these States, the EFC penalised the States which had performed well, introduced reforms and contributed to national development.

Over the last fifty years, Central transfers have mainly been directed to weaker States so that they may come out of the slow growth trap. However, the weaker states have continued to be weak. It is a moot question whether the magnanimity shown by the EFC towards weaker States will be of any help to them.

Even after the transfer to the States of a share of divisible taxes, the resources of some of the States may remain inadequate to meet their needs. Therefore, the Constitution provides for grants-in-aid by the Centre to such States as are in need of assistance. Two types of grants are provided by the Centre to the States: the first under Article 275 which are routed through the Finance Commission, and the second under Article 282 which have traditionally been determined by the Planning Commission.

Grants-in-aid of the Revenues of States (Article 275): These were as follows.

A. Grants-in-aid to Cover Non-Plan Gap on Revenue Account: The EFC recommended grants-in-aid to be given under Article 275(1), **other than those under the proviso to Article 275(1)**, equal to the amount of deficits assessed for each year during the period 2000-2005. The amount of the grant for each State, having non-Plan deficits is indicated in Chapter X of the Report of the Commission.

B. Grants-in-aid for Upgradation of Standards of Administration and Special Problems of States: The EFC recommended grants totalling to Rs. 4,972 crore towards upgradation of standards of administration and special problems of States. The State-wise, year-wise and purpose-wise details of these grants are given in Chapter VII of the Report of the Commission.

C. Grants to States for Financing Local Bodies: EFC was the first to be required by the President, in terms of the 73rd and 74th Amendments to the Constitution, to recommend the measures needed to augment the Consolidated Fund of a State to supplement the resources of the panchayats and municipalities in the State on the basis of the recommendations of the State Finance Commissions.

The EFC recommended grants totalling Rs. 10,000 crore for local bodies during 2000-2005, to be utilised mainly for maintenance of civic services. Of this, Rs. 1,600 crore per annum is for rural local bodies and Rs. 400 crore per annum is for urban local bodies. EFC recommended that the amounts of Rs. 1,600 crore and Rs. 400 crore provided for the panchayats and municipalities respectively, for each of the five years (2000-05) be distributed among the States on the following criteria and weights:

1. Population 40 per cent.
2. Index of decentralisation 20 per cent.
3. Distance from highest per capita income 20 per cent.
4. Revenue effort 10 per cent.
5. Geographical area 10 per cent.

The grants given to local bodies are primarily meant for maintenance of civil services including primary health and family welfare, education as well as other public utility services. Details regarding inter-State distribution are given in Chapter VIII of the Report of the Commission.

It is noteworthy that while a State cannot be denied a part of share in Central taxes even if it has no demonstrated financial need, grants are given upon genuine financial needs of the States. It is possible that even before tax devolution from the Centre, some high-income States have a surplus in their non-Plan revenue account. The Seventh Finance Commission identified Punjab, Haryana, Gujarat, Tamil Nadu, and Karnataka as such States. Thus, grants-in-aid along with share in taxes serve as a levelling up force to promote regional balanced development. From this, it may also be inferred that States as a whole are not affected whether transfers are made by one means (share in Central taxes) or another (grants). It is the total amount transferred which is important for them. However, the sources of transfer become important when it comes to individual States because the formulae applied for various transfers are different. It is not possible to adopt a single formula for all transfers in view of the differing nature of taxes and grants.

Financing of Calamity Relief Expenditure: The EFC recommended the continuance of the existing scheme of Calamity Relief Funds in States with an aggregate size of Rs. 11,008 crore during 2000-2005. This includes the Centre's share of Rs. 8,256 crore and the States' share of Rs. 2,752 crore, worked out in the ratio of 75:25. Details of State-wise distribution and the criterion adopted by the Commission are indicated in Chapter IX of the Report of the Commission.

National Calamity Contingency Fund (NCCF): The EFC recommended that the Central assistance to the States in national calamities should be financed by levy of a special surcharge on Central taxes for a limited period. A surcharge instils a feeling of national participation for a national cause. Collection from such surcharge should be kept in a separate fund, to be known as National Calamity Contingency Fund (NCCF), created in the Public Account of the Government of India.

Debt Relief to States: The EFC proposed the continuance of the existing debt relief scheme, linked to improvement in the ratio of revenue receipts of a State to its total revenue expenditure, with enhanced incentive. Details are given in Chapter XI of the Report of the Commission. EFC was criticised for its restrictive recommendations on the States' borrowings and for providing inadequate debt relief.

Ceiling on Total Revenue Account Transfers: While working out the total quantum of share in Central taxes/duties and grants-in-aid to States, the EFC considered the trends in total transfers from the Centre to the States on revenue account. It recommended that tax devolution and Plan/Non-Plan grants from the Centre to the States should not exceed 37.5 per cent of total Centre's revenues (both tax and non-tax). The rationale of the ceiling was explained by the EFC as follows, "in deciding the level of revenue transfers, all transfers have to be taken in their totality and their components like tax devolution, grants-in-aid and grants in other forms like Plan grants, should be decided in the light of the overall ceiling. Accordingly, after working out the likely profile of the revenue and expenditure of the Centre for the five years 2000-05, we have set a notional limit on the overall revenue transfers, taking into account the legitimate needs of the Centre to meet its revenue expenditure liabilities. In setting this ceiling, we have taken note of the level of transfers that have taken place as a proportion of Centre's revenues in recent years and postulated a proportion of 37.5 per cent in order that there is no disruption in government finances at the two levels. This will serve to raise the volume of resource flow to the States over what has been prevailing of late but not beyond what can be accommodated within the Centre's resource profile, and the contemplated deficit levels." [8]

While accepting this ceiling on total revenue account transfers from the Centre to the States, the Government clarified that the acceptance of this recommendation does not imply the establishment of a principle of mandatory sharing of a fixed percentage of Centre's revenue receipts with the States.

The sharing of the proceeds from almost all Central taxes (global sharing) has been welcomed universally. The earlier arrangement of sharing some of the taxes (itemised sharing) was criticised on the ground that Central Government paid more attention to the administration of non-shareable taxes and was lax in making the shareable taxes buoyant. In the new scheme, no tax, as such, is shareable. A percentage of the total tax proceeds of the Centre is assigned to the States. The total amount assigned has no identifiable parts to it. With the new scheme of tax devolution (effective April 1, 1996), the Central Government can pursue its tax reforms without the need to consider whether a tax is shareable with the States or not.

Notes

1. Apart from its main report, the EFC also submitted an *interim report* on January 15, 2000 for making provisional arrangements for the year 2000-2001. It had recommended the share of States in income tax and Union excise duties for the year 2000-2001 at 80 per cent and 52 per cent respectively.

Again, at the stage of finalisation of its Report, an additional term of reference was added by the Presidential Order dated April 28, 2000 as follows:

"In particular the Commission shall draw a monitorable fiscal reforms programme aimed at reduction of revenue deficit of the States and recommend the manner in which the grants to States to cover the assessed deficit in their non-plan revenue account may be linked to progress in implementing the programme."

Formulation of a fiscal monitorable reforms programme required another round of consultations with the States and the Union Ministry of Finance. Therefore, although the main report was submitted on July 7, 2000, the report on the term of reference notified in the Order dated April 28, 2000 was submitted to the President on August 30, 2000. This *supplementary report* evolved a weightage formula for fiscal discipline in the devolution package for States from the Central taxes.

Following the recommendations of the EFC, the Central Government earmarked Rs. 10,607 crore as Incentive Fund for 5 years to encourage the States to implement monitorable fiscal reforms. To begin with an amount of Rs. 4,243 crore was provided for the Fund for the year 2001-2002 in the budget for the same year.

2. At the time of finalisation of recommendations and preparation of the report of EFC, the Constitution (Eightieth Amendment) Act, 2000 was enacted by the Parliament which had a bearing on the work of the EFC. The amendments made in the Constitution necessitated changes in the terms of reference of the EFC. These were modified by the Presidential Order dated June 19, 2000. By this Order, para 7 of the terms of reference was deleted. This para required the EFC

to suggest changes, if any, in the principles governing the devolution amongst the States of the net proceeds of the additional excise duties leviable under the Additional Duties of Excise (Goods of Special Importance) Act, 1957 in lieu of the sales tax formerly levied by the State Governments, and the grants to be made available to the States in lieu of the tax under the repealed Railway Passenger Fares Act, 1957. Thus, the Report submitted on July 7, 2000, addressed the original terms of reference (excluding paragraph 7). The Constitution (Eightieth Amendment) Act, 2000 provides for sharing of the net proceeds of all Union taxes and duties with the States.

History of Constitution (Eightieth Amendment) Act, 2000: The Constitution (Eightieth Amendment) Act, 2000 was based on a recommendation of the Tenth Finance Commission (TFC) which had recommended an Alternative Scheme of Devolution (ASD) in its report submitted in November 1994. Under this scheme, proceeds of all Central taxes, except surcharges, would constitute a common shareable pool from which a share was to be devolved to the States. The TFC recommended 29 per cent of the proceeds to be devolved to the States under this Scheme. This percentage share included devolution on account of additional excise duties levied in lieu of sales tax as well as the grant-in-lieu of the tax on railway passenger fares.

In December 1996, the Government of India brought out a Discussion Paper on the Alternative Scheme of Devolution spelling out the pros and cons of the proposed scheme. On the basis of a consensus reached in the Third Meeting of the Inter-State Council held on July 17, 1997, the Government accepted the scheme with some modifications. A Constitution (Eighty-fifth Amendment) Bill, 1998 was introduced in the 12th Lok Sabha. The Bill was referred to the Standing Committee of Parliament on Finance. The Standing Committee gave its report to the Parliament in February 1999. However, the Bill lapsed with the dissolution of the Lok Sabha. A modified version of the Bill was introduced in the Lok Sabha as 'The Constitution (Eighty-ninth Amendment) Bill, 2000 on March 9, 2000. The Bill was passed by Parliament and received the assent of the President of India on June 9, 2000 as 'Constitution (Eightieth Amendment) Act 2000.

On the basis of a consensus arrived at the third meeting of the inter-State Council held on July 17, 1997, the Government decided to accept in principle the recommendations of the Tenth Finance Commission regarding the alternative scheme of sharing of taxes between the Centre and the States from a single divisible pool at a uniform rate of 29 per cent. However, instead of freezing this percentage share for 15 years with effect from April 1, 1996 as suggested by the TFC, it was left open to successive Finance Commissions to review it.

The Constitution amendment bill to give effect to this decision was introduced in the Lok Sabha on July 14, 1998. However, it could not be passed due to the dissolution of the Twelfth Lok Sabha.

On February 8, 2000, the Union Cabinet again approved in principle the proposal that would give States a share of 29 per cent of the *net* proceeds of all Central taxes. It is noteworthy that the TFC had envisaged sharing of *gross* proceeds of Central Taxes. The Bill will be introduced again in the Lok Sabha to implement the decision. Since the scheme will come into force with retrospective effect from April 1, 1996, the Centre will have to pay arrears (estimated at Rs. 10,000 crore) to the States.

In short, this amendment brought about the following main changes:

(a) All Central taxes and duties, except those referred in articles 268 and 269 respectively and surcharges and cesses, are to be shared between the Centre and the States.

(b) Only States in which these taxes and duties are leviable in that year are entitled to get a share in these taxes and duties;

(c) A percentage of 'net proceeds' of these taxes and duties as may be prescribed by the

President by order after considering the recommendations of the Finance Commission is to be shared by States.

(d) The percentage of 'net proceeds' of these taxes and duties which is assigned to the States in any financial year shall not form part of the Consolidated Fund of India.

(e) The article 270(2) which referred to taxes on income prior to the amendment contained the following provision:

"Such percentage as may be prescribed, of the net proceeds in any financial year of any such tax, except in so far as those proceeds represent proceeds attributable to Union Territories or to taxes payable in respect of Union emoluments, shall not form part of the Consolidated Fund of India."

In the new article 270 which refers to all taxes the words 'net proceeds' attributable to Union Territories or to 'taxes payable in respect of Union emoluments' have been omitted.

The new article 270 provides as follows:

"270 (1) All taxes and duties referred to in the Union List, except the duties and taxes referred to in articles 268 and 269, respectively, surcharge on taxes and duties referred to in article 271 and any cess levied for specific purposes shall be levied and collected by the Government of India and shall be distributed between the Union and the States in the manner provided in clause (2).

(2) Such percentage, as may be prescribed, of the net proceeds of any such tax or duty in any financial year shall not form part of the Consolidated Fund of India, but shall be assigned to the States within which that tax or duty is leviable in that year, and shall be distributed among those States in such manner and from such time as may be prescribed in the manner provided in clause (3).

(3) In this article, "prescribed" means: -

(i) until a Finance Commission has been constituted, prescribed by the President by order, and

(ii) after a Finance Commission has been constituted, prescribed by the President by order after considering the recommendations of the Finance Commission."

(f) The recommendation of the Tenth Finance Commission regarding sharing of 'gross proceeds' was also not accepted in the new Amendment Act and the words, "the share of net proceeds" was prescribed in order to maintain consistency between articles 270, 279 and 280.

Article 269 has been recast by the Amendment Act. The new article includes only taxes on sale and purchase of goods and taxes on the consignment of goods. All other taxes that were listed under article 269 prior to the amendment have been deleted from this article. It has also drastically changed Article 269 of the Constitution which earlier provided for levy and collection of some taxes by the Government of India but which were assigned to the States

3. Presently, all taxes except the expenditure tax and service tax are leviable in every State of the country. Expenditure tax and service tax are not leviable only in the State of Jammu and Kashmir (EFC, p. 54).

4. As a result of the Eightieth Amendment of the Constitution, the net proceeds of the additional excise duties levied under the Additional Excise Duties (Goods of Special Importance) Act, 1957, cannot be passed on to the States as Article 272 of the Constitution has been deleted. Additional excise duties are now part of the tax revenue of the Central Government and are shareable with the States. In view of these changes, there is a need to review the earlier arrangement. Pending that, the EFC recommended that 1.5 per cent of all shareable Union taxes and duties be allocated to the States separately.

5. *Report of the Eleventh Finance Commission*, June 2000, p. 54.

6. *Ibid.*, p. 58.

7. Expenditure tax and service tax are not presently leviable in the State of Jammu & Kashmir. Hence, share in the net proceeds of these taxes was not assignable to this State. The share of each of the remaining States in the net proceeds of expenditure tax and service tax was worked out separately.

8. *Report of the Eleventh Finance Commission*, op. cit., p. 15.

Appendix 7

Tenth Finance Commission: Alternative Formula of Devolution

The Tenth Finance Commission (TFC) was set up on June 15, 1992 with Mr. K.C. Pant as Chairman. The Government dropped the 'normative approach' (which was in the guidelines of the Ninth Finance Commission) from the terms of reference of the TFC. It was replaced by the 'gap-filling approach'. The TFC submitted its report to the President on November 26, 1994 and it was placed in the Parliament on March 15, 1995. It covers the five year period beginning April 1, 1995. Recommendations of the TFC pertaining to income tax and Union excise duties have already been explained in chapters 4 and 5 respectively.

The Tenth Finance Commission recommended an alternative scheme of devolution, i.e. a system of vertical resource sharing under which Central taxes are to be pooled and a proportion thereof devolved to the States. It recommended a share of 26 per cent for States in the gross receipts of Central taxes. It further recommended that the tax rental arrangement (i.e. additional duties of excise in lieu of sales tax) should be terminated, and additional excise duties merged with basic excise duties. If this is done, a further share of 3 per cent in the gross tax receipts of the Centre should accrue to the States. These share (26 + 3 = 29 per cent), based on the amounts currently accruing to the States, should be suitably provided for in the Constitution and reviewed once in 15 years. The Commission recommended that the alternative scheme of resource sharing suggested by it may be brought into force with effect from April 1, 1996 after necessary amendments to the Constitution.

The TFC claimed the following benefits of the alternative scheme of devolution suggested by it: "(a) With a given share being allotted to the States in the aggregate revenues from Central taxes, States will be able to share the aggregate buoyancy of Central taxes. (b) The Central Government can pursue tax reforms without the need to consider whether a tax is shareable with the States or not. (c) The impact of fluctuations in Central tax revenues would be felt alike by the Central and State Governments. (d) should the taxes mentioned in article 268 and/or 269 form part of this arrangement, there will be a greater likelihood of their being tapped." [1]

However, this scheme of TFC overlooks the standard principles of tax assignment and tax sharing in a federal polity. Moreover, it is not clear whether the contemplated 29 per cent of the States' share will be distributed inter se on the basis of one formula or a separate formula will be followed as hitherto for the distribution of additional duties of excise in lieu of sales tax. The basis for the distribution of additional excise duties among the States has traditionally been different. This is another ticklish issue to be resolved by the Eleventh Finance Commission.

In his 1997-98 budget speech the Finance Minister announced the acceptance of the Tenth Finance Commission's alternative formula for devolution of resources from the Centre to the States.

Note

1. *Report of the Tenth Finance Commission*, 1994, p. 59.

Appendix 8

Ninth Finance Commission: Normative Approach

The Ninth Finance Commission was constituted on June 17, 1987, under the chairmanship of Mr. N.K.P. Salve to go into the question of distribution of non-Plan resources between the Centre and the States. As in the past, the Commission was asked to make recommendations regarding the distribution between the Union and the States of the net proceeds of income tax and Union excise duties and the allocation among the States of the respective shares of such proceeds. It was also asked to recommend the principle which should govern the grants-in-aid of the revenues of the States out of the Consolidated Fund of India.

The terms of reference of the Ninth Finance Commission were wider as compared to previous Commissions. For example, one term of reference provided that the Commission might examine the feasibility of the merger of additional duties of excise in lieu of sales tax with basic duties of excise.

With a view to making the recommendations of the Finance Commissions co-terminus with the Five Year Plans, the Ninth Finance Commission was asked to make two reports, the first covering one year period (1989-90), and the second covering five years of the Eighth Plan (1990-95).

The Commission was asked to adopt a normative approach in assessing receipts and expenditures on revenue account of both the Centre and the States. The normative approach was considered essential to ensure fiscal discipline and adequate efforts to augment revenues.

The Commission presented its first report for the year 1989-90 to the President on July 29, 1988. The second report for the five year period 1990-95 was submitted in December 1989. The report of the Commission was not unanimous as one of its members Justice A. S. Qureshi disagreed with certain recommendations. His note of dissent forms part of the report. The recommendations of the second report pertaining to income tax and Union excise duties have already been explained in chapters 4 and 5 respectively.

The Ninth Finance Commission made a basic departure from the practice of previous Finance Commissions by adopting the normative approach. Under this approach, the 'needs' and 'capacities' of different governments were assessed normatively and such normative assessments were used as the basis for determining the volume and pattern of federal transfers. In other words, the fiscal performance of the governments was judged on the basis of *what ought to be* rather than on the basis of *what it actually is*. To put it differently, the Commission rejected the base year figure on the receipts as well as the expenditure side as the *right* figures. The Commission emphasised that the normative approach would be applied to both the Centre and the States and that the assessment of revenues and expenditures would be done in a manner so as to maintain incentives for greater revenue efforts and economy in spending.

On the revenue side, estimates were derived separately for tax and non-tax revenues. In the words of the Commission, "In respect of taxes, a modified representative tax system approach has been applied in order to determine what a particular State would be able to raise by way of tax revenue had it exploited its tax bases to an average extent. Such 'tax capacity' figures have been derived for a base year and are then projected to the year 1989-90. As regards non-tax revenues, while actuals have been used in the case of fees and user charges, in the case of dividends and interest to be received by the government, normative rates of return have been used.... As in the case of revenues, in regard to a substantial part of non-Plan revenue expenditures, the average behaviour has been taken as the norm." [1] However, considering the request of some State Governments, the application of normative norms by the Commission was moderated and spread over a period of years. Moreover, the Special Category States were kept out of the normative approach and actuals were used to project receipts and expenditure.

The normative approach applied by the Commission generated considerable controversy among fiscal experts. The soundness of the normative approach was questioned by no less a person than Justice Qureshi, a member of the Commission. In his note of dissent appended to the report of the Commission, he observed: "Although the normative approach is in itself a very beneficial thing, there is a practical difficulty in its application. Normative standards can be applied to States easily and effectively, but they cannot be applied to the Centre with the same rigour. It is difficult to set normative standards to certain items, such as, defence expenditure, debts etc. It would, therefore, always be the grouse of the States that the normative approach is applied only to the States and not to the Centre.... I have an objection to the results arrived at by adopting the normative approach in assessing the receipts and expenditures on the revenue account of the States and the Centre. It is on the ground that they have been worked out on the basis of econometric models relying on proxies, dummies, variables etc. in the absence of accurate or reliable data. Moreover, certain considerations have been built in to arrive at the desired results. I am really doubtful about the efficacy of such a mechanical approach towards normative assessment of receipts and expenditures of States, in such a vast country with widely varying social and economic conditions and historical background." [2]

Alternative Terms of Reference

The guidelines issued by the Central Government to the Ninth Finance Commission, such as to follow the normative approach in assessing the revenue and expenditure of the Central and State Governments and keep in view the special requirements like defence, security, debt servicing and other committed expenditures or liabilities of the Centre, were resented by some State Governments.

On January 30, 1988, a group of Chief Ministers met the Prime Minister to present alternative terms of reference for the already set up Ninth Finance Commission. Almost simultaneously the Government released a summary of the report of the Sarkaria Commission on Centre-State relations.

The alternative terms of reference for the Ninth Finance Commission were jointly submitted to the Prime Minister on behalf of the seven non-Congress (I) Chief Ministers who unanimously framed them at their meeting in Bangalore on January 11, 1988. The seven non-Congress (I) States (West Bengal, Haryana, Karnataka, Andhra Pradesh, Kerala, Tripura and Assam) believed that the terms of reference of the Ninth Finance Commission were one-sided in favour of the Centre and the reference in them of 'normative approach' was vague and devoid of operational content. The Chief Ministers demanded the holding of a tripartite meeting between the Ninth Finance Commission, the Centre and the State Governments to evolve the so-called normative approach on the receipts and expenditure.

The alternative terms of reference, *inter alia*, stipulated (i) inclusion of the corporation tax in the divisible pool, (ii) review of the working of the scheme of additional excise duties in lieu of sales tax including the feasibility of reverting to the pre-1957 arrangement, (iii) discontinuation of the grants in lieu of tax on railway passenger fare and the simultaneous reintroduction of tax on railway passenger fare.

The Chief Ministers reiterated their demand for the early constitution of the Inter-State Council as envisaged in the Constitution. They also pleaded that the meetings of the National Development Council should be convened more frequently, at least twice a year.

Notes

1. *Second Report of the Ninth Finance Commission*, p. 4.
2. *Ibid.*, p. 54.

Appendix 9

Main Recommendations of the Commission on Centre-State Relations (Chairman: Justice R. S. Sarkaria), 1988

Government of India appointed in 1983 a Commission on Centre State Relations under the Chairmanship of Mr. Justice R.S. Sarkaria, a retired judge of the Supreme Court. The Commission was set up to review the whole gamut of Centre-State relations in their legislative, administrative, and financial aspects.

The monumental report of the Commission, submitted in 1988, basically accepted the existing framework of the Constitution. It disfavoured any major changes in the provisions of the Constitution including the financial arrangements. It stood for a strong Centre to preserve the unity and integrity of the country.

An important recommendation of the Commission pertained to the residuary power of legislation under the Constitution. Article 248 read with entry 97 of List I (Union List) of the Seventh Schedule vests in Parliament the residuary powers of legislation with respect to any matter not enumerated in List II (State List) or List III (Concurrent List). Such residuary powers include the power of making any law imposing a tax not mentioned in these Lists.

Regarding residuary powers of legislation, the Commission recommended, "that residuary power of legislation in regard to taxation should advisedly remain with Parliament. But, the residuary field other than that of taxation may be transferred to the Concurrent List....The Constitution may be suitably amended to give effect to this recommendation." [1]

Thus, the Commission recommended partial transfer of entry 97 to the Concurrent List. Unfortunately, no action has been taken so far to implement this recommendation of the Commission.

As regards financial relations between the Centre and the States, the Commission recommended as follows.

1. The Commission disfavoured any major modification in the basic scheme of the Constitution dividing the fields of taxation between the Centre and the States.
2. It rejected almost all the suggestions to shift the taxation powers of the Centre to the States. Such suggestions pertained mainly to the shifting of terminal taxes on goods and passengers carried by railways, estate duty, and banking etc.

3. The Commission was not in favour of making the devolution of funds from the Centre to the States automatic. In its view the existing division of functions between the Finance Commission and the Planning Commission was reasonable and must continue.
4. In its opinion the terms of reference of the Finance Commission should be drawn up in consultation with State Governments.
5. Significantly, the Commission recommended the sharing of corporation tax between the Centre and the States. Most other suggestions for enlarging the divisible pool were turned down.
6. It recommended legislation to levy consignment tax and constitutional amendment to enable levy of tax on advertisements in broadcasting.
7. As regards agricultural income tax, the Commission observed that as opinions are divided the matter should be examined further in depth.
8. The Commission recommended the setting up of an expert committee to examine taxation reforms and resource mobilisation.
9. Some other recommendations of the Commission included: review of the royalty paid to the States, modernisation of treasury systems, making available foreign borrowings by States from the banks, the issue of tax free municipal bonds, and assistance for natural calamities, shifting of additional excise duty from fabric to yarn, and setting up of special courts for economic offences.

Note

1. Government of India, *Report of the Commission on Centre-State Relations, 1988*, Part I, p. 31.

Appendix 10

Provisions of Gift Tax Act, 1958 at the Time of its Abolition in 1998

Gift Tax: An Introduction

Gifts from one person to another provide a convenient device to avoid or reduce liability under income tax, wealth tax, and estate duty. Thus, the objective of gift tax is to ensure that transfers of wealth which are effected during the lifetime of a person bear tax liability similar to the levy of estate duty on property passing on the death of a person.

After Independence in 1947, the Taxation Enquiry Commission, 1953-54, considered the proposal for the introduction of gift tax and concluded, "A gift tax is theoretically an attractive proposition, but it requires considerable experience of the operation of estate duty (levied in 1953) before it can be introduced. One of the pre-requisites for operating successfully a tax of this nature would be to introduce the submission by income tax assessees of a statement of assets and liabilities. As more experience is gained of this type of work, the feasibility of introducing a gift tax can be considered. Moreover, the rates of death duty are at present low. The value of the gift tax as a second line of defence for estate duty is greater if the rates of the latter are steeply progressive. We are, therefore, not in favour of introducing the gift tax at this stage." [1] The recommendation of the Commission was framed at a time when there was no wealth tax and estate duty was also in its infancy. The recommendation was influenced by the fact that all gift, *inter vivos*, made within two years of the death of a person were chargeable to estate duty at that time.

Gift Tax Act, 1958: Main Provisions

A tax on *inter vivos* gifts was imposed in India under the Gift Tax Act, 1958 which came into force on April 1 of that year. The Act was enacted as part of an integrated scheme of taxation of income, wealth, expenditure, and gifts, recommended by Professor Nicholas Kaldor. The legislation was intended also to supplement the imposition of estate duty with effect from October 15, 1953. Explaining the philosophy of gift tax in his 1958-59 budget speech, the then Prime Minister and the Minister of Finance Jawahar Lal Nehru had stated, "My first proposal is to introduce a tax on gifts which will fill a gap in the scheme of direct taxation and would not only make evasion or avoidance difficult but also spread the tax burden more equitably.... The transfer of properties through gifts to one's near relations or associates is one of the commonest forms of avoidance of not only the estate duty but also of income tax, wealth tax and even the expenditure tax. The only way of effectively checking this practice is to levy a tax on gifts." [2]

The Gift Tax Act, 1958 (hereinafter called the Act) was amended from time to time by the annual Finance Act and other legislations pertaining to direct taxes. The law of gift tax is stated here as applicable for the assessment year 1998-99.

Persons Liable to Gift Tax: Section 3 of the Act was the charging section. It imposed a tax for every assessment year on the aggregate value of gifts made by any person (individual, Hindu undivided family, firm, company or other association of persons) during the previous year. The 'previous year' was the period of twelve months ending on March 31, immediately preceding the assessment year. However, the following persons were not liable to pay gift tax:

1. A company in which the public are substantially interested.
2. A charitable or religious institution whose income is exempt from income tax (under Sections 11, and 12 of the Income Tax Act).

Definition of Gift: Under Section 2 (xii) of the Act, a gift was defined as a transfer by one person to another of any existing movable or immovable property made voluntarily and without consideration in money or money's worth and includes gifts referred to in Section 4. In other words, before a transfer of property became liable to gift tax, the following conditions must be satisfied: (a) the transfer was voluntary, (b) the transfer was of existing property, and (c) the transfer was without consideration in money or money's worth.

Deemed Gifts. Situations could arise when transfer of property could not be wholly covered within the above-mentioned definition of gift, despite the fact that such transfers passed an element of bounty or benefit in them. To bring such transfers within the purview of the Act, deeming provisions were inserted therein. Under Section 4 of the Act, the following transfers were treated as deemed gifts.

1. Transfers of properties which were not wholly without consideration, but in which the consideration was inadequate. The amount by which the market value of the property exceeded the value of consideration was deemed to be a gift.
2. If the property was transferred for a consideration which had not passed or was not intended to pass, the amount of consideration was deemed to be a gift by the transferor.
3. If there was a release, discharge, surrender or forfeiture or abandonment of any debt, contract, actionable claim or any interest in property in favour of another, the value of release, discharge etc. to the extent it was not found

bonafide, was deemed to be a gift by the person responsible for the release, discharge etc.

4. Where transfers took the form of vesting of property in joint ownership to enable appropriations to be made by another for the benefit of a person other than the person who was absolutely entitled to the property, the value of such appropriations was deemed gifts.
5. Where an individual converted his self-acquired property into Hindu undivided family property by throwing it into the common stock of the family, it was deemed that the individual had made a gift.
6. If a person, who had an interest in property as a tenant for a term or for life, surrendered his interest in the property without consideration or without adequate consideration, the value of interest or the amount by which such value exceeded the consideration received was deemed to be a gift made by such person.

Gifts Exempt from Tax. The Act provided for various exemptions as enumerated in Section 3. Therefore, taxable gifts were defined as the total gifts made during the previous year, less the exemptions allowed under the Act. The following gifts were exempt from gift tax.

1. Gifts of immovable property situated outside India and in the State of Jammu and Kashmir.
2. Gifts made by a person resident outside India out of the moneys standing to his credit in a Non-resident (External) Account maintained in India.
3. Gifts of foreign currency made by an Indian citizen who was not resident in India to any of his relatives in India from a country outside India. The purpose of exemption was to encourage the remittance of foreign exchange into the country.
4. Gifts of notified Special Bearer Bonds, Capital Investment Bonds, Relief Bonds up to prescribed limits.
5. Gifts made to the Central Government, any State Government or any local authority.
6. Gifts to any institution or fund established or deemed to be established in India for charitable purpose and in respect of which deduction was available under Section 80G of the Income Tax Act.
7. Any gift to a temple, mosque, gurudwara, church or any other place as had been notified by the Central Government under Section 80G(2) (b) of the Income Tax Act.
8. Gifts up to a maximum of Rs. 1 lakh in value on the occasion of the marriage of any relation, male or female, dependant on the donor.

9. All gifts made under a will. Such gifts were subject to estate duty (abolished in 1985).
10. All gifts in contemplation of death. Such gifts were subject to estate duty (abolished in 1985).
11. Gifts made by an individual for the education of his children.
12. Gifts of a reasonable amount (subject to the satisfaction of the gift tax officer) by an employer by way of bonus, gratuity or pension to an employee, or to the dependants of a deceased employee.

Basic Exemption and Rate of Tax: Apart from the exemptions referred to above, no gift tax was payable by any person if the total value of the gifts made by him in any one previous year did not exceed Rs. 30,000 [Sec. 5(2)]. In other words, gift tax was payable on the excess of the aggregate value of such gifts over Rs. 30,000. Basic exemption was raised from Rs. 5,000 to Rs. 20,000 from the assessment year 1987-88, and further up to Rs. 30,000 from assessment year 1994-95.

Rates of gift tax were given in the Schedule to the Gift Tax Act. From the assessment year 1987-88, a flat rate of 30 per cent was applicable.

Computation of Gift Tax: The following steps were followed to compute the gift tax liability:

1. The value of all the gifts made during the previous year was computed. There was no difficulty in the valuation of gifts so far as cash gifts were concerned. Problems of valuation arose in the case of gifts other than cash. In such cases, the value was taken to mean the amount which the property could fetch if sold in the open market on the date on which the gift was made.
2. Values of gifts falling under any one of the categories of gifts exempted under Section 5 of the Act were deducted.
3. From the resultant figure, basic exemption of Rs. 30,000 was deducted.
4. The balance represented the value of taxable gifts for which tax liability had to be calculated according to the rates applicable for a particular assessment year.

Why Was Gift Tax Abolished?

At the time of its abolition, gift tax was debated by fiscal experts from three viewpoints: (a) as a revenue-earner, (b) equity promoter, and (c) as an anti-tax avoidance device.

Revenue adequacy is a well-recognised canon of taxation and is particularly relevant in India in view of the need for additional resource mobilisation. Right from its inception in 1958, the share of gift tax had hovered around 0.05 per cent in the Centre's total tax collections. From revenue angle, gift tax was merely a paper tax much less worth the administrative efforts involved in operating it.

The meagre revenue yield made gift tax an ineffective tool of redistributive policy. Prior to the assessment year 1987-88, the rate structure was quite progressive ranging from 5 per cent on the value of taxable gifts not exceeding Rs. 20,000 to 75 per cent on the value of taxable gifts in excess of Rs. 20 lakh. The basic exemption limit was Rs. 5,000. However, from the assessment year 1987-88, the 5 per cent to 75 per cent rate-range was abolished and replaced by a 30 per cent flat rate tax. Hence, whether one made a taxable gift of Rs. 40,000 or Rs. 40 lakh or even Rs. 4 crore, the rate of tax remained the same, i.e. 30 per cent. Moreover, the gift tax legislation did not take into account the two basic indices of taxable capacity of a person, viz. income level and wealth holding. Whether a gift of say Rs. 40,000 was made out of a property of Rs. 50,000 or 50 lakh, the rate applicable remained the same. This violated the principle of vertical equity in taxation.

The utility of gift tax as an anti-tax avoidance device had also been reduced. Estate duty to which gift tax provided the second line of defence was abolished from March 16, 1985. It may be recalled that the Direct Taxes Enquiry Committee, 1971, while suggesting measures to check avoidance of gift tax had recommended aggregation of gifts made by a person from year to year and their integration with estate duty. It observed, "The principle of aggregation of gifts should be extended further so as to achieve complete integration with estate duty. For this purpose the principal value of the estate passing on death should be aggregated with the taxable gifts made during life-time. The estate duty will first be calculated on this aggregate amount, subject to such exemptions as may be available at the time, and then credit allowed for the gift tax paid during life time. This will secure equity between a person who makes gifts in his life-time and another who leaves his property in its entirety on his death to his heirs." [3]

Moreover, the maximum marginal rates of both income tax and wealth tax had been reduced considerably over the years, making splitting of income and wealth among family members less attractive.

Donor-Based Versus Donee-Based Gift Tax: In the 1990-91 budget, the then existing gift tax on donors was proposed to be substituted with a donee-based gift tax. The new provisions proposed a basic exemption of Rs. 20,000 for each year and the levy of gift tax on a graduated scale in case the gifts received in any year exceeded the exemption limit. The rates proposed were: 20 per cent in the slab of Rs. 20,000 to Rs. 50,000; 30 per cent in the slab of Rs. 50,000 to Rs. 2 lakh; and 40 per cent on the value of gifts in excess of Rs. 2 lakh. The purpose of the change from donor-based to donee-based gift tax was stated by the Finance

Minister as follows, "At present, gifts are taxed in the hands of the donor, but there is no limit on the amount which a donee can show as having been received by way of gifts. Because of this, the mechanism of gifts is used to split up capital and launder black money. Some instances have also come to notice recently where attempts have been made to explain away wasteful and ostentatious expenditure on marriage receptions and other functions as having been financed out of gifts. With a view to curbing such practices, I have decided to substitute the present gift tax on donors with a donee-based gift tax." [4] The Minister made it clear that the purpose of the donee-based gift tax was not to raise revenue but check tax evasion and conspicuous consumption. Accordingly, the Gift Tax Bill, 1990, was introduced in the Lok Sabha on March 31, 1990. However, the proposed changes in the Gift Tax Act could not be made when the Bill lapsed due to the dissolution of the Ninth Lok Sabha on March 13, 1991. Hence, gifts continued to be taxed in the hands of the donors.

Integration of Gift Tax and Income Tax: Since gift tax as a separate tax was not serving any useful purpose, it was often suggested that it should be merged with income tax. By treating gifts as a source of income and thus levying income tax on the donee, a separate legislation for gift tax could be dispensed with. The history of income tax reforms in India provided instances when certain incomes (windfall profits like lotteries and gambling wins, and realised capital gains) were brought under the purview of income tax. It was quite feasible to treat gifts received by a person as accretion to his income. The inclusion of gifts in the definition of income or expenditure was also supported by the Meade Committee which observed, "One way of taxing transfers of capital is to incorporate such transfers into the income tax or the expenditure tax itself. Thus, with a comprehensive income tax, gifts received could be taxed as part of the recipient's income and with an expenditure tax gifts made could be taxed as part of the donor's expenditure. Such an arrangement would cause the rate of tax to be adjusted progressively to the recipient's income level in the case of a comprehensive income tax and to the donor's expenditure level in the case of an expenditure tax. The arrangement would have the great advantage of enabling the whole of the apparatus of a separate transfer tax to be dismantled, although there would have to be some averaging arrangements to avoid the unfair effects of progressive tax rates on large lump sum receipts (under a comprehensive income tax) or large lump sum outgoings (under an expenditure tax)." [5]

However, the Indian Committee on Direct Tax Laws did not favour the integration of income tax and gift tax. It observed, "The present provisions for taxing income, wealth, and gifts separately are now well settled in the minds of the taxpayers. The inclusion of gifts as deemed income would be a revolutionary concept and would considerably remove the stability achieved over the past two decades of the operation of the Gift Tax Act. Various other considerations would also result in the income tax law which would outweigh the advantages of integration. We are, therefore, not in favour of treating gifts as income under the Income Tax Act and recommend the continuation of the Gift Tax Act in its present form." [6]

Responding to the realities of the situation, the Finance Minister in his 1998-99 budget discontinued the levy of gift tax on gifts made after September 30, 1998. To ensure that there were no leakages of income tax revenue through the mechanism of gifts, the gifts were made taxable under the Income Tax Act itself in the hands of the recipients. However, replying to the debate on the Finance Bill in the Lok Sabha on July 17, 1998, the Finance Minister announced exemption from all taxes of gifts made on or after October 1, 1998. In other words, his earlier proposal to tax the value of gifts as income of recipient was withdrawn.

Notes

1. Government of India, Ministry of Finance, *Report of the Taxation Enquiry Commission* (Chairman: John Matthai), 1953-54, Vol. II, p. 246.
2. Government of India, Ministry of Finance, *Speeches of Union Finance Ministers, 1947-48 to 1984-85,* p. 168.
3. Government of India, Ministry of Finance, *Final Report of the Direct Taxes Enquiry Committee* (Chairman: Justice K.N. Wanchoo), December 1971, p. 87.
4. Government of India, Ministry of Finance, *Budget Speech of Finance Minister, 1990-91,* Part B.
5. Institute for Fiscal Studies, *The Structure and Reform of Direct Taxation: Report of a Committee Chaired by Professor J.E. Meade* (London: George Allen and Unwin, 1978), pp. 512-13.
6. Government of India, Ministry of Finance, *Final Report of Direct Tax Laws Committee* (Chairman: C.C. Chokshi), 1978, p. 106.

Appendix 11

Provisions of Estate Duty Act, 1953 at the Time of its Abolition in 1985

Justification for Estate Duty

The institution of inheritance is a major contributory factor for inequalities of income and wealth and their perpetuation in capitalist societies. To deal with this problem democratically, estate taxation, if designed properly, can become an instrument for improving the distribution of economic power.

Transfer of property has always been considered an appropriate base for taxation by governments which not only protect privately-owned properties but also supervise their transfers from one generation to another.

Taxation of transfer of wealth at death may take various forms. Tax imposed on the estate as a whole of the deceased at the time of its transfer to his heirs is called estate duty. Tax on each inheritance to which the estate gives rise is known as inheritance tax or succession duty. Estate duty can be avoided if property is transferred by gifts among living persons. To prevent such possibilities, estate tax is generally accompanied by gift tax on the donor. Similarly, inheritance tax is associated with gift tax on the donee. The basic philosophy underlying estate taxation is to curtail an individual's right to acquire property without his own efforts. However, estate taxation does not interfere with the right of a person to use his property during his lifetime.

The role of capital transfer taxes (death duty, inheritance tax, gift tax etc.) is all the more important in countries where real estates have appreciated precipitously in value. Taxation of estate is least objectionable on grounds of efficiency. As Nicholas Kaldor has opined, "Death duties unquestionably represent the least harmful method of making scale levies on capital, largely because in contemplation of death human beings are not perfectly rational, and taxes dependent on death do not in fact lead to the same kind of reaction on conduct as similar taxes which are expected during the taxpayers' lifetime." [1]

Estate duty is often avoided through the use of trusts. A testator may leave to his heir that portion of his assets which are tax free and keep the remainder which are taxable in a trust. He can make arrangements under which his wife and children receive income there from during their lifetime. Such lacunae in the tax law make trust arrangements advantageous for testators of enormous wealth.

Trust arrangements can be curtailed, so far as tax implications are concerned, by limiting trusts to fixed values for each beneficiary or making trusts taxable.

Although bearing a sound social philosophy (to promote a more equitable distribution of wealth) and being least objectionable on efficiency grounds, implementation of estate taxation bristles with difficult technical, social, and economic problems. An appropriate solution of these problems is necessary, primarily on equity considerations.

1. To what extent does society desire to abridge a person's right to transfer property through bequest. The question pertains to exclusions, deductions, exemption limits, and rate progression. For example, if the society wishes to impose a ceiling on such transfers, it may impose a 100 per cent duty on the value of the estate in excess of the ceiling limit.
2. Should the limits imposed on bequests apply irrespective of the family relationship of the recipient with the deceased? It would, of course, be unfair to treat the spouse and a distant relative of the deceased equally under the law of estate duty. In other words, tax treatment of estate should be lenient in case of close, and stricter in case of distant family relationship with the deceased. For this purpose differential rate structures may be prescribed depending on the closeness of the family ties between the testator and the donee.
3. Should an individual's right to pass on wealth be curtailed more severely as successive generations become beneficiaries? According to Italian economist Eugenio Rignano, the level of applicable rates may rise as the property passes through successive bequests. [2] The foregoing issues are value-laden and therefore defy universally acceptable solutions.

Estate Duty in India

Under the Government of India Act, 1935, estate duty was a provincial source of revenue. In the Constitution of independent India, the duty was bifurcated into (a) estate duty on non-agricultural estates, and (b) estate duty on agricultural estates. The former was allocated to the Union Government and the latter to the State Governments.

Estate duty was introduced in India in 1953 when the Estate Duty Act of that year imposed a duty on the capital value of all property passing on the death of any person on or after October 15, 1953. The rationale for the tax was to curb the perpetuation of income and wealth inequalities through inheritance. However, following the recommendations of the Economic Administration Reforms Commission, 1981-83, estate duty was abolished with effect from March 16, 1985. The duty was abolished on the ground that it had failed in both its objectives, viz. to reduce the accumulation of dynastic wealth and raise resources for the Government. The Commission noted that 96.8 per cent of the assessees in 1980-81 related to the estates whose principal value was less than Rs. 3 lakh. [3] In 1985-86, estate duty yielded a paltry sum of Rs. 23 crore (0.08 per cent) out of a total Central tax collection of Rs. 28,671 crore in the same year. However, according to some experts abolition of estate duty was a retrograde fiscal step. Instead of improving and strengthening the duty, the baby was flung out with the bath water.

Provisions of the Estate Duty Act, 1953 at the Time of its Abolition in 1985

Section 5 of the Estate Duty Act was the charging section. It provided for the levy of estate duty on the principal value [4] of all property which passed or was deemed to pass on the death of a person. Estate tax, therefore, was charged directly on the value of property changing hands at death, irrespective of the destination of that property or its distribution among the beneficiaries. [5]

Properties Deemed to Pass on Death: By virtue of sub-section (3) of section 3 of the Act, property passing on death included property deemed to pass on death. Under sections 6 to 17, the following items of property were deemed by law to pass on the death of a person.

1. Property which the deceased was, at the time of his death, competent to dispose of (sec. 6).
2. Property in which the deceased or any other person had an interest ceasing on the death of the deceased (sec. 7).
3. All gifts made in contemplation of death (sec. 8).
4. All gifts of property made within two years [6] of death or gifts which had not been made *bonafide* (sec. 9). However, the following gifts were not deemed to pass on death: (a) gifts made in consideration of marriage up to maximum of Rs. 10,000 and (b) gifts which were proved to have been part of the normal expenditure of the deceased up to a maximum of Rs. 10,000.
5. Gifts made with a reservation of some right (sec. 10).
6. Where an interest, limited to cease on death, had been disposed of within two years of decedent's death and which but for such disposition would have passed on the death under section 5 (sec. 11).
7. Property passing under any settlement made by the deceased where the settler reserves to himself an interest in the settled property or the right to revoke the settlement or to reclaim the absolute interest in such property (sec. 12).
8. Where a person, having been absolutely entitled to any property, had caused it to be transferred to or vested in himself and another person jointly so that the beneficial interest in some part of that property accrued by survivorship to the other person (sec. 13).

9. Money received under a policy of life insurance, kept by a person for the benefit of a donee (sec. 14).
10. Any annuity or other interest, purchased or provided by the deceased to the extent of the beneficial interest accruing or arising on his death (sec. 15).
11. Any annuity or other interest which was attributable to property derived from the deceased (sec. 16).
12. If the deceased had made a transfer of any property to a controlled company and received benefit from the company in the three years ending with his death, the assets of the company were deemed, for the purpose of estate duty, to be included in the property passing on his death in proportion to benefits accrued to him from the company (sec. 17).

Property Exempt from Estate Duty: The provisions relating to exemptions from the charge of estate duty were contained in Part III (Sections 21 to 33) of the Estate Duty Act, 1953. The following were not included in the property passing on the death of the deceased.

1. All immovable property situated out of India – sec. 21(1)(a)
2. All movable property situated out of India at the time of death if the deceased was not domiciled in India – sec. 21(1)(b)
3. Property held by the deceased as trustee for another person subject to the condition that the deceased was not the sole trustee – sec. 22.
4. Settled property in the case of which the interest of the deceased failed before becoming an interest in possession – sec. 23.
5. Income of settled property acquired on death of the spouse if the settlement was effected before the commencement of the Act – sec. 25.
6. Property passing by reason of a *bona fide* purchase for full or partial consideration in money – sec. 26.
7. Settled property in respect of which, since the date of settlement, estate duty had been paid on the death of the deceased's spouse – sec. 29. [7]
8. Certain pensions and annuities payable to the widow and other dependants of the deceased – sec. 29A.
9. Gifts made by the deceased for a public charitable purpose in the vulnerable period (i.e. within a period of six months before death) to the extent of Rs. 2,500 – sec. 33(1)(a). [8]
10. Gifts made by the deceased for any other purpose in the vulnerable period (i.e. within a period of two years before death), to the extent of Rs. 1,500 – sec. 33(1)(b).
11. Household goods to the extent of Rs. 2,500 – sec. 33(1)(c).
12. Book not intended for sale – sec. 33(1)(d)

13. Wearing apparel, but not including any precious stones or ornaments – sec. 33(1)(e)
14. Insurance policies taken out and moneys deposited for the purpose of eventual payment of estate duty subject to a monetary limit of Rs. 50,000 or the amount actually payable as duty, whichever was lower – secs. 31(1)(f) and (g).
15. Moneys payable under one or more policies of insurance effected by the deceased on his life to the extent of Rs. 5,000 – sec. 33(1)(h). [9]
16. Drawings, paintings, photographs etc. which were retained in the family of the deceased and dealt with or disposed of in accordance with the prescribed conditions and were not intended for sale – sec. 33(1)(j)
17. Moneys earmarked under policies of insurance or declaration of trusts or settlements by the deceased for the marriage of female relatives dependent upon him to the extent of Rs. 10,000 in respect of each such relative. – sec. 33(1)(k)
18. Any one building in the occupation of a former ruler declared by the Central Government as his official residence – sec. 33(1)(l)
19. Estate of members of the armed forces killed in action, during operations against an enemy and of members of the police force, including border security force, killed in action in protecting the border - secs. 33(1)(m) and (mm). [10]
20. One house or part thereof exclusively use by the deceased for his residence, to the extent the principal value did not exceed rupees one lakh if such a house was situated in a place with a population exceeding ten thousand, and the full principal value in any other case – sec. 33(1)(n)
21. Property gifted by the deceased to his spouse, son, daughter, brother or sister at least five years before his death provided that the gift was chargeable to gift tax under the Gift Tax Act, 1958 – sec. 33(1)(o)
22. National Defence Gold Bonds, 1980, to the extent of an aggregate weight of fifty kilograms of gold – sec. 33(1)(p)

Aggregation of Properties for Rate Purposes: It should be noted that the properties mentioned in sections 33(1)(a), 33(1)(b), 33(1)(f) and (g), 33(1)(h), and 33(1)(k) though not liable to estate duty were included in the principal value of estate for the purpose of determining the rate of duty. [11]

Deductions and Reliefs: The provisions relating to deductions in computing the principal value of the estate and reliefs from the duty payable were contained in Part VI (Sections 44 to 50B) of the Estate Duty Act, 1953. The following deductions were permissible.

1. Funeral expenses up to Rs. 1,000 – sec. 44 [12]

2. All bonafide debts and encumbrances with some exceptions – sec. 44
3. Relief from estate duty where court fees had been paid for obtaining representation to estate of the deceased – sec. 50.
4. Relief from estate duty where gift tax had been paid – sec. 50A
5. Relief from estate duty where tax has been paid on capital gains – sec. 50B

Quick Succession Relief: An estate which has been subjected to duty may change hands quickly on account of successive deaths and again become liable to payment of duty. In such cases, estate duty puts undue burden on families suffering deaths at short intervals. This problem is mitigated by providing quick succession relief in the law.

To prevent quick diminution of such estates, section 31 of the Estate Duty Act, 1953 provided relief from duty on 'the same property' consequent upon deaths taking place in quick succession. The relief was provided on the basis of fixed percentages laid down in the section itself. The amount of estate duty payable on the second death in respect of the same property was reduced as under:

Where the second death occurs within

3 months of the first death	100 per cent
1 year of the first death	50 per cent
2 years of the first death	40 per cent
3 years of the first death	30 per cent
4 years of the first death	20 per cent
5 years of the first death	10 per cent

It may be observed that duty payable was reduced on account of successive death occurring within 5 years and depended on the interval during which the estate changed hands. Reduction in duty was not allowed where a successive death occurred beyond a period of five years.

Further, in case the value on which the duty was payable on the second death exceeded the value of the property on which the duty was payable on the first death, the latter value was substituted for the former for the purpose of calculating the relief.

Rate-Structure: Estates with a net capital value or principal value of Rs. 50,000 or less were exempt from duty. On estates of a higher value than Rs. 50,000 there was a progressive duty, ranging from 4 per cent to 85 per cent on estates with a net capital value of over Rs. 20 lakh. The progressive rates of estate duty were justified by the Committee on Direct Tax Laws (1978) in the following words, "The fact that income-tax and wealth-tax rates have been brought down does not necessarily imply that there is a case for similar reduction in the estate duty rates. With the deceased's property subject to first charge under section 74 of the Estate Duty Act, there is almost an assumption that there is a prior claim of the State over that of the legal heirs. Besides, the incidence of this levy is felt the least since inheritance is a mere bounty. Estate duty, which thus stands on a different footing, can play a more significant role in the national goal of achieving a socialistic pattern of society." [13]

Notes

1. Nicholas Kaldor, *An Expenditure Tax* (London: George Allen and Unwin Ltd., 1955), p. 95.

2. Quoted in Richard A. Musgrave and Peggy B. Musgrave, *op. cit.*, p. 496.

3. Government of India, Economic Administration Reforms Commission, *Report on Tax Administration, 1981-83*, p. 33.

4. There was no specific definition of 'principal value' in the Estate Duty Act, 1953. The Direct Tax Laws Committee (1978) had recommended the following definition: The term 'principal value of the estate' may be defined to mean the aggregate of market values of all property which passes or is deemed to pass on the death of a person as reduced by the debts and encumbrances and after allowance of the admissible deductions. See, Government of India, Ministry of Finance, *Final Report of Direct Tax Laws Committee* (Chairman: C.C. Chokshi), September, 1978, p. 216.

5. The incidence of estate duty depended on the domicile of the deceased person and location of the property. In case the deceased was domiciled in India, duty was attracted on all properties passing on his death except immovable properties situated outside India. However, if the deceased was not domiciled in India, the duty was payable on all properties passing on death which were situated in India.

6. 6 months in the case of gifts made for charitable purposes.

7. While section 25 dealt with settlements effected before the commencement of the Act, section 29 related to cases in which estate duty had been paid on the death of any one party to a marriage irrespective of when the settlement was made.

8. The Direct Tax Laws Committee had recommended the limits under section 33(1)(a) and 33(1(b) to be raised to Rs. 5,000 and Rs. 3,000 respectively. It had also recommended the period of two years mentioned in section 33(1)(b) to be raised to five years to bring it in line with its another recommendation for increasing the period for gifts under section 9 from two years to five years. See, *Final Report of the Direct Tax Laws Committee*, op. cit., p. 224.

9. The Direct Tax Laws Committee (1978) had recommended this exemption to be raised to Rs. 10,000. It should be noted that provident funds were not being treated on par with insurance moneys for exemption under section 33(1)(h) of the Estate Duty Act whereas in the Income Tax Act, 1961, all long-term savings in the form of insurance policies and provident funds were treated almost alike for tax concessions. The Committee, therefore, found no justification for leaving out provident fund deposits from the scope of exemption under the estate duty law and therefore recommended that moneys payable from provident funds should also be covered by exemption under section 31(1)(h) of the Estate Duty Act within the same consolidated monetary limit of Rs. 10,000 (as recommended by it). See, *Final Report of Direct Tax Laws Committee*, op. cit., p. 225.

10. The Direct Tax Laws Committee (1978) had recommended the enlargement of this exemption to the cases of civil servants and members of National Cadet Corps, Territorial Army,

Home Guards etc. whose employment in the national cause is equally hazardous. For details, see *Final Report of Direct Tax Laws Committee*, op. cit., p. 225.

11. See Part IV, Section 34(1)(a) of the Estate Duty Act, 1953.

12. The Direct Tax Laws Committee (1978) had recommended this limit to be raised to Rs. 2,500. See, *Final Report of Direct Tax Laws Committee*, op. cit., p.230.

13. See, *Final Report of Direct Tax Laws Committee*, op. cit., p. 242.

Appendix 12

Expenditure Tax in India: The Failed Experiment

Following the recommendations of Professor Nicholas Kaldor, a tax on personal expenditure was first imposed in India on April 1, 1958. The tax was introduced as an adjunct to the personal income tax as part of a scheme to evolve a self-checking system of direct taxes in India.

Expenditure tax was withdrawn by Mr. Morarji Desai in his budget for the year 1962-63 on account of insignificant revenue yield and its failure to restrain ostentatious expenditure, and promote savings. [1] It was reintroduced in the 1964-65 budget by Mr. T.T. Krishnamachari with the hope that the tax would help lessen inequalities of income and wealth. However, the tax was repealed again in the 1966-67 budget on the grounds of burden on administration and inconvenience to assesses. [2]

Some of the features of the expenditure tax in the last year of its operation (1965-66) were the following: Corporations were not subject to tax, neither was any taxpayer whose income from all sources did not exceed Rs. 36,000 in the base year (the base year was the same as that for income tax purposes, expiring on March 31). An individual taxpayer and his dependants were entitled to a simple standard expenditure allowance of Rs. 30,000. Also, there was a long list of expenditures exempt from tax: (a) expenditure incurred in earning income, (b) investment expenditure either in connection with a business or in the nature of personal investment in deposits, loans, shares, securities, insurance policies, etc. (c) expenditures covering books, and works of art, (d) charitable expenditures, (e) expenditures by way of gifts, trust and settlements, (f) expenditures on Union, State and Local government taxes, and (g) cost of legal proceedings, expenditure on marriage, medical treatment, maintenance of parents, and education outside India, up to specified limits. [3]

That the tax proved a flop is evident from the small number of assessees falling within its ambit, and the meagre revenue collections. For example, in the first year when the expenditure tax was imposed, the total number of assessees was 7,774 as against 9,83,277 under the income tax. [4]

It is noteworthy that the revenue yield was poor in spite of the high rates of the tax which ranged from 10 per cent on the first Rs. 10,000 of taxable expenditure to 100 per cent on taxable expenditure above Rs. 50,000. The low coverage and low revenue yield of the tax were attributed to the following three factors:

1. High initial income exemption.
2. Generous standard expenditure allowance.
3. Complex and comprehensive series of exempt categories of expenditure. [5]

The introduction of expenditure tax proved abortive in Ceylon (now Sri Lanka) also where it was imposed in 1959, but withdrawn in 1963. The unsuccessful experiments of India, and Sri Lanka have served as a deterrent for other countries to impose expenditure tax.

In 1985, the Government of India appointed a Study Group on Taxation of Expenditure which discounted the practicability of administering a universal classical type of expenditure tax. It observed, "In a developing country, such as India, given the large share of cash transactions, the fact that a substantial number of taxpayers do not maintain proper accounts and the limited capability of the tax administration, the administration of a full-fledged expenditure tax would simply not be feasible." [6]

Expenditure Tax Act, 1987

In 1987, the Government introduced, on a modest scale, a tax on luxury expenditure relating to hotel receipts. The Expenditure Tax Act, 1987 levied a tax at the rate of 20 per cent (reduced to 10 per cent by the Finance, Act, 1994) on expenditure incurred in hotels where the room charge for any unit of accommodation is Rs. 400 or more per day per individual (increased to Rs. 1200 or more by the Finance Act, 1992). This tax is charged on expenditure incurred in a hotel on food or drink, accommodation, and other services. However, expenditure for which payment is made in foreign exchange or any expenditure incurred by a person enjoying diplomatic immunity is exempted from the levy of expenditure tax. The exemption granted in respect of payment made in foreign exchange was withdrawn by the Finance Act, 1992.

The scope of expenditure tax was extended to expenditure incurred in air-conditioned restaurants by the Finance (No. 2) Act, 1991. This tax was levied at the rate of 15 per cent on the expenditure incurred in, or any payment made to such restaurants for the provision of food and drink. However, in a hurried move the Finance Minister announced the withdrawal of the levy of expenditure tax on air-conditioned restaurants in his 1992-93 budget speech.

In the above context, the Task Force on Direct Taxes (Chairman: Vijay Kelkar) observed, "The present tax on expenditure in hotels is in the nature of a consumption tax. It was introduced as a separate tax in the absence of a tax on services. Since tax on services has since been introduced, it is only appropriate that this levy is merged with the service tax." [7] Following the recommendations of the Task Force, expenditure tax was abolished effective from June 1, 2003.

Notes

1. Government of India, Ministry of Finance, *Speeches of Union Finance Ministers, 1947-48 to 1984-85,* p. 216.

2. *Ibid.,* p. 275.

3. James Cutt, *Taxation and Economic Development in India* (New Delhi: Vikas Publications, 1969), p. 197.

4. Government of India, *Report of Direct Taxes Administration Enquiry Committee* (Chairman: Mahavir Tyagi), 1958-59, p. 8.

5. James Cutt, *op. cit.*, p. 200.

6. Government of India, Ministry of Finance, *Study Group on Taxation of Expenditure* (Final Report), 1987, p. 121.

7. Government of India, Ministry of Finance and Company Affairs, *Report of the Task Force on Direct Taxes* (Chairman: Vijay Kelkar), December 2002, p. 178.

Part IX: Glossary of Fiscal Terms

Glossary of Fiscal Terms

—A—

Ability-to-Pay Principle of Taxation: It states that if a given amount of revenue is needed to finance public services, then each taxpayer should contribute in line with his ability-to-pay taxes. Those who possess more economic power (income and wealth) should contribute more to public exchequer and vice versa. The duty to pay taxes is seen as a collective responsibility rather than a personal one. The ability-to-pay principle views tax policy issues in isolation to incidence of public expenditure. This principle is regarded by many as the most equitable and just method of taxation. It is emphasised primarily for its redistributive role.

Accrued Income: It is the income earned during a particular accounting period but not actually received during that period.

Accumulated Depreciation: It is the total depreciation expense accrued from the date of purchase of an asset to the present.

Additional Resource Mobilisation (ARM): It means resources raised through additional efforts such as raising the rates of existing taxes and/or levying new taxes.

Administered Prices: These are prices set consciously by a government rather than being determined by the free play of market forces. Prices of petroleum products in India are a case in point.

Administrative Costs: These are costs incurred by public authorities in administering a tax. These costs (also called expense ratio) include wages of tax officials and expenditure on stores and supplies for running tax administration.

***Ad Valorem* Duty:** An *ad valorem* duty is imposed as a fixed percentage of the price of the product taxed.

Advance Tax Payment: It is a system under which assessees are required to pay tax in advance on incomes which they expect to earn during the current financial year. Advance tax, payable in instalments during the financial year itself, is adjusted against the tax liability determined after proper assessment. Under

Section 208 of the Indian Income Tax Act, 1961, it is obligatory to pay advance tax in every case where the advance tax payable is Rs. 5,000 or more.

Allowances: These are amounts the deductibility of which is statutorily allowed from the tax base, e.g. investment allowance. They have the effect of reducing the tax base.

Amortisation: In finance, it means the gradual repayment of a debt by means of a sinking fund. Thus, amortisation of debt means gradual reduction of a debt through periodic payments. In another context amortisation of an asset (machinery) refers to depreciation in its value over time.

Annuity: It is a fixed sum of money paid to an annuitant yearly, usually for the remaining part of his life. It is a form of pension which provides a regular annual income. An annuity may be purchased by making a lump sum cash payment.

Anti-dumping Tariff: It is imposed to discourage dumping. The tariff rate is usually the difference between the normal selling price and the dumping price. Dumping means the sale of a product in a foreign market at a price much below that at which it is being sold in the domestic market.

Assessee: An assessee is a person by whom a tax is payable under some tax law. It includes every person in respect of whom any proceeding has been taken up for the assessment of his income, wealth, etc. It also includes a person who is assessable in respect of income of another person.

Asset: Ownership of any physical property or right that has money value is called asset. Land, buildings, machinery and other forms of physical property are called *tangible assets*. Goodwill, patents, trademarks, copyrights and other non-material benefits are called *intangible assets*. Similarly, cash in hand, marketable securities, inventories and other assets which can be readily converted into money are called *current assets* while plant, equipment and time deposits are *fixed assets* because they are not readily convertible into money.

Assignment of Tax: Assignment of a tax means transfer of taxation power from a higher level to a lower level government. Taxation power includes the following: right to levy the tax, collect the tax, and appropriate the proceeds from the tax.

Average Tax Rate: It is derived by expressing tax amount as a percentage of taxable income. It is also called effective tax rate.

—B—

Balanced Budget: It is a situation in which current revenue of the government is exactly equal to its current expenditure.

Basic Personal Exemption: Income tax laws of almost all countries conventionally grant exemption of a given portion of income which does not reflect taxpaying capacity of a person. There are two considerations for this exemption. 1. Tax bite into income, barely sufficient for a minimum standard of living, is immoral. 2. It is administratively difficult to deal with low income earners.

Benefit Principle of Taxation: According to this traditional approach, an equitable tax system is one under which tax payments are based on the amount of benefits received from government services. In other words, the cost of government services should be apportioned among individuals according to the relative benefits they enjoy. Clearly, implementation of the benefit principle presupposes determination of the incidence of public expenditure before deciding distribution of tax burden. Thus, it encompasses issues of both tax and expenditure policies.

Best Judgement Assessment: It is an assessment made by a tax officer against a person who is in default of furnishing information as regards his income, wealth etc. Thus, where an assessee fails to file a return or submit documents called for or comply with the terms of a notice, the assessing officer may assess total income, wealth etc. according to the best of his judgement. This he can do after giving the assessee an opportunity of being heard.

Betterment Levy: It is a tax on unearned increment in connection with town improvement (betterment) schemes. Execution of a development scheme by public authorities generally leads to increase in the annual and capital value of land and buildings under the scope of the scheme. Such appreciation is not the result of any individual efforts, but materialises from the corporate activity of the community as a whole. Betterment levy on unearned increment in land values is justified on the ground that it provides additional resources to the government to liquidate partially or fully the capital cost of the development scheme.

Betting Tax: It is levied on horse races. The tax is levied on stakeholder who may be either a race club or a bookmaker. The law governing betting tax is generally regulatory in nature. The main objective is to discourage poorer sections of the population from gambling on horse races.

Bond: A bond is a promise to pay a stated sum of money as interest each year and to repay the face value of bond at some future redemption date. Some bonds, called *perpetuities*, pay a fixed sum of interest each year forever but never repay the principal, i.e. they have no redemption date.

Bonded Warehouse: It is a warehouse licensed and bonded by the government to insure against loss of customs duty. Goods subject to customs duty may be stored there without paying duty. Such goods are said to be under bond. These storage facilities are operated under the lock and key of a country's customs authorities and the owners of these facilities are bonded to ensure that they will satisfy all customs duty obligations. The importer will have to pay the existing duty on the goods if they enter the domestic market.

Bracket Creep: It is a situation when a person's income, rising at the same rate as price level, faces higher rates of taxation.

Budget: It is a financial plan listing expenditure and income expected during some given future period, usually one year. A budget may be prepared by an individual, a family, a company, or a government.

Budget Deficit: It is a situation signifying shortfall of current revenue of the government below its current expenditure.

Budget Incidence: It relates to the combined effects of an equal increase in tax and public expenditure on the distribution of income. It is also called net incidence and is obtained by summing, algebraically, both the tax incidence (negative) and expenditure incidence (positive) for each of the subgroups of the population.

Buffer Stock: It refers to the stock of a commodity (say wheat) kept to meet fluctuations in its demand and/or supply so as to keep its price under check. It is thus a residual between supply and demand. When demand is less than supply it stores the residual and when demand is greater than supply it supplies the residual.

—C—

Canons of Taxation: These are principles or maxims used in the designing or evaluation of a tax or a tax system. Given the level of taxation in a country, fiscal experts can design a tax system which best promotes the objectives of economic policy with due regard to social justice. Adam Smith (1723-1790), the famous 18th century British economist, was the first to set forth such maxims in his book *Wealth of Nations* published in 1776. He laid down the following four general guidelines for designing an ideal system of taxation: equity, certainty, convenience and economy.

Capital: It refers to all those man-made machines and appliances which are used for further production of goods and services rather than being consumed for their own sake.

Capital Allowances: These are deductions from business income for depreciation of assets used in business. These are allowed because fixed assets (like plant and machinery) are gradually used up in the production process. If their wear and tear is not taken into account, the taxable income will be overstated. Annual capital allowances traditionally take the form of a fixed percentage of the cost of an asset.

Capital Expenditure: In the context of taxation of income, the distinction between capital expenditure and revenue expenditure is important because only revenue expenditure is allowed to be deducted while computing income. Capital expenditure is deductible to the extent of depreciation allowance permitted.

Capital Gains Tax: It is a tax on the increase in capital value of an asset.

Capital Levy: It is a one-time tax on existing wealth. It is different from annual tax on wealth. Such a drastic fiscal measure is resorted to during or after a war or some other national emergency. The purpose of capital levy is to reduce the size of national debt and relieve the inflationary pressure associated with it.

Capital Loss: It is a decrease in the value of an asset. In terms of the net accretion principle, capital losses are set off against capital gains and net capital losses are treated as a reduction in income (economic power) of an individual.

Capital Receipts: Those receipts of an organisation which create liability or reduce assets are called capital receipts. Thus, money obtained by way of loan, from the sale of fixed assets, issue of shares and debentures are capital receipts. They are generally of a non-recurring nature. Capital receipts are exempt from income tax unless they are expressly taxable whereas revenue receipts are taxable unless they are expressly exempt from tax.

Cascading Effect: This concept is associated with a traditional turnover tax which is levied on transaction of goods and services at all levels of production and distribution. For example, excise duty may be levied on raw materials, components, semi-finished and finished goods. This system of taxation increases the price of a commodity much more than the tax collected, resulting in *cascading*. The price of a finished product reflects the taxes imposed on inputs used.

Casual Income: Refers to income which is non-recurring in nature. It is produced by chance, accident or fortune. It is neither calculated nor settled nor is there any likelihood of its coming at a certain time. In some countries, casual income up to a certain level is exempt from income tax. For example, under Section 10(3) of the Indian Income Tax Act, 1961, casual income is exempt from tax up to Rs. 5,000.

Cess: A levy, usually on plantation crops (tobacco, jute), to raise funds for research and improvement schemes related to those crops (e.g. high-yielding variety of seeds). A cess is different from a tax in that the proceeds of the former are used for the benefit of industry on which it is levied.

Compensatory Duty: It is a tariff levied on the import of a commodity to match some other tax which a country has imposed on local production of the same commodity. It is levied so that domestic producers are not put to any disadvantage.

Compliance Costs of a Tax: Compliance costs refer to costs incurred by taxpayers or third parties in complying with a tax, over and above the tax payment made to public authorities.

Compounded Levy: Levying of excise duty on the production of small-scale sector is a major problem of tax administration. The procedures adopted for collection of excise from large-scale units are often found expensive and time-consuming when applied to small firms. Under compounded levy, a lump sum payment is made on the basis of some installations, e.g. the number of looms in a textile unit. Once the compounded levy is paid, the producer becomes free from all excise formalities except to maintain a record of looms in operation.

Consignment Tax: It is a levy on inter-state transfer of goods. A consignment is a despatch or a stock-transfer from a company to its branch located in a different state. Since no sale is involved, it is called in-house transaction by a company. Sometimes, unscrupulous parties evade payment of inter-state sales tax by showing virtual sales as consignments from one state to another. By this method, the payment of inter-state sales tax is avoided. This problem was faced by the tax authorities in India. Hence, through a Constitutional amendment the Central Government was empowered to levy taxes on the consignment of goods (whether the consignment is to the person making it or to any other person), where such consignment takes place in the course of inter-state trade or commerce.

Corporate Income Tax: It is levied on the earnings of corporations. A corporation (or a company) is regarded as a separate entity for purposes of income tax. Total income of a corporation is arrived at with reference to its profits shown in its profit and loss account.

Cost-Yield Ratio: It is the cost of collection expressed as a proportion of tax revenue. A lower cost-yield ratio is considered indicative of the efficiency of tax administration. Unusually high cost-yield ratio is a drag on public exchequer. Thus, cost-yield ratios may be used to evaluate administration of competing taxes.

Countervailing Duty: It is a duty in addition to the normal import duty levied on goods imported into a country. The rate of countervailing duty is generally equal to the excise duty imposed on like items produced domestically. The argument is that normal import duty represents the desirable degree of protection to internally produced goods which are not subject to excise duty. When excise duty is levied or the rate of an existing one is increased, a corresponding enhancement in import duty is required to preserve the accepted degree of protection.

Crowding-out: The term is descriptive of any group/section being pushed out of a market. In the context of financial market, the demand for credit by the government and other public sector institutions may be so strong and inflexible that credit requirements of households and companies are crowded-out.

Customs Duty: It is a tax on the import and export of goods levied by a national government and payable to it when the goods cross the customs boundaries of the nation. Hence, it is also called border tax.

—D—

Debt Trap: It is a situation in which a government is unable to repay its past loans without fresh borrowings

Deductions: Deductions mean all amounts which are eligible for subtraction from gross receipts of a business. Strictly speaking, a deduction relates to an actual outlay e.g. expenditure on travelling. Tax laws must clearly specify as to which sums are allowed as deductions from gross receipts in order to determine the amount on which a given set of rates is to be applied.

Deficit Financing: When all types of government receipts fall short of its stipulated total expenditure, then the only alternative left with it is to print more currency. The net effect of deficit financing is to increase money supply in the economy. When money supply increases, it puts pressure on the supply of goods and services. Since supply cannot be increased so easily, prices have a tendency to rise. Price rise is accompanied by its own adverse effects because the burden of price rise falls inequitably on different classes. Deficit financing is a kind of inflation tax which drives the people into involuntary savings.

Deflation: It refers to decrease in the general price level in an economy.

Devaluation: As part of a government's commercial policy, it refers to deliberate reduction in the value of domestic currency in relation to foreign currencies. Devaluation makes domestically produced goods cheaper for the foreigners and foreign goods expensive for the locals. Hence, imports are reduced and exports are promoted to improve the trade balance. For successful devaluation, it is necessary that demand for imports as well as exports is relatively elastic.

Direct Tax: It is a tax the ultimate burden of which falls on the person on whom it is levied. In other words, it is a tax that cannot be shifted from the original payer to someone else. It is contrasted with indirect tax which can readily be shifted to ultimate consumers of the commodity or service taxed.

Discriminating Duty: An import duty levied at a level different from comparable import duties so as to encourage (or discourage) imports of a particular commodity or imports from a particular country.

Dumping: It is a practice of selling goods in a foreign country at a price below their domestic selling price, after allowing for differences due to transportation expenses, tariffs, and other cost justifications. Many governments view the activity as an unfair competitive practice and frequently expose those engaged in dumping to the imposition of an antidumping duty. This generally unfavourable view of the practice stems from the monopoly precondition which underlies it. Economic theory specifies that in order for a producer to discriminate in the pricing of identical goods between markets (or classes of consumers) some element of monopoly power must be present; otherwise, the producer is merely a price-taker forced to adopt the uniform competitive price determined in the overall marketplace.

Duty Drawback: It refers to repayment of import duty, partially or fully, to exporters of commodities in the manufacture of which imported materials and components are used. Duty drawback scheme is a device to encourage exports. Most often, the scheme is used for imported raw materials or semi-finished goods (like raw diamonds) that are incorporated into a finished product (cut and polished diamonds) and then re-exported. Complications arise when exported goods use raw materials and components some of which are imported and some produced domestically. The drawback in such cases means refund of an amount which represents the import duty paid on the imported materials used in the exported goods.

Duty-free Shop: A shop at airports, on ships etc. from where outgoing passengers may buy goods which are free of commodity taxes because the purchases are meant for exports. Similarly, incoming passengers may purchase certain goods from duty-free shop at a cheaper price than usual because they do not have to pay duty that is usually paid when goods are brought into a country.

—E—

Earmarking of Taxes: Earmarking is a fiscal practice under which revenues from one or more sources are pooled into a separate independent fund which is used to finance certain pre-determined public services.

Earned and Unearned Income: Earned income (or employment or labour income) is derived from actual work or services performed and includes wages, salaries and income from professions. Unearned income (or capital or property income) is derived from investment, rent etc.

Entertainment Tax: It is levied on the price charged for admission to various places of entertainment such as a cinema, circus, theatre, exhibition, variety show, cabaret, night-club and casino.

Estate Duty: It is a levy on the value of the entire estate left behind by a decedent before its division among the inheritors. It is contrasted with an inheritance tax which is based on the share of the estate received by each beneficiary. Estate duty (or death duty) is simpler and more productive than inheritance tax because the former avoids the difficult task of determining the value of the share of each inheritor. Estate duty is usually levied at a progressive rate to reduce economic disparities.

Excise Duty: It is a tax on goods produced or manufactured within a country. It is collected from the producers of excisable goods.

Exemptions: Exemptions (or exclusions) are those items which are explicitly and statutorily freed from the scope of a tax and therefore remain untaxed. They may be termed as non-taxable gross receipts. Several considerations weigh on a government to declare a host of receipts exempt, either fully or up to specified limits, from the scope of taxation.

Expenditure Tax: It is a tax on personal expenditure.

Export Subsidies: These are provisions of financial assistance to exporters for encouraging them to export and for making their exports cheaper and competitive in the foreign market.

—F—

Fee: Fee is charged by public authorities for providing certain services such as registration of marriages, births and deaths. Generally, the fee is charged equal to the cost of a service.

Financial Year: It is the year of account for financial purposes, often not coinciding with the calendar year. For example, in India the financial year (or fiscal year) runs from April 1 to March 31 of the following year. In USA, the fiscal year runs from July 1 to June 30.

Fine: A fine is a compulsory payment without any *quid pro quo* to curb certain offence. It is different from a tax because the objective is not to get revenue for the government.

Fiscal Capacity: It refers to the ability of an individual to pay taxes or the ability of a government to raise revenues.

Fiscal Drag: In a period of inflation, the value of money decreases. Therefore, the value of exemptions, deductions, and allowances allowed in the computation of income and tax liability becomes less in real terms. The brackets of taxable income chargeable at progressive rates also shrink in real terms. Taxpayers are pushed into higher income bands (and therefore higher rates) because of increasing money income which in real terms may remain the same. The higher rate of income tax may lead to reduction in real income owing to this fiscal drag.

Fiscal Federalism: A federal set up creates a multiple polity based on divided functions and powers among central, state and local governments. Fiscal federalism deals with financial arrangements and their working in a federal polity.

Fiscal Marksmanship: It refers to the degree of accuracy of budgetary forecasts. Extensive estimates of revenue and expenditure are set forth in the budget of a government for the ensuing financial year. The *actuals* or *accounts* of the revenue and expenditure become available after the expiry of the financial year under consideration. Perfectly accurate estimates of revenue, and expenditure are never possible and therefore some divergence is always there between the *budget estimates* and the *actuals*. The degree of deviation between the two indicates the skill and competence of budget-makers. Excessive deviation reveals the poor fiscal predictability (or marksmanship) of the experts.

Fiscal Monopolies: These are non-financial public enterprises exercising monopoly in the production and/or distribution of such commodities as tobacco, alcoholic beverages, and salt. Using the monopoly power, revenues are raised for the government which may otherwise be gathered through taxes if such commodities are produced/distributed by private units.

Fiscal Policy: It refers to the use of a government's taxation and expenditure policies to influence the level of economic activities at the macroeconomic level.

Flat Rate: Fixed rate of tax regardless of the amount of income.

Free Port: Free port or a free trade zone allows goods to be temporarily imported and held within the port area without paying duty, provided they are re-exported later. The goods may be stored, processed, and/or repackaged in this area, and then either imported in the normal way by paying customs duty or re-exported without paying tariff. Thus, Singapore is a free port and Kandla is a free trade zone.

Free Rider: A free rider is a person who receives benefits of a government service without paying for it.

Future Trading: It refers to commodity or currency trading done on contract for future delivery. The purpose is to insure against risks of price changes, exchange rate changes etc. or to make a profit by speculating on the price trends.

—G—

Gift Tax: It is imposed on the aggregate value of gifts made by a person (donor) during the year. A gift is defined as a transfer by one person to another of any existing movable or immovable property made voluntarily and without consideration in money or money's worth. In other words, before a transfer of property becomes liable to gift tax, the following conditions must be satisfied: (a) the transfer must be voluntary, (b) the transfer must be of existing property and (c) the transfer must be without consideration in money or money's worth.

Gilt-edged Securities: These are government securities free of risk of default.

Grants: Grants are unilateral transfers from one level of government to another (usually lower) level of government. They have the advantage of being targeted towards fiscally disadvantaged state/municipal governments to reduce horizontal fiscal imbalances. They can also be made conditional regarding their utilisation.

—H—

Highway-user Tax: It is a tax levied on the users of highways. The revenue is generally reserved for the construction and maintenance of highways. In USA, highway-user taxes are imposed by both the Federal and the State Governments. They are in the form of a fixed amount per gallon of gasoline sold, and licence fee for motor vehicles.

Horizontal Equity: It is a tax equity criterion advocating similar tax treatment of persons in similar economic circumstances.

—I—

Impact of Tax: It refers to the point at which the burden of a tax falls initially.

Imports: Imports are defined as goods taken into one country from another country in the conduct of foreign trade, with the first country being the importer and the second the exporter.

Imputed Income: Imputed income arises when a taxpayer is himself the producer and the consumer of a given commodity or service. Although no market transaction is involved yet the taxpayer enjoys a certain amount of consumption.

Incidence of Taxation: It refers to the final resting place of tax burden as against the impact which means the first place where a tax is imposed. The incidence of a tax is on the person who ultimately pays it, i.e. who cannot shift it any further.

Income Tax: It is a tax levied on the annual income of various taxable entities, mainly individuals and companies. The taxable income is determined after taking into account certain exemptions and deductions. No tax at all is paid on a basic income that is exempt. Rate schedule of the tax is generally progressive. The larger the taxable income, the higher the tax rate. Higher rates apply not to the total income but to increments of income. The progressive nature of income tax is based on the ability-to-pay principle of taxation.

Indirect Tax: It is a tax which can be shifted from the original payer to the ultimate consumer of the commodity or service taxed. Import duties, excise levies, and sales taxes are generally regarded as indirect taxes. Thus, an excise duty on cigarettes levied on producers is usually passed on to the consumers in the form of higher prices.

Inflation Tax: There are several ways through which resources can be acquired by the government for public use. One such method is deficit financing, i.e. printing more currency. Through deficit financing, it can purchase a part of goods and services available in the economy. Since such a policy usually leads to price rise, it is called *inflation tax*. The effects of such a policy are very disorderly in the sense that the burden of inflation falls inequitably on different classes.

Inheritance Tax: It is a levy on persons who receive property upon the death of a benefactor. It is different from estate duty which is based on the value of the entire estate left behind by a decedent and before it is divided among the heirs. A tax on each inheritance to which the estate gives rise is known as inheritance tax or succession duty.

Inter-corporate Dividends: These are dividends received by a company from another company. Income tax laws generally treat a parent (or a holding) company and its subsidiary company as separate legal entities and therefore tax them separately. Thus, if a holding company receives dividends from its subsidiary, the former has to pay tax on such dividends. Taxation of inter-corporate earnings is designed to prevent concentration of economic power in the hands of corporate giants. However, this provision is said to give rise to treble taxation of such dividends, first in the hands of the earning company, then in the hands of the receiving company, and finally in the hands of individual shareholders. Tax laws often provide certain concessions to facilitate inter-corporate investment.

Inter-governmental Transfers: Transfers (tax sharing and grants) are used to correct vertical imbalances, i.e. mismatch of revenue and expenditure responsibilities of different levels of a government. However, before such transfers are effected, it should be ensured that taxes, duties and levies assigned to a government are being optimally tapped. Thus, tax effort, if not a pre-condition, should at least form part of the formula for transfers. The need for transfers arises because the own revenues of a lower level government (through tax assignments and non-tax sources) are insufficient to meet the expenditure required for providing services allotted to it.

—J—

Joint Assessment: It refers to aggregation of the incomes of husband and wife for joint assessment by tax authorities.

Joint Occupancy of Tax Fields: It relates to concurrent taxation powers enjoyed by different tiers of government in a federal polity. Concurrent taxation powers are a characteristic feature of fiscal federalism in USA, Canada, and Australia. In India, the Central and the State Governments have no concurrent powers of taxation.

—L—

Levy: It is synonymous with tax.

Local Taxation: The term refers to taxes levied at the lower level of government in a federal polity such as municipalities, city corporations, district boards and other local bodies. These local bodies provide certain public services like basic health and education, construction and maintenance of local roads, sanitation, street lighting and parks. Taxes usually levied by local bodies are property tax, octroi, tax on professions and registration and licensing charges.

Lump Sum Tax: It refers to taxation of income, net wealth etc. expressed as a certain fixed sum rather than calculated under the ordinary tax law. This method is used for administrative convenience where facts are difficult to establish. In a lump sum tax, an individual cannot take action to alter his tax liability.

—M—

Marginal Tax Rate: It is the rate of tax, under a progressive rate schedule, applicable to the top slice or bracket of an assessee's income, net wealth or some other taxable item.

Minimum Alternative Tax (MAT): Income tax laws throughout the world generally provide for a number of tax concessions. A clever profit-making company may arrange its affairs in such a manner that the cumulative effect of all tax concessions is to reduce its income declared in the tax return to zero. MAT is a device to keep a zero tax company within the tax net.

Motor Vehicle Tax: It is a tax on vehicles suitable for use on roads. It is levied for granting registration, permit, driving licence etc., and is based on the type of vehicle (truck, bus, car, or scooter). It also means a tax paid periodically for the use of roads. Hence, it is also called road tax.

—N—

Nominal Rate of Tax: Rate of tax approved by the legislature is termed as nominal (or statutory) rate. It can be misleading when one takes into account exclusions, deductions, allowances, tax credits and tax evasion. These erosions in the tax base considerably reduce the average tax rate below the statutory one.

—O—

Octroi: It is a tax on the entry of goods into a local area from other areas for the purpose of consumption or sale. Though an important source of revenue for local bodies, it obstructs the free movement of vehicles carrying goods across the country.

—P—

Pay-As-You-Earn (PAYE): A system of collecting income tax from employees recommended by J.M. Keynes and introduced in Britain in 1944.

Perquisite: It means any casual emolument or benefit attached to an office or position in addition to salary or wages. It does not cover mere reimbursement of necessary disbursements. Perquisites may be provided in cash or in kind.

Poll Tax: Poll tax (also called head tax or capitation tax) is a direct tax of a fixed amount which is levied on individuals irrespective of income, wealth or any other such criterion. Since the amount of a poll tax is fixed, there are no problems of computation. The tax is apparently regressive because it takes a larger percentage of the income of the poor than of the rich.

Preferential Duty: It is an import duty levied at a relatively low level so as to favour imports of a particular commodity or imports from a particular country.

Presumptive Tax: Presumptive tax relates to the use of appropriate indicators of income, wealth etc. instead of the actual records of these tax bases. In the case of income tax, a presumptive tax is imposed on the basis of an estimated taxable income. Presumptive income is exogenously determined. The base for presumptive income tax is fixed and does not depend on the behaviour of individual entrepreneurs. In fact, a presumptive income tax works like a lump sum tax and therefore does not impose marginal tax burden on actual income. The chief advantage of presumptive taxation is its simplicity, both for tax collectors and taxpayers.

Professional Tax: It is a kind of registration fee for practising a profession. In India, State Governments are empowered to levy a tax on professions. However, according to Article 276 of the Constitution, the total amount payable in respect of any one person to the State by way of such tax is not to exceed Rs. 2,500 per annum.

Progressive Tax: A tax schedule is said to be progressive if the ratio of tax to income increases as one moves up the income scale.

Proportional Tax: A tax schedule is said to be proportional if the ratio of tax to income remains constant as one moves up the income scale.

—Q—

Quick Succession Relief: It means a reduction in estate duty if it is paid twice within a few years on the same estate due to a second death. An estate which has been subjected to duty may change hands quickly on account of successive deaths and again become liable to payment of duty. In such cases, estate duty puts undue burden on families suffering deaths at short intervals. This problem is mitigated by providing quick succession relief in the law.

—R—

Refund of Tax: Refund means to pay back. Where the amount of tax paid by a person in respect of any assessment year exceeds the amount of tax properly assessable for that year, he is entitled to a refund of such excess tax paid.

Regressive Tax: A tax schedule is said to be regressive if the ratio of tax to income declines as one moves up the income scale.

Revenue Deficit: It refers to the excess of revenue expenditure over revenue receipts.

Revenue Expenditure: It relates to the normal running of an organisation. Broadly speaking, all those expenditures of an organisation which do not result in the creation of physical or financial assets are treated as revenue expenditures.

Revenue Receipts: Moneys obtained in the normal course of business are called revenue receipts, e.g. sale proceeds, interest on deposits, and dividends on investment. Revenue receipts are normally of recurring nature and are not meant for any specific purpose.

Revenue Sharing: It is a term used in the context of fiscal federalism whereby a higher level of government imposes and collects certain taxes but shares, permissively or mandatorily, the proceeds with lower level governments.

—S—

Sales Tax: It is normally an *ad valorem* levy imposed on the seller with reference to the transaction of sale. Sales tax is generally regressive in nature because being paid by all consumers, it takes a larger proportion of small incomes than of larger ones. On the basis of the stage of collection, sales tax is classified into (a) multi-point sales tax and (b) single-point sales tax.

Securities: The term securities includes shares, bonds, debentures etc. of any body corporate or government. Securities which appear on the official stock exchange list and which may be bought and sold on the stock exchange are called listed securities.

Specific Duty: A specific or volumetric duty represents a fixed amount of tax on a unit of the physical quantity of the product. Customs duties, excise levies and sales taxes on commodities may take specific or *ad valorem* form.

Split Rate System: Under this system, profits distributed as dividends are taxed at a lower rate than retained earnings (i.e. undistributed profits).

Stamp Duty: It is a tax on documents dealing with such matters as transfer of property, shares, debentures and insurance policies. If unstamped, these documents become invalid. Stamp duty (or transfer tax) is generally collected through the sale of revenue stamps which must be affixed or imprinted on the document in question. Stamp duties are often under the jurisdiction of state and local governments.

Standard Deduction: It is common in the income tax laws of countries to allow deduction of expenditures from gross salary income incurred by taxpayers for employment purposes. If the deduction is allowed only on production or proof of having incurred such expenditure, the procedure will obviously be cumbersome for salaried persons. To simplify rules, many countries allow a standard deduction, from aggregate amount of salary, for all types of expenditure incurred towards employment.

Subsidy: A subsidy is a grant of money from an outside third party to either the buyer or the seller of a commodity. Subsidies allow a buyer to procure a commodity /service at a lower price than would otherwise have been necessary. The effect of a subsidy is opposite of the effect of a tax. A business firm will not stay in operation unless revenue is sufficient enough to cover cost plus some return on investment. If revenue from buyers is insufficient, a subsidy from an outside agency may keep the firm in operation.

Sumptuary Tax: It is a kind of excise on goods generally thought to have socially harmful effects. The best examples of such goods are alcoholic beverages and cigarettes. High taxes on these luxury items are imposed with a view to discourage their consumption and also on the ground that those who buy them can afford to pay additional tax.

Surcharge: It is an additional tax calculated on the normal tax liability. In other words, surcharge is assessed on the usual amount of tax due.

—T—

Tariff: It is a tax imposed by authorities on imports with various motives including cut in imports, protection to domestic industries or to earn revenue. Tariff imposed on imported goods according to their value is called *ad valorem* tariff.

Tax: A tax is a compulsory payment made to general government without any direct *quid pro quo*. General government includes central, state and local governments. Tax payments are compulsory and the benefits provided by government to taxpayers are neither direct nor proportional to such payments. Every tax is made up of two elements: a base, i.e. the object to be taxed, and a rate structure indicating how the base is to be taxed.

Tax Amnesty: It refers to an opportunity offered by a government to tax evaders to declare their past concealment of income, wealth etc., without fear of being prosecuted. Tax amnesty (or impunity) is granted only for the past in order to secure better compliance and higher tax yield in the present and future. A tax amnesty brings concealed money in the open, broadens the base of investment and hence accelerates economic development.

Tax Avoidance: It means preventing or reducing one's tax liability through manipulations within the framework of existing tax legislation. Tax avoidance, as against tax evasion, is legally permissible and hence a legitimate aim of taxpayers.

Tax Credit: Tax credit (or tax rebate) is a legal provision permitting taxpayers to deduct specified sums from their tax liability. A tax credit differs from a deduction because the former is subtracted after the total tax liability has been calculated whereas the latter is subtracted from the income subject to tax.

Apparently, a tax credit of a given amount is more valuable to a taxpayer than a deduction of the same amount. For example, a taxpayer who is in the 40 per cent bracket of individual income tax reduces his total burden by Rs. 1,000 if he is allowed a tax credit of Rs. 1,000. However, his tax burden is reduced by Rs. 400 if he is given a deduction of Rs. 1,000.

Tax Evasion: It is an illegal attempt to reduce tax payable through deliberate under-reporting/non-reporting taxable incomes or concealing one's true *state of affairs* from tax authorities. Tax evasion is a criminal offence and if detected is punishable by financial penalties or even by imprisonment or both.

Tax-free Zone: It is an area within the territory of a country in which customs duties and other indirect taxes are not applied. The area is used for export industries based on imported raw materials.

Tax-GDP Ratio: Level of taxation in a country is traditionally judged in terms of the ratio which taxes bear to some measure of national income. This ratio is called tax-GDP ratio and the change in it is determined by variations in both the numerator (total tax revenue) and the denominator (national income).

Tax Haven: It refers to any country or locality which levies very low taxes, or none at all, on foreigners.

Tax Holiday: It is a tax incentive targeted at new firms, and is not available to existing units. Under a tax holiday scheme, new enterprises are allowed a period of time free from the burden of income tax, subject to certain conditions.

Tax Incentives: These are provisions in tax laws which encourage individuals and corporations to undertake activities desired by the government.

Tax Lien: It refers to a government claim on property for which taxes have not been paid when due. In extreme cases, the property may revert to the government.

Toll: A toll (or octroi) is collected on goods that move into or through a local territory.

—U—

Units of Assessment: It means persons or taxable entities chargeable to tax under a tax law. For example, under the Indian Income Tax Act, 1961, there are seven units of assessment: 1. An individual, 2. A Hindu Undivided Family (HUF), 3. A company, 4. A Firm, 5. An association of persons or a body of individuals whether incorporated or not, 6. A local authority and 7. Every artificial juridical person, not falling within any of the preceding categories.

User Charge: It is a fee or charge for use of a government-supplied service, generally transportation service. It is applied so that those who benefit from public transport services repay the cost to the government. User charges are usually in the form of tolls, licence fees and fuel taxes and fall on highway and waterway traffic.

—V—

Value Added Tax (VAT): Value added tax is levied on the sellers of goods and services based on value added by their respective units. The base of VAT is determined by value added at a particular stage of production or distribution.

—W—

Ways and Means Advances: These are short-term loans (also called floating debt) made by the central bank of a country to the government of that country. The purpose of ways and means advances is to accommodate temporary mismatch in the receipts and payments of the government.

Wealth Tax: Wealth represents the command a person has over economic resources at any point of time. Tax base for purposes of wealth tax is normally the taxpayer's net wealth i.e. total assets less liabilities. The base is generally modified by exemptions and deductions.

Withholding Tax: It is a system of collecting income tax whereby money is periodically deducted by the employers, financial institutions, and others from wages of employees, returns on securities, and other payments. Thus, intermediaries (or third parties) do the job on behalf of the government as regards assessment of the taxable base and the collection of tax thereon.

—Z—

Zero-tax Company: Income tax laws usually provide for a host of deductions and incentives to promote socio-economic objectives of state policy. It is likely that a profit-making company may arrange its affairs in such a way that the cumulative effect of all deductions is to reduce its income declared in the tax return to zero. To deal with such situations, some countries have introduced minimum alternative tax.

Part X: Time-series Public Finance Data on India

Table 1: Combined Tax Revenue, Breakdown between Direct and Indirect Taxes with Percentage Shares, and Tax-GDP Ratios: 1950-51 to 2005-06

(Rs. crore)

Year	Combined tax revenue* (3+4)	Direct taxes	Indirect taxes	Col. 3 as % of Col. 2	Col. 4 as % of Col. 2	Col. 2 as % of GDP	Col. 3 as % of GDP	Col. 4 as % of GDP
1	2	3	4	5	6	7	8	9
1950-51	627	231	396	36.8	63.2	6.31	2.33	3.99
1951-52	739	244	495	33.0	67.0	6.99	2.31	4.68
1952-53	678	252	426	37.2	62.8	6.54	2.43	4.11
1953-54	672	242	430	36.0	64.0	5.96	2.15	3.81
1954-55	720	240	480	33.3	66.7	6.74	2.25	4.50
1955-56	768	259	509	33.7	66.3	7.06	2.38	4.68
1956-57	890	288	602	32.4	67.6	6.87	2.22	4.65
1957-58	1,045	327	718	31.3	68.7	7.83	2.45	5.38
1958-59	1,089	344	745	31.6	68.4	7.32	2.31	5.01
1959-60	1,216	378	838	31.1	68.9	7.76	2.41	5.35
1960-61	1,350	402	948	29.8	70.2	7.86	2.34	5.52
1961-62	1,543	449	1,094	29.1	70.9	8.48	2.47	6.01
1962-63	1,865	560	1,305	30.0	70.0	9.53	2.86	6.67
1963-64	2,325	693	1,632	29.8	70.2	10.34	3.08	7.26
1964-65	2,599	743	1,856	28.6	71.4	9.91	2.83	7.08
1965-66	2,922	734	2,188	25.1	74.9	10.56	2.65	7.91
1966-67	3,261	767	2,494	23.5	76.5	10.42	2.45	7.97
1967-68	3,456	780	2,676	22.6	77.4	9.43	2.13	7.30
1968-69	3,759	840	2,919	22.3	77.7	9.68	2.16	7.52
1969-70	4,200	963	3,237	22.9	77.1	9.82	2.25	7.57
1970-71	4,752	1,009	3,743	21.2	78.8	10.40	2.21	8.19
1971-72	5,575	1,171	4,404	21.0	79.0	11.39	2.39	9.00
1972-73	6,436	1,346	5,090	20.9	79.1	11.93	2.50	9.44
1973-74	7,389	1,552	5,837	21.0	79.0	11.26	2.37	8.90
1974-75	9,223	1,834	7,389	19.9	80.1	11.90	2.37	9.54
1975-76	11,182	2,493	8,689	22.3	77.7	13.43	2.99	10.43
1976-77	12,332	2,585	9,747	21.0	79.0	13.74	2.88	10.86
1977-78	13,237	2,680	10,557	20.2	79.8	13.03	2.64	10.39
1978-79	15,528	2,851	12,677	18.4	81.6	14.10	2.59	11.51
1979-80	17,683	3,096	14,587	17.5	82.5	14.63	2.56	12.07
1980-81	19,844	3,268	16,576	16.5	83.5	13.80	2.27	11.53
1981-82	24,142	4,133	20,009	17.1	82.9	14.32	2.45	11.87
1982-83	27,242	4,492	22,750	16.5	83.5	14.47	2.39	12.08
1983-84	31,525	4,907	26,618	15.6	84.4	14.36	2.24	12.13
1984-85	35,814	5,330	30,484	14.9	85.1	14.59	2.17	12.42
1985-86	43,267	6,252	37,015	14.4	85.6	15.56	2.25	13.32
1986-87	49,538	6,889	42,650	13.9	86.1	15.92	2.21	13.71
1987-88	56,977	7,483	49,493	13.1	86.9	16.08	2.11	13.97
1988-89	66,925	9,757	57,168	14.6	85.4	15.88	2.31	13.56
1989-90	77,693	11,165	66,528	14.4	85.6	15.98	2.30	13.68

Contd...

Year	Combined tax revenue* (3+4)	Direct taxes	Indirect taxes	Col. 3 as % of Col. 2	Col. 4 as % of Col. 2	Col. 2 as % of GDP	Col. 3 as % of GDP	Col. 4 as % of GDP
1	2	3	4	5	6	7	8	9
1990-91	87,722	12,260	75,462	14.0	86.0	15.43	2.16	13.27
1991-92	1,03,198	16,657	86,541	16.1	83.9	15.80	2.55	13.25
1992-93	1,14,166	19,387	94,779	17.0	83.0	15.26	2.59	12.66
1993-94	1,21,961	21,713	1,00,248	17.8	82.2	14.19	2.53	11.67
1994-95	1,47,849	28,878	1,18,971	19.5	80.5	14.60	2.85	11.75
1995-96	1,75,259	35,777	1,39,482	20.4	79.6	14.75	3.01	11.74
1996-97	2,01,056	41,061	1,59,995	20.4	79.6	14.69	3.00	11.69
1997-98	2,20,659	50,538	1,70,121	22.9	77.1	14.49	3.32	11.17
1998-99	2,33,017	49,119	1,83,898	21.1	78.9	13.38	2.82	10.56
1999-00	2,74,583	60,864	2,13,719	21.4	78.6	14.02	3.11	10.91
2000-01	3,05,320	71,762	2,33,558	23.5	76.5	14.49	3.40	11.08
2001-02	3,14,535	73,108	2,41,427	23.2	76.8	13.79	3.20	10.58
2002-03	3,56,277	87,365	2,68,912	24.5	75.5	14.54	3.57	10.98
2003-04	4,14,084	1,09,546	3,04,538	26.5	73.5	15.00	3.97	11.03
2004-05	4,94,016	1,39,017	3,55,000	28.1	71.9	15.83	4.45	11.37
2005-06	5,85,626	1,82,134	4,03,492	31.1	68.9	16.58	5.16	11.45

* Total tax revenue of the Central and State Governments.
2004-05 = Revised estimates; 2005-06 = Budget estimates.
Note: The ratios of GDP since 1950-51 are with reference to new series GDP (Base: 1993-94) at current market prices.
Source: Rearranged data from Government of India, Ministry of Finance, *Indian Public Finance Statistics*, 2005-2006, Tables 1.7 and 1.8. Columns 5 and 6 calculations own.

Table 2: Gross Central Taxes, Breakdown between Direct and Indirect Taxes with Percentage Shares, and Tax-GDP Ratios: 1950-51 to 2005-06

(Rs. crore)

Year	Gross Central taxes*(3+4)	Direct taxes	Indirect taxes	Col. 3 as % of Col. 2	Col. 4 as % of Col. 2	Col. 2 as % of GDP	Col. 3 as % of GDP	Col. 4 as % of GDP
1	2	3	4	5	6	7	8	9
1950-51	405	176	229	43.4	56.6	4.08	1.77	2.31
1951-52	512	190	322	37.1	62.9	4.85	1.80	3.05
1952-53	445	186	259	41.8	58.2	4.29	1.79	2.50
1953-54	420	166	254	39.5	60.5	3.72	1.47	2.25
1954-55	455	161	294	35.4	64.6	4.26	1.51	2.75
1955-56	485	171	314	35.2	64.8	4.46	1.57	2.89
1956-57	570	194	376	34.0	66.0	4.40	1.50	2.90
1957-58	692	230	462	33.2	66.8	5.18	1.72	3.46
1958-59	701	238	463	34.0	66.0	4.71	1.60	3.11
1959-60	794	269	525	33.9	66.1	5.07	1.72	3.35
1960-61	895	292	603	32.6	67.4	5.21	1.70	3.51
1961-62	1,054	337	717	32.0	68.0	5.79	1.85	3.94
1962-63	1,285	423	862	32.9	67.1	6.57	2.16	4.41
1963-64	1,634	550	1,084	33.7	66.3	7.27	2.45	4.82
1964-65	1,821	600	1,221	32.9	67.1	6.95	2.29	4.66
1965-66	2,061	598	1,463	29.0	71.0	7.45	2.16	5.29
1966-67	2,307	657	1,650	28.5	71.5	7.37	2.10	5.27
1967-68	2,353	655	1,698	27.8	72.2	6.42	1.79	4.63
1968-69	2,510	698	1,812	27.8	72.2	6.47	1.80	4.67
1969-70	2,822	826	1,996	29.3	70.7	6.60	1.93	4.67
1970-71	3,206	869	2,337	27.1	72.9	7.02	1.90	5.12
1971-72	3,873	1,047	2,826	27.0	73.0	7.92	2.14	5.78
1972-73	4,505	1,233	3,272	27.4	72.6	8.35	2.29	6.07
1973-74	5,070	1,375	3,695	27.1	72.9	7.73	2.10	5.63
1974-75	6,322	1,650	4,672	26.1	73.9	8.16	2.13	6.03
1975-76	7,609	2,205	5,404	29.0	71.0	9.14	2.65	6.49
1976-77	8,271	2,328	5,943	28.1	71.9	9.22	2.59	6.62
1977-78	8,858	2,405	6,453	27.1	72.9	8.72	2.37	6.35
1978-79	10,525	2,528	7,997	24.0	76.0	9.56	2.30	7.26
1979-80	11,974	2,818	9,156	23.5	76.5	9.91	2.33	7.58
1980-81	13,179	2,997	10,182	22.7	77.3	9.17	2.08	7.08
1981-82	15,847	3,786	12,061	23.9	76.1	9.40	2.25	7.15
1982-83	17,696	4,139	13,557	23.4	76.6	9.40	2.20	7.20
1983-84	20,721	4,498	16,223	21.7	78.3	9.44	2.05	7.39
1984-85	23,471	4,798	18,673	20.4	79.6	9.56	1.95	7.61
1985-86	28,670	5,620	23,050	19.6	80.4	10.31	2.02	8.29
1986-87	32,838	6,236	26,602	19.0	81.0	10.55	2.00	8.55
1987-88	37,665	6,752	30,913	17.9	82.1	10.63	1.91	8.72
1988-89	44,474	8,830	35,644	19.9	80.1	10.55	2.09	8.46
1989-90	51,636	10,003	41,633	19.4	80.6	10.62	2.06	8.56

Contd...

Year	Gross Central taxes*(3+4)	Direct taxes	Indirect taxes	Col. 3 as % of Col. 2	Col. 4 as % of Col. 2	Col. 2 as % of GDP	Col. 3 as % of GDP	Col. 4 as % of GDP
1	2	3	4	5	6	7	8	9
1990-91	57,577	11,030	46,547	19.2	80.8	10.12	1.94	8.19
1991-92	67,361	15,353	52,008	22.8	77.2	10.31	2.35	7.96
1992-93	74,636	18,140	56,496	24.3	75.7	9.97	2.42	7.55
1993-94	75,742	20,299	55,443	26.8	73.2	8.82	2.36	6.45
1994-95	92,297	26,973	65,324	29.2	70.8	9.11	2.66	6.45
1995-96	1,11,224	33,564	77,660	30.2	69.8	9.36	2.83	6.54
1996-97	1,29,762	38,898	90,864	30.0	70.0	9.48	2.84	6.64
1997-98	1,39,220	48,282	90,938	34.7	65.3	9.14	3.17	5.97
1998-99	1,43,797	46,601	97,196	32.4	67.6	8.26	2.68	5.58
1999-00	1,71,752	57,960	1,13,792	33.7	66.3	8.77	2.96	5.81
2000-01	1,88,603	68,305	1,20,298	36.2	63.8	8.95	3.24	5.71
2001-02	1,87,060	69,197	1,17,863	37.0	63.0	8.20	3.03	5.17
2002-03	2,15,905	83,363	1,32,542	38.6	61.4	8.81	3.40	5.41
2003-04	2,54,348	1,05,091	1,49,257	41.3	58.9	9.21	3.81	5.41
2004-05	3,06,020	1,34,197	1,71,824	43.8	56.2	9.80	4.30	5.50
2005-06	3,70,025	1,77,080	1,92,945	47.9	52.1	10.48	5.01	5.46

* Before transferring States' share in Central taxes.

2004-05 = Revised estimates; 2005-06 = Budget estimates.

Note: The ratios of GDP since 1950-51 are with reference to new series GDP (Base: 1993-94) at current market prices.

Source: Rearranged data from Government of India, Ministry of Finance, *Indian Public Finance Statistics*, 2005-2006, Tables 1.7 and 1.8. Columns 5 and 6 calculations own.

Table 3: Share of States in Central Taxes, Breakdown between Direct and Indirect Taxes with Percentage Shares, and Tax-GDP Ratios: 1950-51 to 2005-06

(Rs. crore)

Year	States' share in Central taxes (3+4)	Direct taxes	Indirect taxes	Col. 3 as % of Col. 2	Col. 4 as % of Col. 2	Col. 2 as % of GDP	Col. 3 as % of GDP	Col. 4 as % of GDP
1	2	3	4	5	6	7	8	9
1950-51	48	48	--	100.0	0.0	0.48	0.48	0.00
1951-52	53	53	--	100.0	0.0	0.50	0.50	0.00
1952-53	73	56	17	76.7	23.3	0.70	0.54	0.16
1953-54	73	58	15	79.5	20.5	0.65	0.51	0.13
1954-55	71	57	14	80.3	19.7	0.66	0.53	0.13
1955-56	74	57	17	77.0	23.0	0.68	0.52	0.16
1956-57	78	51	27	65.4	34.6	0.60	0.39	0.21
1957-58	116	76	40	65.5	34.5	0.87	0.57	0.30
1958-59	148	75	73	50.7	49.3	1.00	0.50	0.49
1959-60	152	79	73	52.0	48.0	0.97	0.50	0.47
1960-61	165	90	75	54.5	45.5	0.96	0.52	0.44
1961-62	179	98	81	54.7	45.3	0.98	0.54	0.45
1962-63	224	99	125	44.2	55.8	1.14	0.51	0.64
1963-64	260	124	136	47.7	52.3	1.16	0.55	0.60.
1964-65	258	131	127	50.8	49.2	0.98	0.50	0.48
1965-66	276	130	146	47.1	52.9	1.00	0.47	0.53
1966-67	373	142	231	38.1	61.9	1.19	0.45	0.74
1967-68	416	181	235	43.5	56.5	1.14	0.49	0.64
1968-69	491	200	291	40.7	59.3	1.26	0.52	0.75
1969-70	621	300	321	48.3	51.7	1.45	0.70	0.75
1970-71	755	365	390	48.3	51.7	1.65	0.80	0.85
1971-72	945	470	475	49.7	50.3	1.93	0.96	0.97
1972-73	1,062	495	567	46.6	53.4	1.97	0.92	1.05
1973-74	1,170	539	631	46.1	53.9	1.78	0.82	0.96
1974-75	1,225	522	703	42.6	57.4	1.58	0.67	0.91
1975-76	1,599	742	857	46.4	53.6	1.92	0.89	1.03
1976-77	1,690	662	1,028	39.2	60.8	1.88	0.74	1.15
1977-78	1,798	685	1,113	38.1	61.9	1.77	0.67	1.10
1978-79	1,957	717	1,240	36.6	63.4	1.78	0.65	1.13
1979-80	3,406	876	2,530	25.7	74.3	2.82	0.72	2.09
1980-81	3,791	1,014	2,777	26.7	73.3	2.64	0.71	1.93
1981-82	4,274	1,034	3,240	24.2	75.8	2.53	0.61	1.92
1982-83	4,640	1,148	3,492	24.7	75.3	2.46	0.61	1.85
1983-84	5,245	1,188	4,057	22.7	77.3	2.39	0.54	1.85
1984-85	5,777	1,252	4,525	21.7	78.3	2.35	0.51	1.84
1985-86	7,490	1,865	5,625	24.9	75.1	2.69	0.67	2.02
1986-87	8,476	2,170	6,306	25.6	74.4	2.72	0.70	2.03
1987-88	9,597	2,595	7,002	27.0	73.0	2.71	0.73	1.98
1988-89	10,669	2,750	7,919	25.8	74.2	2.53	0.65	1.88

Contd...

Year	States' share in Central taxes (3+4)	Direct taxes	Indirect taxes	Col. 3 as % of Col. 2	Col. 4 as % of Col. 2	Col. 2 as % of GDP	Col. 3 as % of GDP	Col. 4 as % of GDP
1	2	3	4	5	6	7	8	9
1989-90	13,232	3,922	9,310	29.6	70.4	2.72	0.81	1.91
1990-91	14,535	4,121	10,414	28.4	71.6	2.56	0.72	1.83
1991-92	17,197	5,104	12,093	29.7	70.3	2.63	0.78	1.85
1992-93	20,522	6,057	14,465	29.5	70.5	2.74	0.81	1.93
1993-94	22,240	7,767	14,473	34.9	65.1	2.59	0.90	1.68
1994-95	24,843	8,560	16,283	34.5	65.5	2.45	0.85	1.61
1995-96	29,285	11,274	18,011	38.5	61.5	2.47	0.95	1.52
1996-97	35,061	13,516	21,545	38.5	61.5	2.56	0.99	1.57
1997-98	43,548	21,102	22,446	48.5	51.5	2.86	1.39	1.47
1998-99	39,145	14,480	24,665	37.0	63.0	2.25	0.83	1.42
1999-00	43,481	16,523	26,958	38.0	62.0	2.22	0.84	1.38
2000-01	51,945	18,655	33,290	35.9	64.1	2.46	0.89	1.58
2001-02	53,398	21,492	31,906	40.2	59.8	2.34	0.94	1.40
2002-03	56,122	21,473	34,649	38.3	61.7	2.29	0.88	1.41
2003-04	67,366	28,492	38,874	42.3	57.7	2.44	1.03	1.41
2004-05	80,270	n.a.	n.a.	...	...	2.57	n.a.	n.a.
2005-06	96,559	47,298	49,261	49.0	51.0	2.73	1.34	1.39

2004-05 = Revised estimates; 2005-06 = Budget estimates.

Note: The ratios of GDP since 1950-51 are with reference to new series GDP (Base: 1993-94) at current market prices.

Source: Rearranged data from Government of India, Ministry of Finance, *Indian Public Finance Statistics*, 2005-2006, Tables 1.7 and 1.8. Columns 5 and 6 calculations own.

Table 4: Net Central Taxes, Breakdown between Direct and Indirect Taxes with Percentage Shares, and Tax-GDP Ratios: 1950-51 to 2005-06

(Rs. crore)

Year	Net Central taxes* (3+4)	Direct taxes	Indirect taxes	Col. 3 as % of Col. 2	Col. 4 as % of Col. 2	Col. 2 as % of GDP	Col. 3 as % of GDP	Col. 4 as % of GDP
1	2	3	4	5	6	7	8	9
1950-51	357	128	229	35.8	64.2	3.59	1.29	2.31
1951-52	459	137	322	29.8	70.2	4.34	1.30	3.05
1952-53	372	130	242	34.9	65.1	3.59	1.25	2.33
1953-54	347	108	239	31.1	68.9	3.08	0.96	2.12
1954-55	384	104	280	27.1	72.9	3.60	0.97	2.62
1955-56	411	114	297	27.7	72.3	3.78	1.05	2.73
1956-57	492	143	349	29.1	70.9	3.80	1.10	2.69
1957-58	576	154	422	26.7	73.3	4.31	1.15	3.16
1958-59	553	163	390	29.5	70.5	3.72	1.10	2.62
1959-60	642	190	452	29.6	70.4	4.10	1.21	2.88
1960-61	730	202	528	27.7	72.3	4.25	1.18	3.08
1961-62	875	239	636	27.3	72.7	4.81	1.31	3.50
1962-63	1,061	324	737	30.5	69.5	5.42	1.66	3.77
1963-64	1,374	426	948	31.0	69.0	6.11	1.89	4.22
1964-65	1,563	469	1,094	30.0	70.0	5.96	1.79	4.17
1965-66	1,785	468	1,317	26.2	73.8	6.45	1.69	4.76
1966-67	1,934	515	1,419	26.6	73.4	6.18	1.65	4.53
1967-68	1,937	474	1,463	24.5	75.5	5.29	1.29	3.99
1968-69	2,019	498	1,521	24.7	75.3	5.20	1.28	3.92
1969-70	2,201	526	1,675	23.9	76.1	5.15	1.23	3.92
1970-71	2,451	504	1,947	20.6	79.4	5.37	1.10	4.26
1971-72	2,928	577	2,351	19.7	80.3	5.98	1.18	4.80
1972-73	3,443	738	2,705	21.4	78.6	6.38	1.37	5.01
1973-74	3,900	836	3,064	21.4	78.6	5.94	1.27	4.67
1974-75	5,097	1,128	3,969	22.1	77.9	6.58	1.46	5.12
1975-76	6,010	1,463	4,547	24.3	75.7	7.22	1.76	5.46
1976-77	6,581	1,666	4,915	25.3	74.7	7.33	1.86	5.48
1977-78	7,060	1,720	5,340	24.4	75.6	6.95	1.69	5.26
1978-79	8,568	1,811	6,757	21.4	78.9	7.78	1.64	6.14
1979-80	8,568	1,942	6,626	22.7	77.3	7.09	1.61	5.48
1980-81	9,388	1,983	7,405	21.1	78.9	6.53	1.38	5.15
1981-82	11,573	2,752	8,821	23.8	76.2	6.86	1.63	5.23
1982-83	13,056	2,991	10,065	22.9	77.1	6.94	1.59	5.35
1983-84	15,476	3,310	12,166	21.4	78.6	7.05	1.51	5.54
1984-85	17,694	3,546	14,148	20.0	80.0	7.21	1.44	5.76
1985-86	21,180	3,755	17,425	17.7	82.3	7.62	1.35	6.27
1986-87	24,362	4,066	20,296	16.7	83.3	7.83	1.31	6.52
1987-88	28,068	4,157	23,911	14.8	85.2	7.92	1.17	6.75
1988-89	33,805	6,080	27,725	18.0	82.0	8.02	1.44	6.58
1989-90	38,404	6,081	32,323	15.8	84.2	7.90	1.25	6.65

Contd...

Year	Net Central taxes* (3+4)	Direct taxes	Indirect taxes	Col. 3 as % of Col. 2	Col. 4 as % of Col. 2	Col. 2 as % of GDP	Col. 3 as % of GDP	Col. 4 as % of GDP
1	2	3	4	5	6	7	8	9
1990-91	43,042	6,909	36,133	16.1	83.9	7.57	1.21	6.35
1991-92	50,164	10,249	39,915	20.4	79.6	7.68	1.57	6.11
1992-93	54,114	12,083	42,031	22.3	77.7	7.23	1.61	5.62
1993-94	53,502	12,532	40,970	23.4	76.6	6.23	1.46	4.77
1994-95	67,454	18,413	49,041	27.3	72.7	6.66	1.82	4.84
1995-96	81,939	22,290	59,649	27.2	72.8	6.90	1.88	5.02
1996-97	94,701	25,382	69,319	26.8	73.2	6.92	1.86	5.07
1997-98	95,672	27,180	68,492	28.4	71.6	6.28	1.79	4.50
1998-99	1,04,652	32,121	72,531	30.7	69.3	6.01	1.84	4.17
1999-00	1,28,271	41,437	86,834	32.3	67.7	6.55	2.12	4.43
2000-01	1,36,658	49,650	87,008	36.3	63.7	6.48	2.36	4.13
2001-02	1,33,662	47,705	85,957	35.7	64.3	5.86	2.09	3.77
2002-03	1,59,783	61,890	97,893	38.7	61.3	6.52	2.53	4.00
2003-04	1,86,982	76,599	1,10,382	41.0	59.0	6.77	2.78	4.00
2004-05	2,25,803	n.a.	n.a.	...	...	7.23	n.a.	n.a.
2005-06	2,73,466	1,29,782	1,43,684	47.5	52.5	7.74	3.68	4.07

* After transferring States' share in Central taxes.

2004-05 = Revised estimates; 2005-06 = Budget estimates.

Note: The ratios of GDP since 1950-51 are with reference to new series GDP (Base: 1993-94) at current market prices.

Source: Rearranged data from Government of India, Ministry of Finance, *Indian Public Finance Statistics*, 2005-2006, Tables 1.7 and 1.8. Columns 5 and 6 calculations own.

Table 5: States' Own Taxes, Breakdown between Direct and Indirect Taxes with Percentage Shares, and Tax-GDP Ratios: 1950-51 to 2005-06

(Rs. crore)

Year	States' own taxes (3+4)	Direct taxes	Indirect taxes	Col. 3 as % of Col. 2	Col. 4 as % of Col. 2	Col. 2 as % of GDP	Col. 3 as % of GDP	Col. 4 as % of GDP
1	2	3	4	5	6	7	8	9
1950-51	222	55	167	24.7	75.3	2.23	0.55	1.68
1951-52	227	54	173	23.8	76.2	2.15	0.51	1.64
1952-53	233	66	167	28.3	71.7	2.25	0.64	1.61
1953-54	252	76	176	30.2	69.8	2.23	0.67	1.56
1954-55	265	79	186	29.8	70.2	2.48	0.74	1.74
1955-56	283	88	195	31.1	68.9	2.60	0.81	1.79
1956-57	320	94	226	29.4	70.6	2.47	0.73	1.75
1957-58	353	97	256	27.5	72.5	2.64	0.73	1.92
1958-59	388	106	282	27.3	72.7	2.61	0.71	1.90
1959-60	422	109	313	25.8	74.2	2.69	0.70	2.00
1960-61	455	110	345	24.2	75.8	2.65	0.64	2.01
1961-62	489	112	377	22.9	77.1	2.69	0.62	2.07
1962-63	580	137	443	23.6	76.4	2.96	0.70	2.26
1963-64	691	143	548	20.7	79.3	3.07	0.64	2.44
1964-65	778	143	635	18.4	81.6	2.97	0.55	2.42
1965-66	861	136	725	15.8	84.2	3.11	0.49	2.62
1966-67	954	110	844	11.5	88.5	3.05	0.35	2.70
1967-68	1,103	125	978	11.3	88.7	3.01	0.34	2.67
1968-69	1,249	142	1,107	11.4	88.6	3.22	0.37	2.85
1969-70	1,378	137	1,241	9.9	90.1	3.22	0.32	2.90
1970-71	1,546	140	1,406	9.1	90.9	3.38	0.31	3.08
1971-72	1,702	124	1,578	7.3	92.7	3.48	0.25	3.22
1972-73	1,931	113	1,818	5.8	94.2	3.58	0.21	3.37
1973-74	2,319	177	2,142	7.6	92.4	3.53	0.27	3.26
1974-75	2,901	184	2,717	6.3	93.7	3.74	0.24	3.51
1975-76	3,573	288	3,285	8.1	91.9	4.29	0.35	3.95
1976-77	4,061	257	3,804	6.3	93.7	4.53	0.29	4.24
1977-78	4,379	275	4,104	6.3	93.7	4.31	0.27	4.04
1978-79	5,003	323	4,680	6.5	93.5	4.54	0.29	4.25
1979-80	5,709	278	5,431	4.9	95.1	4.72	0.23	4.49
1980-81	6,665	271	6,394	4.1	95.9	4.64	0.19	4.45
1981-82	8,295	347	7,948	4.2	95.8	4.92	0.21	4.71
1982-83	9,546	353	9,193	3.7	96.3	5.07	0.19	4.88
1983-84	10,804	409	10,395	3.8	96.2	4.92	0.19	4.74
1984-85	12,343	532	11,811	4.3	95.7	5.03	0.22	4.81
1985-86	14,597	632	13,965	4.3	95.7	5.25	0.23	5.02
1986-87	16,701	653	16,048	3.9	96.1	5.37	0.21	5.16
1987-88	19,311	731	18,580	3.8	96.2	5.45	0.21	5.24
1988-89	22,452	928	21,524	4.1	95.9	5.33	0.22	5.11
1989-90	26,057	1,162	24,895	4.5	95.5	5.36	0.24	5.12
1990-91	30,145	1,230	28,915	4.1	95.9	5.30	0.22	5.08

Contd...

1991-92	35,837	1,304	34,533	3.6	96.4	5.49	0.20	5.29
1992-93	39,530	1,247	38,283	3.2	96.8	5.28	0.17	5.12
1993-94	46,219	1,414	44,805	3.1	96.9	5.38	0.16	5.21
1994-95	55,552	1,905	53,647	3.4	96.6	5.49	0.19	5.30
1995-96	64,034	2,213	61,822	3.5	96.5	5.39	0.19	5.20
1996-97	71,294	2,163	69,131	3.0	97.0	5.21	0.16	5.05
1997-98	81,439	2,256	79,183	2.8	97.2	5.35	0.15	5.20
1998-99	89,220	2,518	86,702	2.8	97.2	5.12	0.14	4.98
1999-00	1,02,831	2,904	99,927	2.8	97.2	5.25	0.15	5.10
2000-01	1,16,717	3,457	1,13,260	2.9	97.1	5.54	0.16	5.37
2001-02	1,27,475	3,911	1,23,564	3.1	96.9	5.59	0.17	5.42
2002-03	1,40,372	4,002	1,36,370	2.8	97.2	5.73	0.16	5.57
2003-04	1,59,736	4,455	1,55,281	2.8	97.2	5.79	0.16	5.63
2004-05	1,87,996	4,820	1,83,176	2.6	97.4	6.02	0.15	5.87
2005-06	2,15,601	5,054	2,10,547	2.3	97.7	6.11	0.14	5.96

2004-05 = Revised estimates; 2005-06 = Budget estimates.

Note: The ratios of GDP since 1950-51 are with reference to new series GDP (Base: 1993-94) at current market prices.

Source: Rearranged data from Government of India, Ministry of Finance, *Indian Public Finance Statistics*, 2005-2006, Tables 1.7 and 1.8. Columns 5 and 6 calculations own.

Table 6: States' Total Tax Revenue, Breakdown between Direct and Indirect Taxes with Percentage Shares, and Tax-GDP Ratios: 1950-51 to 2005-06

(Rs. crore)

Year	States' total tax revenue* (3+4)	Direct taxes	Indirect taxes	Col. 3 as % of Col. 2	Col. 4 as % of Col. 2	Col. 2 as % of GDP	Col. 3 as % of GDP	Col. 4 as % of GDP
1	2	3	4	5	6	7	8	9
1950-51	270	103	167	38.1	61.9	2.72	1.04	1.68
1951-52	280	107	173	38.2	61.8	2.65	1.01	1.64
1952-53	306	122	184	39.9	60.1	2.95	1.18	1.78
1953-54	325	134	191	41.2	58.8	2.8	1.19	1.69
1954-55	336	136	200	40.5	59.5	3.15	1.27	1.87
1955-56	357	145	212	40.6	59.4	3.28	1.33	1.95
1956-57	398	145	253	36.4	63.6	3.07	1.12	1.95
1957-58	469	173	296	36.9	63.1	3.51	1.30	2.22
1958-59	536	181	355	33.8	66.2	3.60	1.22	2.39
1959-60	574	188	386	32.7	67.3	3.66	1.20	2.46
1960-61	620	200	420	32.3	67.7	3.61	1.17	2.45
1961-62	668	210	458	31.4	68.6	3.67	1.15	2.52
1962-63	804	236	568	29.4	70.6	4.11	1.21	2.90
1963-64	951	267	684	28.1	71.9	4.23	1.19	3.04
1964-65	1,036	274	762	26.4	73.6	3.95	1.05	2.91
1965-66	1,137	266	871	23.4	76.6	4.11	0.96	3.15
1966-67	1,327	252	1,075	19.0	81.0	4.24	0.80	3.43
1967-68	1,519	306	1,213	20.1	79.9	4.14	0.83	3.31
1968-69	1,740	342	1,398	19.7	80.3	4.48	0.88	3.60
1969-70	1,999	437	1,562	21.9	78.1	4.68	1.02	3.65
1970-71	2,301	505	1,796	21.9	78.1	5.04	1.11	3.93
1971-72	2,647	594	2,053	22.4	77.6	5.41	1.21	4.20
1972-73	2,993	608	2,385	20.3	79.7	5.55	1.13	4.42
1973-74	3,489	716	2,773	20.5	79.5	5.32	1.09	4.23
1974-75	4,126	706	3,420	17.1	82.9	5.33	0.91	4.41
1975-76	5,172	1,030	4,142	19.9	80.1	6.21	1.24	4.97
1976-77	5,751	919	4,832	16.0	84.0	6.41	1.02	5.38
1977-78	6,177	960	5,217	15.5	84.5	6.08	0.94	5.13
1978-79	6,960	1,040	5,920	14.9	85.1	6.32	0.94	5.38
1979-80	9,115	1,154	7,961	12.7	87.3	7.54	0.95	6.59
1980-81	10,456	1,285	9,171	12.3	87.7	7.27	0.89	6.38
1981-82	12,569	1,381	11,188	11.0	89.0	7.45	0.82	6.64
1982-83	14,186	1,501	12,685	10.6	89.4	7.54	0.80	6.74
1983-84	16,049	1,597	14,452	10.0	90.0	7.31	0.73	6.58
1984-85	18,120	1,784	16,336	9.9	90.1	7.38	0.73	6.65
1985-86	22,087	2,497	19,590	11.3	88.7	7.95	0.90	7.05
1986-87	25,177	2,823	22,354	11.2	88.8	8.09	0.91	7.18
1987-88	28,908	3,326	25,582	11.5	88.5	8.16	0.94	7.22
1988-89	33,121	3,678	29,443	11.1	88.9	7.86	0.87	6.98
1989-90	39,289	5,084	34,205	12.9	87.1	8.08	1.05	7.04

Contd...

1990-91	44,680	5,351	39,329	12.0	88.0	7.86	0.94	6.92
1991-92	53,034	6,408	46,626	12.1	87.9	8.12	0.98	7.14
1992-93	60,052	7,304	52,748	12.2	87.8	8.02	0.98	7.05
1993-94	68,459	9,181	59,278	13.4	86.6	7.97	1.07	6.90
1994-95	80,395	10,465	69,930	13.0	87.0	7.94	1.03	6.90
1995-96	93,320	13,487	79,833	14.4	85.6	7.86	1.14	6.72
1996-97	1,06,355	15,679	90,676	14.7	85.3	7.77	1.15	6.63
1997-98	1,24,987	23,358	1,01,629	18.7	81.3	8.21	1.53	6.67
1998-99	1,28,365	16,998	1,11,367	13.2	86.8	7.37	0.98	6.40
1999-00	1,46,312	19,427	1,26,885	13.3	86.7	7.47	0.99	6.48
2000-01	1,68,662	22,112	1,46,550	13.1	86.9	8.00	1.05	6.95
2001-02	1,80,873	25,403	1,55,470	14.0	86.0	7.93	1.11	6.81
2002-03	1,96,494	25,475	1,71,019	13.0	87.0	8.02	1.04	6.98
2003-04	2,27,102	32,947	1,94,155	14.5	85.5	8.23	1.19	7.03
2004-05	2,68,213	n.a.	n.a.	...	...	8.59	n.a.	n.a.
2005-06	3,12,160	52,352	2,59,808	16.8	83.2	8.84	1.48	7.36

* States' share in Central taxes plus States' own taxes.

2004-05 = Revised estimates; 2005-06 = Budget estimates.

Note: The ratios of GDP since 1950-51 are with reference to new series GDP (Base: 1993-94) at current market prices.

Source: Rearranged data from Government of India, Ministry of Finance, *Indian Public Finance Statistics*, 2005-2006, Tables 1.7 and 1.8. Columns 5 and 6 calculations own.

Table 7: Income Tax (Including Corporation Tax) Collections*: 1950-51 to 2007-08

(Rs. crore)

Year	Gross Central taxes	Income tax	Col. 3 as % of Col. 2
1	2	3	4
1950-51	405	172	42.5
1951-52	415	185	36.1
1952-53	445	182	40.9
1953-54	420	161	38.3
1954-55	455	156	34.3
1955-56	485	165	34.0
1956-57	570	199	34.9
1957-58	692	215	31.1
1958-59	701	221	31.5
1959-60	794	250	31.5
1960-61	895	277	31.9
1961-62	1,054	316	30.0
1962-63	1,285	407	31.7
1963-64	1,634	533	32.6
1964-65	1,821	580	31.9
1965-66	2,061	576	27.9
1966-67	2,307	637	27.6
1967-68	2,353	636	27.0
1968-69	2,510	678	27.0
1969-70	2,822	801	28.4
1970-71	3,206	843	26.3
1971-72	3,873	1,009	26.1
1972-73	4,505	1,187	26.3
1973-74	5,070	1,328	26.2
1974-75	6,322	1,583	25.0
1975-76	7,609	2,076	27.3
1976-77	8,263	2,178	26.4
1977-78	8,858	2,223	25.1
1978-79	10,525	2,428	23.1
1979-80	11,974	2,731	22.8

Contd...

1980-81	13,179	2,816	21.4
1981-82	15,847	3,446	21.7
1982-83	17,696	3,755	21.2
1983-84	20,721	4,192	20.2
1984-85	23,471	4,484	19.1
1985-86	28,671	5,374	18.7
1986-87	32,837	6,038	18.4
1987-88	37,666	6,620	17.6
1988-89	44,474	8,648	19.4
1989-90	51,636	9,739	18.7
1990-91	57,577	10,606	18.4
1991-92	67,361	14,584	21.6
1992-93	74,636	16,787	22.5
1993-94	75,742	19,183	25.3
1994-95	92,297	25,847	28.0
1995-96	1,10,354	32,090	29.1
1996-97	1,28,762	36,798	28.6
1997-98	1,39,221	37,113	26.7
1998-99	1,43,797	44,764	31.1
1999-00	1,71,752	56,339	32.8
2000-01	1,88,603	67,460	35.8
2001-02	1,87,060	68,613	36.7
2002-03	2,16,266	82,038	37.9
2003-04	2,54,348	1,04,949	41.3
2004-05	3,04,958	1,31,948	43.3
2005-06	3,66,152	1,64,906	45.0
2006-07	4,67,848	2,29,007	48.9
2007-08	5,48,122	2,67,175	48.7

*Before transferring States' share.

2006-07 = Revised estimates; 2007-08 = Budget estimates.

Source: Government of India, Ministry of Finance, *Explanatory Memorandum on the Budget of the Central Government;* and *Receipts Budget* (various years). Column 4 calculations own.

Table 8: Wealth Tax Revenue: 1957-58 to 2007-08

(Rs. crore)

Year	Yield	Year	Yield
1957-58	7	1983-84	93
1958-59	10	1984-85	107
1959-60	12	1985-86	153
1960-61	8	1986-87	174
1961-62	8	1987-88	101
1962-63	10	1988-89	122
1963-64	11	1989-90	179
1964-65	11	1990-91	231
1965-66	12	1991-92	307
1966-67	11	1992-93	468
1967-68	11	1993-94	154
1968-69	11	1994-95	105
1969-70	16	1995-96	74
1970-71	15	1996-97	78
1971-72	25	1997-98	113
1972-73	36	1998-99	162
1973-74	36	1999-00	133
1974-75	39	2000-01	132
1975-76	54	2001-02	135
1976-77	60	2002-03	154
1977-78	48	2003-04	136
1978-79	55	2004-05	145
1979-80	64	2005-06	250
1980-81	67	2006-07	265
1981-82	78	2007-08	315
1982-83	90		

An annual tax on net wealth was introduced in India with the enactment of the Wealth Tax Act, 1957 which came into force from April 1 of that year.

2006-07 = Revised estimates; 2007-08 = Budget estimates.

Source: Government of India, Ministry of Finance, *Explanatory Memorandum on the Budget of the Central Government:* and *Receipts Budget* (various years).

Table 9: Gift Tax Revenue: 1958-59 to 2005-06

(Rs. crore)

Year	Yield	Year	Yield
1958-59	1	1982-83	8
1959-60	1	1983-84	9
1960-61	1	1984-85	11
1961-62	1	1985-86	12
1962-63	1	1986-87	9
1963-64	1	1987-88	8
1964-65	2	1988-89	7
1965-66	2	1989-90	8
1966-67	2	1990-91	3
1967-68	1	1991-92	8
1968-69	2	1992-93	9
1969-70	2	1993-94	·5
1970-71	2	1994-95	15
1971-72	4	1995-96	11
1972-73	4	1996-97	10
1973-74	5	1997-98	9
1974-75	5	1998-99	10
1975-76	5	1999-00	(-) 3
1976-77	6	2000-01	---
1977-78	6	2001-02	(-) 2
1978-79	6	2002-03	(-) 2
1979-80	7	2003-04	1
1980-81	7	2004-05	2
1981-82	8	2005-06	2

A tax on *inter vivos* gifts was imposed in India under the Gift Tax Act, 1958 which came into force on April 1 of that year. The Finance Minister in his 1998-99 budget discontinued the levy of gift tax on gifts made after September 30, 1998.

Source: Government of India, Ministry of Finance, *Explanatory Memorandum on the Budget of the Central Government:* and *Receipts Budget* (various years).

Table 10: Estate Duty* Revenue: 1954-55 to 2001-02

(Rs. crore)

Year	Yield	Year	Yield
1954-55	1	1978-79	13
1955-56	1	1979-80	14
1956-57	2	1980-81	16
1957-58	2	1981-82	20
1958-59	3	1982-83	20
1959-60	3	1983-84	26
1960-61	3	1984-85	24
1961-62	4	1985-86	23
1962-63	4	1986-87	14
1963-64	5	1987-88	8
1964-65	5	1988-89	6
1965-66	7	1989-90	4
1966-67	6	1990-91	3
1967-68	6	1991-92	3
1968-69	7	1992-93	1
1969-70	7	1993-94	...
1970-71	8	1994-95	1
1971-72	9	1995-96	1
1972-73	10	1996-97	1
1973-74	11	1997-98	1
1974-75	11	1998-99	---
1975-76	12	1999-00	(-) 1
1976-77	12	2000-01	---
1977-78	13	2001-02	1

*Estate duty was introduced in India in 1953 when the Estate Duty Act of that year imposed a duty on the capital value of all property passing on the death of any person on or after October 15, 1953. Estate Duty was abolished w.e.f. March 16, 1985. Yields for subsequent years represent collections on estates passing on deaths occurring before the abolition.

Source: Government of India, Ministry of Finance, *Explanatory Memorandum on the Budget of the Central Government:* and *Receipts Budget* (various years).

Table 11: Central Excise Collections*: 1950-51 to 2007-08

(Rs. crore)

Year	Gross Central taxes	Excise revenue	Col. 3 as % of Col. 2
1	2	3	4
1950-51	405	68	16.8
1951-52	512	79	15.4
1952-53	445	79	17.7
1953-54	420	92	21.9
1954-55	455	105	23.1
1955-56	485	142	29.3
1956-57	570	185	32.5
1957-58	692	268	38.7
1958-59	701	307	43.8
1959-60	794	354	44.6
1960-61	895	414	46.3
1961-62	1,054	482	45.7
1962-63	1,285	599	46.6
1963-64	1,634	730	44.7
1964-65	1,821	801	44.0
1965-66	2,061	898	43.6
1966-67	2,307	1,034	44.8
1967-68	2,353	1,148	48.8
1968-69	2,510	1,321	52.6
1969-70	2,822	1,524	54.0
1970-71	3,206	1,758	54.8
1971-72	3,873	2,061	53.2
1972-73	4,505	2,324	51.6
1973-74	5,070	2,602	51.3
1974-75	6,322	3,230	51.1
1975-76	7,609	3,845	50.5
1976-77	8,263	4,221	51.1
1977-78	8,858	4,448	50.2
1978-79	10,525	5,367	51.0
1979-80	11,974	6,011	50.2
1980-81	13,179	6,500	49.3

Contd...

1981-82	15,847	7,421	46.8
1982-83	17,696	8,059	45.5
1983-84	20,721	10,222	49.3
1984-85	23,471	11,151	47.5
1985-86	28,671	12,956	45.2
1986-87	32,837	14,470	44.1
1987-88	37,666	16,426	43.6
1988-89	44,474	18,841	42.4
1989-90	51,636	22,406	43.4
1990-91	57,577	24,514	42.6
1991-92	67,361	28,110	41.7
1992-93	74,636	30,832	41.3
1993-94	75,742	31,697	41.8
1994-95	92,297	37,347	40.5
1995-96	1,10,354	40,187	36.4
1996-97	1,28,762	45,008	34.9
1997-98	1,39,221	47,962	34.4
1998-99	1,43,797	53,246	37.0
1999-00	1,71,752	61,902	36.1
2000-01	1,88,603	68,526	36.3
2001-02	1,87,060	72,555	38.8
2002-03	2,16,266	82,310	38.1
2003-04	2,54,348	90,774	35.7
2004-05	3,04,958	99,125	32.5
2005-06	3,66,152	1,11,226	30.4
2006-07	4,67,848	1,17,266	25.1
2007-08	5,48,122	1,30,220	23.8

*Before transferring States' Share.

2006-07 = Revised estimates; 2007-08 = Budget estimates.

Source: Government of India, Ministry of Finance, *Explanatory Memorandum on the Budget of the Central Government:* and *Receipts Budget* (various years). Column 4 calculations own.

Table 12: Revenue from Customs Duties: 1950-51 to 2007-08

(Rs. crore)

Year	Gross Central taxes	Customs revenue	Col. 3 as % of Col. 2
1		3	4
1950-51	405	157	38.8
1951-52	512	230	44.9
1952-53	445	172	38.7
1953-54	420	156	37.1
1954-55	455	182	40.0
1955-56	485	163	33.6
1956-57	570	170	29.8
1957-58	692	177	25.6
1958-59	701	135	19.3
1959-60	794	152	19.1
1960-61	895	170	19.0
1961-62	1,054	209	19.8
1962-63	1,285	246	19.1
1963-64	1,634	335	20.5
1964-65	1,821	397	21.8
1965-66	2,061	339	16.4
1966-67	2,307	585	25.4
1967-68	2,353	513	21.8
1968-69	2,510	446	17.8
1969-70	2,822	423	15.0
1970-71	3,206	524	16.3
1971-72	3,873	695	17.9
1972-73	4,505	857	19.0
1973-74	5,070	996	19.6
1974-75	6,322	1,332	21.1
1975-76	7,609	1,419	18.6
1976-77	8,263	1,554	18.8
1977-78	8,858	1,824	20.6
1978-79	10,525	2,423	23.0
1979-80	11,974	2,924	24.4
1980-81	13,179	3,409	25.9

Contd...

1981-82	15,847	4,300	27.1
1982-83	17,696	5,119	28.9
1983-84	20,721	5,583	26.9
1984-85	23,471	7,041	30.0
1985-86	28,671	9,526	33.2
1986-87	32,837	11,475	34.9
1987-88	37,666	13,702	36.4
1988-89	44,474	15,805	35.5
1989-90	51,636	18,036	34.9
1990-91	57,577	20,644	35.9
1991-92	67,361	22,257	33.0
1992-93	74,636	23,776	31.9
1993-94	75,742	22,193	29.3
1994-95	92,297	26,789	29.0
1995-96	1,10,354	35,757	32.4
1996-97	1,28,762	42,851	33.3
1997-98	1,39,221	40,193	28.9
1998-99	1,43,797	40,668	28.3
1999-00	1,71,752	48,419	28.2
2000-01	1,88,603	47,542	25.2
2001-02	1,87,060	40,268	21.5
2002-03	2,16,266	44,852	20.7
2003-04	2,54,348	48,629	19.1
2004-05	3,04,958	57,661	18.9
2005-06	3,66,152	65,067	17.8
2006-07	4,67,848	81,800	17.5
2007-08	5,48,122	98,770	18.0

2006-07 = Revised estimates; 2007-08 = Budget estimates.

Source: Government of India, Ministry of Finance, *Explanatory Memorandum on the Budget of the Central Government:* and *Receipts Budget* (various years). Column 4 calculations own.

Table 13: Estimated Additional Resource Mobilisation through Taxation by the Central Government: Selected Years

(Rs. crore)

S. No.	Tax	1990-91	1991-92	1992-93	1993-94	1996-97	1997-98	1998-99	1999-2000	2000-2001
1.	Income tax. (including Corporation tax)	550	1429	895	---	912	---	2400	.3100	6080
2.	Wealth tax	---	25	---	---	---	---	---	---	---
3.	Customs duties	835	-510	-2023	-3273	950	---	2748	1469	-1428
4.	Union excise duties	390	988	2211	-1249	760	---	4290	4765	3252
5.	Central sales tax Union Territory of Delhi	---	---	---	---	---	---	---	---	---
6.	Tax on foreign travel	---	---	---	---	---	---	---	---	---
7.	Interest tax	---	535	---	---	---	-600	---	---	-1000
8.	Stamp duty and excise duty on medical and toilet preparations in Union Territories	---	---	---	---	---	---	---	---	---
9.	Hotel receipts tax	---	---	---	---	---	---	---	---	---
10.	Expenditure Tax Act, 1987	---	150	-100	---	---	---	---	---	---
11.	Other taxes and duties	15	---	---	---	70	900	-233	---	---
12.	Total	1790	2617	983	-4522	2692	300	9205	9334	6904

Source: Rearranged data from Government of India, Ministry of Finance, *Indian Public Finance Statistics*, 2005-06, Table 5.1.

Table 14: Key Deficit Indicators of the Central Government: 1970-71 to 2007-08

(Rs. crore)

Year	Fiscal Deficit	Primary Deficit	Revenue Deficit
1970-71	1,408	803	(-) 163
1971-72	1,727	1,057	100
1972-73	2,179	1,403	15
1973-74	1,733	851	(-) 237
1974-75	2,302	1,301	(-) 765
1975-76	3,029	1,802	(-) 886
1976-77	3,802	2,314	(-) 298
1977-78	3,680	2,034	(-) 430
1978-79	5,710	3,726	(-) 292
1979-80	6,392	4,100	694
1980-81	8,299	5,695	2,037
1981-82	8,666	5,471	392
1982-83	10,627	6,689	1,308
1983-84	13,030	8,235	2,540
1984-85	17,416	11,442	4,225
1985-86	21,858	14,346	5,889
1986-87	26,342	17,096	7,777
1987-88	27,044	15,793	9,137
1988-89	30,923	16,645	10,515
1989-90	35,632	17,875	11,914
1990-91	44,632	23,134	18,562
1991-92	36,325	9,728	16,261
1992-93	40,173	9,098	18,574
1993-94	60,257	23,516	32,716
1994-95	57,703	13,644	31,029
1995-96	60,243	10,198	29,731
1996-97	66,733	7,255	32,654
1997-98	88,937	23,300	46,449
1998-99	1,13,349	35,466	66,976
1999-00	1,04,717	14,467	67,596
2000-01	1,18,816	19,502	85,234
2001-02	1,40,955	33,495	1,00,162

Contd...

2002-03	1,45,072	27,268	1,07,879
2003-04	1,23,272	(-) 816	98,262
2004-05	1,25,202	(-) 1,732	78,338
2005-06	1,46,435	13,805	92,299
2006-07	1,52,328	6,136	83,436
2007-08	1,50,948	(-) 8,047	71,478

2006-07 = Revised estimates; 2007-08 = Budget estimates.

Sources: 1. Reserve Bank of India, *Handbook of Statistics on Indian Economy*, 2004-05, p. 169, Table 103; 2. Government of India, *Economic Survey*, 2006-07, p. 21, Table 2.2; 3. Government of India, Ministry of Finance, *Budget at a Glance*, 2007-08, p. 1.

Table 15: Revenue from Agricultural Income Tax: 1950-51 to 2005-06

(Rs. crore)

Year	Yield	Year	Yield
1950-51	3	1979-80	58
1951-52	4	1980-81	46
1952-53	4	1981-82	38
1953-54	4	1982-83	30
1954-55	5	1983-84	44
1955-56	8	1984-85	84
1956-57	8	1985-86	127
1957-58	8	1986-87	104
1958-59	8	1987-88	63
1959-60	9	1988-89	64
1960-61	10	1989-90	93
1961-62	9	1990-91	198
1962-63	10	1991-92	202
1963-64	9	1992-93	111
1964-65	11	1993-94	107
1965-66	10	1994-95	98
1966-67	11	1995-96	154
1967-68	12	1996-97	103
1968-69	10	1997-98	182
1969-70	14	1998-99	241
1970-71	11	1999-00	150
1971-72	13	2000-01	76
1972-73	12	2001-02	23
1973-74	12	2002-03	14
1974-75	14	2003-04	15
1975-76	29	2004-05	22
1976-77	35	2005-06	55
1977-78	62		
1978-79	80		

2004-05 = Revised estimates; 2005-06 = Budget estimates.

Sources: 1. Reserve Bank of India (a) *Report on Currency and Finance* and (b) *Supplement to Finances of State Governments* (various years); 2. Government of India, Ministry of Finance, *Indian Public Finance Statistics*, 2005-2006, Table 3.2.

Table 16: Land Revenue: 1950-51 to 2005-06

(Rs. crore)

Year	Yield	Year	Yield
1950-51	49	1979-80	152
1951-52	48	1980-81	146
1952-53	57	1981-82	205
1953-54	71	1982-83	189
1954-55	73	1983-84	213
1955-56	78	1984-85	282
1956-57	83	1985-86	353
1957-58	88	1986-87	382
1958-59	92	1987-88	447
1959-60	95	1988-89	594
1960-61	97	1989-90	690
1961-62	95	1990-91	607
1962-63	120	1991-92	636
1963-64	123	1992-93	617
1964-65	120	1993-94	732
1965-66	112	1994-95	1,141
1966-67	90	1995-96	1,326
1967-68	96	1996-97	1,074
1968-69	114	1997-98	1,090
1969-70	103	1998-99	1,031
1970-71	113	1999-00	1,070
1971-72	101	2000-01	1,377
1972-73	93	2001-02	1,717
1973-74	157	2002-03	1,722
1974-75	161	2003-04	2,156
1975-76	230	2004-05	2,362
1976-77	183	2005-06	2,297
1977-78	166		
1978-79	188		

2004-05 = Revised estimates; 2005-06 = Budget estimates.

Sources: 1. Reserve Bank of India (a) *Report on Currency and Finance* and (b) *Supplement to Finances of State Governments* (various years); 2. Government of India, Ministry of Finance, *Indian Public Finance Statistics*, 2005-2006, Table 3.2.

Table 17: Revenue from Sales Tax: 1950-51 to 2005-06

(Rs. crore)

Year	States' own tax revenue	Sales tax	Col. 3 as % of Col.2
1	2	3	4
1950-51	222	58	26.1
1951-52	227	59	26.0
1952-53	233	57	24.5
1953-54	252	66	26.2
1954-55	265	74	27.9
1955-56	283	82	29.0
1956-57	320	98	30.6
1957-58	353	117	33.1
1958-59	388	124	32.0
1959-60	422	137	32.5
1960-61	455	159	34.9
1961-62	489	181	37.0
1962-63	580	208	35.9
1963-64	691	268	38.8
1964-65	778	318	40.9
1965-66	861	368	42.7
1966-67	954	442	46.3
1967-68	1,103	508	46.1
1968-69	1,249	572	45.8
1969-70	1,378	657	47.7
1970-71	1,546	755	48.8
1971-72	1,702	826	48.5
1972-73	1,931	976	50.5
1973-74	2,319	1,143	49.3
1974-75	2,901	1,550	53.4
1975-76	3,573	1,944	54.4
1976-77	4,061	2,270	55.9
1977-78	4,379	2,414	55.1
1978-79	5,003	2,773	55.4
1979-80	5,709	3,211	56.2
1980-81	6,665	3,888	58.3

Contd...

1981-82	8,295	4,893	59.0
1982-83	9,546	5,496	57.6
1983-84	10,804	5,706	52.8
1984-85	12,343	7,060	57.2
1985-86	14,597	8,429	57.7
1986-87	16,701	9,640	57.7
1987-88	19,311	11,183	57.9
1988-89	22,452	13,120	58.4
1989-90	26,057	15,060	57.8
1990-91	30,145	17,667	58.6
1991-92	35,837	21,064	58.8
1992-93	39,530	23,349	59.1
1993-94	46,219	27,638	59.8
1994-95	55,552	33,154	59.7
1995-96	63,865	35,477	55.5
1996-97	71,294	41,896	58.8
1997-98	81,439	45,351	55.7
1998-99	89,220	49,250	55.2
1999-00	1,02,831	57,592	56.0
2000-01	1,16,717	68,386	58.6
2001-02	1,27,475	71,379	56.0
2002-03	1,40,372	79,425	56.6
2003-04	1,59,736	89,658	56.1
2004-05	1,87,996	1,05,562	56.1
2005-06	2,15,601	1,22,796	56.9

2004-05 = Revised estimates; 2005-06 = Budget estimates.

Sources: 1. Reserve Bank of India (a) *Report on Currency and Finance* and (b) *Supplement to Finances of State Governments* (various years); 2. Government of India, Ministry of Finance, *Indian Public Finance Statistics*, 2005-2006, Table 3.2. Column 4 calculations own.

Table 18: Revenue from State Excise Duty: 1950-51 to 2005-06

(Rs. crore)

Year	Yield	Year	Yield
1950-51	48	1979-80	698
1951-52	49	1980-81	824
1952-53	46	1981-82	1,115
1953-54	45	1982-83	1,343
1954-55	45	1983-84	1,384
1955-56	45	1984-85	1,839
1956-57	46	1985-86	2,052
1957-58	46	1986-87	2,421
1958-59	47	1987-88	2,864
1959-60	50	1988-89	3,081
1960-61	53	1989-90	3,864
1961-62	59	1990-91	4,795
1962-63	63	1991-92	5,439
1963-64	73	1992-93	6,365
1964-65	84	1993-94	7,106
1965-66	96	1994-95	7,747
1966-67	109	1995-96	8,516
1967-68	131	1996-97	8,848
1968-69	159	1997-98	11,383
1969-70	174	1998-99	13,438
1970-71	194	1999-00	15,092
1971-72	234	2000-01	15,825
1972-73	279	2001-02	17,150
1973-74	354	2002-03	18,833
1974-75	387	2003-04	19,548
1975-76	435	2004-05	22,537
1976-77	505	2005-06	25,168
1977-78	570		
1978-79	583		

2004-05 = Revised estimates; 2005-06 = Budget estimates.

Sources: 1. Reserve Bank of India (a) *Report on Currency and Finance* and (b) *Supplement to Finances of State Governments* (various years); 2. Government of India, Ministry of Finance, *Indian Public Finance Statistics*, 2005-2006, Table 3.2.

Table 19: Revenue from Entertainment Tax: 1950-51 to 2005-06

(Rs. crore)

Year	Yield	Year	Yield
1950-51	---	1979-80	231
1951-52	6	1980-81	255
1952-53	6	1981-82	304
1953-54	6	1982-83	299
1954-55	6	1983-84	370
1955-56	7	1984-85	412
1956-57	9	1985-86	308
1957-58	9	1986-87	427
1958-59	11	1987-88	382
1959-60	11	1988-89	423
1960-61	13	1989-90	342
1961-62	15	1990-91	412
1962-63	18	1991-92	349
1963-64	23	1992-93	464
1964-65	25	1993-94	426
1965-66	29	1994-95	447
1966-67	35	1995-96	440
1967-68	26	1996-97	796
1968-69	43	1997-98	1,035
1969-70	50	1998-99	926
1970-71	58	1999-00	907
1971-72	63	2000-01	1,203
1972-73	77	2001-02	827
1973-74	100	2002-03	816
1974-75	125	2003-04	755
1975-76	150	2004-05	1,047
1976-77	175	2005-06	1,152
1977-78	181		
1978-79	205		

2004-05 = Revised estimates; 2005-06 = Budget estimates.

Sources: 1. Reserve Bank of India (a) *Report on Currency and Finance* and (b) *Supplement to Finances of State Governments* (various years); 2. Government of India, Ministry of Finance, *Indian Public Finance Statistics*, 2005-2006, Table 3.2.

Select Bibliography

Select Bibliography

Administrative Reforms Commission, *Report of the Study Team on Centre-State Relationships*, Vol. I, 1968.

Alejandro Foxley, Eduardo Aninat, and J.P. Arellano, *Redistributive Effects of Government Programmes - The Chilean Case* (Pergamon Press, 1979).

Alesina, Alberto and R. Perotti, "The Political Economy of Budget Deficits", *IMF Staff Papers*, 1995.

Aronson, Richard, *Public Finance* (New York: McGraw-Hill Book Company, 1985).

Bakshi, P.M., *The Constitution of India* (Delhi: Universal Law Publishing Co. Pvt. Ltd.).

Basu, Durga Das, *Introduction to the Constitution of India* (New Delhi: Prentice-Hall of India Private Ltd., 1987).

Brown, C.V. and Jackson, P.M., *Public Sector Economics* (Oxford: Martin Robertson and Co. Ltd., 1983).

Burkhead, Jesse, *Government Budgeting* (New York: John Wiley and Sons, 1956).

Caiden, Naomi and Wildavsky, Aaron, *Planning and Budgeting in Poor Countries* (New York: John Wiley and Sons, 1974).

Central Board of Excise and Customs, *Guide to MODVAT*.

Danziger, James, *Making Budgets* (London: Sage Publications, 1978).

Gyan Chand, *The Essentials of Federal Finance: A Contribution to the Problem of Financial Re-adjustment in India* (Humphrey Milford, Oxford University Press, 1930).

Government of India, *Report of the Indian Taxation Enquiry Committee*, 1924-25, Vol. I (President: Charles Todhunter).

——*Report of the Income Tax Investigation Commission* (Chairman: Srinivasa Varadachariar), 1948

——*Report of the Taxation Enquiry Commission* (Chairman: John Mathai) 1953-54, Vols. I, II and III.

——*Report of the Customs Reorganisation Committee,* (Chairman: F.C. Budhwar), 1957-58.

——*Report of the Direct Taxes Administration Enquiry Committee* (Chairman: Mahavir Tyagi) 1958-59.

——Central Excise Reorganisation Committee (Chairman: A.K. Chanda), 1963

——*Report of the Committee on Sales Tax* (Chairman: R.G. Saraiya), 1964.

——*Final Report on Rationalisation and Simplification of Tax Structure* (Chairman: S. Bhoothalingam), 1968.

——*Final Report of Direct Taxes Enquiry Committee* (Chairman: K.N. Wanchoo), December 1971.

——Ministry of Finance, R*eport of the Committee on Taxation of Agricultural Wealth and Income* (Chairman: K. N. Raj), 1972.

——*Report of the Central Excise (Self-Removal Procedure) Review Committee* (Chairman: B. Venkatappiah), 1973.

——*Report of the Indirect Taxation Enquiry Committee* (Chairman: L.K. Jha), 1977, Part I.

——*Report of the Indirect Taxation Enquiry Committee* (Chairman: L. K. Jha), Part II, January 1978.

——*Final Report of Direct Tax Laws Committee* (Chairman: C.C. Chokshi), 1978.

——*Report of the Expert Committee on Tax Measures to Promote Employment* (Chairman: V.M. Dandekar), 1980.

——Economic Administrative Reforms Commission, *Report on Tax Administrations*, 1981-83.

——*Report of the Expert Committee on Replacement of Sales Tax by Additional Excise Duty* (Chairman: Kamlapati Tripathi), January 1983.

——*Aspects of the Black Economy in India,* March 1985.

——*Long Term Fiscal Policy* (December, 1985).

——*Report of the Technical Study Group on Central Excise Tariff* (Chairman: J. Datta) Part I, 1985.

——*Study Group on Taxation of Expenditure* (Final Report), 1987.

——*Report of the Commission on Centre-State Relations* (Chairman: R.S. Sarkaria), 1988, Part I.

——*Industrial Policy Statement, 1991.*

——*Interim Report of the Tax Reforms Committee* (Chairman: Raja Chelliah) December 1991.

——*Final Report of the Tax Reforms Committee* (Chairman: Raja Chelliah) Part I, 1992.

——*Advisory Group on Tax Policy and Tax Administration for the Tenth Plan* (Chairman: Parthasarathi Shome), 2001

——*Report of the Task Force on Direct Taxes* (Chairman: Vijay Kelkar), December 2002.

——*Report of the Task Force on Indirect Taxes* (Chairman: Vijay Kelkar), December 2002.

——*White Paper on State-Level Value Added Tax* (Chairman: Asim Kumar Dasgupta), 2005.

——*Rationalisation of Customs and Excise Duties on Edible Oils and Oilseeds* (Chairman: Ashok Lahiri), 2006.

——*Five Year Plans.*

——*Budget Papers* (various years).

——*An Economic and Functional Classification of the Central Government Budget.*

——*Economic Survey* (various issues).

——*Reports of Finance Commissions.*

——*Indian Public Finance Statistics* (various issues).

——*Constitution of India.*

——*Speeches of Union Finance Ministers, 1947-48 to 1984-85; Presenting Central Government Budgets.*

Lee, Robert and Johnson, Ronald, *Public Budgeting Systems* (Baltimore: University Park Press, 1977).

Lok Sabha Secretariat, New Delhi, *Abstracts on Parliamentary Procedures, 1986.*

Mark Krasnick, *Fiscal Federalism* (Toronto: University of Toronto Press, 1986).

Musgrave, Richard and Musgrave, Peggy, *Public Finance in Theory and Practice* (New York: McGraw-Hill Book Company, 1985).

Nicholas Kaldor, *Indian Tax Reform - Report of a Survey* (Government of India, Ministry of Finance, 1956).

Reserve Bank of India, *Report on Currency and Finance* (various years).

——*Handbook of Statistics on the Indian Economy* (various years).

——*Bulletins*

——*Occasional Papers*

——*Supplement on Finances of State Governments.*

Roy T. Gobin, "An Analysis of the System of Sales Taxation in Caribbean Market", *Public Finance*, Vol. XXXV, No. 2, 1980, pp. 272-73.

Shakdher, S.L., *The Budget and the Parliament* (New Delhi: National Publishing House, 1979).

Sury, M.M., Sales Tax in India Since 1938, *Journal of the Indian School of Political Economy*, Vol. 7, No. 1, January-March 1996.

——Customs Duties in India Since 1859, *Journal of the Indian School of Political Economy*, Vol. 7, No. 1, January-March 1995.

——Excise Duties in India: 1894-1994, *Journal of the Indian School of Political Economy*, Vol. 6, No. 1, January-March 1994.

——Income Tax in India Since 1860, *Journal of the Indian School of Political Economy*, Vol. 5, No. 1, January-March 1993.

——Centre-State Financial Relations in India: 1870-1990, *Journal of the Indian School of Political Economy*, Vol. 4, No. 1, January-March 1992.

——South Asia: Trends in Taxation, *Bulletin for International Fiscal Documentation* (Amsterdam), Vol. 46, No. 4, April 1992.

——Tax Structure Developments in India: 1950-90, *Journal of the Indian School of Political Economy*, Vol. 3, No. 1, January-March 1991.

——India: Structure and Evaluation of the Income Tax System, *Asian-Pacific Tax and Investment Bulletin* (Singapore), Vol. 8, Nos. 2 and 3, 1990.

——India: Theoretical and Practical Aspects of Capital Gains Tax, *Bulletin for International Fiscal Documentation* (Amsterdam), Vol. 44, June 1990.

——India: 1989-90 Budget: A Tightrope Walking, *Bulletin for International Fiscal Documentation* (Amsterdam), Vol. 43, June 1989.

——India: Structure and Reform of Indirect Taxes, *Bulletin for International Fiscal Documentation*, (Amsterdam), Vol. 42, October 1988.

——Resources for the Eighth Plan: Constraints and Prospects, *Economic and Social Change*, Vol. 8, No. 3, December 1988.

——Excise Concessions to Small Scale Industries in India: Some Issues, *Small Industry Bulletin for Asia and the Pacific* (United Nations, ESCAP, Bangkok), No. 22, 1987.

——India: Decline of Direct Taxes, *Bulletin for International Fiscal Documentation* (Amsterdam), Vol. 41, June 1987.

——Buoyancy and Elasticity of Union Excise Revenue in India: 1950-51 to 1080-81, *Margin*, Vol. 18, No. 1, October 1985.

——Elasticity of Tax Revenue: Some Measurement Problems, *Indian Economic Journal*, Vol. 26, Part I, 1978.

United Nations, Department of Economic Affairs, *A Manual for Economic and Functional Classification of Government Transactions* (New York, 1958).

Wojthley, John and Ludwin, William, *Zero-Base Budgeting in State and Local Government* (New York: Praeger Publishers, 1979).

Indexes

Name Index

Subject Index